S0-BVE-528

MANAGEMENT
Theory and application

The Irwin Series in Management and
The Behavioral Sciences
L.L. Cummings and E. Kirby Warren *Consulting Editors*
John F. Mee *Advisory Editor*

MANAGEMENT
Theory and application

THIRD EDITION

Leslie W. Rue, Ph.D.

Professor of Management
College of Business Administration
Georgia State University

Lloyd L. Byars, Ph.D.

Professor and Chairman
Department of Management and Organizational Behavior
Graduate School of Business Administration
Atlanta University

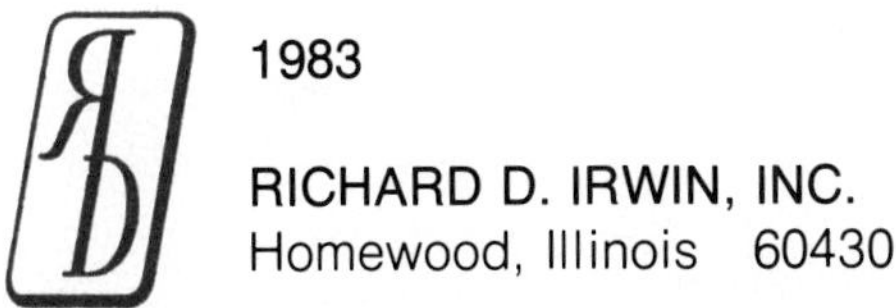

1983

RICHARD D. IRWIN, INC.
Homewood, Illinois 60430

ISBN 0-256-02839-7

Library of Congress Catalog Card No. 82–81950

Printed in the United States of America

3 4 5 6 7 8 9 0 V 0 9 8 7 6 5 4

To Penny and Linda

Preface

The third edition of this book, like the two previous editions, was planned and designed around a simple yet logical model for integrating the various facets of the management process into a conceptual whole. All too often the different aspects of management are presented as if they are entirely separate entities. While each different management-related topic may be well presented, there is often a complete failure to relate the different topics to each other. Rather than take a "process," "behavioral," or any of the other labeled approaches to the study of management, we have tried to analyze and tie together those topics that managers should be aware of in the pursuit of good organizational performance. This has resulted in what we believe is a comprehensive and integrated introduction to the process of management.

As suggested by the subtitle, the book was designed to emphasize the application side of management as well as theory. We hope this has been accomplished by the use of numerous examples scattered throughout the text and by the end-of-chapter materials. In addition to review questions, each chapter is accompanied by several in-depth discussion questions and two minicases, both of which require application of the concepts provided in the chapter. Each major section of the book contains a comprehensive case. The purpose of the section cases is to integrate the various concepts presented in the respective section. A recent incident from a real organization has been added to each chapter to emphasize the practicality of the chapter material. Approximately 20 percent of the minicases, and one of the section cases, are new to this edition.

As with the earlier editions, the book's content is arranged in six major sections. The first three sections are designed to provide the student with the basic foundation necessary to embark on the practice of management. Section One, Introduction and Background, serves as an introduction to the management process.

Section Two, Basic Management Functions, focuses on the basic functions that managers perform. Section Three, Behavioral Aspects, emphasizes the human component in the management process. Section Four, Individual Performance, is concerned with the fact that a manager's success is dependent on the individual performance of his or her subordinates. Section Five, Operations Management, stresses that managers should understand the organizational processes which produce the goods and/or services of the organization. For those adoptors who require a separate operations management course Section Five can be omitted if desired. The final section of the book, Section Six, Contemporary Management, introduces the ingredients necessary to insure responsible management.

The overall length of the book remains at 22 chapters. However, some slight re-ordering of the chapters has been undertaken and several chapters have been significantly altered. In Section One, the chapter on the manager as a decision maker has been almost totally rewritten and updated.

In Section Two, the original chapter dealing with the controlling function of management has been shifted to immediately follow the planning chapters. This makes for a more logical flow because of the similarities between the controlling and planning functions. This change also has the advantage of placing the motivation chapter next to the behavioral section.

In Section Three, the chapters dealing with communication, work groups, and conflict were significantly updated. The management of change and stress were added as major parts of the conflict chapter.

Section Four encountered the least amount of revision in this edition. Section Five, however, received significant attention; all three chapters were significantly updated. Efforts were made to introduce more service-oriented examples. Material requirements planning (MRP) was introduced as a major part of Chapter 20.

In Section Six, a discussion of Japanese management techniques was added to Chapter 22. Other minor changes were implemented where deemed appropriate.

We have revised this edition from the viewpoint of both students and instructors. We have attempted to present major management topics and relate them in a practical, applied format. Management texts too often fall short of adequately integrating the various management topics. We have overcome this problem through the use of our simple model and numerous examples. As are most authors, we are indebted to our families, friends, colleagues, and students for the assistance we have received. Unfortunately, space limits us to mentioning only a few.

Larry Cummings and Kirby Warren, as consulting editors, provided valuable guidance and assistance. Thanks are also extended to Cleveland L. Dennard, president; R. Roosevelt Thomas, dean, Graduate School of Business Administration; and Wayne Wormley, associate dean, Graduate School of Business Administration, all of Atlanta University. Thanks are also due Noah Langdale, president; Bill Suttles, provost-executive vice president; Kenneth Black, Jr., dean, College of Business Administration; and Michael Mescon, chairman, Department of Management, all of Georgia State University. Final thanks go to Linda Byars and Debbie Ales for their assistance in all phases of this revision.

LESLIE W. RUE
LLOYD L. BYARS

Contents

MANAGEMENT
Theory and application

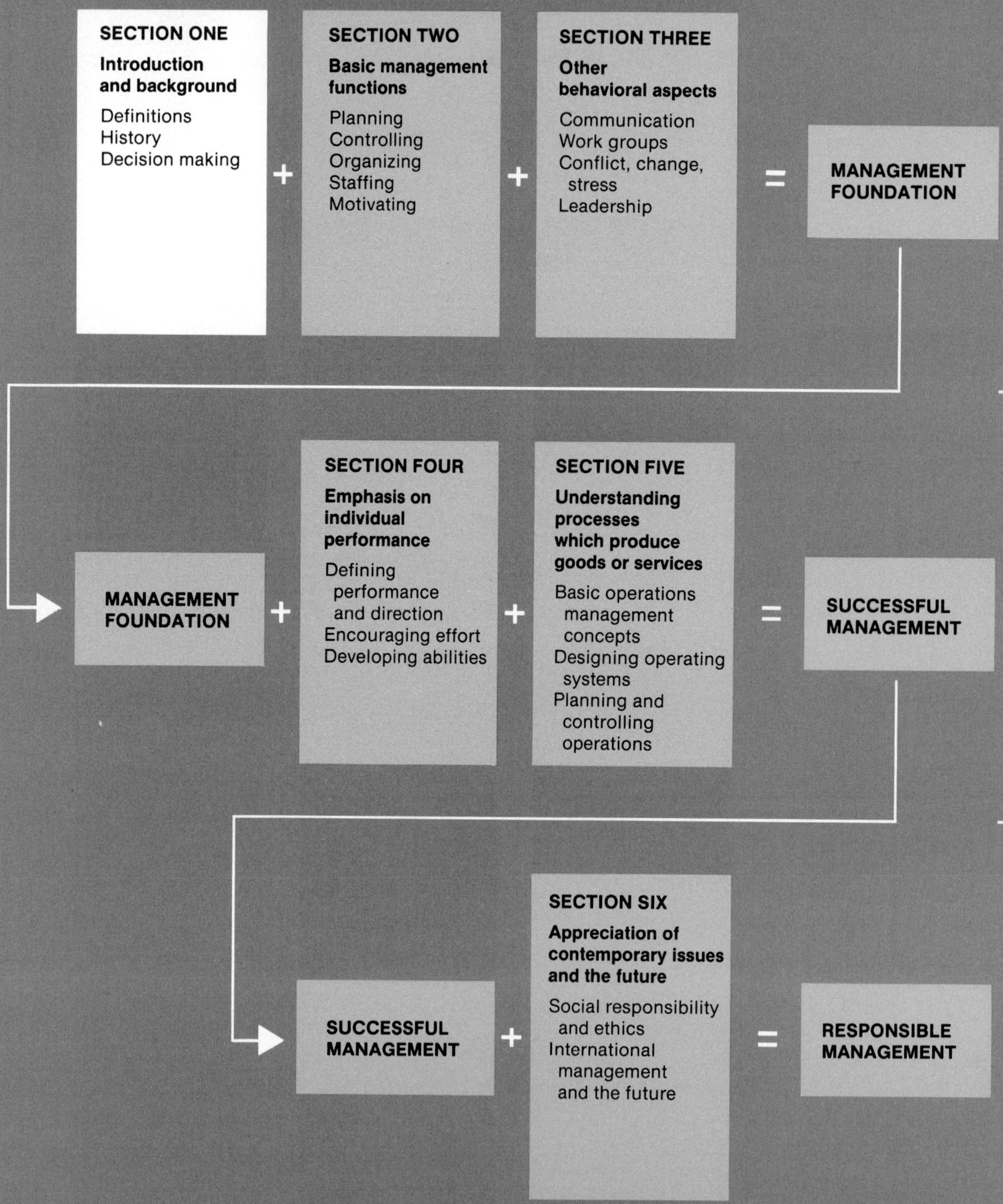

SECTION ONE
Introduction and background
Definitions
History
Decision making

+

SECTION TWO
Basic management functions
Planning
Controlling
Organizing
Staffing
Motivating

+

SECTION THREE
Other behavioral aspects
Communication
Work groups
Conflict, change, stress
Leadership

=

MANAGEMENT FOUNDATION

MANAGEMENT FOUNDATION

+

SECTION FOUR
Emphasis on individual performance
Defining performance and direction
Encouraging effort
Developing abilities

+

SECTION FIVE
Understanding processes which produce goods or services
Basic operations management concepts
Designing operating systems
Planning and controlling operations

=

SUCCESSFUL MANAGEMENT

SUCCESSFUL MANAGEMENT

+

SECTION SIX
Appreciation of contemporary issues and the future
Social responsibility and ethics
International management and the future

=

RESPONSIBLE MANAGEMENT

section one

INTRODUCTION AND BACKGROUND

Section One serves as an orientation for this book. The objectives of Section One are to provide an understanding of the work that a manager does, to develop a historical perspective of how and why management evolved, and to develop an appreciation for the decision-making skills required of a manager.

Chapter 1 discusses the concepts of management and the manager. The work of a manager is discussed in terms of the basic functions that a manager performs—planning, controlling, organizing, staffing, and motivating. Emphasis is placed on the fact that these functions are performed *through people;* thus, a manager must also have an understanding of human behavior. The characteristics of an entrepreneur are discussed and the importance of entrepreneurship in professional management is stressed.

Chapter 2 presents a chronological development of the management discipline. The management pioneers are presented in perspective with the events of their day. Emphasis is placed not so much on what and when events happened as on *why* they happened.

Chapter 3 describes how all managers, regardless of their level in the organization, must make decisions. Both theoretical and practical approaches to decision making are explored. The role of values, as well as the manager's affinity for risk, are discussed. The chapter ends with a discussion of the particular problems associated with making decisions in an organizational context.

1 Introduction

Objectives

1. To define management and describe the functions and activities involved in the management process.
2. To show the relationships among management principles, concepts, and theory.
3. To discuss and explain the design philosophy of this book and how it relates to the management process.

Chapter Outline

Glossary of Terms

Behavioral aspects of management Those areas of the behavioral sciences involved in performing the management process. These areas include such topics as motivation, leadership, group activities, communication, and conflict.

Concepts Commonly agreed upon definitions.

Entrepreneur Person who conceives the idea of what product or service the organization is going to produce, starts the organization, and builds the organization to the point where additional people are needed.

Law A statement of an order or relation of phenomena that, so far as is known, is invariable under the given conditions.

Management A process or form of work that involves the guidance or direction of a group of people toward organizational goals or objectives.

Management functions The activities that a manager performs are called management functions. These are planning, controlling, organizing, staffing, and motivating.

Principle A fundamental, primary, or general truth on which other truths depend.

Theory A systematic grouping of concepts and principles.

The next day Moses sat as usual to hear the people's complaints against each other, from morning to evening.

When Moses' father-in-law saw how much time this was taking, he said, "Why are you trying to do all this alone, with people standing here all day long to get your help?"

"Well, because the people come to me with their disputes, to ask for God's decisions," Moses told him. . . .

"It's not right!" his father-in-law exclaimed. "You're going to wear yourself out—and if you do, what will happen to the people? Moses, the job is too heavy a burden for you to try to handle all by yourself.

"Now listen, and let me give you a word of advice. . . .

"Find some capable, godly, honest men who hate bribes and appoint them as judges, one judge for each 1,000 people; he in turn will have ten judges under him, each in charge of 100; and under each of them will be two judges, each responsible for the affairs of 50 people; and each of these will have five judges beneath him, each counseling ten persons. Let these men be responsible to serve the people with justice at all times. Anything that is too important or complicated can be brought to you. But the smaller matters, they can take care of themselves. That way it will be easier for you because you will share the burden with them."

*The Living Bible**

Many writers have used the above example as one of the earliest written descriptions of a manager at work (utilizing, of course, the ever-present management consultant). Prior to the Industrial Revolution, organizational life was dominated by the military, the church, and the state, and thus the first efforts in management reflected the activities of these organizations. Such an agrarian and craft-oriented society had little need for sophisticated management. However, as the size and complexity of organizations grew, a defined and professional approach to the management process became necessary. Management, as we know it today, exists in all forms of organizations—private, public, and nonprofit.

MANAGEMENT DEFINED

Management has been defined in many ways, and even today there is no universally accepted definition. One frequently used definition is "getting things done through others." Another popular definition holds that management is the efficient utilization of re-

**The Living Bible,* Exod. 18:13–22, copyright 1971 by Tyndale House Publishers, Wheaton, Ill. Used by permission

sources. For the purposes of this book, the following definition of management will be used:

> Management is a process or form of work that involves the guidance or direction of a group of people toward organizational goals or objectives.[1]

MANAGEMENT AND OBJECTIVES

The starting point of the managerial process is the determination of organizational objectives. Objectives are designed to give an organization and its members direction and purpose. It is very difficult to have successful management without well-defined objectives. In fact, evidence suggests that having specific objectives increases both individual employee and organizational performance; and further, if difficult objectives are accepted by the individual employee, the resulting performance is greater than that achieved under less challenging objectives.[2] Managers cannot effectively guide or direct people without well-defined objectives. Precisely what these objectives should be depends on the particular organization and management philosophy.

Although objectives can range widely from organization to organization, they normally fall into one of four general categories: (1) profit-oriented, (2) service to customers, (3) employee needs and well-being, and (4) social responsibility. Peter Drucker has further refined these general categories by stating that there are eight areas in which objectives have to be set: (1) market standing, (2) innovation, (3) productivity, (4) physical and financial resources, (5) profitability, (6) manager performance and development, (7) worker performance and attitude, and (8) public responsibility.[3] Drucker's categorization of objectives in no way implies their relative importance. In fact, various combinations of objectives covering each of these areas are required for successful management.

Peter Drucker 8 areas where org obj must be set

MANAGEMENT FUNCTIONS

It is important to note that management is a form of work. The manager is the person that performs this work; in doing it, the

---

[1]Throughout this book, the terms *goals* and *objectives* will be used interchangeably.

[2]Gary P. Latham and Gary P. Yukl, "A Review of Research on the Application of Goal Setting in Organizations," *Academy of Management Journal*, December 1975, p. 840.

[3]Peter Drucker, *The Practice of Management* (New York: Harper & Row, 1954), pp. 63–87; and in *Management: Tasks, Responsibilities, Practices* (New York: Harper & Row, 1974).

FIGURE 1–1
The Functions of Management

Planning

1. Self audit—determining the present status of the organization.
2. Survey the environment.
3. Set objectives.
4. Forecast future situation.
5. State actions and resource requirements.
6. Evaluate proposed actions.
7. Revise and adjust the plan in light of control results and changing conditions.
8. Communicate throughout the planning process.

Controlling

1. Establish standards.
2. Monitor results and compare to standards.
3. Correct deviations.
4. Revise and adjust control methods in light of control results and changing conditions.
5. Communicate throughout the control process.

Organizing

1. Identify and define work to be performed.
2. Break work down into duties.
3. Group duties into positions.
4. Define position requirements.
5. Group positions into manageable and properly related units.
6. Assign work to be performed, accountability, and extent of authority.
7. Revise and adjust the organization in light of control results and changing conditions.
8. Communicate throughout the organizing process.

Staffing

1. Determine the human resource needs.
2. Recruit potential employees.
3. Select from the recruits.
4. Train and develop the human resources.
5. Revise and adjust the quantity and quality of the human resources in light of control results and changing conditions.
6. Communicate throughout the staffing process.

Motivating

1. Communicate and explain objectives to subordinates.
2. Assign performance standards.
3. Coach and guide subordinates to meet performance standards.
4. Reward subordinates based on performance.
5. Praise and censure fairly.
6. Provide a motivating environment by communicating the changing situation and its requirements.
7. Revise and adjust the methods of motivation in light of control results and changing conditions.
8. Communicate throughout the motivation process.

manager performs certain activities. These activities are often grouped into conceptual categories which are called the *functions of management.* These categories are:

1. Planning—deciding what objectives to pursue during a future time period and what to do in order to achieve those objectives.
2. Controlling—measuring performance against these objectives, determining causes of deviations, and taking corrective action where necessary.
3. Organizing—grouping activities, assigning activities, and providing the authority to carry out the activities.
4. Staffing—determining human resource needs, recruiting, selecting, training, and developing human resources.
5. Motivating—directing and channeling human behavior toward the accomplishment of objectives.

It is important to note that the functions of management are merely categories for classifying knowledge about management. Because of the overlap among the management functions, it is difficult to classify a manager's activities as purely planning, controlling, organizing, staffing, or motivating. In Figure 1–1, several managerial activities are classified under the different functions of management. However, this does not imply that managers engage in each function by sequentially performing each of these steps for each function. Figure 1–2 indicates the relative amount of emphasis placed on each function by different levels of management.

FIGURE 1–2
Relative Amount of Emphasis Placed on Each Function of Management

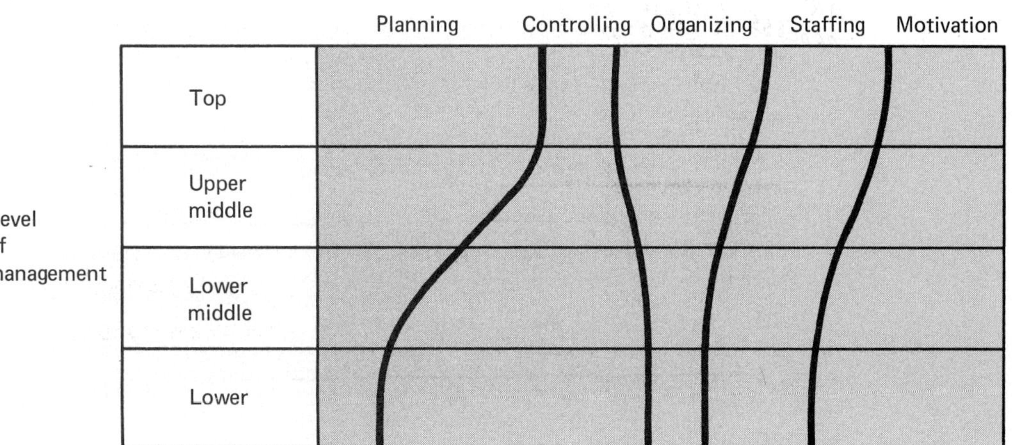

BEHAVIORAL ASPECTS OF MANAGEMENT

Because the process of management involves guiding or directing people, an understanding of the behavioral sciences and human behavior is necessary. The need for such an understanding is suggested by the motivating function as outlined in Figure 1–1. However, an understanding of other behavioral topics not specifically mentioned in Figure 1–1—such as leadership, group activities, communication, and conflict—is also needed.

Many approaches have been suggested to studying the management process. Leading the list are the functional and behavioral approaches. These approaches are usually presented as if they are mutually exclusive; however, a successful manager must understand the work that is to be performed (the management functions) and the people that are to be managed (the behavioral sciences). Thus, the functional and behavioral approaches to management should not be viewed as mutually exclusive but rather as necessary and complementary approaches.

MANAGEMENT—ART OR SCIENCE?

The argument over whether management is an art or science has raged for years.[4] The purpose here is not to enter that battlefield but merely to make the reader aware of the war.

Function of science

The function of science is to "establish general laws covering the behaviors of empirical events or objects with which the science in question is concerned, and thereby to enable us to connect together our knowledge of the separately known events, and to make reliable predictions of events as yet unknown"[5]

The art process has been described as follows:

Art process

> art is the imposition of a pattern, a vision of a whole, on many disparate parts so as to create a representation of that vision; art is an imposition of order on chaos. The artist has to have not only the vision that he or she wants to communicate but also skills or craft with which to present the vision. This process entails choosing the correct art form and within that art form, the correct technique. In good art, the result is a blending of vision and craft that involves the viewer, reader, or listener without requiring that he separate the parts in order to appreciate the whole.[6]

---

[4] See Ronald F. Gibbins and Shelby D. Hunt, "Is Management a Science?" *Academy of Management Review,* January 1978, pp. 139–44; Luther Gulick, "Management Is a Science," *Academy of Management Journal,* March 1965, pp. 7–13; and Waino Suojanen, "Management Theory: Functional and Evolutionary," *Academy of Management Journal,* March 1963, pp. 7–17.

[5] R. Braithwaite, *Scientific Explanation* (Cambridge: Cambridge University Press, 1955), p. 1.

[6] Henry M. Boettinger, "Is Management Really an Art?" *Harvard Business Review,* January–February 1975, pp. 54–55.

MANAGEMENT IN PRACTICE

Cowboys' Stars Start at the Top

DALLAS—That star on the side of their helmets isn't false advertising. The Dallas Cowboys have earned the acclaim, respect and the prestige they continue to enjoy. They've had 16 straight winning seasons and have qualified for the playoffs in all but one of those years.

This is a sterling success story. And what is the formula for such an accomplishment? It's difficult to reduce it to words but Tex Schramm, the Cowboys' articulate and profound president-general manager, attempts to provide an explanation.

"To start with," he said, "we don't always do everything right. We have had some mistakes along the way. But we believe you need three things—the organization, the players and the coaches. If you lack any one of the three, you are not going to be successful.

"The elements have to come together. Players are essential. And coaches are more important, in my opinion, in football than any other sport. If you have a strong organization, you can go through years when you aren't so lucky or have problems with injuries or other factors. If you have a strong base through the organization, you can withstand reversals."

Schramm is a man with powerful motivation. Perceptive, tireless and devoted to a cause, which has dealt with creating the Cowboys from a green expansion franchise in 1960 to the most balanced and mature organization in the National Football League. Six years after their inception, the Cowboys qualified for postseason play and in only one season, 1974, since then have they failed to make the playoffs.

Other clubs have difficulty getting out of their own way. Some have highs and lows. But the Cowboys are a constant. Asked why the team has had so few changes in all phases, from coaching to the ticket department. Schramm answers, "I believe when problems arise it's wrong to start changing people. It's much easier and effective to alter the method."

Schramm is aware that he has an ideal owner in Clint Murchison, the chairman of the board. Murchison, who is involved in the operation of 150 different companies, gives Schramm an autonomy in calling the signals regarding policy and decisions on player trades. But then Schramm works closely with the two men he brought with him. Coach Tom Landry and personnel director Gil Brandt. It's cooperation on all operational fronts. Egos don't get involved.

They have been together since the Cowboys opened for business. This continuity has helped create the solidarity and confidence that goes with being a first-class production. Schramm owes much of his early achievement to the late Dan Reeves, the bright innovator who hired a young sportswriter, Schramm, from the Austin (Tex.) American-Statesman in 1947 to be the publicity director of his Los Angeles Rams.

Except for a three-year span, 1957, '58 and '59, when Schramm was an assistant to Bill MacPhail, the director of CBS Sports, he has been involved in pro football. It was during that time in New York that he got a chance to observe Landry, who was then the defensive coach of the Giants. Schramm was so impressed that he knew he wanted to hire Landry when he heeded the call to get the Cowboys off and running.

"I was confident of Tom's ability," said Tex, "because I was in New York and saw his achievements with the Giants' defense then. You talked to his players and found they had esprit de corps. I felt he could transmit the same qualities as a head coach."

And if you want to know if he had any other names under consideration, the answer is yes. Sid Gillman, a man he had screened and recommended that Reeves hire for the Rams in 1955. Landry was his choice and not because they were alumni of the University of Texas.

Schramm says that he only wishes the press and public would stop inquiring of when Landry might retire. He fears that the coach might hear it so often that he'll start wondering if that's what he should do. "It's odd the way that kind of a thing can work," says Tex. "I still believe Roger Staubach would be playing if the power of suggestion hadn't worked on him. As for Tom, he keeps himself in excellent physical shape. He enjoys coaching and he can mix the two factors of his life, his Christianity and football."

In the three-plus decades that Schramm has been involved in the NFL, he says two players stand out as the finest individuals he ever met—Staubach and Elroy (Crazylegs) Hirsch. "Roger was everything he represented himself to be," commented Schramm. "He has character, fiber and a decency that made you elated to be associated with him. Hirsch is the same. When Elroy played, he was a true star but he never let himself get puffed up. He's just a tremendous gentleman."

The Dallas executive, far from the cold, calculating and aloof figure he is sometimes depicted, is asked if he ever had a hero in the front office of a sports team who impressed him more than any other. "I never met him personally but George Weiss of the New York Yankees was a hidden hero to me. There were a lot of Yankee eras and Weiss guided the club through so many transitions. But they epitomized success and what a winning team should be in all areas of operation."

It just might be that Schramm is a "Weiss" and the Cowboys have become the "Yankees" of football. Called "America's Team," the Cowboys are the envy of their competitors. They have a consistency to their performance and are embraced by fans all over the country.

"The "America's Team" thing isn't something we promoted. But we went along with it. It started when some of the NFL camera people called it to our attention. They said every game they filmed of the Cowboys, regardless of where it was played, there were fans cheering and waving pennants like for no other visiting team."

Dallas puts emphasis on intelligence and character in the players it signs. Not all of them are choir boys but they respond and contribute to the true team concept. They don't always win championships but the organization conducts itself with a professionalism that sets it apart from all the rest. It's not even a contest.

Source: John Steadman, *The Sporting News*, January 9, 1982. Used with permission of The Sporting News Publishing Company.

In other words, an artist has to have imagination and good technical skills. These technical skills are based on science—whether it be in the field of music, composition, engineering, or management. Thus, a good and productive artist uses technical skills that are based on science. Similarly, good managers use principles and concepts (based on science) in their managerial practices (the art of management).

As pointed out above, art and science are not necessarily mutually exclusive; in fact, they can be complementary. A manager must know and understand not only the concepts and principles of management (the science of management) but also how to use them (the art of management). Thus, management may be viewed as an art and a science!

PRINCIPLES OF MANAGEMENT

Henri Fayol, a Frenchman, was one of the first writers to introduce the idea of principles of management. Since that time, numerous concepts have been promulgated as principles of management. Fayol was reluctant to use the term *principle* because it implies law and inflexibility. A principle is defined as "a fundamental, primary, or general truth, on which other truths depend."[7] A law is defined as "a statement of an order or relation of phenomena that so far as is known is invariable under the given conditions."[8] Although the two definitions are similar, the difference is that principles have some degree of flexibility while laws are absolutely rigid.

In the physical sciences, laws exist. Examples include the law of gravity, Ohm's law, and the law of action and reaction. These laws were developed through a careful research process involving controlled experimentation. In this process the researcher sets up an experiment in which control can be maintained on many of the input variables. For instance, in a chemical experiment, the researcher may control input variables such as temperature, humidity, and pressure in order to determine the effect of a change in one of these variables on a chemical. By varying one of the input factors and measuring the corresponding change in the other factors, the researcher can establish a relationship between the changes and the chemical. Figure 1–3 illustrates this process.

After the experiment has been repeated many times with identical results, the initial ideas (called hypotheses in scientific terminology) of the researchers are converted into laws. Furthermore, after an hypothesis has been accepted as law, the law can be used to develop other laws.

---

[7] *The American Collegiate Dictionary,* s.v. "principle."

[8] *Webster's New Collegiate Dictionary,* 8th ed., s.v. "law."

FIGURE 1–3
Controlled Experimentation Process

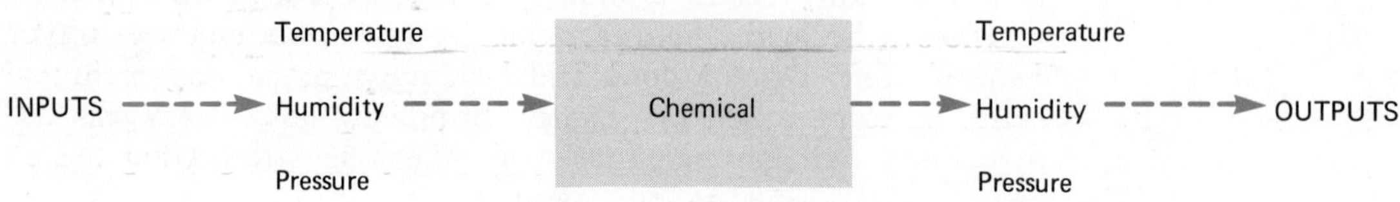

Unfortunately, one of the major problems in developing principles of management is that it is very difficult to conduct a controlled experiment in a management environment. Cost and the inability to place absolute controls on one of the primary inputs—people—make controlled experimentation difficult. Unable to use the time-tested method of scientific experimentation to develop laws, the remaining logical alternative is to use observation and deduction. This is the method by which most principles of management have been developed. For example, Fayol had more than 40 years of practical business experience to draw upon in the development of his principles. However, a word of caution is appropriate. Management principles are much more subject to change and interpretation than are the laws of the physical sciencces. For instance, the management principle of "unity of command" states that an employee should have one and only one supervisor. However, there are examples of organizational structures that violate this principle and seem to work effectively. Thus, management principles must be viewed as guides to action and not laws that must be followed without exception. In summary, management principles should be followed, except where a deviation can be justified on the basis of sound logic.

CONCEPTS AND THEORY OF MANAGEMENT

Concepts have been defined as "abstractions formed by generalizations from particulars."[9] Basically, concepts are commonly agreed upon definitions. Because no progress can be made without a common framework of definitions, concepts are essential for developing principles and theory.

A systematic grouping of concepts and principles related to a discipline such as management creates a theory. In other words, a theory is basically a classification or ordering scheme for principles and concepts. A theory attempts to provide a framework of

[9] Fred N. Kerlinger, *Foundations of Behavioral Research,* 2d ed. (New York: Holt, Rinehart & Winston, 1973), p. 28.

principles and concepts that can be used to further define and refine the theory. Thus, a theory of management involves a systematic synthesis of the concepts and principles of management. The goal of this book is to define the concepts of management as clearly as is possible; to present the principles of management using these concepts; to develop a theory for integrating these concepts and principles; and to encourage the application of the concepts, principles, and theory.

MISCONCEPTIONS ARE COMMON

Management as a field of study, is greatly misunderstood. Everyone seems to have preconceived notions about management, especially its problems. Usually these notions are based on personal experiences and are defended with vigor. Figure 1–4 challenges the reader to test some of his or her own preconceived notions about human behavior.

FIGURE 1–4
True-False Test of Human Behavior

1. People probably never learn anything while they are deeply asleep.
2. Genius and insanity have little or no relationship to each other.
3. Better college students make less money after graduation than average students.
4. A person who learns rapidly remembers longer than a person who learns slowly.
5. All people in America are born equal in capacity for achievement.
6. Teaching a child to roller-skate very early in life will give him a permanent advantage in this skill.
7. People are definitely either introverted or extroverted.
8. After you learn something you forget more of it in the next few hours than in the next several days.
9. Famous men tend to be born of poor but hard-working parents.
10. Lessons learned just before going to sleep are remembered better than those learned early in the morning.
11. On the average, men of 45 are more intelligent than those of 20.
12. The tendency to imitate is probably learned.
13. There is a law of compensation in nature; for example, blind persons are born with a highly developed sense of touch.
14. An especially favorable environment can probably raise the I.Q. a few points.
15. If a person born blind were to have his sight restored as an adult, he would perceive the world as we see it almost immediately.

Answers: (1) T; (2) T; (3) F; (4) T; (5) F; (6) F; (7) F; (8) T; (9) F; (10) T; (11) F; (12) T; (13) F; (14) T; (15) F.

Source: Gregory A. Kimble and Norman Garmezy, *Principles of General Psychology*, (New York: Ronald Press, 1963), p. 4. Copyright © 1963 by the Ronald Press Company.

The answers to the questions in Figure 1–4 have been empirically verified. However, the natural tendency is to believe our intuition even at the expense of refuting scientific investigation. The same is true in management. Many ideas and fads appear which are nothing more than seat-of-the-pants propositions. These propositions have some value in that they lead to hypotheses that can be researched. However, the student and practitioner of management must learn to separate management fact from fiction.

MANAGER AND ENTREPRENEUR

The basic distinction between a manager and an entrepreneur is often said to be the higher degree of financial and personal risk borne by the entrepreneur. The entrepreneur is the person who conceives the idea of what product or service the organization is going to produce, starts the organization, and builds it to the point where additional people are needed. It is at that point that the traditional view of the professional manager comes into focus. The professional manager is the individual who is hired to perform the basic management functions for the on-going organization. Entrepreneurs, therefore, are usually associated with relatively small organizations whereas professional managers are generally associated with medium-to-large-sized organizations. It is important to note, however, that an entrepreneur must perform many, if not all, of the basic management functions in starting and building an organization.

The ability of managers and the style they use in performing their individual jobs are important for organizational success. However, these factors are absolutely crucial for the entrepreneur. If the talent needed for survival and growth is not inherent in the entrepreneur, success is unlikely. Thus, while there are some important differences between entrepreneurs and managers, the ability with which an entrepreneur performs the basic management functions often has a significant impact on the entrepreneur's success. Time and time again, organizations have failed for lack of professional management once the organization reaches a size larger than that which the entrepreneur can effectively manage. The problem is often magnified or intensified by the entrepreneur's reluctance to "let go" and bring in professional management. This is not to imply that an entrepreneur cannot mature with the organization and remain in a top management position, but rather that some entrepreneurs fail to recognize their management shortcomings.

On the other hand, professional managers must have some of the characteristics of the entrepreneur if their organizations are

FIGURE 1–5
Characteristics of a Successful Entrepreneur

The entrepreneur was the first-born child in the family.
Is married, with a supportive spouse.
Began first company at the age of 30 or so (although years ago this happened as late as age 42).
Tendencies to take risks and innovate showed up by the teenage years.
Education varies: the technical entrepreneur often has a master's degree while the garden variety of entrepreneur probably has at least a high school and probably a college degree.
The entrepreneur's primary motivation for becoming an entrepreneur is a psychological inability to work for anyone else.
The entrepreneur's personality developed mainly in interaction with his or her father's personality.
The successful entrepreneur is often lucky.
Entrepreneurs and their financial investors are often in conflict.
The entrepreneur seeks advice, if it is needed, from other entrepreneurs, consultants, and college professors.
Is essentially a doer, not a planner.
Assumes moderate risks, not large or small ones.
Has a never-ending sense of urgency to get things done.

Source: J. R. Mancusco, "What It Takes to Be an Entrepreneur," *Journal of Small Business Management*, October 1974, pp. 16–22; and John A. Welsh and Jeffrey F. White, "Recognizing and Dealing with the Entrepreneur," *S.A.M. Advanced Management Journal*, Summer 1978, pp. 22–24.

to survive and grow. For example, the professional manager must also innovate and take risks when environmental change makes it necessary to do so. It has been suggested that perhaps the greatest weakness of American managers today is their inability to innovate and their unwillingness to take risks.[10] Of course, the ability to innovate and a willingness to take risks are two characteristics of successful entrepreneurs. Figure 1–5 describes some general characteristics of successful entrepreneurs as developed from data collected on 300 entrepreneurs.

DESIGN PHILOSOPHY OF BOOK

The preceding discussions represent an attempt to introduce the reader to the basic terms necessary for embarking on the study of management. The following chapters of this book are designed to introduce and study the concepts and principles necessary for developing a theory of management. The book is divided into six basic sections:

[10] Robert H. Hayes and William J. Abernathy, "Managing Our Way to Economic Decline," *Harvard Business Review*, July–August 1980, pp. 67–77.

Section One—Introduction and background.
Section Two—Basic management functions.
Section Three—Other behavioral aspects.
Section Four—Emphasis on individual performance.
Section Five—Understanding of the processes which produce the organization's goods or services.
Section Six—Appreciation of contemporary issues and the future.

Section One serves as an orientation to the book. The concepts of management and manager are discussed and the functions of management are briefly introduced. A historical perspective of management is also presented along with a discussion of the manager's role as a decision maker.

Section Two analyzes the basic management functions of planning, controlling, organizing, staffing, and motivating. In Section Two, the planning function is discussed in two chapters: Chapter 4 on objectives, policies, and strategy; Chapter 5 on the overall planning process. Chapter 6 discusses the control process. The organizing function is presented in Chapters 7 and 8. Chapter 9 is concerned with staffing. Chapter 10 explores motivation.

Section Three presents an additional set of topics that contribute to the behavioral side of the management process. Beginning with communication, this section discusses work groups, conflict, change, stress, and leadership. It is difficult, if not impossible, to isolate completely the behavioral topics from other management topics. Therefore, many behavioral topics appear throughout this book. For example, Chapters 7 and 8 in Section Two are concerned with the organizing function and contain many behavioral concepts. Other behavioral concepts are interspersed throughout the text. The purpose of Section Three is to present additional behavioral aspects that are not specifically covered elsewhere in this book.

Section Four is designed around the philosophy that the successful manager not only must have knowledge of the functional and behavioral aspects of the management process but also must be able to integrate and apply this knowledge through individuals. This section emphasizes the application and refinement of the management concepts and principles developed in Sections Two and Three in order to attain desired levels of individual performance. Individual performance is presented as being dependent on three major factors: effort, ability, and task direction.

Section Five discusses the production or operations aspects of the organization. The production of goods and/or services ordinarily involves the largest portion of an organization's financial assets, personnel, and expenditures. The processes which produce the goods or services also usually consume an appreciable amount of time. Thus, the manner in which the operations are managed plays a critical role in achieving the organization's goals. Additionally, all management personnel are either a part of or interact with the operations phase of the organization. The design and layout of facilities, scheduling, and inventory control are representative components of operations management.

Section Six looks at the management process from a contemporary viewpoint. The topics of social responsibility, ethics, international management, and the future of management are discussed.

A sequential integration and understanding of the different sections of this book result in a general theory of successful management as summarized in Figure 1–6.

Discussion questions and cases requiring application of the management concepts are provided at the end of each chapter. These questions and cases simulate realistic problem situations that a practicing manager might encounter. Also, a comprehen-

FIGURE 1–6
A Theory of Management

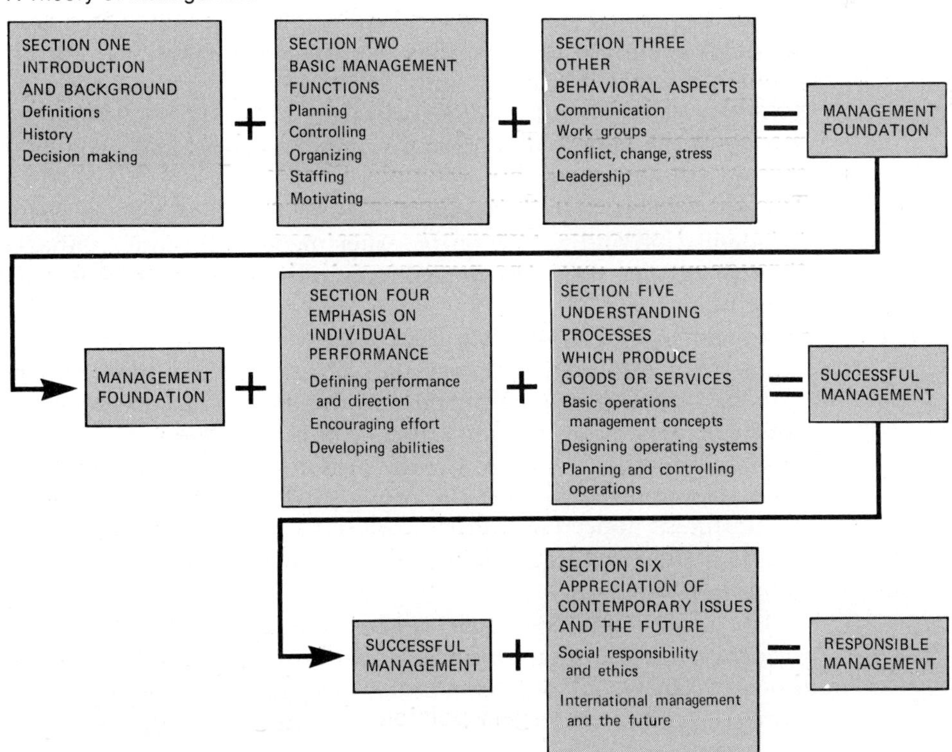

sive case is provided at the end of each section of the book to encourage the reader to integrate the ideas that have been presented in the section chapters.

SUMMARY

Management, as we know it today, exists in all forms of organizations—private, public, and non-profit. As the size and complexity of all types of organizations grew, a defined and professional approach to the management process became a necessity.

Management is a process or form of work that involves the guidance or direction of a group of people toward organizational goals or objectives. In performing this work, the manager uses the functions of management—planning, controlling, organizing, staffing, and motivating. This is frequently called the functional approach to the management process. Because management involves guiding or directing people, an understanding of the behavioral sciences is also essential. Therefore, the functional and behavioral approaches to management should not be viewed as mutually exclusive but rather as necessary and complementary.

The argument concerning whether management is an art or a science has raged for years. Art and science are not necessarily mutually exclusive. In fact, they can be complementary. For example, managers must not only know and understand the concepts and principles of management (the science of management), they must also know how to apply these concepts and principles (the art of management).

Management principles are generally based on observations and deduction and not scientific experimentation. Thus, management principles must be viewed as guides to action rather than inflexible laws.

Concepts are commonly agreed upon definitions within a particular field of study. A theory is a systematic grouping of concepts and principles. The purpose of this book is to use concepts and principles in developing a theory of management.

An entrepreneur is generally the person that conceives the idea of what product or service the organization is going to produce, starts the organization, and builds it to the point where additional people are needed. Several characteristics of entrepreneurs were discussed.

The professional manager is the individual who is hired to perform the basic management functions for the ongoing organization. Professional managers must also have some of the characteristics of the entrepreneur if their organizations are to survive and grow.

REVIEW QUESTIONS

1. What is management?
2. What are the four general categories of organizational objectives?
3. Name and describe the basic management functions.
4. Describe the functional and behavioral approaches to the management process. How do these two approaches relate to each other?
5. What is the difference between an art and a science?
6. What is a principle? How are principles of management developed?
7. What is a law? Does it differ from a principle?
8. What is a concept? What is a theory? How do these terms relate to one another?
9. What is a theory of management?
10. Distinguish between a professional manager and an entrepreneur.

DISCUSSION QUESTIONS

1. Management has often been described as a universal process, meaning that the basics of management are transferable and applicable in almost any environment. Comment on this statement.
2. How does one decide who is and who is not a manager in a given organization?
3. Is the operator of a one-person business, such as a corner grocery store, a manager?
4. Do you think that management can be learned through books and study or only through experience?
5. Discuss the following statement: "All entrepreneurs are managers but not all managers are entrepreneurs."

SELECTED MANAGEMENT AND RELATED PERIODICALS

Selected periodicals from this list are referenced throughout the text. This list is given so the reader will have a listing of the more commonly referenced management and related periodicals.

Academy of Management Journal
Academy of Management Review
Administrative Management
Administrative Science Quarterly
Business Horizons
California Management Review
Canadian Business Review
Columbia Journal of World Business
Decision Sciences
Forbes
Fortune
Harvard Business Review
Human Resource Management
Industrial and Labor Relations Review
Journal of Applied Behavioral Science
Journal of Applied Psychology
Journal of Business
Journal of Human Resources
Journal of Management Studies

Journal of Small Business Management
Journal of Systems Management
Management Accounting
Management of Personnel Quarterly
Management International Review
Management Review
Management Science
Managerial Planning
Michigan Business Review
Monthly Labor Review
Organizational Behavior and Human Performance
Organizational Dynamics
Personnel
Personnel Administration
Personnel Management
Personnel Psychology
Public Administration Review
S.A.M. Advanced Management Journal
Sloan Management Review
Supervisory Management
The Wall Street Journal (newspaper)
Training and Development Journal

SELECTED READINGS

Barnard, Chester I. *The Functions of the Executive.* Cambridge, Mass.: Harvard University Press, 1938.

Bedeian, Arthur. "An Historical Review of the Efforts in the Area of Management Semantics." *Academy of Management Journal,* March 1974, pp. 101–14.

Drucker, Peter. *The Practice of Management.* New York: Harper & Row, 1954.

Fottler, M. D. "Is Management Really Generic?" *Academy of Management Review,* January 1981, pp. 1–12.

Greenwood, William. "Future Management Theory." *Academy of Management Journal,* no. 3, 1974, pp. 503–13.

Gibbins, Ronald F., and Shelby D. Hunt. "Is Management a Science?" *Academy of Management Review,* January 1978, pp. 139–44.

Hayes, J. L. "Making a Professional Manager." *Management Review,* November 1980, pp. 2–3.

Koontz, Harold. "The Management Theory Jungle." *Academy of Management Journal,* December 1961, pp. 174–88.

———. "Management Theory Jungle Revisited." *Academy of Management Review,* April 1980, pp. 175–87.

Lachman, R. "Toward Measurement of Entrepreneurial Tendencies." *Management International Review,* no. 2 (1980), pp. 108–16.

Lawler, E. E., and J. A. Drexler. "Entrepreneurship in the Large Corporation: Is It Possible?" *Management Review,* February 1981, pp. 8–11.

Leffingwell, R. J. "Qualities of Most Productive Managers." *Public Relations Quarterly,* Summer 1980, p. 25.

Mee, John F. "Management Philosophy for Professional Executives." *Business Horizons.* Bloomington, Ind.: Indiana University School of Business, Bureau of Business Research, December 1956, pp. 5–11.

Mintzberg, Henry. "The Manager's Job: Folklore and Fact." *Harvard Business Review,* July–August 1975, pp. 49–61.

———. *The Nature of Managerial Work.* New York: Harper & Row, 1973.

Parker, N. A. "Tongue-in-Cheek Approach to Management Theories." *Personnel Journal,* July 1978, pp. 381–83.

Petrof, J. V. "Entrepreneurial Profile: A Discriminate Analysis (Canada)." *Journal of Small Business Management,* October 1980, pp. 13–17.

Scott, William G. "Organizational Theory: Overview and an Appraisal." *Academy of Management Journal,* April 1961, pp. 7–26.

Smith, H. R., and A. B. Carroll. "Is There Anything New in Management? A Rip Van Winkle Perspective." *Academy of Management Review,* July 1978, pp. 670–74.

This, L. E. "Critical Issues Confronting Managers in the '80s." *Training and Development Journal,* January 1980, pp. 14–17.

Welsh, J. A., and J. F. White. "Recognizing and Dealing with the Entrepreneurs." *S.A.M. Advanced Management Journal,* Summer 1978, pp. 21–31.

Case 1–1

The expansion of Blue Streak

Arthur Benton started the Blue Streak Delivery Company five years ago. Blue Streak initially provided commercial delivery services for all packages within the city of Unionville (population 1,000,000).

Art started with himself, one clerk, and one driver. Within three years Blue Streak had grown to the point of requiring four clerks and 16 drivers. It was then that Art decided to expand and provide statewide service. He figured that this would initially require the addition of two new offices, one located at Logantown (population 500,000) in the southern part of the state and one at Thomas City (population 250,000) in the northern part of the state. Each office was staffed with a manager, two clerks, and four drivers. Because both Logantown and Thomas City were within 150 miles of Unionville, Art was able to visit each office at least once a week and personally coordinate the operations in addition to providing general management assistance. The statewide delivery system met with immediate success and reported a healthy profit for the first year.

The next year Art decided to expand and include two neighboring states. Art set up two offices in each of the two neighboring states. However, operations never seemed to go smoothly in the neighboring states. Schedules were constantly being fouled up, deliveries were lost, and customer complaints multiplied. After nine months Art changed office managers in all four out-of-state offices. Things still did not improve. Convinced that he was the only one capable of straightening out the out-of-state offices, Art began visiting them once every two weeks. This schedule required Art to spend at least half of his time on the road traveling between offices. After four months of this activity the entire Blue Streak operation appeared disorganized and profit had declined dramatically.

1. What is wrong with Blue Streak?
2. Do you think Art is a good entrepreneur? A good manager?
3. What would you suggest that Art do at this point?

Case 1–2

Wadsworth Company

Last year Don Carroll was appointed supervisor of the small parts subassembly department of the Wadsworth Company. The department employed 28 people. Don had wanted the promotion. He felt that his 15 years of experience in various jobs at the company qualified him for the job.

Don decided to have two group leaders report to him. He appointed Evelyn Castalos and Marilyn Degger to these new positions. He made it clear, however, that they retained their present operative jobs and were expected to contribute to the direct productive efforts. Evelyn is ambitious and a highly productive employee. Marilyn is a steady, reliable employee.

Work assignment decisions were to be made by Evelyn. She took on this responsibility with great enthusiasm and drew up work-scheduling plans covering a period of one month. She believed productivity could be increased by eight percent due primarily to work assignment improvements. She went regularly from workplace to workplace checking the finished volume of work at each station. In contrast, Marilyn assumed, at the suggestion and support of Don, the work of training new employees or retraining present employees on new work coming into the department.

Don spent most of his time preparing and reading reports. He also made certain that he kept friendly with most of the other managers. He talked with them frequently and gave them assistance in filling out forms and reports required by their jobs. He also circulated among the employees of his department exchanging remarks which rarely had anything to do with the work. When an employee asked a question concerning work, Don referred the person to either Evelyn or Marilyn.

Some of the employees complained among themselves that the work assignments were most unfair. They contended that favorites of Evelyn got all the easy jobs and although the present volume of work had increased, no extra help was being hired. Several times the employees talked with Don about this, but each time Don excused himself and referred them to Evelyn. Likewise, many of the employees have complained about Marilyn's performance. They base their opinion on the apparent lack of knowledge and skill the new employees have after receiving training from Marilyn.

1. How do you account for the general situation that has developed? Elaborate.
2. In your opinion will waiting and the passing of time tend to correct the current situation? Why?
3. Who should do what at the Wadsworth Company? Discuss.

2 The Management Movement

Objectives

1. To explore the reasons why management did not emerge as a recognized discipline until the 20th century.
2. To develop an understanding of the events and persons that led to the development of modern management.
3. To provide a historical foundation for later chapters in the text.

Chapter Outline

U.S. INDUSTRIAL REVOLUTION
CAPTAINS OF INDUSTRY
SCIENTIFIC MANAGEMENT AND F. W. TAYLOR
OTHER SCIENTIFIC MANAGEMENT PIONEERS
FAYOL'S THEORY OF MANAGEMENT
PERIOD OF SOLIDIFICATION
THE HUMAN RELATIONS THRUST
THE PROFESSIONAL MANAGER
CHANGING STYLES OF MANAGEMENT
MANAGEMENT PROCESS PERIOD
THE MANAGEMENT THEORY JUNGLE
THE SYSTEMS APPROACH
THE CONTINGENCY APPROACH
CURRENT TRENDS

Glossary of Terms

Bottom up management A philosophy of management popularized by William B. Given, which encouraged widespread delegation of authority in order to solicit the participation of all members of the organization from the bottom to the top.

Captains of Industry The name given to a group of men who dominated and built corporate giants during the last 25 years of the 19th century. Captains of Industry included men such as John D. Rockefeller, James B. Duke, Andrew Carnegie, and Cornelius Vanderbilt.

Contingency approach to management An approach to management which theorizes that different situations and conditions require different management approaches.

Management theory jungle This term was developed by Harold Koontz and refers to the division of thought that resulted from the multiple approaches to studying the management process.

McCormick multiple-managment plan This plan, developed by Charles McCormick, uses participation as a training and motivational tool by selecting several promising young men and women from various departments within the company to form a junior board of directors.

Process approach to management An approach to the study of management that focuses on the management functions of planning, controlling, organizing, staffing, and motivating.

Professional manager A career manager who does not necessarily have a controlling interest in the organization for which he or she works and who realizes that he or she has a responsibility to the employees, the stockholders, and the public.

Scanlon plan An incentive plan developed in 1938 by Joseph Scanlon which provided the workers with a bonus for tangible savings in labor costs.

Scientific management A philosophy, popularized by Frederick W. Taylor, concerning the relationship between people and work that sought to increase productivity and simultaneously make the work easier by scientifically studying work methods and establishing standards rather than depending on tradition and custom.

Soldiering A term to describe the actions of employees who intentionally restrict output.

Systems approach to management An approach to management which encourages the manager to view the environmental, psychological, physical, and informational facets of the manager's job as linking together to form an integrated whole.

> History is useful to us not because it provides us with final answers about the fate of man, but because it offers us an inexhaustible storehouse of lifestyles, civilizational modes, and ways of acting that we can draw on as we face the future. History gives us balance, patience, and a deeper understanding of what it means to live and die. History cannot save us in any ultimate sense, but it can deepen our understanding of humanity's potentialities and limitations.
>
> *Arthur N. Gilbert**

As the quote above suggests, an understanding of the history of any discipline is necessary if one is to understand where the discipline currently is and where it is going. Management is no exception. Many of today's managerial problems had their genesis in the early management movement. Understanding the historical evolution of these problems better enables the modern manager to cope with them. The challenge to present and future managers is not to memorize historical names and dates but rather to develop a feel for why and how things happened and to apply this knowledge to the practice of management.

Although some need for management existed centuries ago, sophisticated management was needed in very few places prior to the 19th century. Just as traffic lights were not needed, and therefore not invented, before automobile travel reached a certain level of sophistication, management, as it presently exists, was not needed or even identified before the maturing of the corporate form of organization. The development of management thought and concepts is yet another example of people responding to the needs of their environment. It is this environment leading up to and surrounding the emergence of management thought that is the subject of this chapter.

U.S. INDUSTRIAL REVOLUTION

Professor Daniel Wren has described the Industrial Revolution in America as having three facets: power, transportation, and communication.[1] The steam engine, developed and perfected by James Watt in England in the late 18th century, was transplanted to

*Arthur N. Gilbert, *In Search of a Meaningful Past* (Boston: Houghton Mifflin, 1972), p. 2.

[1] Daniel Wren, *The Evolution of Management Thought*, 2d ed. (New York: Ronald Press, 1979), p. 90.

America shortly thereafter. The steam engine provided more efficient and cheaper power, allowed factories to produce more goods at cheaper prices, and increased the market for goods. An often overlooked contribution of the steam engine was that it allowed factories to be located away from water power. This in itself had a profound effect on the development of this country. Factories could be located near their suppliers, customers, and the most desirable labor markets instead of only near rivers.

The transportation expansion began with the development of canals around 1755. America's first railroad charter was obtained by Colonel John Stevens in 1815. Lacking financial support, Colonel Stevens did not build the first railroad in America until 1830.[2] A railroad boom then followed in the late 1840s. The track mileage increased from just under 6,000 miles in 1848 to over 30,000 miles by 1860.[3] As the railroad network grew so did the size of individual rail companies. By 1855, at least 13 rail companies were operating and maintaining more than 200 miles of track. By the mid-1850s, the railroad industry had clearly established itself as America's first big business and as America's first industry with a scope of operations extending beyond the local area.[4] Although textiles represented America's first entry into the industrial age, textiles were basically a local business with much smaller financial requirements than rail companies.[5] Unlike other local industries, railroad networks often spanned hundreds of miles, creating control and communication problems. Facilities could not be inspected in a matter of hours, decisions had to be made within a relatively rapidly changing framework, and scheduling operations became complicated. Beyond the day-to-day operating decisions, other management decisions became more complex. Long-range decisions had to be made concerning the expansion of facilities, the purchase of new equipment, and the financing of these operations.

Unlike the textile industry, which was transplanted from Europe, few or no precedents were available to guide those charged with managing the country's railroad companies.[6] Thus, rail company managers were the first in this country to need a sophisticated approach to management.

Besides creating the need for sophisticated management tech-

[2] Dorothy Gregg, "John Stevens: General Entrepreneur," in *Men in Business*, ed. William Miller (New York: Harper & Row, 1957), pp. 120–52.

[3] Alfred D. Chandler, Jr., "The Railroads: Pioneers in Modern Corporate Management," *Business History Review*, Spring 1965, p. 17.

[4] Wren, *Management Thought*, pp. 93–94.

[5] Chandler, "The Railroads," pp. 17–19.

[6] Ibid., p. 21.

niques, the railroads made another significant contribution to the development of management. Railroads created national and increasingly urban markets. Urban and industrial centers sprang up all along their miles of tracks. Thus, by providing rapid transportation of raw materials and finished goods, railroads made possible the development of a truly national market.

The third facet of the American Industrial Revolution, communication, was primed in 1844 by Samuel F. B. Morse's invention of the telegraph. The telegraph enabled managers to coordinate and communicate with speed and efficiency.

By 1860, which is the year generally thought of as the start of the Industrial Revolution in this country, it was evident that the power, transportation, and communication fields had advanced to the point that they served as an inducement to the entrepreneur.

CAPTAINS OF INDUSTRY

During the last 25 years of the 19th century, a significant transformation occurred in American industry. The economy shifted from a primarily agrarian economy to an economy more involved with manufactured goods and industrial markets.[7] This was a direct result of the urbanization which was brought about by the completion of a nationwide railroad system.

American business during this transition period was dominated and characterized by "Captains of Industry." These Captains of Industry included men like John D. Rockefeller, James B. Duke, Andrew Carnegie, and Cornelius Vanderbilt. Unlike the laissez-faire attitudes of previous generations, these men often pursued profit and self-interest above all else. Although their methods have been questioned, they did obtain results. Under the guidance of these men, corporate giants grew in industries other than the railroad. Giant companies were formed through mergers in both the consumer and producer goods industries. They created new forms of organizations and introduced new methods of marketing. For the first time nationwide distributing and marketing organizations were brought into existence. The birth of the corporate giant also altered the business decision-making environment.

The empire building and methods of the Captains of Industry had reached a point where previous management methods were no longer applicable. Government began to legislate business reg-

---

[7] Alfred D. Chandler, Jr., "The Beginnings of 'Big Business' in American Industry," *Business History Review*, Spring 1959, p. 3.

ulations. In 1890 the Sherman Antitrust Act, which sought to check corporate practices "in restraint of trade," was passed.

By 1890, U.S. industry had reached a point where previous management methods were no longer applicable. No longer could managers make on-the-spot decisions and maintain records in their heads. Corporations had developed into large-scale enterprises with national markets. Communication and transportation had expanded and greatly facilitated industrial growth. Technological innovations were contributing to industrial growth. Specifically, the invention of the internal combustion engine and the application of electricity as a power source greatly accelerated industrial development at the close of the 19th century.

However, contrary to what might appear to have been an ideal climate for prosperity and productivity, wages were low.[8] Production methods were crude and worker training was almost nonexistent. No methods or standards had been developed for measuring work. Work had not been studied to determine the most desirable way to complete a task. The psychological and physical aspects of a job—such as boredom, monotony, and fatigue—had not been studied or even considered in the design of most jobs.

It was at this point in the development of management that the engineering profession made significant contributions. Because engineers designed, built, installed, and made operative the production systems, it was only natural for them to study the methods used in operating these systems.

SCIENTIFIC MANAGEMENT AND F. W. TAYLOR

The development of departments within organizations and specialized tasks had naturally accompanied the rapid industrial growth and the creation of Big Business. One person no longer performed every task but rather specialized in performing only a few tasks. This created a need to coordinate, integrate, and systematize the work flow. Because of increasing production, the time spent on each item could be very significant if a company was producing several thousand items. Thus the increased production plus the new need for integration and systematizing the work flow caused the engineers of the period to begin to study work flows and job content.

The spark which is generally given credit for igniting the interest of engineers to general business problems was a paper presented in 1886 by Henry Towne, president of the Yale and Towne

[8] Harry Kelsey and David Wilderson, "The Evolution of Management Thought" (Unpublished paper, Indiana University, Bloomington, 1974), p. 7.

Manufacturing Company, to the American Society of Mechanical Engineers. Towne stressed that engineers should be concerned with the financial and profit orientation of the business in addition to their traditional technical responsibilities.[9] A young mechanical engineer named Frederick Winslow Taylor was seated in the audience. As will become evident, Taylor later had a profound impact on the development of management.

Although his father was a successful lawyer, Taylor's first job was as an apprentice with the Enterprise Hydraulic Works of Philadelphia.[10] Here Taylor learned pattern making and machining. Upon finishing his apprenticeship in 1878, Taylor joined Midvale Steel Company as a common laborer. In six short years, Taylor rose through eight positions to chief engineer. During his earlier years at Midvale, Taylor had the opportunity to work with and observe production workers at all levels. It did not take Taylor long to figure out that many workers put forth less than 100 percent effort. Taylor referred to this behavior of restricting output as "soldiering." Because soldiering was in conflict with Taylor's Quaker-Puritan background, it was difficult for him to understand and accept. Taylor, therefore, decided to determine why workers "soldiered."

Taylor quickly perceived that workers had little or no incentive to produce more since most wage systems of that time were based on attendance and position. Piece-rate systems had been tried prior to Taylor's era but generally failed because of poor implementation and weak standards. Taylor believed that a piece-rate system would work if the workers believed that the standard had been fairly set and that management would stick to that standard. Taylor's efforts to scientifically define a full and fair day's standard became the true beginning of scientific management. Taylor wanted to use scientific and empirical methods rather than tradition and custom for establishing work standards. Taylor first formally presented his views to the Society of Mechanical Engineers in 1895.[11] His views were expanded in book form in 1903 and in 1911.[12]

Scientific management, as developed by Taylor, was based upon four main principles:

---

[9] Henry R. Towne, "The Engineer as Economist," *Transactions,* ASME 7 (1886), pp. 428–32.

[10] Frank Barkley Copley, *Frederick W. Taylor: Father of Scientific Management,* vol. 1 (New York: Harper & Row, 1923), pp. 77–79.

[11] Frederick W. Taylor, "A Piece-Rate System," *Transactions,* ASME 16 (1895), pp. 856–83.

[12] Frederick W. Taylor, *Shop Management* (New York: Harper & Row, 1903); and *The Principles of Scientific Management* (New York: Harper & Row, 1911).

1. The development of a scientific method of designing jobs to replace the old rule-of-thumb methods. This involved gathering, classifying, and tabulating data to arrive at the "one best way" of performing a task or a series of tasks.
2. The scientific selection and progressive teaching and development of employees. Taylor realized the value of matching the job to the worker. Taylor also emphasized the need not only for studying worker strengths and weaknesses but also the need to provide training experiences to improve employee performance.
3. The bringing together of scientifically selected employees and scientifically developed methods for designing jobs. Taylor believed that new and scientifically developed methods of job design should not merely be put before an employee but that they should be fully explained by management to the employee. Taylor believed that employees would exhibit little resistance to changes in methods if they understood the reasons for the change and if they perceived an opportunity for greater earnings for themselves.
4. A division of work resulting in an interdependence between management and the workers. Taylor felt that if management and the workers were truly dependent on one another, then cooperation would naturally follow.[13]

Scientific management represented a complete mental revolution on the part of both management and workers toward their respective duties and toward each other.[14] It was a new philosophy and attitude toward the use of human effort. The emphasis was on maximum output with minimum effort through the elimination of waste and inefficiency at the operative level.[15] A methodological approach was used to study job tasks, and standards were established. This approach included research and experimentation methods (scientific methods). The job tasks became the objectives, and standards were set in the areas of personnel, working conditions, equipment, output, and procedures. The managers planned the work while the workers performed the work. This resulted in closer cooperation between managers and workers.

[13] *Scientific Management: Address and Discussions at the Conference on Scientific Management at the Amos Truck School of Administration and Finance* (Norwood, Mass.: Plimpton Press, 1912), pp. 32–35.

[14] John F. Mee, *Management Thought in a Dynamic Economy* (New York: New York, University Press, 1963), p. 411.

[15] John F. Mee, "Seminar in Business Organization and Operation" (Unpublished paper, Indiana University), p. 5.

MANAGEMENT IN PRACTICE

A Steelworker Made Management History

The phenomenal feat of loading 48 tons of pig iron a day was performed by a Bethlehem man 65 years ago in a scientific management experiment conducted by an efficiency expert at Bethlehem Steel Company.

This latter-day Hercules who was called "Schmidt" in a series of experiments conducted by Frederick W. Taylor in 1899 actually was Henry Noll, who died a virtual nonentity February 25, 1925.

His sister, Floranda Noll Lilly, who survived him by almost 20 years, directed his burial under a simple marker in the firemen's plot of Memorial Park Cemetery, Bethlehem, where his remains still rest.

Under the pseudonym "Schmidt," Noll acquired fame in the annals of industrial management for his astonishing accomplishment in pioneer studies conducted by Taylor of the Stevens Institute of Technology.

The Method

The Taylor method—described in his book, *Principles of Scientific Management*—was adopted by firms all over the nation.

It involved a program of high incentive offered to an ambitious workman with a prescribed regime of work and rest. As a result the workman could increase the amount of pig iron he loaded in a day from an average of 13 tons to 48 tons.

This specific job consisted of picking up a pig weighing 92 to 100 pounds and walking with it up an incline leading to a flat car, dropping the pig on a pile and walking back for another pig.

At the time Taylor gave very little information on the subject of his experiment except that he was a healthy, 27-year-old man who was highly ambitious, honest and engaged in building a small house about a mile from the plant during his leisure hours.

Back in Limelight

More than a decade passed and Schmidt was forgotten. Then in 1911 Taylor published a series of articles in the *American Magazine* on his experiments, catapulting "Schmidt" back into the national limelight.

By then Schmidt had become a hot subject in industrial and labor circles. He was even mentioned in a book by Upton Sinclair called "The Octopus," a stinging social commentary on the inhumanity of Taylor's methods. The author commented:

"I shall not soon forget the picture Taylor gave us of the poor old laborer who was trying to build his pitiful little home after hours and who was induced to give 362 percent more work for 61 percent more pay."

The furor piqued the curiosity of a man named P. O. Brown who wanted to know whether Schmidt was still alive and how he had weathered the experiment.

As a result Taylor came to Bethelehem from Philadelphia and conducted an intensive search for Schmidt but failed to find him.

A couple of years later he again tried. By then a bill had been introduced to Congress to utilize Taylor's system in the ordnance department. Strong opposition developed and the erroneous report was circulated that Schmidt had died an early death as a result of the overexertion he suffered.

Very Much Alive

But Schmidt or Noll was still very much alive. Noll's niece, Helen Lilly, who teaches at Broughal Junior High School, Bethlehem, says her uncle lived alone in his small house on Martin's Lane—recently razed by the Redevelopment Authority—and he was a member of the Goodwill Fire Company and the Volunteer Firemen's Relief Association.

Miss Lilly says "I was in high school at the time and I used to take food and baked goods to Uncle Henry when my mother did a little extra cooking.

"At that time he worked for the Pettinos graphic company near the Hill to Hill Bridge. As I remember he was not exceptionally well-built and only average in appearance. He was always rather quiet."

Miss Lilly added that she used her uncle's trunk—a sturdy one—while at college after he died.

Clean Bill of Health

In 1914 Taylor commissioned A. B. Wadleigh to hunt for Schmidt and on June 2 of that year he finally located Henry "Knoll" whose name he misspelled. Taylor had Noll examined by a physician to prove he was still in good health and able to do a good day's work.

When Taylor verified that Noll had not suffered unduly from the experiment, his subject again plunged into obscurity. Taylor died in 1915. Noll died ten years later.

In 1933 students of scientific management again undertook a search for Schmidt. They learned he had died and Morris L. Cooke, a former associate of Taylor, wrote an epitaph—even though the grave could not be located. It read:

"Knolle, we of the scientific management faith salute you. When many a present-day business tycoon has been forgotten, your record as a he-man and a first-class industrial worker will be inspiring to laggards and drones. We trust your last resting place, wherever it may be, is wholly worthy of your prowess. Requiescat in pace."

Latest Search

Just a year ago another search for Schmidt's grave was initiated by Dr. Charles D. Wrege, assistant professor of management at Rutgers University.

This time the hunt was successful—thanks to the cooperation of the Rev. Vernon Nelson of the Moravian Archives; historian Robert Brown; Andrew Maurer Jr. of Nisky Hill Cemetery; and Robert Speck, vice president, and Harold R. Ziegenfuss, manager of Memorial Park Cemetery.

Now perhaps someone will see that Noll's grave is rescued from obscurity and inscribed with a proper epitaph—perhaps the one composed by Cooke.

Source: Ann Kovalenko, *The Sunday Call-Chronicle,* December 6, 1964. Used with permission of the Call-Chronicle Newspapers, Allentown, Pa.

The scientific study of work also placed greater emphasis on specialization and division of labor. Thus the need for an organizational framework became more and more apparent. The concepts of line and staff were developed. In an effort to motivate workers, wage incentives were developed in most scientific management programs. Once standards were set, managers began to monitor actual performance and compare the outcomes with the standards. Thus, the managerial function of control came into being.

Scientific management was actually a philosophy concerning the relationship between people and work, not a technique or an efficiency device. Taylor's ideas and scientific management were based on a concern not only for the proper design of the job but also for the worker. This has often been misunderstood. Taylor and scientific management were (and still are) frequently attacked as being inhumane and interested only in increased output. The key to Taylor's thinking was that he saw scientific management as equally benefiting both management and the worker: management could achieve more work in a given amount of time, and the worker could produce more and hence earn more with little or no additional effort. In summary, Taylor and other scientific managers were concerned with the management of work.

OTHER SCIENTIFIC MANAGEMENT PIONEERS

Several disciples and contemporaries of Taylor helped to popularize and spread the gospel of scientific management. Carl Barth, who is often called the most orthodox of Taylor's followers, worked with Taylor at Bethlehem Steel and followed him as a consultant when Taylor left Bethlehem. Barth did not alter or add to scientific management in any significant manner but rather spent his efforts in popularizing Taylor's ideas.

Morris Cooke was another disciple who worked directly with Taylor on several different occasions. Cooke's major contribution involved the application of scientific management to educational and municipal organizations. Cooke worked hard to bring management and labor together through scientific management. Cooke's rationale was based on the thesis that labor was as responsible for production as management and that increased production would improve the position of both.[16] Thus Cooke broadened the scope of scientific management and helped enlist the support of organized labor.

Henry Lawrence Gantt worked with Taylor at Midvale Steel

[16] Wren, *Management Thought,* p. 188.

and at Bethlehem Steel. Gantt is best known for his contribution in the areas of production control. The "Gantt chart" is still in use today. Gantt was also one of the first management pioneers to recognize publicly the social responsibility of management and business. Gantt believed that the community would attempt to take over business if the business system neglected its social responsibilities.[17]

Frank and Lillian Gilbreth made significant contributions to the early management movement both as a husband and wife team and as individuals. Frank Gilbreth's major area of interest was the study of motions and work methods. Lillian Gilbreth's primary field was psychology. Thus, by combining motion study and psychology, the Gilbreths made significant contributions in the areas of fatigue, monotony, micromotion study, and morale.

Harrington Emerson, who coined the term *efficiency engineer,* was one of the first to recognize the importance of good organization. Emerson felt that waste and inefficiency were eroding the American industrial system. He believed that organization and the application of scientific management could eliminate most waste and inefficiency. Emerson also developed organized management consulting at a time when consulting engineers were still mainly concerned with technical rather than managerial problems.

FAYOL'S THEORY OF MANAGEMENT

Henri Fayol, a Frenchman, was the first person to issue a complete statement on a theory of general management. Born of relatively well-to-do parents, Fayol graduated as a mining engineer and started in 1860 as a junior executive of a coal mining and iron foundry company. In 1888, when the company was near bankruptcy, Fayol took over as managing director and rapidly transformed the company into a financially sound organization. After retirement in 1918, Fayol spent his remaining years lecturing and popularizing his theory of administration. He became especially interested in the application of administrative theory to government. Although he published earlier papers outlining his general thinking, Fayol's major contribution, *Administration Industrielle et Generale,* was published in 1916.[18] Unfortunately, this

[17] Henry L. Gantt, *Organizing for Work* (New York: Harcourt Brace Jovanovich, 1919), p. 15.

[18] Henri Fayol, *Administration Industrielle et Generale* (Paris: La Societe de l'Industrie Minerale, 1916). First translated into English by J. A. Coubrough, *Industrial and General Administration* (Geneva: International Management Institute, 1930). Later translated by Constance Storrs, *General and Industrial Management* (London: Sir Isaac Pitman and Sons, 1949).

work was not translated into English until 1930 and then in only a very limited number of copies. The book was not readily available in English until 1949.

Possibly Fayol's most significant work was his discussion of management principles and elements. Fayol stated the following 14 "principles of management," stressing that managers should be flexible in the application of these principles and that allowances should be made for different and changing circumstances:

1. Division of work.
2. Authority.
3. Discipline.
4. Unity of command.
5. Unity of direction.
6. Subordination of individual interests to the general interest.
7. Remuneration.
8. Centralization.
9. Scalar chain (line of authority).
10. Order.
11. Equity.
12. Stability of tenured personnel.
13. Initiative.
14. Esprit de corps.

Fayol developed his list of principles from those practices which he had used most often in his work. He used them as broad and general guidelines for effective management. The real contribution made by Fayol was not the 14 principles themselves, for many of these were the products of the early factory system, but rather his formal recognition and synthesis of these principles.

In presenting his "elements of management," Fayol was probably the first to outline what today are called the functions of management. Fayol listed planning, organizing, commanding, coordination, and control as elements of management. He placed the greatest emphasis on planning and organizing because he viewed these elements as primary and essential to the other functions.

The works of Taylor and Fayol are essentially complementary. Both believed that proper management of personnel and other resources was the key to organizational success. Both used a scientific approach to management. The major difference in their approaches centered around their orientation. Taylor emphasized the management of the operative work while Fayol emphasized the management of organization.

PERIOD OF SOLIDIFICATION

The 1920s and most of the 1930s represented a period of solidification and popularization of management as a discipline. The recognition of management as a respectable discipline was accomplished through several avenues. Universities and colleges began to acknowledge the subject of management, and by 1925 most schools of engineering were offering classes in management.[19] Professional societies began to take an interest in management. Much of the earlier work of the management pioneers was presented through the American Society of Mechanical Engineers, but after the turn of the century, many other professional societies began to promote management. In 1912, the Society to Promote the Science of Management was founded. The society was reorganized in 1916 as the Taylor Society and in 1936 merged with the Society of Industrial Engineers to form the Society for the Advancement of Management, which is still a viable organization. The American Management Association was founded in 1923.

The first meeting of management teachers, sponsored by the Taylor Society, was held in New York in December 1924.[20] At this meeting the participants agreed that the first course in management should be called Industrial Organization and Management (they could not agree on what should be required in a management curriculum). After this meeting, professors began writing textbooks in the field of management.

During the 1930s, management teachers and practitioners began to stress organization. *Onward Industry!* by J. D. Mooney and A. C. Reiley appeared in 1931 and generated interest in the historical development of organizations. Several other books which

FIGURE 2–1
Significant Events Contributing to the Solidification of Management

First conference on "Scientific Management," October 1911.
First doctoral dissertation on subject of Scientific Management by H. R. Drury at Columbia University, 1915.
Founding of professional management societies: Society to Promote the Science of Management, 1912; Society of Industrial Engineers, 1917; American Management Association, 1923; Society for Advancement of Management, 1936.
First meeting of management teachers, December 1924.

[19] John F. Mee, "Management Teaching in Historical Perspective," *The Southern Journal of Business*, May 1972, p. 21.
[20] Ibid., p. 22.

focused on the organizing function were published in this era. By the mid-1930s, management was truly a respectable discipline. The significant events leading to the solidification of management as a discipline are summarized in Figure 2–1.

THE HUMAN RELATIONS THRUST

After the Great Depression, which saw unemployment in excess of 25 percent, unions sought and gained major advantages for the working class. During this period, known as the Golden Age of Unionism, legislatures and courts actively supported organized labor and the worker. Figure 2–2 contains a summary of the most significant prolabor laws passed during the 1920s and 1930s.

FIGURE 2–2
Significant Prounion Legislation during the 1920s and 1930s

Railway Labor Act of 1926	Gave railway workers the right to form unions and engage in collective bargaining and established a corresponding obligation for employers to recognize and collectively bargain with the union.
Norris-La Guardia Act of 1932.	Severely restricted the use of injunctions to limit union activity.
National Labor Relations Act of 1935 (Wagner Act)	Resulted in full, enforceable rights of employees to join unions and to engage in collective bargaining with their employer who was legally obligated to do so.
Fair Labor Standards Act of 1938	Established minimum wages and required that time-and-a-half wages be paid for hours worked over 40 in one week.

Because organized labor and workers were attracting more attention, emphasis began to be placed on understanding workers and their needs—hence the birth of the human relations movement. The heretofore absence of proper emphasis on human relations was brought to prominence by the now famous Hawthorne Studies.[21]

The Hawthorne Studies began in 1924 when the National Re-

[21] For a detailed description of the Hawthorne Studies, see Fritz G. Roethlisberger and William J. Dickson, *Management and the Worker* (Cambridge, Mass.: Harvard University Press, 1939).

search Council of the National Academy of Sciences undertook a project to determine the relationship between physical working conditions and worker productivity. The Hawthorne Plant of Western Electric in Cicero, Illinois, was the study site. First, the researchers lowered the level of illumination, expecting productivity to decrease. To their astonishment productivity increased. Next they altered such variables as rest periods, length of workday, and noise, and production still increased.

Baffled by the results, the researchers called in a team of psychologists from Harvard University, led by Elton Mayo, to analyze the problem. After much analysis and review, the psychologists concluded that other factors besides the physical environment had effects on worker productivity. They found that workers reacted to the psychological and social conditions at work. These conditions included such things as informal group pressures, individual recognition, and participation in decision making. For the first time, research evidence had indicated the potential impact of the behavioral sciences on management.

While the methodology employed and the conclusions reached by the Hawthorne researchers have been questioned, there is no doubt that they did generate a great deal of interest in the human problems associated with the work place.[22]

Simultaneously, Mary Parker Follett added impetus to the human relations movement. Mary Follett was not a businesswoman in the sense of managing her own business, but her writings and lectures did have a significant impact on many business and government leaders. While she concerned herself with many aspects of the management process, her underlying philosophy was based on the belief that the fundamental problem of any organization was the building and maintenance of dynamic, yet harmonious, human relations within the organization.[23] In 1938, Chester Barnard, who was president of New Jersey Bell Telephone for many years, published a book which combined a thorough knowledge of organization theory and sociology.[24] Barnard viewed the organization as a social structure and stressed the psychosocial aspects of organizations. Because of his effective integration of traditional management and the behavioral sciences, Barnard's work has had a great impact on both practicing managers and teachers of management.

---

[22] For example, see Alex Carey, "The Hawthorne Studies: A Radical Criticism," *American Sociological Review*, June 1967, pp. 403–16.

[23] Henry C. Metcalf and L. Urwick, eds., *Dynamic Administration: The Collected Papers of Mary Parker Follett* (New York: Harper & Row, 1940), p. 21.

[24] Chester I. Barnard, *The Functions of the Executive* (Cambridge, Mass.: Harvard University Press, 1938).

THE PROFESSIONAL MANAGER

The career manager or professional manager was nonexistent until the 1930s. Until this time, managers could be placed into one of three categories: owner-managers, Captains of Industry, or financial managers. The owner-managers predominated until after the Civil War. The Captains of Industry controlled organizations from the 1880s through the turn of the century. The financial managers operated in much the same way as did the Captains of Industry, except they often did not own the enterprises they controlled and operated. The financial managers dominated business organizations from around 1905 until the early 1930s, when public confidence in business organizations was severely weakened as a result of the Great Depression.

It was during this period of weakened public confidence that people began entering managerial positions to perform the functions of management rather than because they owned the business. This marked the emergence of the professional manager. The professional manager can be described as a career person who does not necessarily have a controlling interest in the enterprise for which he or she works. Professional managers realize that they have a responsibility to three groups: the employees, the stockholders, and the public.

As technology expanded and organizations became more complex, the professional manager became more and more prevalent.

CHANGING STYLES OF MANAGEMENT

As organizations grew in size and complexity, managers began emphasizing the importance of workers and their needs. As managers began to study the worker and develop theories concerning worker behavior, new styles and methods of managing began to emerge.

One innovative style of managing was that of James F. Lincoln. The serious illness of his brother forced Lincoln to assume the top management position of the Lincoln Electric Company in 1913.[25] Knowing little about managing a business and having no previous top management experience, Lincoln, remembering his former football days and the cooperation needed on the gridiron, solicited the help of his employees in managing the company. Lincoln realized that effective cooperation would not be achieved without rewards. Therefore he designed a plan which coupled an incentive system with a request for cooperation. Lincoln emphasized the fact that his plan appealed to the basic need of all indi-

[25] Charles W. Brennan, *Wage Administration*, rev. ed. (Homewood, Ill.: Richard D. Irwin, 1963), p. 289. Copyright © 1963 by Richard D. Irwin, Inc.

viduals to express themselves. Specifically the plan contained the following components:

1. An advisory board of employees.
2. A piece-rate method of compensation wherever possible.
3. A suggestion system.
4. Employee ownership of stock.
5. Year-end bonus.
6. Life insurance for all employees.
7. Two weeks paid vacation.
8. An annuity pension plan.
9. Promotion policy.

If the development of the Lincoln Electric Company can be attributed to its innovative management, then it certainly was successful. Over a 30-year period, Lincoln workers have consistently been among the highest paid in their industry in the world; Lincoln's selling price has consistently been lower than any comparable product; and the company has consistently paid a dividend since 1918.

Another innovative manager, Henry Dennison (1877–1952), felt that the strengths of an organization came from its members, and that the sources of power are the incentives, habits, and traditions that influence the men and women of an organization.[26] Dennison believed that an organization's greatest strength is realized if all of its members are strongly motivated; if their actions lose no effectiveness by frictions, conflicts, or unbalance; and if their actions move in a single direction, reinforcing each other. He believed that management's primary purpose was to provide conditions under which men and women work most readily and effectively. Instead of designing organization structure and tasks first, Dennison advocated finding "like-minded" people, grouping them, and then developing the total organizational structure. In summary, Dennison believed that management attention must focus on causes and effects in the field of human behavior. Dennison successfully practiced his management approach in the 1920s and 1930s at the Dennison Manufacturing Company, which was also one of the early companies to practice the Taylor system of Scientific Management.

Charles McCormick and William Given, Jr., were top managers who applied a human relations philosophy to their organizations. Both McCormick's and Given's styles of management were based on worker participation in the decision-making process.

---

[26] Henry S. Dennison, *Organization Engineering* (New York: McGraw-Hill, 1931).

McCormick, the manufacturer of spices and extracts, developed and made famous the McCormick multiple-management plan.[27] This plan used participation as a training and motivational tool by selecting 17 promising young people from various departments within the company to form a junior board of directors. The junior board met with the senior board once a month and submitted its suggestions. Aside from the immediate benefits of providing suggestions, the junior board provided early identification of management talent, opened communication channels, and relieved senior board members of much of the detailed planning and research. The overwhelming success of the junior board led to the creation of a sales board and a factory board which operated in much the same fashion.

Using the term "bottom up management," Given, president of American Brake Shoe and Foundry Company, encouraged widespread delegation of authority in order to solicit the participation of "all those down from the bottom up. . . ."[28] Given's approach promoted considerable managerial freedom in decision making, free interchange of ideas, and the recognition that managerial growth involves some failure. Given's style was based on his belief that the judgment, initiative, and creativeness of all employees in a business organization provide a better end result than the autocratic administration of any single individual.

In 1938, Joseph Scanlon developed a productivity plan which provided employees with a bonus for tangible savings in labor costs. The Scanlon plan was unique in at least three respects: (1) joint management and union committees were established to discuss and propose labor-saving techniques; (2) group rewards, not individual rewards, were made for suggestions; and (3) employees shared in reduced costs as opposed to increased profits.[29] Scanlon believed that participation was desirable not merely to create a feeling of belonging but also to recognize explicitly the role of employees and unions in suggesting improvements.

While many of the emerging styles of management of the 1930s and 1940s had distinct differences, most were based on the human relations thrust, especially on participation. The emergence of the professional manager and the rapidly rising standard of living contributed to a greater concern for the employee and hence the development of participative forms of management. The

---

[27] Charles P. McCormick, *Multiple Management* (New York: Harper & Row, 1949).

[28] William B. Given, Jr., *Bottom Up Management* (New York: Harper & Row, 1949).

[29] Joseph Scanlon, "Enterprise for Everyone," *Fortune*, January 1950, pp. 41, 55–59; and Wren, *Management Thought*, p. 330.

professional manager realized that a greater concern for the worker would most likely result in greater productivity and therefore greater profits. The rising standard of living made workers more mobile, increased the number of employment options open to them, and made them less likely to settle for a strictly authoritarian environment.

MANAGEMENT PROCESS PERIOD

During the late 1940s, management thought began to move toward the idea of a "process for management."[30] This was an attempt to identify and define a process that could be used to attain desired objectives. The "process approach" led management to become primarily concerned with the identification and refinement of the functions or components of the management process. For this reason, the process approach is sometimes referred to as the "functional approach."

As has previously been discussed, Henri Fayol was the first management scholar to present explicitly a functional analysis of the management process. Fayol listed planning, organizing, commanding, coordination, and control as functions of management.

Oliver Sheldon, an Englishman, also presented an early breakdown of the management process.[31] In 1923, Sheldon saw management as the determination of business policy, the coordination of the execution of policy, the organization of the business, and the control of the executive.

Ralph C. Davis was the first American to publish a functional breakdown of the management process.[32] Davis subdivided the management process into three functions: planning, organizing, and controlling.

While all of the above management scholars made early reference to a functional approach to management, the concept was not widely accepted until after Constance Storrs' translation of Fayol's work became readily available in 1949. Thus it is evident that Fayol was truly responsible for fathering the process approach to the study of management.

During this same time, process management was gaining acceptance as a discipline that could be taught. Heretofore, management, while accepted as a discipline, had been modeled after

[30] Mee, *Management Thought*, p. 53.

[31] Oliver Sheldon, *The Philosophy of Management* (London: Sir Isaac Pitman and Sons, 1923).

[32] Ralph C. Davis, *The Principles of Business Organizations and Operations* (Columbus, Ohio: H. L. Hedrick, 1935), pp. 12–13.

certain successful individuals. The functional approach offered a new, logical, and concrete method of presenting management.

A second generation of management process thinkers evolved after the 1949 translation of Fayol's work and capitalized on teaching management via the functional approach. Most management texts published in the 1950s presented management as a series of functions and principles that could be learned and synthesized in a logical fashion.

The early to mid-1950s represented an era of almost complete agreement concerning the composition and teachings of management. The management process or functional approach was the accepted methodological approach to the study of management.

THE MANAGEMENT THEORY JUNGLE

The late 1950s ushered in a new era in the study of management. Many scholars were becoming uneasy with the process approach to management and began to adopt new approaches. Production management and industrial engineering scholars began experimenting with mathematical and modeling approaches in an attempt to quantify management. As a result, a mathematical school of thought and a decision theory school of thought were developed for the study of management. The decision theory school was founded largely on economic theory and the theory of consumer choice. The mathematical school viewed management as a system of mathematical relationships. At the same time, the behavioral scientists were studying management as small group relations, thus depending heavily on psychology and social psychology. Drawing on the work of Chester Barnard and sociological theory, another group developed a social system school which saw management as a system of cultural interrelationships. An empirical school of thought was developed by those management scholars using the case approach. The basic premise of this school was that effective management could be learned by studying the successes and failures of other managers.

Harold Koontz was the first management scholar to verbalize explicitly this fragmentation movement.[33] Koontz accurately referred to this division of thought as the "Management Theory Jungle." Many conferences and discussions followed Koontz's analysis in an attempt to disentangle the theory jungle and to synthesize the various schools of thought. While some progress was made, a unified theory of management has not been realized.

[33] Harold Koontz, "The Management Theory Jungle," *Academy of Management Journal*, December 1961, pp. 174–88.

THE SYSTEMS APPROACH

The fragmentation period of the late 1950s and early 1960s was followed by an era of attempted integration. Many management theorists sought to use a "systems approach" in order to integrate the various management schools. The systems approach was viewed as "a way of thinking about the job of managing . . . [which] provides a framework for visualizing internal and external environmental factors as an integrated whole."[34] The manager was encouraged to view the human, physical, and informational facets of the manager's job as linking together to form an integrated whole.

One popular thrust was to use a systems approach to integrate the other schools of management into the traditional functional approach. The idea here was to integrate the human relations and mathematical approaches into the appropriate functional areas. Thus while studying planning, a systems approach might discuss applicable mathematical forecasting techniques.

Other versions of the systems approach have been much more grandiose and based on general systems theory. These versions have attempted to analyze management in terms of other disciplines and other cultures. Often referred to as "comparative management," this approach evolved as a result of the multinational firms and the need for managing in diverse fields.[35]

While the term *systems approach* has been overused by many, the idea of taking a holistic view of the management process has special merit for today's students and practitioners of management. Students and practicing managers must learn to integrate the different management functions and topics. For example, successful managers must understand both the function of planning and how to relate planning to the other management functions.

THE CONTINGENCY APPROACH

The 1970s were characterized by the so-called contingency approach to management. Basically, the contingency approach theorizes that different situations and conditions require different management approaches. Adherents to this approach believe that there is no one best way of managing but rather that the best way of managing depends on the specific circumstances. Recognizing that it would be rare to find a manager who thinks that one way of managing works best in *all* situations, one might ask, "What is new about this approach?"

---

[34] Richard A. Johnson, Fremont E. Kast, and James E. Rosenzweig, *The Theory and Management of Systems* (New York: McGraw-Hill, 1963), p. 3.

[35] Wren, *Management Thought*, pp. 463–64.

What is new is that contingency theorists have, in many cases, gone much further than simply saying "it all depends." Many contingency theorists outline in detail precisely what style or approach works best under certain conditions and circumstances. Contingency theories (many of which are discussed in this book) have been developed in areas such as decision making, organizational design, leadership, planning, and group behavior.

CURRENT TRENDS

The last chapter of this book is devoted partially to predicting and speculating about the future of management and organizational life. There have been some recent developments which reflect on the past and which will affect the future.

Resource shortages appeared with regularity in the 1970s. These shortages, along with other factors which resulted in slower growth rates and more competitive markets, have rekindled interest in cost-saving methods and techniques as an alternative way of maintaining or increasing profits. The interesting fact is that this has renewed interest in many of Taylor's precepts which focused on cost saving. Chapter 22 will explore several possibilities for the future as managers try to mesh productivity and cost-saving concerns with humanistic programs.

Figure 2–3 presents a summation in chronological order of the major and related events which have contributed to the management movement.

SUMMARY

Management, as we know it today, grew out of the American Industrial Revolution. Not until industry reached a certain level of sophistication was management necessary as a distinct discipline.

The railroads represented the first big industry in this country in terms of sophistication and capital requirements. The railroads also acted as a catalyst to the development of other industries. They provided rapid transportation of raw materials and finished goods, thus allowing companies great flexibility. Taking advantage of the situation, men like Rockefeller, Duke, and Carnegie developed giant corporations in other industries by the end of the 19th century. These new corporate giants, along with the railroads, required new methods of management. No longer could businesses be run out of the home or on an informal basis.

It was at this point that the engineering profession made significant contributions to the development of management thought.

FIGURE 2–3
Major Components and Related Events of the Management Movement

Management movement component	*Relative major events*
U.S. Industrial Revolution (prior to 1875)	Steam power (1790–1810) Railroad boom (1830–50) Telegraph (1844)
Captains of Industry (1875–1900)	Formation of corporate giants: John D. Rockefeller James B. Duke Andrew Carnegie Cornelius Vanderbilt
Scientific Management Era (1895–1920)	Henry Towne, "The Engineer as Economist," 1886 Frederick W. Taylor's work (1895–1915): Carl Barth Morris Cooke Henry Lawrence Gantt Frank and Lillian Gilbreth Harrington Emerson Henri Fayol, *Administration Industrielle et Generale,* 1916
Period of Solidification (1920 to early 1930s)	Founding of professional management societies (1920s) Mooney and Reiley, *Onward Industry!* 1931
Human Relations Movement (1931 to late 1940s)	Hawthorne Studies (1924–32) Mary Parker Follett (1920–33) Chester Barnard, *Functions of the Executive,* 1938
Management Process Period (early 1950s to early 1960s)	Storrs' translation of Fayol's work (1949) Ralph Davis, *Top Management Planning,* 1951 George Terry, *Principles of Management,* 1953 Koontz and O'Donnell, *Principles of Management,* 1955
Management Theory Jungle (early to late 1960s)	Process approach Quantitative approaches Behavioral approaches
The Systems Approach (late 1960s to early 1970s)	Integrating the various approaches to the study of management
The Contingency Approach (1970s)	Theorizes that different situations and conditions require different management approaches
Cost-Saving Methods (late 1970s to early 1980s)	Renewed interest in Taylor's precepts

Challenging previous methods of managing a business, Frederick Taylor devised and popularized scientific management. Although often misunderstood, scientific management as presented by Taylor was a philosophy concerning the relationship of people and work. The basis for this relationship was finding the one best way for doing a job and finding the proper person for each job.

By the 1930s, the field of management had gained general acceptance as a discipline that could be taught and learned. Professional societies and related organizations had been formed and were contributing to the development of the discipline.

Following this period of solidification during the 1920s and early 1930s, the human relations movement made a significant impact on the management discipline. The Hawthorne Studies focused attention on human relations and specifically the psychological and sociological aspects of work. Simultaneously, Mary Parker Follett added impetus to the human relations movement.

Although his work was not readily available in English until 1949, Henri Fayol was the first to present a functional approach to the study of management. Fayol was also one of the first to develop principles of management.

By the mid-1950s, there was general agreement that management should be taught using a process or functional approach similar to that of Fayol. However, this period of general agreement was short-lived and was followed in the early 1960s by a fragmentation era. During this fragmentation period, several different schools of thought were pursued by management scholars.

In an effort to again unify management thought, a systems approach was developed. This approach was an attempt to tie all of the various schools of thought together within an overall "systems framework."

The contingency approach followed the systems approach. The contingency approach theorizes that different situations and conditions require different management approaches. Recent resource shortages have rekindled interest in cost-saving and efficiency approaches.

REVIEW QUESTIONS

1. What were the three facets of the Industrial Revolution in America? Discuss what impact each of these facets had on the development of industry as it is today.
2. What effect did the Captains of Industry have on the relationships between government and industry?
3. What is scientific management? Discuss the four main principles of scientific management.

4. Discuss the major contribution to scientific management of Morris Cooke, Henry Lawrence Gantt, Frank and Lillian Gilbreth, and Harrington Emerson.
5. What was Henri Fayol's major contribution to the management movement?
6. Discuss the impact of the Hawthorne Studies on management thought.
7. Describe in detail the following approaches to the management process: Lincoln Electric Company, McCormick multiple-management plan, bottom up management, and the Scanlon plan.
8. What is the process approach to management? Discuss some of the major contributors to this approach.
9. Discuss the factors which led to the Management Theory Jungle.
10. What is the systems approach to the management process?
11. Describe the contingency approach to managing.

DISCUSSION QUESTIONS

1. Why did the professional manager not emerge until the 20th century?
2. How were Taylor and Fayol's approaches to the management process different and how were they similar?
3. Why do you think Taylor and scientific management have been misunderstood by many people as being inhumane?
4. "Successful managers adopt their style to the situation." Discuss your views on this statement.

SELECTED READINGS

Barnard, Chester I. *The Functions of the Executive.* Cambridge, Mass.: Harvard University Press, 1938.

Bedeian, Arthur. "An Historical Review of the Efforts in the Area of Management Semantics." *Academy of Management Journal,* March 1974, pp. 101–14.

Fayol, Henri L. *General and Industrial Management.* London: Sir Isaac Pitman and Sons, 1949.

Gantt, Henry L. *Organizing for Work.* New York: Harcourt Brace Jovanovich, 1919.

George, Claude S. *The History of Management Thought.* Englewood Cliffs, N.J.: Prentice-Hall, 1972.

Given, William B., Jr. *Bottom Up Management.* New York: Harper & Row, 1949.

McCormick, Charles P. *Multiple Management.* New York: Harper & Row, 1938.

Mee, John F. *A History of Twentieth Century Management Thought.* Columbus, Ohio: Ohio State University, 1959.

———. "Management Teaching in Historical Perspective." *The Southern Journal of Business,* May 1972, pp. 20–24.

———. *Management Thought in a Dynamic Economy.* New York: New York University Press, 1963.

Merrill, C. F., ed. *Classics in Management.* New York: American Management Association, 1960.

Mooney, J. D., and A. C. Reiley. *Onward Industry!* New York: Harper & Row, 1931.

Roethlisberger, Fritz J., and William J. Dickson. *Management and Worker.* Cambridge, Mass.: Harvard University Press, 1939.

Scanlon, Joseph. "Enterprise for Everyone." *Fortune,* January 1950, pp. 41–59.

Sheldon, Oliver. *The Philosophy of Management.* London: Sir Isaac Pitman and Sons, 1923.

Taylor, Frederick W. *Shop Management.* New York: Harper & Row, 1903.

———. *The Principles of Scientific Management.* New York: Harper & Row, 1911.

Wrega, Charles D., and Anne Marie Stotka. "Cooke Creates a Classic: The Story behind F. W. Taylor's Principles of Scientific Management." *Academy of Management Review,* October 1978, pp. 736–49.

Wren, Daniel. *The Evolution of Management Thought.* New York: Ronald Press Company, 1972.

———. "Scientific Management in the U.S.S.R., with Particular Reference to the Contribution of Walter N. Polakov." *Academy of Management Review,* January 1980, pp. 1–12.

Case 2–1

Granddad's company

The J. R. V. Company, which manufactures industrial tools, was founded in 1905 by James R. Vail, Sr. Currently, James R. Vail, Jr., is the president of the company and his son Richard is executive vice president. James Jr., has run the company for the past 30 years in a fashion very similar to that of his father.

When the company was founded, James Sr. had been a big supporter of scientific management. He had organized the work very scientifically with the use of time and motion studies to determine the most efficient method of performing each job. As a result, most jobs at J. R. V. were highly specialized and utilized a high degree of division of labor. In addition, a great deal of emphasis has always been placed on putting people in jobs that were best suited for them and then providing adequate training. Most employees are paid on a piece-rate incentive system with the standards being set by time and motion studies. James Jr. has largely continued the emphasis on scientific management since he took over from James Sr. Currently all employees receive two weeks paid vacation and participate in a company insurance plan. In addition to these benefits, J. R. V. employees are generally considered to be paid an average wage for their industry. The present J. R. V. building was constructed in 1920 but has undergone several minor modifications, such as the addition of fluorescent lighting and an employees' lunchroom.

Recently James Jr., who is planning on retiring in a few years, and Richard, his planned successor, have had disagreements concerning the management of the company. Richard's primary argument is that times have changed and that time and motion studies, specialization, high division of labor, and other company policies are obsolete. On the other hand, James Jr. argues that J. R. V. has been successful under its present management philosophy for many years and to change would be "foolish."

1. Do you agree with Richard?
2. Are the principles of scientific management applicable in today's organizations?

Case 2–2

Return to scientific management

Recently, a professor at State University was lecturing in a management development seminar on the topic of motivation. Each of the participants candidly discussed problems that existed in their respective organizations. Problem areas mentioned included absenteeism, turnover, and poor workmanship. The participants managed a variety of workers such as automobile assembly workers, clerical workers, keypunch operators, sanitation workers, and even some middle-level managers.

During the discussion, one of the participants made the following statement: "What we need to stop all of these problems is a little scientific management."

1. What do you think the person means?
2. Do you agree? Discuss.
3. Take one of the jobs in the above case and show how you could apply scientific management.

3 The Manager as a Decision Maker

Objectives

1. To present several approaches to decision making and to relate these approaches to the job of the manager.
2. To introduce and discuss a general model for making managerial decisions.
3. To emphasize the role that values play in decision making.
4. To develop an appreciation for making decisions within an organizational context.

Chapter Outline

TYPES OF DECISIONS
- Programmed versus Nonprogrammed Decisions
- Organizational versus Personal Decisions

TIMING THE DECISION

THE INTUITIVE APPROACH TO DECISION MAKING

THE RATIONAL APPROACH TO DECISION MAKING
- Limitations of the Rational Approach

A SATISFICING APPROACH

CONDITIONS FOR MAKING DECISIONS
- Certainty
- Risk
- Uncertainty

THE ROLE OF VALUES IN DECISION MAKING

PARTICIPATION IN DECISION MAKING
- Group Decision Making
- A Model for Making Managerial Decisions

THE DECISION MAKER'S ENVIRONMENT

Glossary of Terms

Certainty situation Decision situation in which the decision maker knows the state of nature and can calculate exactly what will happen.

Decision making A process that involves searching the environment for conditions requiring a decision, developing and analyzing possible alternatives, and then selecting a particular alternative.

Intuitive approach to decision making Approach to making decisions based on hunches and intuition.

Level of aspiration The level of performance that a person expects or hopes to attain.

Optimizing The practice of selecting the best possible alternative.

Rational approach to decision making A structured approach to decision making that involves the following steps: recognize the need for a decision; establish, rank, and weight criteria; collect data; identify alternatives; evaluate alternatives; and make the final choice.

Risk situation Decision situation in which the decision maker has some information and can calculate probabilistic estimates concerning the outcome of each alternative.

Satisficing The practice of selecting the first alternative that meets the decision maker's minimum standard of satisfaction.

Uncertainty situation Decision situation in which the decision maker has no knowledge concerning the relative probabilities associated with the different possible outcomes.

Value Conception, explicit or implicit, defining what an individual or a group regards as desirable.

"Executive" derives from a Latin word meaning "to do," and the Oxford dictionary defines it in terms of "the action of carrying out or carrying into effect." Neither of these approaches would suggest that the main responsibility and function of the executive is to make decisions. Yet in modern business and industry this is precisely what is expected of him. He is rewarded and evaluated in terms of his success in making decisions.

*David W. Miller and Martin K. Starr**

Some authors use the term *decision maker* as if it were synonymous with manager. Although managers are decision makers, the converse is not necessarily true. Not all decision makers are managers. For example, a person sorting fruit or vegetables is required to make decisions, but not as a manager. However, all managers, regardless of their position in the organization, must make decisions in the pursuit of organizational objectives. In fact, decision making pervades all of the basic management functions: planning, controlling, organizing, staffing, and motivating. Although different types of decisions are required in performing the respective management functions, they all require decisions. Thus, in order for a manager to be a good planner, controller, organizer, staffer, and motivator, he or she must first be a good decision maker.

Herbert Simon, a Nobel prize winner, has described the manager's decision process in three stages: (1) intelligence, (2) design, and (3) choice.[1] The intelligence stage involves searching the environment for conditions requiring a decision. The design stage entails inventing, developing, and analyzing possible courses of action. The final stage, choice, refers to the actual selection of a particular course of action. Analyzing the decision process by stages emphasizes the difference between management and nonmanagement decisions. Nonmanagement decisions are concentrated in the last (choice) stage.

The fruit or vegetable sorter has only to make a choice as to the size or quality of the goods. Management decisions place greater emphasis on the intelligence and design stages. If the decision-making process is viewed as being composed only of the

*David W. Miller and Martin K. Starr, *Executive Decisions and Operations Research* (New York: Harper & Row, 1960), p. 10.

[1] Herbert A. Simon, *The New Science of Management Decision* (New York: Harper & Row, 1960), p. 2.

choice stage, then managers spend very little time making decisions. If, however, decision making is viewed as encompassing not only the actual choice but also the intelligence and design work necessary for making the choice, then managers spend most of their time making decisions.

TYPES OF DECISIONS

Programmed versus Nonprogrammed Decisions

Decisions are often classified as programmed or nonprogrammed. Programmed decisions are reached by following an established or systematic procedure. Normally, the decision maker is familiar with the situation surrounding a programmable decision. Routine and repetitive type decisions usually fall into this category. Managerial decisions covered by organizational policies, procedures, and rules are programmed in that preestablished guidelines must be followed in arriving at the decision.

Nonprogrammed decisions are unique and have little or no precedent. These decisions are relatively unstructured and generally require a more creative approach by the decision maker. When dealing with nonprogrammed decisions, the decision maker must develop the procedure to be used. Naturally, nonprogrammed decisions are generally more difficult to make than are programmed decisions. Deciding on a new product, selecting a new piece of equiment, or deciding on next year's objectives are all examples of nonprogrammed decisions.

It should be realized that both programmed and nonprogrammed decisions can have either major or minor consequences depending on the nature of the decisions. For example, many personnel-related decisions are programmed. However, a personnel-related decision involving disciplinary action could easily have major consequences. On the other hand, the nonprogrammed decision of deciding how to arrange your office furniture would probably have minor consequences.

Organizational versus Personal Decisions

Organizational decisions are those that managers make as a part of their organizational responsibilities. Organizational decisions ultimately relate to the organization's purposes and objectives. Personal decisions, on the other hand, are decisions that a manager makes that relate to individual goals. For example, a decision to leave one organization and join another would be a personal decision. Personal decisions may affect the organization and vice versa; however, the basis for making the decision determines whether the decision is organizational or personal. Personal decisions are made from the standpoint of the individual; organizational decisions are made from the standpoint of the organization.

TIMING THE DECISION

A prerequisite for properly timing a decision is recognizing the need for a decision. Recognizing the need to make a decision is not always easy. The manager may simply not be aware of what is going on, or the problem requiring a decision may be camouflaged. Once the need to make a decision is realized, the decision must be properly timed. Some managers always seem to make decisions on the spot, while others tend to take forever in deciding even a simple matter. Another familiar type of manager just seems to ignore the entire situation, acting as if it doesn't exist. The manager who takes pride in making quick decisions is also running the risk of making bad decisions. Failure to gather and evaluate available data, to consider people's feelings, and to anticipate the impact of the decision can result in a very quick but poor decision. Of course, the other extreme is just as risky—the manager who listens to problems and promises to get back to the employee but never does. Nearly as bad is the manager who gets back to the employee only after an inordinate amount of time. Other familiar types are: the manager who never seems to have adequate information to make a decision; the manager who frets and worries over even the simplest decisions; and the manager who refers everything to superiors.

Knowing when to make a decision is complicated by the fact that different decisions must be made within different time frames. For instance, a manager generally has more time in deciding on committee appointments than when deciding what to do when three employees call in sick. Unfortunately, no magic formula exists to tell managers when a decision should be made or how long it should take. The important thing is to develop an awareness for the importance of properly timing decisions.

THE INTUITIVE APPROACH TO DECISION MAKING

Chapter 1 addressed the question of whether management was an art or a science. When managers make decisions solely on hunches and intuition, they are practicing management as if it were wholly an art based primarily on feelings. Unfortunately, this happens in many situations. Managers sometimes become so emotionally attached to certain positions that almost nothing will change their minds. Under such circumstances, managers, develop the "don't bother me with the facts—my mind is made up" attitude. George

Odiorne has isolated the following emotional attachments which can adversely affect decision makers:

1. They fasten on the big lie and stick with it.
2. They are attracted to scandalous issues and heighten their significance.
3. They press every fact into a moral pattern.
4. They overlook everything except the immediately useful.
5. They have an affinity for romantic stories and find such information more significant than any other kind, including hard evidence.[2]

Such emotional attachments can be very real and can have serious consequences for the organization. They can lead to poor decisions. Emotional attachments most often affect managers or decision makers who are living in the past and either will not or cannot modernize. An example is the manager who insists on making decisions just as the founder of the company did 50 years ago.

Odiorne offers two suggestions for managers and decision makers engulfed by emotional attachments.[3] The first suggestion is for the decision maker to become aware of biases and make allowances for them. Undiscovered biases do the most damage. The second suggestion is for the decision maker to seek out independent opinions. It is always good practice to ask the opinion of some person who has no vested interest in the decision.

THE RATIONAL APPROACH TO DECISION MAKING

Fortunately, the physical sciences provide an alternative approach to decision making which is readily adaptable to management problems. The rational approach (sometimes called the scientific approach) to decision making is outlined in Figure 3–1.

Once the need for making the decision has been recognized, criteria must be established in terms of results that are expected from the decision. These criteria should then be ranked and weighted according to their relative importance.

Next, factual data relating to the decision should be collected. After the data have been collected, all alternatives that meet the criteria are identified. After all alternatives have been identified, each is then evaluated with respect to all the criteria. The final selection or choice is then made based on the alternative which

[2] George S. Odiorne, *Management and the Activity Trap* (New York: Harper & Row, 1974), pp. 128–29.

[3] Ibid., pp. 142–43.

FIGURE 3–1
The Rational Approach to Decision Making

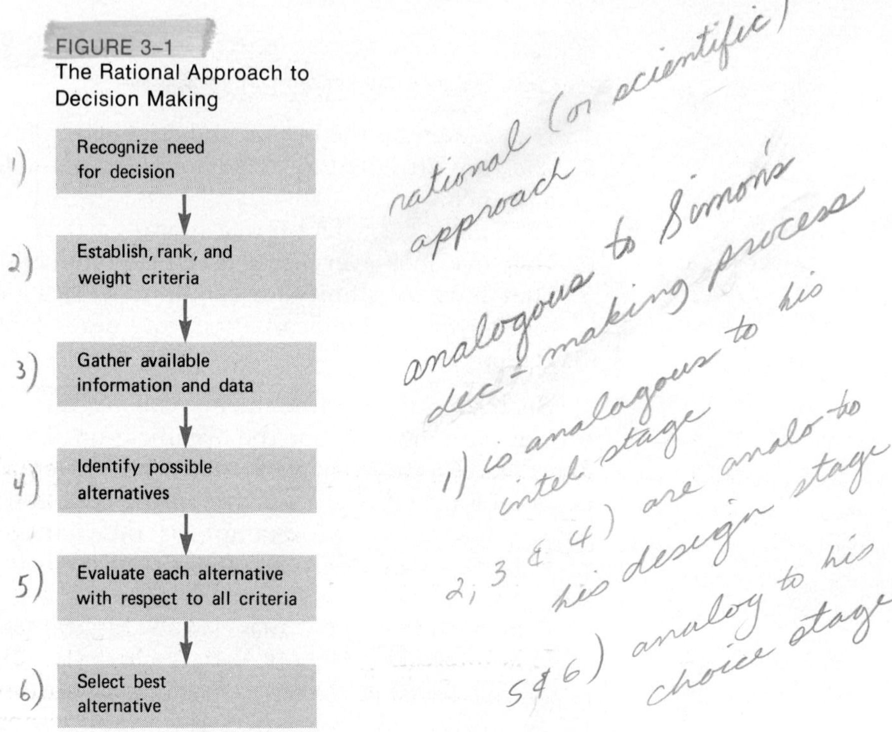
Recognize need for decision
Establish, rank, and weight criteria
Gather available information and data
Identify possible alternatives
Evaluate each alternative with respect to all criteria
Select best alternative

best meets the criteria. The following example illustrates the scientific approach to decision making.

Suppose Ms. Ryan, who is office manager for the TDY Company, is trying to reach a decision concerning the selection of a new supplier of office materials for her insurance business. The need for a new supplier has gradually become evident over the last six months. During this time, the present supplier has been late on deliveries with seven out of nine orders. After consulting with the members of the office staff, Ms. Ryan selected the following criteria for the decision: dependability, price, delivery time, location of the suppliers, and variety of products offered. After further consultation with her staff, Ms. Ryan establsihed the priorities, weights (or relative importance of each item), and limits for the criteria, as shown in Table 3–1.

After looking through the city directory and talking with the managers of the local Office Suppliers Association, Ms. Ryan identified the companies listed in Table 3–2 as possible candidates. After identifying the possible suppliers and collecting available data concerning these companies, Ms. Ryan evaluated each with respect to each criterion. Table 3–2 also shows the results of this evaluation using a scale of one (low) to nine (high).

TABLE 3–1
Priorities, Weights, and Limits of Office Supplier

Criteria	*Priority*	*Weight (1–5)*	*Limit, if any*
Dependability	1	5	—
Variety of products offered	2	4	A full line of products
Price	3	4	Competitive
Delivery time	4	2	Less than four weeks
Location of supplier	5	1	Have at least one branch in the city

The total for each line was found by multiplying each individual criterion evaluation by its respective weight and then summing all of these scores for the respective alternative.

Now that each alternative has been evaluated with regard to the criteria, it is evident that Ms. Ryan should select Acme Supply Company because it received the highest point total.

It is interesting to note that the first step of the scientific approach to decision making is analogous to Simon's intelligence stage; the next three steps of the scientific approach are analogous to Simon's design stage; and the final two steps are analogous to Simon's choice stage.

TABLE 3–2
Evaluation of Alternative Suppliers

Weight	*5*	*4*	*4*	*2*	*1*	*Total*
Criteria / Alternative	*Dependability*	*Variety of products*	*Price*	*Time to delivery*	*Location of supplier*	
Office Supply, Inc.	6	7	8	3	6	102
ABC Company	7	4	5	8	5	92
Acme Supply	9	3	9	8	5	114
University Supply	4	6	7	3	7	85
QTR Company	3	6	6	4	7	78

Limitations of the Rational Approach

While the rational approach to decision making is certainly an improvement over the intuitive approach, it is not without its problems and limitations.

The rational approach to decision making is based on the concept of the "economic man." The economic man concept postulates that people behave rationally and that their behavior is based on the following four major assumptions:

1. People have clearly defined criteria, and the relative weights which they assign to these criteria are stable.
2. People have knowledge of all relevant alternatives.
3. People have the ability to evaluate each alternative with respect to all the criteria and arrive at an overall rating for each alternative.
4. People have the self-discipline to choose the alternative which rates the highest (they will not manipulate the system).

In many instances, these assumptions are not very realistic. First, difficulties arise in setting decision objectives because the decision maker may not always know the criteria used in evaluating the decision. Factors considered important by the person making the decision may not be viewed as important by his or her superiors and subordinates. In the example of Ms. Ryan selecting a new office supplier, it is entirely possible that Ms. Ryan and her staff may not have been able to agree on the proper criteria for selecting a new supplier. Even if they could agree on the criteria, they might have disagreed on the priorities, weights, or limits. Just because Ms. Ryan has the authority to overrule her subordinates doesn't mean that the situation is simplified; they may very well try to undermine her decision at a later time.

Another problem is that most decisions are based on limited knowledge. In the example above, one or several alternatives could have been omitted due to a lack of knowledge (for instance, other suppliers who meet all the criteria may not even have been considered). Although most decisions are based on less than perfect information, in many situations a manager has very limited or no control over the information used to make the decision. Information over which the manager has no control might be generated by outside sources or even by a competitor. With new products or innovative ideas, information may be nonexistent. In such instances, the ability to evaluate each alternative and to reach the best decision may be hampered by a lack of information.

Probably the most difficult step in the decision process is the evaluation or the prediction of outcomes for the various alternatives. Even in the relatively simple example given earlier, it would be hard to evaluate accurately each criteria for each alternative.

Since the final selection is based on predicted outcomes, inaccurate predictions may lead to poor decisions. A final problem is the temptation to manipulate the information and choose a favored—but not necessarily the best—alternative. This temptation may come from within the decision maker or it may come from external forces. Again referring to the office supplies example, Ms. Ryan's staff might persuade her to select Office Supply, Inc., "just because they have the friendliest salesperson."

Because of the inherent limitations with the rational approach, it should be evident that most decisions, even when the rational approach is followed, still involve some degree of judgment. Thus, in making decisions, the manager generally uses a combination of science and art.

A SATISFICING APPROACH

Believing that the assumptions concerning the "economic man" are generally unrealistic, Herbert Simon developed the *principle of bounded rationality,* which states: The capacity of the human mind for formulating and solving complex problems is very small compared with the size of the problems whose solution is required for objectively rational behavior—or even for a reasonable approximation to such objective rationality.[4]

Thus, the principle of bounded rationality states that there are definite empirical limits to human rationality. As an outgrowth of the principle of bounded rationality, Simon has proposed a decision theory based on what he labeled the "administrative man." The administrative man theory is based on the following assumptions:

1. There are limitations to a person's knowledge of alternatives and criteria.
2. People act on the basis of a simplified, ill-structured, mental abstraction of the real world, and this abstraction is influenced by personal perceptions, biases, and so forth.
3. People do not attempt to optimize but will select the first alternative which satisfies their current level of aspiration. This is called *satisficing.*
4. An individual's level of aspiration concerning a decision fluctuates upward and downward depending on the values of the most recently found alternatives.

---

[4]Herbert A. Simon, *Model of Man* (New York: John Wiley & Sons, 1957), p. 198.

The first assumption is a synopsis of the principle of bounded rationality. The second assumption follows naturally from the first. If limits do exist to human rationality, then an individual must make decisions based on limited and incomplete knowledge. The third assumption also naturally follows from the first assumption. If the decision maker's knowledge of alternatives is incomplete, then the individual cannot optimize, only satisfice. Optimizing refers to the practice of selecting the best possible alternative; satisficing refers to the practice of selecting the first alternative that meets the decision maker's minimum standard of satisfaction. Assumption four is based on the belief that the criteria for a satisfactory alternative is determined by the current level of aspiration. The level of aspiration refers to the level of performance that a person expects to attain and is determined by the person's prior successes and failures.

Figure 3–2 represents the satisficing approach to decision making. If the decision maker is satisfied that an acceptable alternative has been found, that alternative is selected. Otherwise, the decision maker searches for an additional alternative. In the office supplier example, the office manager would select the first satisfactory supplier rather than looking at all possibilities. If an additional alternative is required, its value to the decision maker is evaluated. This evaluation is influenced by the value of the previous best alternative and by the current level of aspiration. In the office supplier example, the last supplier used and the last one

FIGURE 3–2
Model of the Satisficing Approach

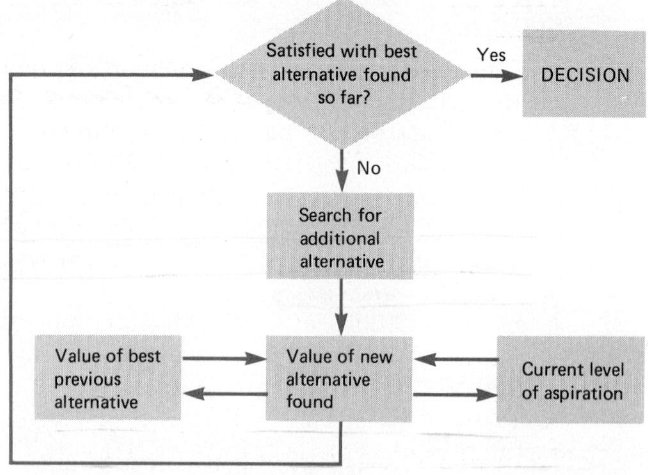

Source: Adapted from James G. March and Herbert A. Simon, *Organizations* (New York: John Wiley & Sons, 1958), p. 49.

considered for use would both influence the office manager's evaluation of a new supplier.

In Figure 3–2 the double arrows indicate a two-way relationship; that is, the value of the new alternative is influenced by the value of the previous best alternative, and the value of the best previous alternative is, in turn, influenced by the value of the new alternative. As indicated by the arrows, a similar two-way relationship exists between the value of the new alternative and the current level of aspiration. The net result of this evaluation determines whether or not the decision maker is satisfied with the alternative. Thus, the administrative man selects the first alternative that meets the minimum satisfaction criteria and makes no real attempt to optimize.

CONDITIONS FOR MAKING DECISIONS

Regardless of the approach used, decisions are not always made under the same conditions with regard to the amount of information available. The best decision is often dependent on what happens at a later point in time. Take for instance the simple decision of whether or not to take an umbrella when going outside. The more desirable alternative is determined by whether or not it rains, and this is something that is not under the control of the decision maker.

Table 3–3 represents the various combinations of alternatives and states of nature with their respective outcomes for the individual who is going outside and trying to decide whether or not to take an umbrella.

TABLE 3–3
Alternatives and States of Nature

Alternative	*State of nature*	
	No rain	*Rain*
Take umbrella	Dry, but inconvenient	Dry
Do not take umbrella	Dry	Wet

Certainty

Knowing exactly what will happen places the decision maker in a situation of certainty. In a situation of certainty the decision maker can often calculate the precise outcome associated with each alternative. Referring to the previous example, if it is rain-ing when the person goes out, the person knows the state of nature and therefore knows the most desirable alternative (take an umbrella).

Risk

Unfortunately, the state of nature is not always known in advance. The decision maker can often obtain, at some cost, information relating to the state of nature. The desirability of obtaining the information is determined by weighing the costs of obtaining the information against the value of the information. A decision maker is operating in a situation of risk if the relative probabilities associated with each state of nature are known. Again referring to the previous umbrella example, the decision maker is operating in a situation of risk if the weather forecaster has said there is a 40 percent chance of rain.

For most practical problems, the precise probabilities of the various states of nature are not known. However, reasonably accurate probabilities based on historical data and past experiences can often be calculated. When no historical data exists, it is difficult to estimate probabilities. One approach taken in such circumstances is to survey individual opinions.

When making decisions in conditions of risk, expected value analysis can be used to assist the decision maker. By using expected value analysis, the expected payoff of an act can be mathematically calculated. One shortcoming of expected value analysis is that it represents the average outcome if the event is repeated a large number of times. Such an approach is of little help if the act only takes place once rather than a large number of times. For example, airplane passengers are not interested in the average fatality rates, but rather are interested in what happens on their particular flight. Appendix A at the end of this book contains a more detailed explanation of expected value analysis.

Uncertainty

When decision makers have no knowledge of the relative probabilities associated with the respective states of nature, they are operating in a situation of uncertainty. For example, if a person taking a trip to New York has never been there before and has not heard a weather forecast concerning New York, the individual would have no knowledge about the likelihood of rain and, hence, whether or not to carry an umbrella.

If the decision maker has little or no knowledge about which state of nature will occur, one of three basic approaches to making a decision may be taken. The first approach is to choose the alternative whose best possible outcome is the best of all possible outcomes for all alternatives. This is an optimistic or gambling approach (sometimes called the maximax approach). Referring to the umbrella example, a decision maker using this approach would not take the umbrella since the best possible outcome is no rain and no umbrella.

A second approach to dealing with uncertainty is to compare the worst possible outcomes of each of the alternatives and select the alternative whose worst possible outcome is least bad. This is a pessimistic approach (sometimes called the maximin approach). Using the umbrella example, the decision maker would compare the worst possible outcome of taking an umbrella to that of not taking an umbrella. The decision maker would then decide to take an umbrella, since it is better to carry an unneeded umbrella than to get wet.

The final approach is to choose the alternative which has the least variation among its possible outcomes. This is a risk-averting approach and makes for more effective planning. If the decision maker chooses not to take an umbrella, the outcomes can vary from staying dry to getting wet. By choosing to take an umbrella, the outcomes can vary from being dry, but inconvenienced to dry. Thus, the risk-averting decision maker would take an umbrella to be sure of staying dry. Figure 3–3 summarizes the different approaches to making a decision under conditions of uncertainty.

FIGURE 3–3
Possible Approaches to Making Decisions under Uncertainty

Approach	*How it works*	*Related to the umbrella example*
Optimistic or gambling approach (maximax)	Choose the alternative whose best possible outcome is the best of all possible outcomes for all alternatives.	Do not take umbrella.
Pessimistic approach (maximin)	Compare the worst possible outcomes of each of the alternatives and select the alternative whose worst possible outcome is least bad.	Take umbrella.
Risk-averting approach	Choose the alternative which has the least variation among its possible alternatives.	Take umbrella.

MANAGEMENT IN PRACTICE

"There Was No Other Way"

Back in 1978 Chairman Orin E. Atkins of Kentucky's $8.1 billion (sales) Ashland Oil sold most of the company's crude oil producing reserves and some chemical businesses for $1.2 billion. Since then, with crude oil prices up from $13 to $38 a barrel, those assets may have risen in value to $1.7 billion. Did Atkins make a $500 million blunder?

"We had to do it," he replies. "We didn't have a choice." Ashland didn't have enough crude to become a full-fledge independent or enough cash and talent to become a major. That's obvious when one considers that in 1978 Ashland had to buy 335,000 barrels of oil per day on the open market as against the 23,000 produced from its own resources. And while Ashland had a cash flow of $460 million in 1978 and assets of $2.9 billion that's still far too little to play in the same league with $52 billion (revenues) Texaco, let alone $110 billion (revenues) Exxon.

What Atkins now says is that Ashland had to sell because of more pressing financial reasons. "If we hadn't sold out then, we'd be in serious financial trouble now," he says. "Our situation was untenable although we didn't admit it at the time. In 1978 Ashland had committed itself to spend $393 million more than it could earn over the next three years." It would have had to borrow to close the gap. "That would have sent our debt-equity ratio from 36 percent to 49 percent."

Certainly Ashland's debt, including lease obligations, was then $935 million, precariously supported by shareholders' funds of $1 billion—the highest in the petroleum industry at the time. "Our debt facility had been pushed to the limit of an A rating on our bonds," he says. "Losing that rating would have materially increased the cost of capital." How did Ashland get itself into that situation? "Unfortunately our production operation had developed a major-company complex. It was attempting to emulate the majors. We spent a tremendous amount of money with absolutely no results." In fact, Ashland spent $365 million in five years up to 1978 but added no oil or gas reserves at all.

With some of the proceeds of the sale, Atkins cut Ashland's debt-to-equity ratio to 25 percent or 20 percent. He also spent $565 million buying up 42 percent of Ashland's own stock. He claims it was the biggest corporate stock repurchase ever. Says Atkins, "By retiring our stock we guaranteed earnings improvement while we were attempting to restructure. It was more of a financial exercise than a business exercise, but the result is the same." There was another probable reason: A $1.2 billion cash hoard is a magnet for predators. By reducing Ashland's float he made the company less vulnerable to takeover. In 1980, without its oil properties, Ashland had operating earnings of $6.49 a share versus $3.52 in 1978, when it still owned them.

After the oil and gas divestitures, Ashland was left with a major independent refining and marketing operation, and substantial coal holdings and chemicals. It was still a big company: Revenues last year were $8.1 billion. The trouble was that Atkins was left with the least profitable part of the oil industry and the part most vulnerable to a supply glut: While crude prices are kept high by OPEC fiat, there is no floor under the prices of refined products. Thus, Ashland barely broke even in the first quarter of 1981. "We expected the decline in profitability, but we didn't expect it to be as precipitous as it has been," Atkins concedes.

Trouble is, U.S. oil consumption dropped 8 percent last year, pulling refining capacity usage down from over 90 percent in 1979 to 70 percent in 1980. Oil in the ground, however, has appreciated. Atkins: "The way I like to think of it is we traded oil and gas properties for the company's common stocks." Fair enough, but the trick now is to show he can get better earnings out of the remaining assets.

High among those assets was nearly $650 million in cash left over from the oil and gas sales. Much depended on how he used that money. Certainly the $243 million spent on $612 million (revenues) U.S. Filter, a maker of pollution-control equipment, looks sensible. So does the $252 million purchase of the $226 million (revenues) Integon Corp. insurance business with its healthy cash flow. Ashland has also plowed $150 million into a refining process that gets more gasoline from a barrel of crude. Says Atkins, "We would much prefer to do something on a larger scale, but acquisitions are not like buying neckties."

His current aim: "Our basic objective is to reduce earnings from petroleum to one third of our total [versus four fifths now] in the next three to five years. We want to expand in the entire financial services area and in high technology like software computer services." Ashland Oil—a sixties-type conglomerate? "Look, every business is a conglomerate," laughs Atkins.

Has it all been worth it? Says Atkins, "There is no question that if we had held those [oil and gas] assets we could have got more for them." But then, he adds sheepishly, "We simply had no choice."

Source: Reprinted by permission from Maurice Barnfather, *Forbes* Magazine, March 30, 1981, p. 41. Copyright 1981, Forbes, Inc.

The specific approach used by the decision maker under conditions of uncertainty is contingent on the individual's aversion to risk and the consequences of making a bad decision.

THE ROLE OF VALUES IN DECISION MAKING

A value is a conception, explicit or implicit, defining what an individual or group regards as desirable.[5] Values play an important role in the decision-making process. People are not born with values but acquire and develop them early in life. Parents, teachers, relatives, and others influence an individual's values. As a result, every manager and employee brings a certain set of values to the workplace.

A person's values have an impact on the selection of performance measures, alternatives, and choice criteria in the decision

[5] William D. Guth and Renato Tagiuri, "Personal Values and Corporate Strategy," *Harvard Business Review*, September–October 1965, pp. 124–25.

process. Differences in values often account for the use of different performance measures. For example, a manager primarily concerned with economic values would probably measure performance differently from a manager primarily concerned with social values. The former might measure performance strictly on profit where the latter might be more concerned with customer complaints. Differences in values might also cause decision makers to generate different alternatives. A viable alternative to one person might be completely unacceptable to another because of differences in values. Because the final choice criteria depend on the performance measures used, they are also affected by values.

FIGURE 3–4
England's Major Categories of Values

The pragmatic mode—Suggests that an individual has an evaluative framework that is primarily guided by success-failure considerations.

The ethical-moral mode—Implies an evaluative framework consisting of ethical considerations influencing behavior toward actions and decisions which are judged to be right and away from those judged to be wrong.

The affect or feeling mode—Suggests an evaluative framework which is guided by hedonism. One behaves in ways that increase pleasure and decrease pain.

Professor George England, who has conducted very extensive research on the role that values play in the decision-making process, has identified three major categories of values (see Figure 3–4).[6] In summarizing his research, Professor England reported the following:

1. There are large individual differences in personal values within every group studied. Among managers in the different countries studied, some have a pragmatic orientation, some have an ethical-moral orientation, and some have an affect or feeling orientation. Some managers have a very small set of values, while others have a large set and seem to be influenced by many strongly-held values.

2. Personal value systems of managers are relatively stable and do not change rapidly. Edward Lusk and Bruce Oliver repeated one of England's earlier studies and reported that values of managers had changed very little between 1966 and 1972.[7]

---

[6] George England, "Personal Value Systems of Managers and Administrators," *Academy of Management Proceedings*, August 1973, pp. 81–94.

[7] Edward J. Lusk and Bruce L. Oliver, "American Managers' Personal Value Systems Revisited," *Academy of Management Journal*, September 1974, p. 549–54.

3. Personal value systems of managers are related to and/or influence the way managers make decisions. Those who have profit maximization as an important goal are less willing to spend money on cafeteria and rest room facility improvements than those who do not have profit maximization as an important value.

4. Personal value systems of managers are related to their career success as managers. With regard to American managers, it was found that successful managers favor pragmatic, dynamic, achievement-oriented values while less successful managers prefer more static and passive values.

5. There are differences in the personal values of managers working in different organizational contexts. For example, in the United States the personal values of managers were found to be different from those of labor leaders.

6. There are both differences and similarities in the value systems of managers in the different countries studied.[8]

The work of England and others clearly establishes the importance that values play in the decision-making process of managers. In order to make sound decisions, today's managers must be aware not only of their own values but also those of the other members of the organization. Closely related to values is the topic of business ethics. Business ethics is a topic discussed at length in Chapter 21.

PARTICIPATION IN DECISION MAKING

Most managers have opportunities to involve their subordinates and others in the decision-making process. One pertinent question is: "Do groups make better decisions than individuals?" Another is "When should subordinates be involved in making managerial decisions?"

Group Decision Making

Everyone is familiar with the old axiom that two heads are better than one. Empirical evidence generally supports this view, with a few minor qualifications. It has been found that group performance is frequently better than that of the average group member.[9] It has also been found that groups take longer to solve prob-

[8] England, "Personal Value Systems," pp. 82–87.

[9] I. Lorge et al., "A Survey of Studies Contrasting the Quality of Group Performance and Individual Performance, 1930–1957," *Psychological Bulletin*, November 1958, pp. 337–72; and Ross A. Weber, "The Relation of Group Performance to the Age of Members in Homogeneous Groups," *Academy of Management Journal*, September 1974, pp. 570–74.

lems than does the average individual.[10] Thus, group decisions are generally advantageous in situations where avoiding mistakes is of greater importance than speed.

Group performance is generally superior to that of the average group member for two basic reasons. First, the sum total of the group's knowledge is greater and, secondly, the group possesses a much wider range of alternatives in the decision process.

Group decision making also has other benefits. Participation in the decision-making process increases acceptance of the decision by group members and decreases the problem of persuading the group to accept the decision. This is especially true when change is being implemented in an organization. A more complete understanding of not only the decision but also the alternatives that were considered results from group decision making. This is especially helpful when the individuals who must implement the decision participate in the decision process.

However, some potential drawbacks can drastically limit the effectiveness of group decision making. One individual may dominate or control the group. This situation occurs frequently when the president or other "higher-ups" in the organization participate in the decision process. Because of their presence, many members become inhibited. The social pressures of conformity can also inhibit group members.

Competition can develop within the group to such an extent that winning an issue becomes more important than the issue itself. A final hazard results from the dynamics involved in group decision making. Groups can tend to accept the first potentially positive solution and give little attention to other solutions.

One additional interesting characteristic of group decision making concerns the risk that individuals are willing to take alone as compared with the risk taken by the same individuals in a group. Laboratory experiments have shown that decisions taken on a unanimous group basis are consistently more risky than the average of the individual decisions.[11] This is somewhat surprising in view of the fact that group pressures often inhibit the members. One possible explanation is that individuals feel less responsible for the outcome of a group decision than when acting alone.

[10] M. E. Shaw, "A Comparison of Individuals and Small Groups in the Rational Solution of Complex Problems," *American Journal of Psychology*, July 1932, pp. 491–504; and I. Lorge et al., "A Survey of Studies."

[11] M. Wallach, N. Kogan, and D. J. Bem, "Group Influence on Individual Risk Taking," *Journal of Abnormal and Social Psychology*, August 1962, pp. 75–86; and N. Kogan and M. Wallach, "Risk Taking as a Function of the Situation, the Person, and the Group," in *New Directions of Psychology*, vol. 3 ed. G. Mardler (New York: Holt, Rinehart & Winston, 1967).

FIGURE 3–5
Positive and Negative Aspects of Group Decision Making

Positive aspects of group decision making:
1. The sum total of the group's knowledge is greater.
2. The group possesses a much wider range of alternatives in the decision process.
3. Participation in the decision-making process increases the acceptance of the decision by group members.
4. Group members better understand the decision and the alternatives considered.

Negative aspects of group decision making:
1. One individual may dominate and/or control the group.
2. Social pressures to conform can inhibit group members.
3. Competition can develop to such an extent that winning becomes more important than the issue itself.
4. Groups have a tendency to accept the first potentially positive solution while giving little attention to other possible solutions.

Figure 3–5 summarizes the positive and negative aspects of group decision making. Committees, which are a form of group decision making, are discussed at length in Chapter 8.

A Model for Making Managerial Decisions

One key to making effective managerial decisions is the ability of the manager to select the appropriate decision-making style for each decision that is faced. Research and practice have demonstrated that no single style of decision making works best in all situations. Successful managers learn to match the appropriate decision-making style with the situation.

Victor Vroom and Philip Yetton have addressed the problem and have suggested a very practical and useful model.[12] In their work Vroom and Yetton developed the set of alternative decision styles shown in Table 3–4. Each style is represented by a code that is used to refer to each respective process. Each successive style is increasingly more participative: style AI involves no subordinate participation, whereas style GII is almost totally participative.

Vroom and Yettan selected three variables as having a significant bearing on the appropriateness of a given decision-making style: (1) the quality or rationality of the decision; (2) the accep-

[12] Victor H. Vroom, "A New Look at Managerial Decision Making," *Organizational Dynamics*, Spring 1973, pp. 66–80; and Victor H. Vroom and Philip W. Yetton, *Leadership and Decision-Making* (Pittsburg: University of Pittsburgh Press, 1973).

TABLE 3–4
Types of Management Decision Styles

AI:	You solve the problem or make the decision yourself, using information available to you at that time.
AII:	You obtain the necessary information from your subordinate(s), then decide on the solution to the problem yourself. You may or may not tell your subordinates what the problem is while getting the information from them. The role played by your subordinates in making the decision is clearly one of providing the necessary information to you, rather than generating or evaluating alternative solutions.
CI:	You share the problem with your subordinates as a group, collectively obtaining their ideas and suggestions. Then you make a decision that may or may not reflect your subordinates' influence.
GII:	You share a problem with your subordinates as a group. Together you generate and evaluate alternatives and attempt to reach agreement (consensus) on a solution. Your role is much like that of chairperson. You do not try to influence the group to adopt your solution and you are willing to accept and implement any solution that has the support of the entire group.

Source: Victor Vroom, "A New Look at Managerial Decision Making," *Organizational Dynamics*, Spring 1973.

tance or commitment on the part of subordinates to execute the decision effectively; and (3) the amount of time required to make the decision.

Figure 3–6 shows Vroom and Yetton's model expressed in the form of a decision tree. The particular problem attributes are shown across the top of the figure. To use the decision model for a particular decision situation, start at the left-hand side and work toward the right until a terminal node is reached. When more than one decision-making style is feasible, this model chooses the style requiring the least amount of time.

Vroom and Yetton found that in actual practice most managers do use different decision-making styles in different situations. They also found that managers are much more likely to violate decision rules dealing with acceptance or commitment of the decision than they are to violate decision rules designed to protect the quality or rationality of the decision. One might then conclude that decisions made by typical managers are more likely to prove ineffective due to a lack of acceptance by subordinates than to the quality of the decision. Similarly, managers who learn what decision styles work best in what situations are usually going to make better decisions than those that don't.

Vroom and Yetton Decision Model

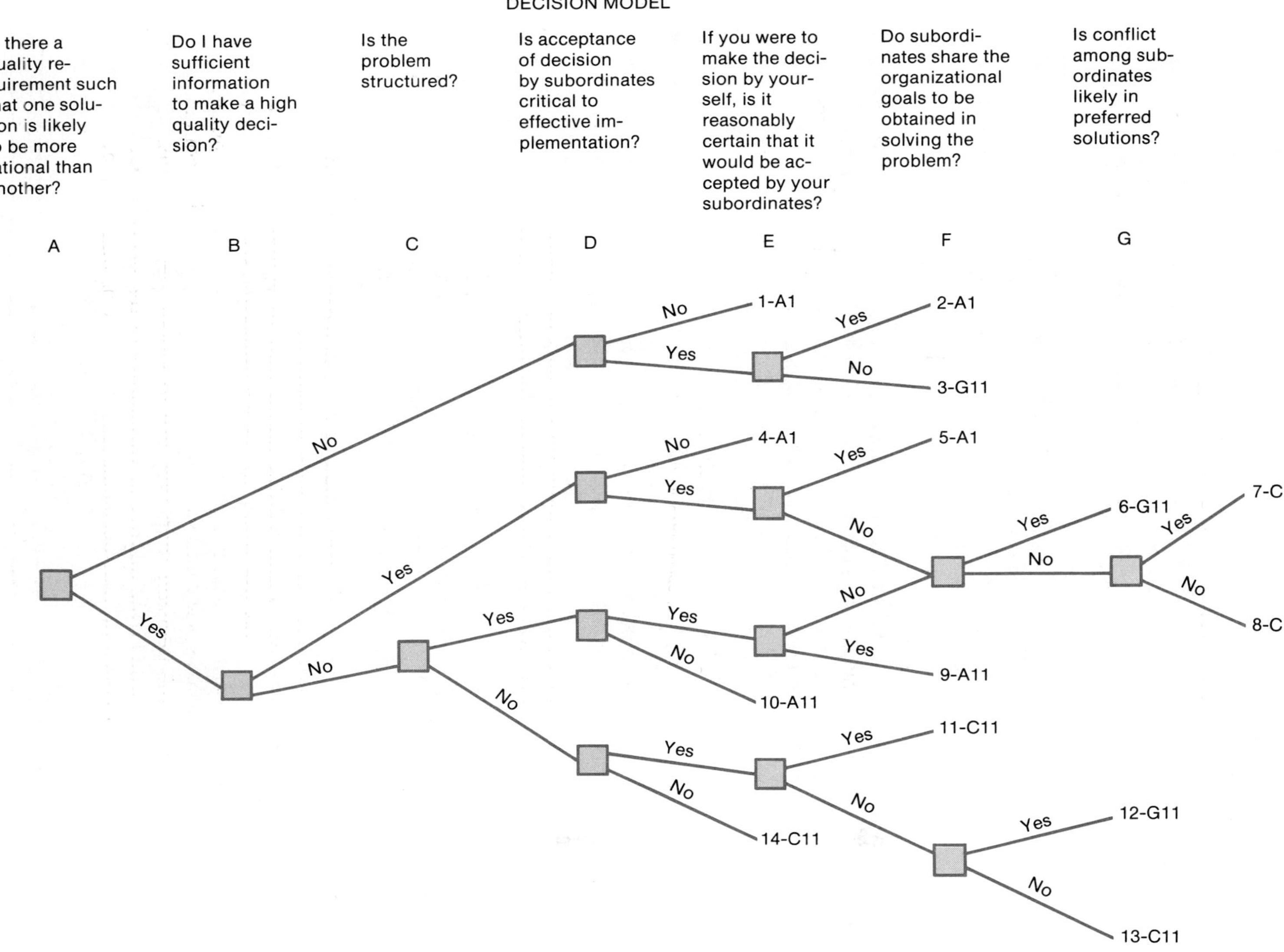
DECISION MODEL
Is there a quality requirement such that one solution is likely to be more rational than another?
Do I have sufficient information to make a high quality decision?
Is the problem structured?
Is acceptance of decision by subordinates critical to effective implementation?
If you were to make the decision by yourself, is it reasonably certain that it would be accepted by your subordinates?
Do subordinates share the organizational goals to be obtained in solving the problem?
Is conflict among subordinates likely in preferred solutions?
A
B
C
D
E
F
G
Yes
No
1-A1
2-A1
3-G11
4-A1
5-A1
6-G11
7-C
8-C
9-A11
10-A11
11-C11
12-G11
13-C11
14-C11

Source: Victor Vroom, "A New Look at Managerial Decision Making," *Organizational Dynamics*, Spring 1973.

THE DECISION MAKER'S ENVIRONMENT

In addition to the specific situational factors considered by the Vroom and Yetton model, a decision maker's style is often influenced by the environment. This environment includes the organization itself, groups within the organization, and individuals within the organization.

The freedom which a manager has in making a decision depends to a large extent on the manager's position within the organization and the organization structure. In general, higher-level managers have more flexibility and discretion in making decisions. The patterns of authority outlined by the formal organization structure also influence the flexibility afforded the decision maker.

Another important factor which influences decision-making style is the purpose and tradition of the organization. For example, a military organization requires a different style of decision making than does a volunteer organization.

The formal and informal group structures within the organization affect decision-making styles. These groups may range from labor unions to advisory councils.

A final subset of the environment includes all the decision maker's superiors and subordinates. The personalities, backgrounds, and expectations of these individuals influence the decision maker. Figure 3–7 summarizes the major environmental factors that affect the decision maker in an organization.

Thus, successful managers must develop an appreciation for the different environmental forces that influence them and that are in turn influenced by their decisions. They must develop a

FIGURE 3–7
Environmental Factors Influencing Decision Making in an Organization

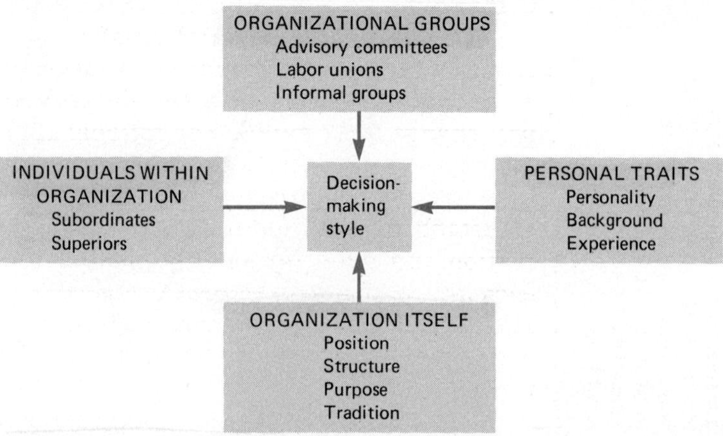

multilevel perspective (organization, group, and individual) toward decision making. To continually view decisions from a single-level perspective, whether it be from the organization's perspective, a group perspective, or the individual's perspective, will not result in optimal decisions. Managers who view decisions only from the organizational perspective, with no appreciation for the groups and individuals making up the organization, will eventually experience behavioral problems. "Country club" managers, who are concerned only about their employees and neglect the organization's objectives in their decisions, will probably not keep their jobs. The same is true of managers who become overly concerned with organizational groups and neglect either the individual's or the organization's objectives. The key to good decision making is a balanced multilevel perspective and the ability to match the decision situation with the appropriate decision making style.

SUMMARY

Decision making pervades all management functions, and therefore all managers are decision makers. Decision making is a process that involves searching the environment for conditions requiring a decision, developing and analyzing possible alternatives, and then selecting a particular alternative.

Programmed decisions are reached by following an established or systematic procedure. Nonprogrammed decisions are unique and have little or no precedent. Organizational decisions are those that managers make in carrying out their organizational responsibilities. Properly timing a decision is a major requirement for its success. Knowing when to make a decision is complicated by the fact that different decisions must be made within different time frames.

There are many potential pitfalls associated with making decisions strictly from intuition. Decision makers can become so emotionally attached to a certain position that almost nothing will change their minds. The rational approach to decision making provides a structured method for making decisions. The steps in the rational approach are: (1) recognize the need for a decision; (2) establish, rank, and weight criteria; (3) gather available information and data; (4) identify possible alternatives; (5) evaluate each alternative with respect to all criteria; and (6) select the best alternative. However, the rational approach also has certain inherent weaknesses because of its reliance on the "economic man" concept.

The satisficing approach to decision making is based on Herbert Simon's principle of bounded rationality, which states that there are empirical limits to a person's rationality. The basic premise of this theory is that a person does not attempt to optimize in the decision process but rather selects the first alternative that satisfies.

The state of nature coupled with the chosen alternative determine the outcome of a decision. Conditions of certainty exist when the state of nature is known. A situation of risk exists when the relative probabilities of the various states of nature are known. Conditions of uncertainty exist when nothing is known concerning the probabilities of the various states of nature. The personal value systems of managers also play an important role in the decision-making process.

Groups can be effective decision-making bodies and are especially advantageous in situations where avoiding mistakes is of greater importance than speed. Victor Vroom and Philip Yetton have developed a very practical model for matching decision-making style to the decision situation. Their model is based on the fact that different decision-making styles work best in different decision situations. In addition to the specific situational factors considered by the Vroom and Yetton model, a decision maker's style is often influenced by his or her environment. This environment includes the organization itself, groups within the organization, and individuals within the organization. Successful managers develop a multilevel perspective toward decision making. This multilevel perspective includes the ability to evaluate a decision from an organizational, group, and individual perspective.

REVIEW QUESTIONS

1. What are three stages in the decision-making process?
2. What are the differences between programmed and nonprogrammed decisions? Between organizational and personal decisions?
3. Describe the intuitive approach to decision making.
4. Describe the rational approach to decision making.
5. What criticisms can be made concerning the rational approach to decision making?
6. Describe the satisficing approach to decision making.
7. What is the difference between satisficing and optimizing?
8. What are values? Is there any relationship between values and managerial success?
9. Distinguish between the decision situations of certainty, risk, and uncertainty.

10. Describe some positive and negative aspects of group decision making.
11. According to Vroom and Yetton what three variables have a significant bearing on the appropriateness of a given decision-making style?

DISCUSSION QUESTIONS

1. Do you subscribe to the belief that many managers only attempt to satisfice rather than optimize in making decisions? Support your answer with examples.
2. Specifically, how can managers' values affect their decisions?
3. What factors do you think affect the amount of risk that a manager is willing to take when making a decision?
4. Comment on the following statement: "Groups always make better decisions than individuals acting alone."
5. How does decision making within an organization differ from individual or personal decision making? Support your answer with examples.

SELECTED READINGS

Cooper, M. R., and M. T. Wood. "Effects of Member Participation and Commitment in Group Decision Making on Influencing Satisfaction and Decision Riskiness." *Journal of Applied Psychology,* no. 2 (1974), pp. 127–34.

Edwards, M. O. "Solving Problems Creatively." *Systems and Procedures Journal,* January–February 1966, pp. 16–24.

England, George. "Personal Value Systems of Managers and Administrators." *Academy of Management Proceedings,* August 1973, pp. 81–94.

Guth, W. D., and R. Tagiuri. "Personal Values and Corporate Strategy." *Harvard Business Review,* September–October 1965, pp. 123–32.

Hall, J. "Decisions, Decisions, Decisions." *Psychology Today,* November 1971, p. 51.

Kelley, George. "Seducing the Elites: The Politics of Decision Making and Innovation in Organizational Networks." *The Academy of Management Review,* July 1976, pp. 66–74.

Kepner, Charles J., and Benjamin B. Tregoe. *The Rational Manager.* New York: McGraw-Hill, 1965.

Marquis, D. G. "Individual and Group Decisions Involving Risk." *Industrial Management Review,* Spring 1968, pp. 69–75.

Odiorne, George S. *Management and the Activity Trap.* New York: Harper & Row, 1974, pp. 127–43.

Peterson, Richard B. "A Cross-Cultural Perspective of Supervisory Values." *Academy of Management Journal,* March 1972, pp. 105–17.

Radford, K. J. *Management Decision Making.* Reston, Va.: Reston Publishing, 1975.

Roach, John M. "Simon Says: Decision Making Is a Satisficing Experience." *Management Review,* January 1979, pp. 8–17.

Shull, F. A. *Organizational Decision Making.* New York: McGraw-Hill, 1970.

———. "Theories of Decision Making in Economics and Behavioral Science." *American Economic Review,* 1959, pp. 253–83.

Simon, H. A. *The New Science of Management Decision.* New York: Harper & Row, 1960.

Vroom, Victor. "A New Look at Managerial Decision Making," *Organizational Dynamics,* Spring 1973, pp. 66–80.

Case 3–1

Getting out of the army

Jay Abbott is confident that his future will be secure and financially rewarding should he decide to remain in the army. He entered the army more than 10 years ago as a commissioned officer after completing his college education on an ROTC scholarship. Jay, who is 31 years old, has progressed to the grade of captain and is currently being considered for promotion to major. He has no reason to believe he will not be promoted to the grade of major. He has been successful in all of his appointments, is well liked by everyone—his peers, superiors, and subordinates—and has an unblemished record.

However, upon reaching the 10-year mark, Jay had second thoughts regarding whether he should stay in or leave the army, and has been thinking about leaving ever since. He has felt increasingly resentful that the army has affected a large part of his personal life. Although he had always preferred to wear his hair shorter than that of most young men, he resented the fact that even if he wanted to let it grow out or have sideburns, he couldn't do it. It was the principle of the whole idea—the intrusion of the army into his personal life. The fact that this intrusion extended beyond himself, to the behavior of his wife and children, bothered him even more.

Jay's wife, Ellen, was finishing up her master's thesis. This took up a substantial portion of her free time; yet her lack of involvement in the officers' clubs was inevitably frowned upon. There was just no such thing as a private family life in his position. He didn't even have much time to spend with the family. His job required long hours of work, including weekend duty, which left little time for his wife and two daughters, aged seven and nine. Another problem constantly on his mind was the fact that Ellen, holding a degree in design engineering, was unable to pursue any kind of real career—something that was important to both of them.

These thoughts raced through Jay's mind over and over again as he tried to decide what would be best for him and his family. There were a lot of positive factors about the army, he kept reminding himself: he was already earning $21,000 a year, and with his near-certain promotion, this would be raised to $25,000. He could not forget the fact that he was being recommended for the Army's Command and General Staff College. There was little chance he would not be approved, and upon completing the program, his future would be even brighter. If he stayed, he'd be able to retire in just 10 more years (at age 41) with a permanent retirement income of half his final salary plus free medical and dental coverage. By then, he figured he would probably be a lieutenant colonel with a base pay of around $37,000; at worst he would retire a major. At 41, there would be plenty of time to devote to a second career should he so desire.

But then, Jay could argue that regardless of how attractive the benefits seemed, it was a fact that salaries in the armed services had not kept pace with the rising rate of inflation: Congress had held the lid on raises at five percent. Furthermore, he did not anticipate any change in their posture in the next few years. In fact, Jay had read several newspaper articles indicating that Congress was considering reducing benefits for the armed services—the 20-year retirement specifically.

Jay had done some checking around and learned that the training and experience received in the army was valuable to civilian employers. Having been commissioned in the signal corps, he had vast experience in the area of telecommunications. He had recently completed a tour as an instructor in a service school. He had also been in many positions of leadership during his term in the army. At 31, he probably had more firsthand managerial experience than most civilian managers. He knew that large organizations were currently hiring young ex-military officers at salaries of $5,000 higher than recent college graduates.

Jay knew he had to make a decision soon. The closer he got to the 20-year mark, the more he stood to lose by leaving the army. He knew that if he was going to make a change, it had to be soon.

1. What should Jay do?
2. What factors should be considered in Jay's decision?
3. What role would values play in Jay's decision?

Case 3–2

Going abroad*

You are supervising the work of 12 engineers. Their formal training and work experience are very similar, permitting you to use them interchangeably on projects. Yesterday, your manager informed you that a request had been received from an overseas affiliate for four engineers to go abroad on extended loan for a period of six to eight months. For a number of reasons, he argued and you agreed that this request should be met from your group.

All your engineers are capable of handling this assignment and, from the standpoint of present and future projects, there is no particular reason why any one engineer should be retained over any other. The problem is somewhat complicated by the fact that the overseas assignment is in what is generally regarded as an undesirable location.

1. How would you select who should go abroad on extended loan?
2. Analyze this situation using the Vroom and Yetton model.

*This case is from Victor Vroom, "A New Look at Managerial Decision Making," *Organizational Dynamics*, Spring 1973. © 1973 by AMACOM, a division of American Management Associations, p. 73. Reprinted by permission of the publisher. All rights reserved.

SECTION ONE
CASE

Burred panels *

The Afco plant manufactures quarter panels—the body parts that cover the front quarters of a car, including the wheels. The quarter panel is the successor to the fender and is the part most often damaged in collisions in traffic accidents. This plant has 3,000 employees and makes not only quarter panels but many other smaller parts and components for two of the models sold by one of the Big Three auto companies.

The panels are made on four separate production lines, each line headed by a huge hydraulic press that stamps the panels out of short-steel blanks. When the flat steel arrives at the plant from various suppliers by rail, it is unloaded and carried to a machine which cuts identical-size blanks for all four hydraulic presses. Blanks go to the presses by forklift trucks in pallet stacks of 40 each, and the schedule is so arranged that there is always a supply on hand when the presses are started up on the morning shift.

The Principals

Since this problem, like any other management problem, involves different types of people, the following brief descriptions of the characters, whose names have been disguised, may be useful:

Oscar Burger, plant manager—a tough manager in his late fifties known for his willingness to listen to others; considered antiunion by his employees.

Robert Polk, production chief—a hard-nosed driver, very able technically, but quick-tongued and inclined to favor certain subordinates; also considered antiunion by the employees.

Ben Peters, quality control manager—reserved, quiet, and cautious when dealing with others; extremely confident in his figures.

Ralph Coggin, industrial relations manager—a fairly typical personnel manager; sympathetic to employees, relies on human relations techniques in dealing with the union.

Andy Patella, shop steward—antagonistic to management and eager to prove his power; has developed rapport with industrial relations manager, Coggin.

George Adams, supervisor on line 1—steady, solid, and well respected by his men.

* Reprinted with minor changes by permission of *Harvard Business Review*, Perrin Stryker, "Can You Analyze This Problem?" May–June 1965.

James Farrell, supervisor on line 2—irrascible, ambitious, and somewhat puritanical, very antiunion.

Henry Dawson, supervisor on line 3—patient, warmhearted, and genuinely liked by his men.

Otto Henschel, supervisor on line 4—aloof, cool, and a bit ponderous; neither liked nor disliked by his men.

Morning Emergency

The situation opens at 11:00 A.M. on a Wednesday in the office of the plant manager, Oscar Burger, who has called an emergency meeting. About 30 minutes ago he learned from production chief Bob Polk that nearly 10 percent of the panels coming off lines number 1 and number 2 were being rejected by quality control because of burrs and other rough spots.

Burger: I've called you in here because we're in real trouble if we can't lick this reject problem fast. The company needs all the panels we can ship, and more, if it's going to catch up with this new-model market. Both new models of the Panther and the Cheetah are going over big, and if we slow down in panels, the old man in Detroit will be on my neck fast. So let's get all the facts out on the table and run this thing down before lunch. Bob here tells me line 1 started putting out rejects about three minutes after the end of the 10:00 A.M. relief break and line 2 went wild about one and one-half hours after starting time, which was 8:00 A.M. Bob, suppose you tell us just what you've found out so far.

Polk: You've about covered it, Oscar. Farrell, the supervisor now on line 2, says he's checked several times to see if these burrs in the panels are being caused by something in the sheets, but he hasn't found anything suspicious. Sheets all look nice and clean going into the press, but many come out rough as hell. He says the inspectors report that rejects rose from the normal one or two an hour to eight or nine in the last hour. On line 1, George Adams says it's about the same story, and he can't figure it out. It just started up suddenly after the relief break.

Burger: Doesn't Farrell or Adams have *any* idea why it started?

Polk: Well, Farrell is sure it's deliberate sabotage by the drawpress operators, but he can't catch them at it. He says it's not hard to produce burrs and rough spots if a man positions a sheet just slightly wrong. He says the men on his line are mad as hell over his suspending Joe Valenti yesterday, and he had another argument when Valenti came in this morning against orders and tried to take back his press job. Farrell called the guard and had Valenti escorted to the gate.

Burger: What's that? I never heard about this. What's wrong with Valenti? [*He turns to industrial relations manager Coggin.*] Ralph, what about this?

Coggin: Oh, I don't think it's all Valenti's fault. He and Farrell have been at it for a long time, as you no doubt know, arguing over management's rights. Farrell says he saw Valenti go behind the tool crib yesterday afternoon during the relief break, and Farrell swears Valenti had a bottle with him. He caught Valenti drinking on the job last year, you remember, and says he wishes he'd fired Valenti then instead of suspending him. You know how Farrell is about liquor, especially on the job. Anyway, he accused Valenti of drinking on the job again, and after some hot words he sent Valenti home for the rest of the week. Andy Patella, the shop steward, protested Farrell's action immediately, of course.

Polk: Farrell's OK, Ralph; he's doing his job.

Burger: Let's get back to this reject problem. What has Valenti got to do with it?

Coggin: Well, I talked with Patella, and he reports the men on all four lines are sore as hell. They made some sharp cracks about Farrell being a union-buster yesterday after the argument and again this morning when he threw Valenti out. When the drawpress on 2 started putting out a lot of rejects on Panther panels, and Quality Control reported this to Farrell, he went over to the press operator and made some suggestions on placing the sheets, or something like that. The man just glared at him and said nothing, Patella tells me, and Farrell finally walked away. The reject rate stayed high, and during the whole 15 minutes of the relief break, the men from all the lines were talking together about Valenti's case. Patella says Valenti's younger brother, Pete, a spot welder who works on line 3 under Dawson, called for a walkout, and quite a few seemed to think it was a good idea—contract or no contract. Then right after the men went back to work, line 1 started to throw off rejects at a high rate.

Burger: What does Adams think about this, Ralph?

Coggin: He won't completely buy that sabotage theory of Farrell's, but he admits there doesn't seem to be any other explanation. The maintenance troubleshooters have been all over the press and can't find anything wrong. The die is OK, and the hydraulic system is OK. They made some adjustments on the iron claw that removes the piece from the press, but that's all.

Burger: [*Turning to quality control manager Ben Peters.*] Ben, what is your idea about this?

Peters: It's hard to say what might be causing it. We've been checking the sheets from Zenith Metals we started using this morning, and they looked perfect going through the blanker. Besides, it's only on lines 1 and 2 that we're getting burrs, so maybe we've got trouble with those presses.

Polk: I'll check it with Engineering, but I'm willing to bet my last dollar the presses are OK.

Burger: Yes, I think you can forget about trouble in the presses, Ben. And the blanker's never given us a hard time, ever. Still, you'd better have Engineering check that too, Bob, just in case. Meanwhile, I'd like to . . . [*He pauses while the door opens and Burger's secretary slips in and hands Peters a note.*]

Peters: I'll be damned! My assistant, Jerry, tells me that line 4 has just begun turning out a mess of burred rejects! I wouldn't have thought that slow old line could go haywire like that—those high-speed presses on the other lines, maybe, but not on Henschel's steady old 4 rocking along at 50 panels an hour.

Polk: Well, that seems to knock out a theory I was getting ready to offer. With 4 acting up, too, it looks like the press speeds aren't to blame. Now I guess we won't have long to wait before Dawson's line also starts bugging up the blanks.

Coggin: Maybe 3 won't go sour if what Patella says about Dawson is true. He says Dawson's men would go all out for him if he asked them, and I gather Patella hasn't had much success selling them on his anticompany tactics.

Burger: What's he peddling now?

Coggin: Same old stuff. He claims the company is trying to discredit the union with the men, especially now that contract negotiations are coming up next month. This year he's also tossed in the rumor that the company will threaten to abandon this plant and move out of the state if the union does not accept the local package of benefits management offers in negotiations.

Burger: That's stupid. Hell, when will the union wake up and give us a fair day's work for the pay they're getting? But let's stop this chatter and get after these rejects. Check anything and everything you can think of. We can't afford to shut any line down with the factory as tight as it is on Panther panels. Let's meet back here at 4:00 this afternoon.

Informal Get-Together

The meeting breaks up, and Polk goes to the shop floor to check on the presses and the blanker. Peters goes to his quality-control records to see when the reject rate last hit its current level. Industrial relations manager Coggin seeks out Patella to check on Farrell's handling of Valenti and the other men on his line. During the lunch hour in the cafeteria, an informal meeting of the four supervisors and production chief Bob Polk takes place.

Supv Line 2

Farrell: I suppose you got the boss all straightened out on those rejects, Bob. That Valenti has a lot of buddies, and we'll need to keep our eyes peeled to actually catch them fouling up the stampings.

Supv line 4

Henschell: You can say that again! I've got a couple of Valenti's old buddies on my line, and ever since the burrs started showing up about 11:30, they've been extra careful. I've traced at least three rejects that I think I can attribute to them.

Polk: Keep a count on who makes the most rejects, and maybe we can pin this down to a few soreheads.

Adams: You fellas sound like you're on a manhunt. As for me, I think Engineering will come up with the answer. The press on my line has been making more noise than usual today, and I think there's something fishy there. Right now, Bob, I'd like your help in getting the night shift to cut down on the number of stacks of blanks they leave us for the morning runs. It'd help a lot if they'd keep it down to two stacks of 40 each. Again this morning, I had four stacks cluttering up my area.

Polk: I'll see what we can do with Scheduling.

Henschel: I'm with you there Adams. I've been loaded with four stacks for the last five days running. With my slow-speed old equipment, I could manage nicely with only one stack to start off. I noticed that Farrell had two stacks and Dawson had only one to start his line today, and why should they be getting favors?

Dawson: Now, Otto, you're just jealous of my new high-speed press. You got an old clunker, and you know it. What you need is to get off that diet of Panther panels and join me banging out those shallow-draw panels for the Cheetah. Also, it might help you to smile now and then when one of your men cracks a joke. Remember that old proverb, "He that despiseth small things shall fall by little and little."

Farrell: I can think of another proverb that you might consider, Dawson. "Spare the rod and spoil the child." Is it true that your crew is going to win a trip to Bermuda if they're all good boys and make nothing but good panels?

Adams: OK, cut it out Farrell. We can't all be tough guys.

Farrell: Well, anyway, I'm glad Dawson didn't have to cope with Valenti today. That boozer is finally out of my hair. I can't forget last year when he helped Patella spread the word that if the men would burr a lot of the stampings, they could pressure management into a better contract. I wouldn't be surprised if Valenti and Patella were in cahoots now, trying the same angle before negotiations start.

Adams: Relax, Farrell. You can't prove that's so. The men aren't as dumb as all that, as last year proved when they refused to believe Patella. What bugs me is those rejects this morning. Never saw so many bad burrs show up so fast.

Henschel: They sure surprised me, too, but you know I think Quality Control may be a little bit overexcited about the burrs. I figure all of them could be reamed and filed out with a little handwork. Put two extra men on the line, and it would be all taken care of.

Farrell: Maybe so, but you know how Burger would feel about the extra costs on top of the lower output. And don't forget, Henschel, our high-speed presses are banging out 30 more an hour than yours. Well, I gotta get back and see what's with Valenti's buddies on my line.

Aside Conversation

All the supervisors get up and leave together. They pay no attention to industrial relations manager Coggin talking to shop steward Patella in a corner of the cafeteria.

Coggin: What I want to know, Patella, is why did Valenti try to get back on the line this morning against Farrell's orders?

Patella: Why not? Farrell was miles off base sending Joe home yesterday without telling me or you or anyone else. I was glad Joe came back and faced that s.o.b. Farrell's been getting jumpier and jumpier lately, and do you know what they say? They say he's cracking up over that poor kid of his—the little teenager who's turned out to be such a tramp. I feel sorry for him, but that's no reason why he has to take his feelings out on his men. His crew won't take it much longer, and the other crews are sore, too. You know Valenti's brother this morning over on line 3 began talking about a walkout?

Coggin: Yes, I heard he did. So why didn't they go out?

Patella: Oh, that crew of Dawson's is too company-minded, and there are some older men there who almost worship Dawson. But they'll go out if management doesn't wise up and respect their rights.

Coggin: What about that man who got hurt last night on overtime while unloading those sheets?

Patella: He's been on the job for a couple of months, but he tells me he wasn't familiar with the method of blocking that Zenith Metals uses. He's not hurt bad, but he'll get workmen's compensation OK.

Coggin: Sure. Now how certain are you about Farrell not finding any bottle behind the tool crib after he suspended Valenti? And are you sure you're right that there were no witnesses? You know you've got to be positive of your evidence.

Patella: OK, Ralph. I'm certain, I'm sure. I'm positive.

Afternoon Meeting

Three hours later, plant manager Burger is again in a meeting with production chief Polk, quality control manager Peters, and industrial relations manager Coggin.

Burger: Let's hear from you first, Bob, about that check on the presses and the blanker. Any clues to those burrs?

Polk: Nope. Everything is OK with the machinery, according to Engineering. They even thought I was nuts to be questioning them and making them double check.

Burger: I can imagine. But we can't overlook anything, no matter how impossible Engineering may think it is. By the way, Ben, are the rejects still running as high this afternoon?

Peters: Higher. Line 1 is lousing up nine or ten an hour, line 2 is ruining about a dozen, and line 4 is burring about seven an hour.

Burger: What about line 3?

Peters: Nothing so far. Dawson's line has been clean as a whistle. But, with Valenti's brother on the line, we can expect trouble any time.

Polk: Maybe not. Dawson's reject rates have always been a bit lower than the others.

Burger: That so? How do you account for that?

Coggin: How about better supervision accounting for it? Dawson's men always seem to take more pride in their work than the other men do, and they really operate as a team. The other day I heard two of his men talking about one of their crew who apparently was getting careless, and they decided to straighten him out themselves, without bothering Dawson. When you get that kind of voluntary discipline, you've got real supervision.

Burger: Glad to hear that some of our men feel responsible for doing good work.

Polk: Dawson's crew is OK. One of his men will always tip me off early if they're getting low on blanks, but the night shift on that line is mighty careless. That crew left Dawson's line with only a half-hour's stack of blanks to start up with this morning.

Peters: By the way, Bob, have you heard that some of the men on the other crews are calling his men "Dawson's Darlings"? The rumor is that those shallow Cheetah panels are easier to make, and someone played favorites when they gave that production run to Dawson's crew.

Polk: That's crazy. We gave those panels to Dawson's line because this makes it easier for the Shipping Department, and they just aren't any easier to make; you know that.

Peters: I know, but that's what the men say, and I thought you'd like to be cut in on the grapevine.

Coggin: If the men think the deep panels are a harder job, maybe there's something to it. I've heard this story, too, and there's a chance the union may try to review our rates and standards one of these days.

Polk: Yeah? Well, I say nuts to it. If those items go on the agenda, then Patella might as well be running this shop. Why don't we ask the union: "How about making up for that half hour line 2 lost this morning while Valenti argued with Farrell about his suspension?"

Coggin: While you're asking, ask Farrell why he didn't call me before suspending Valenti yesterday. What a mess Farrell put us in!

Burger: What do you mean, Ralph?

Coggin: Just that we've got a real big grievance coming up for sure. Patella tells me that after Farrell suspended Valenti yesterday, he went looking behind the tool crib and couldn't find any sign of a liquor bottle. Also, Patella claims there were no witnesses around when Farrell accused Valenti of drinking on the job. It's going to be impossible for Farrell to prove he wasn't acting merely on his suspicions, without evidence. And the union is sure to hit us hard with this, especially with contract negotiations coming up.

Burger: Damn it. Farrell should have known better! This isn't the first time he's been tough with a man, but he's got to learn to use better judgment. Bob, you'd better have a talk with him right away. See if anything special is chewing him. Maybe a little firm advice from you will sharpen him up.

Polk: OK, Oscar, but Farrell's a very good man, and we ought to back him up on this completely.

Coggin: If you do, you're going to have real trouble with the union. Patella says if we don't drop the charge against Valenti and reinstate him, he's going to propose a strike vote and he claims the men will positively go out. It looks like they have a clear case against Farrell, and except for Dawson's men, a lot of them seem plenty sore. And those rejects they're producing are telling you so, loud and clear.

Polk: Oscar, we can't undercut Farrell! If we do, we're playing right into the union's hands. It's obvious that Valenti is in collusion with Patella on this, and they're framing Farrell to get themselves a hot issue for the contract negotiations. I say we should charge the union with framing Farrell and willfully producing rejects. If they try to strike, get an injunction immediately so we can keep production up and satisfy Detroit.

Burger: Not so fast, Bob. I'd rather first try to get the union off our backs before they seriously start talking about a strike. Ralph, what about that demand the local union agent told you he was going to make—something like four minutes extra wash-up time? If we gave in to him on this, do you think he could hold Patella in line on this Farrell-Valenti problem?

Coggin: Probably. But you would want to find some way for Patella to save face, as well as Farrell.

Burger: You may be right, but we can't let Patella think he can go on using this sabotage technique of his. I want to mull this over some more before deciding what our answer will have to be. Meanwhile, Ben, you keep a close check on the reject rates. And you, Bob, check on the operation on line 3 to see if there really is anything to that rumor about our favoring Dawson's crew. Ralph, see what you can find out about that extra wash-up time deal and how Patella feels about it. That's about all I can suggest for now. Let's meet again tomorrow at 10:00 and wind this thing up.

Burger's Dilemma

The meeting breaks up and the managers go back to their respective jobs. Plant manager Burger spends some time by himself trying to resolve the dilemma. He sees two choices facing him: (1) back up Farrell and risk a strike that might be stopped by injunction, or (2) avoid a strike by undercutting Farrell, reinstating Valenti, and asking the men to cooperate in eliminating excess rejects. He does not like either of the alternatives and hopes he can think of some better way to get out of this jam. At least, he tells himself, he has a night to sleep on it.

1. What would you recommend that Mr. Burger do?
2. What is causing the burrs?

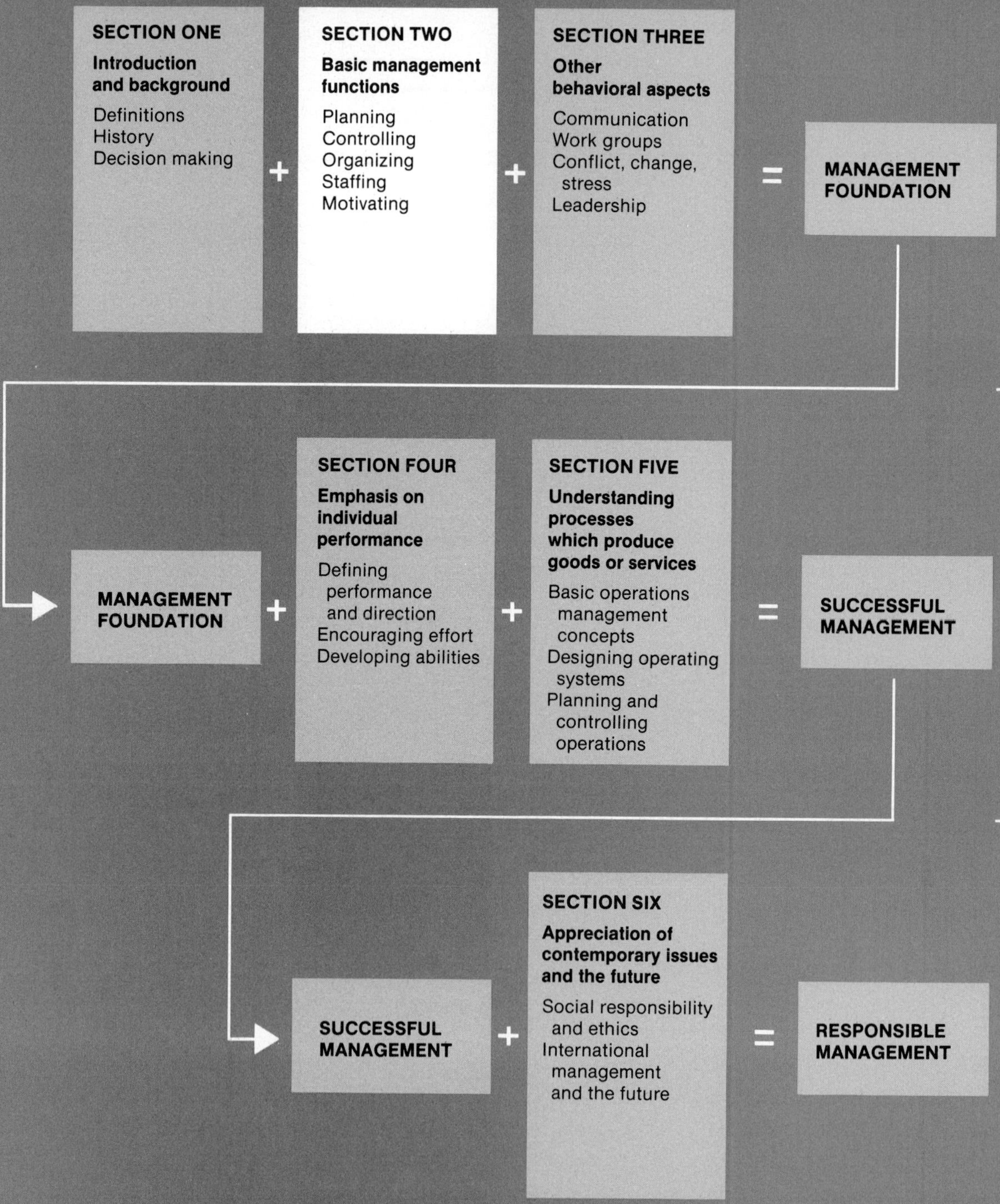

SECTION ONE

Introduction and background

Definitions
History
Decision making

+

SECTION TWO

Basic management functions

Planning
Controlling
Organizing
Staffing
Motivating

+

SECTION THREE

Other behavioral aspects

Communication
Work groups
Conflict, change, stress
Leadership

=

MANAGEMENT FOUNDATION

MANAGEMENT FOUNDATION

+

SECTION FOUR

Emphasis on individual performance

Defining performance and direction
Encouraging effort
Developing abilities

+

SECTION FIVE

Understanding processes which produce goods or services

Basic operations management concepts
Designing operating systems
Planning and controlling operations

=

SUCCESSFUL MANAGEMENT

SUCCESSFUL MANAGEMENT

+

SECTION SIX

Appreciation of contemporary issues and the future

Social responsibility and ethics
International management and the future

=

RESPONSIBLE MANAGEMENT

section two

BASIC MANAGEMENT FUNCTIONS

4. Objectives, policies, and strategies
5. Planning: The fundamental function
6. Controlling: The containment function
7. Organizing: The ordering function
8. Organization structure
9. Staffing: The securing function
10. Motivating: The moving function

Section One introduced the work that a manager does. Section Two deals specifically with the basic functions of planning, controlling, organizing, staffing, and motivating that a manager must engage in while doing this work.

Chapter 4 is the first of two chapters related to the planning function. This chapter introduces and discusses the planning-related concepts of objectives, strategy, and policy. The primary intent is to define the concepts and clarify the relationships between each of these concepts as preparatory work before discussing the overall planning process in chapter 5.

Chapter 5 discusses the various dimensions of the planning process as well as a step-by-step discussion of how to plan. Chapters 4 and 5 both emphasize that today's manager must be future oriented.

Chapter 6 is concerned with the controlling function. The reasons for management control are discussed along with the requirements of a control system. Several management control methods and techniques are discussed and illustrated.

Chapter 7 is the first of two chapters related to the organizing function. It introduces the organizing function through a discussion of division of labor. Authority is presented as the concept most central to the organizing function. The delegation process and its importance in the management process are discussed.

Chapter 8 builds on the basic concepts of Chapter 7 and presents several types of organizational structures. This chapter also develops the idea that the most appropriate organizational structure depends on the organizational objectives, the particular technology employed, the rate of change in the environment, and many other dynamic factors.

Chapter 9 deals with the staffing function. Personnel (human resource) planning, recruitment, selection, and other personnel-related activities are discussed.

Chapter 10 introduces the motivating function of management. Current concepts and approaches to motivating people are discussed. The relationship between motivation and satisfaction is analyzed.

4 Objectives, Strategies, and Policies

Objectives

1. To define and discuss the importance of organizational objectives and to illustrate various types of objectives.
2. To define and illustrate the concept of strategy.
3. To explain the reasons for and the use of organizational policies.
4. To clarify the relationships among organizational objectives, strategy, and policy.

Chapter Outline

Glossary of Terms

Goal A statement (used interchangeably with objective) designed to give an organization and its members direction and purpose.

Long-range objectives Objectives that extend beyond the current fiscal year of the organization.

Management by objectives (MBO) A management system in which the superior and subordinate jointly define the objectives and responsibilities of the subordinate's job and then the superior uses these as criteria in periodically evaluating the subordinate's performance.

Master strategy Refers to the entire pattern of the organization's basic missions, purposes, objectives, policies, and specific resource deployment.

Objective A statement (used interchangeably with goal) designed to give an organization and its members direction and purpose.

Organizational purpose Term that refers to identifying an organization's current and future business. It can be viewed as the primary objective of the organization.

Policies Broad, general guides to action which relate to goal attainment.

Procedures A series of related steps or tasks expressed in chronological order to achieve a specific purpose.

Program strategies Refer to the specific deployment of resources to achieve basic organizational purposes.

Rules Guidelines that require that specific and definite actions be taken or not be taken with respect to a given situation.

Short-range objectives Objectives that are generally tied to a specific time period of a year or less and are derived from an in-depth evaluation of long-range objectives.

Substrategies More detailed than program strategies and are concerned with the deployment of resources in order to achieve specific objectives.

Tactics Short-range, detailed, step-by-step methods used to accomplish a given objective.

Of course, objectives are not a railroad timetable. They can be compared to the compass bearing by which a ship navigates. The compass bearing itself is firm, pointing in a straight line toward the desired port. But in actual navigation the ship will veer off its course for many miles to avoid a storm. She will slow down to a walk in a fog and heave to altogether in a hurricane. She may even change destination in mid-ocean and set a new compass bearing toward a new port—perhaps because war has broken out, perhaps only because her cargo has been sold in mid-passage. Still, four fifths of all voyages end in the intended port at the originally scheduled time. And without a compass bearing, the ship would neither be able to find the port nor be able to estimate the time it will take to get there.

*Peter F. Drucker**

Before studying the planning process in depth it is necessary to have a clear understanding of the terms *objective, strategy,* and *policy*. All of these terms are either a part of or relate directly to the planning process.

Unfortunately, many semantic and conceptual differences exist with regard to the meanings of these terms. As will become evident, not only are there wide variations in the definitions and meanings of these terms but there is also considerable confusion concerning how the terms relate to each other. Hopefully this chapter will help in clarifying some of this confusion.

OBJECTIVES

If you don't know where you're going, how will you know when you get there? Objectives or goals, as stated in chapter 1, are used interchangeably in this book. It is recognized that some authors describe objectives as being somewhat more specific and short range than are goals. Few managers question the importance of objectives, only what the objectives should be.

Management is a process or form of work that involves the guidance or direction of a group of people toward organizational goals or objectives. Thus, the management process centers around organizational objectives. Management cannot be properly practiced without pursuing specific objectives.

Too many managers become so involved in the day-to-day routine of the job that they forget the major reasons for performing their work. Having the proper physical and human resources are prerequisites for successful performance; however, these re-

* Peter F. Drucker, *The Practice of Management* (New York: Harper & Row, 1954), pp. 60–61.

sources must be properly channeled and directed toward defined objectives. Managers of today and perhaps even more in the future must concentrate on where they and their organizations are headed.

A Cascade Approach

One approach to setting objectives is to have the objectives "cascade" down through the organizational hierarchy.

1. The objective-setting process begins at the top with a clear, concise statement of the central purpose of the enterprise.
2. Long-range organizational goals are formulated from this statement.
3. The long-range goals lead to the establishment of more short-range performance objectives for the organization. When tied to a specific time period, such as a year, these performance objectives become the basis for and an integral part of the objectives of the chief executive and the top management team.
4. Derivative objectives are then developed for each major division or department.
5. Objectives are then established for the various subunits in each major division or department.
6. The process continues on down through the organizational hierarchy.[1]

The cascade approach to goal setting, as outlined above and as depicted in Figure 4–1, does not imply autocratic or "top down" management. It merely ensures that the objectives of individual units within the organization are in phase with the major objectives of the organization and that the entire objective-setting process is coordinated.

Organizational Purpose

Defining the organizational purpose is crucial. It is also more difficult than one might initially think. Peter Drucker emphasizes the point that an organization's purpose should be examined and defined not only at its inception or during difficult times but also during successful periods.[2] If the railroad companies of the early 1900s or the wagon makers of the 1800s had defined their organizational purpose as developing a firm position in the transportation business rather than limiting themselves strictly to the rail or wagon business, they might today hold the same economic positions that they earlier held.

[1] Anthony Raia, *Managing by Objectives* (Glenview, Ill.: Scott, Foresman, 1974), p. 30.

[2] Drucker, *The Practice of Management*, p. 51.

FIGURE 4–1
Cascade Approach to Objective Setting

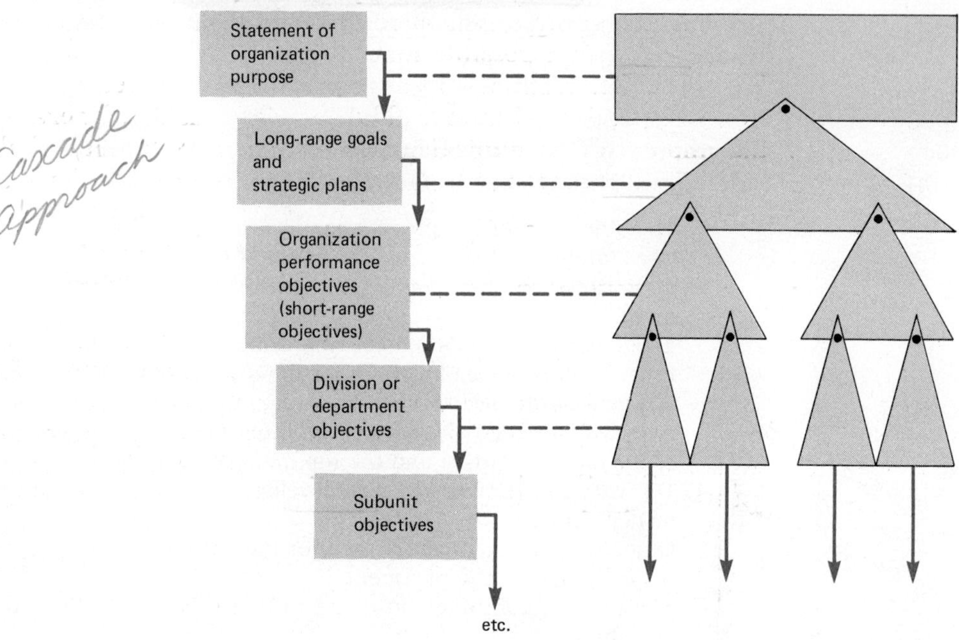

Drucker argues that an organization's purpose is not determined by the organization itself but by the organization's customers.[3] The satisfaction the customer gains from buying an organization's product or service defines the purpose more than does the organization name, statutes, or articles of incorporation.

In identifying the present business, Drucker outlines three questions that need to be answered. First, management must identify the customer—where the customer is, how the customer buys, and how the customer can be reached (is the customer *retail* or *wholesale*). Second, management must determine what the customer buys. Does the Rolls-Royce owner buy transportation or prestige? Finally, what is the customer looking for in the product? For example, does the homeowner buy an appliance from Sears, Roebuck because of price, quality, or service?

In addition to defining the present business, management must also identify what the future business will be and what it should be. Drucker presents four areas to be investigated in identifying the future business. The first is market potential—what does the long-term trend look like? Second, what changes in market struc-

[3] Ibid., pp. 50–57.

ture might occur as a result of economic developments, changes in styles or fashions, or moves by the competition? For example, how has the energy crisis affected the automobile market structure? Third, what possible innovations will alter the customers' buying habits? What new ideas or products might create new customer demands or eliminate old demands? Consider, for example, the impact of the minicalculator on the marketability of slide rules. Finally, what needs does the customer presently have that are not being adequately served by available products and services? The success of the Xerox Corporation is a well-known example of identifying and filling a current customer need.

Long-Range and Short-Range Objectives

Long-range objectives generally extend beyond the current fiscal year of the organization. Long-range objectives must support and not be in conflict with the stated organizational purpose. However, long-range objectives may be quite different from the organizational purpose and still support it. For instance, the organizational purpose of a fast food restaurant might be to provide rapid hot food service to a certain area of the city. One long-range objective might be to increase sales to a specific level within the next four years. Obviously, this objective is quite different from the organizational purpose but still supportive of the purpose.

Short-range objectives should be derived from an in-depth evaluation of long-range objectives. Such an evaluation should result in a listing of priorities of the long-range objectives. Once the priorities have been established, short-range objectives can be set to help achieve the long-range objectives.

Departments, other subunits, and even individuals within the organization should set objectives based on the long-range and short-range objectives of the organization. Organizational objectives at any level of the organization must be coordinated with and subordinated to the objectives of the next higher level. Such a system ensures that all objectives are synchronized and not working against each other.

Specifically, objectives should be clear, concise, and quantified whenever possible. They should be detailed enough so that the affected personnel clearly understand what is expected. Objectives should span all significant areas of the organization and not just a single area. The problem with one overriding objective is that it is often achieved at the expense of other desirable objectives. While objectives in different areas may serve as checks on each other, they should be reasonably consistent with each other. Objectives should be dynamic in that they should be reevaluated as the environment and opportunities change. Finally, objectives should represent a mix of business skills and personal management values. This is especially true with today's increasing concern for the environment and other social concerns. As stated earlier in Chapter 1, objectives for organizations normally fall into one of four general categories: (1) profit oriented; (2) service to customers; (3) employee needs and well-being; and (4) social responsibility. It should be noted that even non-profit organizations must be concerned with profit in the sense that they generally must operate within a budget. The following items represent potential areas for establishing objectives in most organizations.[4]

1. *Profitability* can be expressed in terms of profits, return on investment, earnings per share, or profit-to-sales ratios, among others. Objectives in this area may be expressed in such concrete and specific terms as "to increase return on investment to 15 percent after taxes within five years" or "to increase profits to $6 million next year."

2. *Markets* may also be described in a number of different ways, including share of the market, dollar or unit volume of sales, and niche in the industry. To illustrate, marketing objectives might be "to increase share of market to 28 percent within three years," or "to sell 200,000 units next year," or "to increase commercial sales to 85 percent and reduce military sales to 15 percent over the next two years."

3. *Productivity* objectives may be expressed in terms of ratio of input to output; for example, "To increase the number of units to *x* amount per worker per eight-hour day." The objectives may also be expressed in terms of cost per unit of production.

4. *Product* objectives, aside from sales and profitability by product or product line, may be stated as, for example, "to introduce a product in the middle range of our product line within two years" or "to phase out certain products by the end of the next year."

5. *Financial resource* objectives may be expressed in many different ways, depending upon the company, such as capital structure, new issues of common stock, cash flow, working capital, dividend payments, and collection periods. Some illustrations include "to decrease the collection period to 26 days by the end of the year," "to increase working capital to $5 million within three years" and "to reduce long-term debt to $8 million within five years."

6. *Physical facilities* may be described in terms of square feet, fixed costs, units of production, and many other measurements.

[4] Raia, *Managing by Objectives,* p. 38.

Objectives might be "to increase production capacity to eight million units per month within two years" or "to increase storage capacity to 15 million barrels next year."

7. *Research and innovation* objectives may be expressed in dollars as well as in other terms: "to develop an engine in the (specified) price range, with an emission rate of less than 10 percent, within two years at a cost not to exceed $150,000."

8. *Organization* changes in structure or activities are also included, and may be expressed in any number of ways, such as "to design and implement a matrix organizational structure within two years" or "to establish a regional office in the South by the end of next year."

9. *Human resource* objectives may be quantitatively expressed in terms of absenteeism, tardiness, number of grievances, and training, such as "to reduce absenteeism to less than four percent by the end of next year" or "to conduct a 20-hour in-house management training program for 120 front-line supervisors by the end of 1978 at a cost not to exceed $200 per participant."

10. *Customer service* objectives may be expressed in explicit terms such as "to reduce the number of customer complaints by 30 percent by the end of the year" or "to reduce delivery time from three to two weeks by the end of this quarter."

11. *Social responsibility* objectives may be expressed in terms of types of activities, number of days of service, or financial contributions. An example might be "to hire 120 hard-core unemployables within the next two years."

Management by Objectives (MBO)

One approach to setting objectives that has enjoyed considerable popularity is the concept of management by objectives. MBO is a philosophy of management that is based on converting organizational objectives into personal objectives. It is based on the assumption that establishing personal objectives elicits employee commitment, which leads to improved performance. The MBO process is summarized in Figure 4–2. MBO has also been called "management by results," "goals and control," "work planning and review," and "goals management." All these programs are similar and follow the same basic process.

The objective-setting process in MBO is best accomplished by using the cascade approach to objective setting that was outlined in Figure 4–1. Establishing objectives from the top to bottom creates an integrated hierarchy of objectives throughout the entire organization. It ensures that the various levels within the organization have a common direction. At the same time, however,

FIGURE 4–2
The MBO Process

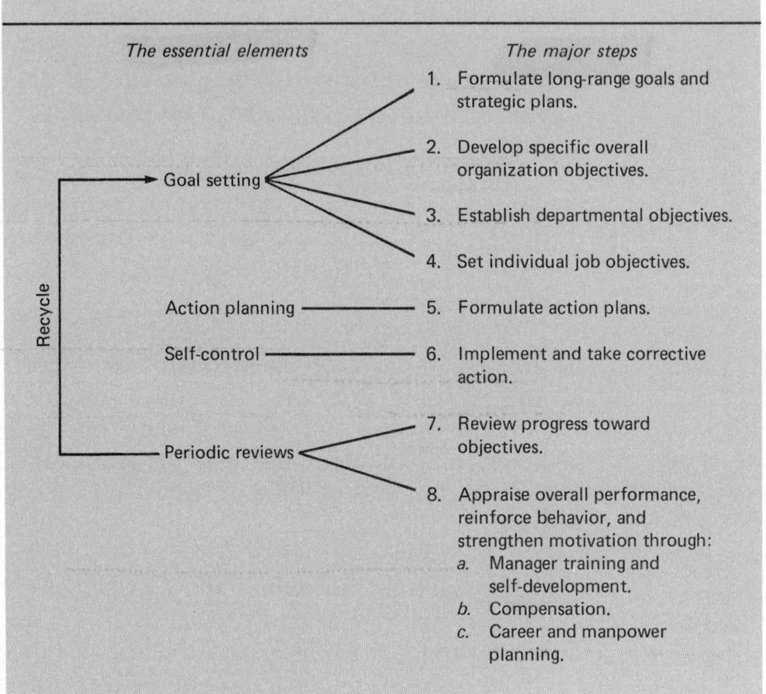
The essential elements
The major steps
Recycle
Goal setting
Action planning
Self-control
Periodic reviews
1. Formulate long-range goals and strategic plans.
2. Develop specific overall organization objectives.
3. Establish departmental objectives.
4. Set individual job objectives.
5. Formulate action plans.
6. Implement and take corrective action.
7. Review progress toward objectives.
8. Appraise overall performance, reinforce behavior, and strengthen motivation through:
a. Manager training and self-development.
b. Compensation.
c. Career and manpower planning.

Source: Anthony P. Raia, *Managing by Objectives.* (Glenview, Ill.: Scott, Foresman). Copyright © 1974 by Scott, Foresman and Company. Reprinted by permission of the publisher.

goals at each level are somewhat tentative, subject to their establishment at the next lower level. For example, a goal set at a lower level might logically expand or alter goals at a higher level.

In MBO, the objective-setting process requires a high degree of participation and collaboration among the various levels of the organization. This results in several benefits. First, the individuals at each level in the organization become more aware of overall objectives. The better individuals understand the overall objectives, the better their understanding of their role in the total organization will be. MBO also requires that the objectives for an individual be jointly set by the individual and the superior. Such an approach results in give-and-take negotiating sessions between the individual and the superior. Furthermore, achieving self-formulated objectives can improve motivation and, thus, job performance.

Setting objectives in MBO is not always easy, and problems

occur frequently. Often the largest problem is deciding the specific areas in which to set objectives. The guidelines offered in Figure 4–3, should help in this process.

After the objectives have been jointly established by the superior and the subordinate, a plan of action for achieving the objectives should be developed. This involves the following:

1. Determine the major activities necessary to accomplish the objective.
2. Establish subactivities necessary for accomplishing the major activities.
3. Assign primary responsibility for each activity and subactivity.
4. Estimate time requirements necessary to complete each activity and subactivity.
5. Identify additional resources required for each activity and subactivity.

FIGURE 4–3
Guidelines for Establishing Individual Objectives

1. Adapt your objectives directly to organizational goals and strategic plans. Do not *assume* that they support higher level management objectives.
2. Quantify and target the results whenever possible. Do not formulate objectives whose attainment cannot be measured or at least verified.
3. Test your objectives for challenge and achievability. Do not build in cushions to hedge against accountability for results.
4. Adjust the objectives to the availability of resources and the realities of organizational life. Do not keep your head either in the clouds or in the sand.
5. Establish performance reports and milestones that measure progress toward the objective. Do not rely on instinct or crude benchmarks to appraise performance.
6. Put your objectives in writing and express them in clear, concise, and unambiguous statements. Do not allow them to remain in loose or vague terms.
7. Limit the number of statements of objectives to the *most* relevant key result areas of your job. Do not obscure priorities by stating too many objectives.
8. Communicate your objectives to your subordinates so that they can formulate their own job objectives. Do not demand that they do your goal setting for you.
9. Review your statements with others to assure consistency and mutual support. Do not fall into the trap of setting your objectives in a vacuum.
10. Modify your statements to meet changing conditions and priorities.
11. Do not continue to pursue objectives which have become obsolete.

Source: Anthony P. Raia, *Managing by Objectives.* (Glenview, Ill.: Scott, Foresman).

After establishing objectives and outlining the actions necessary to accomplish the objectives, individuals are allowed to pursue their objectives essentially in their own manner. Therefore, MBO is largely a system of self-control. Obviously, there are policy constraints on individuals but basically people achieve goals through their own abilities and effort.

Periodic progress reviews are an essential ingredient of MBO. This includes providing each employee with feedback on actual performance as compared to planned performance (objectives). The importance of this personal feedback cannot be overestimated.

The manner in which the feedback is given is important. If the manager provides the feedback in a hostile manner, then performance may be reduced. The purpose of these reviews is to compare planned performance to actual performance and should not be used to degrade the individual. Performance appraisal under MBO is discussed at length in Chapter 15, "Defining Performance and Direction."

Before departing from the subject of MBO, its basic requirements should be summarized. Many organizations proudly proclaim to have successfully implemented MBO when, in fact, they have met very few of the actual requirements. In its simplest form an MBO system must meet the following three minimum requirements:

1. Individual objectives are jointly set by the subordinate and the superior.
2. Individuals are periodically evaluated and receive feedback concerning their performance.
3. Individuals are evaluated and rewarded on the basis of objective attainment.

STRATEGY

The word *strategy* originally came from the Greeks around 400 B.C. and pertained to the art and science of directing military forces.[5] Only in modern times has the word found its way into the management field. A 1974 survey asked corporate planners what the word strategy meant to them. The conclusion of the 111 respondents was that "a near-consensus view would be that it includes the determination and evaluation of alternative paths to

[5] George A. Steiner, *Top Management Planning* (New York: Macmillan, 1969), p. 237.

an already established mission or objective and, eventually, choice of the alternative to be adopted."[6] It is important to note that under this definition the mission, or objective, has already been set and is not part of the strategy process.

In recent times the meaning and definition of strategy has been considerably broadened by many writers and practitioners. For example, George Steiner and John Miner define strategy as "the formulation of basic organizational missions, purposes, and objectives; policies and program strategies to achieve them; and the methods needed to assure that strategies are implemented to achieve organizational ends."[7] Obviously, this definition encompasses much more than the previous definition. Under this definition strategy is viewed as primarily the concern of top management. Determining the organizational purpose, which was discussed earlier under objectives, would be a part of strategy under this definition.

In an attempt to reconcile the exisitng misconceptions related to strategy, Steiner and Miner introduced three categories or types of strategies: master or grand strategies, program strategies, and substrategies. Master strategies are basically analogous to the second strategy definition given above; i.e., they refer to the "entire pattern of the company's basic mission, purpose, objectives, policies, and specific resource deployment."[8] The process of formulating master strategy is analogous to the long-range (also called strategic) planning process which is discussed in depth in the next chapter. Program strategies are more specific and refer to the "choice of specific methods to achieve an already established mission or objective."[9] Program strategies are closely related to the first definition of strategy given above, i.e., they are concerned with the specific deployment of resources, in order to achieve basic organizational purposes. Substrategies are even more detailed and oriented toward the deployment of resources in order to achieve specific objectives.

The decision of a company to enter into a new market with the objective of capturing 10 percent of the market within 18 months represents a master strategy. The decision to accomplish this through an extensive advertising campaign represents a pro-

---

[6] James K. Brown and Rochelle O'Connor, *Planning and the Corporate Planning Director* (New York: National Industrial Conference Board, 1974).

[7] George A. Steiner and John B. Miner, *Management Policy and Strategy,* (New York: Macmillan, 1977), p. 7.

[8] Ibid., p. 20.

[9] George A. Steiner and John B. Miner, *Management Policy and Strategy,* 2d ed. (New York: Macmillan, 1981), p. 20.

gram strategy. A possible substrategy would be to use the ABC Advertising Company to manage the advertisng campaign.

The differences between program strategies and substrategies are merely a matter of degree, whereas the differences between master strategies and program/substrategies are more fundamental. Master strategies are top level in nature and include the formulation of the organizational purpose; program and substrategies are more action oriented, can occur at many levels of the organization, and are primarily concerned with specifically how to attain objectives. It should be noted that a master strategy may include program strategies.

Tactics versus Strategy

Whenever strategy is discussed, the term *tactics* invariably arises. The military has always discussed things in terms of strategies and tactics. Some authors equate strategy to what was previously defined as master strategy and tactics to what was previously defined as program and/or substrategies. The primary differences between tactics and strategy are that tactics are more short range in nature and have a lesser impact on the total organization. In terms of the three types of strategies discussed in the previous section, tactics can be viewed as a typc of substrategy (see Figure 4–4). In general, it is safe to view tactics as involving the short-range, detailed, step-by-step methods used to accomplish a given objective.

FIGURE 4–4
Pyramid of Strategies

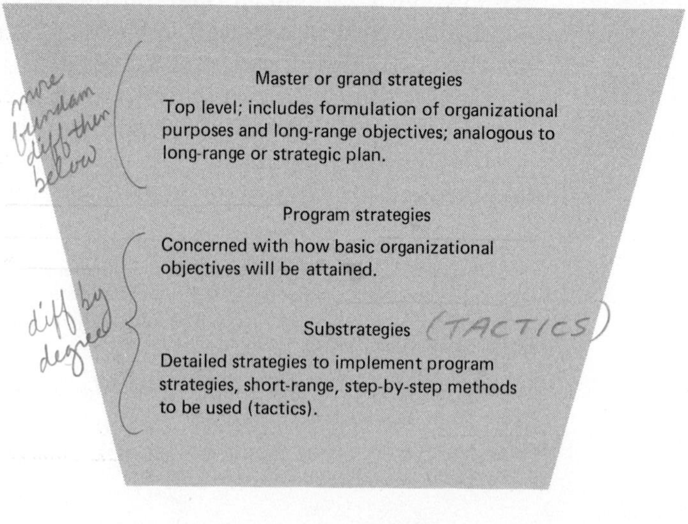

Master or grand strategies

Top level; includes formulation of organizational purposes and long-range objectives; analogous to long-range or strategic plan.

Program strategies

Concerned with how basic organizational objectives will be attained.

Substrategies

Detailed strategies to implement program strategies, short-range, step-by-step methods to be used (tactics).

Types of Strategies

William Glueck has outlined four basic types of strategies of which three are fundamental, and the fourth is a combination of the other three.[10]

1. Retrenchment strategies. Retrenchment strategies can be one of three types: to reduce the level of operation of the organization; to become a captive of another organization; or to sell or dissolve the organization. Retrenchment strategies usually are chosen by default when no better alternative exists.

Retrenchment to reduce the level of operation is most common in recessionary or difficult times. The general intention is to eliminate the "excess fat" and operate more efficiently. Retrenchment strategies of this type may include laying-off personnel, replacing higher-paid employees with lower-paid employees, eliminating marginal or unprofitable products, reducing expense accounts, and even cutting back marketing efforts. The overall idea is to retain the present level of service or production and operate more efficiently. Retrenchment to reduce the level of operation is generally a short-range strategy.

Retrenchment to become a captive of another organization has more permanent ramifications than a cutback strategy. This is the situation whereby an independently owned organization allows another organization's management to make certain decisions for it in return for a guarantee that the managing organization will buy a certain amount of the captive organization's product. Generally such arrangements are made between a small- to medium-sized manufacturer or supplier and a larger retailer. The captive organization may give up decisions in the areas of sales, marketing, product design, and even personnel. Retrenchment to become a captive can take place unconsciously as well as consciously. A small manufacturer can slowly do more and more business with one large retailer until it no longer has a choice about becoming a captive. Although retrenchment to become a captive can work out well for both parties, it usually occurs either by default or because of a long and gradual increase in dependence of one organization on another.

The final retrenchment strategy is to sell out or dissolve the organization. The decision to sell or dissolve may come by choice or by force. Frequently the owners of an organization decide to sell out because they are tired of the business or because they are near retirement. The chance to get rich quick has lured many owners of small, closely held organizations into selling. In other situations the owners may have a negative view of the organization's future potential and, therefore, desire to sell while they can

[10] William F. Glueck, *Business Policy and Strategic Management*, 3d ed. (New York: McGraw-Hill, 1980), pp. 202–31.

still get a good price. If an organization is forced to sell out, the decision usually occurs because of a deteriorated financial condition. Obviously, such circumstances leave the seller in a weak bargaining position. Certain organizations may also be dissolved because the products or services they offer are no longer needed.

2. Stability strategies. Stability strategies are followed when the organization is satisfied with its present course of action. Management may make efforts to eliminate minor weaknesses, but generally its actions will be such as to maintain the status quo. As long as the organization is doing well, many managers are very reluctant to change anything. This strategy works for many organizations in both the short and long run. However, problems can arise if a stability strategy is followed too closely and management becomes complacent. In good economic times it is easy to make money—even with poor management practices. However, when economic conditions deteriorate, organizations guided by weak management are the first to flounder. Organizations conditioned to a stability strategy have difficulty reacting to sudden or radical changes.

Stability strategies are most likely to be successful in unchanging or very slowly changing environments. Organizations employing a stability strategy are usually staffed by executives who feel comfortable with a slow-going, stable operation.

3. Growth strategies. Growth strategies are followed when the organization makes a conscious effort to grow or expand as measured by sales, product line, number of employees, or other similar measures. Growth strategies have dominated the philosophy of many American organizations since World War II. It has been a widely held opinion that an organization must grow to survive. This opinion is most often based on the belief that a smaller organization cannot be competitive and will eventually be gobbled up by larger organizations. Thus, many organizations have followed growth strategies because they were afraid not to grow. Furthermore, growth strategies have been socially very acceptable, especially in the postwar era.

Another reason for pursuing growth strategies may be the personality and personal goals of the chief executive. There is some inherent pleasure in seeing an organization grow and become larger. The thought of providing new direction and growth to the organization is very satisfying to many executives.

Finally, growth strategies may be chosen out of necessity. This usually occurs in rapidly changing environments where the product or service life cycle is relatively short. If the organization does not engage in a growth strategy its product line may be obsolete within a few years.

MANAGEMENT IN PRACTICE

Avco Seeks a Long-Term Strategic Plan as Several of Its Operations Turn Sour

GREENWICH, Conn.—"Who makes wings for the L-1011 and operates 1,800 financial services offices worldwide?" Avco Corp. used to ask in its advertisements.

The big conglomerate, with $2.3 billion in annual revenue and interests including consumer loans and insurance, jet engines and land development, liked to boast that diversification would protect its earnings from the cyclical swings of a single market. But the strategy isn't working.

High interest rates and increased credit losses have hurt its extensive consumer lending operations. Avco's defense and commercial aircraft engine and structures divisions lost $23 million last year, because of high start-up costs, a one-time charge for the discontinued L-1011 program, and delays in meeting some contract deadlines. These and other problems sent Avco's profits plunging 39 percent last year.

As a result, Avco is retrenching on several fronts. Last year, its big Avco Financial Services unit closed 535 consumer-loan offices. And this year, Chairman Robert P. Bauman said in an interview, it will shut 100 to 200 more. In January, the company sold Avco Embassy Pictures Corp., its money-losing motion-picture subsidiary. Now Mr. Bauman says its troubled farm-machinery unit will go on the block, too.

Despite such steps, some remain skeptical that the company knows where it's headed. "They are going to have to determine what their long-term strategy is," says Carol Neves, a vice president and analyst, at Merrill Lynch, Pierce, Fenner & Smith Inc. "Do they want to be a manufacturing company or a finance-insurance company?"

The man responsible for improving Avco's gloomy picture is almost an outsider. Mr. Bauman, who will turn 51 years old tomorrow, spent 23 years at General Foods Corp., and became Avco chairman and chief executive officer last fall in a top-level shakeup. His appointment followed the sudden resignation in September of Ross M. Hett after less than two years as president. Avco chairman James R. Kerr, 64, stepped down a year before his scheduled retirement to make way for Mr. Bauman, who had served as an Avco director since 1980.

Mr. Bauman defends Avco's current posture: essentially one foot in insurance and financial services and the other in aerospace and defense. "These aren't in compatible businesses," he says. But the new chairman also adds that the company is developing a long-term strategic plan and will look at "disposing of those assets" that don't fit or don't meet targeted returns. "We have got to determine what this company should be," he says. This may signal that more divestitures lie ahead.

Source: Daniel Hertzberg, *The Wall Street Journal*, March 26, 1982, p. 8.

A growth strategy can be pursued either internally or externally and can be either vertical or horizontal. Internal growth is realized through expansion of present products or services. External growth is usually accomplished through mergers and/or acquisitions. Vertical growth is attained by adding to or expanding the current operations and functions relating to the present products or services. A manufacturer of radios might expand vertically by making more of the component parts itself or by opening its own stores for marketing the radios. Horizontal growth is accomplished by expanding the products or services offered. The manufacturer of radios could expand horizontally by making stereos and television sets.

Organizations following strict growth strategies are often headed by "fast movers" or aggressive executives who like a challenge. With the shortages of raw materials that are becoming more and more common, growth strategies may become less and less popular.

4. Combination strategies. Combination strategies are followed when the organization uses any combination of the aforementioned strategies. For example, it is certainly feasible for an organization to follow a retrenchment strategy for a short period of time due to general economic conditions and then pursue a growth strategy once the economy strengthens. The obvious combination strategies include (1) retrench, then stability; (2) retrench, then growth; (3) stability, then retrench; (4) stability, then growth; (5) growth, then retrench; and (6) growth, then stability.

It can be argued that some of the combination strategies would never be conscientiously selected by management [such as (5) above] but could occur by default. The same argument might be made regarding the selection of any strategy. Although most organizations do adhere to one of the general strategies outlined above, many never formally acknowledge that such a strategy exists.

Formulating Strategy

The process of determining strategy may take place at many different levels in the organization. For example, once top management has formulated the master strategy, different organizational units may be asked to formulate program and/or substrategies in light of the master strategy. The basic steps followed in the formulation and development of strategy are similar regardless of the level of strategy being formulated. Although very complex, strategy formulation can be broken down into four major stages. First, those charged with strategy formulation must identify opportunities and threats. This involves analyzing the organizational environment including everything from pertinent organizational policies to the competition.

After opportunities and threats have been identified, the risk associated with the various possible opportunities and threats must be estimated. Essentially this involves estimating the probability that an event will occur and assessing the consequences of that occurrence. An event estimated to have a high probability of occurrence but a small effect on the organization would result in a small risk to the organization. On the other hand, an event with a medium probability of occurrence but a major impact on the organization would represent a major risk.

Third, the strategy formulators must appraise the organization's strengths and weaknesses based on current organizational resources. What are the organization's primary strengths in sales and marketing, production, personnel, and so forth? A good strategy will build on the organization's strengths and minimize the impact of its weaknesses.

Matching opportunities with capabilities in the pursuit of organizational objectives at an acceptable level of risk is the final step in the strategy formulation process. This matching process is actually an integration of each of the previous three steps. There is no defined or set manner for deciding what is an acceptable level of risk. An acceptable level of risk depends on management values and philosophy and might vary with the specific opportunity. The end result is an outline of the general approach to be followed in attaining certain goals by appropriately mixing opportunities and capabilities.

The very nature of the strategy formulation process makes it dynamic and iterative. For example, the results of a current strategy could change the environment to such an extent that the val-

FIGURE 4–5
The Strategy Formulation Process

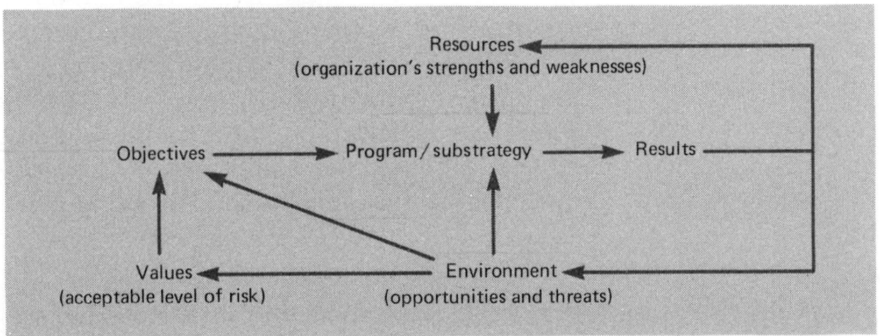

Source: Frank T. Paine and William Naumes, *Organizational Strategy and Policy* (New York: Holt, Rinehart and Winston), p. 13. Copyright 1974 by W. B. Saunders Company. Reprinted by permission of Holt, Rinehart and Winston, CBS College Publishing.

ues of management would change and lead to a revised strategy. Figure 4–5 summarizes this process.

POLICIES

Unfortunately, the term *policy* suffers from many of the same definitional problems as does strategy. Some people view policy in much the same light as master strategy. For instance, a company document might state, "The primary purpose of top management is to establish corporate policy." Under this interpretation the policy process is viewed strictly as top-level and as encompassing the objective-setting processes.

The more popular definition views policies as broad, general guides to action which relate to goal attainment. In this light, policies give guidance as to how management should order its affairs and its attitude toward major issues: they dictate the intentions of those who guide the organization. In other words, policies define the universe from which future strategies and plans are derived. "It is the policy of the public relations department to answer in writing all written customer complaints" is an example of a policy under this interpretation.

Policies are generally not as action oriented as strategies and usually have a longer life. Policies generally do not indicate precisely how to attain an objective but rather outline the framework within which the objectives must be pursued.

Policy statements often contain the words *to ensure, to follow, to maintain, to promote, to be, to accept,* and similar verbs. For example, the ABC Company may have a policy "to accept all returns that are accompanied by a sales slip." Such a policy outlines a general guideline to be followed in pursuing company objectives related to profit and sales.

Policies exist at all levels of an organization. A typical organization has some policies that relate to everybody in the organization and some policies that relate only to certain parts of the organization. A policy such as "this company will always try to fill vacancies at all levels by promoting present employees" would relate to everyone in the organization. On the other hand, the previously described policy of a public relations department requiring that all customer complaints be answered in writing is a policy which relates only to departmental personnel.

Procedures and Rules

Procedures and rules differ from policies only in degree. In fact, procedures and rules may be thought of as low-level policies. A procedure is a series of related steps or tasks expressed in chronological order to achieve a specific purpose. Procedures define in step-by-step fashion the methods by and through which policies are achieved. They outline precisely the manner in which a recurring activity must be accomplished. Procedures generally allow for little flexibility and deviation. A company's policy may be to accept all customer returns submitted within one month of purchase; company procedures would outline exactly how a return should be processed by the salespeople. Well-established and formalized procedures are often known as standard operating procedures (SOP's). For example, standard operating procedures may be established for handling customer complaints.

Rules require that specific and definite actions be taken or not taken with respect to a given situation. Rules leave little doubt concerning what is to be done. They permit *no* flexibility and deviation. Unlike procedures, rules do not necessarily specify sequence. For example, "no smoking in the conference room" is a rule.

As can be gleaned from the above discussion, procedures and rules are actually subsets of policies. All provide guidance in solving a particular problem. The differences lie in the ranges of applicability and the degree of flexibility. A no smoking rule is much less flexible than a procedure for handling customer complaints, which is likewise less flexible than a hiring policy.

Reasons for Policies

Policies aid in preventing deviations from the desired course of action by providing definite guides to follow. Policies provide communication channels between the organizational units, thus facilitating the delegation process. Policies ensure that the different elements within the organization are all operating under the same ground rules and within the same boundaries. Policies promote closer coordination and cooperation among the organizational elements. More delegation and closer coordination permit a greater degree of decentralization within the organization. Policies foster individual initiative and eliminate the need to reanalyze important decisions each time they arise. Personnel are more likely to take action and voluntarily assume greater responsibility when they are aware of organizational policies. If personnel are confident that their actions are consistent with organizational policy, they are more likely to take action than to do nothing.

Origin of Policies

Policies can also be classified into one of three categories depending on how the policy evolved.[11] The first category includes poli-

[11] Alan Filley, Robert House, and Steven Kerr, *Managerial Process and Organizational Behavior*, 2d ed. (Glenview, Ill.: Scott, Foresman, 1976), p. 310.

cies formed by tradition. Traditional policies emerge from history, tradition, and earlier events. In the worst case, traditional policies may be very static and inflexible. In other cases, they may be very desirable. Such policies usually evolve for some justifiable reason. However, the reason for the policy, along with the surrounding circumstances, often disappear, yet the policy remains in effect. In modern organizations, outdated, traditional policies may be of little consequence and affect the organization only in minor ways. On the other hand, they can inhibit organizational performance.

The second category includes those policies that are arbitrarily announced by an individual or group of individuals. These are referred to as policies by fiat. Policies by fiat emerge from situations lacking precedence or clear-cut rationale. For instance, it may be necessary for an individual to improvise policies so as to ensure some degree of order. In most instances, however, policy by fiat has undesirable effects. The potential problem is twofold. First, policy by fiat binds the subordinate to the policy maker. Such a situation makes it difficult for the subordinate to be his or her own person as opposed to a "yes person" for the policy maker. Second, because the policy maker can redefine and/or change the policy at any time, the subordinate never knows what to expect next. Policy by fiat is potentially very satisfying for the policy maker but very frustrating for those subject to the policy.

The final category, called rational policies, includes policies that are initiated by the board of directors or a policy committee. Unlike traditional policies and policies by fiat, rational policies may be altered depending upon conditions and the situation. Rational policies provide general guides to action and general guides for avoiding undesirable behavior. One danger is that a rational policy, through time and neglect, may turn into a traditional policy. Effective guards against such deterioration are to record the assumptions, conditions, and reasons used in the original formulation of the policy and to reevaluate the policy periodically.

Formulating and Implementing Policy

When formulating policies, the policy maker must analyze several factors. First and foremost, the policy maker must appraise the organizational objectives in order to have a complete understanding of where the organization is going before setting the guides to action. In order to avoid conflict, the policy maker must consider both long-term and short-term objectives.

Because the organization must be concerned with its public image, formulators of policy must be cognizant of the social and ethical responsibilities of the organization. Today's emphasis on social responsibility has focused increased attention on the image of business organizations. Because the policies of the organization directly reflect the ethical philosophy of the company, they often dictate how employees, customers, competitors, the government, and others view the organization. For example, a company policy to actively support the United Way campaign might contribute positively to the public's view of the corporation.

The organizational structure also affects policy formulation. A multi-location or a multinational company may have different policies for each location because of environmental differences. The policies of a U.S. plant regarding working hours, employee selection, and so on may not be appropriate for a Brazilian plant.

The policies of the competition may have a great impact on an organization's policies. This is particularly true with personnel policies, such as employee benefits and reward structure, management development, and working conditions.

The final factor affecting policy formulation involves the analysis of the general organizational environment. This includes the identification and consideration of such factors as economic trends, social and political trends, the competitive environment, technological breakthroughs, and so forth. The establishment of policies without first considering such factors could be disastrous.

During the policy formulation process, the affected personnel should be consulted. The people to be affected by a policy should participate in making the policy. Consulting the affected personnel does not imply that the affected individuals should have the right to dictate the policy, but rather that they have a right to be heard.

Proper use of participation by the affected individuals greatly aids in the implementation of a policy. If the affected individuals feel that they at least have some input into the formulation of the policy they are much more likely to accept the policy.

How Much Policy?

It has already been pointed out that policies can have positive effects on the organization. However, the degree of structure and formality imposed by policies can be overdone. While individuals desire and need a certain amount of structure in the environment, too much can have bad effects. Ralph Stogdill has proposed a curvilinear relationship between the degree of structure, control, or formality in a situation and productivity, individual freedom, and job satisfaction (see Figure 4–6).[12]

Ralph Stogdill

[12] Ralph Stogdill, *Individual Behavior and Group Achievement* (New York: Oxford University Press, 1959), pp. 284–85.

FIGURE 4–6
Relationship between Productivity and Control

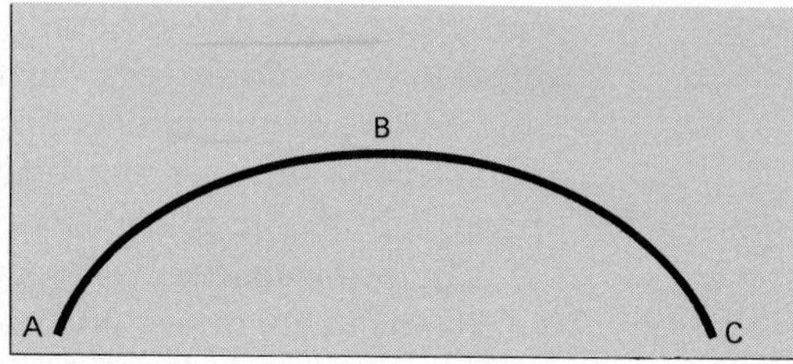

At Point A, one has no guidelines and is unsure of what one's behavior should be; therefore, one flounders around or does nothing. At Point B, one has a firm idea of what is expected of oneself and others. Having a good understanding of these expectations, the individual takes the initiative and thus feels greater satisfaction and freedom. At Point C, the individual once again feels restricted and tends to withdraw or fight the system.

One point should be made clear. The proper blend of policy and structure is a necessary but not sufficient condition for organizational performance. Without policies, the organization will almost certainly not function properly and efficiently, but having policies does not, in itself, ensure desired performance.

INTEGRATING OBJECTIVES, STRATEGIES, AND POLICIES

Organizational objectives, strategies, and policies are not mutually exclusive components of the management process. They are highly interdependent and inseparable. One cannot talk about attaining objectives without knowing the policy guidelines that must be followed. Similarly, a program strategy cannot be determined without first knowing the objectives to be pursued and the policies to be followed. David Rogers provided the basis for the following analogy which demonstrates the interdependencies among objectives, strategies, and policies.[13]

Consider the situation of a boat going up a river toward some predetermined harbor (see Figure 4–7). The decision to make the trip and the selection of the destination would emerge from the master strategy (long-range plan). The organizational purpose represents the surrounding terrain; it influences the general flow and direction of the river. The primary objective is a harbor or

[13] David C. D. Rogers, *Corporate Strategy and Long-Range Planning* (Ann Arbor, Mich.: Landis Press, 1973), p. 13.

FIGURE 4–7
Conceptual Analogy for Integrating Objectives, Policies, and Strategies

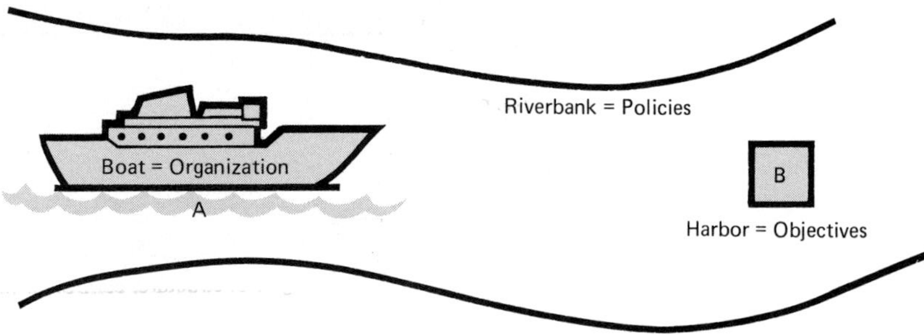

Source: Adapted from David C. D. Rogers, *Corporate Strategy and Long-Range Planning* (Ann Arbor, Mich.: Landis Press, 1973), p. 18.

stopping point some distance up the river to be reached by a certain time (point B in Figure 4–7). Organizational performance objectives and other subordinate goals can be represented by other milestones between the boat's present position and the harbor. Policies are the riverbanks which help guide the boat toward the harbor. Like the riverbanks, policies remain in effect after the primary objective is reached. They are independent of time and must be reviewed as to applicability and consistency whenever new objectives are set. A program strategy defines a major pattern of action for getting to the harbor (point B) from where the boat currently is (point A). This would involve stipulating such things as what kind of boat to use and what route to follow. Obviously, the strategy selected depends on the specific harbor (objective) to be reached and the flow of the river (purpose and policies) between the boat and the harbor.

SUMMARY

Unfortunately, many semantic and conceptual differences exist with regard to the meanings of the terms *objective, policy,* and *strategy*. The management process centers around predetermined organizational objectives. The objective-setting process should begin at the top with a clear statement of the organization's purpose and should cascade down through the organizational hierarchy. In order to ensure continuity, short-range, departmental, sectional, and individual objectives should be derived only after an in-depth evaluation of the long-range objectives.

One approach to setting objectives that has enjoyed considerable popularity in recent years is management by objectives

(MBO). MBO is a philosophy of management that is based on converting organizational objectives into personal objectives. The three minimum requirements of an MBO system are that (1) individual objectives are jointly set by the subordinate and the superior; (2) individuals are periodically evaluated and receive feedback concerning their performance; and (3) individuals are evaluated and rewarded on the basis of objective attainment.

Master strategies refer to the entire pattern of an organization's basic mission, purposes, objectives, policies, and specific resource deployment. Program strategies are more specific and are concerned with the deployment of resources to achieve basic organizational purposes. Substrategies are even more detailed than program strategies and are concerned with the attainment of specific objectives. The primary differences between tactics and strategies are that tactics are more short range in nature and have a less wide-ranging impact on the organization.

The process of determining strategy can be broken down into four major stages: (1) identifying the opportunities for and threats to the organization; (2) estimating the risk associated with the various possible opportunities and threats; (3) appraising the organization's strengths and weaknesses; and (4) matching the opportunities with capabilities at an acceptable level of risk in the pursuit of organizational objectives.

The term *policy* suffers from many of the same definitional problems as does strategy. Some interpretations view policy in much the same light as master strategy. The more popular definition views policies as broad, general guides to action which relate to goal attainment. Policies are not as action oriented as strategies and generally have a longer life. Procedures and rules differ from policies only in degree. A procedure is a series of related steps or tasks expressed in chronological order to achieve a specific purpose. Rules require that specific and definite actions be taken or not taken with respect to a given situation.

When formulating policy, policy makers must analyze several factors. They must appraise the organizational objectives, must be cognizant of the social and ethical responsibilities of the organization, must know the general policies of the competition, and must identify current economic trends in the environment.

REVIEW QUESTIONS

1. What is the purpose of organizational objectives or goals?
2. Describe the cascade approach to setting objectives.
3. What questions must be answered in identifying an organization's present business? What areas must be investigated in identifying an organization's future business?

4. List several areas in which objectives might be set by an organization.
5. What is management by objectives? What are the three minimum requirements of an MBO system?
6. What is master strategy, program strategy, and substrategy?
7. Describe the strategy formulation process.
8. Describe four basic types of strategies.
9. Describe the difference between strategy and tactics.
10. What are policies?
11. Define the following types of policies: traditional policies, policies by fiat, and rational policies.
12. What factors must be analyzed in formulating policies?

DISCUSSION QUESTIONS

1. What percentage of managers do you think have a clear understanding of what they are supposed to do? How might this percentage be improved?
2. Is it possible to have policies that inhibit the attainment of organizational objectives? Explain. Give an example.
3. "Policy should always be made at the top" is the belief of many managers. What do you think?
4. "How can we develop long-range objectives and strategies when we do not know where we are going tomorrow?" is a question often posed by managers. How would you answer this question?

SELECTED READINGS

Bracker, Jeffrey. "The Historical Development of the Strategic Management Concept." *The Academy of Management Review,* April 1980, pp. 219–24.

Camillus, John C. "Corporate Strategy and Executive Action: Transition Stages and Linkage Dimensions." *The Academy of Management Review,* April 1981, pp. 253–60.

Carroll, Stephen J., and Henry L. Tosi, Jr. *Management by Objectives.* New York: Macmillan, 1973.

Drucker, Peter F. *The Practice of Management.* New York: Harper & Row, 1954.

Glueck, William F. *Business Policy and Strategic Management,* 3d ed. New York: McGraw-Hill, 1980.

Higginson, M. Valliant. *Management Policies I: Their Development as Corporate Guides.* New York: American Management Association, 1966.

———. *Management Policies II: Sourcebook of Statement.* New York: American Management Association, 1966.

Hofer, Charles W. "Toward a Contingency Theory of Business Strategy." *Academy of Management Journal,* December 1975, pp. 784–810.

———. "Research on Strategic Planning: A Survey of Past Studies and Suggestions for Future Efforts." *Journal of Economics and Business,* Spring–Summer 1976, pp. 261–86.

Hughes, Charles L. *Goal Setting, Key to Individual and Organizational Effectiveness.* New York: American Management Association, 1965.

Humble, J. W. *Management by Objectives.* London: Industrial Education and Research Foundation, 1967.

Jauch, Laurence R., and Richard N. Osborn. "Toward an Integrated Theory of Strategy." *The Academy of Management Review,* July 1981, pp. 491–98.

Kalman, J. C., and Richard M. Cyert. "Strategy Formulation, Implementation, and Monitoring." *Journal of Business,* July 1973, pp. 349–67.

Kondrasuk, J. N. "Studies in MBO Effectiveness." *The Academy of Management Review,* July 1981, pp. 419–30.

Litschert, Robert J., and T. W. Bonham. "A Conceptual Model of Strategy Formulation." *Academy of Management Review,* April 1978, pp. 211–19.

Odiorne, George. *Management by Objectives.* Marshfield, Mass.: Pitman Publishing, 1964.

Raia, Anthony. *Managing by Objectives.* Glenview, Ill.: Scott, Foresman, 1974.

Rogers, David C. D. *Corporate Strategy and Long-Range Planning.* Ann Arbor, Mich.: Landis Press, 1973.

Schendel, D., and C. W. Hofer. *Strategic Management: A New View of Business Policy and Planning.* Boston: Little, Brown, 1978.

Steiner, George A., and John B. Miner. *Management Policy and Strategy,* 2d ed. New York: Macmillan, 1981.

Case 4–1

The Hudson Shoe Company

Mr. John Hudson, president of the Hudson Shoe Company, and his wife spent the month of February in Santo Oro in Central America on a long vacation. After two weeks, Mr. Hudson became restless and started thinking about an idea he had considered for several years but had been too busy to pursue—entering the foreign market.

Mr. Hudson's company, located in a midwestern city, was started some 50 years ago by his father, now deceased. It has remained a family enterprise, with his brother David in charge of production, his brother Sam the comptroller, and his brother-in-law Bill Owens taking care of product development. Bill and David share responsibility for quality control, and Bill often works with Sam on administrative matters and advertising campaigns. Many competent subordinates are also employed. The company has one of the finest reputations in the shoe industry. Their integrity of product and behavior is to be envied and is a source of great pride to the company.

During John's stay in Santo Oro, he decided to visit some importers of shoes. He spoke to several and was most impressed with Señor Lopez of Bueno Compania. After checking Señor Lopez's bank and personal references, his impression was confirmed. Señor Lopez said he would place a small initial order if the samples proved satisfactory. John immediately phoned his office and requested that they rush samples of their best numbers to Señor Lopez. These arrived a few days before John left for home. Shortly after arriving home, John was pleased to receive an order for 1,000 pairs of shoes from Señor Lopez.

John stayed in touch with Lopez by telephone and within two months after the initial order Hudson Shoe received an order for 5,000 additional pairs of shoes per month. Business continued at this level for about two years until Señor Lopez visited the plant. He was impressed and increased his monthly order from 5,000 to 10,000 pairs of shoes.

This precipitated a crisis at Hudson Shoe Company, and the family held a meeting. They had to decide whether to increase their capacity with a sizeable capital investment or drop some of their customers. They did not like the idea of eliminating loyal customers but did not want to make a major investment. David suggested that they run a second shift which solved the problem nicely.

A year later Lopez again visited and left orders for 15,000 pairs per month. He also informed them that more effort and expense was now required on his part for a wide distribution of the shoes. In addition to his regular 5 percent commission, he asked John for an additional commission of $1 per pair of shoes. When John hesitated, Lopez assured him that Hudson could raise their selling price by $1 and nothing would be lost. John felt uneasy but went along because the business was easy, steady, and most profitable. A few of Hudson's smaller customers had to be dropped.

By the end of the next year, Lopez was placing orders for 20,000 pairs per month and asked that Hudson bid on supplying boots for the entire police force of the capital city of Santo Oro. Hudson received the contract and within a year was also supplying the army and navy of Santo Oro and three other Central American countries with their needs.

Again, several old Hudson customers could not get their orders filled. Other Hudson customers were starting to complain of late deliveries. Also, Hudson seemed to be less willing to accept returns at the end of the season or to offer markdown allowances or advertising money. None of this was necessary with their export business. However, Hudson Shoe did decide to cling to their largest domestic customer—the largest mail order chain in the United States.

In June of the following year Lopez made a trip to Hudson Shoe. He informed John that in addition to his $1 per pair, it would also be necessary to give the Minister of Revenue $1 per pair if he was to continue granting import licenses. Moreover, the defense ministers, who approved the army and navy orders in each country where they did business, also wanted $1 per pair. Again, selling prices could be increased accordingly. Lopez informed John that shoe manufacturers in the United States and two other countries were most anxious to have this business at any terms. John asked for ten days to discuss this with his partners. Lopez agreed and returned home to await their decision. The morning of the meeting of the board of directors of the Hudson Shoe Company a wire was received from the large domestic chain stating that they would not be buying from Hudson next season. John Hudson called the meeting to order.

1. What were the objectives of Hudson Shoe?
2. What policies existed?
3. Do you agree with Hudson's strategy?
4. What would you do if you were John Hudson?

Case 4–2

The privileged few

Jan Morgan was faced with a perplexing situation. Six months ago, Madison Business Machines had implemented a corporate-wide no smoking policy. There were, as anticipated, loud complaints voiced by the smokers at the southeast divisional headquarters where Jan was director of employee relations. But gradually this vocal minority accepted the policy and even attended the "stop smoking" clinics made available to them by the company. For the first three months after the policy was announced, smoking was allowed in the general office area. After that, the employee lounge was partitioned off, creating a smoking area, and smokers were permitted to smoke only on break periods. But this room was, as scheduled and announced earlier, done away with after the second three-month period following the announcement of the policy. That was just two weeks ago.

Jan was quite surprised with the growing acceptance of the policy. Some employees had competed with each other, seeing who could quit first. Others had even begun to form jogging groups who ran either before or after working hours.

All was fine until this morning. A sales manager's meeting had just been completed at the corporate offices in Chicago. Dan Wetcott, the southeast division sales manager, returned from the meeting in an uproar. It was evident that while Dan was in Chicago, he learned that the corporate officers were not complying with the new no smoking policy. In fact, Dan claimed that smoking was permitted in the executive lounge and that "they didn't even try to conceal it"—not that concealing it would have made any difference to Dan. He had come storming into Jan's office early this morning, lit up a cigarette and stated that he was all for the new "health kick," but "what was good for the rest of them was good for those turkeys up in Chicago—no matter who they were, right on up to the president!"

The news traveled fast, and by early afternoon, ash trays appeared in their old places on desks and in the lounge areas. Even the nonsmokers appeared to be somewhat distraught with the apparent double standard that existed in the organization. Jan overheard one employee comment, "Why, that's enough to make me want to start smoking."

1. Should double standards exist in organizations such as depicted in this case? no!
2. What implications does the existence of double standards have for the behavior of the members of the organization?
3. What should be done in this case?

5 Planning: The Fundamental Function

Objectives

1. To emphasize the importance of planning in the management process.
2. To compare and contrast formal and informal planning as well as strategic and tactical planning.
3. To outline the role and responsibilities of an organization planner or a planning department.
4. To suggest a systematic approach to planning.

Chapter Outline

Glossary of Terms

Budget A statement of expected results or requirements expressed in financial or numerical terms.

Forecasting The fourth step in the planning process; it involves making predictions about the future.

Formal plan A written, documented plan developed through an identifiable process.

Functional plans Plans that originate from the functional areas of an organization such as production, marketing, finance, and personnel.

Long-range plans Plans that generally pertain to a period which starts at the end of the current year and extends forward into the future.

Planning A process of deciding what objectives to pursue during a future time period and what to do in order to achieve those objectives.

Pro forma statements Statements which forecast the future financial impact of a particular course of action.

Self-audit The first step in the planning process; it answers the question "Where are we now?" and is an evaluation of all relevant factors internal to the organization.

Short-range plans Plans that can generally be defined as covering up to one year.

Strategic planning Planning that covers a relatively long period of time, affects many parts of the organization, includes the formulation of objectives and the selection of the means by which the objectives are to be attained.

Survey environment The second step in the planning process; it answers the question "Where are we now?" and involves surveying factors which may influence the operation and success of the organization but are not under the control of the organization.

Tactical planning Planning that presupposes a set of objectives handed down by a higher level in the organization and determines ways of attaining them.

Zero-base budgeting Form of budgeting which requires managers to justify their entire budget request in detail and shifts the burden of proof to each manager for justification of money spent.

Once upon a time there were two pigs (a third one had gone to market and disappeared) who were faced with the problem of protecting themselves from a wolf.

One pig was an old-timer in this wolf-fending business, and he saw the problem right away—just build a house strong enough to resist the huffing and puffing he had experienced before. So, the first pig built his wolf-resistant house right away out of genuine, reliable lath and plaster.

The second pig was green at this wolf business, but he was thoughtful. He decided he would analyze the wolf problem a bit. He sat down and drew up a matrix (which, of course, is pig latin for a blank sheet of paper) and listed the problem, analyzed the problem into components and possibilities of wolf strategy, listed the design objectives of his wolf-proof house, determined the functions that his fortress should perform, designed and built his house, and waited to see how well it worked.

All this time, the old-timer pig was laughing at the planner pig and vehemently declined to enter into this kind of folly. He had built wolf-proof houses before, and he had lived and prospered, hadn't he? He said to the planner pig, "If you know what you are doing, you don't have to go through all of that jazz." And with this, he went fishing, or rooting, or whatever it is that pigs do in their idle hours.

The second pig worked on his system anyway, and designed for predicted contingencies.

One day the mean old wolf passed by the two houses (they both looked the same—after all, a house is just a house). He thought that a pig dinner was just what he wanted. He walked up to the first pig's house and uttered a warning to the old-timer, which was roundly rejected, as usual. With this, the wolf, instead of huffing and puffing, pulled out a sledge hammer, knocked the door down, and ate the old-timer for dinner.

Still not satisfied, the wolf walked to the planner pig's house and repeated his act. Suddenly, a trap door in front of the house opened and the wolf dropped into a deep, dark pit, never to be heard from again.

Morals:
1. They are not making wolves like they used to.
2. It's hard to teach old pigs new tricks.
3. If you want to keep the wolf away from your door, you'd better plan ahead.

*Roger A. Kaufman**

Planning is the process of deciding what objectives to pursue during a future time period and what to do in order to achieve those objectives. Thus, the process is composed of two major segments: (1) setting objectives and (2) determining the course of action to be used in achieving those objectives. Planning is the management function that produces and integrates objectives, strategies, and policies. Planning answers three basic questions:

1. Where are we now?
2. Where do we want to be?
3. How can we get there from here?

*Roger A. Kaufman, "Why System Engineering? A Fable," (original source unknown).

The first question calls for an assessment of the present situation. The second question involves determining the desired objectives. The final question requires an outline of actions and an analysis of the financial impact on those actions. It should be stressed that planning is concerned with *future implications of current decisions,* not with decisions to be made in the future.[1] The planner should examine how current decisions will limit the scope of future actions.

Many authors separate the objective-setting process from the planning process. In such cases, planning is viewed in the more narrow sense of determining a course of action toward some predetermined goal or objective. For example, it is not uncommon for top management to dictate the objectives for a division or department and then ask the respective manager to develop a plan for attaining the objectives. In this light, planning is analogous to the formulation of program and/or substrategy as defined in the previous chapter. At the upper levels of management, the planning process usually does involve the setting of objectives. When this occurs at the very top levels of management, planning is analogous to the formulation of master strategy. Whether or not the objective-setting process is viewed as an integral part of the planning process or as a precedent of the planning process, objectives must be set before the planning process can be completed. Obviously, it is not possible to outline a course of action for reaching some objective if one does not know what the objective is.

WHY PLAN?

The fable at the beginning of the chapter provided some insights into the reasons for planning. Planning is the primary management function and is inherent in everything a manager does. It is futile for a manager to attempt to perform the other management functions without having a plan. Managers who attempt to organize without a plan will find themselves reorganizing on a regular basis. The manager who attempts to staff without a plan will be constantly hiring and firing employees. Motivation is almost impossible in an organization characterized by continuous reorganization and excessive employee turnover.

Planning enables a manager or organization to affect rather than accept the future. By setting objectives and charting a course of action, the organization commits itself to "making it happen."

[1] David C. D. Rogers, *Corporate Strategy and Long-Range Planning* (Ann Arbor, Mich.: Landis Press, 1973), p. 12.

Such a commitment allows the organization to affect the future. Without a planned course of action, the organization is much more likely to sit back, let things happen, and then react to these happenings in a crisis mode.

Planning provides a means for actively involving personnel from all areas of the organization in the management of the organization. Involvement produces a multitude of benefits. First, soliciting inputs from throughout the organization improves the quality of the plans. Good suggestions concerning the future of the organization can come from any level in the organization. Involvement in the planning process also enhances the overall understanding of the organization's directions. Understanding the big picture can minimize friction between departments, sections, and individuals. Planning enables the sales department to understand and appreciate the objectives of the production department and their relationship to organizational objectives. Involvement in the planning process fosters a greater personal commitment to the plan because it develops an attitude toward the plan as "our" plan rather than "their" plan. Positive attitudes created by involvement also improve overall organizational morale and loyalty.

An additional reason for planning is that it can have positive effects on managerial performance. Laboratory studies have demonstrated that employees who stressed planning earn very high performance ratings from supervisors.[2] Field studies have also shown that planning has a positive impact on the quality of work produced.[3] While some studies have reported inconclusive results, several studies have reported a positive relationship between planning and certain measures of organizational success such as profits and goals.[4] One explanation that would fit all the findings to date is that *good* planning, as opposed to the mere presence or absence of a plan, is related to organizational success. Additional evidence has shown that the positive relationship between planning and performance appears to hold at all levels: the individual manager, decision-making groups, and the organization as a whole.[5]

---

[2] J. J. Hemphill, "Personal Variables and Administrative Styles," in *Behavioral Science and Educational Administration* (National Society for the Study of Education, 1964), chap. 8.

[3] A. L. Comrey, W. High, and R. C. Wilson, "Factors Influencing Organization Effectiveness: A Survey of Aircraft Workers," *Personnel Psychology* 8 (1955), pp. 79–99.

[4] For a discussion of these studies see, Charles W. Hofer, "Research on Strategic Planning: A Survey of Past Studies and Suggestions for Future Effort," *Journal of Economics and Business*, Spring 1976, pp. 262–64.

[5] Alan C. Filley, R. J. House, and Steven Kerr, *Managerial Process and Organizational Behavior*, 2d ed. (Glenview, Ill.: Scott, Foresman, 1976), p. 457.

A final reason for planning is the mental exercise that is required in developing a plan. Many people believe that the experience and knowledge gained throughout the development of a plan is more important than the plan itself. Preparing and developing a plan requires managers to think in a future and contingency-oriented manner, and this can result in great advantages over managers who are static in their thinking.

A DILEMMA

Planning is easiest where environmental change is least. Planning is most useful where environmental change is greatest. The environmental change since the Industrial Revolution has been unparalleled in human history. The increasing rapidity of change can well be appreciated if the entire span of human evolution is compressed into a 50-year time scale:

> It took man 49 years to get over being a nomad and settle down into established communities. It took a bit longer than that for us to get our first pair of pants. Only six months ago we learned to read and write. Two weeks ago, the first printing press was built. And only in the last three or four days we learned how to use electricity.
>
> Yesterday was a very busy day. We developed radio, television, diesel power, rayon, nylon, motion pictures, and high octane gasoline. Since breakfast this morning, we have released atomic energy, built jet planes, and produced several dozen new antibiotics. We may now add that a few minutes ago we sent a man to the moon.[6]

There is no doubt that the rate of change of technology and the economy has been increasing at a staggering pace. This rapid rate of change has made planning much more difficult but also much more necessary. John Argenti, a British planning consultant, has described the present phenomenon as creating a vicious cycle which results in an ever-lengthening planning horizon accompanied by increased risks:

> All types of planning, including strategic, have lately entered this vicious circle. Decisions are becoming more difficult; so it is necessary to spend longer on planning. If one spends longer on planning one must plan further ahead. If one plans further ahead it means making forecasts further into the future. The further ahead one forecasts the greater will be the level of uncertainty. The greater the uncertainty the more difficult the decision—and so back to the start of the vicious circle of spending longer on the planning, planning still further ahead with still more errors in the forecast and so on.[7]

John Argenti

[6] "Future Shock Arrived Yesterday," source unknown.

[7] John Argenti, *Systematic Corporate Planning* (New York: Halsted Press, 1974), p. 23.

Any good plan has built-in contingencies and alternatives. One real payoff in planning comes from the search and identification of contingencies. The search process causes the planners to consider events and evaluate their potential impact on the organization. If and when such events occur, the organization is in a much better position to take the proper actions. The fable presented at the beginning of this chapter very clearly exemplifies the need for contingency planning.

FORMAL PLANNING

All managers plan. The difference lies in the methods they employ and the extent to which they plan. Most planning is carried out on an informal or casual basis. This occurs when planners do not record their thoughts but rather carry them around in their heads. A formal plan can be defined as a written, documented plan developed through an identifiable process. Figure 5–1 highlights the strengths of formal planning as compared to informal planning.

FIGURE 5–1
General Characteristics of Formal Planning versus Informal Planning

Formal planning	*Informal planning*
Rational	Emotional
Systematic	Disorganized
Regular intervals	Sporadic episodes
Future improvement	Past evaluation
Hard document	Memory

The absence of a formal planning system often results in continuous fire-fighting behavior by managers. Unless a formal system has been established with objectives and schedules, daily problems generally receive precedence over planning.

Additionally, formal planning enhances the integration of managerial activity in organizations. A formal planning process forces collaboration between organizational subunits, such as the functional areas of marketing, production, finance, and accounting.

The need and desirability for formal planning is not limited to large organizations. Managers of small organizations can realize the same benefits. Of course, the sophistication of formal planning processes can vary greatly from large to small organizations and even among similar-sized organizations. One organization might have a two-page formal plan while another has a 200-page document. The appropriate degree of sophistication depends on the needs of the individual managers and the organization itself. The environment, size, and type of business are factors which typically affect the planning needs of an organization.

PLANNING HORIZON: SHORT-RANGE VERSUS LONG-RANGE

Short-range plans can generally be defined as those plans covering up to one year. Long-range planning pertains to a period which starts at the end of the current year and extends forward into the future. The question of "How long should a long-range plan be?" cannot be answered specifically. Circumstances vary from organization to organization, and the appropriate time frame varies with the nature of the specific environment and activity. What may be long range for an organization operating in a rapidly changing environment may be short range for an organization operating in a relatively static environment. In practice, most long-range plans span three to five years into the future (see Figure 5–2).[8] While long-range planning can theoretically take place at any level in the organization, it is primarily carried out at the top levels of the organization.

Formal long-range planning did not become popular until after World War II. A 1939 survey conducted by Stanford University found that about half of the 31 companies interviewed made plans in some detail up to a year in advance.[9] However, only 2 of the 31 firms established plans for as long as five years. A 1956 survey by the National Industrial Conference Board found that 142 out of 189 responding organizations employed planning programs further than one year ahead.[10] A 1973 survey by one of the authors revealed that 328 out of 398 organizations (84 percent) did prepare some form of documented long-range plan covering at least three years.[11] A follow-up survey conducted in 1979 found that 120 out of 142 organizations (also 84 percent) did prepare some form of documented long-range plan.[12]

Several developments have contributed to the increased attention given to long-range planning. First, the rate of technological change has increased continually since World War II. Expenditures for research and development have increased almost expo-

---

[8] Leslie W. Rue, "The How and Who of Long-Range Planning," *Business Horizons,* December 1973, p. 29.

[9] Paul E. Holden, Lounsbury S. Fish, and Hubert I. Smith, *Top-Management Organization and Control* (New York: McGraw-Hill, 1941), p. 405.

[10] Arthur D. Baker, Jr., and G. Clark Thompson, "Long-Range Planning Pays Off," *Conference Board Business Record,* October 1956, pp. 435–43.

[11] Leslie W. Rue, "Tools and Techniques of Long-Range Planners," *Long-Range Planning,* October 1974, p. 1.

[12] William R. Boulton et al., "How Are Companies Planning Now? A Survey," *Long-Range Planning,* February 1982, pp. 82–86.

FIGURE 5–2
Short-Range versus Long-Range Planning

	Short range—up to one year (quantified—included in quarterly budgets and action programs)	*Long range—more than one year (broadly quantified as long-range plans in corporate development)*
Basic objectives, guidelines, and policy	Profits and sales Costs Finance	Growth Reduction Finance
Capital expenditures	Minor items, expendables, and short-life equipment	Basic equipment, buildings, infrastructures, and land
Sales	By salesman, products, customers and current markets, home sales and promotions	By potential markets and industries Exports
Personnel	Operating and clerical classes	Supervisory, middle and top management
R&D, design	Fashion goods, short-life items, etc.	Basic research, especially associated with human, animal, and plant health, and items of high capital cost

Source: Adapted from Harry Jones, *Preparing Company Plans* (New York: Halsted Press, 1974), p. 39.

nentially during the past 30 years. The postwar era has also resulted in continuous expansion in the size and complexity of firms. Such rapid growth in size and complexity requires extensive forward planning. More recently, the development and refinement of computers and sophisticated mathematical models have added to the potential and precision of long-range planning. Finally, the postwar economy has succeeded in avoiding the radical fluctuations experienced in the earlier decades of the 20th century. This phenomenon has made longer term planning more realistic.

STRATEGIC VERSUS TACTICAL PLANNING

Many writers and practitioners frequently use the terms *strategic planning* and *tactical planning*. Strategic planning is synonymous with the formulation of a master strategy (which was defined in Chapter 4) and is also the same as top level long-range planning.

The terms *strategic plan, master strategy,* (top level) *long-range plan,* and *corporate planning* basically mean the same thing and are used interchangeably. Strategic planning covers a relatively long period of time, affects many parts of the organization, includes the formulation of objectives, and the selection of the means by which the objectives are to be attained.

Tactical planning refers to short-range planning and includes the formulation of substrategy (which was defined in Chapter 4). Production schedules and day-to-day operational plans are examples of tactical plans. It should be noted, however, that the distinctions made between strategic and tactical planning are relative and not absolute. Figure 5–3 categorizes the different terms that are frequently used to describe plans.

FIGURE 5–3
Planning Terms and Their Respective Characteristics

Terminology used	*Characteristics*
Master strategy Long-range plan (top level) Strategic plan Corporate plan	Covers a relatively long period of time; includes the formulation of objectives; affects many facets of the organization; general in nature.
Tactical plan Short-range plan Action plan Operational plan	Covers a relatively short period of time; primarily concerned with how to attain objectives (substrategy formulation); may affect a small part of the organization; specific in nature.

FUNCTIONAL PLANS

In addition to being categorized as long-range or short-range, strategic or tactical, plans are often classified according to their function or use. The most frequently encountered types of functional plans are sales and marketing plans, production plans, financial plans, and personnel plans. Sales and marketing plans are concerned with plans for developing new products/services and with selling both present and future products/services. Production plans are concerned with producing the desired products/services on a timely schedule. Production planning is discussed in depth in Chapter 20. Financial plans primarily deal with meeting the financial commitments and capital expenditures of the organization. Personnel plans, which are discussed at length in Chapter 9, relate to planning the human resource needs of the organization. Many functional plans are interrelated and interdependent. For example, a financial plan would obviously be dependent on the production, sales, and personnel plans.

MANAGEMENT IN PRACTICE

GM's Chairman Smith Has Company Moving, but in What Direction?

DETROIT—Roger B. Smith, the 56-year-old chairman and chief executive of General Motors Corp., likes to spend his weekends cruising around town in his 1959 Corvette.

The mint-condition sports car provides a welcome change from the burdens of steering the world's largest manufacturing company. It also is a nostalgic reminder of a simpler era for a corporation that once dominated its industry with astonishing ease.

In the little more than a year that Mr. Smith has been chairman, he has run up against an array of troubles never dreamed of by his predecessors. Occurring in the midst of the worst industry slump in 50 years, they include a dwindling share of the U.S. market, a deteriorating balance sheet and a still-growing competitive threat from the Japanese.

The problems have severely tested the leadership of Mr. Smith, a sandy-haired, squeaky-voiced finance expert whom some GM executives refer to as "Jolly Roger." The nickname parodies his ruthless efforts to cut costs and streamline management. Those actions have helped GM return to profitability at a time when other U.S. auto makers are suffering huge losses.

But while respected for his hard-bitten approach to the bottom line, the chairman has yet to convince some insiders of his ability to lead the company on a clear course. "He's given a lot of orders and done some good things," says one middle manager at GM headquarters, "but there isn't any real sense of direction."

Blaming much of the company's current troubles on an auto market that has become as unreliable as a dashboard clock, Mr. Smith hopes that a trimmer management will help GM respond faster to swings in demand.

Another solution, he believes, is to improve GM's strategic planning. Before he took over, most of the company's long-range forecasting and analysis were done by four separate groups reporting to different arms of the corporation. But the system, designed to provide a range of opinions, didn't work well because top executives were never sure which group to believe. "It was just like Russian roulette," says one insider. "The planning groups were all like armed camps vying for management's attention."

To get better results, Mr. Smith has been consolidating the groups and assigning different specialties. He also insists they develop alternative pictures of the future rather than a single outlook. One result: GM now sets production plans based on a range of projected sales, as opposed to its past practice of using a set forecast.

The Computer Model

Mr. Smith also has stayed closely involved with the development of a computer model of the corporation, a secret project he started as an executive vice president. Tucked away in a high-security office and updated each day by a staff of Ph.D. mathematicians, the computer is programmed to forecast the effects of management decisions on everything from production demand for steering wheels to GM's stock price.

Mr. Smith says that the first time he ran the computer four years ago, it "spewed out so much information we couldn't find the answer we wanted." Now it has been considerably refined, and he says he is using it to double-check important decisions.

Where forecasting is more difficult, Mr. Smith has been working to develop contingency plans. Uncertain about future demand for subcompact and mini cars—and GM's ability to produce them at competitive cost—he is lining up supplies from the company's two Japanese partners, Isuzu Motors Ltd. and Suzuki Motor Co., as well as negotiating with Toyota. The arrangements reduce GM's risk, if small cars remain in excess supply, and they provide a backup in the event another oil shortage causes a sudden demand for fuel-thrifty autos.

The idea, according to Mr. Smith, is to be prepared for anything. "I don't like people running into my office saying, 'Jeez, this just happened. What do we do next?' " he says. "I want to have a plan for just about everything. I don't have one for a nuclear attack, but, of course, we have all the usual security precautions for that, too."

Putting much of his faith in the new system, Mr. Smith remains confident that the company will regain its competitive advantage. And he believes that progress will be much easier once the market begins to pick up.

"Have you seen our new Camaro and Firebird and looked at our new A-cars?" he says excitedly. "Holy Toledo, there's just no way we can miss."

Source: John Koten, *The Wall Street Journal*, April 8, 1982, pp. 1, 20.

WHO SHOULD PLAN

Planning is not something reserved strictly for top-level managers. Planning should be practiced by all levels of management—from first-line supervisors right up to the chairman of the board. Of course, the detail and type of plan developed will vary greatly depending on the level and responsibility of the manager. For example, first-line supervisors should normally prepare short-range plans to aid in meeting the objectives of their department. Such plans might even include a day-by-day breakdown of what needs to be done. Middle-level managers should also prepare plans to aid in the accomplishment of their objectives. Normally, the plans of middle management are for a longer duration and are more comprehensive than the plans of those managers working beneath them. Top-level managers should develop the strategic (long-range) plans for the organization. The important thing is to plan and to coordinate the planning efforts of the different levels of management.

THE ORGANIZATION PLANNING SYSTEM

The organization planning system is the framework that ties the various plans and levels within the organization together. The organization planning system ensures that short-range plans are in agreement with long-range plans and that the various plans of the different organizational units mesh together in an effort to accomplish the objectives of the organization as a whole.

In large organizations, an organization planner or planning department is generally used for the purpose of directing the organization planning system. Many think it a mistake to have a full-time employee function as an organization planner in addition to other duties and responsibilities. The reasoning is that day-to-day problems often seem more urgent than longer term problems, and thus inevitably take precedence. The end result often is that the part-time organization planner spends all of the time with daily problems and rarely plans for the long term. Figure 5–4 outlines the functions and related activities of the organization planner. In small organizations, a top manager often directs the planning efforts, although a part-time advisor or consultant sometimes fills the role.

Although the organization planner and planning department have the wide-ranging duties and responsibilities outlined in Figure 5–4, their overriding objective is to systematize and coordinate all the planning efforts of the organization. Therefore, their activities require constant interaction with the other elements of the organization.

PLANNING IN PRACTICE

Although the practice of planning may vary from industry to industry, firm to firm, and even within the different components of the same organization, certain steps must be followed in developing and implementing all plans, regardless of the type of plan being prepared or the level of the organizational unit preparing the plan. The relative attention devoted to each step may vary but not the value of their presence. The following steps for developing a plan should not be treated as mutually exclusive events but rather should be viewed as overlapping and interacting components of the planning system.

Prepare Self-Audit

Where are we now?

The first step in the planning process is a self-audit which is designed to answer part of the question "Where are we now?" A self-audit is actually an evaluation of all relevant factors internal to the organization. Before an organizational unit can set realistic objectives it must know where it stands. In practice, a checklist of factors should be used in auditing the organization on a periodic basis. A typical checklist might include the following factors:

1. Financial position.
2. Condition of facilities and equipment.

FIGURE 5–4
Functions and Activities of the Organization Planner

Basic function:
To ensure that plans are made at all levels.

Organizational relationships:
1. Reports to: chief executive.
2. Supervises: staff assistants.
3. Other contacts: corporate executives, heads of business divisions and functions, and through them the appropriate members of their staffs.

Activities and responsibilities:

Methodology
1. Prepare an agreed-upon planning system, appropriate to the organization and the interests of the firm, in which the participation of the heads of key departments is specified.
2. Ensure that the planning system and the roles of the participants are known and understood through their presentation in a corporate planning manual which embraces detailed formats, instructions, and timetables for the annual cycles of planning and for the monitoring and control of activities.
3. Continuously revise and update the manual so that it always reflects the planning needs of the company and developments in planning techniques.

Formal activities:
As a staff executive, act on behalf of the chief executive at all the key stages of planning, and assist:
1. In the preparation of planning documents.
2. In the coordination and integration of unit plans.
3. In the preparation of the corporate plan.
4. In the control procedures for reporting on progress toward goals.

Functional activities:
1. Participate in the determination of basic corporate objectives, guidelines, and policy.
2. Propose basic economic and general assumptions.
3. Propose specific business objectives, primarily at corporate level but also for business divisions and functions.
4. Assist the chief executive and others in the identification and selection of strategies to achieve the objectives.
5. Participate in the development of unit plans and ensure that they are consistent with the overall objectives of the company.
6. Through liaison between executives, ensure coordination between the plans of different units.
7. Integrate unit plans in the preparation of the corporate plan.
8. Assist and advise all executives in the preparation and presentation of their plans.
9. Organize and participate in periodic reviews and reporting of progress toward objectives.

Specific functional activities:
1. Prepare the information base for the company as a whole, particularly concerning political, economic, sociological, legal, fiscal, and monetary matters; also concerning general trends in business, industry, and markets.
2. Identify corporate opportunities for the growth of profitability in the context of external trends, especially in technology, competition developments, and diversification expansion goals. Recognize internal improvement opportunities in the light of strengths, weaknesses, and resources.
3. Propose objectives and strategies to exploit the growth opportunities in the preceding activity.
4. Keep abreast of developments in management techniques which are of assistance in planning.

Source: Adapted from Harry Jones, *Preparing Company Plans* (New York: Halsted Press, 1974), p. 44.

3. Quantity and quality of personnel.
4. Appropriateness of organizational structure.
5. Major policies and strategies in the past history of the organization.
6. Competitive position.
7. Profitability of various product lines.

Survey the Environment

The second step in the planning process is a survey of the environmental and external factors of the organizational unit preparing the plan. This step also answers the question "Where are we now?" Generally this includes factors which may influence the operation and success of the organizational unit but are not under the control of that unit. For top levels in the organization, the environmental factors include those factors external to and not under the control of the organization. For a department, the environment might include other departments within the organization in addition to factors outside the organization. By developing an awareness of the external environment, the organization can better respond to change. Some general areas which might be surveyed are:

1. Population growth and movement.
2. Economic conditions and their effect on product or service demand.
3. Government regulation (taxes, wage and price controls, Occupational Safety and Health Act [OSHA], pollution control, equal opportunity, etc.).
4. Labor supply.
5. Competitors.
6. Suppliers.
7. Financial community.
8. Social attitudes.

Set Objectives

After the self-audit and environmental survey have been completed, management can set objectives. The acutal process of selecting objectives involves the application of the decision-making concepts of Chapter 3. Many different objectives are considered in the process of selecting the combination that best reflects the aims of the entire organization. Chapter 4 discussed in detail the objective setting process.

Forecast the Future Situation

Almost all managers have some way of forecasting the future, especially as it relates to their job and areas of responsibility. For example, a top-level manager may be concerned with forecasting the future demand for a certain product. A first-line supervisor may be concerned with forecasting next week's production. Generally, a forecast tells the manager what to expect in view of the current situation, what performance the manager can expect to achieve given the current facilities and personnel.

The method and level of sophistication of the forecasting methods used vary greatly from situation to situation. Many managers forecast the future based on their experience and what has happened in the past. Typically, a manager might examine what happened during the last few years and then extrapolate this into the future. One obvious drawback to this method is that the past may not be representative of the future.

Another popular method of forecasting is to use a jury of opinion. This method is practiced whenever several managers get together and devise a forecast based on their pooled opinions. Such a method has the advantage of being simple but the disadvantage of not necessarily being based on facts.

Statistics and mathematical methods represent the most sophisticated and reliable approach to forecasting. The advent and growth of the electronic computer has made statistical and mathematical forecasting not only possible but accessible. Such methods include time series analyses, regression and correlation analyses, and simulation experiments. A major drawback to the use of statistical and mathematical methods is the cost of gathering and analyzing data. Another drawback is that many statistical and mathematical analyses require expertise in the field of mathematics, statistics, and the computer.

There are many specialized methods of forecasting depending on the type of forecast desired. Sales forecasts, for instance, are often obtained through a sales force composite. A sales force composite is obtained by combining the views of salesmen and sales managers as to expected sales. This method is based on the belief that those actually doing the selling should have the best knowledge of the market.

Setting objectives and preparing a forecast answer the second basic planning question, "Where do we want to go?"

State Actions and Resources Required

After the objectives have been set and the forecasts made, the planner must then determine what actions and resources are necessary in order to bring the forecast in line with the objectives. Suppose one objective is to increase sales by 15 percent and that the forecast, based on the current sales force and advertising budget, predicts an 8 percent increase. The manager would then determine how many additional salespeople would be needed and how much the advertising budget must be increased in order to bring the forecasted sales increase (8 percent) up to the objective (15 percent). This step of the planning process answers part of the basic question "How do we get there from where we are?" The planner should determine both *what* actions and resources are needed and *when* the actions and resources are needed. It is often helpful to graphically portray, on some type of time scale, just when certain actions and resources will be needed. Such a graphical presentation allows the manager to better grasp the timing requirements of carrying out a plan.

It is in this step and the next—evaluate proposed actions—that different contingency approaches are considered. There may be several different mixes of resources that could lead to the attainment of a given objective(s). The idea is to identify the most desirable mix of resources.

Evaluate Proposed Actions

After objectives have been set, forecasts made, and resource requirements determined, the proposed actions should be evaluated to determine their feasibility and desirability. In most instances, the evaluation phase involves the preparation of a budget for the proposed actions and resource requirements. A budget is a statement of expected results or requirements expressed in financial or numerical terms. Zero-base budgeting is one approach to budgeting. It requires each manager to justify an entire budget request in detail, from scratch, and shifts the burden of proof to each manager to justify why any money should be spent.[13] Under zero-base budgeting each activity under a manager's discretion is identified, evaluated, and ranked in order of its importance. Then each year every activity in the budget is on trial for its life and is matched against all the other claimants for an organization's resources.

In addition to budgets, other pro forma statements such as income statements, balance sheets, and cash flow statements may be prepared as part of the evaluation step. Basically, pro forma statements are designed to forecast the future financial impact of a particular course of action.

Control the Plan

All too often a plan is developed and placed in a bottom file drawer never to be looked at again. The plan should be periodically reviewed and compared with actual events to determine any major

[13] Stanton C. Lindquist and R. Bryant Mills, "Whatever Happened to Zero-Base Budgeting?" *Managerial Planning*, January–February 1981, pp. 31–35.

deviations between the plan and reality. If major deviations have occurred, they should be analyzed and proper adjustments should be made. It may be that certain environmental factors beyond the control of the organization have changed and thus the plan needs updating. On the other hand, it may be that certain problems have arisen within the organization that need to be corrected. The frequency with which a plan is formally reviewed varies with the application, but a good rule of thumb is to review it at least quarterly.

Figure 5–5 outlines the sequence of events included in the planning process.

FIGURE 5–5
The Planning Process

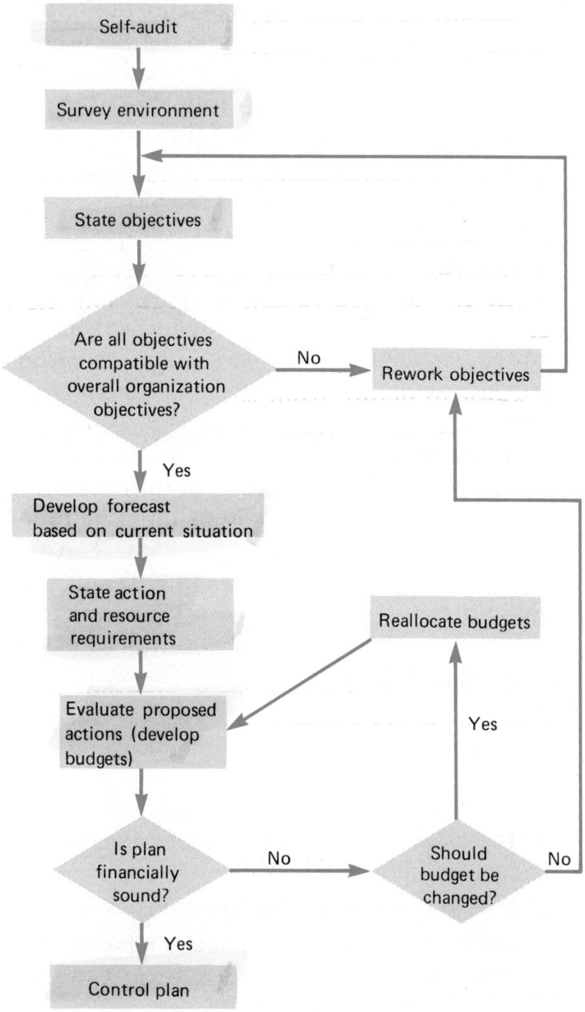

Self-audit
Survey environment
State objectives
Are all objectives compatible with overall organization objectives?
No
Rework objectives
Yes
Develop forecast based on current situation
State action and resource requirements
Reallocate budgets
Evaluate proposed actions (develop budgets)
Yes
Is plan financially sound?
No
Should budget be changed?
No
Yes
Control plan

SUMMARY

Planning is the process of deciding what objectives to pursue during a future time period and what to do in order to achieve those objectives. Planning is concerned with the future implications of current decisions and how the current decisions might limit the scope of future actions.

When properly practiced, planning has many positive effects on an organization. It allows management to affect rather than accept the future; provides a means for actively involving personnel from all areas of the organization; and can positively affect individual and organizational performance. Implementation of planning presents a serious dilemma for the planner. It is easiest where environmental change is least, yet it is most useful where environmental change is greatest.

Formal planning results in a written, documented plan and has several advantages over informal planning. Short-range plans are generally defined as those plans covering up to one year. Long-range planning pertains to a period which starts at the end of the current year and extends into the future.

Strategic planning covers a relatively long period of time, affects many parts of the organization, and includes the formulation of objectives and the selection of the means by which the objectives are to be attained. Tactical planning is concerned with a short time span and emphasizes the means and actions necessary to attain a given set of objectives.

In addition to being categorized as either long-range, short-range, strategic, or tactical, plans are often classified according to their function or use. The most frequently encountered types of functional plans are sales and marketing plans, production plans, financial plans, and personnel plans.

Although the practice of planning may vary from organization to organization, certain steps must be followed in developing and implementing a plan. These steps consist of performing a self-audit; surveying the environment; setting objectives; forecasting the future situation; stating the actions and resource requirements; evaluating the proposed actions and resource usage; and controlling the plan.

REVIEW QUESTIONS

1. What is planning? What questions does planning answer?
2. Discuss the relationship between objectives and planning. Give an example of this relationship.
3. Why is it necessary to plan?
4. Distinguish between formal and informal planning. How is most planning conducted?

5. Explain the difference between strategic and tactical planning.
6. Define the most popular types of functional plans.
7. Discuss the steps in the planning process.

DISCUSSION QUESTIONS

1. Can you resolve the dilemma that planning is easiest where environmental change is least but more useful where environmental change is greatest?
2. If you were serving as a planning consultant how might you answer the question "How can I plan for next year when I don't even know what I'm going to do tomorrow?"
3. With the rapid pace of change in today's world, why should management try to plan ahead?
4. What are some of the problems that an organization planner might experience in attempting to coordinate the plans of various subunits?
5. Discuss the following statement: "Planning is something managers should do when they have nothing else to do."

SELECTED READINGS

Ackoff, Russell. "A Concept of Corporate Planning." *Long Range Planning,* September 1970, pp. 2–8.

Allen, L. A. "Managerial Planning: Back to Basics." *Management Review,* April 1981, pp. 15–20.

Ansoff, H. I. "Managing Strategic Surprise by Reponse to Weak Signals." *California Management Review,* Winter 1975, pp. 21–33.

Boulton, William R., et al. "How are Companies Planning Now? A Survey." *Long-Range Planning,* February 1982, pp. 82–86.

Glueck, William. *Business Policy and Strategic Management,* 3d ed. New York: McGraw-Hill, 1980, chap. 1.

Hobbs, J. M., and D. F. Heany. "Coupling Strategy to Operating Plans." *Harvard Business Review,* May–June 1977, pp. 119–26.

Hofer, C. W. "Research on Strategic Planning: A Summary of Past Studies and Suggestions for Future Efforts." *Journal of Economics and Business,* Spring–Summer 1976, pp. 261–86.

Jones, Harry. *Preparing Company Plans.* New York: Halsted Press, 1974.

Kahalas, H. "Look at Major Planning Methods: Development, Implementation, Strengths, and Limitations." *Long-Range Planning,* August 1978, pp. 84–90.

Koontz, H. "Making Strategic Planning Work." *Business Horizons,* April 1976, pp. 37–47.

Larange, P., and R. F. Vancil. "How to Design a Strategic Planning System." *Harvard Business Review,* September–October 1976, pp. 75–81.

Linneman, R. E., and J. D. Kennell. "Shirt-Sleeve Approach to Long-Range Plans." *Harvard Business Review,* March–April 1977, pp. 141–50.

Most, K. S. "Wanted: A Planning Model for the Firm." *Managerial Planning,* July–August 1973, pp. 1–6.

Naylor, T. H. "Integrating Models into the Planning Process." *Long-Range Planning,* December 1977, pp. 11–15.

Rue, Leslie W. "The How and Who of Long-Range Planning." *Business Horizons,* December 1973, pp. 23–30.

Thune, S. S., and R. J. House. "Where Long-Range Planning Pays Off." *Business Horizons,* August 1970, pp. 81–87.

Wheelright, S. C., and D. G. Clarke. "Corporate Forecasting: Promise and Reality." *Harvard Business Review,* November–December 1976, pp. 40–42.

Woodward, H. N. "Management Strategies for Small Companies." *Harvard Business Review,* January–February 1976, pp. 113–21.

Case 5–1

First in the market

Johnny Peron is a process engineer employed by Vantage Engineering, Inc., and assigned to the research laboratory in the Advanced Products Division (APD). Vantage is a well-established manufacturer of military hardware. The general purpose of APD is to conduct research for improving the military hardware products of Vantage. However, the laboratory director was recently given permission to develop spin-off products for possible sale on the open market.

Johnny spent his first year in APD assisting on various project assignments. At the end of his first year he was put in charge of a special project which was to research a chemically processed wood for specialty applications. During the initial stages of the project, Johnny spent the majority of his time in the laboratory becoming familiar with the basic aspects of the treatment process. However, he soon became tired of the long and tedious experimental work and became more and more anxious to move quickly into the promotion and marketing of the product. This desire was soon realized. An article in a recent national trade publication had generated keen interest in a similar wood product, and as a result, Vantage immediately allocated several thousand dollars to the development and marketing of the chemically processed wood. Simultaneously, a minor reorganization occurred, placing Johnny and his project under the direction of Greg Waites, a close friend of Johnny's. Thus, Johnny's opportunity to get out of the lab and become involved in the more desirable promotion and marketing aspects arose.

Johnny and Greg soon began traveling nationally, discussing the new product with potential customers. Traveling enabled Johnny to spend less and less time in the lab, and as a result many of the experiments required to determine the performance characteristics of the new product were left unfinished. As the number of companies that demonstrated an interest in purchasing small quantities for trial applications grew, Johnny suggested to Greg that a small pilot plant be constructed. In answering Greg's concerns regarding the performance characteristics of the wood, Johnny assured him that the preliminary tests indicated the wood could be successfully produced. It was Johnny's contention that Vantage had to get a head start on the newly created market before everyone else got into the game, that they should build the pilot plant immediately to fill the sudden influx of orders and then worry about completing the performance tests. Greg, seeing the advantages associated with getting into the market first, finally agreed and construction of the pilot plant began shortly thereafter.

During construction, Johnny and Greg continued traveling around promoting the wood. When the pilot plant was near completion, Johnny went to Vantage's personnel department and requested that three laborers be hired to operate the plant. Johnny intended to personally direct the technical operations and thus saw no need to establish elaborate job descriptions for the positions.

A week later, Johnny had his three employees. Due to a work load reduction in the Electronics Division of Vantage, the employees filling these positions had taken the laborer jobs in order to avoid being laid off. One had been a purchasing agent and the others had been electronics technicians. At the beginning of the workday, Johnny would drop by the plant and give directions to the crew for the entire day before departing to make sales calls. No formal leader had been appointed, and the three laborers, knowing little about the chemical process involved, were instructed to "use common sense and ingenuity."

A month after the plant operations had gotten underway, a major producer of archery bows requested an order for 2,000 bow handles to be delivered in time to be sold for the upcoming hunting season. It was too good to be true. Johnny knew if they accepted the order, the first year of operations would be guaranteed to be in the black. Upon receiving the product specifications, Johnny persuaded Greg to sign the contract, arguing that they would be throwing all their hard work down the drain if they didn't. Subsequently, a crash program was established at the plant to get the order out on time.

One month after the final shipment of handles had been made, Johnny hired a junior engineer, Steve Adams, to conduct the performance experiments that had been disbanded while the plant had been getting the rush order out. Steve examined some of the experimental handles and discovered hairline cracks at various stress points that had not appeared during the initial examination. He immediately went to Johnny's office to inform him of the problem and found Johnny and Greg sitting there with a telegram from the archery company. It stated that several retailing merchants had returned bows with hairline cracks in the handles and that the archery company would seek a settlement for their entire investment in the handles.

Vantage paid the settlement and subsequently cancelled the wood project.

1. What caused the wood project to fail?
2. Would more effective decision making on the part of Johnny and Greg have aided in insuring the success of the project?
3. At what stage of the planning process did the breakdown occur?
4. What general observations can be made so as to prevent such a situation from occurring again?

Case 5–2

Planning by a student

Susan Good is a senior majoring in management at the local university. She has been an excellent student with a 3.4 out of a 4.0 grade-point average. However, she really hasn't decided on what she wants to do. Her interviews for jobs through the university placement office have confused her even more. Each interviewer has asked her what she wanted to do, and she really had no adequate answer. Because of her dilemma, Susan went by to see Professor Chapman, one of her management professors, and discussed the problem with him. His reply was: "Your problem is not all that unusual. Many students feel the same way. Why don't you use some of the planning concepts you have learned in management and develop a personal career plan?"

1. Can general planning concepts be used for personal career planning?
2. Develop a five-year career plan for your own career.

6 Controlling: The Containment Function

Objectives

1. To define the management control process and discuss the major elements of the process.
2. To develop an appreciation for the economic and behavioral aspects of a management control system.
3. To introduce and describe several specific management control methods and techniques.

Chapter Outline

Glossary of Terms

Audit A method of control that is normally involved with financial matters but also can include other areas of the organization.

Behavioral (personal) control Control method that is based on direct, personal surveillance.

Break-even chart Chart used to depict graphically the relationship of volume of operations to profits.

Budget A statement of expected results or requirements expressed in financial or numerical terms.

Control A process of insuring that organizational activities are going according to plan. Control is accomplished by comparing actual performance to predetermined standards or objectives and then taking action to correct for any deviations.

Critical Path Method (CPM) A planning and control technique that graphically depicts the relationships between the various activities that make up a project. CPM is used when time durations of activities in the project are accurately known and have little variance.

Flexible budget A special type of budget which allows certain expenses to vary with the level of sales or output.

Gantt chart A control device that graphically shows work planned and work accomplished in their relation to each other and in relation to time.

Management audit An attempt to evaluate the overall management practices and policies of the organization.

Management by objectives (MBO) A management system in which the superior and subordinate jointly define the objectives and responsibilities of the subordinate's job and then the superior uses these as criteria in periodically evaluating the subordinate's performance.

Output (impersonal) control Control method that is based on the measurement of outputs.

Performance Evaluation and Review Technique (PERT) A planning and control technique that graphically depicts the relationships between the various activities that make up a project. PERT is used when the durations of the project activities are not accurately known.

Standard A value used as a point of reference for comparing other values.

> In many circumstances the more managers attempt to obtain and exercise control over the behavior of others in the organization, the less control they have. Furthermore, often the less control they have, the more pressure they feel to exert greater control, which in turn often decreases the amount of control they have, etc., etc.
>
> *Gene Dalton and Paul Lawrence* *

The basic premise of organizations is that all activities will function smoothly; however, the possibility of this being false gives rise to the need for control. Control simply means knowing what is actually happening in comparison to predetermined standards or objectives. The basic idea behind all management controls is to alert the manager to a problem or a potential problem before the problem becomes critical. Control is accomplished by comparing actual performance to predetermined standards or objectives and then taking action to correct any deviations from the standard. However, as the quote above implies, control is a sensitive and complex component of the management process.

Controlling is similar to planning in that it addresses the basic questions of: Where are we now? Where do we want to be? How can we get there from here? The difference is that controlling takes place after the planning has been completed and after the organizational activities have begun. Comparatively speaking, controlling is after the fact, whereas planning is before the fact. This does not mean that control is practiced only after problems occur. Control can be preventive. Control decisions can also affect future planning decisions.

WHY PRACTICE MANAGEMENT CONTROL?

As stated in the opening paragraph, management controls alert the manager to potentially critical problems. At top management levels, a problem occurs whenever the organization's objectives are not being met. At middle and lower levels of management, a problem occurs whenever the objectives for which the manager is responsible are not being met. These objectives may be in the

*Gene Dalton and Paul Lawrence, *Motivation and Control in Organizations* (Homewood, Ill.: Richard D. Irwin, 1971), p. 5. Copyright © 1971 by Richard D. Irwin, Inc.

form of departmental objectives, production standards, or other performance indicators. All forms of management controls are designed to provide the manager with information regarding progress. Once the manager has this information it can be used for several purposes:

1. To prevent crises: If a manager does not know what is going on, it is easy for small, readily correctable problems to turn into crises.
2. To standardize outputs: Products and services provided can be standardized in terms of quantity and quality through the use of good controls.
3. To appraise employee performance: Proper controls can provide the manager with objective information concerning employee performance.
4. To update plans: Remember from chapter 5 the final step in the planning process was to control the plan. Controls allow the manager to compare what is happening with what was planned.
5. To protect an organization's assets: Controls can protect an organization's assets from inefficiency, waste, and pilferage.

TWO CONCERNS OF CONTROL

stability & objective realization

In performing the function of controlling the manager must simultaneously balance two major concerns: stability and objective realization. In order to maintain stability the manager must be sure that the organization is operating within its established boundaries of constraint. The boundaries of constraint are determined by policies, budgets, ethics, laws, and so on. The second concern of control, objective realization, requires continual monitoring to ensure that adequate progress is being made toward the accomplishment of established objectives.

The danger exists that a manager will become overly worried about one of the two concerns at the expense of the other. The most common example of this behavior occurs when a manager becomes preoccupied with the stability of the operation and neglects the goal. Such behavior can lead to excessive activity but very little output. A manager obsessed with the manner or style with which a job is accomplished exemplifies this behavior. On the other hand, a manager may lose sight of stability and experience glamorous but short-lived success. A manager who sets production records by eliminating safety checks is an example of this behavior.

FIGURE 6–1
The Control Process

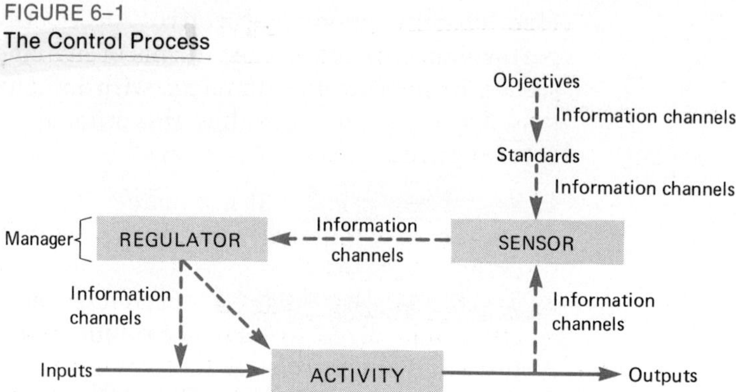

THE MANAGEMENT CONTROL PROCESS

Figure 6–1 is a simple model of the management control process. Activities and outputs from the activity are monitored by some type of sensor and compared to preselected standards (normally set during the planning process). The manager acts as the regulator and takes corrective action when the outputs do not conform to the standards. The manager's actions may be directed at the inputs to the activity or to the activity itself.

Such a system—where outputs from the system affect future inputs or future activities of the system—is called a feedback or closed system. In other words, a feedback system is a system influenced by its own past behaviors.[1] The heating system of a house is a common example of a mechanical feedback system. The thermostat sensor compares the temperature resulting from heat previously generated by the system to some predetermined standard (the desired temperature setting) and responds accordingly.

Feedback is a necessary component of the control process. Although precautionary, before-the-fact steps can often be taken to aid the control process, total control cannot be practiced without feedback. Managers may receive and act on information concerning the inputs or the activity itself; however, they ultimately must know what is happening in the organization and feedback provides them with this information.

THREE REQUIREMENTS FOR CONTROL

The process of control has three basic requirements: (1) establish standards; (2) monitor results and compare to standards; and (3) correct deviations. The first requirement (setting standards) is de-

[1] Jay W. Forrester, *Principles of Systems,* 2d ed. (Cambridge, Mass.: Wright-Allen Press, 1968), pp. 1–5.

rived from the planning process while the latter two (monitoring and correcting) are unique to the control process. All three requirements are essential to maintaining effective control.

Setting Standards

A standard is a value used as a point of reference for comparing other values. Standards, when used in management controls, are derived directly from objectives. As such, a standard outlines what is expected of the job and/or individual. In some instances, objectives may be used directly as standards. In other instances, performance indicators may be derived from the objectives. In either case standards should be easily measurable and definable. The more specific and measurable an objective is the more likely that it can be directly used as a standard. Standards may deal with output per hour, quality level, inventory level, or other indicators of individual and/or organizational performance. The same guidelines presented in chapter 4 for setting objectives should be followed for establishing standards.

Monitoring Performance

Monitoring performance is often considered to be synonymous with control. In fact, it is only part of the total control process. The overriding purpose of monitoring performance is to isolate problem areas. Once actual performance has been determined and compared to standards, the proper corrective action can be determined. The nature and type of standard being used often dictates the type of checks to be made. Obviously, the entire control system is no better than the information on which it operates, and much of this information is gathered from the monitoring process.

The major problem of monitoring performance is deciding when, where, and how often to inspect or check. Checks must be made often enough to provide adequate information. However, if overdone, the monitoring process can become expensive, and can also result in adverse reactions when employees are being monitored. It is not uncommon for a manager to become obsessed with the checking process. Timing is equally important in the monitoring of performance. The manager must recognize a deviation in time to correct it. For example, inventory control personnel must reorder stock before the inventory has been depleted. Several specific techniques for monitoring performance are presented later in this chapter.

Correcting for Deviations

All too often managers set standards and monitor results but do not follow up with appropriate actions. The first two steps are of little value if corrective action is not taken. It is entirely possible that the corrective action that is needed may be to maintain the status quo. Action of this type would be contingent upon standards being met in a satisfactory manner. If standards are not being satisfactorily met, the manager must find the cause of the deviation and correct it. It is not enough simply to eliminate the deviation itself or treat only the symptoms. This action is analogous to replacing a car battery when the real problem is a faulty generator. In a short time, the battery will go dead again. It is also possible that a careful analysis of the deviation will require a readjustment of the standard. The standard may have been improperly set initially or conditions may have changed so as to require a readjustment. Figure 6–2 lists some potential causes of deviations between desired and actual performance.

FIGURE 6–2
Potential Causes of Performance Deviations

- Faulty planning
- Lack of communication within the organization
- Personal ineptness or negligence
- Need for training
- Lack of motivation
- Forces outside the organization such as government regulation or competition

CONTROL TOLERANCES

Actual performance rarely conforms exactly to standards or plans. A certain amount of variation will normally occur as a result of chance. Therefore, the manager must set limits concerning the acceptable degree of deviation from standard. In other words, how much variation from standard is tolerable? The manner in which the manager sets control tolerances depends on the particular standard being used for comparison. Frequently, the manager must make subjective judgments as to when the system or factor being monitored is out of control. If the activity being monitored lends itself to numerical measurement, statistical control techniques can be used. In any case, one element influencing how much deviation is acceptable is the risk of being out of control and not realizing it. In general, the lower the risk, the wider the tolerances. Figure 6–3 illustrates the idea of control tolerances. It should be noted that the tolerance levels may be formalized, or they may merely exist in the mind of the manager. The important point is that the manager must develop some guidelines as to what

FIGURE 6–3
Control Tolerance Limits

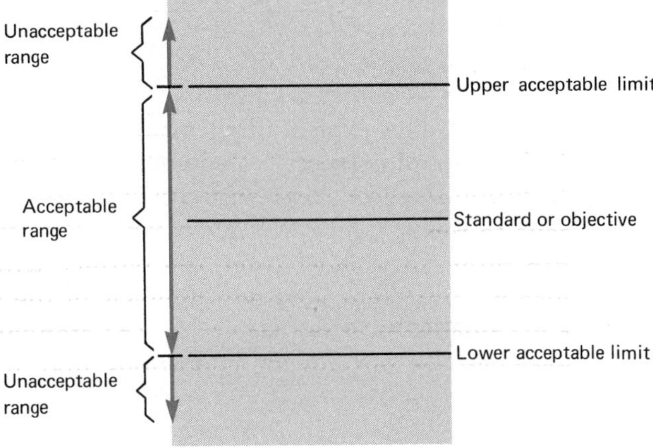

is acceptable (in control) and what is not acceptable (out of control).

HOW MUCH CONTROL?

When deciding how much control should be exercised in an organization, two major factors must be appraised: (1) economic considerations and (2) behavioral considerations.

Economic Considerations

Installing and operating control systems cost money. A good quality control system, for instance, requires additional labor if nothing else. The equipment costs of sophisticated electronic and mechanical control systems can be very high. Ideally, control systems should be installed as long as they save more than they cost. The costs of implementing a control system can usually be estimated or calculated much more accurately than the benefits. For example, it is difficult to quantify and measure the true benefits of a quality control system. A good quality control system supposedly increases goodwill, but how does one measure this attribute? The decision is obviously much easier in situations where the costs of not maintaining control are either very high or very low. Despite the problems associated with measuring the economic benefits of a system of controls, management should periodically undertake such a study to ensure that gross misapplications do not occur.

Behavioral Considerations

Negative behavioral reactions are a frequently encountered result of the control function. The major problem is deciding how much control is necessary. Very few people like to work in an environment where there is no control. An absence of control creates an uncertain environment in which people do not know what is expected of them. On the other hand, most people do not like to work in an overly controlled environment.

Figure 6–4 shows a simplified version of a model developed by Alvin Gouldner which illustrates a dilemma related to control. This dilemma often occurs when management has little or no feel for the appropriate degree of control.

FIGURE 6–4
Simplified Gouldner Model of Organization Control

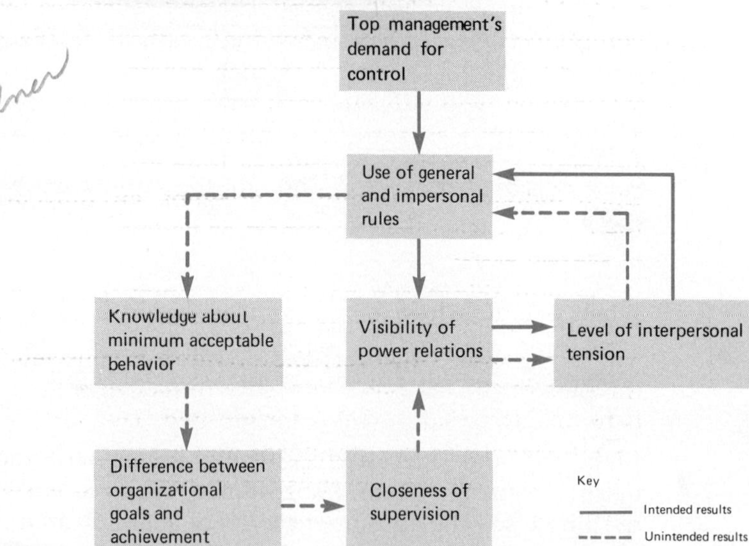

Source: James G. March and Herbert A. Simon, *Organizations* (New York: John Wiley & Sons, 1958), p. 45.

Gouldner's model begins with top management's demand for control over operations. This is attempted through the use and enforcement of general and impersonal rules regulating work procedures. These rigid rules provide intentional guides for the behavior of the organization members, but they also have the unintentional effect of indicating minimum acceptable behavior. In organizations where there is not a high level of congruence between individual and organizational objectives or there is not a high acceptance of organizational objectives, the effect is a reduction of performance to the minimally acceptable level (people not highly committed to organizational objectives will perform at the minimally acceptable level). Management views such behavior as the result of inadequate control and therefore responds with closer supervision. This closer supervision increases the visibility of power which in turn raises the level of interpersonal tension in the organization. A raising of the tension level elicits even closer enforcement of the general and impersonal formal rules and hence the cycle repeats itself. The overall effect is increased control, increased interpersonal tension, and a lowering of performance.

One difficulty in determining the appropriate degree of control is that different individuals react differently to similar controls. Research has suggested that individual reactions to patterns of organizational control differ according to personality and prior experiences.[2] Problems can occur from unanticipated reactions to control because of both compliance and resistance.[3] Problems from compliance arise when individuals adhere to the behavior prescribed by controls even when such behavior is inappropriate. The salesperson who will not vary from prescribed procedures in order to satisfy a customer complaint is a common example of overcompliance. Problems resulting from resistance to controls arise when individuals attempt to preempt, circumvent, or sabotage the controls. Distorting a report or padding the budget is a form of control resistance.

Several things can be done to minimize negative behavioral reactions to controls. Most of these suggestions are based on good common sense. However, they require a conscientious effort on the part of the manager to assure implementation. The tendency is to take these suggestions for granted. They are:

1. Make sure the standards and associated controls are realistic. Standards set unrealistically high or low turn people off. Make the standards attainable but challenging.

2. Involve subordinates in the control-setting process. Many of the behavioral problems associated with controls result from a lack of understanding of the nature and purpose of the controls. It is natural for people to resist anything new, especially if they do not understand why it is being used. Solicit and listen to suggestions from subordinates.

3. Use controls only where needed. There is a strong tendency to overcontrol, to be sure that all bases are covered. Periodically evaluate the need for different controls. A good rule of thumb is to evaluate every control at least annually. Things change which make certain controls obsolete. Remember overcontrol can produce some very negative results.

---

[2] For a discussion of some relevant studies see Arnold S. Tannenbaum, "Control in Organizations Individual Adjustment in Organization Performance," *Administrative Science Quarterly*, September 1962, pp. 241–46.

[3] Dalton and Lawrence, *Motivation and Control*, p. 8.

MANAGEMENT IN PRACTICE

How a President Can Get Control of the White House

Can a President really control his own White House? Yes, if he insists on a basic restructuring. But if President-elect Reagan accepts the traditional pattern and fills all the job slots that will be available, he will be frustrated eventually, just as his predecessors have been.

I believe that the White House staff group has become much too large, that the excess staffing contributes to loading the president's in-basket with many items that might better be handled elsewhere, and that the staff's size invites intrigue and tends to add to confusion throughout government.

The bottom-line issue involves preserving the president's time for those items that must have his personal attention, gaining the time he needs for study and reflection—which he must have if he is to lead and not merely react—and providing him with ready access to the thinking of the best brains in government.

Nearly all, if not all, recent presidents have announced that they would make broad delegations for decision making to the members of the cabinet and to the vice president, and that they would become involved in the affairs of departments only in exceptional instances where concerns extend far beyond normal operations. Recent administrations, both Republican and Democratic, have begun that way, but invariably, decision making has begun to flow back to the White House—not necessarily because of any overt action or policy expressed by the president, but because the structure surrounding the White House encourages it.

Paul Nitze, in the context of foreign policy and national defense, has spoken to this point in a paper published by the University of Virginia's White Burkett Miller Center. He favors, as I do, transferring back some or all of the staff functions that have been going to the White House to the operating departments, and he states:

"Frankly, I think the White House staff is too big, deals with too many diverse questions and isn't focused on the control issues. . . ." He concludes: "The main problem with the presidency is the economy of time. What we have is one man with a 12-hour day. . . . How do you prevent everything going to the President? I think you prevent it mainly through decentralization of authority."

Something needs to be done also with the independent federal agencies. I don't think the answer lies in grouping them all into a new Department of Potpourri, but perhaps they could, on a selective basis, be made part of appropriate existing departments.

Span of control is only part of the problem. Associated with it is the quality of staff work and background papers. Increasingly, the background material and the option papers are originating within the White House staff. The system is not only funneling more decisions into the White House, but more and more of the staffing out is being done there also.

Yet the experience, expertise and general capability for developing position papers in both foreign policy and domestic areas exist, to a much greater degree, in the departments than they do in the White House staff. As a matter of fact, in every cabinet department there are a few top career people who can only be described as superb.

They are mature and "game-wise," and they have long memories. Typically, they are nonpolitical. They are the kind of people who can be helpful on a professional basis and who are able to transfer their loyalties to succeeding administrations.

The president needs the input of these unusual professionals. They are part of the glue that holds government together; they provide for continuity when there is a change of administration.

As with so many things that happen, it is relatively easy to be critical or to analyze with the benefit of hindsight.

Reform will not come easily, but the stakes are high. As we begin the decade of the 80s, the leadership of the United States is being challenged. The need for a strong and clear voice from the White House is paramount. A well-disciplined staff that focuses on the control issues may not guarantee an effective presidency, but it will greatly increase the likelihood of success.

Source: Adapted from Clifford M. Hardin, *Nation's Business*, Chamber of Commerce of the United States, January 1981, pp. 67–69. Excerpted by permission.

A CONTINGENCY APPROACH

For years, management and behavioral scholars maintained that control in organizations was a fixed commodity that should rest only in the hands of top management. Arnold Tannenbaum has formulated a theory which states that the total amount of control in an organization may increase or decrease.[4] Tannenbaum's theory postulates that increased control, when exercised by both managers and subordinates, can lead to more effective organizational performance. Building on Tannenbaum's work, Timothy McMahon and G. W. Perritt have formulated a contingency theory of control.[5] They state "that organizational effectiveness will be enhanced to the extent that there is a high amount of control exerted within the management system, and that this control is distributed in a power equalized fashion and that there is agreement among managerial echelons as to the amount and distribution of control within the system."[6] Essentially, McMahon and Perritt are saying that the more control, the better, provided the control is shared by individuals close to the work and that there are no disagreements concerning the distribution of the controls.

[4] Arnold S. Tannenbaum, *Control in Organizations* (New York: McGraw-Hill, 1968), pp. 12–25.

[5] J. Timothy McMahon and G. W. Perritt, "Toward a Contingency Theory of Organizational Control," *Academy of Management Journal*, December 1973, pp.624–35.

[6] Ibid., p. 634.

Sharing the controls with individuals close to the work can be accomplished by placing the controls as far down in the organizational structure as possible. Involving the lower echelons in the control process minimizes communication problems and also elicits support. The second contingency of McMahon and Perritt—concerning the distribution of the controls—is necessary to avoid conflicts as to who has the controls. Such conflicts can adversely affect the processes of communicating, organizing, and motivating.

CONTROL METHODS AND SYSTEMS

Control methods can be classified in either of two categories: (1) behavior control or (2) output control. Behavior control, which is sometimes called personal control, is based on direct, personal surveillance. The first-line foreman who maintains a close personal watch over subordinates is using behavior control. Output control, which is sometimes called impersonal control, is based on the measurement of outputs. Tracking production records or sales figures represent uses of output control. Recent research has shown that these two categories of control are not substitutes for each other in the sense that a manager uses one or the other.[7] The evidence suggests rather that output control occurs in response to a manager's need to provide unquestionable evidence of performance. On the other hand, behavior control is exerted when performance requirements are well known and personal surveillance is needed to promote efficiency. Therefore, because output control is impersonal, it is used for communicating the performance of subunits in a large and complex organization. By using output control, the performance of different subunits can be fairly compared. At the subunit level, however, behavioral control is necessary to promote efficiency and to guide the employee. Thus, organizations need to use a mix of output and behavioral controls because they each serve different organizational needs.

One of the most common mistakes made by management is to assume that a new method or system of control will in itself solve problems. Methods and systems in themselves do not control! Control methods and systems in conjunction with good administration and intelligent interpretation provide control. The most appropriate control system is almost worthless if not properly ad-

---

[7] William G. Ouchi and Mary Ann Maguire, "Organizational Control: Two Functions," *Administrative Science Quarterly*, December 1975, pp. 559–71; and William G. Ouchi, "The Transmission of Control Through Organizational Hierarchy," *Academy of Management Journal*, June 1978, pp. 174–76.

ministered. Furthermore, an appropriate control system which is properly administered can only produce information which requires intelligent interpretation. Thus the methods and systems presented in this section should not be viewed as solutions to control problems but rather as potential aids in the control process. It should also be realized that many control tools (such as budgets) are developed as part of the planning process but administered on a regular basis as part of the control process.

Before or after the Fact?

In general, methods of exercising control can be described as either before the fact or after the fact. Before-the-fact methods of control are anticipatory in nature and attempt to prevent a problem from occurring. Requiring prior approval for purchases of all items over a stipulated dollar value is a before-the-fact method of control. After-the-fact methods of control are designed to detect an existing or potential problem before it gets out of hand. Written or periodic reports represent after-the-fact control methods. Most controls are based on after-the-fact methods.

Budgets

Budgets are probably the most widely-used control devices. A budget is a statement of expected results or requirements expressed in financial or numerical terms. Budgets express plans, objectives, and programs of the organization in numerical terms. While preparation of the budget is primarily a planning function (as discussed in Chapter 5), its administration is a controlling function.

Many different types of budgets are in use (Figure 6–5 outlines some of the most common). Although the dollar is usually the common denominator, budgets may be expressed in other terms. Equipment budgets may be expressed in numbers of machines. Material budgets may be expressed in pounds, pieces, gallons, and so on. Budgets not expressed in dollars can usually be translated into dollars for incorporation into an overall budget.

Inflexible budgets. While budgets are useful for planning and control they are not without their dangers. Perhaps the greatest potential danger is inflexibility. Inflexibility is a special threat to organizations operating in an industry characterized by rapid change and high competition. Rigidity in the budget can also lead to a subordination of organizational goals to budgetary goals. The financial manager who won't go $5 over budget in order to make $500 is a classic example. Budgets can hide inefficiencies. The fact that a certain expenditure was made in the past often becomes justification for continuing the expenditure, when in fact the sit-

FIGURE 6–5
Types and Purposes of Budgets

Type of budget	Brief description or purpose
Revenue and expense budget	Provides details for revenue and expense plans
Cash budget	Forecasts cash receipts and disbursements
Capital expenditure budget	Outlines specific expenditures for plant, equipment, machinery, inventories, and other capital items
Production, material, or time budget	Expresses physical requirements of production, or material, or the time requirements for the budget period
Balance sheet budgets	Forecasts the status of assets, liabilities, and net worth at the end of the budget period

uation has changed considerably. Budgets can also become inflationary and inaccurate when managers pad their budgets because they know they will be cut by their superiors. Since the manager is never sure of how severe the cut will be, the result is often an inaccurate if not unrealistic budget.

Flexible budgets. In order to overcome many of the shortcomings resulting from inflexibility in budgets, flexible or variable budgets are designed to vary with the volume of sales or some other measure of output. Because of their nature, flexible budgets are generally limited in application to expense budgets. The basic idea is to allow material, labor, advertising, and other related expenses to vary with the volume of output. Because the actual level of sales or output is not known in advance, flexible budgets are more useful for evaluating what the expenses should have been under the circumstances but have limited value for

TABLE 6–1
Simplified Flexible Budget

Sales (in units)	5,000	6,000	7,000	8,000	9,000
Product cost	$10,000	$12,000	$14,000	$16,000	$18,000
Advertising cost	5,000	5,000	6,000	6,000	7,000
Shipping costs	5,000	5,500	6,000	6,500	7,000
Sales commissions	2,500	3,000	3,500	4,000	4,500
Budgeted expenses	$22,500	$25,500	$29,500	$32,500	$36,500

providing planning information to the overall budgeting program. Table 6–1 illustrates a simplified flexible budget.

Direct Observation

A store manager's daily tour of the facility, a company president's annual visit to all branches and a methods study by a staff industrial engineer are examples of control by direct observation. Although it is time-consuming, personal observation is sometimes the only way to get an accurate picture of what is really happening. A hazard of personal observation is the possibility that the subordinates may misinterpret a superior's visit and consider such action meddling or eavesdropping. A potential inaccuracy associated with personal observation is that behaviors change when they are being watched or monitored. When the boss or methods engineer walks into the room, behaviors may change. Another potential inaccuracy lies in the interpretation of the observation. The observer must be careful not to read into the picture events that did not actually occur. Visits and direct observation can have very positive effects when viewed by the workers as a display of the superior's interest.

Written Reports

Written reports can be prepared on a periodic or "as necessary" basis. There are two basic types of written reports, analytical and informational. Analytical reports interpret the facts they present, whereas informational reports only present the facts. Preparing a report is a four- or five-step process depending on whether it is informational or analytical. The steps are: (1) planning the attack on the problem; (2) collecting the facts; (3) organizing the facts; (4) interpreting the facts (this step is omitted with informational reports); and (5) writing the report.[8] It should be kept in mind that most reports are prepared for the benefit of the reader, not the writer. The reader wants useful information not previously available. The need for a report should be carefully evaluated. Periodic reports have a way of continuing long past their usefulness. Such unnecessary reports represent a substantial waste of organizational resources. Another tendency, even with necessary reports, is to include much useless information.

Audits

Audits can be conducted either by internal or external personnel. An external audit is normally conducted by outside accounting

---

[8] C. W. Wilkinson, Peter B. Clarke, and Dorothy C. M. Wilkinson, *Communicating through Letters and Reports*, 7th ed. (Homewood, Ill.: Richard D. Irwin, 1980), p. 445. Copyright © 1980 by Richard D. Irwin, Inc.

personnel and is limited to financial matters. Such an audit is generally performed to certify the fairness, consistency, and conformity with existing rules of the organization's accounting methods. Most audits performed by outside accounting firms do not delve into nonfinancial matters such as management practices. The internal audit is normally similar to the external audit except it is performed by the organization's own personnel.

When the auditing procedure evaluates areas other than finances and accounting, it is known as a management audit. Management audits attempt to evaluate the overall management practices and policies of the organization. Management audits can be conducted by outside consultants or inside staff; however, a management audit conducted by inside staff can easily result in a biased report.

Break-Even Charts

Break-even charts are used to depict graphically the relationship of volume of operations to profits. Specifically, the break-even point (BEP) is the point at which sales revenues exactly equal expenses. Total sales below the BEP result in a loss; total sales above the BEP result in a profit.

Figure 6–6 illustrates a typical break-even chart. The horizontal axis represents output, the vertical axis represents expenses and revenues. Although not a requirement, most break-even charts assume that there are linear relationships and that all costs are either fixed or variable. Fixed costs are those that do not vary with output, at least in the short run. Examples include rent, insurance, and administrative salaries. Variable costs are those that vary with output. Typical variable costs include direct labor and materials. The purpose of the chart is to show the exact break-even point and the effects of changes in output. A break-even chart

FIGURE 6–6
Break-Even Chart

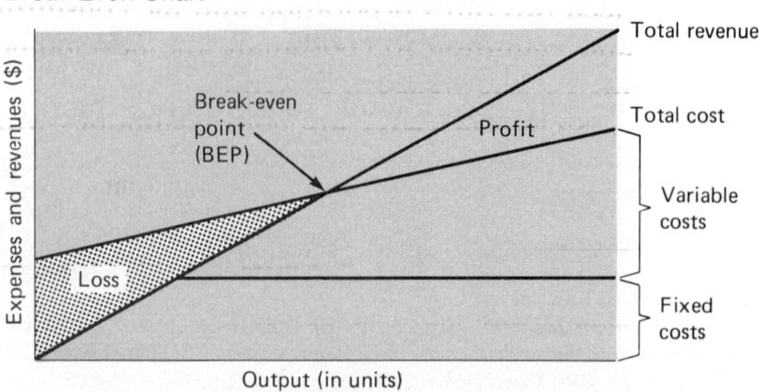

is useful for indicating whether revenue and/or costs are running as planned.

Appendix B at the end of this text contains a more detailed discussion of break-even analysis.

Time-Related Charts and Techniques

"Plan your work and work your plan" has long been a credo for many organizations. Several useful graphical and analytical techniques have been developed to aid in the planning and controlling processes. The overriding purpose of such techniques is to permit the manager to see how the various segments of the operation interrelate and to evaluate the overall progress being made.

The Gantt chart is the oldest and simplest method of graphically showing both anticipated and completed production. Developed by Henry L. Gantt in the early 1900s, the distinguishing feature of the Gantt chart is that work planned and work accomplished are shown in their relation to each other and in relation to time. Figure 6–7 presents a typical Gantt chart.

Gantt charts emphasize the element of time by readily pointing out any actual or potential slippages. One criticism of the Gantt chart is that it can require considerable time to incorporate scheduling changes such as rush orders. To accommodate such scheduling changes rapidly, mechanical boards using movable pegs or cards have been developed.

The Gantt chart concept—identifying work to be done and graphing it against time—formed the foundation for network analysis.[9] The most popular network analysis approaches are Critical Path Method (CPM) and Program Evaluation and Review Technique (PERT). These two techniques were developed almost simultaneously in the late 1950s. CPM grew out of a joint study undertaken by DuPont and Remington Rand Univac to determine how to best reduce the time required to perform routine plant overhaul, maintenance, and construction work.[10] PERT was developed by the Navy in conjunction with representatives of Lockheed Aircraft Corporation and the consulting firm of Booz, Allen, and Hamilton to coordinate the development and production of the Polaris weapons system.

CPM and PERT are both techniques which result in a graphical network representation of a project. The graphical network is composed of activities and events. An activity is the work neces-

[9] There is evidence that there were other forerunners to CPM and PERT. See Edward R. Marsh, "The Harmonogram of Karol Adamiecki," *Academy of Management Journal,* June 1975, pp. 358–64.

[10] Joseph J. Moder and Cecil R. Phillips, *Project Management with CPM and PERT* (New York: Van Nostrand Reinhold, 1970), p. 6.

FIGURE 6–7
Gantt Chart with Heavy Lines Indicating Work Completed

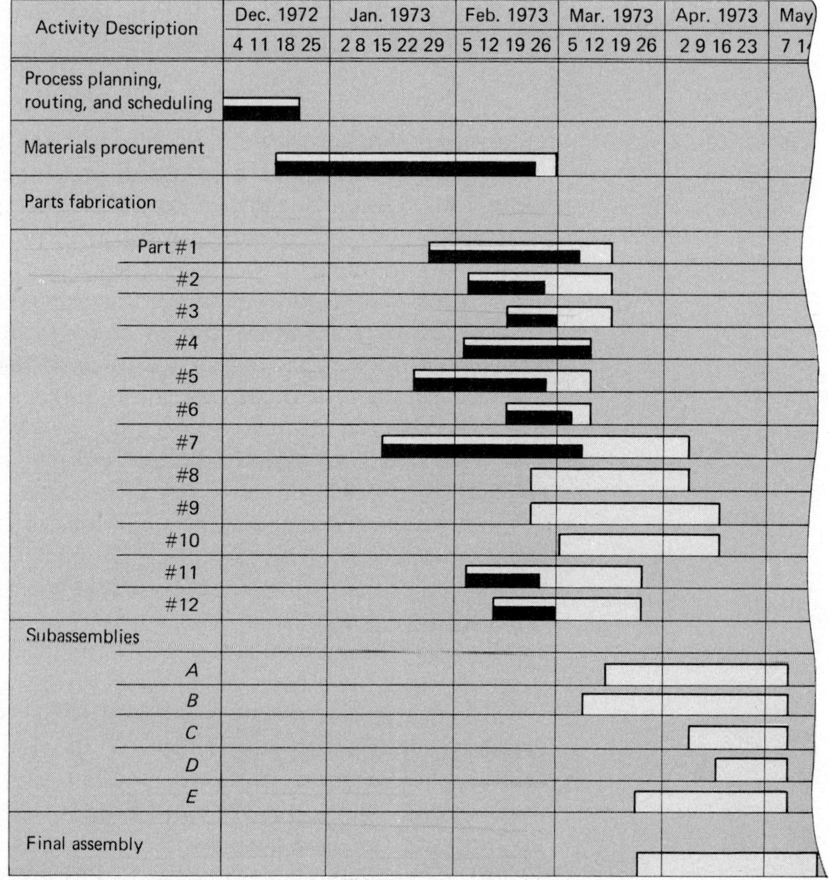

Source: Adapted from Elwood S. Buffa, *Modern Production Management*, 4th ed. (New York: John Wiley & Sons, 1973), p. 576.

sary to complete a particular event, and it usually consumes time. Events denote a point in time, and their occurrence signifies the completion of all activities leading into the event. All activities originate and terminate at events. Activities are normally represented by arrows in a network, while events are represented by a circle. The dashed arrows in a project network, called dummies, show dependencies or precedence relationships. They simply denote that the starting of an activity or set of activities depends on the completion of another activity or set of activities.

Figure 6–8 shows a simple project represented by a Gantt chart and a project network. The project network has two distinct advantages over the Gantt chart: (1) the dependencies of the activities on each other are noted explicitly; and (2) the activities are shown in greater detail.

The path through the network which has the longest duration (based on a summation of estimated individual activity times) is referred to as the critical path. If any activity on the critical path lengthens, then the entire project duration lengthens.

The major difference between CPM and PERT centers around the activity time estimates. CPM is used for projects whose activity durations are accurately known and whose variance in performance time is negligible. On the other hand, PERT is used when the activity durations are more uncertain and variable. CPM is based on a single estimate for an activity duration, where PERT is based on three time estimates for each activity: an optimistic (minimum) time, a most likely (modal) time, and a pessimistic (maximum) time.

Project network analysis can provide information beyond simple project planning and control. By knowing the critical activities, the project manager can best allocate limited resources and

FIGURE 6–8
Project Represented by Gantt Chart and a Project Network

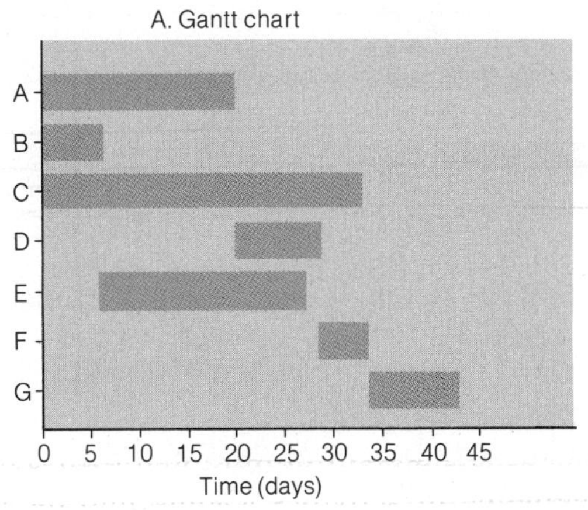

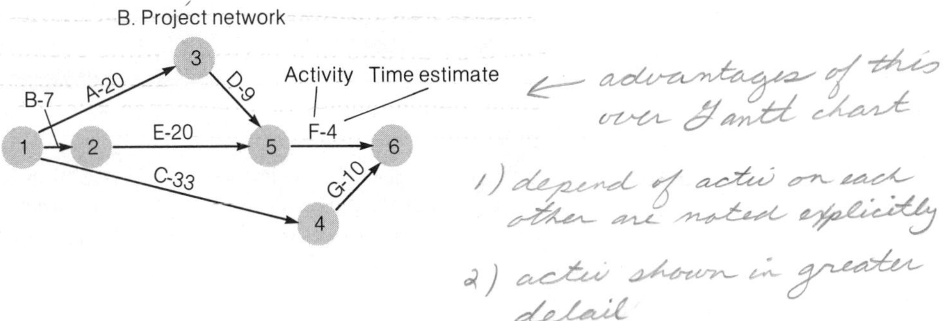

make more accurate time-cost trade-offs. Appendix C at the end of this text contains a more detailed discussion of CPM and PERT.

Management by Objectives (MBO)

Management by objectives (MBO), (discussed in Chapter 4 as an effective means for setting objectives), is another method which can be used for control purposes. As with many of the control techniques discussed in this chapter, the development of an MBO system is part of the planning function. However, once MBO is implemented, it can be used for control purposes. MBO emerged in the late 1950s, and has been described in the following manner:

> A process whereby the superior and subordinate managers of an organization jointly identify its common goals, define each individual's major areas of responsibility in terms of the results expected of him, and use these measures as guides for operating the unit and assessing the contribution of each of its members.[11]

MBO is the control process applied on an individual basis. Standards (objectives) are set, performance is monitored, and corrective action taken where necessary.

Management Information Systems

In recent years the term *management information system* (MIS) has become popular. A management information system is a formal system for providing information to managers. While not absolutely essential, most management information systems incorporate the use of a computer. The basic idea behind a MIS, regardless of its sophistication, is to provide managers with information in a systematic and integrated manner rather than in a sporadic and piecemeal manner. A good MIS naturally enhances managerial control by providing managers with better information on a timely basis.

Unfortunately, many management information systems have been utter failures, often due to the fact that the supposed users didn't know how to use the system. The first rule for any MIS is to design the system to fit the users, not the designers (who are typically computer-oriented). A second rule is to design the MIS

[11] George Odiorne, *Management by Objectives* (Marshfield, Mass.: Pitman Publishing, 1965). Copyright © 1965 by Pitman Publishing Corp. Reprinted by permission of the publisher.

to provide needed information; don't produce information and then attempt to find uses for it.

With the advent and proliferation of small business and personal computers, it may not be long before even most small organizations have an MIS.

SUMMARY

The basic idea behind all management controls is to alert the manager to a problem or potential problem before the problem becomes critical. Management controls are used for several reasons: (1) to prevent crises; (2) to standardize outputs; (3) to appraise employee performance; (4) to update plans; and (5) to protect an organization's assets. The process of control has three basic requirements: (1) establish standards or objectives; (2) monitor results and compare to standards; and (3) correct for deviations. All three requirements are essential to maintaining effective control.

Because actual performance rarely conforms exactly to standards or plans, the manager must set limits as to which deviations from standards are acceptable and which are not. Such deviations are referred to as control tolerances.

Two major factors must be appraised when deciding the degree of control that should be exercised in an organization: (1) economic (cost) considerations and (2) behavioral considerations. Although the benefits from a particular system are often hard to calculate precisely, management should periodically attempt to measure the cost benefit of controls. Such an investigation ensures that gross misapplications do not occur. In order to lessen negative behavioral reactions to control, the manager should make sure that the purpose and nature of the controls are fully understood by all affected employees. A contingency theory of control states that the amount of control exerted within an organization is contingent on the degree to which the control is shared by individuals close to the work and the degree of agreement concerning the distribution of the controls.

Control methods can be classified as one of two types: (1) behavioral control or (2) output control. Behavioral control is based on direct personal surveillance while output control is based on the measurement of outputs.

Several control methods and systems were discussed. These included budgets, personal observation, written reports, audits, break-even charts, time-related charts, management by objectives, and management information systems.

REVIEW QUESTIONS

1. What is management control? What are the two major concerns in management control?
2. Describe a model of the management control process.
3. Outline the three basic requirements of control.
4. How much control should be exercised in an organization?
5. Describe two categories of control methods.
6. Describe the following control methods and systems:
   a. Budgets.
   b. Direct observation.
   c. Written reports.
   d. Audits.
   e. Break-even charts.
   f. Time-related charts and techniques.
   g. Management by objectives.
   h. Management information systems.

DISCUSSION QUESTIONS

1. What factors should you consider before installing tighter controls, and how might you evaluate these factors?
2. If you were implementing a new control system designed to check more closely the expenses of your salespeople, what actions might you take in order to minimize negative reactions?
3. Why are many managers reluctant to take the actions necessary to correct for deviations?
4. How should you deal with managers who are so "married" to their departmental budget that they will not let you spend one dollar in order to make ten dollars?

SELECTED READINGS

Bacon, J. *Managing the Budget Function.* New York: National Industrial Conference Board, 1970.

Barrett, M. E., and L. B. Fraser III. "Conflicting Roles in Budgeting for Operations." *Harvard Business Review,* July–August 1977, pp. 137–46.

Cammann, C., and D. A. Nadler. "Fit Control Systems to Your Managerial Style." *Harvard Business Review,* January–February 1976.

Erlon, Samuel. *Management Control.* London: Macmillan, 1971.

Gibons, C. C. "The Psychology of Budgeting." *Business Horizons,* June 1972, pp. 47–58.

Giglioni, G. B., and A. G. Bedeian. "A Conspectus of Management Control Theory: 1900–1972." *Academy of Management Journal,* June 1974, pp. 292–305.

Hofstade, Geert. "The Poverty of Management Control Philosophy," *Academy of Management Review,* July 1978, pp. 450–61.

Koontz, H., and R. W. Bradspies. "Managing through Feedforward Control." *Business Horizons,* June 1972, pp. 25–36.

Lawler, E. E., and J. G. Rhode. *Information and Control in Organizations.* Santa Monica, Calif.: Goodyear Publishing, 1976.

Mantz, R. K., and F. L. Neumann. "The Effective Corporate Audit Committee." *Harvard Business Review,* November–December 1970, pp. 57–65.

McMahon, J. Timothy, and G. Perritt. "Toward a Contingency Theory of Organization Control." *Academy of Management Journal,* December 1973, pp. 624–35.

Newman, William. *Constructive Control: Design and Use of Control Systems.* Englewood Cliffs, N.J.: Prentice-Hall, 1975.

Odiorne, George. *Management by Objectives.* Marshfield, Mass.: Pitman Publishing, 1965.

Ouchi, William G. "The Transmission of Control through Organization Hierarchy." *Academy of Management Journal,* June 1978, pp. 173–92.

Ouchi, William, and Mary Ann Maguire. "Organizational Control: Two Functions." *Administrative Science Quarterly,* December 1975, pp. 559–69.

Reimann, Bernard, and Anant Negandhi. "Strategies of Administrative Control and Organizational Effectiveness." *Human Relations* 28, no. 5 (1975), pp. 475–86.

Schonberger, R. J. "Custom-Tailored PERT/CPM Systems." *Business Horizons,* December 1972, pp. 64–66.

Tosi, Henry. "The Human Effects of Budgeting Systems on Management." *MSU Business Topics,* Autumn 1974, pp. 53–63.

Case 6–1

"Bird dogging" the employee

Ace Radio, Inc., is a small company located in Centerville. The company is owned and operated by Al Abrams. Abrams, a highly experienced electronics man, founded the company in 1972.

Ace Radio's basic product is a walkie-talkie which is sold primarily to the U.S. military. The walkie-talkie units are relatively simple to produce; Ace merely purchases the parts—cables, wires, transistors, and so on—and assembles them with hand tools. Because of this moderate level of complexity, Ace employs semiskilled workers at low wages.

Although Ace has made a profit each year since production started in 1972, Abrams has become increasingly concerned. Over the past six years he has noticed a general decline in employee morale; concomitantly, he has observed a decline in his employee's productivity and his company's profit margin.

Concerned, Abrams asked his supervisors to keep a closer watch on the hour-to-hour activities of the workers. In the first week they discovered two workers in the restroom reading magazines. This "bird dogging" technique, as it was called by management, or "slave driving," as it was called by the workers, failed to increase production or productivity.

Abrams realized that the lack of performance on the part of some of the workers affected the production of everyone. This phenomenon was caused by the balanced assembly line under which the walkie-talkies were assembled. If an employee next to a normally productive employee did not work fast enough, walkie-talkies would back up on the line. Instead of a backup occurring, however, what usually occurred was a readjustment of the assembly line to the production rate of the slower workers.

In addition, another situation developed which lowered productivity and increased unit costs. Ace was required by the government to meet monthly production and delivery schedules. If they failed, there was a very substantial financial penalty. In recent years the production and delivery schedule had become increasingly difficult to meet. As a matter of fact, for the last eight months Abrams had scheduled overtime in order to meet the production and delivery schedule and thus avoid the financial penalty. This overtime not only increased unit production costs but as a result of this consistent use of overtime many employees began to realize that if they worked slower at the beginning of the month, they could receive more overtime at the end of the month.

This strategy to increase overtime wages was practiced by even senior employees. Abrams was very reluctant to fire anyone especially senior employees. Even if he was inclined to do so, it was difficult to catch employees slowing down, or to provide any reasonable evidence for such rash action.

Abrams was frustrated and perplexed.

1. Describe in detail the control dilemma that exists.
2. Are Abrams and the workers getting the same feedback?
3. What should Abrams do?

Case 6–2

Mickey Mouse controls

Bill: Hey, John, I could sure use some help. We regional supervisors are caught in the middle. What do you do about all this red tape we're having to put up with? The accounting department is all bothered about the way people are padding their expenses and about the cost of luncheons and long-distance calls. You know—their answer is nothing but more red tape.

John: Well, Bill, I don't know. I'm feeling the heat too. Upper management wants us to maintain our contacts with our brokers and try to get the money out in loans. So we push the district supervisors to see our best contacts or at least call them frequently. Yet, lately I've been having a heck of a time getting my men reimbursed for their expenses. Now the accounting department is kicking because we spend a few bucks taking someone to lunch or making a few long-distance calls.

Bill: I really don't know what to do, John. I'll admit that some of my people tend to charge the company for expenses that are for their personal entertainment. But how can I tell whether they're buttering up a broker or just living it up on the company? The accounting department must have some receipts and records to support expenses. Yet I think that getting a receipt from a parking lot attendant is carrying this control stuff too far. As a matter of fact, the other day, I caught a taxi at the airport and failed to get a receipt—I'll bet I have a hard time getting that money from the company even if I sign a notarized affidvait.

John: Well, the way I handle those things is to charge the company more for tips than I actually give—and you know they don't require receipts for tips. I just don't know how to decide whether those reimbursement requests that I sign for my boys are legitimate. If I call a guy up and ask him about some items on a reimbursement request, he acts as though I'm charging him with grand larceny. So far, I've decided to sign whatever requests they turn in and leave the accounting department to scream if it wants to. The trouble is that I don't have any guidelines as to what is reasonable.

Bill: Yeah, but I don't want to ask questions about that because it would just result in more controls! It isn't up to me to be a policeman for the company. The accounting department sits back looking at all those figures—it should watch expenses. I ran into someone from the department the other day on what she called an internal audit trip, and she told me that they aren't in a position to say whether a $25 lunch at a restaurant is necessary to sell a loan. She said that the charge was made by one of my men and that I should check it out! Am I a regional production man or am I an accountant? I've got enough to do meeting my regional quota with my five district sales people. I can't go snooping around to find out whether they're taking advantage of the company. They may get the idea that I don't trust them, and I've always heard that good business depends on trust. Besides, our department makes the company more money than any other one! Why shouldn't we be allowed to spend a little of it?

John: Well, I must say that the brass is getting hot about a relatively small problem. A little fudging on an expense account isn't going to break the company. I learned the other day that the accounting department doesn't require any receipts from the securities department people. They just give them a per diem for travel and let them spend it however they want to, just so long as they don't go over the allotted amount for the days that they're on trips.

Bill: Now that sounds like a good idea. Why can't we do that? It sure would make my life easier. I don't want to get a guilt complex about signing reimbursement requests that may look a little out of line. Why should I call a district man on the carpet for some small expense he swears really was the reason that he got the deal? Production is our job, so why can't the company leave us alone? They should let us decide what it takes to make a deal. If we don't produce the loans, we should catch flak about something that's important—not about these trifling details.

John: Bill, I've got to run now, but honestly if I were you, I wouldn't worry about these Mickey Mouse controls. I'm just going to do my job and fill in the forms in order to stay out of trouble on the details. It's not worth getting upset about.

1. Has the company imposed overly restrictive controls?
2. Do you think the company has a good conception of control tolerances?
3. What should Bill do?

7 Organizing: The Ordering Function

Objectives

1. To introduce the organizing function and show how organization is achieved through division of labor.
2. To discuss the delegation process and its importance in the management process.
3. To present several principles of organization that are related to authority.
4. To explore the advantages and disadvantages of centralization and decentralization.

Chapter Outline

Glossary of Terms

Authority The right to command and expend resources.

Centralized organization A type of organization in which little authority is delegated to lower levels of management.

Decentralized organization A type of organization in which a great deal of authority is delegated to lower levels of management.

Departmentation A form of division of labor that involves grouping activities into related work units.

Exception principle States that managers should concentrate their efforts on matters which deviate significantly from normal and let their subordinates handle routine matters.

Informal organization The aggregate of the personal contacts and interactions and the associated groupings of people working within the formal organization.

Job depth Refers to the freedom of workers to plan and organize their own work, to work at their own pace, and to move around and communicate as desired.

Job scope Refers to the number of different types of operations performed on the job.

Organization A group of people working together in some type of concerted or coordinated effort to attain objectives.

Organizing The grouping of activities necessary to attain common objectives and the assignment of each grouping to a manager who has the authority necessary to supervise the people performing the activities.

Parity principle States that authority and responsibility must coincide.

Power The ability to command or apply force and is not necessarily accompanied by authority.

Responsibility Accountability for the attainment of objectives, the use of resources, and the adherence to organizational policy.

Scalar principle States that authority in the organization flows, one link at a time, through the chain of managers ranging from the highest to lowest ranks.

Span of management Refers to the number of subordinates a manager can effectively manage.

Unity of command principle States that an employee should have one and only one immediate boss.

> If the employer fails to apportion the work among his assistants, it is likely that they will duplicate one another's work. If he neglects to distinguish between the kinds of work as promptly as the amount of endeavor permits, he will lose the advantages of specialization. If he delays too long in appointing supervisors, with the result that the task of oversight exceeds his capacity, the work will not be as well done as it might. Any of these errors reduces, if it does not prevent, the success of the enterprise. In each case, organization has been neglected; it has not performed its mission as a means to a more effective concerted endeavor.
>
> *Alvin Brown**

Most work today is accomplished by organizations. An organization is a group of people working together in some type of concerted or coordinated effort to attain objectives. As such, an organization provides a vehicle for accomplishing objectives that could not be achieved by individuals working separately. The process of organizing is the grouping of activities necessary to attain common objectives and the assignment of each grouping to a manager who has the authority necessary to supervise the people performing the activities.[1] Thus, organizing is basically a process of division of labor accompanied by appropriate delegation of authority. As illustrated in the above introductory quote, proper organizing results in the better use of resources. The framework which defines the boundaries of the formal organization and within which the organization operates is the organization structure. A second and equally important element of an organization is the informal organization. The informal organization refers to the aggregate of the personal contacts and interactions and the associated groupings of people working within the formal organization.[2] The informal organization has a structure but it is not formally and consciously designed.

REASONS FOR ORGANIZING

One of the primary reasons for organizing is to establish lines of authority. Establishing lines of authority creates order within the

*Alvin Brown, *Organization of Industry* (Englewood Cliffs, N.J.: Prentice-Hall, 1947), p. 15.

[1] Harold Koontz and Cyril O'Donnell, *Management: A Systems and Contingency Analysis of Managerial Functions*, 6th ed. (New York: McGraw-Hill, 1976), p. 274.

[2] Chester L. Barnard, *Functions of the Executive* (Cambridge, Mass.: Harvard University Press, 1938), pp. 114–15.

group. The absence of authority almost always leads to chaotic situations in which everyone is telling everyone else what to do.

Secondly, organizing improves the efficiency and quality of work through synergism. Synergism occurs when individual or separate units work together to produce a whole greater than the sum of the parts. Synergism results when three people working together produce more than four people working separately. Synergism can result from division of labor or from increased coordination, both of which are products of good organization.

A final reason for organizing is to improve communication. A good organization structure clearly defines channels of communication among the members of the organization. Such a system also ensures more efficient communications. The role of communication in the management process will be discussed in Chapter 11.

DIVISION OF LABOR

Organizing is basically a process of division of labor. The merits of dividing labor have been known for centuries. Taking the very simple task of manufacturing a pin, Adam Smith in 1776 demonstrated how much more efficiently the task could be performed through division of labor.[3]

Labor can be divided either vertically or horizontally. Vertical division of labor is based on the establishment of lines of authority and defines the levels that make up the vertical organizational structure. In addition to establishing authority, vertical division of labor facilitates the flow of communication within the organization.

Horizontal division of labor is based on specialization of work. The basic assumption underlying horizontal division of labor is that by making each worker's task specialized, more work can be produced with the same effort through increased efficiency and quality. Specifically, horizontal division of labor can result in the following advantages:

1. Fewer skills required per person.
2. Easier to specify the skills required for selection or training purposes.
3. Repetition or practice of the same job develops proficiency.
4. Efficient use of skills by primarily utilizing each worker's best skills.
5. The ability to have concurrent operations.

[3] Adam Smith, *The Wealth of Nations* (New York: Modern Library, 1917); originally published in 1776.

6. More conformity in the final product if each piece is always produced by the same person.

The major problem with horizontal division of labor is that it can result in job boredom and even degradation of the worker. An extreme example of horizontal division of labor is the automobile assembly line. It is not hard to imagine the behavioral problems associated with such an assembly line. When examining horizontal division of labor, it is necessary to identify two dimensions of the job: scope and depth.[4]

Job scope refers to the number of different types of operations performed. In performing a job with narrow scope the worker would perform few operations and repeat the cycle frequently. The negative effects of jobs lacking in scope vary with the person performing the job but can result in more errors and lower quality.

Job depth refers to the freedom of workers to plan and organize their own work, to work at their own pace, and to move around and communicate as desired. A lack of job depth can result in job dissatisfaction and work avoidance which can in turn lead to absenteeism, tardiness, and even sabotage.

A job can be high in job scope and low in job depth or vice versa. For example, newspaper delivery involves the same few operations each time, but there is considerable freedom in organizing and pacing the work. Thus, the job is low in scope but high in depth. Of course, many jobs are low (or high) in both job scope and job depth.

Division of labor is not more efficient or even desirable in all situations. At least two basic requirements must exist for the successful use of division of labor. The first requirement is a relatively large volume of work. Enough volume must be produced to allow for specialization and also to keep each worker busy. A second basic requirement is stability in the volume of work, worker attendance, quality of raw materials, product design, and production technology.

DEPARTMENTATION

Departmentation is the most frequently used method for implementing division of labor. Departmentation involves grouping activities into related work units. The work units may be related on the basis of work functions, product, customer, geography, technique, or time.

[4]Alan Filley, Robert House, and Steven Kerr, *Managerial Process and Organizational Behavior*, 2d ed., (Glenview, Ill.: Scott, Foresman, 1976), p. 339.

Functional Departmentation

Functional departmentation occurs when organization units are defined by the nature of the work. Although different terminology may be used, most organizations have three basic functions—production, sales, and finance. Production refers to the actual creation of something of value, either goods or services or both. The distribution of the goods or services created is usually referred to as sales or marketing. Finally, any organization, whether manufacturing or service, must provide the financial structure necessary for carrying out its activities.

Each of these basic functions may be further subdivided as necessary. For instance, the production department may be departmentalized into maintenance, quality control, engineering, manufacturing, and so on. The marketing department may be grouped into advertising, sales, and market research. Figure 7-1 illustrates a typical organization with functional departmentalization.

FIGURE 7–1
Functional Departmentation

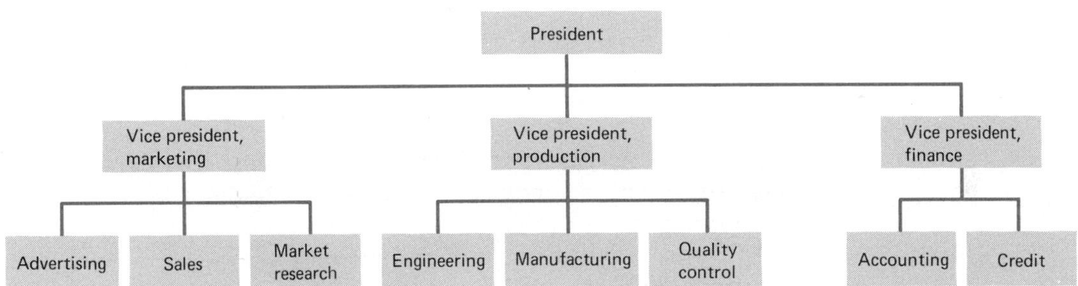

The primary advantage of functional departmentalization is that it allows for specialization within functions. It also provides for efficient use of equipment and resources. Functional departmentation, however, can be accompanied by some negative effects. Members of a functional group may develop more loyalty to the functional group's goals than to the organization's goals. If the group's goals and the organization's goals are not mutually supportive, such activity can lead to suboptimization. Conflict may also develop between different departments striving for different goals. This type of conflict is discussed in greater depth in Chapter 13.

Product Departmentation

Under departmentation by product or service, all the activities necessary to produce and market a product or service are usually under a single manager. Product departmentation allows individuals to identify with a particular product and thus develop esprit de corps. It also facilitates managing each product as a different profit center. Product departmentation provides opportunities for training executive personnel by allowing them to experience a broad range of functional activities. Problems can arise under product departmentation if departments become overly competitive to the detriment of the overall organization. A second potential shortcoming of product departmentation is that duplication of facilities and equipment may be necessary. Product departmentation is most adaptable to large, multiproduct organizations (see Figure 7–2).

FIGURE 7–2
Product Departmentation

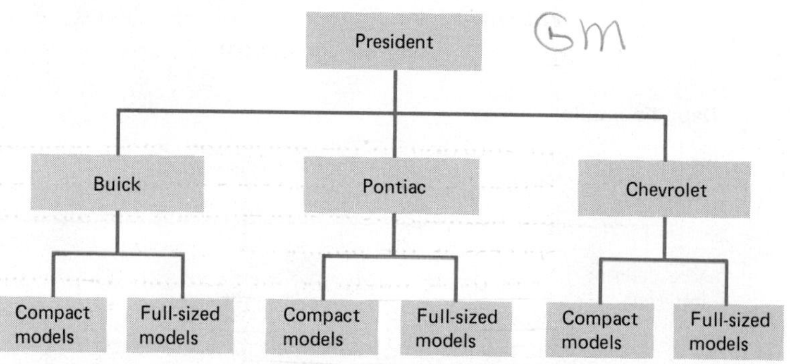

Geographic Departmentation

Departmentation by territories is most likely to occur in organizations which maintain physically dispersed and autonomous operations or offices. Geographic departmentation permits the use of local workers and/or salespeople. This can create customer goodwill and an awareness of local feelings and desires. Geographic departmentation can also provide a high level of service. Of course, operating too many geographic locations can be extremely costly.

Customer Departmentation

Another type of departmentation is based on division by customers served. A common example is an organization which has one department to handle retail customers and one to handle wholesale or industrial customers. Figure 7–3 represents departmentation by customer for a large insurance company. Customer departmentation is subject to the same advantages and dis-

FIGURE 7–3
Customer Departmentation

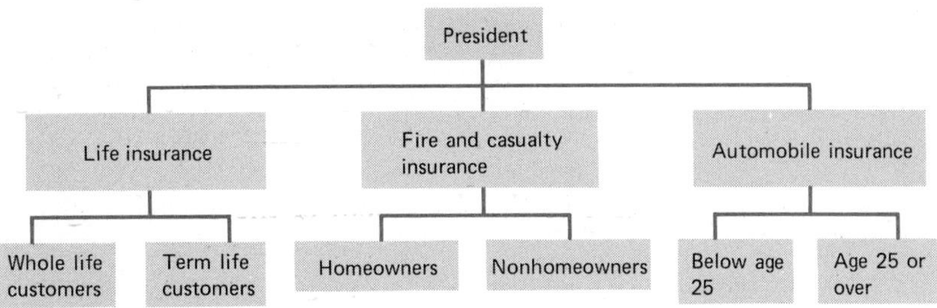

advantages as product departmentation. For example, if the life insurance division and fire and casualty division in Figure 7–3 became overly competitive with each other in regard to the allocation of organizational resources, the organization's overall performance could be damaged.

Other Types of Departmentation

In addition to the preceding, most popular, types of departmentation, several other types are possible. Departmentation by simple numbers is practiced when the most important ingredient to success is the number of workers. Organizing for a local United Way drive might be an example. Departmentation by process or equipment is another possibility. Not totally different from functional departmentation, activities can be grouped according to the equipment or process used. A final type of departmentation is by time or shift. Organizations that work around the clock may departmentalize according to shift.

Departmentation is practiced not only as a means of implementing division of labor but also to improve control and communications. Typically, as an organization grows in size it adds levels of departmentation. A small organization may initially have no departmentation. As it grows it may first departmentalize according to function, then according to product, then according to geography. As illustrated in Figure 7–4, many different department mixes are possible for a given organization. Which one is best depends on the specfic situation and circumstances.

AUTHORITY, POWER, AND RESPONSIBILITY

Authority is the right to command and expend resources. Lines of authority serve to link the various organizational components together. Unclear delegation of authority is a major source of confusion and conflict within an organization.

FIGURE 7–4
Possible Departmentation Mixes for a Sales Organization

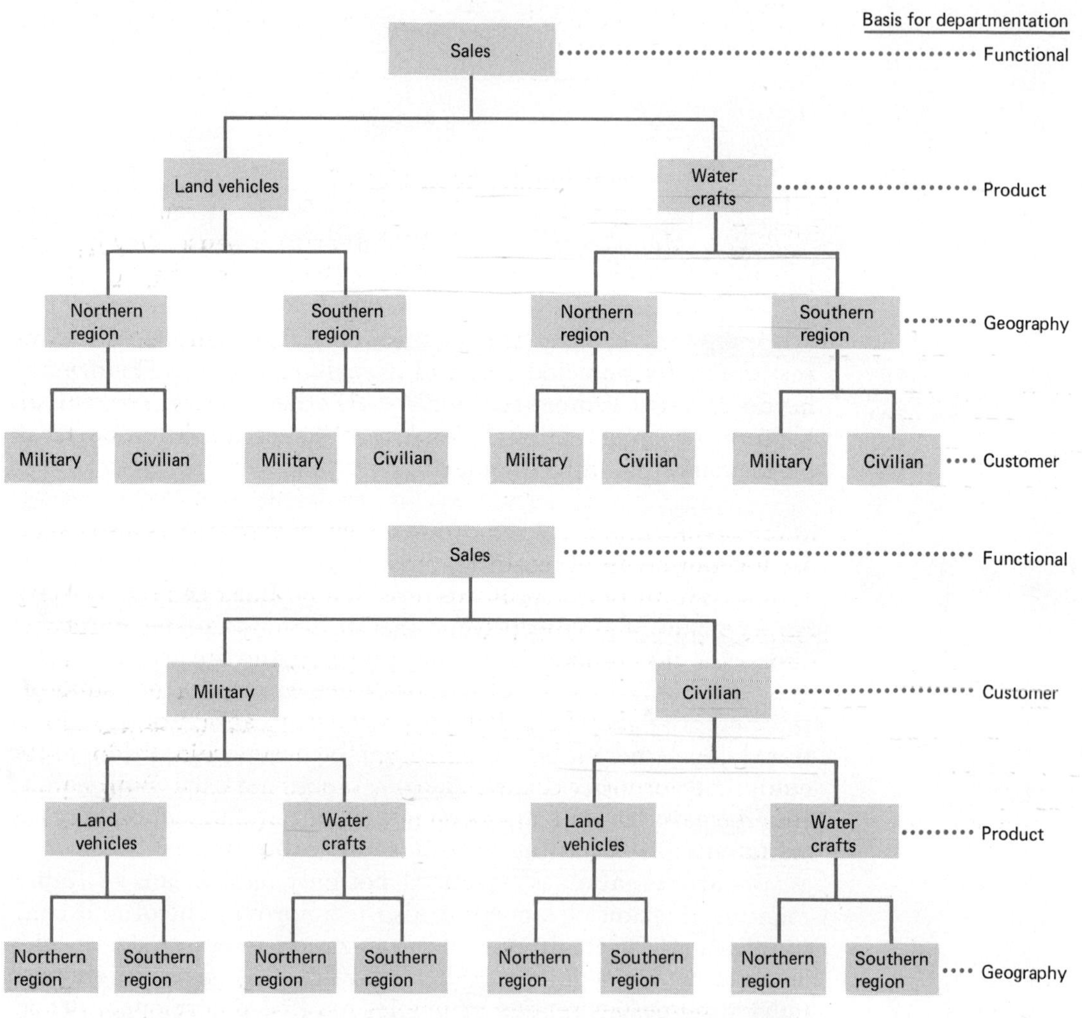

Many people confuse power with authority. Power is the ability to command or apply force and is not necessarily accompanied by authority. Power is derived from the control of resources. A man with a pistol may have the power to shoot another, but he does not have the right to do so. Similarly, managers may have the power to make frivolous expenditures, but they do not have the right to do so. However, it is true that authority and power often accompany each other.

Responsibility is accountability for the attainment of objectives, the use of resources, and the adherence to organizational policy. Once responsibility is accepted, it becomes an obligation to perform assigned work. The term *responsibility* as used here should not be confused with the term *responsibilities* as in the context of defining job duties.

SOURCES OF AUTHORITY

Authority has traditionally been viewed as a function of position, flowing from top to bottom through the formal organization. According to this view, people hold authority because they occupy a certain position; once removed from the position they lose their authority. Taking this theory one step further, one can say that the American people, through the Constitution and laws, represent the ultimate source of authority in this country. The Constitution and laws guarantee the right of free enterprise. The owners of a free enterprise organization have the right to elect a board of directors and top management. Top management selects middle-level managers. This process continues down to the lowest person in the organization. This traditional view of authority is also called the formal theory of authority.

A second theory of authority was first outlined in 1926 by Mary Parker Follett and later popularized in 1938 by Chester Barnard.[5] Called the acceptance theory of authority, this theory maintains that a manager's source of authority lies with his or her subordinates because they have the power to either accept or reject the manager's command. Presumably, if the subordinate does not accept the authority of the manager, it does not exist. Both Follett and Barnard viewed disobedience of a communication from a manager as a denial of authority by the subordinate.

PRINCIPLES BASED ON AUTHORITY

Because authority is a key element in management and organizations, numerous related principles have been developed. Before proceeding, recall from chapter 1 that management principles are suggested guides rather than ironclad laws.

Delegation—The Parity Principle

Can authority be delegated? Can responsibility be delegated? There is little debate concerning the delegation of authority—it can and should be delegated. For example, a manager might very well choose to delegate the authority to subordinates to make ex-

[5] Mary Parker Follett, *Freedom and Co-Ordination* (London: Management Publication Trust, 1949), pp. 1–15 (the lecture reproduced in *Freedom and Co-ordination* was first delivered in 1926); and Barnard, *Functions of the Executive*, p. 163.

penditures, without approval, up to a stipulated amount. However, considerable debate often arises with regard to the delegation of responsibility. A close analysis of this debate generally reveals that the debate is more the result of semantics rather than a misunderstanding of the concepts involved. Those contending that responsibility cannot be delegated support their answer by stating that managers can never shed the responsibilities of their jobs by passing them on to subordinates. Those contending that responsibility can be delegated justify their position by pointing out that managers can certainly make subordinates responsible to them for certain actions. Both parties are correct! Managers can delegate responsibilities to subordinates in the sense of making subordinates responsible to them. However, this delegation to subordinates does not make managers any less responsible to their superiors. Delegation of responsibility does not mean abdication of responsibility by the delegating manager. Responsibility is not like an object which can be passed from individual to individual. Suppose a loan manager for a bank decided to delegate to the loan officers the responsibility for insuring that all loans are processed within a 10-day limit as stated by bank policy. The loan manager can certainly make the loan officers accountable (responsible) to him or her regarding this matter. At the same time the loan manager is no less accountable to his or her boss.

The parity principle states that authority and responsibility must coincide. Management must delegate sufficient authority so subordinates can do their jobs. At the same time subordinates can be expected to accept responsibility only for those areas within their authority.

Both authority and responsibility must be accepted by subordinates before the delegation process has been completed. Management sometimes expects employees to seek and assume responsibility that they have not been asked to assume and then to bid for the necessary authority. Such a system leads to guessing games which do nothing but create frustration and waste energy.

Resisting the delegation of authority is natural. There are several reasons why many managers are reluctant to delegate authority. Unfortunately, many managers subscribe to the old saying "If you want something done right do it yourself!" Such an attitude reveals that the manager does not have a grasp of the management process, and demonstrates that the manager has done a poor job of selecting and developing subordinates. Managers who attempt to do everything themselves find that their time is continually consumed by rather unimportant tasks and that they do not have time to do important tasks. Newly appointed managers often have a tendency to adopt this attitude. They fear failure unless they do each task personally.

A second reason often given for not delegating is that it is easier for a manager to do a task than to teach a subordinate how to do it. This might be true the first time a particular task has to be done, but what about the tenth or twentieth time? Delegating often does involve some initial investment of time; however, this investment is usually quickly recouped through subsequently saved time.

A third reason why managers are reluctant to delegate is the fear that a subordinate will look so good that he or she might replace the manager. To good managers, such fears are totally unfounded. A manager's performance is, for the most part, a reflection of the performance of subordinates. If a manager's subordinates look good, the manager looks good; if the subordinates look bad, the manager looks bad.

A fourth reason that causes managers to shy away from delegating is the human attraction for power. Most humans like the feel of power which often accompanies authority. To many managers there is a certain degree of satisfaction in having the power and authority to grant or not grant certain requests.

In spite of all the reasons for not delegating, there are some very strong reasons why a manager should delegate. Several phenomena occur when a manager successfully delegates. The manager's time is freed to pursue more important tasks, and the subordinates gain feelings of belonging and being needed. These feelings often lead to a genuine commitment on the part of the subordinates. An additional reason to delegate is that it is one of the best methods for developing subordinates.

Unfortunately, the tendency of many delegating managers is to delegate only simple, unimportant tasks. The following quote from Robert Townsend illustrates this point:

> Many give lip service, but few delegate authority in important matters. And that means all they delegate is dog-work. A real leader does as much dog-work for his people as he can: He can do it, or see a way to do without it, 10 times as fast. And he delegates as many important matters as he can because that creates a climate in which people grow.[6]

Successful delegation involves delegating matters which stimulate the subordinates.

How to delegate William Newman has listed three components of the delegation process: (1) the assignment of duties by managers to their immediate subordinates; (2) the granting of permission (authority) to make commitments, use resources, and

[6] Robert Townsend, *Up the Organization* (New York: Alfred A. Knopf, 1970), p. 46.

MANAGEMENT IN PRACTICE

Profile: Sanford N. McDonnell

Shortly after Sanford N. McDonnell was promoted to chief executive officer of McDonnell Douglas Corporation nine years ago, he attended a monthly dinner meeting of his management personnel from the St. Louis facilities of the giant aerospace manufacturing company.

Officers of the club escorted Sandy McDonnell, as he likes to be called, into a special room where the top executives of the company were enjoying before-dinner refreshments. Sandy McDonnell accepted a drink and kept on walking—into the much larger area where hundreds of the company's foremen and middle managers were gathering.

There he began shaking hands, calling many of the men and women by their first names. The remainder of his executives soon followed suit, and that was the end of special rooms at management club meetings.

This story is typical of the lanky six-footer who does not stand on ceremony and who has practiced "hands-on" management throughout his more than three decades with McDonnell Douglas.

A soft spoken Southerner, he has helped propel this jet-age company into the fore-front of space-age technology with keen perception and acute analytical ability. With annual sales in excess of $6 billion, McDonnell Douglas is the nation's second largest defense contractor and the world's third largest commercial aircraft supplier.

From microcircuits to software designs, from guidance systems to composites, from wide-body jets to fighter planes, Sandy McDonnell has helped the company build a reputation for being in the vanguard of the aerospace industry. Under the leadership of CEO McDonnell, McDonnell Douglas has displayed the designing and building capability of America's premiere defense contractor.

Born in Little Rock, Arkansas in 1922, Sandy McDonnell attended Princeton University where he earned a B.A. in economics. He then attended the University of Colorado, earning a B.S. in mechanical engineering. He was awarded an M.S. in applied mechanics at Washington University.

In 1948, degrees in hand, he approached his uncle, founder of the then-nine-year-old McDonnell Aircraft Corporation. "I went to him to ask for a job," he explains. "Mr. Mac wanted me to start at the lowest wage paid," he chuckles, "That of a floor sweeper. I refused. I wanted to start at the going rate for a person with my background." After much bargaining, his high-flying career was launched—at the rate of $1.26 an hour.

Armed with a slide rule and a calculator, Sandy McDonnell began his ascent to the top of the corporation. After completing the company-wide training program, he served as stress engineer, aerodynamicist, design engineer, group leader, project manager, vice president, president and, ultimately, chairman of the board and chief executive officer. "Mr. Mac gave me a broad base of experience before I started moving up," he explains. "But," he adds, "I had to prove myself all along the way before I had the opportunity to climb to the next rung on the ladder."

Advancement under fire in no way changed the easygoing manner and country charm of this executive ignited with the zeal to succeed. To this day, 59-year-old Sandy McDonnell is known in the industry as a "nice guy." He believes "you don't have to be a table-pounding, shouting, overbearing tyrant to be a good executive. You can be firm and tough in an empathetic way."

Geographically and functionally decentralized, the success of McDonnell Douglas rests firmly upon the delegation of decision making. "I'm a team player," McDonnell explains. "I like to think of myself not as someone sitting on top telling everybody what to do but someone who tries to put together the best combination of individuals to come up with the most synergistic team we can put together. A company this size cannot function with decisions being handed down from one office. I concentrate on bringing out the potential of our executives—to get them to work together toward the common goals of the corporation."

Delegation, however, does not mean hands-off. Each day at 8:20 a.m., the company's top corporate executives gather in Sandy McDonnell's office atop the company's bronze steel and glass office tower to discuss projects and problems. The stand-up meeting, which lasts approximately 15 minutes, serves as a base for communication among the various parts of the corporation, he asserts.

Source: Karol White, *Sky*, March 1982, p. 27. Reprinted by permission.

take all actions which are necessary to perform the duties; and (3) the creation of an obligation (responsibility) on the part of each subordinate to the delegating manager to perform the duties satisfactorily.[7]

In order to best assign duties to subordinates, managers must be well acquainted with the skills of their immediate subordinates. The manager must also be able to determine the functions and duties that can be delegated and those that cannot.

The second and third components of Newman's delegation process stress the parity principle. The still unanswered question is "How much authority should be delegated?" As mentioned previously, management must delegate sufficient authority to allow the subordinate to perform the job. Precisely what can and what cannot be delegated depends on the commitments of the manager and the number and quality of subordinates.

Unity of Command

The principle of unity of command states that an employee should have one and only one immediate manager. The difficulty of serving more than one superior has been recognized for thousands of years. Recall the Sermon on the Mount, when Jesus said, "No man can serve two Masters."[8] Experts have speculated that vio-

[7] William H. Newman, *Administrative Action*, 2d ed. (Englewood Cliffs, N.J.: Prentice-Hall, 1963), pp. 185–86.

[8] *The Holy Bible*, Revised Standard Version, Matt. 6:24.

lation of this one concept accounts for as many as 30 percent of the human relations problems in American industry.[9] In its simplest form, this problem arises when two managers tell the same subordinate to do different jobs at the same time. The subordinate is thus placed in a no-win situation. Regardless of which manager the employee obeys, the other will be dissatisfied. Violation of the principle of unity of command is generally caused by unclear lines of authority and poor communication.

Scalar Principle

The scalar principle states that authority in the organization flows one link at a time, through the chain of managers ranging from the highest to lowest ranks. Commonly referred to as the chain of command, the scalar principle is based on the need for communication and the principle of unity of command.

The problem with circumventing the scalar process is that the link bypassed in the process may have very pertinent information. For example, suppose that Jerry goes directly above his immediate boss, Ellen, to Charlie for permission to take his lunch break 30 minutes earlier. Charlie, believing the request to be reasonable, approves Jerry's request only to later find out that the other two people in Jerry's department had also rescheduled their lunch breaks. Thus, the department would be totally vacant from 12:30 to 1:00. Ellen, the bypassed manager, would probably have known about the other rescheduled lunch breaks.

A common misconception is that every action must painfully progress through every link in the chain, whether its course is upward or downward. Lyndell Urwick has refuted this point:

> Provided there is proper confidence and loyalty between superiors and subordinates, and both parties take the trouble to keep the other informed in matters in which they should have a concern, the "scalar process" does not imply that there should be no shortcuts. It is concerned with authority and provided the authority is recognized and no attempt is made to evade or to supercede it, there is ample room for avoiding in matters of action the childish practices of going upstairs one step at a time or running up one ladder and down another when there is nothing to prevent a direct approach on level ground.[10]

As Fayol stated, years before Urwick, "it is an error to depart needlessly from the line authority, but it is an even greater one to

---

[9] E. T. Eggers, "Authority and Responsibility," *Atlanta Economic Review*, February 1970, p. 32.

[10] L. F. Urwick, *The Elements of Administration* (New York: Harper & Row, 1943), p. 46.

keep to it when detriment to the business ensues."[11] Both men are simply saying that in certain instances one can and should shortcut the scalar chain if it is not done in a secretive or deceitful manner.

Span of Management

The span of management (also called the span of control) refers to the number of subordinates a manager can effectively manage. Although the concept was discussed by Fayol, Sir Ian Hamilton, the World War I-British general, is usually given credit for developing the first popular version of the concept of a limited span of management. Sir Ian argued that a narrow span of management (with no more than six subordinates reporting to a manager) would enable the manager to get the job accomplished in the course of a normal working day.[12]

In 1933, V. A. Graicunas published a classical paper which analyzed subordinate-superior relationships in terms of a mathematical formula.[13] This formula was based on the theory that the complexities of managing increase geometrically as the number of subordinates increases arithmetically. Graicunas's reasoning was that not only did the number of direct single relationships increase but so did the number of direct group relationships and cross relationships. Table 7–1 shows the total number of potential relationships envisioned by Graicunas.

TABLE 7–1
Graicunas's Direct, Cross, and Group Relationships

Number of subordinates	Number of direct single relationships	Number of cross relationships	Number of direct group relationships	Number of total relationships
1	1	0	0	1
2	2	2	2	6
3	3	6	9	18
4	4	12	28	44
5	5	20	75	100
6	6	30	186	222
7	7	42	441	490
8	8	56	1016	1080

[11] Henri Fayol, *General and Industrial Management* (London: Sir Isaac Pitman and Sons, 1949), p. 36. (First published in 1916.)

[12] Sir Ian Hamilton, *The Soul and Body of an Army* (London: Edward Arnold, 1921), p. 229.

[13] V. A. Graicunas, "Relationship in Organization," *Bulletin of the International Management Institute* (Geneva: International Labour Office, 1933), reprinted in *Papers on the Science of Administration*, (ed. L. Gulick and F. L. Urwick (New York: Institute of Public Administration, 1937), pp. 181–87.

Based on personal experiences and the works of Sir Ian Hamilton and Graicunas, Lyndall Urwick first stated the concept of span of management as a management principle in 1938: "No superior can supervise directly the work of more than five or, at the most six subordinates whose work interlocks."[14] As will be seen, Urwick's concept is not exactly applicable in all situations.

Since the publication of Graicunas's and Urwick's works, the upper limit of five or six subordinates has been continuously criticized as being too restrictive. Many practitioners and scholars contend that there are situations in which more than five or six subordinates can be effectively supervised. Their beliefs have been substantiated by considerable empirical evidence showing that the limit of five or six subordinates has been successfully exceeded in many situations.[15] Urwick has suggested that these exceptions can be explained by the fact that senior workers often function as unofficial managers or leaders.[16]

In view of recent evidence the span of management concept has been revised to state that the number of people who should report directly to any one person should be based upon the complexity of the jobs, the variety of the jobs, the proximity of the jobs, the quality of the people filling the jobs, and the ability of the manager. Complexity basically refers to the job scope and job depth of the jobs being managed. Naturally, the more complex the jobs being managed, the lower the appropriate span of management. Variety relates to the number of different types of jobs being managed. For example, are all the subordinates doing the same or similar jobs or are they doing very different jobs? The more variety that is present, the lower the appropriate span of management. The physical dispersion or the proximity of the jobs being managed also influences the span of management. If the subordinates are all working in rather close proximity, such as in one room, the span of management would be greater than if they are spread over the city or state. Quality of the people refers to the fact that some people need and require closer supervision than do others. The final contingent factor, the ability of the manager, refers to the skill of the manager in performing managerial duties.

Thus, in situations where workers are engaged in simple, re-

---

[14] L. F. Urwick, "Scientific Principles and Organizations," *Institute of Management Series no. 19* (New York: American Management Association, 1938), p. 8.

[15] For a brief discussion of such situations see Leslie W. Rue, "Supervisory Control in Modern Management," *Atlanta Economic Review,* January–February 1975, pp. 43–44.

[16] L. F. Urwick, "V. A. Graicunas and the Span of Control," *Academy of Management Journal,* June 1974, p. 352.

petitive operations in close proximity, the span of management could be very large. In situations involving highly diversified and technical work, the span of management might be as low as three or four.

While much thought is given to ensuring that a manager's span of management is not too great, the opposite situation is often overlooked. All too frequently, situations develop in organizations in which only one subordinate is reporting to a particular manager. While this situation might very well be justified under certain circumstances, it often results in an inefficient and "top-heavy" organization. The pros and cons of flat (wide span of management, few levels) organizations versus tall (narrow span of management, many levels) organizations are discussed at length in the next chapter. Figure 7–5 summarizes the factors affecting the manager's span of management.

FIGURE 7–5
Factors Affecting the Span of Management

Factor	*Description*	*Relationship to span of control*
Complexity	Job scope Job depth	Inverse*
Variety	Number of different types of jobs being managed	Inverse*
Proximity	Physical dispersion of jobs being managed	Direct†
Quality of subordinates	General quality of the subordinates being managed	Direct†
Quality of manager	Ability to perform managerial duties	Direct†

*As the factor of complexity (or variety) increases, the span of management decreases.
†As the factor of proximity (or quality) increases, the span of management increases.

The Exception Principle

The exception principle (also known as management by exception) is closely related to the parity principle. The exception principle states that managers should concentrate their efforts on matters which deviate significantly from normal and let subordinates handle routine matters. The idea here is that managers should concentrate on those matters that require their abilities and not become bogged down with duties that their subordinates should be doing. The exception principle can be abused by incompetent and insecure subordinates who refer everything to their superiors because they are afraid to make a decision. On the other hand, the superior should refrain from making everyday decisions which have been delegated to a subordinate.

CENTRALIZATION VERSUS DECENTRALIZATION

There are limitations to the authority of any position. These limitations may be external, in the form of laws, politics, or social attitudes, or they may be internal, as delineated by the organization's objectives or by the job description. The tapered concept of authority states that the breadth and scope of authority become more limited as one descends the scalar chain (see Figure 7–6).

The top levels of management establish the shape of the funnels in Figures 7–6 and 7–7. The more authority that top management chooses to delegate, the less conical the funnel becomes. The less conical the funnel, the more decentralized is the organization. Centralization or decentralization refers to the degree of authority delegated by upper management. This is usually reflected by the numbers and kinds of decisions made by the lower levels of management. As the number and importance of decisions made at the lower levels of the organization increase, the degree of decentralization also increases. Thus, an organization is never totally centralized or totally decentralized: it falls along a continuum ranging from highly centralized to highly decentralized. Looking at Figure 7–7, the organization represented by the left-hand side diagram is much more centralized than that represented by the right-hand side diagram.

The answer to the question of how much an organization should decentralize depends on the specific situation and organization. Decentralization allows for more flexibility and quicker action. It also relieves executives from time-consuming detail work. It often results in higher morale by allowing lower levels of management to be actively involved in the decision-making process. The major disadvantage of decentralization is the potential

FIGURE 7–6
Tapered Concept of Authority

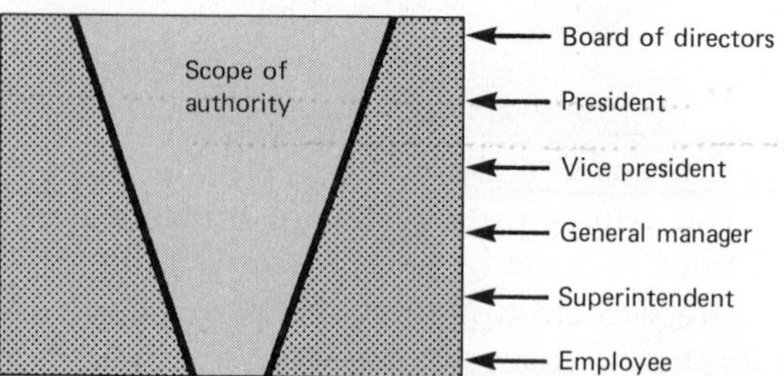

FIGURE 7–7
Centralized versus Decentralized Authority

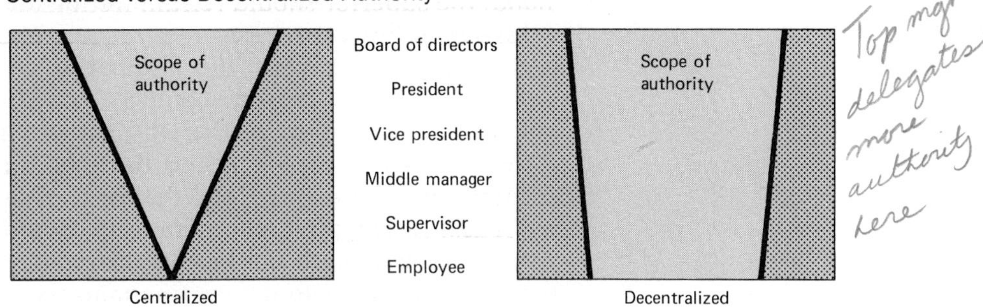

loss of control. Duplication of effort can also accompany decentralization.

Because no magic formula exists for determining the appropriate degree of decentralization, top management must periodically evaluate its particular situation in light of the advantages and disadvantages of greater decentralization.

SUMMARY

An organization is a group of people working together in some type of concerted or coordinated effort to attain common objectives. As such, an organization provides a vehicle for accomplishing objectives that could not be achieved by individuals working separately. Specific reasons for organizing include the need to establish lines of authority, improve efficiency and quality of work through synergism, and increase communication.

Horizontal and vertical division of labor are the means by which organization is accomplished. Departmentation is the most frequently used method for implementing division of labor. Departmentation refers to the grouping of activities into related work units. The work units may be related on the basis of work function, product, customer, geography, techniques, or time.

Authority is the right to command and expend resources. Power is the ability to command or apply force. Responsibility is accountability for the attainment of objectives, the use of resources, and the adherence to organizational policy.

Many management principles are based on the concept of authority. These principles include:

1. The parity principle: authority and responsibility must coincide.
2. Unity of command: an employee should have one and only one immediate manager.

3. The scalar principle: authority in the organization flows, one link at a time, through the chain of managers ranging from highest to lowest ranks.
4. Span of management: the number of people who directly report to any one person should be based on the complexity of the jobs, the variety of the jobs, the proximity of the jobs, the quality of the people filling the jobs, and the ability of the manager.
5. The exception principle: managers should concentrate on matters which deviate significantly from normal and let their subordinates attend to the routine matters.

While all managers should be familiar with the basic management and organization principles, they should be used as guides for action, not as laws.

Delegation is one key to successful management. Yet there are several reasons why managers are often reluctant to delegate. Fear of the subordinate failing, the "If you want it done right, do it yourself" attitude, fear of the subordinate 'looking too good,' and the human attraction for power are some of the more frequently encountered reasons for failure to delegate.

Centralization or decentralization refers to the degree of authority delegated by upper management. This is usually reflected by the numbers and kinds of decisions made by the lower levels of management.

REVIEW QUESTIONS

1. What is an organization? Define the management function of organizing. Define organizational structure. What is the informal organization?
2. Discuss the reasons for organizing.
3. What is the difference between horizontal and vertical division of labor? What is the difference between job scope and job depth?
4. Explain:
   a. Functional departmentation.
   b. Product departmentation.
   c. Geographic departmentation.
   d. Customer departmentation.
5. Define authority, power, and responsibility.
6. Discuss two approaches to viewing the sources of authority.
7. What is the parity principle?
8. Describe three components of the delegation process.
9. Why are many managers reluctant to delegate authority?
10. What is the unity of command principle?

11. What is the scalar principle?
12. What is the span of management?
13. What is the exception principle?
14. What is the difference between a highly centralized and highly decentralized organization?

DISCUSSION QUESTIONS

1. Do you think that division of labor has been emphasized too much in today's highly mechanized and efficient society?
2. Comment on the following statement which is attributed to Robert Heinlein:

   > A human being should be able to change a diaper, plan an invasion, butcher a hog, conn a ship, design a building, write a sonnet, balance accounts, build a wall, set a bone, comfort the dying, take orders, give orders, cooperate, act alone, solve equations, analyze new problems, pitch manure, program a computer, cook a tasty meal, fight efficiently, die gallantly. Specialization is for insects.

3. The Que Company has 712 employees and annual sales of $11.2 million. The entire company is located in one office building on Main Street. Based on this information, what can you say about the degree of centralization of authority in this organization?
4. As a manager, do you think you would prefer a relatively large (more than seven) or small (seven or less) span of management? Why and what are the implications of your choice?

SELECTED READINGS

Albanese, Robert. "Substitutional and Essential Authority." *Academy of Management Journal,* June 1966, pp. 136–44.

Barnard, Chester. *The Functions of the Executive.* Cambridge, Mass.: Harvard University Press, 1938.

Brill, A. E. "Delegation: It's Harder Than It Looks." *Journal of Systems Management,* February 1979, pp. 36–37.

Child, John. "Organization Structure and Strategies of Control." *Administrative Science Quarterly,* June 1972, pp. 163–77.

Dale, Earnest. *Organization.* New York: American Management Association, 1967.

Filley, Alan C.; Robert House; and Steven Kerr. *Managerial Process and Organizational Behavior.* 2d ed. Glenview, Ill.: Scott, Foresman, 1976.

Harrell, Thomas W., and Alpert Bernard. "The Need for Autonomy Among Managers." *Academy of Management Review,* April 1979, pp. 259–67.

Lawrence, Paul, and Jay Lorsch. *Organization and Environment.* Homewood, Ill.: Richard D. Irwin, 1969.

Litterer, Joseph A. *The Analysis of Organizations.* New York: John Wiley & Sons, 1965.

Murphy, David. "Decentralization: The Effects of Complexity." *Southern Journal of Business* 7, no. 4 (1972), pp. 79–86.

Newman, William H. *Administrative Action.* 2d ed. Englewood Cliffs, N.J.: Prentice-Hall, 1963.

Oncker, W., and D. L. Wass. "Getting Those Monkeys Off Your Back." *Management World,* August 1980, pp. 22–25.

Ouchi, William, and John Dowling. "Defining the Span of Control." *Administrative Science Quarterly,* September 1974, pp. 357–65.

Suojanen, Waino. "The Span of Control—Fact or Fable?" *Advanced Management,* November 1955, pp. 5–13.

Urwick, Lyndell F. "The Manager's Span of Control." *Harvard Business Review,* May–June 1956, pp. 39–47.

Van Fleet, D. D., and A. G. Bedeian. "A History of the Span of Management." *Academy of Management Review,* July 1977, pp. 356–72.

Woodward, Joan. *Industrial Organization: Theory and Practice.* London: Oxford University Press, 1965.

Case 7–1

Taking over dad's business

The Casey Ice Company had been in operation for over 50 years manufacturing ice for all purposes, ranging from crushed ice for sale in convenience stores to 300-pound block ice for industrial use. As with all seasonal industries, the company's daily operations were in a state of flux, with long hours of work required during the busy season. The company employed anywhere from 75 to 125 people ranging from unskilled labor to sales and supervisory personnel.

Mr. Albert had managed the plant for the past 30 years, ever since he had purchased it from an old friend. He performed all of the jobs in the plant, working right along with the workers and spending very little time in the office looking at "those figures and crazy ideas that have no business in an ice plant." Mr. Albert's philosophy was aptly described by his frequently made observation that "this is an old-fashioned business and we're going to run it in an old-fashioned way." Mr. Albert's words were law. That he knew everything there was to know about making ice could not be disputed. He used his expertise and position to run all aspects of the operation, trusting few if any of the other employees. Recently he had fired Ben Porter on the spot for "laying out" on Labor Day. Ben tried to explain he had worked 33 days straight with no time off and, further, that his supervisor had given him permission to take the day off. But his explanation was to no avail. Mr. Albert simply stated that no supervisor had the authority to give him the day off.

Two months ago, Mr. Albert suffered a heart attack and died while loading a truck with ice. His daughter, Christie, who had been living on the West Coast, had been considering going into business for herself for some time and was now considering the possibility of replacing her father. She hadn't been home much during the past few years as she had been busy pursuing her own career in advertising. But she remembered how much the company had meant to her father and felt somewhat obligated to carry on and expand his organization.

In October, Christie arrived at the Casey Ice Company, walked in the door and saw a sign posted on the wall directly in front of her: "We got one rule—do what you're told." It had been a long time since she'd walked through that door, but she knew she'd never seen the sign before. Tearing it down, she proceeded to walk through the plant talking to the employees and supervisors.

The situation was bordering on chaos; nobody seemed to be working. As the day progressed, she learned that nobody really knew what they were supposed to do. "Mr. Albert had always assigned the jobs first thing each morning" was the most common answer she received when asking what was going on. Absenteeism and tardiness were major problems; there were no policies, procedures, or rules for her to refer to; and when she tried to get information from the supervisors, she learned that her father hadn't really used supervisors as subordinates who directed the work force.

Christie retreated to the office for the rest of the day to study the records regarding company operations. The investigation proved even more alarming than her conversations with the employees. Her father had kept all the books with the help of an old friend who was a CPA. It took some time to decipher the meaning behind the figures she found.

The annual turnover rate averaged about 75 percent over the past five years, which explained why the daily work log revealed that many employees spent a substantial part of their time training new employees. The financial statements revealed that the company had lost a considerable amount of money due to decreasing sales over the past two years. In fact, sales for last year were down $327,000 from the previous year. On the other hand, Christie knew that the Casey Ice Company was the only large ice company in the major metropolitan area (550,000 population). She later learned that many vendors, dissatisfied with late deliveries and even forgotten deliveries, discontinued buying ice from Casey and purchased ice machines. Further, one employee of Casey revealed to Christie that during the July 4 ice shortage last year, Casey Ice Company's prices rose 100 percent for a two-week period because Mr. Albert believed "if they want it bad enough, they'll pay for it." This, the employee suggested, resulted in even more vendors discontinuing use of the company's services.

The records also revealed a significant problem existed in the industrial market for ice. Casey Ice Company once served a large number of industrial users; in fact, over half of Casey's customers used to be industrial users. However, the number of industrial users had gradually dwindled over the years. Today, industrial ice services comprised a little under 12 percent of the total business.

Christie sat back in the leather chair, resting her feet on the desk. Her father had been so proud of the Casey Ice Company. None of this made any sense—how could he have let things get into such a state? But more importantly, what could she do to get things moving again?

1. What can Christie do to straighten things out?
2. What principles of organization have been violated?

Case 7–2

The vacation request

Tom Blair has a week's vacation coming and really wants to take it the third week in May, which is the height of the bass fishing season. The only problem is that two of the other five members of his department have already requested and received approval from their boss, Luther Jones, to take off that same week. Afraid that Luther would not approve his request, Tom decided to forward his request directly to Harry Jensen, who is Luther's boss and who is rather friendly to Tom (Tom has taken Harry fishing on several occasions). Not realizing that Luther has not seen the request, Harry approves it. Several weeks pass before Luther finds out, by accident, that Tom has been approved to go on vacation the third week of May.

The thing that really "bugs" Luther is that this is only one of many instances in which Luther's subordinates have gone directly to Harry and gotten permission to do something. In fact, just last week he overheard a conversation in the washroom to the effect that "if you want anything approved, don't waste time with Luther, go directly to Harry."

1. What should Harry have done?
2. Who is at fault, Harry or Tom?
3. Suppose Luther confronts Harry with the problem and he simply brushes it off by saying that he is really only helping?

8 Organization Structure

Objectives

1. To describe several types of organizational structures.
2. To outline methods for the effective use of committees in organizations.
3. To discuss the relationship between organization structure, environment, and technology.
4. To present a contingency approach for the design of organization structures.

Chapter Outline

Glossary of Terms

Committee A type of organization structure in which a group of people are formally appointed, organized, and superimposed on the line or line and staff structure in order to consider or decide certain matters.

Contingency approach to organization structure An approach for designing organization structures which states that the most appropriate organization structure depends on the particular technology employed, the rate of change in the environment, and many other dynamic forces.

Line and staff organization A type of organization structure that results when staff specialists are added to a line organization.

Line functions Those functions and activities of the organization that are directly involved in producing and marketing the organization's goods or services.

Line organization A type of organization structure that is characterized by direct vertical links between the different levels of the organization.

Matrix organization A hybrid type of organization structure in which individuals from different functional areas are assigned to work on a specific project or task.

Organization structure The framework which defines the boundaries of the formal organization and within which the organization operates.

Staff functions Functions that are advisory and supportive in nature and are designed to contribute to the efficiency and maintenance of the organization.

One man draws out the wire, another straightens it, and a third cuts it, a fourth points it, a fifth grinds it at the top for receiving the head; to make the head requires two or three distinct operations; to put it on is a peculiar business, to whiten the pins is another; it is even a trade by itself to put them into the paper; and the important business of making a pin is, in this manner, divided into 18 distinct operations, which, in some manufactory, are all performed by distinct hands, though in others the same man will sometimes perform two or three of them. I have seen a small manufactory of this kind where ten men only were employed, and where some of them consequently performed two or three distinct operations. But though they were very poor, and therefore but indifferently accommodated with the necessary machinery, they could, when they exerted themselves, make among them about 12 pounds of pins a day.

*Adam Smith**

The previous chapter discussed the basic organizational concepts of division of labor as implemented through departmentation and the establishment of appropriate authority relationships. Departmental units and authority relationships must then be fused together in such a manner as to form an organizational structure which aids in the accomplishment of organizational objectives.

Many people believe that a good manager or a good employee should be able to perform satisfactorily regardless of the organization structure and environment. The belief is that if managers or employees are good enough then they can overcome whatever obstacles the organization structure might present. Others believe that given the right organization structure, anyone should be able to perform in an acceptable fashion. The truth lies somewhere in between the above propositions. An appropriate organization structure certainly helps in achieving good performance in organizations. Clear and appropriate lines of authority coupled with proper departmentation provide the basis for the organization structure. The organization structure forms the framework within which the organization operates. While thousands of different organization structures exist, all are variations or combinations of three basic types: the line organization; the line and staff organization; and the matrix organization.

* Adam Smith, *An Inquiry into the Nature and Causes of the Wealth of Nations*, vol. 1 (London: A. Strahan and T. Cadell, 1776), pp. 7–8.

LINE ORGANIZATION

The line organization is the simplest organization structure. It is characterized by direct vertical links between the different levels of the organization. All members of the organization receive instructions through the scalar chain. The most important aspect of the line organization is that the work of all organizational units is directly involved in producing and marketing the organization's goods or services. One advantage of the line organization is a clear authority structure which promotes rapid decision making and prevents the practice of passing the buck or blaming someone else. A disadvantage of the line organization is that it may overextend managers by forcing them to perform a broad range of duties. The line organization structure may also cause the organization to become overly dependent on one or two key individuals who are capable of performing many duties. Because of its simplicity, the line organization exists most frequently in small organizations. Figure 8–1 represents a simplified line organization structure.

FIGURE 8–1
A Simplified Line Organization Structure

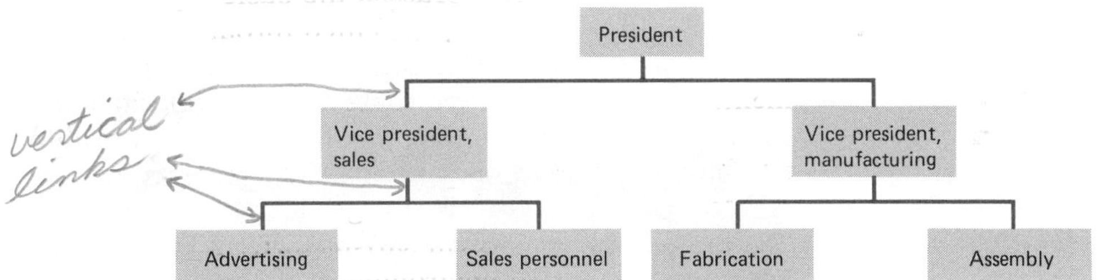

LINE AND STAFF ORGANIZATION

The addition of staff specialists to a line organization creates a line and staff organization. As a line organization grows in size, staff assistance often becomes necessary. Staff functions are advisory and supportive in nature and are designed to contribute to the efficiency and maintenance of the organization; whereas line functions are directly involved in producing and marketing the organization's goods or services. Line functions generally relate directly to the attainment of major organizational objectives whereas staff functions facilitate the accomplishment of major objectives in an indirect manner. Staff people are generally specialists in a particular field and their authority is normally limited to that of making recommendations to the line people. Typical staff functions include research and development, personnel

FIGURE 8–2
A Simplified Line-Staff Organization Structure

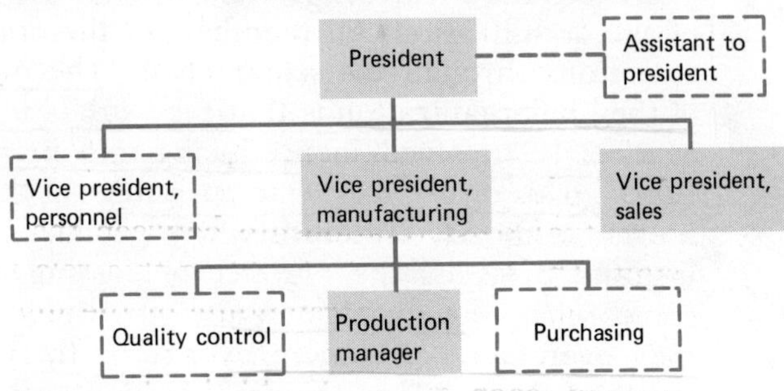

management, employee training, and various "assistant to" positions. Figure 8–2 shows a simplified line and staff organization structure.

Line and Staff Conflict

The line and staff organization allows for much more specialization and flexibility than the line organization; however it sometimes creates conflict. The potential problem of a line-staff conflict should not be taken lightly. A study conducted by the American Management Association in the 1960s found that 41 out of 100 companies reported some form of a line-staff conflict.[1] There is no reason to believe that this is any less of a problem today.

Some staff specialists resent the fact that they may be acting only as advisors to line personnel and have no real authority over the line. At the same time, line managers, knowing that they have ultimate responsibility for the results produced, are often reluctant to listen to staff advice. Many staff specialists feel that they should not be placed in a position of having to sell their ideas to the line. They feel that the line managers should openly listen to their ideas. If the staff specialist persists in such situations, the line manager often builds up additional resentment of the staff as "always trying to interfere and run my department." If the staff specialist does not persist, he or she often becomes discouraged because "no one ever listens."

Another factor that contributes to line and staff conflict is that line and staff personnel may be different in personal characteristics and behavior. For example, line managers are often older individuals who have worked their way up through the ranks and

[1] Dale, Earnest, *Organization* (New York: American Management Association, 1962), p. 67.

who do not have a college education.[2] On the other hand, staff specialists usually are young and highly educated. Because they often lack line experience, staff personnel are frequently accused of not knowing anything about what the line does and therefore living in ivory towers.

The reduction and subsequent elimination of line-staff conflict that is destructive to the organization depends on the building of a mutual trust relationship between the line managers and the staff. The first step in building this relationship is the development of a clear understanding of the lines of authority and the responsibilities of each group. If this is successfully accomplished, each group should develop an appreciation of the fact that the only way they can both maximize their performance is through cooperation.

In some organizations staff specialists are encouraged to obtain some line experience. This is accomplished by working on projects or committee assignments with the line departments, or by working on a temporary assignment in a line department.[3] By obtaining some experience in line management, staff specialists can better understand the problems facing the line managers that they work with and support.

MATRIX ORGANIZATION

The matrix (also called project organization) form of organization has recently evolved as a way of forming project teams within the traditional line-staff organization. A project is "a combination of human and nonhuman resources pulled together in a temporary organization to achieve a specified purpose."[4] The marketing of a new product and the construction of a new building are examples of projects. Because projects have a temporary life, a method of managing and organizing them was sought so that the existing organization structure would not be totally disrupted and would maintain a degree of efficiency.

Under the matrix structure, individuals working on a project are officially assigned to the project *and* to their original or base department. A manager is given the authority and responsibility

---

[2] M. Dalton, "Conflict between Staff and Line Managerial Officers," *American Sociological Review*, June 1950, pp. 342–51; and James A. Belasco and Joseph A. Alutto, "Line-Staff Conflicts: Some Empirical Insights," *Academy of Management Journal*, December 1969, p. 477.

[3] Lloyd L. Byars and Leslie W. Rue, *Personnel Management: Concepts and Applications* (Philadelphia: W. B. Saunders, 1979), p. 28.

[4] David Cleland and William King, *Systems Analysis and Project Management*, 2d ed. (New York: McGraw-Hill, 1975), p. 184.

for meeting the project objectives in terms of cost, quality, quantity, and time of completion. The project manager is then assigned the necessary personnel from the functional departments of the parent organization. Thus, a horizontal line organization develops for the project and leaves the parent vertical line functions in a support relationship to the project organization.[5] Under such a system, the functional personnel are assigned and evaluated by the project manager while they work on the project. Upon completion of the project or completion of their contribution to the project, the functional personnel return to their functional departments. Figure 8–3 illustrates a matrix organization.

A major advantage of matrix organization is that the combination of people and resources used on the project can readily be changed to correspond to changing project needs. Other advantages include the emphasis placed on the project by establishing

FIGURE 8–3
Illustrative Matrix Organization

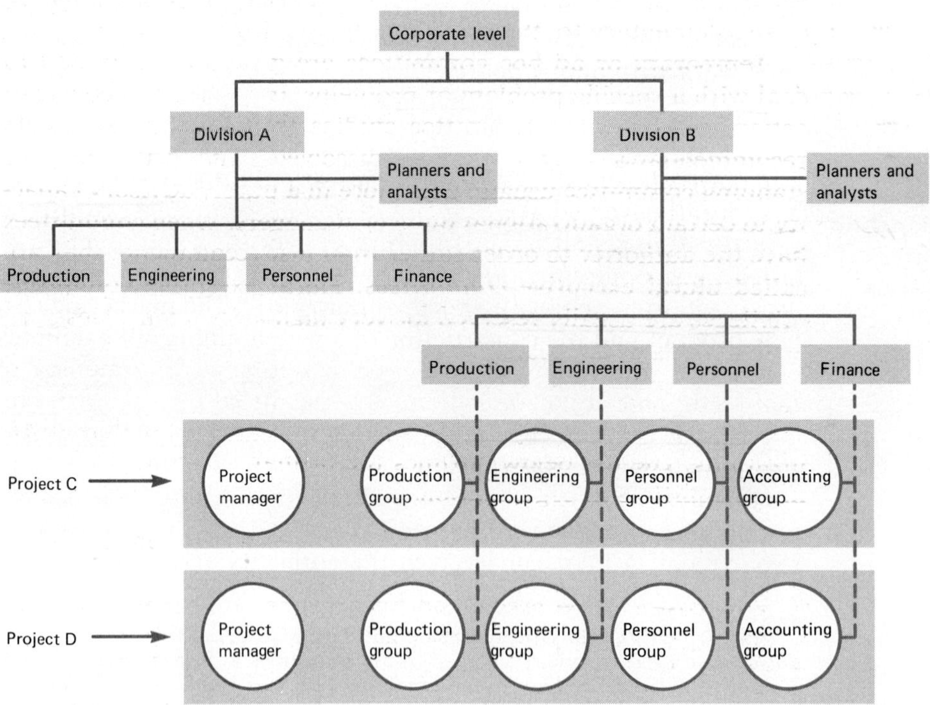

Source: David Cleland and William King, *Systems Analysis and Project Management,* 2d ed. (New York: McGraw-Hill, 1975), p. 184.

[5] John F. Mee, "Matrix Management," *Business Horizons,* June 1969, p. 60.

a project team and the relative ease with which project members can be absorbed back into the functional organization once the project has been completed. One serious potential disadvantage is that matrix organization can result in a violation of the principle of unity of command. A role conflict can develop if the authority of the project manager is not clearly delineated from that of the functional managers. In such a case the personnel assigned to the project might receive conflicting assignments from their project manager and their functional manager. A second problem occurs when the personnel assigned to a project are still evaluated by their functional manager, who has little opportunity to observe their work on the project.

COMMITTEE ORGANIZATION

A committee is a group of people formally appointed and organized to consider or decide certain matters. Actually, committees are a form of matrix organization in that they are superimposed on the existing line or line and staff structure. Committees can be permanent (standing) or temporary and are usually in charge of, or supplementary to, the line and staff functions.

Temporary or ad hoc committees are generally appointed to deal with a specific problem or problems. In the normal course of action, a temporary committee studies the problem, makes its recommendations, and then is dissolved. The permanent or standing committee usually acts more in a purely advisory capacity to certain organizational units or managers. When committees have the authority to order rather than just recommend, they are called plural executive committees. Plural executive committee privileges are usually reserved for very high-level committees such as the board of directors.

Advantages of Committees

Committees have many of the same advantages as matrix organizations. The list below outlines the primary advantages for using committees in organizations.

1. The formation of a committee places emphasis on the problem.
2. Expertise can be assembled by drawing from many areas of the organization; thus, better solutions often result.
3. Group decisions are often better than individual decisions.
4. Committee members are often motivated by being involved.
5. Better coordination and communication often result because all affected parties can be represented.
6. Consolidation of authority from several areas of the organization exists to make decisions.

Disadvantages of Committees

Everyone has heard the old sayings, "A committee is a collection of the unfit appointed by the unwilling to do the unnecessary" and "A camel is a horse invented by a committee." While committees can have many positive features they can also have many drawbacks if not properly managed. Some of the potential drawbacks of committees are listed below.

1. They can be excessively time consuming and costly.
2. Committees have a tendency to compromise when agreement is not easily reached. Such compromised decisions are often mediocre in quality.
3. They can result in divided responsibility with no one feeling personally responsible.
4. A committee can result in a tyranny of the minority. For example, one very strong-minded and vocal committee member can often control the entire committee.

Effectively Using Committees

There are many things that managers can do to avoid the pitfalls associated with committees and increase the efficiency of the committee. The first step is to define clearly its functions, scope, and authority. Obviously the committee members must understand the purpose of the committee if they are to be effective. If the committee is a temporary committee, the members should be informed of the committee's expected life duration. This should aid in unnecessarily prolonging the life of the committee.

In addition, careful thought should be put into the selection of the committee members and the committee chairperson. Size is an important variable with any committee. Generally, committees become increasingly inefficient as they grow in size. A good rule of thumb to follow when setting up a committee is to use the smallest group necessary to get the job done. It is more important to select capable members than representative members. It is also important to select members from the same approximate organizational level. The problem with a committee whose members represent several organizational levels is that the members from the higher levels may inhibit the actions and participation from the other members. Figure 8–4 lists several methods for selecting committee members and chairpeople and outlines potential advantages and disadvantages of each method.

Once a committee has been properly established there are other things a manager can do to ensure that the committee functions effectively. The manager should encourage participation from all members. All too often, one or two members do 90 percent of the work. Because a large percentage of committee work involves

FIGURE 8–4
Methods of Selecting Committees

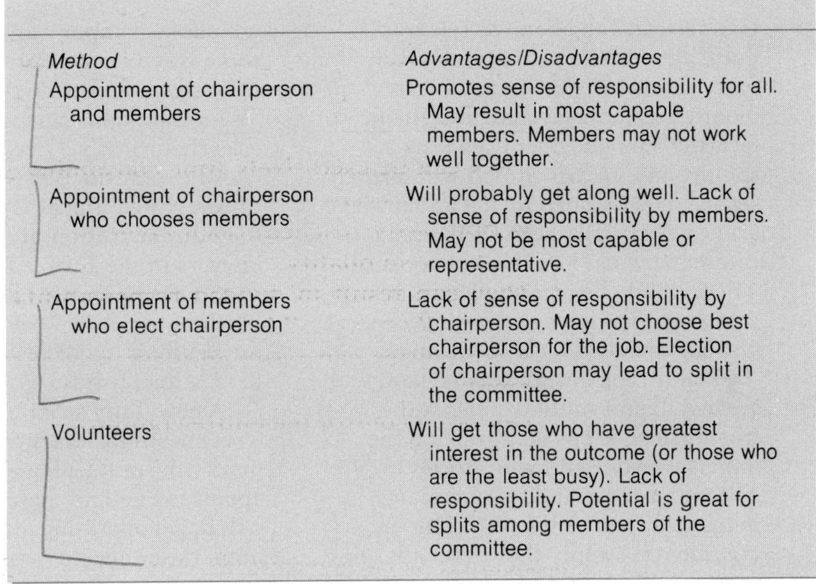

Method	*Advantages/Disadvantages*
Appointment of chairperson and members	Promotes sense of responsibility for all. May result in most capable members. Members may not work well together.
Appointment of chairperson who chooses members	Will probably get along well. Lack of sense of responsibility by members. May not be most capable or representative.
Appointment of members who elect chairperson	Lack of sense of responsibility by chairperson. May not choose best chairperson for the job. Election of chairperson may lead to split in the committee.
Volunteers	Will get those who have greatest interest in the outcome (or those who are the least busy). Lack of responsibility. Potential is great for splits among members of the committee.

meetings, emphasis should be placed by the chairperson on the conduct of all committee meetings. Each meeting should be carefully planned with an agenda distributed in advance. This helps the committee members prepare for the meeting and also communicates to them that the meeting is not going to be a waste of time. It is equally important to stick to the agenda and not run the meeting past the allotted time. Once the meeting is in progress, careful minutes should be taken covering the major points and recommendations. These minutes should be distributed to all committee members after the meeting. Once a meeting has been concluded, there is a great tendency for members to relax and neglect to take necessary follow-up actions. The committee chairperson should design a reporting system to ensure that all follow-up actions are taken. A final recommendation is that the committee periodically re-evaluate the need for the committee.

Boards of Directors

A board of directors is in reality a type of committee that is responsible for the major policy and strategy formulation of the organization. Although most boards restrict their inputs to the policy and strategy level and do not participate in the day-to-day operation of the organization, the degree of involvement of the

MANAGEMENT IN PRACTICE

Ma Bell Gets Ready for the 80s

Is American Telephone & Telegraph Corp. about to be broken into several parts? Is that the meaning of last month's announced changes? No. In fact, the announcement suggests a compromise by which Bell will formally separate its manufacturing and utility arms, yet actually keep them under common ownership. If that happens it will certainly be a great victory for common sense over an obsolete concept of what constitutes competition.

Bell, which has played its hand with great skill and subtlety against the trustbusters, keeps emphasizing the importance of Bell Laboratories to national defense and to American industrial competitiveness. The argument is simply that Bell Labs' pure research efforts can be sustained only by the vast earning power of an integrated Bell system.

Says AT&T Chairman Charles L. Brown: "The Defense Department is very concerned about the rupture of the integrated Bell system for national defense purposes." Strictly military work was 3 percent of Bell Labs' revenues of $1.1 billion last year. But that conceals its real importance. When solutions have had to be found quickly, "The U.S. Government has, over the years, found it desirable, if not necessary, to turn to Bell Laboratories," argues Solomon Buchsbaum, a Bell Laboratories executive vice president.

Bell Labs' credentials as one of the finest private-industry research establishments in the world are impressive. It invented the transistor and the basic technology that underpins the laser and data communications, the new industry AT&T is fighting hard to enter.

Bureaucrats in the Justice Department in 1974 launched an antitrust suit that seeks to rip the telephone company apart. Aside from some greedy competitors the suit has little support outside the bureaucracy. "Who wants this suit, anyway?" Brown asks rhetorically. "Certainly Congress doesn't want the Bell System disintegrated, the FCC doesn't, nor does the Administration. It comes down to lawyers in the Justice Department."

Confident that it has a strong case in Washington, AT&T set the stage in August for a major restructuring of its $114 billion assets:

A new, fully separate $10 billion (revenues) subsidiary for nationwide marketing of telephone terminal apparatus and all manner of services will begin operating after 1982. In preparation for the separation some corporate loose ends are being tied by buying minority interests in four telephone companies for $1 billion.

AT&T International Inc. has been formed. AT&T opted out of telephone equipment sales overseas in the 1920s. It went back into several countries, including Saudi Arabia and South Korea, in the mid-1970s. As the world's almost unchallenged leader in technology and quality, Bell has tremendous prospects in the export field. Like the U.S. banks in the 1960s, AT&T is following its multinational clients around the globe.

The $28 billion (assets) of 33 pension funds are being lumped into two schemes in order to ease staff transfers during the corporate restructure.

Management responsibilities were realigned to run the new AT&T. James E. Olsen, vice chairman of the board, will run the new, fully separated subsidiary.

Source: Adapted from Maurice Barnfather, *Forbes*, September 15, 1980, pp. 38–39. Used with permission.

board varies widely from organization to organization. Boards are used strictly as figureheads in some organizations, contributing little to the organization. However, because of the potential contribution that the board can make, its members should be carefully chosen. Directors do not necessarily need to own stock and should be chosen primarily on the basis of what they can and will contribute to the organization. Usually boards of directors are paid a nominal fee for their services. Recent lawsuits against boards of directors concerning their liabilities regarding the day-to-day operation of the organization have increased the risks of serving on boards. Thus, boards are becoming more active than they have been in the past. Moreover, some people now require liability insurance coverage before they will serve on a board of directors.

FIGURE 8–5
Organization Growth and Change

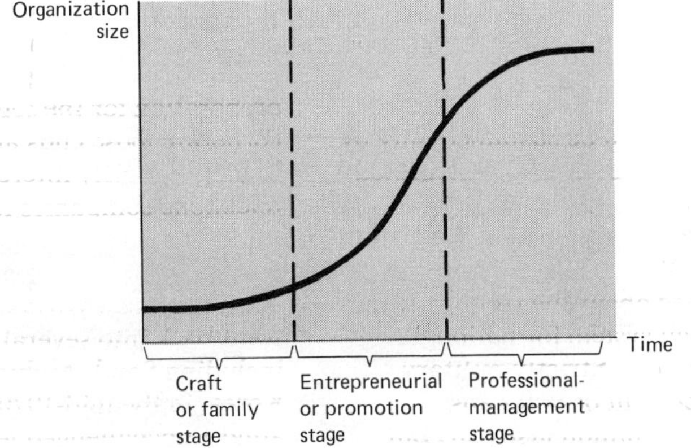

ORGANIZATION STRUCTURE, ENVIRONMENT, AND TECHNOLOGY

Figure 8–5 depicts the different stages of an organization as it grows and matures. The craft stage is characterized by the absence of formal policies, objectives, and structure.[6] The operations of the organization at this stage generally center around one individual and one functional area. During the entrepreneurial or promotion stage, the organization grows first at an increasing and then a decreasing, rate. An atmosphere of optimism pervades the entire organization as sales and profits rise rapidly. By the third stage of growth, the entrepreneur has been replaced by or has evolved into a professional manager who performs the processes of planning, controlling, organizing, staffing, and motivating.[7]

[6] Alan Filley, Robert House, and Steven Kerr, *Managerial Process and Organizational Behavior*, 2d ed. (Glenview, Ill.: Scott, Foresman, 1976). pp. 519–20.

[7] Ibid.

Profits are realized more from internal efficiency and less from external exploitation of the market. At this stage the organization becomes characterized by written policies, procedures, and plans.

As the organization moves through the craft stage and into the entrepreneurial stage, an organization structure must be developed. This is a critical stage for the organization. If an appropriate structure is not established and utilized, the entrepreneur may lose control and the entire organization may collapse. The organization structure that is developed must allow the organization to adapt to changes in its environment.

Organization and Environment

A landmark study relating organization to environment was conducted by Tom Burns and G. M. Stalker in the United Kingdom.[8] By examining some 20 industrial firms, both in a dynamic, changing industry and in a more stable, established industry, Burns and Stalker focused on how a firm's pattern of organization was related to certain characteristics of the external environment. The researchers identified two distinct organizational systems. One, labeled "mechanistic systems," is characterized by a rigid delineation of functional duties, precise job descriptions, fixed authority and responsibility, and a well-developed organizational hierarchy through which information filters up and instructions flow down. The other, labeled "organic systems," is characterized by less formal job descriptions, greater emphasis on adaptability, more participation, and less fixed authority. Burns and Stalker found that successful firms in stable and established industries tended to be "mechanistic" in structure. Successful firms in dynamic and changing industries tended to be "organic" in structure.

Paul Lawrence and Jay Lorsch conducted a later study dealing with organizational structure and its environment.[9] Their original study included 10 firms in three distinct industrial environments. Reaching conclusions similar to Burns and Stalker, Lawrence and Lorsch found that in order to be successful firms operating in a dynamic environment needed a relatively flexible structure; firms operating in a stable environment needed a more rigid structure; and firms operating in an intermediate environment needed a structure somewhere between the two extremes.[10]

---

[8] Tom Burns and G. M. Stalker, *The Management of Innovation* (London: Tavistock Institute, 1962).

[9] Paul Lawrence and Jay Lorsch, "Differentiation and Integration in Complex Organizations," *Administrative Science Quarterly*, June 1967, pp. 1–47; and Paul Lawrence and Jay Lorsch, *Organization and Environment* (Homewood, Ill.: Richard D. Irwin, 1969). Originally published in 1967 by Harvard University Graduate School of Business Administration, Division of Research.

[10] Ibid.

Several other studies investigating the relationship between organization structure and environment have been conducted in the past few years.[11] In general, most have concluded that the best organization structure for a given organization is contingent to some degree on the conditions of its environment.

Organization and Technology

Numerous studies have also been conducted investigating potential relationships between technology and organizational structure. One of the most significant of these studies was conducted by Joan Woodward in the late 1950s.[12] Her study was based on an analysis of 100 manufacturing firms in the southeast Essex area of England. The general approach taken by Woodward was to classify firms along a scale of "technical complexity" with particular emphasis on three modes of production: (1) unit or small batch production (e.g., custom-made machines); (2) large batch or mass-production (e.g., an automotive assembly plant); and (3) continuous flow or process production (e.g., a chemical plant). The unit of small batch production mode represents the lower end of the technical complexity scale while the continuous flow mode represents the upper end.

After classifying each firm into one of the above categories, Woodward investigated a number of organizational variables. Some of her findings are presented below:

1. The number of levels in an organization increased as technical complexity increased.
2. The ratio of managers and supervisors to total personnel increased as technical complexity increased.
3. Using Burns and Stalker's definition of organic and mechanistic systems, organic management systems tended to predominate in firms at both ends of the scale of technical complexity, while mechanistic systems predominated in firms falling in the middle ranges.
4. No significant relationship existed between technical complexity and organizational size.

A similar study was undertaken a few years later by Edward Harvey.[13] Rather than use Woodward's "technical complexity" scale, Harvey grouped firms along a continuum from technical diffuseness to technical specificity. Technically diffused firms have

---

[11] For a review of these, see: Mariann Jelinek, "Technology, Organizations and Contingency," *Academy of Management Review*, January 1977, pp. 17–26.

[12] Joan Woodward, *Industrial Organization: Theory and Practice* (London: Oxford University Press, 1965).

[13] Edward Harvey, "Technology and the Structure of Organizations," *American Sociological Review*, April 1968, pp. 247–59.

a wider range of products, produce products that vary from year to year, and produce more "made-to-order" products. Harvey's findings were similar to Woodward's in that he found significant relationships between technology and several organizational characteristics.

The general conclusion reached in the Woodward and the Harvey studies was the presence of a relationship between organizational technology and a number of aspects of organizational structure. Many additional studies have been conducted investigating the relationship between technology and structure.[14] While there have been some conflicting results reported, most studies have found a relationship between technology and structure, and most researchers suggest that technology, per se, determines structure.

Flat versus Tall Organizations

Many studies have been undertaken relating to the desirability of flat organizations versus tall organizations. A flat organization is characterized by relatively few levels and relatively large spans of management at each level; a tall organization is characterized by many levels with relatively small spans of management (see Figure 8–6). A classic study in this area was conducted several years ago by James Worthy.[15] Worthy studied the morale of over 100,000 employees at Sears, Roebuck and Company during a 12-year period. One implication that emerged from Worthy's study was that organizations with fewer levels and wider spans of management tend to create the potential for greater job satisfaction. Another potential advantage for organizations characterized by a wide span of management is that the manager is forced to delegate authority and to develop more direct links of communication. On the other hand, Carzo and Yanouzas found that groups operating in a tall organization had significantly better performance than those operating in a flat organization.[16] Other studies have also revealed conflicting results. Therefore, one cannot conclude that all flat organizations are better than all tall organizations (or vice versa).[17] Recalling from Chapter 7 that the most

James Worthy: Sears Study

Carzo & Yanouzas

[14] For a summary, see: David F. Gillespie and Dennis S. Mileti, "Technology and the Study of Organizations: An Overview and Appraisal," *Academy of Management Review*, January 1977, pp. 7–16.

[15] James Worthy, "Organization Structure and Employee Morale," *American Sociological Review*, 15 (1956), pp. 169–79.

[16] Rocco, Carzo, Jr. and John Yanouzas, "Effects of Flat and Tall Organization Structure," *Administrative Science Quarterly*, 14 (1969), pp. 178–91.

[17] Dan R. Dalton et al., "Organization Structure and Performance: A Critical Review," *The Academy of Management Review*, January 1980, pp. 49–54.

FIGURE 8–6
Flat versus Tall Organizations

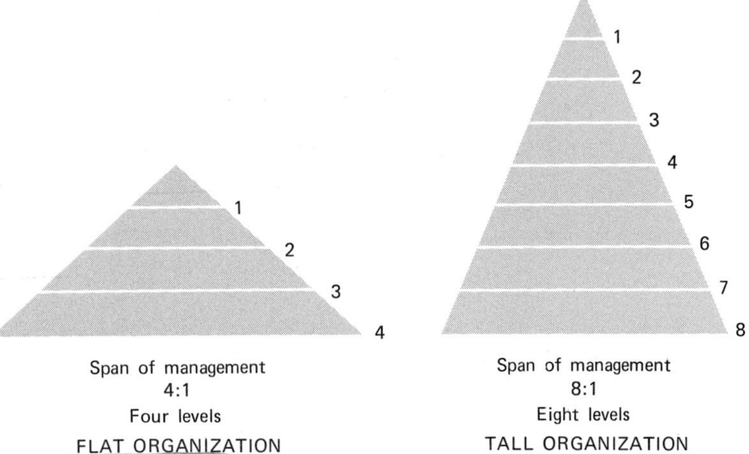

appropriate span of management is dependent on several situational variables, this is exactly what one would expect to find. There are advantages and disadvantages associated with both flat and tall structures. Which is most appropriate depends on the specific situational variables.

A CONTINGENCY APPROACH

The studies discussed above support what practicing managers have been saying for years—there is no organization structure applicable to all situations. The most appropriate organization structure depends primarily on organizational objectives but also on the particular technology employed, the rate of change in the environment and many other dynamic forces.

Recognition by management practitioners and scholars that there is no universal best way to organize but that the design is conditional has led to the evolution of a contingency or situational approach to organizing. Paul Lawrence and Jay Lorsch concluded in their study dealing with organization structure and environment (which was discussed in the "Organization and Environment" section of this chapter) that different organizations in different environments require different kinds of organization structures at different stages in their growth.[18] Figure 8–7 de-

[18] Lawrence and Lorsch, "Complex Organizations."

FIGURE 8–7
Variables Affecting Appropriate Organization Structure

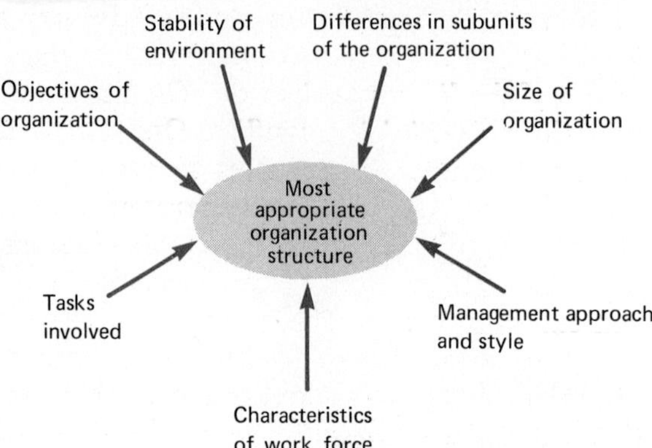

picts many of the potential variables that can have an impact on determining the most appropriate organization structure.

Once management adopts a contingency view, it will begin to thoroughly analyze the relevant variables and then identify the appropriate pattern of structure. The result is essentially a matching process. Because each of the interacting forces is dynamic, top management should periodically analyze and appraise their organization structure in light of any relevant changes. Fremont Kast and James Rosenzweig have offered the following clarification of the contingency approach:

> The general tenor of the contingency view is somewhere between the simplistic, specific principles and complex, vague notions. It is a mid-range concept which recognizes the complexity involved in managing a modern organization but uses patterns of relationships and/or configurations of subsystems in order to facilitate improved practice.[19]

SUMMARY

The organization structure forms the framework within which the organization operates. An appropriate organization structure helps in achieving good performance. The line organization is the simplest organization structure. It is characterized by direct vertical links between the different levels of the organization. The addition of staff specialists to a line organization creates a line and

[19] Fremont Kast and James Rosenzweig, "General Systems Theory: Applications for Organization and Management," *Academy of Management Journal*, December 1972, p. 463.

staff organization. Line functions are functions directly involved in the production and marketing of the organization's goods or services while staff functions are advisory and supportive in nature and are designed to contribute to the efficiency and maintenance of the line organization. The line and staff organization creates the potential for conflict. One of the major reasons for this potential conflict is that staff specialists have no direct authority over the line personnel and therefore must convince the line personnel to implement their ideas. Also line and staff personnel often have different personal characteristics and backgrounds and this can cause problems. The matrix organization has recently evolved as a way of forming project teams within the traditional line-staff organization. Committees are a form of matrix organization in that they are superimposed on the existing line and staff structure. A committee is a group of people formally appointed and organized to consider or decide certain matters. Several advantages and disadvantages of committees were outlined. In addition, several steps were suggested for effectively using committees. A board of directors is in reality a type of committee that is responsible for the major policy and strategy formulation of the organization.

Most studies conducted on the relationship between organization structure and environment have concluded that the best organization structure is contingent to some degree on the conditions of the organization's environment. Several studies have also found a relationship between technology and structure and most researchers suggest that technology, per se, determines structure. The results of these studies and others have led to a contingency approach to organization structure. This approach states that the most appropriate organization structure depends not only on the organizational objectives but also on the particular technology employed, the rate of change in the environment, and many other dynamic forces.

REVIEW QUESTIONS

1. What are line functions? What are staff functions?
2. Explain:
   a. Line organization.
   b. Line and staff organization.
   c. Matrix organization.
   d. Committee organization.
3. What factors contribute to the potential conflict between line and staff personnel in a line and staff organization? How can the potential for destructive conflict be reduced?

4. What are the advantages of the matrix organization? What problems does the matrix organization pose?
5. What are the advantages associated with committee organization? What are the disadvantages? How can committee organization be made more effective?
6. Discuss the relationship between organization structure and environment.
7. Discuss the relationship between organization structure and the type of technology employed.
8. What are the stages of organizational growth?
9. What are the advantages of a flat organization? What are the advantages of a tall organization?
10. What is the contingency approach to organizing?

DISCUSSION QUESTIONS

1. How can you justify the use of a matrix organization structure since it clearly violates the unity of command principle?
2. Do you think that the contingency approach to organzing is a useful concept that can be implemented or is it really a cop out?
3. Discuss this statement: "When the appropriate organization structure is determined, the firm no longer has to worry about it."

SELECTED READINGS

Aldrich, H. E. "Technology and Organization Structure: A Reexamination of the Findings of the Aston Group." *Administrative Science Quarterly* 17 (1972), pp. 26–43.

Belasco, James A., and Joseph A. Alutto. "Line-Staff Conflict: Some Empirical Insights." *Academy of Management Journal,* December 1969, pp. 469–78.

Carzo, Rocco, Jr., and John Yanouzas. "Effects of Flat and Tall Organization Structure," *Administrative Science Quarterly* 14 (1969), pp. 178–91.

Chandler, Alfred. *Strategy and Structure.* Cambridge, Mass.: MIT Press, 1961.

Child, J. "Predicting and Understanding Organization Structure," *Administrative Science Quarterly* 18 (1973), pp. 168–85.

Child, J., and R. Mansfield. "Technology, Size, and Organization Structure." *Sociology* 6 (1972), pp. 369–93.

Dalton, Dan R. et al. "Organization Structure and Performance: A Critical Review," *The Academy of Management Review,* January 1980, pp. 49–54.

Dalton, M. "Conflict between Staff and Line Managerial Officers." *American Sociological Review,* June 1950, pp. 342–51.

Ford, Jeffrey D., and John W. Slocum, Jr. "Size, Technology, Environment and the Structure of Organizations." *Academy of Management Review,* October 1977, pp. 561–74.

Galbraith, Jay and D. A. Nathanson. *Strategy Implementation: The Role of Structure and Process.* St. Paul, Minn.: West Publishing, 1978.

Jelinek, Mariann. "Technology, Organization and Contingency." *Academy of Management Review,* January 1977, pp. 17–26.

Kolodny, Harvey K. "Managing in a Matrix," *Business Horizons,* March–April 1981, pp. 17–35.

McKelvey, Bill, and Ralph Kilman. "Organization Design." *Administrative Science Quarterly,* March 1975, pp. 24–36.

Mintzberg, Henry. "Organization Design: Fashion or Fit?," *Harvard Business Review,* January–February 1981, pp. 103–17.

Perrow, Charles. "The Short and Glorious History of Organization Theory." *Organizational Dynamics,* Summer 1973, pp. 2–15.

Pigh, Derek. "The Measurement of Organization Structure." *Organization Dynamics,* no. 2 (1975), pp. 19–34.

Scott, William G. "Organization Theory: A Reassessment." *Academy of Management Journal,* June 1974, pp. 242–54.

Shelly, Y. K., and H. M. Carlise. "A Contingency Model of Organization Design." *California Management Review,* Fall 1972, pp. 38–45.

Walton, Eric J., "The Comparison of Measures of Organization Structure," *The Academy of Management Review,* January 1981, pp. 155–60.

Case 8–1

Who dropped the ball?

In October 1975, the Industrial Water Treatment Company (IWT) introduced KELATE, a new product that was 10 times more effective than other treatments in controlling scale buildup in boilers. The instantaneous demand for the new water treatment, KELATE, required that IWT double its number of service engineers within the following year.

The sudden expansion caused IWT to reorganize their operations. Previously, each district office had been headed by a district manager who was assisted by a chief engineer and two engineering supervisors. In 1976, this structure was changed. The district manager now had a chief engineer and a manager of operations. Four engineering supervisors (now designated as "group leaders") were established. They were to channel all work assignment matters through the manager of operations, while all engineering-related problems were to be handled by the chief engineer. Each group leader supervised eight to ten field service engineers (see Exhibit 1).

EXHIBIT 1
Partial Organizational Chart for IWT

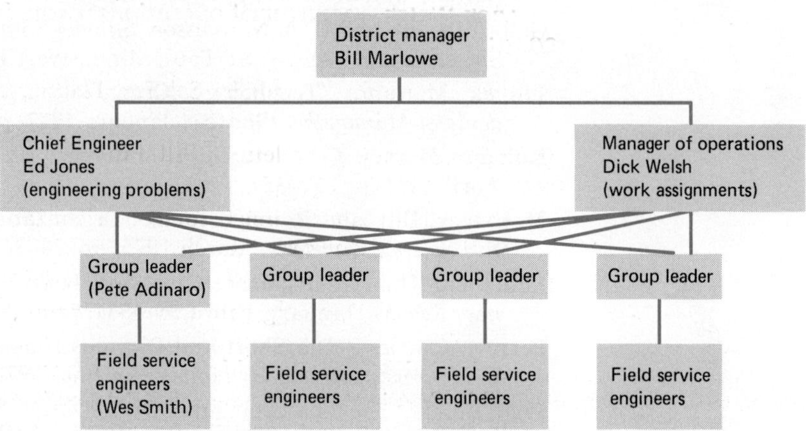

Bill Marlowe, district manager for the southeast district, has just received a letter from an old and very large customer, Sel Tex, Inc. The letter revealed that when Sel Tex inspected one of their boilers last week, they found that the water treatment was not working properly. When they contacted IWT's service engineer for their area, Wes Smith, they were told "he was scheduled to be working in the Jacksonville area the rest of the week but would get someone else down there the next day." When no one showed up, Sel Tex was naturally upset—after all, they were only requesting the engineering service they had been promised.

Bill Marlowe, upset over the growing number of customer complaints that seemed to be crossing his desk in recent months, called Ed Jones, chief engineer, into his office and showed him the letter he had received from Sel Tex.

Ed: Why are you showing me this? This is a work assignment foul-up?

Bill: Do you know anything about this unsatisfactory condition?

Ed: Sure, Wes called me immediately after he found out. Their concentration of KELATE must have gone up, since they're getting corrosion and oxygen on their tubes. I told Peter Adinaro, Wes' group leader, about it and I suggested he schedule someone to visit Sel Tex.

Bill: OK, Ed, thanks for your help. [Bill then calls Peter Adinaro into his office.]

Bill: Peter, two weeks ago Ed asked you to assign someone to visit Sel Tex because of a tube corrosion problem they are having. Do you remember?

Peter: Oh sure! As usual, Wes Smith called Ed instead of me. I left a message for Dick to assign someone there because my whole group was tied up and I couldn't spare anyone. I thought Dick would ask another group leader to assign someone to check it out.

Bill: Well, thanks for your help. Tell Dick to come on in here a second.

Dick Welsh, manager of operations, came into Bill's office about 20 minutes later.

Bill: Dick, here's a letter from Sel Tex. Please read it and tell me what you know about the situation.

Dick: [After reading the letter.] Bill, I didn't know anything about this.

Bill: I checked with Pete, Wes's group leader, and he tells me he left a message for you to assign someone since his group was all tied up. Didn't you get the message?

Dick: Have you taken a look at my desk lately? I'm flooded with messages. Heck, I'm the greatest message handler of all times. If I could schedule my people without having all the engineering headaches unloaded on me, I wouldn't have all these messages. Sure, it's possible that he left a message but I haven't seen it. I will look for it though. Anyway, that letter sounds to me like they've got an engineering problem and Ed should contact them to solve it.

Bill: I'll write Sel Tex myself and try to explain the situation to them. You and I will have to get together this afternoon and talk over some of these difficulties. See you later, Dick.

1. What are the problems that Bill Marlowe faces?
2. Are the problems related to the way IWT is organized or are they related to the employees?
3. How could these problems be resolved?

Case 8–2

A new organizational structure

Yesterday, Tom Andrews was officially promoted to his new job as hospital administrator for Cobb General Hospital. Cobb General is a 600-bed hospital located in a suburban area of New Orleans. Tom is extremely excited about the promotion, but at the same time has some serious doubts about it.

Tom has worked at Cobb General for three years and had previously served as the associate administrator of the hospital. Although associate administrator was his official job title, he was really more of a "go-fer" for the former administrator, Bill Collins. Because of Tom's educational background (which includes a master of hospital administration degree) and his enthusiasm, Tom was offered the administrator's job last week after the hospital's board of directors had asked for Bill Collins' resignation.

Tom was now looking at the organization chart for the hospital which had been pieced together over the years by Bill Collins

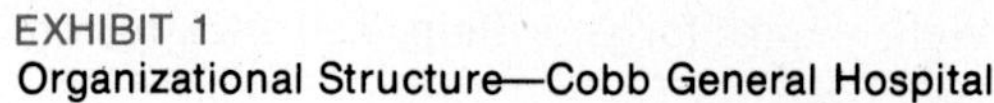

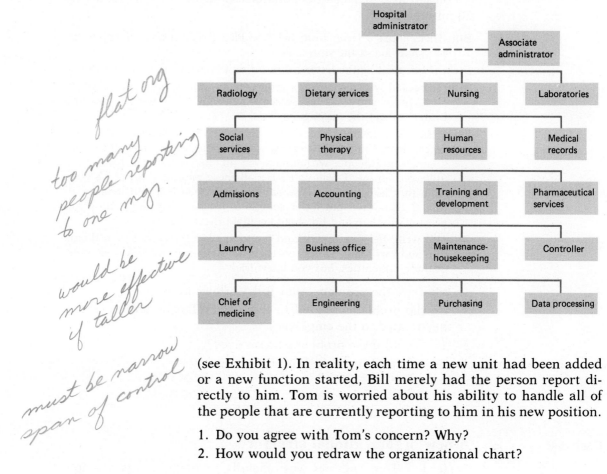

EXHIBIT 1
Organizational Structure—Cobb General Hospital

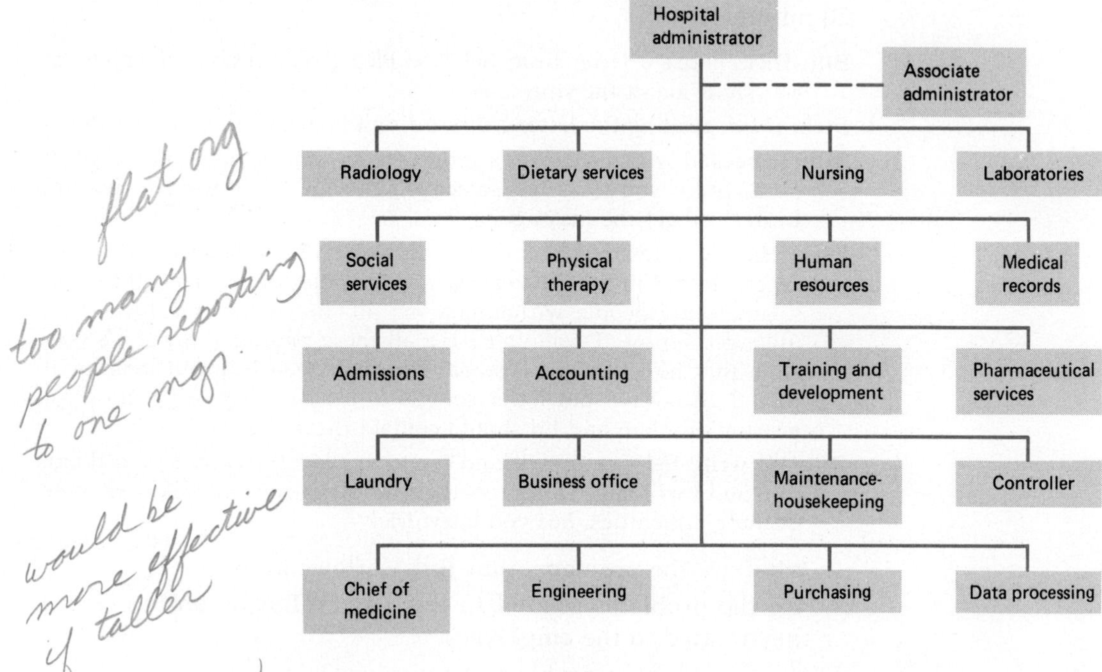

(see Exhibit 1). In reality, each time a new unit had been added or a new function started, Bill merely had the person report directly to him. Tom is worried about his ability to handle all of the people that are currently reporting to him in his new position.

1. Do you agree with Tom's concern? Why?
2. How would you redraw the organizational chart?

featherbedding - displacing inds from one job by creating another

9 Staffing: The Securing Function

Objectives

1. To develop an appreciation for the importance of staffing.
2. To describe and illustrate the personnel planning process.
3. To discuss some significant government legislation related to staffing.
4. To explore the processes of recruitment, selection, employee development, transfers, promotions, and separations.

Chapter Outline

PERSONNEL (HUMAN RESOURCE) PLANNING
- Job Analysis and Skills Inventory
- Personnel Forecasting
- Personnel Transition
- Special Considerations in Personnel Planning

INTEGRATING ORGANIZATIONAL OBJECTIVES, POLICIES, AND PERSONNEL PLANNING

RECRUITMENT
- Promotion from within
- External Sources
- Legal Influences on Recruitment

SELECTION
- Who Makes the Selection Decision?
- Legal Influences on Selection
- The Selection Procedure
- Testing
- Reference Checking
- Employment Interview
- Physical Examination
- Personal Judgment

EMPLOYEE DEVELOPMENT

TRANSFERS, PROMOTIONS, AND SEPARATIONS

THE DYNAMICS OF STAFFING

Glossary of Terms

Age Discrimination in Employment Act of 1967 An act which went into effect on June 12, 1968, later amended in 1978, designed to protect individuals from 40 to 70 years of age from discrimination in hiring, retention, compensation, and other conditions of employment.

Civil Rights Act of 1964 Title VII of this act was designed to eliminate discrimination in employment related to race, color, religion, sex, or national origin in organizations that conduct interstate commerce.

Criterion A measure of job success or performance.

Employee development A process concerned with the improvement and growth of the capabilities of individuals and groups within the organization.

Equal Pay Act of 1963 Law which became effective in June 1964, and prohibits wage discrimination on the basis of sex.

Federal Rehabilitation Act of 1973 Law which prohibits discrimination in the hiring of the handicapped by federal agencies and federal contractors.

Halo effect Occurs when managers allow a single prominent characteristic to dominate their judgment of all traits.

Human resource planning Term that is synonymous with personnel planning.

Job analysis Process of determining, through observation and study, the pertinent information relating to the nature of a specific job.

Job description Written statement which identifies the tasks, duties, activities, and performance results required in a particular job.

Job specification Written statement which identifies the abilities, skills, traits, or attributes that are necessary for successful performance in a particular job.

Peter Principle An idea popularized by Lawrence Peter which states that managers tend to be promoted to their level of incompetence.

Promotion The act of moving an employee to a job involving higher pay, status, and thus higher performance requirements.

Recruitment The process of seeking and attracting a supply of people from which qualified candidates for job vacancies can be selected.

Reverse discrimination Alleged preferential treatment of one group (minority or sex) over another rather than merely providing equal opportunity.

Separation Either voluntary or involuntary termination of an employee.

Staffing Involves securing and developing personnel for the jobs which were created by the organizing function.

Tests Instruments used in the selection process which provide a sample of behavior that is used to draw inferences about the future behavior or performance of an individual.

Test reliability The consistency or reproducibility of the results of a test.

Test validity The extent to which a test measures what it purports to measure; generally, this refers to the extent that a test predicts future job success or performance.

Transfer The act of moving an employee to another job at approximately the same level in the organization with basically the same pay, performance requirements, and status.

All the activities of any enterprise are initiated and determined by the persons who make up that institution. Plants, offices, computers, automated equipment, and all else that a modern firm uses are unproductive except for human effort and direction. Human beings design or order equipment: they decide where and how to use computers; they modernize or fail to modernize the technology employed; they secure the capital needed and decide on the accounting and fiscal procedures to be used. Every aspect of a firm's activities is determined by the competence, motivation, and general effectiveness of its human organization.

*Rensis Likert**

Staffing involves securing and developing personnel for the jobs which are created by the organizing function. The objective of staffing is to obtain the best available people for the organization and to develop the skills and abilities of those people. Obtaining the best available people for the organization generally involves forecasting personnel requirements and recruiting and selecting new employees. Developing the skills and abilities of an organization's employees involves the general area of employee development as well as the proper use of promotions, transfers, and separations. The staffing function is complicated by numerous government regulations. Furthermore, many of these regulations are subject to frequent change.

Unfortunately, many of the staffing activities have traditionally been conducted by personnel or human resource departments and have been considered relatively unimportant by line managers. However, obtaining and developing qualified personnel should be a major concern of all managers, as it involves the most valuable asset of an organization—human resources.

PERSONNEL (HUMAN RESOURCE) PLANNING

Personnel planning has been defined as "the process by which an organization ensures that it has the right number of people and the right kind of people, at the right places, at the right time, doing things for which they are economically most useful."[1]

Basically, personnel planning involves the application of the

*Rensis Likert, *The Human Organization* (New York: McGraw-Hill, 1967), p. 1.

[1]Thomas H. Patten, Jr., *Manpower Planning and the Development of Human Resources* (New York: John Wiley & Sons, 1972), p. 14.

planning concepts discussed in Chapter 5 to the human resources of the organization.

Once organizational plans are made and specific objectives set, the personnel planning process attempts to define the human resources necessary to meet the organization's objectives. The need to fully integrate personnel planning with organizational planning activities is important because having the right people at the right time has a major impact on the overall success or failure of an organization.[2]

The first basic question addressed by the planning process Where are we now?, is frequently answered in personnel planning by using job analyses and skills inventories.

Job Analysis and Skills Inventory

Job analysis is the process of determining, through observation and study, the pertinent information relating to the nature of a specific job. The end products of a job analysis are a job description and a job specification. A job description is a written statement which identifies the tasks, duties, activities, and performance results required in a particular job. A job specification is a written statement which identifies the abilities, skills, traits, or attributes that are necessary for successful performance in a particular job. In general, it can be said that a job description identifies the work that is performed in a job, while a job specification identifies the qualifications of an individual who could perform the job. Job analyses are frequently conducted by specialists from the personnel department. However, managers should provide input for developing the final job descriptions for the jobs they are managing.

Through conducting job analyses, an organization defines what its current resource needs are on the basis of current and/or newly created jobs. The purpose served by a skills inventory is to consolidate information about the organization's current human resources. The skills inventory contains basic information on all the employees of an organization giving a comprehensive picture of the individual. Through analyzing the skills inventory, the organization can state what the current quantity and quality of its human resources are.

Thomas H. Patten has outlined seven broad categories of information that should be included in a skills inventory:

---

[2] Keith Allen, Jim Cannon, Keith Carby, and Neil Johnston, "Personal Planning—the Key to Future Business Success," *Personnel Management*, October 1978, pp. 50–53.

1. Personal data history: age, sex, marital status, etc.
2. Skills: education, job experience, training, etc.
3. Special qualifications: memberships in professional groups, special achievements, etc.
4. Salary and job history: present salary, past salary, dates of raises, various jobs held, etc.
5. Company data: benefit plan data, retirement information, seniority, etc.
6. Capacity of individual: test scores on psychological and other tests, health information, etc.
7. Special preferences of individual: location or job preferences, etc.[3]

Some organizations maintain a separate inventory of information concerning managerial employees. While similar in nature to a skills inventory, a management inventory also contains brief assessments of the managers' past performances, their strengths and weaknesses, and their potential for advancement.[4]

The popularity of skills inventories has risen in recent years with the development of the computer. While most of the information provided by a skills inventory was available to organizations before the computer, compiling it manually was time consuming. Today, many large organizations such as IBM, RCA, Cummins Engine, U.S. Civil Service Commission, and the Canadian Public Service have computerized skills inventory systems. The primary advantage of a computerized skill inventory is that it enables a quick and accurate evaluation of the skills that are available within the organization. Combining the information provided by job analyses and the skills inventory enables the organization to evaluate the present status of its human resources.

In addition to appraising the current status of its human resources, managers should consider anticipated changes in the current work force due to retirements, deaths, discharges, promotions, transfers, and resignations. While some anticipated events are more easily estimated than others, certain information is available to aid in estimating these changes. For example, an organization's personnel records should provide information to calculate the average number of deaths, discharges, resignations, and so on that have occurred in the organization in the past. Amendments to the Age Discrimination in Employment Act in 1978, prohibiting mandatory retirement at age 65 in most cases, will also make this aspect of assessing the current status of human resources even more important.

---

[3] Patten, *Manpower Planning*, p. 243.
[4] Ibid.

Now that most individuals cannot be required to retire at age 65, traditional promotion patterns and job vacancies will be altered. For example, Sears, Roebuck & Co. estimates that on the average when one salaried employee retires, four hourly and six salaried promotional opportunities open up.[5] The total impact of the Age Discrimination in Employment Act is yet unknown, but many organizations have voiced concern over its potential impact on the staffing function.

Personnel Forecasting

The second basic question addressed in the planning process is "Where does the organization want to be?" Personnel forecasting attempts to answer this question with regard to the organization's human resource needs. Personnel forecasting is a process that attempts to determine the future human resource needs of the organization in light of the organization's objectives. Some of the many variables that are considered in forecasting human resource needs include future sales projections, skills required in potential new business ventures, composition of the present work force, technological changes, and general economic conditions. Due to the critical role human resources play in attaining organizational objectives, all levels of management should be involved in the personnel forecasting process.

Personnel forecasting is presently conducted largely on the basis of intuition. The experience and judgment of the manager is used to determine future personnel needs. Of course, this assumes that all managers in the organization are aware of the future plans of the total organization. Unfortunately, this is not true in many cases. For instance, a decision to increase the number of sales representatives in an organization could very likely have personnel implications for all units of the organization. Ideally, an increase in the number of sales representatives would generate more sales, which would then require increased production and increased invoicing to customers. Thus, the production and accounting departments would need to increase their personnel.

Various mathematical and statistical techniques are also used to project future personnel needs. A simple example of such a method is the use of sales forecasts to determine personnel needs.

Personnel Transition

The personnel forecast results in a statement of what the organization's human resource needs are in light of its plans and objectives. These human resource needs are referred to as gross person-

[5] "The Sears Suit: Goliath Meets Goliath," *The Atlanta Constitution*, February 1, 1979, p. 4–A.

nel requirements. The skills inventory, management inventory, and job descriptions derived from job analyses define what the current quantity and quality of the organization's human resources are. The final phase of personnel planning is to determine how the organization can obtain the quantity and quality of human resources required to meet its objectives as reflected by the personnel forecast. The difference between the gross personnel requirements and the current level of human resources available to the organization is referred to as the net personnel requirements. The net personnel requirements may be either positive or negative.

The organization engages in several different activities in order to bring its current level of human resources in line with forecasted requirements. These activities include recruiting and selecting new employees, developing current and/or new employees, promoting or transferring employees, laying off employees, and discharging employees. Other factors that must be considered when determining how forecasted human resources will be attained include organizational policies on promotions, transfers, layoffs, and discharges. Generally, the coordination of these activities is delegated to a personnel or human resource department within the organization.

Special Considerations in Personnel Planning

Government legislation now plays a vital role in personnel planning. Alleged discriminatory personnel practices by many organizations led to this legislation. Four significant government bills in this area are the Equal Pay Act of 1963; the Civil Rights Act of 1964; the Age Discrimination in Employment Act of 1967, as amended in 1978; and the Federal Rehabilitation Act of 1973.

The Equal Pay Act of 1963, which became effective in June 1964, prohibits wage discrimination on the basis of sex. The law states: "No employer . . . shall . . . discriminate . . . between employees on the basis of sex by paying wages . . . at a rate less than the rate at which he pays wages to employees of the opposite sex . . . for equal work on jobs the performance of which requires equal skill, effort, and responsibility and which are performed under similar working conditions. . . ."[6]

Title VII of the Civil Rights Act of 1964 is designed to eliminate discrimination in employment related to race, color, religion, sex, or national origin in organizations that conduct interstate commerce. The 1978 Civil Rights Act Amendment to Title VII

[6] "Equal Pay for Equal Work under the Fair Labor Standards Act," *Interpractices Bulletin* (Washington, D.C.: U.S. Department of Labor, 1967), Title 29, pt. 800.

prohibits discrimination in employment because of pregnancy, childbirth, or related medical conditions.

The Age Discrimination in Employment Act was passed by Congress in 1967 and went into effect on June 12, 1968. Initially, it was designed to protect individuals from 40–65 years of age from discrimination in hiring, retention, compensation, and other conditions of employment. In 1978, the act was amended, and coverage was extended to individuals up to age 70. Specifically, the act now forbids mandatory retirement at age 65 except in certain circumstances. The Federal Rehabilitation Act of 1973 prohibits discrimination in hiring of the handicapped by federal agencies and federal contractors.

Union contracts also influence personnel planning when they contain clauses regulating transfers, promotions, discharges, and so on.

INTEGRATING ORGANIZATIONAL OBJECTIVES, POLICIES, AND PERSONNEL PLANNING

Figure 9–1 graphically illustrates the basic relationships among organizational objectives, policies, and personnel planning. As discussed in chapter 4, organizational policies outline the ground rules and define the boundaries within which organizational objectives must be formulated and within which personnel planning must operate. Once the organizational objectives have been established, they are translated into a forecast of gross personnel requirements.

The net personnel requirements are determined by comparing the gross personnel forecasts to the present human resources in light of anticipated changes. If the net requirements are positive, the organization implements the process of recruitment, selection, and training and development. If the requirements are negative, proper adjustments must be made through attrition, layoffs, or discharges. As these changes take place, they should be recorded in the skills inventory.

RECRUITMENT

Recruitment involves the activities of seeking and attracting a supply of people from which qualified candidates for job vacancies can be selected. The amount of recruitment that must be done by an organization is determined by the difference between the forecasted personnel needs and the talent available within the organization as outlined by the skills inventory.

After the decision to recruit has been made, the sources of supply must be explored.

FIGURE 9–1
Organizational Objectives, Policies, and Personnel Planning

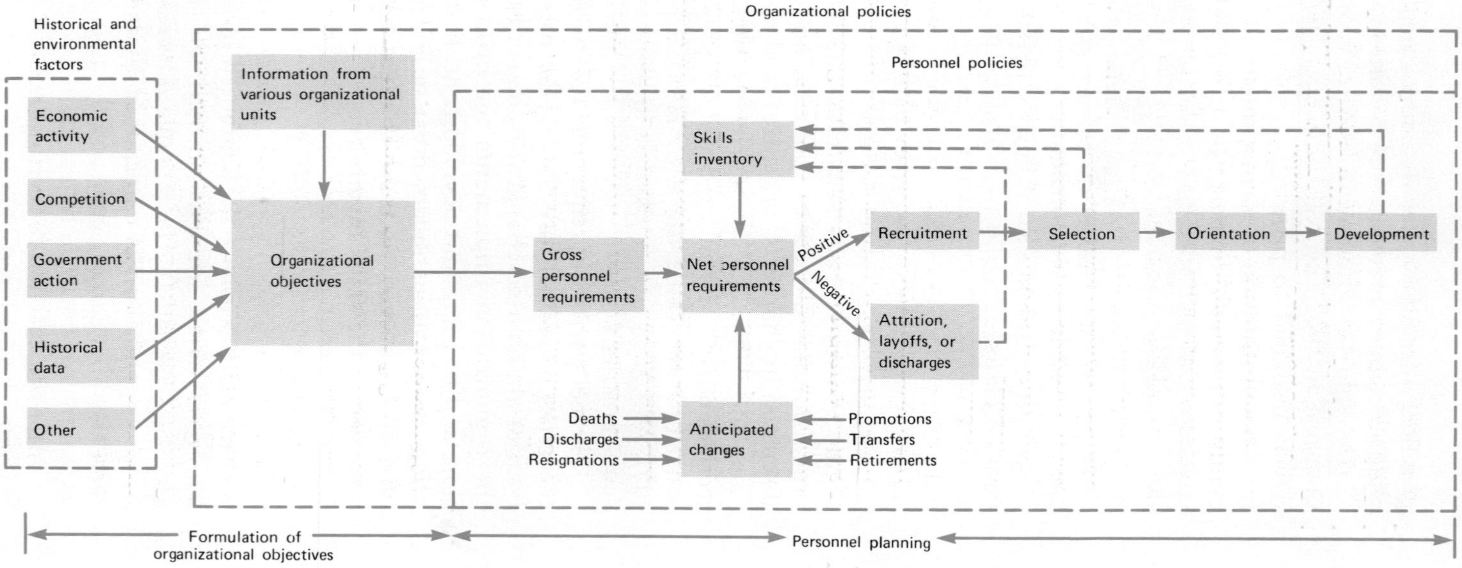

Historical and environmental factors

Economic activity

Competition

Government action

Historical data

Other

Organizational policies

Information from various organizational units

Organizational objectives

Personnel policies

Skills inventory

Gross personnel requirements

Net personnel requirements

Positive

Negative

Recruitment

Selection

Orientation

Development

Attrition, layoffs, or discharges

Deaths

Discharges

Resignations

Anticipated changes

Promotions

Transfers

Retirements

Formulation of organizational objectives

Personnel planning

Promotion from within

If an organization has been doing an effective job of selecting employees, one of the best sources of supply for job openings is its own employees. Promotion from within is a policy that many organizations follow. Obviously, this policy is only applicable for jobs above the entry level.

Promotion from within has several advantages. First, an organization should have a good idea about the strengths and weaknesses of its own employees. Employee morale and motivation are positively affected by internal promotions, assuming such promotions are perceived as being equitably related to performance. Finally, most organizations have a sizable investment in their employees, and using the abilities of present employees to their fullest extent improves the organization's return on its investment.

However, certain potential dangers must be acknowledged before adopting a policy of promotion from within. One danger has been popularized by Lawrence Peter and states that managers tend to be promoted to their level of incompetence.[7] According to the Peter Principle, successful managers are continually promoted until they finally reach a level at which they are unable to perform.

The Peter Principle can and does occur in organizations. Knowing the present skills of employees (skills inventory) and knowing the skills required by a new job (job analysis) minimizes the occurrence of the Peter Principle.

A second danger involves the inbreeding of ideas. When all vacancies are filled from within, caution must be taken to ensure that new ideas and innovations are not stifled by attitudes such as "we've never done it before," or "we did all right without it."

External Sources

Organizations have a wide range of external sources available for obtaining personnel. Probably the most widely used method for obtaining external personnel is the "Help Wanted" advertisement. Recruitment on college and university campuses is also used by many organizations. Other sources for obtaining personnel include employment agencies (public and private), management consulting firms, employee referrals, and labor unions.

The primary requisite for effective recruitment is that the organization must know the requirements for the particular jobs that it is attempting to fill. Only then can it seek qualified candidates.

---

[7] Lawrence J. Peter and R. Hall, *The Peter Principle* (New York: Bantam Books, 1969).

Legal Influences on Recruitment

For many years, some organizations were proud of the fact that they did not have to recruit since they could find many qualified applicants by merely spreading the word of a vacancy among current employees who in turn recruited friends and relatives. However, the government has made it clear that this form of recruiting is not acceptable when the current work force is predominantly white or male since it tends to perpetuate the present composition of the work force.[8] The rationale for the government's viewpoint is based on the belief that the friends and relatives of a primarily white work force will also be white in most cases and that the social environments within which much job vacancy information is transmitted is male-oriented.

SELECTION

The purpose of selection is to choose individuals that are most likely to succeed on the job from those that are available. The process is entirely dependent on proper personnel planning and recruitment. Only when an adequate pool of qualified candidates is available can the selection process function effectively. The ultimate objective of the selection process is to match the requirements of the job with the qualifications of the individual.

Who Makes the Selection Decision?

The responsibility for hiring is assigned to different levels of management in different organizations. In many organizations, the personnel department does the initial screening of recruits but the final selection decision is left to the manager of the department with the job opening. Such a system relieves the manager of the time-consuming responsibility of screening out unqualified and uninterested applicants. Less frequently, the personnel department is responsible for both the initial screening and the final decision. Many organizations leave the final choice to the immediate manager subject to the approval of higher levels of management. In small organizations, the owner or the top manager often makes the choice.

An alternate approach is to involve peers in the selection decision. Traditionally, peer involvement has been used primarily with professionals and those in upper levels of management, but it is becoming more popular at all levels of the organization. Un-

[8] Mary Green Miner and John B. Miner, *Employee Selection and the Law* (Washington, D.C.: Bureau of National Affairs, 1978), p. 331.

der this approach, co-workers have an input into the final selection decision.

Peer and managerial involvement normally are desirable not only for identifying talent but also for facilitating the acceptance of the new employee by the work group. Experience has shown that co-workers may have negative reactions toward the new employee if the selection is made solely by the personnel department. On the other hand, supervisors and peer groups are often more committed to helping new workers succeed if they have some input into their selection.

Legal Influences on Selection

The selection process has been of primary interest to the government in recent years, as evidenced by the number of laws and regulations in effect that prohibit discrimination in the selection of employees. The government can require an organization to develop an affirmative action plan; the purpose of which is to ensure that minority groups are not discriminated against.

However, the growing number of reverse discrimination suits (which results from preferential treatment for one group over another for reasons other than equal opportunity) may have a significant impact on affirmative action programs. The first real test case in this area was the Bakke case of 1978. Allen Bakke, a white male, brought suit against the medical school of the University of California at Davis, charging that he was unconstitutionally discriminated against when he was denied admission to the medical school while some minority applicants with lower qualifications were accepted. The Supreme Court ruled in Bakke's favor but at the same time upheld the constitutionality of affirmative action programs.

In another case in 1979, the Supreme Court heard a challenge to an affirmative action plan, collectively bargained by a union and an employer, brought by a white worker, Brian F. Weber.[9] This case questioned whether Title VII of the Civil Rights Act of 1964 as amended prohibited private employers from granting racial preferences in employment practices. The Court, in a 5-to-2 opinion, held that it did not, and that the voluntary quota was permissible.[10] At present, the issue of reverse discrimination has not been resolved, but it will have a significant impact on selection procedures in the future.[11]

---

[9] *United Steelworkers of America* v. *Brian F. Weber* 61 LEd 2d 480(1979).

[10] N. D. McFeeley, "Weber versus Affirmative Action?" *Personnel*, January 1980, pp. 47–48.

[11] Miner and Miner, *Employee Selection*, p. 42.

The Selection Procedure

Figure 9–2 is a suggested procedure for selecting employees. The preliminary screening and preliminary interview eliminate candidates who are obviously not qualified for the job. In preliminary screening application blanks, personnel data sheets, school records, work records, and similar sources are reviewed to determine characteristics, abilities, and the past performance of the individual. The preliminary interview is then used to screen out unsuitable or uninterested applicants who passed the preliminary screening phase. If caution is not exercised by the organization during the preliminary interview, some qualified applicants may be eliminated. The danger of this happening can be minimized by using structured interviews with specific screening criteria.

Testing

One of the most controversial areas of staffing is employment testing. Tests generally provide a sample of behavior that is used to draw inferences about the future behavior or performance of an individual. Tests used by organizations can be grouped into five general categories: personality, interest, aptitude (potential ability), achievement (knowledge), and mental ability (general intelligence).[12]

Employment testing is legally subject to the requirements of validity and reliability. Test validity refers to the extent to which a test predicts a specific criterion. For organizations, the criterion generally used is performance on the job. Thus, test validity generally refers to the extent to which a test predicts future job success or performance. The selection of criteria to define job success or performance is a most difficult problem, and its importance cannot be overstated. Obviously, test validity cannot be measured unless satisfactory criteria exist.

Test reliability refers to the consistency or reproducibility of the results of a test. Three methods are commonly used to determine the reliability of a test. The first method, called test-retest, involves testing a group of people and then retesting them at a later date. The degree of similarity between the sets of scores determines the reliability of the test. The second method, called parallel forms, entails giving two separate but similar forms of the test. The degree to which the sets of scores coincide determines the reliability of the test. The third method, called split-halves, divides the test into two halves to determine if performance is similar on both halves. Again, the degree of similarity determines the reliability. All of these methods require statistical

---

[12] A large number of tests are described in detail in O. K. Buros, *The Sixth Mental Measurements Yearbook* (Highland Park, N.J.: Gryphon Press, 1964).

FIGURE 9–2
Steps in the Selection Process

Steps in the selection process	*Possible criteria for eliminating potential employee*
Preliminary screening from application blank, résumé, employer records, etc.	Inadequate educational level or performance/experience record for the job and its requirements.
Preliminary interview	Obvious disinterest and unsuitability for job and its requirements.
Testing	Failure to meet minimum standards on job-related measures of intelligence, aptitude, and/or personality, etc.
Reference checks	Unfavorable reports from references regarding past performance.
Employment interview	Inadequate demonstration of ability or other job-related characteristics.
Physical examination	Lack of physical fitness required for job.
Personal judgment	Intuition and judgment resulting in the selection of a new employee.

calculations for determining the degree of reliability of the test.

In the past, organizations have frequently used tests without establishing their validity or reliability. As a result of such practices, testing has come under a great deal of attack. The previously discussed Civil Rights Act of 1964 includes a section specifically related to the use of tests:

> nor shall it be an unlawful employment practice for an employer to give and to act upon the results of any professionally developed ability test provided that such a test, its administration or action upon the results is not designed, intended, or used to discriminate because of race, color, religion, sex, or national origin.[13]

Two Supreme Court decisions have had a profound impact on the use of testing by organizations. First, in the case of *Griggs* v. *Duke Power Company*, the court ruled that any test which has an adverse effect on women or minority group applicants must be validated as job related, regardless of whether an employer intended to discriminate.[14] In *Albermarle Paper Company* v. *Moody*,

[13] Title VII, Sections 703(h), Civil Rights Act of 1964.
[14] *Griggs* v. *Duke Power Company*, U.S. Supreme Court (1971).

MANAGEMENT IN PRACTICE

Many Bosses Already Have Decided Who Successors Will Be and Why

Speculation about likely heirs to the top jobs in corporate America may be mostly academic.

Two thirds of the chief executives of the largest U.S. companies say they already have a clear idea who their successors will be. Half of these executives say they believe their top subordinates share that knowledge.

But the smaller the company, the less certain the chief executive is likely to be about a successor. And the smaller the company, the shorter the list of prospects the incumbent chief considers capable of doing his job.

What sort of person should a successor be? "Someone in our image," says the head of a medium-sized company in the West. "A person sensitive to the needs of his people who can motivate and lead by example. A hard worker who takes time to have fun with his employes."

These are among the major findings of a Wall Street Journal/Gallup survey of 782 chief executives. Results are based on interviews with heads of 282 of the country's largest corporations (including 102 Fortune 500 companies), heads of 300 medium-sized companies and owners of 200 small companies.

In companies of all sizes, chief executives say they would choose a successor on the basis of integrity, ambition, commitment, judgment, capacity for work and ability to motivate others. A majority of executives in large and medium-sized companies also mention knowledge of the industry or technical skills.

Personal character apparently matters most to heads of companies when they evaluate their possible successors. More than half the chiefs of large and medium-sized companies specifically mention such traits as honesty, intelligence, good judgment and self-reliance, as do 43 percent of chiefs of small companies.

"I would say he'd have to be more sophisticated than I, with more formal education dedicated to strategic planning," says the head of a large company in the Midwest. The chief of a large nonindustrial company cities "public relations ability, political awareness" and the skills to "represent the company in the public and political arenas." Adds the chief of a large company in the East: "First of all, integrity . . . and the ability to determine the proper course of action for the company."

SUITABLE SUCCESSORS

Q. How many people in your company are capable of doing your job as chief executive?

	Large firms	*Medium firms*	*Small firms*
One person	6%	10%	22%
Two	14	27	30
Three	24	26	18
Four or five	30	21	8
Six or more	22	11	4
Don't know	4	5	18

About half the heads of large companies also cite the abilities to get along with other employees and to lead and motivate as essential qualifications. In medium-sized companies, about 4 of every 10 chiefs mention these abilities, but in small companies, only about 1 in every 5 mention them.

The chief of a medium-sized company in the Midwest, for example, says his successor must have "a good, well-balanced personality . . . an appreciation of people and an ability to recognize their value."

A nonindustrial boss says he wants his successor to be able to "communicate with all people—workers, staff, the public" and to have a sense of humor.

Someone in Mind

The head of a small publishing company says he would select "a person who has a romantic vision of what he's doing, who gets a great kick out of it without expecting great financial return."

In the largest companies, 64 percent of chief executives say they have a clear idea who their successor will be. In medium-sized companies, 49 percent say they have a clear idea. In small companies, only 36 percent do.

Similarly, half the chief executives in large companies say they believe their top subordinates already know who will be the next chief. But in medium-sized companies, the proportion drops to 39 percent, and among small companies, it dips to 31 percent.

The number of eligible candidates for the top position apparently increases with company size.

In the large companies, about a third of chief executives say there are at least five prospects who could handle the top job after a reasonable learning period, compared with a fifth of chief executives in medium-sized companies. In small companies, more than half the chiefs say only one or two individuals would make a suitable successor.

Strength and Depth

The results indicate particular management strength and depth in the very largest corporations. Among chief executives of companies that rank among the 200 largest in the United States for example, 42 percent say they have six or more suitable successors, compared with 22 percent for all large companies and 11 percent for medium-sized companies. Another 21 percent of the chiefs of the 200 largest concerns say they have five qualified prospects.

The chief of one of those companies says the person he selects from those candidates "must have vision and understanding, the ability to see the big picture and yet know details so as not to be naive or easily misled, and secure enough in himself that he can admit when he's wrong."

But the chief of another large company with plenty of prospects to choose among offers a different view of the process:

"I don't feel that I should pick my successor. My personality was right for this company during a time of growth. But as executives tend to pick their successors in their own image, because of their egos, it would not be in the best interests of the company for me to pick him. I think it should be done by the second-tier management as a group."

Note: For this survey, the Gallup Organization interviewed 782 chief executives by telephone between October 13 and October 27. Large companies were respresented by a sample of 282 companies drawn from *Fortune* magazine's listings of 1,300 large companies. Medium and small companies were drawn from a commercial listing of about 3.5 million companies. The margin of sampling error is plus or minus six percentage points for responses from large and medium companies, and plus or minus seven percentage points for small companies.

Source: Frank Allen, *The Wall Street Journal*, May 18, 1980.

the Supreme Court ruled that the guidelines issued in 1966 by the Equal Opportunity Commission must be followed in validating tests.[15] While requiring a specified methodology, the Court did not require organizations to give up testing.[16]

However, one study revealed that the use of tests for hiring and promotions has declined and that tests are most frequently used for clerical jobs.[17] The decline in the use of tests can be attributed to the legal requirements of testing. Basically, many organizations have decided the benefits received from testing are not worth the effort required to satisfy the legal requirements.

Table 9–1 summarizes the findings of a 1977 study concerning the use of tests for hiring and promotions. Generally tests should be used in conjunction with other data and should be used as an aid in the selection process and not as the sole deciding factor.

Reference Checking

Reference checking involves the gathering and use of information about applicants in the selection process. It includes information about former work experience, past work performance, school performance, physical and mental health, character, public records (litigation, bankruptcies, etc.), workers' compensation claims, and the general accuracy of information supplied by the applicant. This information must be supplied by sources other than the applicant in order to be called reference checking.

Most prospective employers contact individuals from three reference categories: personal, academic, and past employment.[18] The thoroughness of reference checks generally depends on the position being filled. As a rule, the higher the position, the more thorough the verification should be. For the most part, contacting personal references has limited value because no applicant lists someone as a reference who will not give a positive recommendation. Contacting academic references may also have little value for similar reasons. Previous employers are the most-used source and are clearly in a position to supply the most objective information.

One problem associated with reference checks is concerned with the Privacy Act of 1974. Under this act, individuals have a legal right to examine letters of reference about themselves unless they have waived their right to do so. As a result of this act and

---

[15] *Albemarle Paper Company* v. *Moody*, U.S. Supreme Court (1965).

[16] J. Ledvinka and L. F. Schoenfeldt, "Legal Developments in Employment Testing: Albemarle and Beyond," *Personnel Psychology*, Spring 1978, p. 12.

[17] *The Personnel Executive's Job* (Englewood Cliffs, N.J.: Prentice-Hall/ASPA, 1977), p. 215; see also Hal Lancaster, "Failing System: Job Tests are Dropped by Many Companies," *The Wall Street Journal*, September 3, 1975.

[18] George M. Blason and John A. Belt, "Verifying Applicants' Backgrounds," *Personnel Journal*, July 1976, pp. 345–48.

TABLE 9–1
Incidence of Testing for Hiring and Promotion Decisions

A. Incidence of testing for hiring and promotion (by employer category)*

	Manufacturers	Public utilities	Hospitals	Banks	Insurance	Other offices	Retail stores	Transportation and communications	Other	All respondents
Test for hiring	41.2%	59.1%	41.8%	47.5%	67.9%	69.2%	44.2%	75.5%	55.1%	49.1%
Test for promotion	24.9	49.2	17.4	16.0	25.5	19.7	22.5	42.2	19.7	24.0
Don't test	42.3	22.4	46.6	36.5	21.8	25.0	42.5	18.3	33.8	36.5

B. Incidence of testing for hiring and promotion (by size of employer)*

	Fewer than 100 employees	100–499 employees	500–999 employees	1,000–4,999 employees	5,000–9,999 employees	10,000–25,000 employees	More than 25,000 employees	All respondents
Test for hiring	30.4%	43.4%	46.8%	55.4%	62.7%	54.9%	57.1%	49.1%
Test for promotion	17.9	17.3	24.0	29.3	27.4	32.7	32.4	24.0
Don't test	61.0	49.2	45.1	40.4	32.9	38.4	39.6	36.5

*Percentages total more than 100 percent because some respondents test for both hiring and promotion.

Source: Adopted from "The Personnel Executive's Job," *Personnel Management Policies and Practice* (Englewood Cliffs, N.J.: Prentice-Hall, Inc., ASPA, 1977).

court interpretations of the act, reference letters are often hard to obtain. In fact, many employers will now verify in writing only the last salary, job title, and date of employment for previous employees.[19]

Employment Interview

The interview is one of the most widely used selection tools. One study reported that 56 percent of the responding companies viewed the interview as the most important aspect of selecting employees while 90 percent stated that they had more confidence in interviews than all the other possible information sources.[20] The employment interview should focus all of the information obtained in the previous stages of the selection process toward the ultimate objective of selecting and hiring the best individual for the job.

[19] Lawrence Wangler, "Employee Reference Request Revisited," *The Personnel Administrator*, November 1975; and "References Dry Up," *The Wall Street Journal*, January 6, 1976, p. 1.

[20] Bureau of National Affairs, *Personnel Policies Forum*, survey no. 114, September 1976.

Interviews can either be structured or unstructured. In a structured interview, the interviewer knows in advance the questions that are to be asked and generally merely proceeds down a list of questions while recording the interviewee's responses. Structured interviews give a common body of knowledge on all interviewees; allow for a systematic coverage of all information deemed necessary by the organization; and provide a means of minimizing the personal biases and prejudices of the interviewer.

Unstructured interviews have no definite checklist or preplanned strategy for the interview. The interviewee largely determines the path of the interview. Questions such as "Tell me about your previous job," are asked. Unstructured interviews generally require a greater participation on the part of the interviewee than in the case of a structured interview.

Three other types of interviewing techniques have been used by organizations to a more limited extent. The stress interview places interviewees on the defensive and attempts to confuse them as to their progress. The purpose of this type of interview is to detect the highly emotional individual. Panel or board interviews have also been used. Here a group of people question the interviewee using either a structured or unstructured technique. Finally, group interviews have been used where a group of job candidates are observed in group discussions.

It is highly unlikely that any one type of interview is appropriate for all situations. The most appropriate type of interview depends on the type of information that the organization wants to obtain from the interviewee and the nature of the job to be filled.

Interviews have the same basic problems of validity and reliability as do tests. Research has shown that interviewers often report extreme differences in evaluating the same individual.[21] Regardless of the criticism, interviewing is still a widely used technique in the selection process. Cross validation of the interview with other data obtained in the selection process is one method of attempting to solve validity and reliability problems. Presently, the structured interview has the most promise for high validity.[22]

Interviews are also subject to numerous legal questions. Figure 9–3 outlines permissible questions and questions to be avoided in an interview with a job applicant.

---

[21] Herbert Heneman III, "The Impact of Interviewer Training and Interview Structure on the Reliability and Validity of the Selection Interview," *Academy of Management Proceedings*, 1975, pp. 231–233.

[22] Wendell French, *The Personnel Management Process*, 5th ed. (Boston: Houghton Mifflin, 1982), p. 231.

FIGURE 9–3
Pre-Employment Inquiry Guide

This guide is *not* a complete definition of what can and cannot be asked of applicants. It is illustrative and attempts to answer the questions most frequently asked about equal opportunity law. It is hoped that in most cases the given rules, either directly or by analogy, will guide all personnel involved in the pre-employment processes of recruiting, interviewing, and selection. This guide pertains only to inquiries, advertisements, etc., directed to all applicants prior to employment. Information required for records such as race, sex, and number of dependents may be requested after the applicant is on the payroll provided such information is not used for any subsequent discrimination, as in upgrading or layoff.

These laws are not intended to prohibit employers from obtaining sufficient job-related information about applicants, as long as the questions do not elicit information which could be used for discriminatory purposes. Applicants should not be encouraged to volunteer potentially prejudicial information. The laws do not restrict the rights of employers to define qualifications necessary for satisfactory job performance, but require that the same standard of qualifications used for hiring be applied to all persons considered for employment.

It is recognized that the mere routine adherence to these laws will not accomplish the results intended by the courts and Congress. Employment discrimination can be eliminated only if the laws and regulations are followed in the spirit in which they were conceived.

Subject	*Permissible inquiries*	*Inquiries to be avoided**
1. Name	"Have you worked for this company under a different name?" "Is any additional information relative to change of name, use of an assumed name or nickname necessary to enable a check on your work and educational record? If yes, explain."	Inquiries about name which would indicate applicant's lineage, ancestry, national origin, or descent. Inquiry into previous name of applicant where it has been changed by court order or otherwise. Inquiries about preferred courtesy title: Miss, Mrs., Ms.
2. Marital and family status	Whether applicant can meet specified work schedules or has activities, commitments, or responsibilities that may hinder the meeting of work attendance requirements. Inquiries as to a duration of stay on job or anticipated absences which are made to males and females alike.	Any inquiry indicating whether an applicant is married, single, divorced, or engaged, etc. Number and age of children. Information on child-care arrangements. Any questions concerning pregnancy. Any such questions which directly or indirectly result in limitation of job opportunities.
3. Age	Requiring proof of age in the form of a work permit or a certificate of age—if a minor. Requiring proof of age by birth certificate after being hired. Inquiry as to whether or not the applicant meets the minimum age requirements as set by law, and requirement that upon hire proof of age must be submitted in the form of a birth certificate or other forms of proof of age. If age is a legal requirement, "if hired, can you furnish proof of age?," or statement that hire is subject to verification of age.	Requirement that applicant state age or date of birth. Requirement that applicant produce proof of age in the form of a birth certificate or baptismal record. *The Age Discrimination in Employment Act of 1967 forbids discrimination against persons between the ages of 40 and 70.*

FIGURE 9–3 (*continued*)

Subject	*Permissible inquiries*	*Inquiries to be avoided**
	Inquiry as to whether or not an applicant is younger than the employer's regular retirement age.	
4. Handicaps	For employers subject to the provisions of the Rehabilitation Act of 1973, applicants may be "invited" to indicate how and to what extent they are handicapped. The employer must indicate that: (1) compliance with the invitation is voluntary; (2) the information is being sought only to remedy discrimination or provide opportunities for the handicapped; (3) the information will be kept confidential; and (4) refusing to provide the information will not result in adverse treatment. All applicants can be asked if they are able to carry out all necessary job assignments and perform them in a safe manner.	An employer must be prepared to prove that any physical and mental requirements for a job are due to "business necessity" and the safe performance of the job. Except in cases where undue hardship can be proven, employers must make "reasonable accommodations" for the physical and mental limitations of an employee or applicant. "Reasonable accommodation" includes alteration of duties, alteration of work schedule, alteration of physical setting, and provision of aids. *The Rehabilitation Act of 1973 forbids employers from asking job applicants general questions about whether they are handicapped or asking them about the nature and severity of their handicaps.*
5. Sex	Inquiry or restriction of employment is permissible only where a *bona fide occupational qualification* exists. (This BFOQ exception is interpreted very narrowly by the courts and the EEOC.) The burden of proof rests on the employer to prove that the BFOQ does exist and that *all* members of the affected class are incapable of performing the job. Sex of applicant may be requested (preferably not on the employment application) for affirmative action purposes but may not be used as an employment criterion.	Sex of applicant. Any other inquiry which would indicate sex. Sex is *not* a BFOQ because a job involves physical labor (such as heavy lifting) beyond the capacity of *some* women nor can employment be restricted just because the job is traditionally labeled "men's work" or "women's work." Applicant's sex cannot be used as a factor for determining whether or not an applicant will be satisfied in a particular job. Questions about an applicant's height or weight, unless demonstrably necessary as requirements for the job.
6. Race or color	General distinguishing physical characteristics such as scars, etc., to be used for identification purposes. Race may be requested (preferably not on the employment application) for affirmative action purposes but may not be used as an employment criterion.	Applicant's race. Color of applicant's skin, eyes, hair, etc., or other questions directly or indirectly indicating race or color.

FIGURE 9–3 (*continued*)

Subject	*Permissible inquiries*	*Inquiries to be avoided**
7. Address or duration of residence	Applicant's address. Inquiry into length of stay at current and previous addresses. "How long a resident of this State or city?"	Specific inquiry into foreign address which would indicate national origin. Names and relationship of persons with whom applicant resides. Whether applicant owns or rents home.
8. Birthplace	"Can you after employment submit a birth certificate or other proof of U.S. citizenship."	Birthplace of applicant. Birthplace of applicant's parents, spouse, or other relatives. Requirement that applicant submit a birth certificate before employment. Any other inquiry into national origin.
9. Religion	An applicant may be advised concerning normal hours and days of work required by the job to avoid possible conflict with religious or other personal conviction. However, except in cases where undue hardship can be proven, employers and unions must make "reasonable accommodation" for religious practices of an employee or prospective employee. "Reasonable accommodation" may include voluntary substitutes, flexible scheduling, lateral transfer, change of job assignments, or the use of an alternative to payment of union dues.	Applicant's religious denomination or affiliation, church, parish, pastor, or religious holidays observed. Any inquiry to indicate or identify religious denomination or customs. Applicants may not be told that any particular religious groups are required to work on their religious holidays.
10. Military record	Type of education and experience in service as it relates to a particular job.	Type of discharge.
11. Photograph	May be required for identification after hiring.	Requirement that applicant affix a photograph to his application. Request that applicant, at his option, submit photograph. Requirement of photograph after interview but before hiring.
12. Citizenship	"Are you a citizen of the United States?" "Do you intend to remain permanently in the U.S.?" "If not a citizen, are you prevented from becoming lawfully employed because of visa or immigration status?" Statement that, if hired, applicant may be required to submit proof of citizenship.	"Of what country are you a citizen?" Whether applicant or his parents or spouse are naturalized or native-born U.S. citizens. Date when applicant or parents or spouse acquired U.S. citizenship. Requirement that applicant produce his naturalization papers. Whether applicant's parents or spouse are citizens of the U.S.

FIGURE 9–3 (*continued*)

Subject	*Permissible inquiries*	*Inquiries to be avoided**
13. Ancestry or national origin	Languages applicant reads, speaks, or writes fluently. (If another language is necessary to perform the job.)	Inquiries into applicant's lineage, ancestry, national origin, descent, birthplace, or native language. National origin of applicant's parents or spouse.
14. Education	Applicant's academic, vocational, or professional education; school attended. Inquiry into language skills such as reading, speaking, and writing foreign languages.	Any inquiry asking specifically the nationality, racial or religious affiliation of a school. Inquiry as to how foreign language ability was acquired.
15. Experience	Applicant's work experience, including names and addresses of previous employers, dates of employment, reasons for leaving, salary history. Other countries visited.	
16. Conviction, arrest, and court record	Inquiry into actual *convictions* which relate reasonably to fitness to perform a particular job. (A conviction is a court ruling where the party is found guilty as charged. An arrest is merely the apprehending or detaining of the person to answer the alleged crime.)	Any inquiry relating to arrests. Any inquiry into or request for a person's arrest, court, or conviction record if not *substantially related* to functions and responsibilities of the particular job in question.
17. Relatives	Names of applicant's relatives already employed by this company. Names and address of parents or guardian (if applicant is a minor).	Name or address of any relative of adult applicant.
18. Notice in case of emergency	Name and address of persons to be notified in case of accident or emergency.	Name and addres of *relatives* to be notified in case of accident or emergency.
19. Organizations ...	Inquiry into any organizations which an applicant is a member of providing the name or character of the organizations does not reveal the race, religion, color, or ancestry of the membership. "List all professional organizations to which you belong. What offices do you hold?"	"List all organizations, clubs, societies, and lodges to which you belong." The names of organizations to which the applicant belongs if such information would indicate through character or name the race, religion, color, or ancestry of the membership.
20. References	"By whom were you referred for a position here?" Names of persons willing to provide professional and/or character references for applicant.	Requiring the submission of a religious reference. Requesting reference from applicant's pastor.

FIGURE 9–3 (*concluded*)

Subject	*Permissible inquiries*	*Inquiries to be avoided**
21. Credit rating	None.	Any questions concerning credit rating, charge accounts, etc. Ownership of car.
22. Miscellaneous	Notice to applicants that any misstatements or omissions of material facts in the application may be cause for dismissal.	Any inquiry should be avoided which, although not specifically listed among the above, is designed to elicit information concerning race, color, ancestry, age, sex, religion, handicap, or arrest and court record unless based upon a bona fide occupational qualification.

Source: Clifford M. Koen, Jr., "The Pre-Employment Inquiry Guide," *Personnel Journal,* Costa Mesa, Calif., October 1980, pp. 826–28.

Several common pitfalls may be encountered in interviewing a job applicant. Managers may have personal biases, and should be careful not to let those biases play a role in the interviewing process. For example, a qualified male applicant should not be rejected merely because he has long hair.

Closely related is the problem of the halo effect. The halo effect occurs when a manager allows a single prominent characteristic to dominate judgment of all traits. For instance, it is easy to ignore other characteristics when a person has a pleasant personality, but merely having a pleasant personality does not necessarily mean the person will be a good employee.

Overgeneralizing is another pitfall. It must be remembered that the interviewee is under pressure during the interview, and may not act exactly the same way on the job as during the interview.

Certain things can be done to overcome many of the pitfalls in interviewing. First, all of the information that has been obtained in the previous steps of the selection process should be reviewed. Next, a plan should be developed for the interview. For example, if a structured interview is to be used, all of the questions that are to be asked should be written down before the interview takes place. Part of the plan should also include room arrangements. Privacy and some degree of comfort are important. If a private room is not available, the interview should be conducted in a place where other employees are not within hearing distance. The applicant should also be put at ease. The interviewer should not argue with the applicant or attempt to put the applicant on the spot. Engaging in a brief conversation about a general topic of broad interest or offering the applicant a cup of coffee can help ease the tension. However, the interviewer should always keep in mind that the primary goal of the interview is to get information that will aid in the selection decision. Finally, notes from the interview should be taken to ensure that the facts are not forgotten.

One of the best ways to determine the success of an organization's interviewing program is to compare the performance ratings of individuals hired against their appraisal based on the interviewing process. This cross validation can prove quite beneficial not only to the interviewer but to the total organization.

Physical Examination

After the potential employee has cleared the preceding hurdles, most organizations require a physical examination. The physical examination is given not only to determine the potential employee's eligibility for group, life, health, and disability insurance but also to determine if the individual is physically capable of performing the job. As with most of the steps in the selection process, changes are also occurring in this area. New definitions and policies are emerging for hiring handicapped people. Many jobs are also being reexamined to determine the exact physical requirements of the job.

Personal Judgment

The final step in the selection process is the personal judgment that is required in selecting one individual for the job. Of course, the assumption made at this point is that there will be more than one individual qualified for the job. If this is true, a value judgment using all of the data obtained in the previous steps of the selection process must be made in selecting the best individual for the job. If the previous steps have been performed successfully, the chances of success in this personal judgment are dramatically improved.

The individual making the personal judgment should also recognize that in some cases none of the applicants are satisfactory. If this occurs, the job should be redesigned, more money should be offered to attract more qualified candidates, or other actions should be taken. Caution should be taken against accepting the best individual that has been seen if the individual is not what is needed to do the job.

EMPLOYEE DEVELOPMENT

Employee development is a process that is concerned with the improvement and growth of the capabilities of individuals and groups within the organization. The goal of employee development is to facilitate the achievement of organizational goals. Included in this process are such activities as determining employee development needs, training and development programs, performance reviews, and employee counseling.

The importance of employee development cannot be overstated. Employee development is frequently viewed by management as a nicety that is encouraged in good economics times but quickly reduced or eliminated in bad economic times. Such a short-term position often causes the organization to suffer in the long run.

Chapter 17, which focuses on developing individual abilities, discusses specific methods and techniques of employee development.

TRANSFERS, PROMOTIONS, AND SEPARATIONS

Recalling Figure 9–1, the final step in the personnel planning process involves transfers, promotions, and separations. Transferring an employee merely involves moving an employee to another job at approximately the same level in the organization with basically the same pay, performance requirements, and status. Planned transfers can serve as an excellent development technique. Transfers can also be helpful in balancing varying departmental work load requirements. The most common problem relating to transfers occurs when a "problem" employee is unloaded on an unsuspecting manager. Training, counseling, or corrective punishment of the delinquent employee may eliminate the need for such transfers. If the employee cannot be rehabilitated, discharge is usually preferable to transfer.

A promotion involves moving an employee to a job involving higher pay, status, and thus higher performance requirements. The two basic criteria used by most organizations in promotions are merit and seniority. Union contracts often require that seniority be considered in promotions. Many organizations prefer to base promotions on merit as a way of rewarding and encouraging performance. Obviously, this assumes that the organization has a method for evaluating performance and determining merit. An organization must also consider the requirements of the job for which an individual is being considered and not just performance in previous jobs. Both potential and past performance must be considered. Success in one job does not automatically ensure success in another job. Furthermore, evaluating potential in addition to past performance lessens the probability of the occurrence of the Peter Principle.

A separation involves either voluntary or involuntary termination of an employee. In voluntary terminations, many organizations attempt to determine why the employee is leaving by using exit interviews. This type of interview provides insights into problem areas in the organization that need to be corrected. Involuntary separations should be made only as a last resort. When a company has hired an employee and invested resources in the employee, termination results in a low return on the organization's investment. Training and counseling often are tried before firing an individual. However, when rehabilitation fails, the best course of action is usually termination because of the negative impact a disgruntled or misfit employee can have on others in the organization.

THE DYNAMICS OF STAFFING

Because organizations are dynamic, the staffing process is subjected to continual changes. The activities involved in the staffing function must be continuously reevaluated in light of changing conditions, both internal and external. Internal conditions include changing job requirements, changing technology, retirements, deaths, resignations, terminations, and promotions. External conditions include government regulations, general economic conditions, industry competition, and resource availabilities. These conditions and the changes they cause must be adequately considered so that the level of human resources can be maintained in order to achieve organizational objectives. The critical link between an organization's human resources and the achievement of organizational goals is reflected in the general consensus that even if the physical assets of an organization were suddenly destroyed, the human organization, if properly staffed, could rebuild and maintain a viable firm.[23]

This chapter has presented what could be considered an ideal staffing model. It should not be concluded, however, that most organizations follow this model: many do not.

SUMMARY

Staffing involves securing and developing personnel to fill the jobs that have been created by the organizing function.

Personnel planning is the process by which an organization ensures that it has the right number of people and the right kind of people, at the right places, at the right time, doing things for which they are economically most useful. The following activities

[23] Joseph L. Massie and John Douglas, *Managing: A Contemporary Introduction* (Englewood Cliffs, N.J.: Prentice-Hall, 1977), p. 315.

and information are required in performing the personnel planning process: job analyses, skills inventories, personnel forecasts, recruitment, selection, employee development, promotions, transfers, and separations.

Job analysis is a process of determining through observation and study, the pertinent information relating to the nature of a specific job. The end products of a job analysis are a job description and a job specification. A job description is a written description of a job and its requirements. A job specification is a written statement of the necessary qualifications of the prospective employee. A skills inventory provides basic information on all the employees of an organization. Combining the skills inventory with the job analyses enables the organization to determine its present position with regard to its human resources. Personnel forecasting is an attempt to determine the future personnel needs of an organization. Recruitment involves the activities of seeking and attracting a supply of people from which qualified candidates for job vacancies can be selected.

The purpose of the selection process is to choose the individuals that are most likely to succeed from those that have been recruited. Steps involved in the selection process are preliminary screening and interviewing, testing, reference checks, employment interviews, physical examination, and personal judgment. Several suggestions were made for improving the interviewing process.

Employee development is a process that is concerned with the improvement and growth of the capabilities of individuals and groups within the organization. The goals of employee development are to facilitate the achievement of organizational objectives.

Transfers, promotions, and separations are the final steps that influence the personnel planning process. Transferring an employee involves moving the employee to another job at approximately the same level in the organization with basically the same pay, performance requirements, and status. A promotion involves moving an employee to a job involving higher pay, status, and thus higher performance requirements. A separation involves either voluntary or involuntary termination of an employee.

REVIEW QUESTIONS

1. How does staffing relate to the organizing function?
2. What is personnel planning?
3. What is a job analysis? A job description? A job specification? A skills inventory?

4. What is personnel forecasting?
5. Describe a model of the personnel planning process.
6. Describe the purpose of the following government legislation:
   a. Equal Pay Act of 1963.
   b. Civil Rights Act of 1964.
   c. Age Discrimination in Employment Act of 1967, as amended in 1978.
   d. Federal Rehabilitation Act of 1973.
7. What is recruitment? Describe some sources of recruitment.
8. What is selection? Describe the steps in the selection process.
9. What is test reliability? What methods are commonly used to determine test reliability?
10. What is test validity?
11. What is reference checking?
12. Describe two basic types of interviews.
13. Discuss some common pitfalls in interviewing.
14. What is employee development? Cite some of the activities involved in employee development.
15. What is a transfer? A promotion? A separation?

DISCUSSION QUESTIONS

1. Discuss the following statement: "If an individual owns a business, he or she should be able to hire anyone and shouldn't have to worry about the government."
2. Discuss your feelings on "reverse discrimination."
3. Many managers believe that line managers should not have to worry about personnel needs and that this should be handled by the personnel department. What do you think?
4. One common method of handling problem employees is to transfer them to another department of the organization. Discuss your feelings on this practice.

SELECTED READINGS

Alpander, G. G. "Human Resource Planning in U.S. Corporations." *California Management Review,* Spring 1980, pp. 24–32.

Clague, J. R. "Impact of Human Rights Legislation on Recruitment (Canada)." *C A Magazine,* March 1979, pp. 76 ff.

Ellig, B. R. "Impact of Legislation on the Personnel Function." *Personnel,* September –October 1980, pp. 49–53.

Frank, J. G. "Recruiting in a Changing Environment (Canada)." *Canadian Business Review,* Spring 1981, pp. 37–40.

Gatewood, R. D., and J. Ledvinka. "Selection Interviewing and EEO: Mandate for Objectivity." *Personnel Administrator,* December 1979, pp. 51–54.

Greenlaw, P. S., and J. P. Kohl. "Selection Interviewing and the New Uniform Federal Guidelines." *Personnel Administrator,* August 1980, pp. 74–79.

Jacobs, R. B. "Confusion Remains Five Years after *Alexander* v. *Gardner–Denver.*" *Labor Law Journal,* January 1980, pp. 623–36.

Kaumeyer, R. A., Jr. "Taking Inventory of Employees' Skills, with an Eye Towards Affirmative Action." *Management World,* September 1976, pp. 15–16.

Koen, C. M., Jr. "Pre-Employment Inquiry Guide." *Personnel Journal,* October 1980, pp. 825–29.

Latterell, J. D. "Planning for the Selection Interview." *Personnel Journal,* July 1979, pp. 466–67.

Ledvinka, J., and L. F. Schoenfeldt. "Legal Developments in Employment Testing: Albemarle and Beyond." *Personnel Psychology,* Spring 1978, pp. 1–13.

Levine, E. L. "Legal Aspects of Reference Checking for Personnel Selection." *Personnel Administrator,* November 1977, pp. 14–16 ff.

Manning, W. H. "Test Validation and EEOC Requirements: Where We Stand." *Personnel,* May 1978, pp. 70–77.

McFeeley, N. D. "*Weber* v. *Affirmative Action?*" *Personnel,* January 1980, pp. 38–51.

Miner, Mary Green, and John B. Miner. *Employee Selection and the Law.* Washington, D.C.: Bureau of National Affairs, 1978.

Patten, Thomas H., Jr. *Manpower Planning and the Development of Human Resources.* New York: John Wiley & Sons, 1972.

Pati, G. C. "Reverse Discrimination: What Can Managers Do?" *Personnel Journal,* July 1977, pp. 334–38 ff.

Sewell, C. "Pre-Employment Investigations: The Key to Security in Hiring." *Personnel Journal,* May 1981, pp. 376–79.

Smith, R. H. "Let Your Employees Choose their Co-Workers." *S.A.M. Advanced Management Journal,* Winter 1981, pp. 27–30 ff.

Stone, J. E. "Age Discrimination in Employment Act: A Review of Recent Changes." *Monthly Labor Review,* March 1980, pp. 32–36.

Williams, H. E. "Eight Question Interview." *Management World,* June 1978, pp. 17–18.

Case 9–1

To promote or not to promote?

Tom Roper, president of Quine Company, which is a manufacturer of highly technical components, was contemplating events that had transpired over the past several months. Six months ago, it became apparent that Quine needed to create a position of executive vice president. This person was to be responsible for many of the day-to-day operations of the company so that Tom could concentrate more on strategy formulation and long-range planning. Tom felt that this was imperative since the company was beginning to expand rapidly and move into new areas.

At the time, Tom thought long and hard about offering the job to Jake Barnes. Jake had been with the company 19 years and had worked his way up from a junior engineer to chief engineer. Although Jake only had two years of college, he is practically a genius when it comes to engineering. Also, Tom was told that Jake would really be disappointed, or maybe even violently mad, if he was not given a shot at the job. Tom was sympathetic to Jake's feelings. After all, he had been extremely loyal to the company and he had done a good job over the years.

On the other hand, Tom had some real doubts concerning Jake's ability to handle a true management job. Tom knew that being a top-notch engineer did not guarantee that Jake would be a good manager. Tom had heard complaints from several of the junior engineers concerning their feelings that Jake was narrow-minded and tried to handle people the same way that he handled machines.

1. Should Tom promote Jake?
2. What are the potential consequences of promoting Jake? Of not promoting Jake?

Case 9–2

The employment interview

Jerry Sullivan is the manager of underwriting for a large insurance company located in the southeast. Recently, one of his best employees had given him two weeks' notice of her intention to leave. She was expecting a baby within a very short time period, and she and her husband had decided that she was going to quit work and stay home with her new baby and her other two young children.

Today, Jerry was scheduled to start interviewing applicants for this job. The first applicant was Barbara Riley. She arrived at the company's office promptly at 9:00 *a.m.*, the time scheduled for her interview. Unfortunately, just before she arrived, Jerry received a phone call from his boss, who had just returned from a three weeks' vacation. He just wanted Jerry to bring him up-to-date on what had been going on. The telephone conversation lasted 30 minutes. During this time, Ms. Riley was seated in the company's reception room.

At 9:30, Jerry went to the reception room and invited Ms. Riley into his office. The following conversation occurred:

Jerry: Would you like a cup of coffee?

Barbara: No, I've already had one.

Jerry: You don't mind if I have a cup, do you?

Barbara: No, go right ahead. [*Jerry pauses and rings his secretary, Dorothy Cannon.*]

Jerry: Dorothy, would you fix me a cup of coffee?

Dorothy: I'll bring it in shortly. You have a call on line one.

Jerry: Who is it?

Dorothy: It's Tom Powell, our IBM representative. He wants to talk to you about the delivery date on our new word processor.

Jerry: I'd better talk to him. [*Turning to Barbara.*] I'd better take this call. I'll only be a minute. [*He picks up his phone.*] Well, Tom, when are we going to get our machines?

This phone conversation goes on for almost 10 minutes. After hanging up, Jerry turns again to Barbara to resume the interview.

Jerry: I'm sorry, but I needed to know about those machines. We really do need them. We only have a short time, so why don't you just tell me about yourself.

At that point, Barbara tells Jerry about her education, which includes an undergraduate degree in psychology and an MBA which she will be receiving shortly. She also explains to Jerry that this will be her first full-time job. Just then the phone rings and Jerry's secretary tells him that his next interviewee is waiting.

Jerry: [*Turns to Barbara.*] Thank you for coming in. I'll be in touch with you as soon as I interview two more applicants for this job.

1. Outline the inadequacies of this interview.
2. What information did Jerry learn?
3. How do you think Barbara Riley feels?

10 Motivation: The Moving Function

Objectives

1. To develop an understanding of the motivation process.
2. To present and clarify the relationships among the current theories of motivation.
3. To explore the relationships between motivation, satisfaction, and performance.

Chapter Outline

Glossary of Terms

Achievement-power-affiliation theory A theory which holds that all people have three needs—a need to achieve, a need for power, and a need for affiliation; that the level of intensity of these needs varies among individuals; and that people are motivated in situations which allow them to satisfy their most intense need(s).

Job enlargement Involves making a job structurally larger by giving a worker more similar operations or tasks to perform.

Job enrichment Upgrading a job with factors such as more meaningful work, more recognition, more responsibility, and more opportunities for advancement.

Job satisfaction An individual's general attitude about his or her job.

Morale Refers to an individual's feeling of being accepted by and belonging to a group of employees through common goals, confidence in the desirability of these goals, and progress toward these goals.

Motivation A causative sequence, illustrated by the following diagram, which elicits increased effort.

Needs ⟶ Drives or motives ⟶ Achievement of goals

Motivation-maintenance theory A theory of motivation which states that all work-related factors can be grouped into one of two categories: maintenance factors, which will not produce motivation but can prevent motivation; and motivators, which can encourage motivation.

Need hierarchy Refers to the five different levels of individual needs (physiological, safety, social, esteem or ego, and self-actualization) which were identified by Abraham H. Maslow.

Preference-expectancy theory A theory which holds that motivation is based on a combination of the individual's expectancy that increased effort will lead to increased performance; increased performance will lead to rewards and the individual's preference for the rewards being offered.

Reinforcement theory An approach to motivation based on the idea that behavior which is reinforced will be repeated and behavior that is not reinforced is less likely to be repeated.

Traditional theory of motivation Theory of motivation based on the assumption that money is the primary motivator.

The early bird catches the worm. That fact
Has been into every young cranium packed
It's really absurd the talk that is heard
Of the wonderful thrift of that wonderful bird
And not the least mention is made of the worm
That equally early set out on a squirm
Except that within that most provident bird
The poor little fellow was thus early interred
Now it seems there's a word on both sides to be said
For had he but snugly remained in his bed
Or curled up for a nap
In mother earth's lap
The poor little chap
Would doubtless have lived to Methuselah's age
And another tale figured in history's page.

Moral: Maxims and rules
That are taught in the schools
Are excellent truly for governing fools
But you of your actions get up early of course
But if you're a worm don't be so absurd
As to get up at dawn to be caught by a bird.*

"Our employees are just not motivated." "Half the problems we have are due to a lack of personal motivation." "How do I motivate my employees?" Statements and questions such as these are often expressed by managers at all levels in organizations.

The problem of motivation is not a recent development. Research conducted by William James in the late 1800s indicated the importance of motivation.[1] James found that hourly employees could keep their jobs by using approximately 20 to 30 percent of their ability. James also found that highly motivated employees will work at approximately 80 to 90 percent of their ability. Figure 10–1 illustrates the potential influence of motivation on performance. Highly motivated employees can bring about substantial increases in performance and substantial decreases in problems such as absenteeism, turnover, tardiness, strikes, grievances, and so forth.

**The Early Bird,* source unknown.

[1] Cited in Paul Hersey and Kenneth H. Blanchard, *Management of Organizational Behavior,* 4th ed. (Englewood Cliffs, N.J.: Prentice-Hall, 1982), p. 4.

FIGURE 10–1
Potential Influence of Motivation on Performance

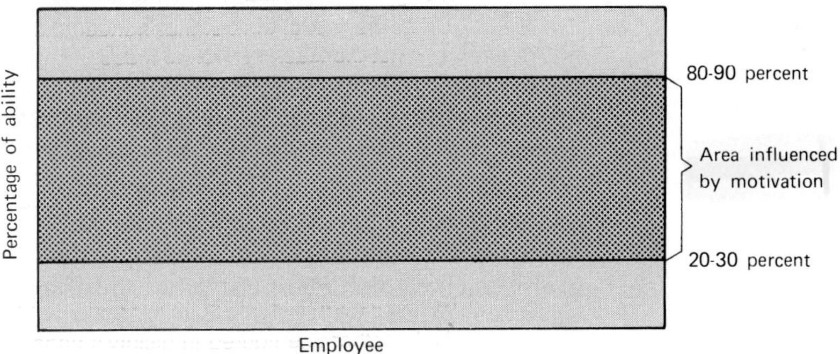

Source: Paul Hersey and Kenneth H. Blanchard, *Management of Organizational Behavior: Utilizing Human Resources,* 4th ed., (Englewood Cliffs, N.J.: Prentice-Hall, 1982), p. 4. Copyright © 1982 by Prentice-Hall, Inc. Adapted by permission.

THE MEANING OF MOTIVATION

Numerous definitions are given for the word *motivation.* Usually included in these definitions are such words as *aim, desire, end, impulse, intention, objective,* and *purpose.* The word *motivation* comes from the Latin word *movere,* which means to move. Two formal definitions of motivation are as follows:

> all those inner striving conditions described as wishes, desires, drives, etc. . . . It is an inner state that activates or moves.[2]
>
> the combination of forces which initially direct and sustain behavior toward a goal.[3]

The process of motivation can best be understood in the following causative sequence.

Needs ⟶ Drives or motives ⟶ Achievement of goals

In the motivation process, needs produce motives which lead to the accomplishment of goals. Needs are caused by deficiencies, which can be either physical or psychological. For instance, a physical need exists when an individual goes without sleep for 48 hours. A psychological need exists when an individual has no friends or companions. Individual needs will be explored in much greater depth in a later section of this chapter.

A motive is a stimulus which leads to an action that satisfies the need. In other words, motives produce action. Lack of sleep

motives produce action

[2] Bernard Berelson and Gary A. Steiner, *Human Behavior* (New York: Harcourt Brace Jovanovich, 1964), p. 240.

[3] Donald B. Lindsley, "Psychophysiology and Motivation," *Nebraska Symposium on Motivation,* ed. Marshall R. Jones (1957), p. 48.

(the need) activates the physical changes of fatigue (the motive) which produces sleep (the action or, in this example, inaction).

Achievement of the goal in the motivation process satisfies the need and reduces the motive. When the goal is reached, balance is restored. However, other needs arise which are then satisfied by the same sequence of events. Understanding the motivation sequence in itself offers the manager little help in determining what motivates people. The following theories of motivation will be described in this chapter to help provide a broader understanding of what motivates people: traditional theory, need hierarchy theory, achievement-power-affiliation theory, motivation-maintenance theory, preference-expectancy theory, and reinforcement theory.

TRADITIONAL THEORY

The traditional theory of motivation evolved from the work of Frederick W. Taylor and the Scientific Management movement which took place at the turn of this century. Taylor's ideas were based on his belief that existing reward systems were not designed to reward a person for high production. Taylor felt that when a highly productive person discovered that he or she was being compensated basically the same as someone producing less, this individual's production would decrease. Taylor's solution was quite simple. He designed a system whereby a worker was compensated according to the individual's production.

One of Taylor's problems was determining a reasonable standard of performance. Taylor solved the problem by breaking jobs down into components and measuring the time necessary to accomplish each component. In this way, Taylor was able to establish standards of performance "scientifically."

Taylor's plan was unique in that he had one rate of pay for units produced up to the standard. Once the standard was reached, a significantly higher rate was paid not only for the units above the standard, but for all units produced during the day. Thus under Taylor's system, workers could, in many cases, significantly increase their pay for production above the standard.

The traditional theory of motivation is based on the assumption that money is the primary motivator. Under this assumption, financial rewards are directly related to performance in the belief that if the reward is great enough, workers will produce more.

NEED HIERARCHY THEORY

The need hierarchy theory is based on the assumption that workers are motivated to satisfy a number of needs and that money

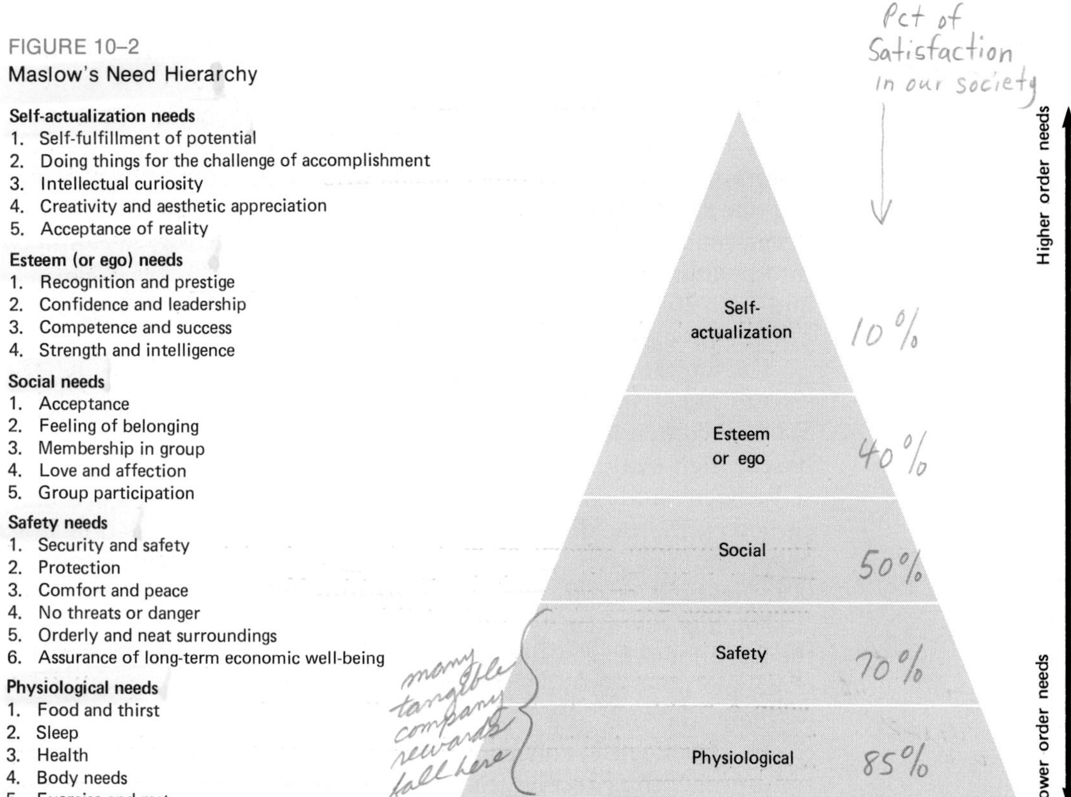

FIGURE 10–2
Maslow's Need Hierarchy

can satisfy directly or indirectly only some of these needs. The need hierarchy theory is based largely on the work of Abraham Maslow.[4]

Maslow's Need Hierarchy

Maslow felt that several different levels of needs exist within individuals and these needs relate to each other in the form of a hierarchy. Maslow's hierarchy of needs consists of the five levels of needs shown in Figure 10–2.

The physiological needs are basically the needs of the human body that must be satisfied in order to sustain life. These needs include food, sleep, water, exercise, clothing, shelter, and so forth. Safety needs are concerned with protection against danger, threat, or deprivation. Since all employees have to some degree, a dependent relationship with the organization, safety needs can be critically important. Favoritism, discrimination, and arbitrary ad-

[4] Abraham H. Maslow, *Motivation and Personality* (New York: Harper & Row, 1954).

ministration of organizational policies are all actions which arouse uncertainty and therefore affect the safety needs.

The third level of needs is composed of the social needs. Generally categorized under the social needs are the needs for love, affection, belonging—all of which are concerned with establishing one's position relative to others. This need is satisfied by the development of meaningful personal relations and by acceptance into meaningful groups of individuals. Belonging to organizations and identifying with work groups are means of satisfying these needs in organizations.

The fourth level of needs is composed of the esteem needs. The esteem needs include both self-esteem and the esteem of others. Maslow contended that all people have needs for a stable, firmly based, high evaluation of themselves, that is, for self-respect and self-esteem and for the esteem of others. These needs are concerned with the development of various kinds of relationships based on adequacy, independence, and the giving and receiving of indications of self-esteem and acceptance.

The highest order need in Maslow's hierarchy is concerned with the need for self-actualization or self-fulfillment, that is, the need of people to reach their full potential in terms of the application of their abilities and interests in functioning in their environment. This need is concerned with the will to operate at the optimum and thus receive the rewards that are the result of that attainment. The rewards may be not only in terms of economic and social remuneration, but also in terms of psychological remuneration. As Maslow terms it, "What a man can be, he must be."[5] The need for self-actualization or self-fulfillment is never completely satisfied; one can always reach one step higher.

Maslow believed that only one level of need motivates a person at any given time. Furthermore, he believed that humans start with the lower-order needs of the hierarchy and move up the hierarchy one level at a time as the needs at their present level become satisfied. In Figure 10–3 the physiological needs are shown as having the highest strength; they tend to dominate all other needs until they are substantially satisfied. Once the physiological needs have been satisfied, the safety needs become dominant in the need structure. This process continues with different needs emerging as each respective level of need is satisfied. Figure 10–4 shows a situation in which safety has become the dominant need.

It is important to note that in our society the physiological and safety needs are more easily and therefore more generally satisfied than other needs. In fact, Maslow estimated the percentage of satisfaction of all needs as follows: physiological—85 per-

[5] Ibid., p. 91.

FIGURE 10–3
Maslow's Need Hierarchy

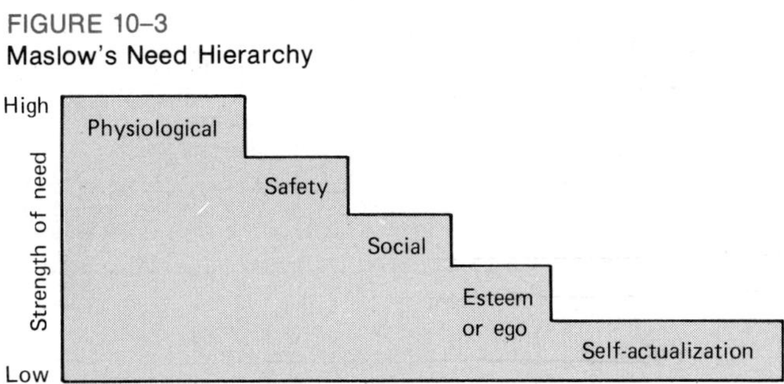

FIGURE 10–4
Dominant Safety Need

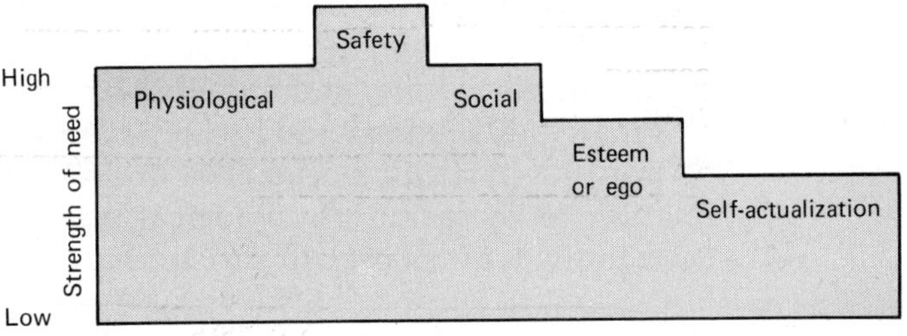

cent; safety—70 percent; social—50 percent; ego—40 percent; and self-actualization—10 percent. Many of the tangible rewards (pay, fringe benefits, etc.) dispersed by today's organizations are used to satisfy primarily the physiological and safety needs.

Although the needs of the majority of the people are arranged in the sequence shown in Figure 10–2, differences in the sequence can occur depending on an individual's learning experience, culture, social upbringing, and numerous other aspects of an individual's personality.

The strength or potency of an individual's needs may shift back and forth under different situations. For instance, during bad economic times, the physiological and safety needs might tend to dominate an individual's behavior; whereas, in good economic times, higher-order needs might dominate an individual's behavior.

Another major assumption of the need theory—that as one need is satisfied, then and only then does another need emerge—is not always correct. Some needs may be partially but not completely met. Such instances can result in an opportunity for another need to present itself. For instance, it is possible to be motivated by the social and esteem needs at the same time. Figure 10–5 illustrates such a situation.

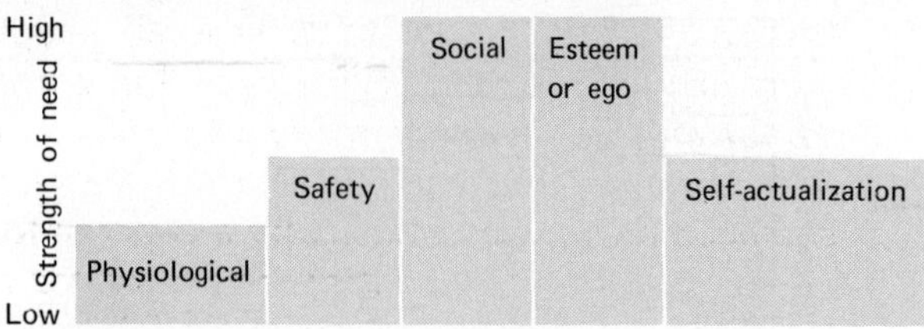

FIGURE 10–5
Need Hierarchy Dominated by Two Needs

The unconscious character of the various needs should also be recognized. In addition, there is a certain degree of cultural specificity of needs. In other words, the ways by which the various needs can be met tend to be controlled by cultural and societal factors. For example, the particular culture may dictate one's eating habits, social life, and numerous other facets of life.

Finally, different methods can be used by different individuals to satisfy a particular need. Two individuals may be deficient in relation to the same physiological need, but the way in which each individual chooses to satisfy that need may vary considerably.

As far as the motivation process is concerned, the thrust of the need hierarchy theory is that a satisfied need is not a motivator. Consider the basic physiological need for oxygen. Only when an individual is deprived of oxygen can it have a motivating effect on his or her behavior. Many of today's organizations are applying the logic of the need hierarchy. For instance, compensation systems are generally designed to satisfy the lower-order needs—physiological and safety. On the other hand, interesting work and opportunities for advancement are designed to appeal to higher-order needs. So the job of a manager is to determine the need level that any individual employee is attempting to attain and then provide the means by which the employee can satisfy that need. Obviously, determining the need level of one particular individual can be a difficult process. All people do not operate at the same level on the need hierarchy, and all people do not react similarly to the same situation. In addition, it must be pointed out that little research has been conducted to test the validity of the need hierarchy theory.[6] Its primary value seems to be that it provides a structure for analyzing needs and, as will be seen later in this chapter, is used as a basis for other theories of motivation.

---

[6] Edwin A. Locke, "The Nature and Causes of Job Satisfaction," in *The Handbook of Industrial and Organizational Psychology,* ed. Marvin D. Dunnette (Skokie, Ill.: Rand McNally, 1976), p. 1309.

ACHIEVEMENT-POWER-AFFILIATION THEORY

Closely related to the need hierarchy theory is the achievement-power-affiliation theory primarily developed by David McClelland.[7] This theory holds that all people have three needs—(1) a need to achieve, (2) a need for power, and (3) a need for affiliation. The need for achievement is a desire to do something better or more efficiently than it has been done before—to achieve. The need for power is basically a concern for influencing people—to be strong and influential. The need for affiliation is a need to be liked—to establish or maintain friendly relations with others. McClelland maintains that most people have a degree of each of these needs but that the level of intensity varies. For example, an individual may be high in the need for achievement, moderate in the need for power, and low in the need for affiliation. This individual's motivation to work will vary greatly from that of another person who has a high need for power and low needs for achievement and affiliation. According to this theory, it is the responsibility of managers to recognize the dominating needs in both themselves and their employees and to integrate effectively these differences. An employee with a high need for affiliation would probably respond positively to demonstrations of warmth and support by the manager. Similarly, an employee with a high need for achievement would likely respond positively to increased responsibility. Through self-analysis, managers can gain insight as to how they tend to respond to employees. They may then want to alter their response to employees to best fit the employees' needs. Figure 10–6 shows the effect of certain characteristics on the need for achievement, the need for power, and the need for affiliation.

FIGURE 10–6
Responses to Different Characteristics

Characteristic present in organization	*Need for achievement*	*Need for power*	*Need for affiliation*
Warmth	No effect	No effect	Aroused
Support	Aroused	No effect	Aroused
Conflict	Aroused	Aroused	Reduced
Reward	Aroused	No effect	Aroused
Responsibility	Aroused	Aroused	No effect

Source: Adapted from George Litwin and Robert Stringer, *Motivation and Organization Climate* (Cambridge, Mass.: Harvard University Press, 1968), chapter 8. Copyright © 1968 by the President and Fellows of Harvard College. All rights reserved.

[7] D. C. McClelland and D. H. Burnham, "Power Is the Great Motivator," *Harvard Business Review,* March–April 1976, pp. 100–10.

MANAGEMENT IN PRACTICE

Rules and Discipline, Goals and Praise Shape IBMers' Taut World

When Thomas J. Watson, Sr. died in 1956, some might have thought the IBM spirit of the stiff white collar was destined to die with him. But indications are that the founder's legacy of decorum to International Business Machines Corp. still burns bright. Consider the way an IBM man on a witness stand in San Francisco the other day replied when questioned about an after-hours encounter with a competitor:

Q. "All of you were in the hot tub with the Qyx district manager?"

A. "The party adjourned to a hot tub, yes. Fully clothed, I might add."

That an IBMer invited to a California hot tub should fear that propriety demanded a swimsuit wouldn't surprise many people who have ever worked for the giant company. For, besides its great success with computers, IBM has a reputation in the corporate world for another standout trait: an almost proprietary concern with its employees' behavior, appearance and attitudes.

What this means to employees is a lot of rules. And these rules, from broad, unwritten ones calling for "tasteful" dress to specific ones setting salesmen's quotas, draw their force at IBM from another legacy of the founder: the value placed on loyalty. Mr. Watson believed that joining IBM was an act calling for absolute fidelity to the company in matters big and small.

Esprit de Corps

And just in case an IBM employee isn't a self-starter in the loyalty department, the company has a training regimen geared to instilling it. In brief, this consists of supervising new trainees closely, grading them, repeatedly setting new goals for them, and rewarding them amply for achievement. Suffused in work and pressure to perform, employees often develop a camaraderie, an esprit de corps.

What it all amounts to is a kind of IBM culture, a set of attitudes and approaches shared to a greater or lesser degree by IBMers everywhere. This culture, as gleaned from talks with former as well as current employees, is so pervasive that, as one nine-year (former) employee puts it, leaving the company "was like emigrating."

Rising Quotas

One way to stand out at training school is to finish work in time to help slower classmates. Those who help the most may be elected class officers. Then they may get choice sales territories when they return to the field.

Once out in the field, salesmen get a quota of IBM machines to be placed in their territories. Each year the quota is raised or the territory cut or both, partly to test employees' ingenuity in selling more products to the same people. Customers need to be sold hard; IBM takes back the commission if a customer decides to return rented equipment after a year or so.

The Performance Plan is law. Extensions to deadlines for handing in reports are given for good reasons only. (A broken leg will do.) Employees get an overall rating based on the various points in their plans. A "1" means exceeding expectations; a "5" is unsatisfactory.

Achievement is followed by immediate rewards. Insiders say the most cherished of these isn't money. It's having your name and quota on the bulletin board with a notation saying "100 percent." It's having a party thrown for you at your branch because you have satisfied a prickly customer. It's a steady flow of letters of commendation. Says one ex-IBMer: "If you burp the right way, they sent you a certificate."

Thank You Notes

Gina Rulon-Miller was a "1" who burped the right way. Her file overflowed with notes. "Dear Gina, thank you . . . for the excellent job you did in setting up our case studies at your branch last month" or "for helping to make this business show a success." Or, "Your performance in purchase and new equipment placements has been tremendous." Congratulations "for qualifying for your third 100 percent club. . . . May the force be with you."

The notes and the quotes, the training and the praise are very effective. "People work their brains out," says Miss Rulon-Miller's brother Todd, an IBM veteran who now works for an American Express Company unit. The results please IBM, too. Asked whether company officials ever wonder if IBM has too many rules, a spokesman replies: "IBM has an adequate number of rules. We think they are proper and necessary. But we always try to challenge bureaucracy, so that any time we felt a rule was extraneous or unnecessary, we would seek to eliminate it."

The hard work that the IBM atmosphere inspires has another effect, Todd Rulon-Miller believes. "A close clique forms from the pressure everyone feels," he says. "The first thing they want to do at night is go out and have drinks with each other. Then they start blending business and social life. They rent cabins in Tahoe together, buy a sailboat, join a softball team, play golf."

Source: *The Wall Street Journal,* April 8, 1982, p. 1.

MOTIVATION-MAINTENANCE THEORY

Frederick Herzberg has developed a theory of work motivation which has had a wide acceptance in management circles. His theory is referred to by several names: motivation-maintenance theory, dual factor theory, or the motivation-hygiene theory.

The initial stages in the development of the theory involved extensive interviews with approximately 200 engineers and accountants from 11 industries in the Pittsburgh area. The initial purpose of this work was summarized as follows:

> To industry, the payoff for a study of job attitudes would be increased productivity, decreased absenteeism, and smoother working relations. To the individual, an understanding of the forces that lead to improved morale would bring greater happiness and greater self-realization.[8]

[8] Frederick Herzberg, Bernard Mausner, and Barbara Snyderman, *The Motivation to Work* (New York: John Wiley & Sons, 1959), p. ix.

critical incident method

In conducting the interviews, Herzberg and his colleagues, Bernard Mausner and Barbara Snyderman, used what is called the critical incident method. This method involved interviewing subjects and asking them to recall work situations in which they had experienced periods of high and low motivation. They were asked to recount specific details about the situation and the effect of the experience over time.

It was found through analysis of the interviewees' statements that different factors were associated with good and bad feelings. The findings fell into two major categories. Those factors that were most frequently mentioned in association with a favorably viewed incident concerned the work itself. These factors were achievement, recognition, responsibility, advancement, and the characteristics of the job. But when subjects felt negatively oriented toward a work incident, they were more likely to mention factors associated with the work environment, such as status; interpersonal relations with supervisors, peers, and subordinates; technical aspects of supervision; company policy and administration; job security; working conditions; salary; and aspects of personal life that were affected by the work situation. Herzberg referred to the latter set of factors as "hygiene" or "maintenance" factors. These terms were used because of the researchers' feelings that these factors are preventive in nature. In other words, they will not produce motivation but can prevent motivation from occurring. Thus, proper attention to hygiene factors is a necessary but not sufficient condition for motivation. The first set of factors were called "motivators." Herzberg contends that these factors, when present in addition to the hygiene factors, provide true motivation. In summary, Herzberg maintains that motivation comes from the individual not from the manager. At best, proper attention to the hygiene factors will keep an individual from being highly dissatisfied but will not make that individual motivated. Both hygiene and motivator factors must be present in order for true motivation to occur. Figure 10–7 lists some examples of hygiene-motivator factors.

FIGURE 10–7
Hygiene-Motivator Factors

Hygiene factors (environmental)	*Motivator factors (job itself)*
Policies and administration	Achievement
Supervision	Recognition
Working conditions	Challenging work
Interpersonal relations	Increased responsibility
Personal life	Advancement
Money, status, security	Personal growth

As a solution to motivation problems, Herzberg developed an approach called "job enrichment." Unlike "job enlargement," which merely involves giving a worker more of a similar type of operation to perform, or "job rotation," which is the practice of periodically rotating job assignments, job enrichment involves an upgrading of the job by adding motivator factors. Designing jobs that provide for meaningful work, achievement, recognition, responsibility, advancement, and growth is the key to job enrichment.

As can be seen from Figure 10–8 Herzberg's motivation-maintenance theory is very closely related to the need hierarchy theory of motivation and so is subject to many of the same criticisms.

In terms of application, there have been a large number of studies concerning the motivation-maintenance theory. These studies have produced mixed, positive, and negative outcomes. The majority of the studies have shown that when the subjects are very similar to Herzberg's initial subjects, accountants and engineers, and when a similar methodology is used, the results

FIGURE 10–8
A Comparison of Maslow's Need Hierarchy Theory with Herzberg's Motivation-Maintenance Theory

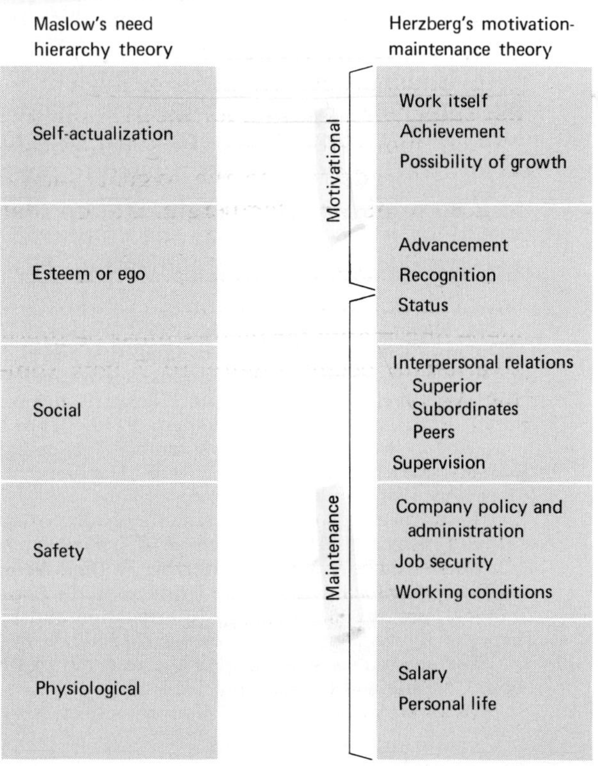

are supported.[9] In terms of lower management, blue-collar workers, and low-level, routine, white-collar workers, the results have been confounding and nonconfirming.[10] Also, Herzberg's methodology (especially his use of the critical incident method) has been criticized considerably.[11] Without doubt, however, Herzberg has made a major contribution to motivation theory by his emphasis on the relationship between the job content and the feelings of the worker.

VROOM

5) PREFERENCE-EXPECTANCY THEORY

An additional theory of motivation was developed by Victor H. Vroom.[12] Called the preference-expectancy (or expectancy) theory, Vroom's theory is based on the belief that people act in such a manner as to increase pleasure and decrease displeasure. According to this theory, a person is motivated to work if (1) they believe their efforts will be rewarded and (2) they value the rewards that are being offered. The first requirement that persons believe that their efforts will be rewarded can be further broken down into two separate components: (1) the expectancy that increased effort will lead to increased performance and (2) the expectancy that increased performance will lead to increased rewards. These expectancies are developed largely from an individual's past experiences. For example, a person may feel that working harder does not seem to produce any better results. On the other hand, even if employees believe that working harder does result in higher performance, they may believe that higher performance is not directly related to rewards.

The second part of the preference-expectancy theory is concerned with the value that the employee places on the rewards that are offered by the organization. Historically, organizations

---

[9] M. Myers, "Who Are the Motivated Workers?" *Harvard Business Review* 42 (1965), pp. 73–88; M. M. Swartz, E. Janusaits, and H. Stark, "Motivational Factors among Supervisors in the Utility Industry," *Personal Psychology* 16 (1963), pp. 45–53; F. Friedlanger and E. Walton, "Positive and Negative Motivations toward Work," *Administrative Science Quarterly* 9 (1965), pp. 194–207; T. M. Lodahl, "Patterns of Job Attitudes in Two Assembly Technologies," *Administrative Science Quarterly,* March 1964, pp. 482–519; F. Herzberg, *Work and the Nature of Man* (Cleveland: World Publishing, 1966).

[10] R. B. Ewen, "Some Determinants of Job Satisfaction: A Study of the Generality of Herzberg's Theory," *Journal of Applied Psychology* 47 (1963), pp. 246–50; R. J. House and L. A. Wigdor, "Herzberg's Dual-factor Theory of Job Satisfaction and Motivation: A Review of the Evidence and a Criticism," *Personnel Psychology* 20 (1967), pp. 369–90; N. King, "Clarification and Evaluation of the Two-factor Theory of Job Satisfaction," *Psychological Bulletin* 74 (1970), pp. 18–31.

[11] For a complete discussion of the research related to Herzberg's theory, see Locke, "Nature and Causes," pp. 1314–19.

[12] Victor H. Vroom, *Work and Motivation* (New York: John Wiley & Sons, 1967).

have assumed that whatever rewards that are provided will be valued by employees. Even if this were true, certainly some rewards are more valued than others. In fact, certain rewards, such as a promotion which involves a transfer to another city, may be viewed negatively.

Expectancy theorists believe that individual expectancies and preferences are formed either consciously or unconsciously but that they definitely exist for most people.

The preference-expectancy theory is shown in model form in Figure 10–9.

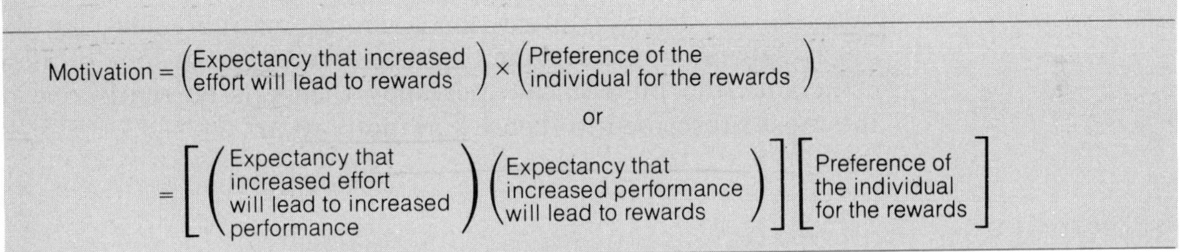

FIGURE 10–9
Model of Preference-Expectancy Theory

The following example is intended to illustrate the preference-expectancy theory. Assume that John Stone is an insurance salesman for the ABC Life Insurance Company. John has learned over the years that he makes one sale for approximately every six calls he makes. John definitely perceives a direct relationship between his effort and performance. Since John is on a straight commission, he also perceives a direct relationship between performance and rewards. Thus his expectation that increased effort will lead to increased rewards is relatively high. Further, suppose that John's income is currently in a high tax bracket such that he gets to keep, after taxes, only 50 percent of his commissions. This being the case, he may not look upon the additional money that he gets to keep (the reward) as being very attractive. The end result is that John's preference for the additional money may be relatively low, and even when this is multiplied by his relatively high expectation of receiving the additional money, his motivation to do additional work may be relatively low.

Each of the separate components of the preference-expectancy model can be affected by the organization's practices and management. The expectancy that increased effort will lead to increased performance can be positively influenced by providing proper selection, training, and clear direction to the work force.

The expectancy that increased performance will lead to rewards is almost totally under the control of the organization. Does the organization really attempt to link rewards to performance, or are rewards based on some other variable, such as seniority? The final component, the preference for the rewards being offered, is usually taken for granted by the organization. Organizations should solicit feedback from their employees concerning the types of rewards that are valued. Since an organization is going to spend a certain amount of money on rewards (salary, fringe benefits, and so on), it should ensure the maximum return on its investment.

The development of the preference-expectancy theory is still in its infancy, and many questions remain that must be answered. For example, more critics attack the theory as being overly rational, i.e., humans often don't act rationally. Others say the theory ignores impulsive and expressive behavior. In spite of these criticisms, the preference-expectancy theory is currently one of the most subscribed-to theories of motivation.

REINFORCEMENT THEORY

The final theory of motivation to be explored in this chapter is reinforcement theory, which is closely related to the preference-expectancy theory.[13] Reinforcement theory is based primarily on the work of B. F. Skinner.[14] The general idea behind the theory is that reinforced behavior will be repeated, and behavior that is not reinforced is less likely to be repeated. For instance, if an employee is given a pay increase when performance is high, then the employee is likely to continue to strive for high performance. Reinforcement theory assumes that the consequences of an individual's behavior determine the level of motivation. An individual's motives are considered to be relatively minor in this approach.

Reinforcers are not necessarily rewards and do not necessarily have to be positive in nature. For instance, the desire of an employee to avoid disciplinary action would be an avoidance reinforcer. Similarly, decreasing a salesperson's salary when their sales fall illustrates a negative reinforcer. The word *negative reinforcer* is used because in order for the individual to stop the action that is being taken (decreasing salary), the person's behavior must change (increase sales).

[13] McGregor's Theory X and Theory Y, which some authors consider to be basic theories of motivation, are discussed in Chapter 14 (Leadership Behavior). The authors of this text feel that they more logically fit into a discussion of leadership than basic motivation theories.

[14] B. F. Skinner, *Beyond Freedom and Dignity* (New York: Alfred A. Knopf, 1971).

The current emphasis in management practices on the use of reinforcers revolves around positive reinforcement. Unfortunately, the experimental research provides little guidance as to how to identify reinforcers.[15] Furthermore, little applied research has been conducted on reinforcement theory, and therefore, organizations should be cautious with its application.

INTEGRATING THE THEORIES OF MOTIVATION

All of the motivation theories presented previously contain the common thread that motivation is goal-directed behavior. Although the theories may appear to be quite different, most of them are not in conflict with one another but rather look at a different segment of the overall motivational process or look at the same segment from a different perspective. Figure 10–10 presents a model which reflects the overall motivational process and indicates relationships among major motivational theories.

FIGURE 10–10
The Overall Motivational Process

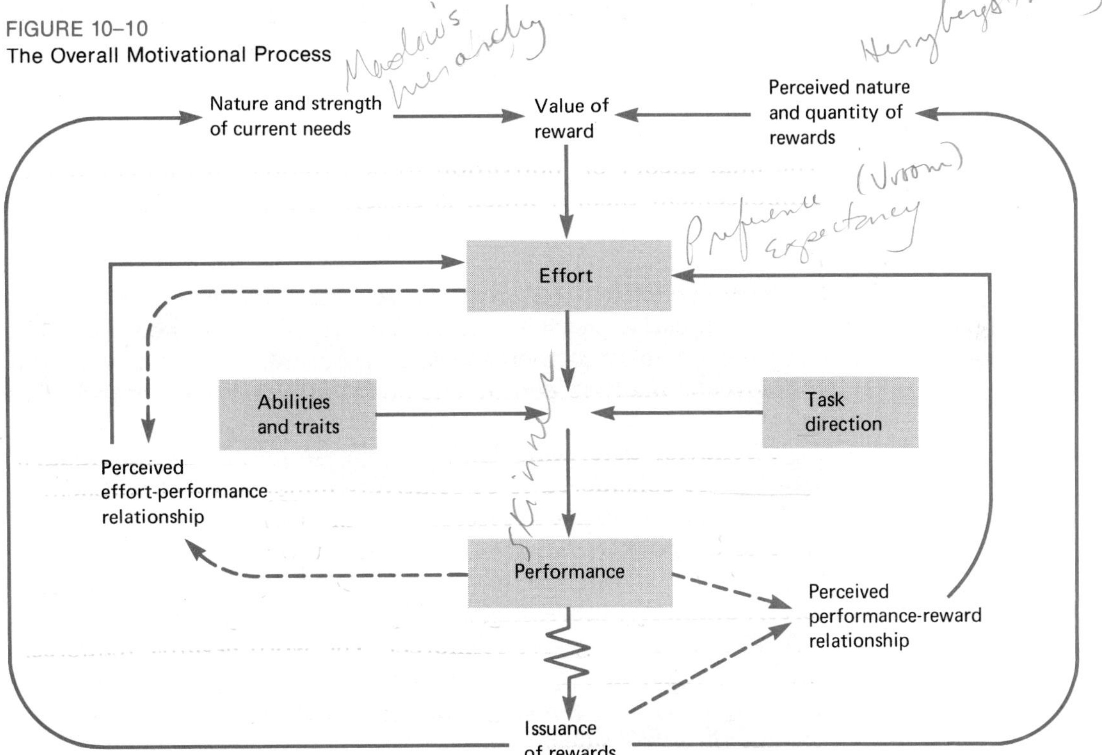

[15] John P. Campbell and Robert D. Pritchard, "Motivation Theory in Industrial and Organizational Psychology," in *Handbook of Industrial and Organizational Psychology*, ed. Marvin D. Dunnette (Skokie, Ill.: Rand McNally, 1976), pp. 63–130.

Vroom's preference-expectancy theory is shown at the heart of the model by the three factors that are shown to influence effort; note the arrows leading to the effort box. Maslow's need theory and the achievement-power-affiliation theory are represented in the upper left-hand corner of the model by the variable labeled "nature and strength of current needs." The nature and strength of current needs reflect where the individual is in terms of his or her needs, and this in turn affects the value that the individual places on the reward being offered. If the reward matches the individual's needs, that person will place more value on the reward than if it does not match the need level. Herzberg's theory is represented by the variable "perceived nature and quantity of rewards," which is found in the upper right-hand corner of the model. Both of these variables reflect the need for rewards to consist of both hygiene and motivator factors. For example, if only hygiene factors are provided, then the perceived nature and quantity of the rewards would be only marginal, which would in turn result in a marginal or low value placed on the reward by the individual. Reinforcement theory is represented through the effort-performance-reward relationship (note the middle and lower portions of the model). As shown in Figure 10–10, no single motivation theory provides all the answers.

JOB SATISFACTION

Closely related to motivation is the concept of job satisfaction. In fact, many managers often view motivated employees as being synonymous with satisfied employees. There are, however, important differences between motivated employees and satisfied employees.

Job satisfaction is concerned with an individual's general attitude about his or her job. Phillip Applewhite has listed the five major components of job satisfaction as "(1) attitude toward work group, (2) general working conditions, (3) attitude toward company, (4) monetary benefits, and (5) attitudes toward supervision."[16] Other major components that should be added to these five are the individual's attitudes toward the work itself and toward life in general. The individual's health, age, level of aspiration, social status, and political and social activities can all contribute to job satisfaction. Therefore, job satisfaction is an attitude that results from other specific attitudes and factors.

Job satisfaction refers to the individual's mental set about the

[16] Phillip B. Applewhite, *Organizational Behavior* (Englewood Cliffs, N.J.: Prentice-Hall, 1965), p. 22.

job. This mental set may be positive or negative depending on the individual's mental set concerning the major components of job satisfaction. Job satisfaction is not synonymous with organizational morale. Organizational morale refers an individual's feeling of being accepted by and belonging to a group of employees through common goals, confidence in the desirability of these goals, and progress toward these goals. Morale is related to group attitudes, while job satisfaction is more of an individual attitude. However, the two concepts are interrelated in that job satisfaction can contribute to morale and morale can contribute to job satisfaction.[17]

The Satisfaction-Performance Controversy

For many years, managers have believed, for the most part, that a satisfied worker will automatically be a good worker. In other words, if management could keep all the workers "happy," then good performance would automatically follow. Charles Greene has suggested that many managers subscribe to this belief because it represents "the path of least resistance."[18] Greene's thesis is that increasing employees' happiness is far more pleasant than confronting employees with their performance if a performance problem exists. Before exploring the satisfaction-performance controversy further, it might be wise to point out that there are subtle but real differences between being satisfied and being happy. Although happiness eventually results from satisfaction, satisfaction goes much deeper and is far less tenuous than happiness.

Greene

The incident below presents two propositions concerning the satisfaction-performance relationship.

> As Ben walked by smiling on the way to his office, Ben's boss remarked to a friend, "Ben really enjoys his job, and that's why he's the best damn worker I ever had. And that's reason enough for me to keep Ben happy." The friend replied, "No, you're wrong! Ben likes his job because he does it so well. If you want to make Ben happy, you ought to do whatever you can to help him further improve his performance."[19]

The first is the traditional view that satisfaction causes performance. The second proposition is that satisfaction is the effect rather than the cause of performance. In this proposition, perfor-

[17] Milton L. Blum, *Industrial Psychology and Its Social Foundations* (New York: Harper & Row, 1956), p. 126.

[18] Charles N. Greene, "The Satisfaction-Performance Controversy," *Business Horizons*, October 1972, p. 31.

[19] Ibid., p. 32.

mance leads to rewards which result in a certain level of satisfaction. Thus, rewards constitute a necessary intervening variable in the relationship. Another position considers both satisfaction and performance to be functions of rewards. This position not only views satisfaction as being caused by rewards, but also postulates that current performance affects subsequent performance if rewards are based on current performance.

Research evidence generally rejects the more popular view that satisfaction causes performance. The evidence does, however, provide moderate support for the view that performance causes satisfaction. The evidence also provides strong indications that: (1) rewards constitute a more direct cause of satisfaction than does performance and (2) rewards based on current performance cause subsequent performance.[20]

Recent research has investigated the relationship between intrinsic and extrinsic satisfaction and performance for jobs categorized as being either stimulating or nonstimulating.[21] The studies found that the relationship did vary depending on whether the job was stimulating or nonstimulating. This and other studies further emphasize the complexity of the satisfaction-performance relationship. One relationship that has been clearly established is that job satisfaction does have a positive impact on turnover, absenteeism, tardiness, accidents, grievances, and strikes.[22]

In addition, recruitment efforts by employees are generally more successful if the employees are satisfied. Satisfied employees are preferred simply because they make the work situation a more pleasant environment. So, even though a satisfied employee is not necessarily a high performer, there are numerous reasons for cultivating satisfied employees.

As mentioned earlier, a wide range of both internal and external factors affect an individual's level of satisfaction. The top portion of Figure 10–11 summarizes the major factors which determine an individual's level of satisfaction (or dissatisfaction). The lower portion of the figure shows the organization behaviors generally associated with satisfaction and dissatisfaction. Individual satisfaction leads to organizational commitment, while dissatisfaction results in behaviors detrimental to the organization (turn-

---

[20] Ibid., p. 40.

[21] John M. Ivancevich, "The Performance to Satisfaction Relationship: A Causal Analysis of Stimulating and Nonstimulating Jobs," *Organizational Behavior and Human Performance* 22 (1978), pp. 350–64.

[22] Donald P. Schwab and Larry L. Cummings, "Theories of Performance and Satisfaction: A Review," *Industrial Relations*, October 1970, pp. 408–29; also see Locke, "The Nature and Causes of Job Satisfaction," p. 1343 for a complete summary of the related research.

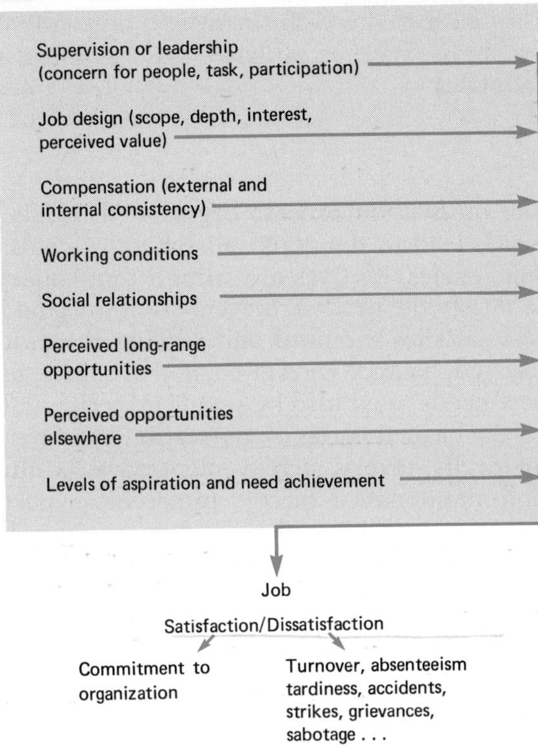

FIGURE 10–11
Determinants of Satisfaction and Dissatisfaction

over, absenteeism, tardiness, accidents, etc.). For example, employees who like their jobs, supervisors, and other job-related factors will probably be very loyal and devoted employees. However, employees who strongly dislike their jobs or any of the job-related factors will probably be disgruntled and will often exhibit these feelings by being late, absent, or by taking more covert actions to disrupt the organization.

It must be remembered that satisfaction and motivation are not synonymous. Motivation is a drive to perform, while satisfaction reflects the individual's attitude or happiness with the situation. The factors that determine whether an individual is satisfied with the job differ from those that determine whether the individual is motivated. Satisfaction is largely determined by the comfort offered by the environment and the situation. Motivation, on the other hand, is largely determined by the value of rewards and their contingency on performance. The result of motivation is increased effort which in turn increases performance if the individual has the ability and if the effort is properly directed.

The result of satisfaction is increased commitment to the organization which may or may not result in increased performance. This increased commitment will normally result in a decrease in problems, such as absenteeism, tardiness, turnover, strikes, and so forth.

SUMMARY

The motivation process begins with needs which cause motives which lead to the accomplishment of goals. Needs are caused by deficiencies. Motives are stimuli that cause an action to be taken to satisfy the need. Achievement of the goal in the motivation process satisfies the need and reduces the motive. When the goal is reached, balance is restored, and of course, other needs arise. These new needs must also be satisfied by the motivation process.

Six basic theories of motivation are the traditional theory, need hierarchy theory, achievement-power-affiliation theory, motivation-maintenance theory, preference-expectancy theory, and reinforcement theory. Traditional theory is based on the assumption that money is a primary motivator. Employees will produce more to get a greater financial gain.

The need hierarchy theory is based on the assumption that workers are motivated to satisfy a variety of needs only some of which can be satisfied by money. The needs of an individual exist in a hierarchy and range from low to high as follows: physiological, safety, social, esteem, and self-actualization. Once a need has been sufficiently satisfied, it can no longer be used to motivate an individual.

The achievement-power-affiliation theory holds that all people have three needs—a need to achieve, a need for power, and a need for affiliation. Furthermore, the level of intensity of these needs varies among individuals. People are motivated in situations that allow them to satisfy their most intense needs.

The motivation-maintenance model states that there are two categories of factors which relate to motivation. The first category, called "hygiene" or "maintenance" factors, relate to the work environment and include status, interpersonal relations, supervision, company policy and administration, job security, working conditions, salary, and personal life. The hygiene factors are important and must be present in the job, or motivation cannot occur. However, providing the hygiene factors does not motivate employees but rather keeps them from being dissatisfied. The second category of factors, called "motivators," relates to the work itself. These factors include such things as recognition, advancement, achievement, growth potential, and responsibility. Only if both the hygiene and motivator factors are properly provided will motivation occur.

The preference-expectancy theory of motivation implies that motivation depends on the preferences and expectations of an individual. The preference-expectancy theory emphasizes the need for organizations to relate rewards directly to performance and to ensure that the rewards provided are desired by the recipients.

The reinforcement theory of motivation is based on the idea that reinforced behavior will be repeated and behavior that is not reinforced will not be repeated. The theory assumes that the consequences of an individual's behavior determine his or her level of motivation.

Although each of the basic motivation theories may appear to be quite different, most of them are not in conflict with one another but rather look at a different segment of the overall motivational process or look at the same segment from a different perspective.

Job satisfaction is an individual's general attitude about the job and is influenced by many factors. The relationship between job satisfaction and job performance is complex and has been debated for years. Current theory holds that performance should determine rewards. Rewards in turn affect an individual's level of satisfaction through their impact on current needs and desires. Research has shown that job satisfaction can have a direct impact on managerial concerns, such as absenteeism, turnover, tardiness, grievances, and sabotage.

REVIEW QUESTIONS

1. Explain the motivation sequence.
2. Describe the following theories of motivation:
   a. Traditional theory
   b. Need hierarchy theory
   c. Achievement-power-affiliation theory
   d. Motivation-maintenance theory
   e. Preference-expectancy theory
   f. Reinforcement theory
3. What is job satisfaction? What are the major components of job satisfaction?
4. What is organizational morale?
5. Discuss the satisfaction-performance controversy.
6. From a managerial standpoint, what are the real benefits of having satisfied employees?

DISCUSSION QUESTIONS

1. "Most people can be motivated with money." Discuss your views on this statement.
2. Do you think that a very loyal employee is necessarily a good employee?
3. As a manager would you prefer a motivated or a satisfied group of employees?
4. The XYZ Company has just decided to take all of its employees (200 in number) to Las Vegas for a three-day expense paid weekend to show its appreciation for their high level of performance this past year. What is your reaction to this idea?
5. Discuss the following statement: "A satisfied employee is one that is not being pushed hard enough."

SELECTED READINGS

Alber, A., and M. Blumberg. "Team vs. Individual Approaches to Job Enrichment Programs." *Personnel,* January–February 1981, pp. 63–75.

Argyris, Chris. *Personality and Organization.* New York: Harper & Row, 1957.

Bobko, P. "Concerning the Non-Application of Human Motivation Theories in Organizational Settings." *Academy of Management Review,* October 1978, pp. 906–13.

Davis, Keith. "Low Productivity? Try Improving the Social Environment." *Business Horizons,* June 1980, pp. 27–29.

———. *Human Relations at Work.* New York: McGraw-Hill, 1978.

Fisher, C. D. "On the Dubious Wisdom of Expecting Job Satisfaction to Correlate with Performance." *Academy of Management Review,* October 1980., pp. 607–12.

Gayle, J. B., and F. R. Searle. "Maslow, Motivation and the Manager." *Management World,* September 1980, pp. 18–20 ff.

Guzzo, R. A. "Types of Rewards, Cognitions, and Work Motivation." *Academy of Management Review,* January 1979, pp. 75–86.

Herzberg, Frederick. *The Managerial Choice: To Be Efficient and To Be Human.* Homewood, Ill.: Richard D. Irwin, 1976.

———. "The Wise Old Turk." *Harvard Business Review,* September–October 1974, pp. 70–80.

Ivancevich, John M. "The Performance to Satisfaction Relationship: A Causal Analysis of Stimulating and Nonstimulating Jobs." *Organizational Behavior and Human Performance* 22 (1978), pp. 350–64.

Lawler, E. E. *Motivation in Work Organizations.* Monterey, Calif.: Brooks/Cole Publishing, 1973.

Maslow, A. H. *Motivation and Personality.* New York: Harper & Row, 1970.

McClelland, D. C., and D. H. Burnham. "Power is the Great Motivator." *Harvard Business Review,* March–April 1976, pp. 100–10.

McGregor, Douglas. *The Human Side of Enterprise.* New York: McGraw-Hill, 1960.

Mitchell, Vance F., and Provin Moudgill. "Measurement of Maslow's Need Hierarchy." *Organizational Behavior and Human Performance,* August 1976, pp. 334–49.

Schwab, Donald P., and Larry L. Cummings. "Theories of Performance and Satisfaction: A Review." *Industrial Relations,* October 1970, pp. 408–29.

Sheridan, J., and J. W. Slocum. "The Direction of the Causal Relationship between Job Satisfaction and Work Performance." *Organizational Behavior and Human Performance* 14 (1975), pp. 159–72.

Skinner, B. F. *Reflections on Behaviorism and Society.* Englewood Cliffs, N.J.: Prentice-Hall, 1978.

Taylor, M. S. "Motivational Effects of Task Challenge: A Laboratory Investigation." *Organizational Behavior and Human Performance,* April 1981, pp. 255–78.

Vroom, Victor H. *Work and Motivation.* New York: John Wiley & Sons, 1967.

Case 10–1

Our engineers are just not motivated

Situation: You are a consultant to the manager of mechanical engineering for a large company (8,000 employees, $200 million annual sales) that manufactures industrial equipment. The manager has been in this position for six months, having moved from a similar position in a much smaller company.

Manager: I just can't seem to get these guys to perform. They are all extremely competent, but they just don't seem to be willing to exert the kind of effort that we need and expect to have if this company is going to remain successful.

Consultant: What type of work do they do?

Manager: Primarily designing minor modifications to existing equipment lines to keep up with our competition and to satisfy special customer requirements.

Consultant: How do you evaluate their performance?

Manager: Mainly on whether they meet project deadlines. It's hard to evaluate the quality of their work, since most of it is fairly routine and the designs are frequently altered later by the production engineers to facilitate production processes.

Consultant: Are they meeting their deadlines reasonably well?

Manager: No, that's the problem. What's worse is that they don't really seem too concerned about it.

Consultant: What financial rewards do you offer them?

Manager: These people are all well-paid—some of the best salaries for mechanical engineers that I know of anywhere. Base pay is determined mainly on the basis of seniority, but there is also a companywide profit sharing plan. At the end of each year, the company distributes 10 percent of its profit after taxes to the employees. The piece of the pie that you get is in proportion to your basic salary. This kind of plan was used in the company I used to work for, and it seemed to have a highly motivating effect for them. They also get good vacations, insurance plans, and all the other usual goodies. I know of no complaints about compensation.

Consultant: How about promotion possibilities?

Manager: Well, all I know is that I was brought in from the outside. .

Consultant: If they are so lackadaisical, have you considered firing any of them?

Manager: Are you kidding? We need them too much, and it would be difficult and expensive to replace them. If I even threatened to fire any of them for anything short of blowing up the building, my boss would come down on me like a ton of bricks. We are so far behind on our work as it is. Besides, I'm not sure that it's really their fault entirely.

1. Why are the engineers not motivated?
2. What should management do to correct the situation?

Case 10–2

The long-term employee

Bill Harrison is 57 years old and has been with Ross Products for 37 years. He is on a top-paying machine-operator job and has been for the last 20 years. Bill is quite active in community affairs and takes a genuine interest in most employee activities. He is very friendly and well-liked by all employees, especially the younger ones, who often come to him for advice. He is extremely helpful to these younger employees and never hesitates to help when called on. When talking with the younger employees Bill never talks negatively about the company.

Bill's one shortcoming, as his manager Tom Williams sees it, is his tendency to spend too much time talking with other employees. This not only causes Bill's work to suffer, but perhaps more important, it hinders the output of others. Whenever Tom confronts Bill with the problem, Bill's performance improves for a day or two. It never takes long, however, for Bill to slip back into his old habit of storytelling and interrupting others.

Tom considered trying to have Bill transferred to another area where he would have less opportunity to interrupt others. However, Tom concluded that he needs Bill's experience, especially since he has no available replacement for Bill's job.

Bill is secure in his personal life. He owns a nice house and lives well. His wife works as a librarian, and their two children are grown and married. Tom has sensed that Bill feels he is as high as he'll ever go in the company. This doesn't seem to bother him since he feels comfortable and likes his present job.

1. What would you do to try and motivate Bill if you were Tom Williams?
2. Suppose Tom could transfer Bill, would you recommend that he do it?

SECTION TWO CASE:

The Edsel story*

In 1948, Ford Motor Company was faced with a significant problem. It was well known in the automobile industry that lower-income car owners traded in their lower-priced cars for higher-priced cars as soon as their yearly income exceeded $5,000. Ford had kept pace quite well with the other members of the Big Three (General Motors, Chrysler, and Ford) in the lower-priced market. But what was perplexing to Ford was that as the lower-income Ford car owners moved up the income ladder, they traded up to medium-priced cars made by Ford's competitors. Specifically, they traded up to General Motors' medium-priced cars.

Two years earlier, Henry Ford II had assumed the reins at Ford. Realizing the critical need for a qualified, forward-thinking top management team, he quickly brought on board several young Air Force officers and ex-General Motors executives. With the new influx of managers, a sweeping reorganization of the company was undertaken. The reorganization established two operating divisions on a profit center basis: the Ford Division and the Lincoln-Mercury Division.

With the new managerial guidance from the executive committee and its new organization structure, Ford Motor Company displayed remarkable gains in both market share and profits during the post-World War II years. A forward products planning committee was established to assess the desirability of introducing a new middle-priced car with the overall objective of gaining greater advantage in the market (i.e., hitting at General Motors' market in the medium-priced car range).

The final report drafted by the forward products planning committee was presented to the executive committee in December 1954. The report predicted that by 1965, the market for medium- and higher-priced cars would increase to nearly 40 percent of the car-owning population. It was rather obvious that Ford had to come up with a successful medium-priced car or it would be left without a car to compete in this growing market.

Ford's executive committee was well aware of the risks associated with introducing a new car. Past experience showed that of the 2,900 cars ever introduced in America, only about 20 were

---

*The facts in this case were derived from William H. Reynolds, *Products and Markets* (New York: Appleton-Century-Crofts, 1969); William H. Reynolds, "The Edsel Ten Years Later," *Business Horizons*, Fall 1967, pp. 39–46; and John Brooks, *The Fate of the Edsel and Other Business Adventures* (New York: Harper & Row, 1963).

still being produced and marketed in 1954, and neither General Motors nor Chrysler had attempted to introduce a new car since the late 1920s. However, Ford Motor Company had fared relatively well during 1954. The new management team had things running fairly smoothly, and the favorable profit situation had enabled new and modernized facilities to be built. Additionally, Ford was firmly entrenched in the lower-priced car market. For the industry as a whole, Ford's sales captured 25 percent of the market; Chevrolet accounted for another 25 percent; Buick-Oldsmobile-Pontiac cars accounted for the third quarter of the market; and all other makes shared the last 25 percent. After considering all of these factors, the executive committee decided to approve the forward products planning committee's recommendations and set out to produce a successful, medium-priced car.

Lewis Crusoe, an ex-General Motors executive and member of Ford's executive committee, knew full well that trying to cut into GM's market was not going to be easy. He was responsible for developing the overall plan for Ford. He set out a long-range plan designed to hit at all three levels—GM's low-priced car (the Chevrolet); the three GM mid-range cars (Buick-Oldsmobile-Pontiac); and GM's high-priced car (the Cadillac). However, the mid-range area was to receive the greatest amount of Ford's attention.

In order to ensure that these three areas of the overall plan would be effectively carried out, Crusoe reorganized the company into five, rather than two, profit centers: Ford (low-priced cars); Mercury (medium-priced cars); Continental, Lincoln (both higher-priced cars); and Special Products (later called the Edsel).

The Special Products Division, headed up by Richard Krafve (formally the assistant general manager of the old Lincoln-Mercury Division) immediately began developing plans for the new mid-range priced car. The division's mission was to create a new mid-priced car that was unique in that it would be readily recognizable from the other 19 cars currently on the road and yet still maintain a feel of familiarity.

The design efforts were carried out under conditions of utmost secrecy and were finished and revealed to the executive committee in August of 1955. During the design stage, over 4,000 design decisions were made.

The Special Products Division met its objective of designing a car that was distinct from those currently on the market and yet familiar. The final product had a horse-collar-shaped radiator grille placed in a vertical position dead center on the front end. Some members of the executive committee likened the grille to the classic cars of the 1930s; others saw a close resemblance to certain European sports cars; and at least one member likened the grille to the front end of the Navy Grumman fighter plane. The rear end was unique in that its widespread horizontal wings were distinctly different from the longitudinal fins that were so popular at that time. The steering wheel, perhaps the most fascinating part of the new car, was surrounded by a cluster of automatic transmission push buttons.

The executive committee applauded the design efforts of the Special Products Division. The next step undertaken by the division was to give the car a "personality" that could be marketed. The division contracted with research organizations to assess the personalities of currently marketed medium- and low-priced cars. Eight hundred recent car buyers in both Peoria, Illinois, and San Bernardino, California, were polled in an attempt to discover their impressions of the characteristics or profiles of people who owned existing automobiles. The results of these surveys fell somewhat short of the division's expectations but confirmed the general belief that automobile lovers are unable to analyze cars in a rational manner. Thus, it was recommended to Krafve and his associates that the personality of the new car should capitalize on the assumed weaknesses of its competitors.

The next step was to name the car. Early on, the three Ford brothers (Henry, Benson, and William Clay) rejected Krafve's suggestion that it be named Edsel in honor of their father. So elaborate surveys and other techniques were employed in an attempt to derive the right name, but these proved to be futile. Finally, the name Edsel was agreed to, and with the formal naming of the new car, the Special Products Division became known as the Edsel Division.

Momentum gained, and an extensive campaign was initiated to set up Edsel dealers. These dealers were to be special and independent of those selling other Ford cars. The major fear was that if dealers who already handled other Ford cars were to also handle the Edsel, the minute they were faced with price resistance on the part of a potential customer, they would attempt to sell another, cheaper Ford. By the middle of 1957, nearly 1,200 independent dealers had been established for the Edsel on a nationwide basis. Krafve made it clear that only dealers whose records demonstrated that they had the ability to successfully sell cars without using high pressure tactics were desired. The task of finding so many qualified dealers was monumental. The average dealer had at least \$100,000 invested in his agency; had salespeople, mechanics, and office help; had his own tools, technical literature, and signs, which alone cost as much as \$5,000 a set; and had to pay the factory spot-cash for cars received.

Within Ford Motor Company itself, hundreds of millions of

dollars were being poured into converting existing plants to meet the production requirements of the Edsel—special tooling was required—and advertising and promotional activities were begun. The Edsel Division had some 1,800 salaried employees and 15,000 factory workers when production began on July 15, 1957.

At this same time, the U.S. started on an economic downturn (what is now referred to as the recession of 1958). The decline in the sales of medium-priced cars (the market for the Edsel) was so great that dealers of all makes were closing out the season with the second largest number of unsold cars in history. However, the Edsel Division proceeded full speed ahead with continued high expectations regarding the Edsel's success. On September 4, 1957, the Edsel was revealed for the first time to the public in the dealers' showrooms. The visual impact of the Edsel is described in the following paragraphs:

> The most striking physical characteristic of the Edsel was, of course, its radiator grille. This, in contrast to the wide and horizontal grilles of all 19 other American makes of the time, was slender and vertical. Of chromium-plated steel and shaped something like an egg, it sat in the middle of the car's front end and was embellished by the word "EDSEL" in aluminum letters running down its length. It was intended to suggest the front end of practically any car of 20 or 30 years ago and of most contemporary European cars and thus to look at once seasoned and sophisticated. The trouble was that whereas the front ends of the antiques and the European cars were themselves high and narrow—consisting, indeed, of little more than radiator grilles—the front end of the Edsel was broad and low, just like the front ends of all its American competitors. Consequently, there were wide areas on either side of the grille that had to be filled in with something, and filled in they were—with twin panels of entirely conventional horizontal chrome grillwork. The effect was that of an Oldsmobile with the prow of a Pierce-Arrow implanted in its front end or, more metaphorically, of the charwoman trying on the duchess' necklace. The attempt at sophistication was so transparent as to be endearing.
>
> But if the grille of the Edsel appealed through guilelessness, the rear end was another matter. Here too, there was a marked departure from the conventional design of the day. Instead of the notorious tail fin, the car had what looked to its fanciers like wings and to others, less ethereal-minded, like eyebrows. The lines of the trunk lid and the rear fenders, swooping upward and outward, did somewhat resemble the wings of a gull in flight, but the resemblance was marred by two long narrow tail lights, set partly in the trunk lid and partly in the fenders, which followed those lines and created the startling illusion, especially at night, of a slant-eyed grin. From the front, the Edsel seemed, above all, anxious to please, even at the cost of being clownish; from the rear it looked crafty, Ori-

> ental, smug, one-up, and maybe a little cynical and contemptuous too. It was as if, somewhere between the grille and rear fenders, a sinister personality change had taken place.
>
> In other respects, the exterior styling of the Edsel was not far out of the ordinary. Its sides were festooned with a bit less than the average amount of chrome and distinguished by a gouged-out bullet-shaped groove extending forward from the rear fender for about half the length of the car. Midway along this groove, the word "EDSEL" was displayed in chrome letters, and just below the rear window was a small grille-like decoration on which was spelled out—of all things—"EDSEL." (After all, hadn't [they] declared [their] intention to create a vehicle that would be readily recognizable?) In its interior, the Edsel strove mightily to live up to the prediction of Krafve that the car would be "the epitome of the push-button era." The push-button era in medium-priced cars being what it was, Krafve's had been a rash prophecy indeed, but the Edsel rose to it with a devilish assemblage of gadgets such as had seldom, if ever, been seen before. On or near the Edsel's dashboard was a push button that popped the trunk lid open; a lever that popped the hood open; a lever that released the parking brake; a speedometer that glowed red when the driver exceeded his chosen maximum speed; a single-dial control for both heating and cooling; a tachometer in the best racing-car style, buttons to operate or regulate the lights, the height of the radio antenna, the heater-blower, the windshield wiper, and the cigarette lighter; and a row of eight red lights to wink warnings that the engine was too hot, that it wasn't hot enough, that the generator was on the blink, that the parking brake was on, that a door was open, that the oil pressure was low, that the oil level was low, and that the gasoline level was low, the last of which the skeptical driver could confirm by consulting the gas gauge mounted a few inches away. Epitomizing this epitome, the automatic-transmission control box—arrestingly situated on top of the steering post in the center of the wheel—sprouted a galaxy of five push buttons so light to the touch that, as Edsel men could hardly be restrained from demonstrating, they could be depressed with a toothpick.[1]

Early on, the Consumers Union declared in its January 1958 issue of *Consumer Reports* that "the Edsel has no important basic advantages over other brands. The car is almost entirely conventional in construction . . . as a matter of simple fact, combined with the car's tendency to shake like jelly, Edsel handling represents retrogression rather than progress . . . the 'luxury-loaded' Edsel—as one magazine cover described it—will certainly please anyone who confuses gadgetry with true luxury."

---

[1] John Brooks, *The Fate of the Edsel and Other Business Adventures* (New York: Harper & Row, 1963), pp. 53–55.

While any new car has its bugs, the Edsel, having been brought to the height of public attention as a result of Ford's continuous advertising and promotion activities, was no exception—just a bigger public spectacle.

The first day's sales totaled more than 6,500 Edsels—a good showing. However, sales dropped sharply over the next few days. As this decline continued, Ford pumped more and more time, effort, and money into promoting the Edsel in order to meet the necessary 200,000 cars that was calculated as the breakeven point. Sales continued to move in a downward direction until January 14, 1958, when the Ford Motor Company announced that it was consolidating the Edsel Division with the Lincoln-Mercury Division to form the Mercury-Edsel-Lincoln Division under the management of the former manager of the Lincoln-Mercury Division.

All told, 110,810 Edsels were produced, and 109,466 were sold. While exact estimates cannot be found, it is generally estimated that Ford lost something like $200 million on the Edsel after it appeared on the market. In addition to the initial investment of about $250 million, a net loss of about $350 million resulted after accounting for salvageable plant and equipment. According to these rough estimates, every Edsel produced lost about $3,200 which was just about equal to the cost of an Edsel. In other words, Ford Motor Company would have saved itself money if, back in 1955, it had decided not to produce the Edsel at all but had simply given away 110,810 specimens of its comparably priced car—the Mercury.

1. How effective was the Ford Motor Company in implementing their plan for the Edsel?
2. Were the basic functions of management carried out properly in this case? If not, which functions were not?
3. What should the Ford Motor Company have done differently?

SECTION ONE

Introduction and background

Definitions
History
Decision making

+

SECTION TWO

Basic management functions

Planning
Controlling
Organizing
Staffing
Motivating

+

SECTION THREE

Other behavioral aspects

Communication
Work groups
Conflict, change, stress
Leadership

=

MANAGEMENT FOUNDATION

MANAGEMENT FOUNDATION

+

SECTION FOUR

Emphasis on individual performance

Defining performance and direction
Encouraging effort
Developing abilities

+

SECTION FIVE

Understanding processes which produce goods or services

Basic operations management concepts
Designing operating systems
Planning and controlling operations

=

SUCCESSFUL MANAGEMENT

SUCCESSFUL MANAGEMENT

+

SECTION SIX

Appreciation of contemporary issues and the future

Social responsibility and ethics
International management and the future

=

RESPONSIBLE MANAGEMENT

section three

OTHER BEHAVIORAL ASPECTS

All of the basic management functions discussed in Section Two are implemented through people and depend on people for their success. Therefore an understanding of human behavior in organizations is another requirement for building a sound management foundation.

It is difficult if not impossible to isolate completely the behavioral aspects from other management topics. For example, appropriate managerial controls and organization can only be determined in light of certain behavioral considerations. Therefore, many behavioral concepts are interspersed throughout all sections of the text. However, the purpose of this section is to isolate and emphasize other important aspects of human behavior in organizations.

Chapter 11 deals with the topic of communication, which is relevant to all managers and employees. Both the formal and informal communication systems in organizations are analyzed.

Because both formal and informal work groups exist in most organizations, Chapter 12 discusses them both. Informal work groups are shown to be assets of the organization if properly managed. The topics of conformity and creativity are also introduced.

Chapter 13 focuses on organizational conflict, change, and stress. Conflict is presented as a normal and natural organizational activity which can produce positive results if properly managed. Organizational change and stress are treated as inevitable occurrences. Suggestions are offered for managing both change and stress.

Chapter 14 discusses the topic of leadership. Different styles of leadership are discussed and evaluated. Several contemporary leadership theories are also presented. A strong argument is made for a situational approach to leadership.

11 Communication in Organizations

Objectives

1. To analyze the interpersonal communication process.
2. To describe downward, upward, and horizontal communication systems in organizations.
3. To discuss the nature of the grapevine in organizations.
4. To present several suggestions for improving communication in organizations.

Chapter Outline

Glossary of Terms

Communication The transfer of information that is meaningful to those involved, the transmittal of understanding.

Downward communication The transmitting of information from higher to lower levels of the organization through the chain of command within the organizational structure.

Feedback An essential element in effective communication that involves determining whether the receiver has received the intended message and produced the intended response.

Grapevine Informal channels of communication resulting from casual contacts between friends or acquaintances in various organizational units.

Horizontal (lateral) communication Communication across organizational units which are at the same approximate level in the organizational hierarchy.

Interpersonal communication Communication between individuals.

Nonverbal communication Conscious or unconscious behavior on the part of the individual sending a message that occurs in the presence of the receiver and is perceived either consciously or unconsciously by the receiver.

Organizational communication Communication occurring within the formal organizational structure.

Perception Refers to how an individual processes a message; is influenced by the individual's personality and previous experience and is thus unique for each individual.

Semantics The science of the meaning and study of words and symbols.

Upward communication Communication originating at the lower levels of the organization and flowing toward the top.

A naturalist discovered that baboons have a language consisting of shrill alarm cries, contented chucklings and grunts, dissatisfied barks, silly happy chatterings, mourning wails for their dead, cries denoting pain, groans of dread, and calls for assembly and for action. He observed that at night there was a continuous soft mumbling among them which sounded so much like human talk that he was almost convinced that they were capable of articulated speech. A native confirmed this for him: "Baboons can talk," he said. "But they won't do it in front of white men for fear you will put them to work."

*John Denton Scott**

Breakdowns in the communication process are said to cause divorces, wars, racial problems, business failures, and other problems too numerous to mention. Within organizations, there are endless places where poor communication can be costly if not disastrous. It is therefore not surprising that poor communication is often named the culprit when any organizational problem arises. Poor communication may very well be the cause of the problem, but it is sometimes only a symptom of a more complex problem. Poor communication is sometimes used as a scapegoat for other problems. Good communication is not a panacea for all organizational problems. It will not, for instance, make up for poor planning. However, even good plans must eventually be communicated. Thus, communicating is a very important skill required in the management process, and its significance cannot be overstated.

In fact, communication has been estimated to occupy between 50 and 90 percent of the manager's time.[1] Unfortunately, however, research has revealed that as much as 70 percent of all business communications fail to achieve their intended purpose.[2]

WHAT IS COMMUNICATION?

The difficulty in defining communication is best illustrated by the fact that one study found over 95 definitions of communication.[3] Many of these definitions were from articles whose purpose was

*John Denton Scott, "Speaking Wildly," *The Reader's Digest,* May 1977, p. 144.

[1] Henry Mintzberg, *The Nature of Managerial Work* (New York: Harper & Row, 1973), p. 38.

[2] Ralph W. Weber and Gloria E. Terry, *Behavioral Insights for Supervisors* (Englewood Cliffs, N.J.: Prentice-Hall, 1975), p. 138.

[3] F. E. X. Dance, "The Concept of Communication," *The Journal of Communication* 20 (1970), pp. 201–10.

to find "the one true" definition of communication. In this book, communication is defined as the transfer of information that is meaningful to those involved.[4] In a more general sense, communication is the transmittal of understanding.[5] Communication can occur in many forms ranging from face-to-face contact involving facial expressions and body movements to written messages. The pervasiveness of communication was explained by one author who states that communication occurs when an individual takes something into account, whether that something was something someone did or said or did not do or say, whether it was some observable event, some internal condition, the meaning of something being read or looked at, some feeling intermingled with some past memory—literally anything that can be taken into account by human beings in general and that individual in particular.[6]

Communication in organizations can be viewed in one of two perspectives: communication between individuals (interpersonal communication) and communication within the formal organizational structure (organizational communication). These two basic forms of communication are interdependent in that interpersonal communication is almost always a part of organizational communication.

INTERPERSONAL COMMUNICATION

Effective communication between individuals, particularly between a manager and subordinates, is critical to achieving organizational goals and, as a result, to effectively managing people. Interpersonal communication is an interactive process that involves an individual's effort to attain meaning and to respond to it. It involves the transmission and reception of verbal and nonverbal signs and symbols which come not only from other people but also from the physical and cultural settings of both the sender and the receiver.[7]

One approach to analyzing the nature of interpersonal communication can be seen in the following example.[8] In any two-

[4] Fred Luthans, *Organizational Behavior* (New York: McGraw-Hill, 1973), p. 236.

[5] John H. Ivancevich, Andrew G. Szilagyi, and Marc G. Wallace, *Organization Behavior and Performance* (Santa Monica, Calif.: Goodyear Publishing, 1977), p. 400.

[6] L. Thayer, *Communication and Communication Systems* (Homewood, Ill.: Richard D. Irwin, 1968), pp. 26–27. Copyright © 1968 by Richard D. Irwin, Inc.

[7] Lyman W. Porter and Karlene H. Roberts, "Communication," in *Handbook of Industrial and Organizational Psychology*, ed. Marvin D. Dunnette (Skokie, Ill.: Rand McNally, 1976), p. 1558.

[8] L. Thayer, "Communication and Organization Theory," in *Human Communication Theory: Original Essays*, ed. F. E. X. Dance (New York: Holt, Rinehart & Winston, 1967), pp. 70–115.

person conversation, each person exists in his or her own world. One person's world is defined by his or her self-concept, his or her concept of the other person, and his or her concept of the purpose of the communication. On the other hand, the other person's world is defined by his or her self-concept, his or her concept of the other person, and his or her concept of the purpose of the communication. As these two people communicate, each processes the messages transmitted in a way that is consistent with his or her own world and then behaves on the basis of these processed messages. The resulting behavior exhibited by one person is then a potential message for the other person. Obviously, at several points in this example, the potential exists for a breakdown in the communication process. Some of the causes of interpersonal communication failure are different interpretations of the meaning of words (semantics), differences in perception, poor listening habits, inadequate feedback, and differences in the interpretation of nonverbal communications.

Semantics

Semantics is the science or study of the meaning of words and symbols. Words themselves have no real meaning. Words have meaning only in terms of peoples' reactions to them. A particular word may mean very different things to different people depending on how it is used. In addition, a word may be interpreted differently, depending on the facial expressions, hand gestures, and voice inflection used.

The problems involved in semantics are of two general types. Some words and phrases invite multiple interpretations. Figure 11–1 gives an illustration of different interpretations of the word *fix*. Another problem is that groups of people in particular situations frequently develop their own technical language which may or may not be understood by others outside the group. For example, physicians, government, and military employees are often guilty of using acronyms and abbreviations that only they understand. Words are the most common form of interpersonal communication, and because of the real possibility of misinterpretation, effective communication requires that words be carefully chosen and clearly defined.

Perception

Perception also plays an important role in interpersonal communication. Perception basically refers to how a message is processed by a particular individual. Each individual's perception is unique and influenced by his or her own world. As a result, people often perceive the same situation in entirely different ways.

FIGURE 11–1
Interpretations of the Word *Fix*

An Englishman visits America and is completely awed by the many ways we use the word *fix*. For example:

1. His host asks him how he'd like his drink fixed. He meant *mixed*.
2. His hostess calls to everyone to finish their drinks because dinner is all fixed. She means *prepared*.
3. As he prepares to leave, he discovers that he has a flat tire and calls a repairman who says he'll fix it immediately. He means *repair*.
4. On the way home, he is given a ticket for speeding. When he calls his host, he says, "Don't worry, I'll fix it." He means *nullify*.
5. At the office the next day, he comments on the cost of living in America, and one of his cohorts says, "It's hard to make ends meet on a fixed income." He means *steady* or *unchanging*.
6. Later, he remarks that he doesn't know what to do with his college diploma. A colleague says, "I'll fix it on the wall for you." He means *attach*.
7. He has an argument with a co-worker. The latter says, "I'll fix you." He means *seek revenge*.
8. Another of his cohorts remarks that he is in a "hell of a fix." He means *condition or situation*.
9. He meets a friend at this boarding house who offers to "fix him up" with a girl. You know what that means.

For instance, the following story shows how two individuals have completely different perceptions of the same situation.

> A woman of 35 came in one day to tell me that she wanted a baby but that she had been told that she had a certain type of heart disease which might not interfere with a normal life but would be dangerous if she ever had a baby. From her description, I thought at once of mitral stenosis. This condition is characterized by a rather distinctive rumbling murmur near the apex of the heart and especially by a peculiar vibration felt by the examining finger on the patient's chest. The vibration is known as the "thrill" of mitral stenosis.
>
> When this woman had been undressed and was lying on my table in her white kimono, my stethoscope quickly found the heart sounds I had expected. Dictating to my nurse, I described them carefully. I put my stethoscope aside and felt intently for the typical vibration which may be found in a small but variable area of the left chest.
>
> I closed my eyes for better concentration and felt long and carefully for the tremor. I did not find it, and with my hand still on the woman's bare breast, lifting it upward and out of the way, I finally turned to the nurse and said: "No thrill."
>
> The patient's black eyes snapped open, and with venom in her voice she said: "Well, isn't that just too bad? Perhaps it's just as well you don't get one. That isn't what I came for."

My nurse almost choked, and my explanation still seems a nightmare of futile words.[9]

Perception in the communication process is primarily dependent on three factors: individual personality, previous experience, and a stimulus (see Figure 11–2). The combination of these factors creates perception which is unique for each individual. In perception development, the stimulus refers to the information received, whether it is conveyed in writing, conversation, or another way. The information that is received is modified on the basis of the individual's personality, previous experience, and other factors. Therefore, different people react differently to the same message because no two individuals have the same personal experiences, memories, likes, and dislikes. One study at the Texas

FIGURE 11–2
Perception Development in Communication

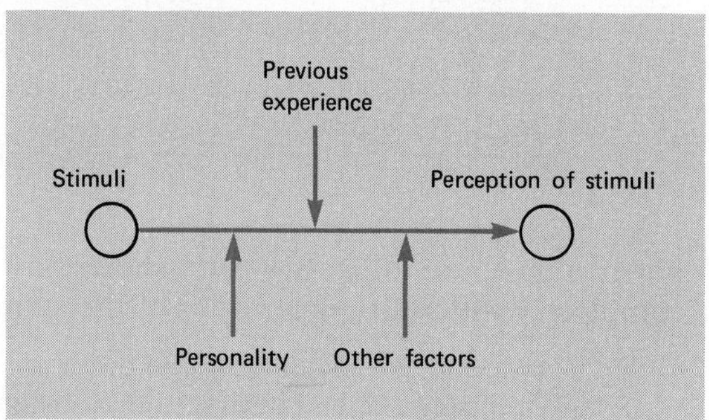

Instruments Company found that messages from management reach less than 15 percent of the intended audience because of the erroneous assumption that all employees think alike and that the same message or methods of communication work equally well for everyone. This same study identified seven different value systems that influenced how individual employees reacted to situations, including communications from their supervisors.[10] These variations in the value systems cause individuals to respond to the same message in different ways. In addition, the phenomenon of selective perception often distorts the intended message in that people tend to listen to only part of the message, blocking out other information for a variety of reasons.

---

[9] Frederic Loomis, *Consultation Room* (New York: Alfred A. Knopf, 1939), p. 47.

[10] "Hitting the Communication Bull's Eye," *The Personnel Administrator,* June 1974, p. 16.

Two illustrations that are found in many introductory psychology texts demonstrate the influence of perception. Please answer the following questions before proceeding.

1. In Figure 11–3, what characteristics do you perceive of the woman in the figure?
2. In Figure 11–4A, what shape is the largest?
3. In Figure 11–4B, which line—*AX, CX, CB,* or *XD*—is the longest?

About 60 percent of the people who see Figure 11–3 for the first time see an attractive, apparently wealthy, young woman. About 40 percent see an ugly, poor, old woman. Figure 11–5 clearly indicates the two figures. In Figure 11–4, both shapes in A are the same size, and in B, the lines *AX, CX, CB,* and *XD* are of equal length. Obviously, if differences in perception exist in viewing physical objects, more subtle forms of communication, such as facial expression and hand gestures, leave much room for differences in perception.

FIGURE 11–3
Picture of a Woman

Source: Edwin G. Boring, "A New Ambiguous Figure," *American Journal of Psychology,* July 1930, p. 444. Also see Robert Leeper, "A Study of a Neglected Portion of the Field of Learning—The Development of Sensory Organization," *Journal of Genetic Psychology,* March 1935, p. 62. Originally drawn by cartoonist W. E. Hill and published in *Puck,* November 8, 1915.

FIGURE 11–4
Shapes for Perception

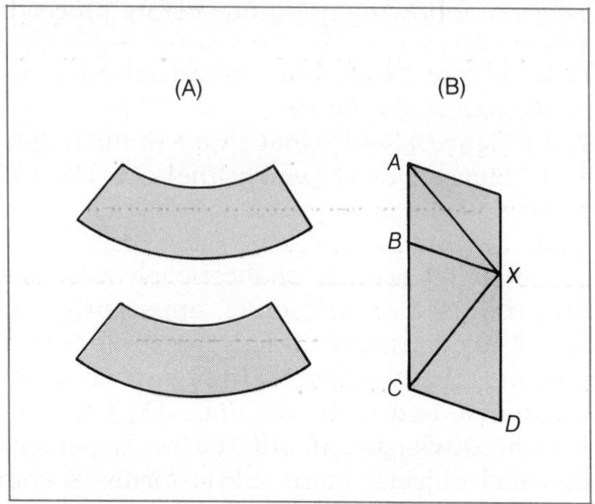

Source: Gregory A. Kimble and Norman Garmezy, *General Psychology* (New York: Ronald Press, 1963), pp. 324–25.

FIGURE 11–5
Clear Picture of the Young and Old Woman

Source: Robert Leeper, "A Study of a Neglected Portion of the Field of Learning—The Development of Sensory Organization," *Journal of Genetic Psychology,* March 1935, p. 62.

Listening—An Important Factor in Interpersonal Communication

Since communication depends on the ability not only to send but also to receive messages, the ability to listen effectively greatly enhances the communication process. Studies have concluded that 45 percent of the total time spent in verbal communication is devoted to listening.[11] Unfortunately, studies have also revealed that most people are not very good listeners in that they only retain about 25 percent of all the information they hear.[12]

Effective listening is not natural to most people. How well a person listens is very much dependent on the attitude of the listener toward the speaker. When the listener respects the intelligence of the speaker and believes he or she will profit from the communication, the likelihood increases that the person will listen more effectively to that person.

Daydreaming and preoccupation with other matters also often preclude individuals from listening to what a speaker is saying. It has been suggested that at any given instant in a college lecture hall, 20 percent of both men and women are thinking about sex, 60 percent are off on some mental trip of their own, and only the remaining 20 percent are concentrating on the professor.[13] Other barriers to effective listening include mentally arguing with points made by the speaker before the talk is finished, becoming impatient with listening and preferring active involvement by talking, lack of interest in the message, and other negative reactions toward the speaker.

Effective listening habits can be developed. Ralph Nichols has proposed a pattern of thought to follow in improving listening habits.[14]

1. Anticipate what a person is going to talk about. On the basis of what has already been said, ask yourself: What point is the person trying to make?
2. Summarize what the person has been saying. What point(s), if any, have been made?
3. Mentally question the person's evidence. Ask yourself: Am I getting the full picture or only what will prove the person's point?

---

[11] Ralph G. Nichols, "Do We Know How to Listen? Practical Helps in a Modern Age," in *Communication Concepts and Processes*, ed. Joseph De Vito (Englewood Cliffs, N.J.: Prentice-Hall, 1971), p. 206.

[12] Phillip V. Lewis, *Organizational Communication. The Essence of Effective Management* (Columbus, Ohio: Grid, 1975), p. 9.

[13] David R. Hampton, Charles E. Summer, and Ross A. Webber, *Organizational Behavior and the Practice of Management* (Glenview, Ill.: Scott, Foresman, 1978), p. 117.

[14] Ralph G. Nichols, "Listening is a 10-Part Skill," in *Readings in Interpersonal and Organizational Communication*, ed. Richard C. Huseman, Cal M. Logue, and Dwight L. Freshley (Boston, Mass.: Holbrook Press, 1977), p. 560.

FIGURE 11–6
Effective Listening Guides

1. *Stop talking.* Unfortunately, most of us prefer talking to listening. Even when we are not talking, we are inclined to concentrate on what to say next rather than on listening to others. So you must stop talking before you can listen.
2. *Put the talker at ease.* If you make the talker feel at ease, he will do a better job of talking. Then you will have a better input to work with.
3. *Show the talker you want to listen.* If you can convince the talker that you are listening to understand rather than oppose, you will help to create a climate for information exchange. Specifically, you should look and act interested. Doing things like reading, looking at your watch, and looking away distracts the talker.
4. *Remove distractions.* Things you do can also distract the talker. So don't doodle, tap with your pencil, shuffle papers, or the like.
5. *Empathize with the talker.* If you will place yourself in the talker's position and look at things from his point of view, you will help to create a climate of understanding. With such a climate established, a true exchange of information can result.
6. *Be patient.* You will need to allow the talker plenty of time. Remember that not everyone can get to the point as quickly and clearly as you. And do not interrupt him. Interruptions merely serve as barriers to information exchange.
7. *Hold your temper.* From our review of the workings of our mental filters, we know that angry minds do not contribute to communication. Angry people build walls between themselves. They harden their positions and block their minds to the words of others.
8. *Go easy on argument and criticism.* Argument and criticism tend to put the talker on the defensive. Thus, he tends to "clam up" or get angry. Even if you win the argument, you lose. Rarely does either party benefit from such controversy.
9. *Ask questions.* By frequently asking questions, you display an open mind. You show that you are listening. And you assist in developing the message and in improving correctness of meaning.
10. *Stop talking!* The last guideline is to stop talking. It was also the first. All other guidelines depend on it.

Source: Raymond V. Lesikar, *Communication Theory and Application* (Homewood, Ill.: Richard D. Irwin, 1976), p. 480. Copyright © 1976 by Richard D. Irwin, Inc.

4. Listen between the lines. Voice tone and volume, facial expressions, hand gestures, and body movements also may have meaning.

The 10 guides for effective listening shown in Figure 11–6 enumerate some additional ways for improving listening habits.

Feedback

Effective communication is a two-way process. Information must flow back and forth between the sender and the receiver. The flow of information from the receiver to the sender is called feedback. It allows the sender to know if the receiver has received the cor-

MANAGEMENT IN PRACTICE

How Sperry Made People Listen

It all started as an advertising gimmick. And as advertising gimmicks go, it was not even original. Other companies had used the theme of listening to customers' problems in their advertising campaigns. So Sperry Rand Corp., a U.S. engineering and computer company, was taken aback when its campaign began to develop a life of its own.

The campaign was the result of 20 months' research aimed at producing the kind of corporate image that would set Sperry aside from the rest of the pack of computer companies snapping at the heels of the market leader, International Business Machines Corp. (IBM).

Sperry's chairman and chief executive J. Paul Lyet, had in mind the success with which Avis Corp. established its position as the number two car hire firm with the slogan: "We try harder." He instructed the executives in charge of advertising and public relations to find a theme that would emulate the Avis story.

The researchers interviewed everyone they could think of, from customers and suppliers to managers at all levels in the company, asking what they thought Sperry did differently to other computer companies. The suggestion, "We listen," came from a branch manager in Houston.

Having accepted the concept, fired its advertising agency, and hired another one, Sperry decided that its campaign should not be hollow. It would have to make some efforts to ensure that people in the company really did listen to customers.

The search for expert advice on how to educate employees in good listening habits led Sperry to Dr. Lyman K. Steil who, by coincidence worked at the University of Minnesota close to corporate headquarters. Steil, it turned out, had already run a number of *ad hoc* classes in listening for Sperry managers over the past 10 years. The company hired him as a consultant to tour its major locations in the U.S. and Europe.

At each location, Steil gave a seminar to senior managers. Over 1½ months, the 500 most senior U.S. managers and the 200 most senior European managers all attended Steil's seminars.

Once the advertisements stressing Sperry's commitment to good listening and to training good listeners appeared on television, however, the pot started bubbling much more vigorously than Sperry had expected. The advertisements concentrated not on how well Sperry listened, but on how important it was for everyone to develop good listening habits.

The employees, who had already heard about the top management seminars, began clamouring to know when it would be their turn. Marketing manager Del Kennedy found that so many employee inquiries were coming into his office that he had to give the switchboard a special briefing on the details of the programme. The operators, too, made it clear that they also wanted to attend a listening seminar as soon as possible.

Peter Hynes, now director of international communications at the company's European headquarters in the UK, was one of the team handling the programme. "What started out as an advertising and corporate image programme turned into something else," he says. "It began to involve all sorts of people."

The company's training staff were given instruction in how to present a one-day listening seminar which had been designed with Steil's help. However, to put 80,000 employees through a course takes a long time. So Sperry elected to concentrate first on those employees, such as salesmen, customer engineers and receptionists, who dealt with the public.

To keep the rest of the employees happy, the concept was introduced by a videotape of Lyet explaining why listening was important in their work, followed rapidly by a record covering the basics of good and bad listening, and a booklet posted to all 55,000 U.S. employees' homes.

The booklet contains much the same information as the record plus a number of exercises to help employees work out where they should improve their own listening behaviour. More recently, the seminar has been condensed into three 20-minute cassettes, available on loan to any employee who wants to preempt the course.

By the end of September last year, 10,000 people had attended the formal seminars. All employees in West Germany and Switzerland have been through the course as have all the people with direct customer contact in the UK. Even so, the company's response time in dealing with employee interest has not been fast enough for many people. Says Kennedy: "We have had some negative feedback from employees in Europe who say, 'when are we going to take the course? The advertisement says it is available to all employees'."

When I attended one of the courses recently in London, there were 11 other participants, although some marketing territories have opted for considerably larger groups. The session begins with a brief self-introduction by each participant, followed by a brief unexpected quiz by the session leader to demonstrate how little of the information supplied in this way had been retained by people. I found I could scarcely remember half of the participants' middle names, for example.

A series of video-films illustrate poor listening habits and demonstrate the four phases of effective listening—sensing, interpreting, evaluating, and responding—and how the good listener handles each. The information portions of the seminar are followed by roleplaying exercises in small groups where everyone has the opportunity to practise those skills.

Analysis of the exercises afterwards

The 10 bad listening habits that the Sperry Training Programme tries to eradicate:

1. Calling the subject uninteresting
2. Criticizing the speaker's delivery or mannerisms
3. Getting stimulated by something the speaker says
4. Listening primarily for facts
5. Trying to outline everything
6. Faking attention to the speaker
7. Allowing interfering distractions
8. Avoiding difficult material
9. Letting emotion-laden words arouse personal antagonism
10. Wasting the advantage of thought speed (daydreaming)

allows the participants to see where their poor listening habits had interfered with communication. Each was encouraged to draw up action plans to overcome their principal weaknesses with the aid of other participants.

One of my identified weaknesses was not taking enough action to prevent outside interruptions. Another was allowing my mind to wander to other pressing matters when the speaker's words did not seem to be immediately relevant. The mind, the course leader explains, can usually cope with, at least twice the information rate of a person talking at normal speed. The excess capacity should be used to analyse and assess what the person is saying, but rarely is. The cures worked out for these failings were to stop all calls during meetings in my office and to ensure as far as possible that all other urgent business is dealt with before the meeting starts.

One of the clear lessons from the seminar is that we are much less efficient listeners than we imagine.

Source: *International Management,* February 1981, pp. 20–21. Reprinted by special permission from the February 1981 issue of *International Management,*

rect message and also lets the receiver know if he or she has the correct message. For example, instead of asking a person if he or she understands a message, it is much better to request that the receiver explain what he or she has heard. Asking a person if he or she understands a message often places the person on the defensive and can result in little feedback.

In an experiment designed to illustrate the importance of feedback, an individual was asked to describe a series of rectangles (see Figure 11–7) to a group of individuals.[15] The experiment was conducted under two distinctly different conditions. First, the sender described the rectangles, and the listeners could not ask questions or see the sender. Thus, feedback was nonexistent. In the second trial, the sender could see the listeners, and the listeners could ask questions. Thus, feedback was present.

The results showed that lack of feedback increased the speed of transmission. However, feedback caused the accuracy and the degree of confidence the listeners had in the accuracy to improve significantly. In summary, the results showed that feedback in the communication process takes more time but significantly improves the quality of the communication.

[15] Harold J. Leavitt, *Managerial Psychology* (Chicago: University of Chicago Press, 1972), p. 116.

FIGURE 11–7
Rectangles in Communication Experiment

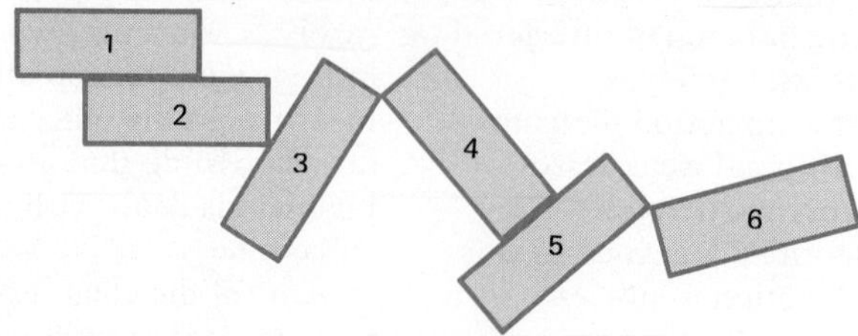

Source: Harold J. Leavitt, *Managerial Psychology* (Chicago: University of Chicago Press, 1972), p. 116.

Nonverbal Communication

Nonverbal communication is the conscious or unconscious behavior on the part of the sender that occurs in the presence of the receiver and is perceived either consciously or subconsciously by the receiver. Humans have a unique capacity for conveying meaning through speech as well as through silence and other nonverbal means of expression. Gestures, vocal intonations, facial expressions, and body posture are all used to communicate at the nonverbal level.[16] Randall Harrison, an expert on nonverbal communication, has estimated that no more than 35 percent of the meaning of a message is communicated by the words used in face-to-face communication.[17] The influence of nonverbal communication over verbal communication suggests that people are not good "nonverbal liars." In other words, people communicate nonverbally that part of the message which they wish least to communicate.[18] Further, visual cues have been found to lead to more accurate judgments regarding the meaning of a message than vocal cues.[19]

ORGANIZATIONAL COMMUNICATION SYSTEMS

Analyzing the communication process from an organizational perspective views the organizational structure as a network through which the communication process functions. In general,

[16] A. Mehrabian, "Inference of Attitudes from the Posture, Orientation, and Distance of the Communicator," *Journal of Consulting Psychology* 31 (1967), pp. 248–52.

[17] Randall Harrison, "Non-Verbal Communication," in *Dimensions in Communication*, ed. J. H. Campbell and P. W. Harper (Belmont, Calif.: Wadsworth, 1970).

[18] P. Ekman and W. V. Friesen, "Nonverbal Leadage and Clues to Deception," *Psychiatry* 32, no. 1 (1969), pp. 88–105.

[19] K. L. Burns and E. G. Beier, "Significance of Vocal and Visual Channels in the Decoding of Emotional Meaning," *Journal of Communication* 23 (1973), pp. 118–30.

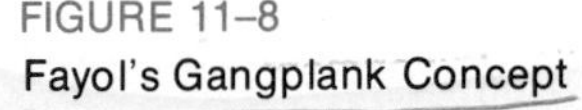

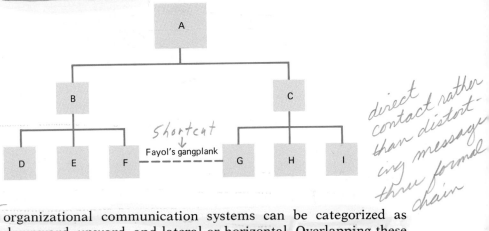

FIGURE 11–8
Fayol's Gangplank Concept

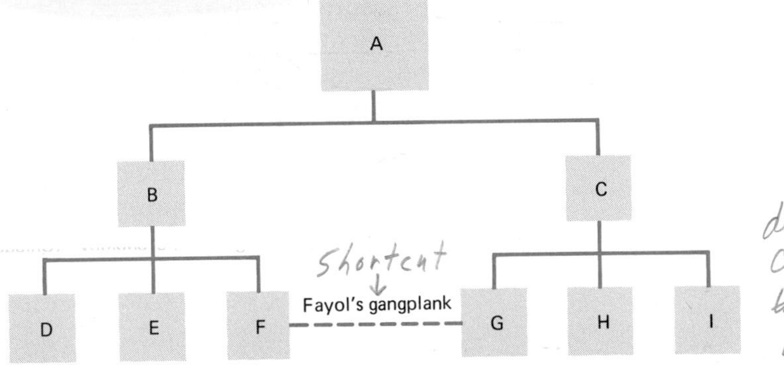

organizational communication systems can be categorized as downward, upward, and lateral or horizontal. Overlapping these three formal systems is the informal communication system called the grapevine.

Two Early Approaches to Organizational Communication

The management pioneer Henri Fayol, who was introduced in Chapter 2, was one of the first writers to analyze the communication process. Fayol recognized that communication via the formal chain of command could produce unnecessary distortion. In Figure 11–8, suppose that F would like to transmit a message to G. Following the formal chain of command, the message would go from F-B-C-G. It is easy to see from the number of steps in the process the potential for distortion. Fayol proposed that a shortcut be taken between F and G. Called Fayol's gangplank or bridge, this concept is illustrated in Figure 11–8. Fayol summarized the need for the gangplank as follows:

> allow the two employees . . . to deal at one sitting, and in a few hours, with some question or other which via the scalar chain would . . . inconvenience many people, involve masses of paper, lose weeks or months to get to a conclusion less satisfactory generally than the one which could have been obtained via direct contact.[20]

Chester Barnard also stressed the importance of the communication process in organization.[21] In fact, he felt that communication was one of the basic elements necessary for the existence

[20] Henri Fayol, *General and Industrial Management,* trans. Constance Storrs (London: Sir Isaac Pitman and Sons, 1949), p. 35.

[21] Chester I. Barnard, *The Functions of the Executive* (Cambridge, Mass.: Harvard University Press, 1938).

of an organization. Barnard felt that the communication process was essential for establishing the authority structure of the organization. His contention was that an individual can and will accept a communication as authoritative only if four conditions are met. The individual (1) understands the communication, (2) believes it to be consistent with the purpose of the organization, (3) believes it to be compatible with his or her personal interest as a whole, and (4) is physically and mentally able to comply with the communication. Barnard's coupling of authority with the communication process led to his development of the acceptance theory of authority which was discussed in Chapter 7.

Communication Patterns

Figure 11–9 shows several different communication patterns which can exist in an organization.[22] Each of the patterns in Figure 11–9 falls into one of two classes depending on the presence or lack of feedback. No pair of individuals can exchange messages in patterns A, B, and C. In other words, no feedback can occur. Any pair of individuals in patterns D, E, and F can exchange messages either directly or indirectly. Thus feedback can occur. Patterns A,

FIGURE 11–9
Communication Patterns

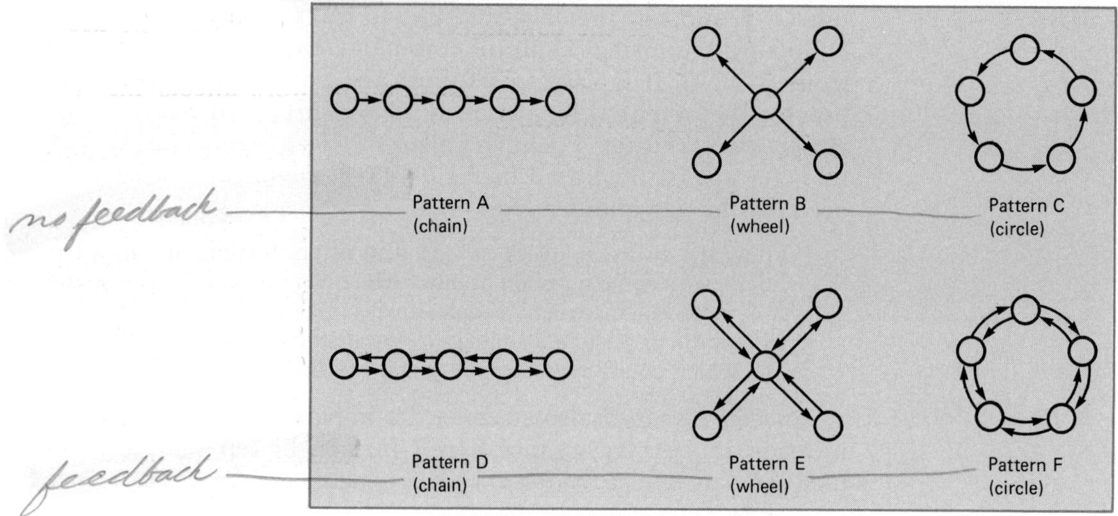

[22] Alex Bavelas and Dermot Barrett, "An Experimental Approach to Organizational Communication," *Personnel,* March 1951, pp. 366–71.

FIGURE 11–10
Advantages and Disadvantages of Communication Patterns

Characteristics	Chain	Wheel	Circle
Speed	Fast	Fast	Slow
Accuracy	Good	Good	Poor
Organization	Slowly emerging but stable organization	Almost immediate and stable organization	No stable form of organization
Emergence of leader	Marked	Very pronounced	None
Morale	Poor	Very poor	Very good

B, and C do not lend themselves to good coordination or the exchange of ideas.

Patterns which allow feedback or two-way communication (patterns D, E, and F in Figure 11–9) have advantages and disadvantages as outlined in Figure 11–10.

The following conclusions can be drawn from Figure 11–10:

1. The pattern of the communication network affects the accuracy and speed of messages.
2. The pattern of the communication network affects the task performance of the group.
3. The pattern of the communication network affects the satisfaction of group members.[23]

Thus, no one communication pattern is best for all situations. The most effective communication pattern for a given situation depends on the required speed, accuracy, morale, and organization structure. For instance, the wheel pattern is most desirable in situations requiring a clear-cut leader and rapid decisions.

Numerous research studies have been conducted on the relationships between the pattern of the network and the communication process. Primarily, these studies have indicated that the network configuration is important in determining the effectiveness of the communications process.

[23] James L. Gibson, John M. Ivancevich, and James H. Donnelly, Jr., *Organizations: Structure, Processes, Behavior* (Plano, Tex.: Business Publications, 1973), p. 174.

Downward Communication Systems

Traditional views of the communication process in organizations are dominated by downward communication systems. Such systems involve transmitting information from higher to lower levels of the organization. The chain of command within the organizational structure determines the flow of downward information. Policy manuals, bulletins, organizational magazines, job descriptions, orders, and directions are all examples of the downward communication system.

Frequently, downward communication systems are assumed to be better than they actually are. Unfortunately, many studies indicate that this assumption may be invalid. One study established that there is considerable disagreement between first-line managers and their superiors regarding the authority of the first-line managers.[24] Another study indicated that there was considerable filtering of information down through the chain of command.[25] Furthermore, it has also been reported that much of the material in employee handbooks and manuals is not understandable to the average employee.[26]

One important decision that must be made in downward communication systems is the choice of the medium to use. Written communication is less likely to be filtered, provides an official record, but does not enable immediate feedback. On the other hand, oral communication provides no record, is subject to filtering, but does facilitate immediate feedback. Figure 11–11 offers some suggestions to aid in deciding when to use oral and written communications.

In addition, several general suggestions for improving downward communications are summarized in Figure 11–12.

Upward Communication Systems

Upward communication originates at the lower levels of the organization and flows toward the top. An upward communication system in an organization should aid management in evaluating the effectiveness of their downward communication efforts and enable them to learn about organizational problems. In general, four major areas of information should be communicated from

[24] Bradford B. Boyd and J. Michael Jensen, "Perceptions of the First-Line Supervisor's Authority: A Study in Superior-Subordinate Communication," *Academy of Management Journal,* September 1972, pp. 331–42.

[25] Keith Davis, "Success of Chain-of-Command Oral Communication in a Manufacturing Management Group," *Academy of Management Journal,* December 1968, pp. 379–87.

[26] Keith Davis, "Readability Changes in Employee Handbooks of Identical Companies during a 15 Year Period," *Personnel Psychology* 21, no. 4 (1968), pp. 413–20.

FIGURE 11–11
Effective Communication Methods

Method of communication	*Situations* — *Most effective*	*Least effective*
Oral communication by itself	1. Reprimanding employees. 2. Resolving work-centered disputes.	1. Communicating information requiring future action. 2. Communicating information of a general nature. 3. Communicating directives or orders. 4. Communicating information about an important policy change. 5. Communicating with your immediate superior about work problems. 6. Promoting a safety campaign.
Written communication by itself	1. Communicating information requiring future action. 2. Communicating information of a general nature.	1. Communicating information requiring immediate action. 2. Commending an employee for noteworthy work performance. 3. Reprimanding an employee for poor performance. 4. Resolving work-related disputes.
Oral then written communication	1. Communicating information requiring immediate action. 2. Communicating directives or orders. 3. Communicating information about an important policy change. 4. Communicating with your immediate superior about work-related problems. 5. Promoting a safety campaign. 6. Commending an employee for noteworthy work performance.	

Source: Dale Level, Jr., "Communication Effectiveness: Method and Situation," *Journal of Business Communication,* Fall 1972, pp. 19–25.

below: (1) the activities of subordinates in terms of their achievements, progress, and future plans, (2) unresolved work problems in which subordinates may need help currently or in the future, (3) suggestions or ideas for improvements within work groups or the organization as a whole, and (4) the feelings of subordinates about their jobs, associates, and the organization.[27] Figure 11–13 lists several forms of upward communication.

[27] Earl Planty and William Machaner, "Upward Communication: A Project in Executive Method," in *Readings in Interpersonal and Organizational Communication,* eds. Richard C. Huseman, Cal M. Logue, and Dwight L. Freshley (Boston: Holbrook Press, 1977), pp. 102–3.

FIGURE 11–12
Techniques for Improving Downward Communication

1. Establish an objective for communicating.
2. Consider the content of the message to be communicated.
   a. Is it accurate?
   b. Is it definite and specific in meaning?
   c. Is it forceful in indicating that management cares about any actions taken that may affect the company?
   d. Is it oriented to the receiver?
   e. Is it stated simply?
   f. Does it contain hidden meanings?
3. Use the communication technique that will most effectively transmit the message.
4. Consider value differences between management and employees.
5. Present organizational goals to employees so they can see how these goals coincide with their goals.
6. Provide for regular and frequent meetings between managerial and nonmanagerial personnel.

Source: Andrew B. Chase, Jr., "How to Make Downward Communication Work," *Personnel Journal,* June 1970, pp. 478–83. Copyright *Personnel Journal,* Costa Mesa, California; all rights reserved. Reprinted with permission.

The key to developing effective upward communication systems appears to be a superior-subordinate relationship in which subordinates do not feel that they will be penalized for disclosure. In their relationships with superiors, subordinates often conceal and distort their real feelings, problems, opinions, and beliefs because they fear disclosure may cause the superior to punish them in some way.[28] In fact, trust in one's superior appears to be one

FIGURE 11–13
Techniques Used in Upward Communication

Informal inquiries or discussion with employees.
Exit interviews.
Discussion with first-line supervisors.
Grievance or complaint procedures.
The grapevine.
Union representatives.
Counseling.
Formal meeting with employees.
Suggestion system.
Formal attitude surveys.
Question and answer column in employee publication.
Gripe boxes.
Hot line or recording system.

[28] Gary Gemmie, "Managing Upward Communication," *Personnel Journal,* February 1970, pp. 107–9.

of the key variables in effective upward communication systems.[29]

Ideally, the organizational structure should provide a basis for an upward communication system as well as a downward system. In other words, communication should flow in both directions through the formal organizational structure. Unfortunately, communication from the bottom does not flow as freely as communication from the top.

Some of the deterrents to effective upward communication are:

1. Management fails to respond to communication from the bottom. When subordinates bring information or problems to management, failure to respond will ultimately result in the termination of communication.
2. Managers tend to be defensive about their actions which have been less than perfect. When subordinates recognize that managers are being defensive about their actions, information will be withheld.
3. The manager's attitude plays a critical role in the upward communication process. If the manager is really concerned and really listens, then upward communication improves.
4. Physical barriers can also inhibit the upward communication process. Physically separating a manager from his or her immediate subordinates creates communication problems.
5. Time lags from the time of the communication to the time of action can inhibit upward communication. For example, if an employee makes a suggestion and it takes months for the various levels of management to approve the suggestion, upward communication is hindered.

Figure 11–14 gives some general guidelines for improving upward communication systems within organizations.

Horizontal or Lateral Communication Systems

LATERAL & HORIZ.

The upward and downward communication systems generally follow the formal chain of command within the organization. However, in large and complex organizations, communication across the lines of the various organizational units has become more important. Commication across organizational units which are at the same approximate level in the organizational hierarchy is referred to as lateral or horizontal communication.

Interdepartmental committee meetings (committees were dis-

[29] Karlene H. Roberts and Charles A. O'Reilly III, "Failures in Upward Communication in Organizations: Three Possible Culprits," *Academy of Management Journal,* June 1974, pp. 205–15.

FIGURE 11–14
Guides for Improving Upward Communication

1. There must be systematic, balanced coverage. Free communications upward can't be left to chance but must be stimulated, encouraged, and facilitated by superiors.
2. Continuity must be present. The flow of information upward cannot be turned on and off at the whim or to the advantage of either party.
3. The flow of communications must be directed. Communications should move step by step upward through the organization until it reaches the individual who can take action.
4. Listening must be sensitive and not condescending. A sincere effort must be made to get employee interpretations and ideas and to learn the real causes for complaints.
5. Listening must be objective. A constructive, receptive attitude toward direct or implicit criticism must be displayed; the manager should not state his or her own opinion when seeking those of subordinates. He or she should have an open mind and a willingness to change if shown to be wrong.
6. Listening implies action. Where adjustments are necessary, listening in the absence of corrective action is not effective. The manager should not verbally agree or appear to do so if he or she does not intend to take corrective action.

Source: Adapted from Earl Planty and William Machaner, "Upward Communication: A Project in Executive Development," in *Readings in Interpersonal and Organizational Communication*, eds. Richard D. Huseman, Cal M. Logue, and Dwight L. Freshley (Boston: Holbrook Press, 1977), pp. 105–9.

cussed in depth in Chapter 8) and distribution of written reports are two of the more commonly used methods in horizontal communication.

A word of caution should be given about the distribution of memorandums across departmental lines. Too many memos and reports can create an excess of paperwork that can, of itself, lead to new communication problems. The recipient of too many messages may end up not reading even the important ones.

Grapevine

In addition to the formal channels, many informal paths of communication exist in organizations. These informal channels of communication are generally referred to as the grapevine. The term *grapevine* arose during the Civil War when intelligence telegraph lines were hung loosely from tree to tree, in an appearance similar to a grapevine. The messages transmitted over these lines were often garbled, and thus any rumor was said to be "from the grapevine."[30] In organizations, the grapevine often exists as a result of informal work groups which are found in every organization and which are discussed in detail in Chapter 12.

Although the grapevine generally is not sanctioned as a part of the formal organizational structure, it always exists. As the name suggests, the grapevine does not follow the organizational hierarchy. It may go from secretary to vice president or from engineer to clerk. Because it is not limited to nonmanagement personnel, the grapevine also operates among managers and professional personnel.

One study of the grapevine in an organization reached the following conclusions:

1. Males and females participated equally in the activities of the grapevine.
2. Full-time employees were more active in the grapevine than part-time employees.
3. Managers were more knowledgeable about information on the grapevine than were nonmanagers.
4. Although managers accounted for only a small percentage of the employees studied, they initiated nearly 50 percent of the grapevine information and, on the average, told about eight other people. The average employee told only four other people.[31]

The grapevine generally has a poor reputation in organizations because it is regarded as a rumor factory. However, rumors and the grapevine are not identical. Rumors are only part of the grapevine—the part not based on fact or authority. Managers should correct all rumors as quickly as possible.

It has been estimated that between 75 and 95 percent of grapevine information is correct, even though most of the information is incomplete in detail.[32] This 5 to 25 percent error can, of course, completely change the information. So it can safely be concluded that the grapevine probably produces more misunderstanding than its small percentage of wrong information indicates.[33]

---

[30] Keith Davis, *Human Relations at Work,* 3d ed. (New York: McGraw-Hill, 1967), p. 222.

[31] Jay Knippen, "Grapevine Communication: Management Employees," *Journal Of Business Research,* January 1974, pp. 47–58.

[32] Keith Davis, "The Care and Cultivation of the Corporate Grapevine," in *Readings in Interpersonal and Organizational Communication,* 3d ed., Richard C. Huseman, Cal M. Logue, and Dwight L. Freshley (Boston, Mass.: Holbrook Press, 1977), p. 136.

[33] Ibid., p. 136.

Summarized below are several suggestions to aid management in effectively using the grapevine.

1. The grapevine is a permanent part of the formal organizational structure and should be used to facilitate effective communication.
2. Managers should have a knowledge of what the grapevine is communicating and its reasons for doing so.
3. Inputs into the grapevine at the management level are spread to a greater number of employees, and a majority of employees hear grapevine information for the first time from management. As a result, all levels of management should be provided with total and accurate information to ensure that the messages they communicate through the grapevine are accurate.

SUMMARY

Communication is defined as the transfer of information that is meaningful to those involved—the transmittal of understanding. Two forms of communication were discussed: interpersonal communication and organizational communication.

Interpersonal communication involves communication between individuals and is an interactive process involving the transmission and reception of verbal and nonverbal signs and symbols which come from other people as well as from the physical and cultural settings of both the sender and the receiver. Obstacles to effective interpersonal communication can result from semantics, perception, poor listening, inadequate feedback, and nonverbal communication.

Analyzing the communication process from the organizational perspective involves viewing the organizational structure as the primary network through which the communication process flows. Several different communication patterns that occur in organizations were presented and evaluated. Downward communication, upward communication, horizontal or lateral communication, and the grapevine were discussed as forms of organizational communication. Suggestions were given for making each of these forms of communication more effective.

REVIEW QUESTIONS

1. What is communication?
2. Define interpersonal communication.
3. What is semantics?
4. What is perception, and what role does it play in communication?

5. What is feedback, and how does it affect the communication process?
6. Give some suggestions for improving listening habits.
7. What is the importance of nonverbal communication in interpersonal communication?
8. Identify the contributions of Henri Fayol and Chester Barnard to the understanding of the communication process.
9. Describe three conclusions which can be drawn concerning communication patterns in organizations.
10. Describe the following organizational communication systems:
    a. Downward communication systems.
    b. Upward communication systems.
    c. Horizontal or lateral communication systems.
    d. Grapevine.

DISCUSSION QUESTIONS

1. Describe some ways in which the grapevine can be used effectively in organizations.
2. Explain why the following question is raised frequently by many managers: Why didn't you do what I told you to do?
3. Discuss the following statement: "Meanings are in people not words."
4. "Watch what we do, not what we say." Is this good practice? Explain.
5. Poor communication of the organization's goals is often given as the reason for low performance of the organization. Do you think that this is usually a valid explanation?

SELECTED READINGS

Baird, J. E., Jr., and G. K. Wieting. "Nonverbal Communication Can Be a Motivational Tool." *Personnel Journal,* Spring 1979, pp. 607–10.

Clinard, H. "Interpersonal Communication Skills Training." *Training and Development Journal* August 1979, pp. 34–38.

Davidson, J. P. "Communicating Company Objectives." *Personnel Journal* April 1981, pp. 292–93.

Ewing, D. W., and P. M., Banks. "Listening and Responding to Employees' Concerns (Interview with A. W. Clausen)." *Harvard Business Review,* January–February 1980, pp. 101–14.

Foltz, R. G. "Internal Communications: What's Ahead." *Public Relations Journal,* December 1979, p. 47.

Huseman, R. C.; M. James Lahiff; and John D. Hatfield. *Interpersonal Communications in Organizations.* Boston: Holbrook Press, 1976.

Huseman, R. C.; C. Logue; and D. Freshley. *Readings in Interpersonal and Organizational Communication,* 3d ed. Boston: Holbrook Press, Inc., 1977.

Josefowitz, N. "Management Men and Women: Closed vs. Open Doors." *Harvard Business Review,* September–October 1980, pp. 56ff.

Kikoski, J. F. "Communication: Understanding It, Improving It." *Personnel Journal,* February 1980, pp. 126ff.

Loffreda, R. "Employee Attitude Surveys: A Valuable Motivating Tool." *Personnel Administrator,* July 1979, pp. 41–43.

McMaster, M. D., and J. Grinder. "Art of Communicating." *Administrative Management,* December 1980, pp. 56–60.

Miller, J. T. "Communication or Getting Ideas Across." *S. A. M. Advanced Management Journal,* Summer 1980, pp. 32–38.

O'Reilly, C. A. "Individuals and Information Overload in Organizations: Is More Necessarily Better?" *Academy of Management Journal,* December 1980, pp. 794–96.

Penley, L. S., and B. L. Hawkins. "Communicating for Improved Motivation and Performance." *S.A.M. Advanced Management Journal,* Spring 1980, pp. 39–44.

Roberts, K. H., and C. A. O'Reilly. "Some Correlations of Communication Roles in Organizations." *Academy of Management Journal,* March 1979, pp. 42–57.

Samaras, J. T. "Two-way Communication Practices for Managers." *Personnel Journal,* August 1980, pp. 645–48.

Sharma, J. M. "Organizational Communications: A Linking Process." *Personnel Administrator,* July 1979, pp. 35–39.

Wooten, B. E. "Organizational Communication: The Channel vs. the Grapevine." *Management World,* March 1981, pp. 39–40.

Case 11–1 Who calls the shots?

The financial reports for the last quarter of operations for the Brighton Cabinet Company have just been received by the company's president, John Branner. After looking over the reports, John has decided that the purchasing department is paying too much for the company's raw materials, which include plywood, paneling, and flakeboard. He immediately called Joe Scott, vice president of manufacturing, and informed him of the decision.

Joe called Bill Sloane, the supervisor of purchasing, and said, "Bill, Mr. Branner is upset over the cost figures for raw materials last quarter. You were well above budget. He wants them brought down, this quarter!"

As Bill hung up the phone, he wondered to himself who figured out the budget for his department and if they realized that plywood had gone up from $6.05 to $6.75 a sheet.

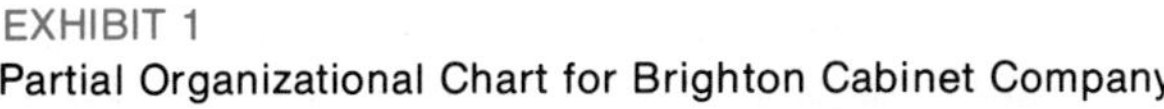

EXHIBIT 1
Partial Organizational Chart for Brighton Cabinet Company

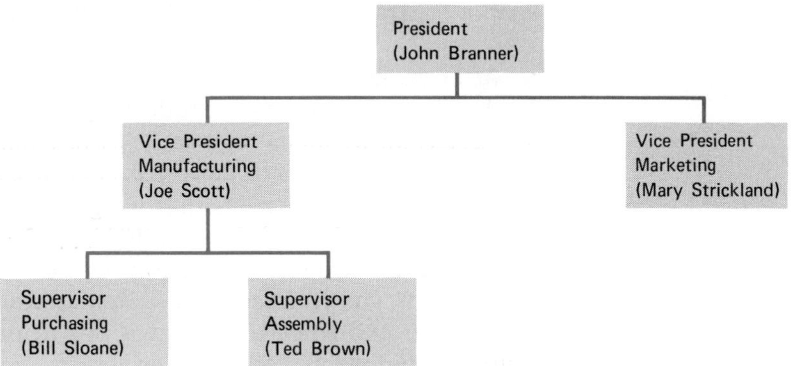

Instructed to cut costs, Bill was determined to do so. Two days later, Bill found a supplier who would sell Brighton Cabinet plywood for $5.95 a sheet. He ordered a two-week supply. Upon delivery, Bill's suspicions were confirmed. The plywood was a poorer quality, but it would work. Bill decided to continue to buy the less-expensive plywood.

A month later, Bill was approached by Ted Brown, supervisor of the assembly department, who asked, "Bill, what's with this plywood? All of a sudden we've been having a lot of it split on us while trying to nail and staple the pieces together."

Bill replied, "Well Ted, Mr. Branner sent orders down for me to cut costs. I don't know how else to do it other than purchasing the lower-grade plywood. It was the only way out."

Things were left as they were, and the quarter ended. The financial reports for the quarter showed a drop in sales and profits. According to forecasts and trends of previous years, the profits and sales should have been higher. John Branner immediately called Mary Strickland, vice president of marketing, to his office and demanded an explanation. Mary explained, "It seems that we have lost a couple of major builders as customers. They seem to think that our competitors have something better to offer. I have investigated the situation and have found that our cabinets are splitting more on installation due to the fact that we are using a lower-grade plywood now. I talked to Joe Scott, and he told me you had ordered him to cut costs. And the purchase of the lower-grade plywood was one of the few ways that costs could be reduced."

Branner immediately ordered Scott to begin purchasing plywood of the necessary quality. Scott then informed Sloan. Later that day, Bill asked Joe what should be done with the three-week supply of the lower-grade plywood. "That's your problem," Joe snapped. Apparently, he had gotten a good chewing out from Branner.

After making several calls, Bill decided that the only good offer for the plywood was made by the company who sold it to Brighton. But they would only pay 60 percent of what it cost Brighton. Bill agreed to the price, wanting to get rid of it to make room for the new supplies that would be coming in.

Three days later, Bill was called into Scott's office. Scott asked, "Bill, who gave you permission to sell that plywood at that price?"

"No one sir, it was my decision. It was the best deal that I could find, and I needed to get it out to make room for the new supplies coming in," Bill replied.

"Well Bill, with decisions like that, this company won't last very long," Scott commented. "You should have used up the other plywood a little at a time by mixing it in with the higher grade plywood. Don't let this happen again!"

1. How did this problem actually begin, and how could it have been avoided?
2. Describe the communication failures that occurred in this case.
3. Is Bill really responsible? Who else, if anyone, is responsible?
4. Comment on Scott's talk with Bill at the end of the case.

Case 11–2 Unions—why?

George Abbott, 53 years old, sat back in his chair totally bewildered. He had just been told by his first-shift supervisor (Alice Moore) that the paperworkers union was rapidly gaining support in the mill that he had managed for over 20 years and that, the way things were going, it looked like they would have enough supporters to demand an election within the next week's period. He couldn't believe it. The Marlan Textile Mill was a small mill, employing about 50 relatively unskilled employees. The work force was predominantly comprised of middle-aged females living in the small, rural, southern town of Tyson where the mill was located.

Abbott could not understand why they would do this to him. He had always thought his employees were happy with the conditions at the mill. It was a small operation and was more like a large family than a place of employment. Surely, if there was something causing them to be so dissatisfied that they felt they had to turn to a union, he would have been aware of it. It made no sense whatsoever to him.

George: Alice, I just can't understand it. I can't help but take it personally. Why I've done everything I could to see that they would get a fair deal. What could it be?

Alice: Well George, I don't really know for sure, but rumor has it that it's not more money that they're after. Shoot, half of them couldn't earn near what you pay them anywhere else, and they know it. And I can tell you, they do appreciate it. I can't figure it out either. Everyone that's talked to me about the whole situation has agreed that you've been real fair with them.

George: Then why the union? I mean, they just didn't wake up one morning and say "Hey let's unionize!" Something must be wrong—it just doesn't make sense.

Alice: You know George, I've only been at the mill two months now. But I've heard that they've been asking for years for more washroom facilities. This may sound crazy, but I wonder what that might have had to do with it. I've heard a lot of talk about that lately.

George: No, we're in compliance with the OSHA standards. Sure, at least once a month someone suggests that additional washroom facilities be made available and the existing ones be made "prettier." But I don't take those suggestions seriously. You know, when I implemented the suggestion box. I knew people would feel like they had to participate. Asking for more washrooms is just one of the first things that would come into a woman's mind. You know how those ladies are—they want to be sure that I know they're interested in the company, and so they feel like they have to make their share of the suggestions. They don't *really* need another washroom.

1. What communication system has failed?
2. What do you think of George's perception of the situation? Is his perception typical of some managers?

12 Work Groups in Organizations

Objectives

1. To learn to distinguish between formal and informal work groups in organizations.
2. To explore why informal work groups form in organizations.
3. To discuss some factors common to all informal work groups.
4. To describe the impact that informal work groups can have on individuals and on managing individuals.
5. To introduce the concept of creativity in organizations.

Chapter Outline

Glossary of Terms

Brainstorming A process designed to produce creative ideas by presenting a group with a problem and then eliciting their ideas for solutions; no criticisms of solutions are initially allowed so as not to inhibit the group members.

Conformity Refers to the degree to which the members of a group accept and abide by the norms of the group.

Creative problem solving Involves bringing about useful changes within the organization by introducing and putting into action new elements or new combinations of existing elements.

Creativity Total thinking process involved in the production of an idea, concept, innovation, or discovery that is original, useful, or satisfying to its creator or someone else.

Formal work groups Groups in organizations which generally have a defined structure and established goals and are formally recognized by the organization.

Gordon technique An aid to producing creative ideas in which no one but the group leader knows the exact nature of the real problem under consideration. The group leader uses a key word to describe the problem area as a starting point for exploring solutions to the problem.

Group A number of persons who interact with one another often over a period of time, communicate with all the other members on a face-to-face basis, and perceive themselves to be a group.

Group cohesiveness The degree of attraction that each member has for the group.

Group norm An agreement among members of the group concerning how the members should behave.

Idiosyncracy credit A form of credit or liberties which a group gives to certain members of the group who have made or are making significant contributions to the group's goals.

Informal work groups Groups in organizations which result from personal contacts and interactions and the associated groupings of people working within the formal work groups of the organization; such groups are usually not formally recognized by the organization.

Nominal grouping technique Highly structured technique for solving group tasks; designed to minimize personal interactions so as to encourage creativity and reduce pressures toward conformity.

Primary group A group that meets all of the characteristics of a group but also has feelings of loyalty, comradeship, and a common sense of values among its members.

Team building Process that involves developing an awareness on the part of the work group of those conditions that keep the group from functioning effectively and then requires the work group to take those actions that will eliminate those conditions.

Work groups A term used to describe groups in organizations.

Joe Marm was a young second lieutenant serving in South Vietnam. In the fall of 1965, he grabbed up two side arms and a pile of grenades and ran up a hill alone. He attacked and destroyed a machine gun nest killing eight Viet Cong. Afterwards, Lieutenant Marm was recommended for the Congressional Medal of Honor for his heroic actions. When asked why he had made the attack on his own, Marm replied, "What would the fellows have thought of me if I had been afraid to do it?"

*The New York Times**

The quote above describes the effect of a group on one individual. The importance of belonging to a group and its effect on human behavior in organizations was emphasized early by Elton Mayo in the famous Hawthorne studies in which he concluded that much of human behavior and attitudes can be better explained by looking at the informal work group rather than individuals themselves.[1] The major conclusion reached by the Hawthorne researchers was that workers react to the psychological and social conditions at work as well as to the physical conditions and that group pressures directly affect an individual's actions. A significant contribution of these studies was the recognition that an organization consists of individuals, groups, and intergroup relationships and that these components greatly influence the productivity and stability of the organization.

WORK GROUPS DEFINED

There are many ways of defining a group. George Homans defined a group as "a number of persons who communicate with one another often over a span of time, and who are few enough so that each person is able to communicate with all the others, not at secondhand through other people but face-to-face."[2] Edgar Schein has described a group as "any number of people who (1) interact with one another, (2) are psychologically aware of one another, and (3) perceive themselves to be a group."[3] Thus, small size,

---

**The New York Times*, November 17, 1966.

[1] Elton Mayo, *The Human Problems of an Industrial Civilization* (Cambridge, Mass.: Harvard University Graduate School of Business Administration, 1946).

[2] George C. Homans, *The Human Group* (New York: Harcourt Brace Jovanovich, 1950), p. 1.

[3] Edgar H. Schein, *Organizational Psychology* (Englewood Cliffs, N.J.: Prentice-Hall, 1965), p. 67.

physical and psychological awareness, and interaction are all characteristics of groups.

Sociologists have further refined the definition of groups by distinguishing between a small group and a primary group. A small group must merely meet all of the characteristics outlined in the previous paragraph. A primary group, in addition to meeting the above characteristics, must also have feelings of loyalty, comradeship, and a common sense of values among its members. Therefore, all primary groups are small groups, but all small groups are not necessarily primary groups. Both types of groups exist within organizations.

For the purposes of this chapter, the term *work groups* will be used to describe groups in organizations. A further distinction will be made between formal and informal work groups. Formal work groups result primarily from the organizing function of management which was discussed in Chapters 7 and 8. Generally, formal work groups are defined by officially prescribed relationships between employees and a prescribed plan of effort directed toward the attainment of specific objectives. Two popular forms of formal work groups are command and task groups.[4] These groups can be either small or primary. Command groups are almost always shown on an organization chart. The vice presidents reporting to the president comprise a command group. The department heads reporting to a vice president comprise another command group. A task group is formed by employees that collaborate in order to accomplish a work task assigned by the organization. Engineers working on a particular project and committees are both examples of task groups.

Overlapping the formal work groups in organizations are informal work groups. These groups are not defined by the organizing function of management. Yet, all organizations have them. Groups of employees that regularly lunch together and office "cliques" are examples of informal work groups.

THE LINKING-PIN CONCEPT

Rensis Likert has proposed the linking-pin concept to describe management's role in work groups. Likert suggests that as an individual interacts with the organization, these interactions should contribute to maintaining the sense of personal worth and importance. Both formal and informal work groups are important

[4] Leonard R. Sayles, "Work Group Behavior and the Larger Organizations," in *Research in Industrial Human Relations*, Industrial Relations Research Association, no. 17 (New York: Harper & Row, 1957), pp. 131–45.

FIGURE 12–1
Linking-Pin Concept

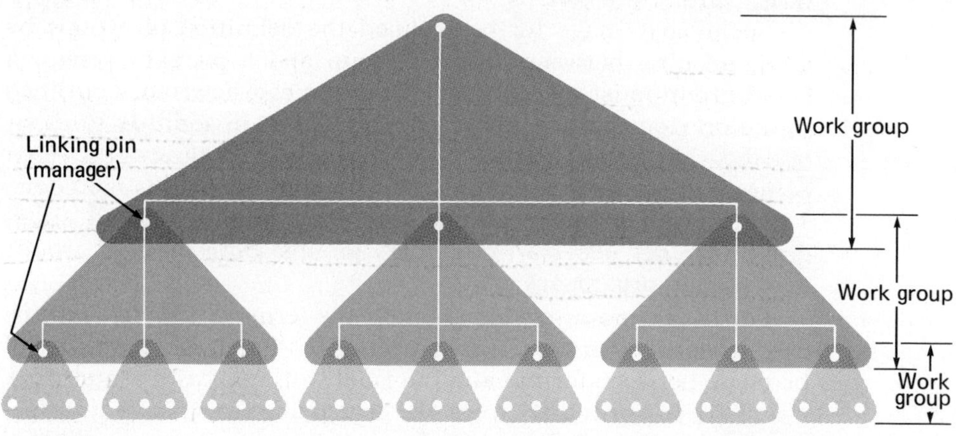

Source: Rensis Likert, *New Patterns of Management* (New York: McGraw-Hill, 1961), p. 104.

sources of satisfaction in maintaining an employee's sense of personal worth and importance. Likert concludes:

> Management will make full use of the potential capacities of its human resources only when each person in an organization is a member of one or more effectively functioning work groups that have a high degree of group loyalty, effective skills of interaction, and high performance goals.[5]

Likert further contends that management should consciously attempt to build these groups. Managers have overlapping group memberships and link these groups to the total organization. Thus, the manager is viewed as a linking pin in the organization. The linking-pin concept is depicted in Figure 12–1.

TEAM BUILDING

Building the kind of work groups that Rensis Likert described in the previous section is often called team building. Team building is a process that involves developing an awareness on the part of the work group of those conditions that keep the group from functioning effectively and then requires the workers to take those actions that will eliminate those conditions.

To build an effective team, the manager must first establish a working environment that is considered to be fair and equitable.

[5] Rensis Likert, *New Patterns of Management* (New York: McGraw-Hill, 1961), p. 104.

This cannot be done by one manager alone. All levels of management must contribute. However, if a manager does not establish this environment in his or her work unit, the efforts of higher levels of management will usually be wasted. Second, participation by the employees in working out changes and keeping them informed about what is taking place also helps build an effective team. An effective manager also attempts to see and understand issues from the employees' point of view. However, the manager needs to be careful here. A manager who is always siding with the employees and taking an attitude of "it's us against them" can create a negative environment. The point is not to side with employees against management but to attempt to understand the issues from the employees' point of view. Finally, the manager should strive to gain acceptance as the group's leader. Certainly, a manager has formal authority that is delegated from higher levels of management. However, formal authority does not guarantee effective team building. Figure 12–2 summarizes these suggestions for effective team building.

FIGURE 12–2
Suggestions for Effective Team Building

1. Establish a working environment that is considered to be fair and equitable by employees.
2. Practice participation—listen to employees' ideas and get them involved in planning.
3. Show the employees that you, the manager who represents higher levels of management, also see issues from the employees' side.
4. Attempt to gain acceptance as the group's leader.

WHY INFORMAL WORK GROUPS EXIST

Work is a social experience and provides an opportunity for employees to fulfill many needs. When people are brought together in an office or plant, they interact and work together in their formal job duties. Friendships naturally emerge out of these continuous contacts and from areas of common interest. Mutual interests, friendships, and the need to fulfill social needs are three reasons that help to explain both the formation of informal work groups and the desire of employees to become members of such groups. Informal work groups provide a sense of security to the individual members because group members usually exhibit a strong sense of loyalty and share common values. Further, membership in informal work groups facilitates social interaction and affiliation and fosters a feeling of pride or esteem by enabling the individual to be part of the "in-group." In general, one of the reasons why informal work groups evolve is to satisfy many of the needs that were described in Maslow's need hierarchy in Chapter 10.

The physical work conditions can also encourage the formation of informal work groups. People in close proximity to each other are almost forced to interact. The arrangement of furniture, desks, and offices can either encourage or discourage the formation of informal work groups.[6] Generally, a physical work setting which facilitates social interaction increases the likelihood not only that an informal work group will exist, but also that new employees will join.

Technology, which is closely aligned with the physical work conditions, also heavily influences informal work group formation. Technology in this broad sense refers to how the overall work flows through the organization. The technology of an organization positions people in the work system, prescribes their activities, and determines their interactions. Technology can also influence the negotiating power of the group. For example, one study found that informal work groups in the electrical equipment industry did not engage in wildcat strikes and other disruptive acts as frequently as informal work groups in the rubber tire industry.[7] The researchers attributed this dissemblance to the differences in the technology used by the two industries. In the tire manufacturing industry, employees worked under adverse working conditions and were positioned so that a few employees could stop the entire work flow. These conditions did not exist in the electrical equipment industry. Thus, because of the technology used, informal work groups in the tire manufacturing industry had more power than did those in the electrical equipment industry.

Like technology, management can influence the formation of informal work groups. For instance, if management decides to organize on a functional basis—accounting department, marketing department, and so forth—this facilitates the formation of informal work groups comprised of people performing similar functions. If, on the other hand, management organizes by product, customer, or geographical area, then people performing different functions are likely to form into groups.

In addition, the style of leadership employed by a manager can influence the formation of informal work groups. For instance, an autocratic manager and a participative manager would

[6] Fred I. Steele, "Social Contact," *Physical Settings and Organization Development* (Reading, Mass.: Addison-Wesley Publishing, 1973), chap. 5.

[7] J. W. Kulin, *Bargaining in Grievance Settlement* (New York: Columbia University Press, 1961).

probably cause entirely different informal work group behavior.[8]

In summary, there are many reasons for the formation of informal work groups within organizations. The reasons discussed above are by no means mutually exclusive or all-inclusive. The important point to remember is that overlapping the formal work groups in an organization are informal work groups which can have a significant impact on both individual and organizational performance.

FACTORS COMMON TO ALL INFORMAL WORK GROUPS

Once informal groups are formed, they evolve in such a manner that they take on a life of their own, separate and distinct from the work processes in which they originated.[9] Informal group development is viewed as a self-generating process. Individuals who are formally required to interact with each other soon build favorable sentiments toward certain people. These sentiments serve to facilitate interactions and activities above and beyond those required by the job description, such as eating lunch together, discussing problems, etc. Simultaneously, these individuals become closer, and the group becomes an identifiable entity rather than just a collection of people. Over time, the informal group develops a set way of doing things and possesses several factors which seem to be common to all informal work groups. The implications of these factors on effective management can be better understood by examining them in more detail.

Group Norms

A group norm is an agreement among the members of the group concerning how the members should behave.[10] The various forms of informal group norms are limitless. Examples of informal group norms that relate to the work place are setting certain performance levels that may be either above, below, or the same as those set by management. Playing a joke or trick on all new employees is another example. Unfortunately, little is known about what factors determine whether an informal group will establish

---

[8] R. E. Miles, *Theories of Management: Implications for Organizational Behavior and Development* (New York: McGraw-Hill, 1975).

[9] David R. Hampton, Charles E. Summer, and Ross A. Webber, *Organizational Behavior and the Practice of Management* (Glenview, Ill: Scott, Foresman, 1978), p. 192.

[10] Joseph A. Litterer, *The Analysis of Organizations* (New York: John Wiley & Sons, 1973), pp. 243–48.

a pro- or antiorganization norm.[11] However, a significant factor that determines whether group norms are closely adhered to by group members is the group's cohesiveness.[12]

Group Cohesiveness

Cohesiveness basically refers to the degree of attraction that each member has for the group, or the stick togetherness of the group. Cohesiveness is important for the group because the greater the cohesiveness of the group, the more likely it will be that members will pursue the group norms and not individual norms. That is, the greater the cohesiveness, the greater the individual members will conform to group norms.

One variable affecting the cohesiveness of the group is its size. As discussed earlier, individuals in the group must interact in order for the group to exist. This interaction requirement limits the size of the group.[13] In other words, group cohesiveness decreases as the size of the group increases.[14] It is impossible to specify an upper limit on the size of informal work groups. However, the interaction requirement generally limits the size of the group to a maximum of 15 to 20 members. Generally, if the informal work group becomes larger than 20, subgroups begin to form.

The success and status of the group also play an important part in group cohesiveness. The more successful a group is in achieving its goals, the more cohesive the group becomes. The relationship is circular in that success breeds cohesiveness and cohesiveness in turn breeds more success. Numerous factors contribute to the status of work groups. Some of these include: the skill required in performing the job (skilled versus semiskilled jobs); opportunities for promotion out of the group (some groups develop reputations such as "the way to the top is through marketing"); the degree of supervision required (groups requiring less supervision have a higher status); and the type of work that is performed by the group (the more dangerous or more financially rewarding the work, the greater the status). Several other factors can also contribute to the status of the group. However, the important point is that groups that are successful in achieving their goals and that have higher status generally exhibit more cohesiveness.

[11] J. Richard Hackman, "Group Influences on Individuals," in *Handbook of Industrial and Organizational Psychology*, ed. Marvin D. Dunnette (Skokie, Ill.: Rand McNally, 1976), p. 1517.

[12] Ibid.

[13] Stanley E. Seashore, *Group Cohesiveness in the Industrial Work Group* (Ann Arbor: University of Michigan Institute for Social Research, 1954), pp. 90–95.

[14] N. Trichy, "An Analysis of Clique Formation and Structure in Organizations," *Administrative Science Quarterly* 18, no. 2 (1973), pp. 194–208.

Outside pressures, stability of membership, ability to communicate, and degree of physical isolation are also variables that can influence group cohesiveness. For instance, if demands or requests made by management are perceived as threats by informal work groups, group cohesiveness increases to offset the perceived threat. Higher cohesion results from stable membership in the group because the group members have a longer time to know each other, to learn the norms of the group, and to learn how to behave according to group norms. Production lines and office layouts designed to inhibit conversation can reduce group cohesiveness.[15] Furthermore, coal miners in their geographical isolation from the rest of the community have demonstrated in numerous strikes the cohesiveness that can result from the physical isolation from other groups.

Stanley Seashore studied the relationship between group cohesiveness and worker attitudes and production in a large, heavy-equipment manufacturing company.[16] Seashore found that workers in highly cohesive groups had less anxiety about job-related matters. In other words, workers in highly cohesive groups felt less pressure on the job. Seashore also found that highly cohesive groups are more likely to have output records that diverge in either direction from plant averages. Thus, if the goals of a highly cohesive group are compatible with the organization's productivity goals, then the group's output will be above average. However, if the group's goals are incompatible with the organization's performance goals, the group's output will be below average.

Other variables can also influence the degree of group cohesiveness. Figure 12–3 summarizes many of the conditions that can either increase or decrease group cohesiveness.

Group Leadership

Informal group leadership has been the subject of numerous research studies. Several of the studies on both informal and formal work group leadership are examined in much greater detail in Chapter 14. However, two of the general conclusions that have been reached on informal group leadership are:

1. The group selects as its leader the individual the group perceives to have the most competence in helping the group achieve its objectives.[17]
2. The group selects as its leader the individual with strong com-

[15] M. Krain, "Communication as a Process of Dyadic Organization and Development," *The Journal of Communication*, December 1973, pp. 392–408.

[16] Seashore, *Group Cohesiveness*, pp. 90–95.

[17] E. P. Hollander, "Style, Structure and Setting in Organizational Leadership," *Administrative Science Quarterly* 16 (1971), pp. 1–8.

FIGURE 12–3
Conditions for Increasing or Decreasing Cohesiveness

Increasing cohesiveness	*Decreasing cohesiveness*
1. Smaller groups tend to have more cohesiveness. When the group becomes too large (generally larger than 20), subgroups begin to form.	1. When interpersonal conflict results from members' disagreements over ways to achieve group goals or solve group problems, the attractiveness of the group decreases. Members of highly cohesive groups may often have disagreements but they try to eliminate the disagreements quickly.
2. The success and prestige of the group increases cohesiveness. Groups that are successful in achieving their goals are more cohesive. Higher status groups are also more cohesive.	2. If participation in the group results in unpleasant experiences for an individual, the attractiveness of the group decreases. When group activities result in embarrassment for an individual, the individual's attraction is usually reduced.
3. Physical isolation from other groups increases group cohesiveness.	3. If membership in the group places limits on the individuals' participation in other activities or groups, cohesiveness may be lowered. In other words, if the group restricts the freedom of its members' activities outside the group, the attraction of the group may decrease.
4. The group becomes more attractive for individuals who gain prestige or status within the group.	4. If conditions exist in the group which prevent or restrict effective communication, cohesiveness decreases. Reduced communication may result if some members are too dominating or if some members are unpleasant or obnoxious in their communication behavior.
5. Cohesiveness is higher under conditions where group members are in cooperative relationships than under conditions where there is internal competition.	5. The cohesiveness may be reduced if group members feel the activities involve too great a personal risk. The risks could be physical danger or psychological threats. Risk could involve the group engaging in activities which individuals feel may be illegal or immoral. Risk could involve group actions in an organization that the individual feels might result in getting disciplined or fired.

FIGURE 12–3 (*concluded*)

Increasing cohesiveness	*Decreasing cohesiveness*
6. When group members can fulfill more needs through participating in the group, the attraction of the group increases.	6. If the evaluation of the group by outsiders who are respected becomes negative, this can result in the group becoming unattractive to its members.
7. When the group is attacked from the outside, the cohesiveness usually increases as the members deal with the external threat. When the group shares a common fate as a result of external attack, the reaction is usually to focus the group's resources on protecting the group. The response to an outside threat is reflected in the statement, "United we stand, divided we fall."	

Source: Adapted from: Dan L. Costley and Ralph Todd, *Human Relations in Organizations* (St. Paul, Minn.: West Publishing, 1978), pp. 229–30. Copyright © 1978 by West Publishing Company. Reprinted by permission. All rights reserved.

munication skills especially in the areas of setting objectives for the group, giving direction, and summarizing information for the group.[18]

It has also been suggested that many informal work groups may require two leaders—a task and social leader.[19] The task leader pushes the group toward the accomplishment of its objectives; while the social leader is primarily concerned with maintaining harmony within the group.

Task & Social Leader

CONFORMITY AND INFORMAL WORK GROUPS

The earlier sections of this chapter were designed to give an understanding of the nature of informal work groups in organizations. The purpose of this section is to examine the role of informal work groups in obtaining conformity of individuals to group norms.

[18] Beatrice Schultz, "Characteristics of Emergent Leaders of Continuing Problem-Solving Groups," *Journal of Psychology* 88 (1974), pp. 167–73; and Beatrice Schultz "Predicting Emergent Leaders, an Exploratory Study of the Salience of Communicative Functions," *Small Group Behavior,* February 1978, pp. 109–14.

[19] G. H. Lewis, "Role Differentiation," *American Sociological Review* 37 (1972), pp. 424–34.

MANAGEMENT IN PRACTICE

Savings at Hatfield Are the Real McCoy

Getting everybody into the act has always been important in cost reduction. It's absolutely vital in industry today—and that's just what the Hatfield Wire & Cable Division of Continental Copper & Steel Industries, Inc. has accomplished. Cranked up two years ago, the firm's cost improvement program has these features:

Departmental teams that include just about all nonunion employees at Cranford, N.J. HQ and the operating plants.

Individual and team goals, against which progress is regularly monitored.

Authentication of savings claims, by engineering and financial executives.

A variety of incentives and rewards for real "go-getters."

The program is run by a three-man cost improvement council. One of the three is director of purchasing Ron Watson. "This isn't just a give-away program for employees," Watson stresses. "Ordinary, routine performance doesn't qualify as a true saving toward individual or team goals. We are trying to motivate our people to go above and beyond normal duties. The awards are to assure recognition for extra performance."

An imaginative approach to a negotiation, for example, recently qualified as a saving for buyer Richie Jannuzzi and for the purchasing team—which, along with other key functions, has carried out significant improvement goals. Extraordinary efforts in their particular fields are likewise credited to others in the program. There are about 180 employees in the effort, divided into 31 teams ranging in members from 3 to 12, and each led by a team captain.

Everybody shares. "One of the program's biggest pluses," says Watson, "is that the credit for a saving can be shared not only among one team's members, but among several teams. That makes for healthy cooperation. Suppose purchasing spots a chance to substitute an equivalent material. We'll share the saving with the chemist who makes tests or anyone else involved in functional studies. Other teams will share their ideas' savings with us as appropriate."

The savings report form on which individuals outline their claims has a section in the lower right corner where credit is apportioned. Say a saving claimed was $10,000. The divvying-up might find six or eight people, from two or three teams, listed in varying amounts that total $10,000.

Team captains break out the amounts credited to each of their team members, depending on creativity involved in coming up with the idea and doggedness in following through on it. They also negotiate the team-to-team sharing with one another, calling on the cost improvement council to mediate if necessary.

Source: Somerby Dowst, *Purchasing,* July 24, 1980, p. 71. Reprint from *Purchasing* Magazine.

Conformity refers to the degree to which the members of a group accept and abide by the norms of the group. Conformity in one situation might be viewed as deviant behavior in another situation; therefore, conformity is situationally determined. Probably the most important variable in the situation is the individual's relationships with other people and their relationships with each other. Thus, the group defines conformity for any given situation.

Knowing that the group defines conformity does not offer much help to the practicing manager. The manager needs to know how the group maintains conformity and the effect it has on the individual in the group. The following sections explore these concerns.

Group Pressures on the Individual

Informal work groups seek to control the behavior of their members for many reasons. One reason the group desires uniform, consistent behavior from each individual member is so that members can predict with reasonable certainty how the individual members will behave. This certainty is necessary in order to achieve some degree of coordination in working toward the group's goals. On the other hand, groups are organizations in and of themselves, and as a result, conformity is often required in order to maintain the group. Individualistic behavior among group members can threaten the survival of the group by causing internal dissension.[20] Individual members tend to conform to group norms under the following conditions:

1. When the norm is congruent with the personal attitudes, beliefs, and behavioral predispositions of the members.
2. When the norm is inconsistent with the personal attitudes, beliefs, or behavioral predispositions, but strong pressures to comply are exerted by the group and the rewards of complying are valued or the sanctions imposed for noncompliance are devalued.[21]

One study on the influence of group pressures on individuals placed college students in groups ranging in size from seven to nine people.[22] The members of the groups were told that they would be comparing lengths of lines on white cards. Figure 12–4 illustrates the cards and lines. The individuals in the study were

---

[20] J. Davis, "Group Decision and Social Interaction," *Psychological Review* 80 (1973), pp. 97–125.

[21] Hackman, "Group Influences," p. 1503.

[22] Solomon Asch, "Opinions and Social Pressure," *Scientific American*, November 1955, pp. 31–34.

FIGURE 12–4
Cards in Asch Experiment

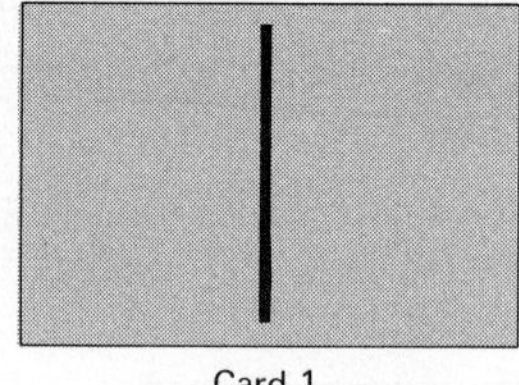
Card 1

Card 2

then asked to pick the line on the second card that was identical in length to the line on the first card.

In the experiment, all but one member of each group were told to pick one of the two wrong lines on card 2. In addition, the uninformed member of the group was positioned so that this person was always one of the last individuals to respond. Under ordinary circumstances individuals make mistakes on the line selection less than 1 percent of the time. However, in this experiment, the uninformed member made the wrong selection in 36.8 percent of the trials.

The study further showed that when an uninformed member was confronted with only a single individual who contradicted the choice, the uniformed member continued to answer correctly in almost all trials. When the opposition was increased by two, incorrect responses increased to 31.8 percent.

The experiment demonstrated that the group's behavior affected the behavior of the individual members; although some individuals remained independent in their judgments, others acquiesced on almost every judgment. Overall group pressure caused individuals to make incorrect judgments in over one third of the cases. The experiment also showed that the more members that disagreed with the individual the more likely the individual was to succumb to the judgment of the group.

In the late 1940s, Lester Coch and John R. P. French conducted studies at a textile firm, Harwood Manufacturing Company, in Marion, Virginia. Figure 12–5 illustrates a major finding of their study. In this case, a woman textile worker started to exceed the group norm of 50 units per day. On the 13th day, the group exerted pressure on the woman, and thus, the woman's output was quickly reduced to conform with the group norm. On the 20th day, the group was disbanded by moving all group members, except the woman, to other jobs. Once again, her production, quickly climbed to almost double the group norm.

FIGURE 12–5
Effect of Group Norms on Member Productivity

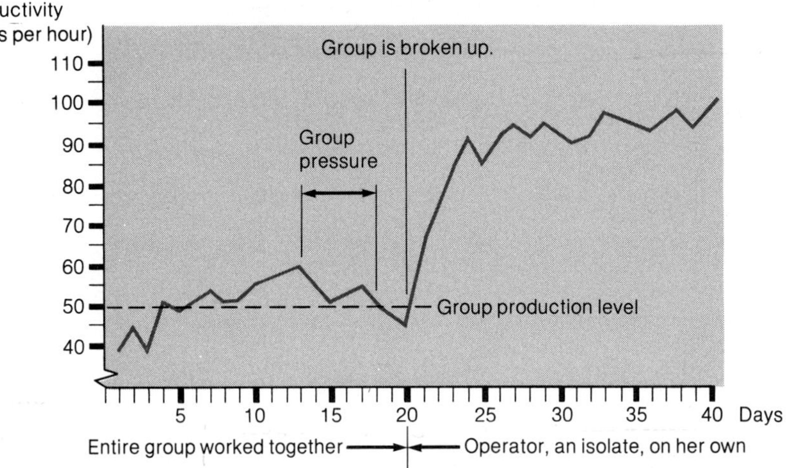

Source: Lester Coch and J. R. P. French, Jr., "Overcoming Resistance to Change," *Human Relations*, 1948, pp. 519–20.

Idiosyncrasy Credit

While evidence of conformity is abundant in all group situations, there are also those members who deviate from group norms and are allowed to do so by group members. Certain members who have made or are making significant contributions to the group's goals are allowed to take certain liberties within the group. The phenonmenon is called idiosyncrasy credit.[23]

People who contribute a great deal to the group also play a major role in developing group norms. Consequently, the group's norms largely reflect the attitudes of the major givers. This means that those who accumulate the most idiosyncrasy credit do not have to use it because the group norms largely reflect their own attitudes. Therefore, people who make large contributions to the group are allowed to deviate from the group norms, but they are not likely to do so because of the similarity between their norms and group norms. Conversely, those members who make little or no contribution to the group must learn to conform to norms which they had little or no part in establishing. Conformity, therefore, may be more difficult and more rigorously demanded from these members.

[23] E. P. Hollander, "Conformity, Status, and Idiosyncrasy Credit," *Psychological Review* 65 (1958), pp. 117–27.

FIGURE 12–6
Potential Benefits from Informal Work Groups

1. Informal work groups blend with the formal organization to make a workable system for getting work done.
2. Informal work groups lighten the workload for the formal manager and fill in some of the gaps in the manager's abilities.
3. Informal work groups provide satisfaction and stability to the organization.
4. Informal work groups provide a useful channel of communication in the organization.
5. The presence of informal work groups encourages managers to plan and act more carefully than they would otherwise.

Source: Keith Davis, *Human Behavior at Work*, 5th ed. (New York: McGraw-Hill, 1978), pp. 275–76.

MANAGEMENT AND INFORMAL WORK GROUPS

As this chapter has discussed, much individual behavior is influenced by the informal work groups to which individuals belong. Unfortunately, many managers view informal work groups as being only negative in their orientation toward organizational objectives. However, as summarized in Figure 12–6, informal work groups can be beneficial to management.

In order to realize the potential benefits outlined in Figure 12–6, the manager must be aware of the impact of informal work groups on individuals. Figure 12–7 indicates several key factors the manager should keep in mind in dealing with informal work groups.

CREATIVITY IN ORGANIZATIONS

Conformity is necessary if an organization is to function efficiently. However, too much conformity can result in little or no innovation which can have a detrimental effect on the organization. Thus, both conformity and creativity are required in an organization. Providing an environment that fosters a healthy mix of conformity and creativity is difficult at best. But the manager who is cognizant of the components of both characteristics is better able to recognize the trade-off involved and better prepared to successfully manage this trade-off. The following sections of this chapter describe the creative process and some aids for improving creativity in organizations.

The Creative Process

Creativity is the total thinking process involved in the production of an idea, concept, innovation, or discovery that is new, original,

FIGURE 12–7
Key Factors in Dealing with Informal Work Groups

1. Participation in groups is a basic source of social need satisfaction for employees.
2. Informal groups try to protect their members and provide security. They will try to protect members from perceived threats from management.
3. Groups develop communication systems to provide information that members want. If management does not provide the information employees want, the informal group will try to obtain it.
4. Both formal and informal groups obtain status and prestige within an organization. Groups may use their status and prestige as a power base to influence others in the organization.
5. Groups develop and enforce norms for the behavior of members. The group norms may be supportive of management or may work against management objectives.
6. The more cohesive a group is, the more control it has over the behavior of its members. The highly cohesive group can produce high achievement of organizational goals. But it can work just as effectively against organizational objectives when the group opposes management.
7. Both formal and informal groups within an organization establish roles that affect the activities and responsibilities of members. Accepting role responsibilities in an informal group may require that an individual violate the role expectations of management.

Source: Dan L. Costley and Ralph Todd, *Human Relations in Organizations* (St. Paul, Minn.: West Publishing, 1978), pp. 234–35.

useful or satisfying to its creator or someone else. Normally, the creative process impacts management through solving problems. Creative problem solving involves bringing about useful changes within the organization by introducing and putting into action new elements or new combinations of existing elements.

The creative process generally takes place in four basic stages: (1) preparation, (2) incubation, (3) illumination, and (4) verification.[24] Preparation involves the hard, conscious, systematic, and often fruitless examination of a problem or area of study. The preparation stage involves getting ready to solve a particular problem. Preparation requires not only being aware of a problem area but also requires study of the problem area. The stage during which the individual or group is not consciously thinking about the problem forms the incubation stage. Unconscious mental exploration of the problem occurs during incubation. The illumination stage occurs with the appearance of the solution and is generally a very sudden occurrence. Finally, the verification stage of creativity involves testing and refining the solution.

[24] Graham Walles, *The Art of Thought* (New York: Harcourt Brace Jovanovich, 1976), p. 80.

For most people, the above four stages overlap each other as different problems are explored. A business executive reading the morning mail may be accumulating knowledge in preparation for solving one problem, may be at the incubation stage on another problem, and may also be verifying another problem.

Aids in Creativity

Several techniques exist which can serve as aids for creative problem solving in organizations. Three of these techniques are brainstorming, the Gordon technique, and the nominal grouping technique.

Alex F. Osborn developed brainstorming as an aid to producing creative ideas for an advertising agency. Basically, brainstorming involves presenting a problem to a group of people and allowing them to present ideas for solution to the problem. Brainstorming is intended to produce a large quantity of ideas or alternatives and generally follows a definite procedure. In the first phase, members of the group are asked to present ideas off the top of their heads. The group is told that quantity is desired and that they should not be concerned about the quality of their ideas. Four basic rules followed in the first phase are:

1. No criticism of ideas is allowed.
2. No praise of ideas is allowed.
3. No questions or discussion of ideas is allowed.
4. Combinations and improvements on ideas that have been previously presented are encouraged.

During the second phase, the merits of each idea are reviewed. This review often leads to additional alternativws. Furthermore, alternatives with little merit are eliminated in this phase. In the third phase, one of the alternatives is selected. Frequently, the alternative is selected through group consensus.

William J. J. Gordon developed a technique to spur creative problem solving for the consulting firm of Arthur D. Little, Inc. The technique was initially devised to get creative ideas on technical problems. The Gordon technique differs from brainstorming in that no one but the group leader knows the exact nature of the real problem under consideration. A key word is used to describe a problem area and the group then explores the problem area using the key word as a starting point. For instance, the word *conservation* might be used to start a discussion on energy conservation. The key word would direct discussion and suggestions on conservation in other areas in addition to the one under question. Proponents of the Gordon technique argue that it gives better quality ideas because the discussion is not limited to one particular area as with the brainstorming technique. Some rules and suggestions for conducting sessions using brainstorming and the Gordon technique are summarized in Figure 12–8.

The nominal grouping technique is a highly structured technique designed to keep personal interactions at a minimum and involves the following steps:

1. Listing: each group member, working alone, develops a list of possible solutions to a group task.
2. Recording: each member offers an item from his or her list in a round-robin manner to the group leader who records the ideas on a master list in full view of the group. The round-robin process continues until all items on each person's list have been recorded by the leader.
3. Voting: each member records on an individual ballot his or her preference with respect to the priority or importance of the items appearing on the master list.

No verbal interaction is allowed during the first three steps. The results of the voting are tabulated and scores are posted on the master list.

4. Discussion: each item is then discussed for clarification as well as evaluation.
5. Final voting: each member votes a second time with respect to the priority of the ideas generated.[25]

The nominal grouping technique has been found to generate more unique ideas than brainstorming. However, both the nominal grouping technique and brainstorming suffer from the problem that occurs when the participants are so close to the problem that they are blind to what appear to be obvious solutions.[26]

Much controversy exists regarding the effectiveness of brainstorming, the Gordon technique, and the nominal grouping technique.[27] None of the techniques is a complete answer for creative problem solving. Each is merely a tool to serve a limited purpose. Probably the best suggestion for building a creative organization is to (1) build an effective work team using the ideas discussed in this chapter, (2) recognize the importance of the informal work group and manage it properly, and (3) selectively use the aids to creativity discussed in this chapter.

[25] Gene E. Burton, Dev S. Pathak, and David B. Burton, "The Gordon Effect in Nominal Grouping," *University of Michigan Business Review*, July 1978, p. 8.

[26] Ibid., p. 7.

[27] T. Richards and B. L. Freedman, "Procedures for Managers in Idea- Deficient Situations: An Examination of Brainstorming Approaches," *Journal of Management Studies*, February 1978, pp. 43–55.

FIGURE 12–8

Rules and Suggestions for Brainstorming and the Gordon Technique

Osborn brainstorming

Rules:

1. Judicial thinking or evaluation is ruled out.
2. Freewheeling is welcomed.
3. Quantity is wanted.
4. Combinations and improvements are sought.

Suggestions for the Osborn technique:

1. Length: 40 minutes to one hour, sessions of 10 to 15 minutes can be effective if time is short.
2. Do not reveal the problem before the session. An information sheet or suggested reference material on a selected subject should be used if prior knowledge of a general field is needed.
3. Problem should be clearly stated and not too broad.
4. Use a small conference table which allows people to communicate with each other easily.
5. If a product is being discussed, samples may be useful as a point of reference.

Gordon technique

Rules:

1. Only the group leader knows the problem.
2. Free association is used.
3. Subject for discussion must be carefully chosen.

Suggestions for the Gordon technique:

1. Length of session: two to three hours are necessary.
2. Group leader must be exceptionally gifted and thoroughly trained in the use of the technique.

General suggestions that apply to both techniques

1. Selection of personnel: a group from diverse backgrounds helps. Try to get a balance of highly active and quiet members.
2. Mixed groups of men and women are often more effective, especially for consumer problems.
3. Although physical atmosphere is not too important, a relaxed pleasant atmosphere is desirable.
4. Group size: groups of from 4 to 12 can be effective. We recommend 6 to 9.
5. Newcomers may be introduced without disturbing the group, but they must be properly briefed in the theory of creative thinking and the use of the particular technique.
6. A secretary or recording machine should be used to record the ideas produced. Otherwise they may not be remembered later. Gordon always uses a blackboard so that ideas can be visualized.
7. Hold sessions in the morning if people are going to continue to work on the same problem after the session has ended; otherwise hold them late in the afternoon. (The excitement of a session continues for several hours after it is completed, and can affect an employee's routine tasks.)
8. Usually it is advisable not to have people from widely differing ranks within the organization in the same session.

Source: Charles S. Whiting, "Operational Techniques of Creative Thinking," *S.A.M. Advanced Management Journal*, October 1955, p. 26.

SUMMARY

Small size, physical and psychological awareness, and interaction are all characteristics of groups. Sociologists have further refined the definition of groups by distinguishing between a small group and a primary group. A small group meets all of the requirements given above. A primary group in addition to meeting the above requirements must also have feelings of loyalty, comradeship, and a common sense of values among its members. Both types of groups exist within organizations.

The term *work groups* is used to describe groups in organizations. Both formal and informal work groups exist in organizations. Formal work groups result primarily from the organizing function of management. Team building is a process that involves developing an awareness on the part of the work group of those conditions that keep the group from functioning effectively and then requires the work group to take those actions that will eliminate those conditions. Overlapping the formal work groups in organizations are informal work groups.

Informal work groups form for many reasons. Some of these reasons include mutual interests, friendships, the need to fulfill social needs, the physical work conditions, technology, and management practices.

Once informal work groups are formed they possess several factors which seem to be common to all informal work groups. Some of these factors analyzed in this chapter were group norms, group cohesiveness, and group leadership. A group norm is an agreement among the members of the group concerning how the members should behave. Group cohesiveness refers to the degree of attraction that each member has for the group. Variables that affect group cohesiveness are size, success and status of the group, outside pressures, stable membership, ability to communicate, and degree of physical isolation from other groups.

Conformity refers to the degree to which the members of a group accept and abide by the norms of the group. Individual members tend to conform to group norms when the norm is congruent with the personal attitudes, beliefs, and behavioral predispositions of the members. Individual members also tend to conform even if the group norm is inconsistent with their personal attitudes, beliefs, and behavioral predispositions, when strong pressures to comply are applied by the group and the sanctions imposed for noncompliance are devalued. While conformity is necessary to some degree in all organizations, it must not be at the expense of eliminating creativity. A balance of conformity and creativity is required in organizations, and management must provide an environment that fosters a healthy mix.

Creativity is the total thinking process involved in the production of an idea, concept, innovation, or discovery that is new, original, useful or satisfying to its creator or someone else. The creative process generally takes place in four stages: (1) preparation, (2) incubation, (3) illumination, and (4) verification. Brainstorming, the Gordon technique, and the nominal grouping technique were described as aids for fostering creativity in organizations.

REVIEW QUESTIONS

1. Define the following terms:
   a. Group.
   b. Small group.
   c. Primary group.
   d. Work group.
2. What is team building?
3. Outline some of the reasons why informal work groups exist in organizations.
4. What is a group norm?
5. What is group cohesiveness?
6. Describe some of the variables that affect the cohesiveness of a group.
7. What is conformity?
8. Describe the results of two studies dealing with the influence of groups on individual behavior.
9. What is idiosyncrasy credit?
10. What is creativity? Describe the creative process.
11. Describe the following aids to creativity:
    a. Brainstorming.
    b. Gordon technique.
    c. Nominal grouping technique.

DISCUSSION QUESTIONS

1. Do you think it is possible to eliminate entirely the need for informal work groups?
2. Discuss the following statement: "Goals of informal work groups are never congruent with the goals of the formal organization."
3. Some employees are described as "marching to the beat of a different drummer." In light of the discussion in this chapter, what does this statement mean to you?
4. "Creativity is born in an individual and cannot be developed." Do you agree?

SELECTED READINGS

Baker, H. K. "How and Whys of Team Building." *Personnel Journal,* June 1979, pp. 367–70.

Blau, J. R., and W. McKinley. "Ideas, Complexity, and Innovation." *Administrative Science Quarterly,* June 1979, pp. 200–19.

Bradley, Patricia Hayes. "Pressure for Uniformity: An Experimental Study of Deviate Responses in Group Discussions of Policy." *Small Group Behavior,* February 1978, pp. 149–60.

Burton, G. E. "Group Processes: Key to More Productive Management." *Management World,* May 1981, pp. 12–15.

Burton, G. E.; Dev S. Pathek; and David B. Burton. "The Gordon Effect in Nominal Grouping." *University of Michigan Business Review,* July 1978, pp. 7–10.

Cummings, T. G. "Self-Regulating Work Groups: A Socio-Technical Synthesis." *Academy of Management Review,* July 1978, pp. 625–34.

Dyer, William G. *Team Building: Issues and Alternatives.* Reading, Mass.: Addison-Wesley Publishing, 1977.

Fisher, M. S. "Work Teams: A Case Study." *Personnel Journal,* January 1981, pp. 42–45.

Glover, John A., and Terry Chambers. "The Creative Production of the Group: Effects of Small Group Structure." *Small Group Behavior,* August 1978, pp. 387–92.

Gorman, R. H., and H. K. Baker. "Brainstorming Your Way to Problem Solving Ideas." *Personnel Journal,* August 1978, pp. 438–440.

Hayes, J. L. "Creativity and the Group Effort." *Management Review,* May 1979, pp. 2–3.

Nadler, D. A. "Effects of Feedback on Task Group Behavior: A Review of the Experimental Research." *Organizational Behavior and Human Performance,* June 1979, pp. 309–338.

Rabinowitz, Stuart E., and Muhyi A. Shakoar. "Person-Group Relations: A Conceptual Model in a Group Where Membership Is Sought." *Small Group Behavior,* August 1978, pp. 325–329.

Randsepp, E. "Nurturing Managerial Creativity." *Administrative Management,* October 1980, pp. 32–33.

Richards, T., and B. L. Freedman. "Procedures for Managers in Idea-Deficient Situations: An Examination of Brainstorming Approaches," *Journal of Management Studies,* February 1978, pp. 43–55.

Sherwood, John J., and Florence M. Haylman. "Individual versus Group Approaches to Decision Making." *Supervisory Management,* April 1978, pp. 2–9.

Stumpe, S. A.; R. D. Freedman; and D. E. Zand. "Judgmental Decisions: A Study of Interactions among Group Membership, Group Functioning, and the Decision Situation." *Academy of Management Journal,* December 1979, pp. 765–82.

Summers, Irvin, and Major David E. White. "Creativity Techniques: Toward Improvement of the Decision Process." *Academy of Management Review,* April 1976, pp. 99–107.

Willis, R. E. "Simulation of Multiple Selection Using Nominal Group Procedures." *Management Science,* February 1979, pp. 171–81.
Zander, Alvin F. *Groups at Work.* San Francisco: Jossey-Bass, 1977.

Case 12–1

Company man or one of the gang?

Recently Gary Brown was appointed as the supervisor of a group of machine operators in which he was formerly one of the rank and file. When he was selected for the job, the department head told him the former supervisor was being transferred because he could not get sufficient work out of the group. He said also that the reason Gary was selected was because he appeared to be a natural leader, that he was close to the group, and that he knew the tricks they were practicing in order to restrict production. He told Gary that he believed he could lick the problem and that he would stand behind him.

He was right about Gary knowing the tricks. When he was one of the gang, not only did he try to hamper the supervisor, but he was the ringleader in trying to make life miserable for him. None of them had anything personally against the supervisor, but all of them considered it a game to pit their wits against his. There was a set of signals to inform the boys that the supervisor was coming so that everyone would appear to be working hard. As soon as he left the immediate vicinity, everyone would take it easy. Also the operators would act dumb to get the supervisor to go into lengthy explanations and demonstrations while they stood around. They complained constantly and without justification about the materials and the equipment.

At lunchtime the boys would ridicule the company, tell the latest fast one they had pulled on the supervisor, and plan new ways to harass him. All this seemed to be a great joke. Gary and the rest of the boys had a lot of fun at the expense of the supervisor and the company.

Now that Gary has joined the ranks of management, it is not so funny. He is determined to use his managerial position and his knowledge to win the group over to working for the company instead of against it. Gary knows that, if this can be done, he will have a topnotch group. The operators know their stuff, have a very good team spirit, and if they would use their brains and efforts constructively, they could turn out above-average production.

Gary's former buddies are rather cool to him now, but this seems to be natural, and he believes he can overcome this in a short time. What has him concerned is that Joe James is taking over his old post as ringleader of the group, and the group is trying to play the same tricks on him as they did on the former supervisor.

1. Did the company make a good selection in Gary?
2. What suggestions would you make to Gary?
3. Are work groups necessarily opposed to working toward organizational goals? Explain.

Case 12–2

Talkative Mike

Mike was an exceptionally friendly and talkative man to the extent that he bothered his supervisor by frequently stopping his whole work crew to tell them a joke or story. It didn't seem to bother Mike that it was during working hours or that somebody other than his crew might be watching. He just enjoyed telling stories and being the center of attention. The trouble was that the rest of the crew enjoyed him too.

The supervisor had just recently taken over the department and he was determined to straighten the crew out. He felt that he would have no problem motivating Mike, since he was such a friendly person. The crew was on a group incentive, and the supervisor felt that he could get them to see how much they were losing by standing around and talking. But there was no question about it, Mike was the informal leader of the crew, and they followed him just as surely as if he was the plant manager.

Mike's crew produced extremely well. When they worked, and that was most of the time, they couldn't be equaled in their output. But the frequent nonscheduled breaks for storytelling did bother the supervisor. Not only could their nonproductive time be converted into badly needed production but also they wouldn't be setting a poor example for the other crews and the rest of the department.

The supervisor called Mike in and discussed the situation with him. But the primary emphasis was on the fact that Mike's crew could be making more money by better using their idle time. Mike's contention was, "What good is money if you can't enjoy it. You sweat your whole life away to rake in money and then all you've got is a lot of miserable years and no way of knowing how to enjoy what's left. Life's too short to spend every minute of it trying to make more money." This discussion ended with Mike stating that the group would quiet down, and if their production didn't keep up to let him know.

Things did improve for a while, but within a week or so the old pattern was right back where it had been so the supervisor arranged to talk with the other members of the crew individually. Their reactions were the same as Mike's, and as before, some improvements were noted at first. Then they gradually reverted back to their old habits.

1. Do you agree with Mike and his group?
2. Does the supervisor really have a complaint in light of the fact that Mike's group produces well above average?
3. If you were the supervisor what would you do next?

13 Managing Conflict, Change, and Stress

Objectives

1. To develop an understanding of the types of conflict that can occur in organizations.
2. To explore several possible methods of resolving conflict in organizations.
3. To present several methods for reducing resistance to change.
4. To discuss stress and methods of managing stress.

Chapter Outline

Glossary of Terms

Conflict Refers to overt behavior arising out of a process in which one party seeks the advancement of its own interests in its relationship with others.

Dissonance A feeling of disharmony within an individual.

Frustration A form of intrapersonal conflict which results when a drive or motive is blocked before the goal is reached.

Goal conflict A form of intrapersonal conflict which results when a goal that an individual is attempting to achieve has both positive and negative features or when two or more competing goals exist.

Interpersonal conflict A form of conflict between two or more individuals which can be caused by many factors.

Intrapersonal conflict A form of conflict which is internal to the individual and relates to the need-drive-goal motivational sequence.

Strategic conflict A form of conflict which usually results from the promotion of self-interests on the part of an individual or a group and is often deliberately planned.

Stress An interaction between a person and an environment which presents a demand threatening to exceed the person's capabilities and resources for meeting it, under conditions where the person expects a substantial difference in the rewards and costs resulting from meeting the demand versus not meeting it.

Structural conflict A form of conflict which exists as a result of the organizational structure and is relatively independent of the individuals occupying the roles within the organizational structure.

As conflict—difference—is here in the world, as we cannot avoid it, we should, I think, use it. Instead of condemning it, we should set it to work for us. Why not? What does the mechanical engineer do with friction? Of course his chief job is to eliminate friction, but it is true that he also capitalizes friction. The transmission of power by belts depends on friction between the belt and the pulley. The friction between the driving wheel of the locomotive and the track is necessary to haul the train. All polishing is done by friction. The music of the violin we get by friction. We left the savage state when we discovered fire by friction. We talk of the friction of mind on mind as a good thing. So in business, too, we have to know when to try to eliminate friction and when to try to capitalize it, when to see what work we can make it do.

*Mary Parker Follet**

Conflict in organizations is often assumed to be an unnatural and undesirable situation that is to be avoided at all costs. Conflict can lead to rigidity in the system in which it operates, can distort reality, and can debilitate the participants in the conflict situation.[1] Therefore, many organizations approach the management of conflict based on the following assumptions:

1. Conflict is avoidable.
2. Conflict is the result of personality problems within the organization.
3. Conflict produces inappropriate reactions by the persons involved.
4. Conflict creates a polarization of perception, sentiments, and behavior within the organization.[2]

Recent studies in the behavioral sciences have caused a reexamination of the assumptions concerning organizational conflict. These studies suggest that conflict is perfectly natural and should be expected to occur. The key point in the study of conflict, however, is not that it is natural or unavoidable, but that, as Mary Parker Follet states in the introduction to this chapter, management must know when to eliminate conflict and when to build on it.

* Mary Parker Follett, "Constructive Conflict," in *Dynamic Administration,* ed. Henry C. Metcalf and L. Urwick (New York: Harper & Row, 1940), pp. 30–31.

[1] Richard E. Walton, *Interpersonal Peacemaking* (Reading, Mass.: Addison-Wesley Publishing, 1969), p. 5.

[2] Joe Kelly, *Organizational Behavior* (Homewood, Ill.: Richard D. Irwin and the Dorsey Press, 1969), p. 501. © 1969 by Richard D. Irwin, Inc., and the Dorsey Press.

WHAT IS CONFLICT?

Conflict refers to overt behavior arising out of a process in which one party seeks the advancement of its own interests in its relationship with others.[3] Conflict begins when one party perceives that a second party has frustrated, or is about to frustrate, some concern of the first party[4] In this definition, the parties involved denote social units in a conflict situation and can be referring to individuals, groups, organizations, or nations. In one survey, managers reported that they spend 20 percent of their time dealing with conflict and that their ability to manage conflict has become more increasingly important.[5]

Today's managers must accept the existence of conflict and realize that attempting to eliminate all conflict is a mistake. The general consensus today is that conflict itself is not undesirable but rather is a phenomenon that can have constructive or destructive effects. The favorableness of the conflict often depends on the particular participant's point of view; however, the results of a conflict should also be evaluated from the organization's point of view. For example, in a struggle between two people to gain a promotion, the winner will probably feel that the conflict was most worthwhile, while the loser will probably reach the opposite conclusion. However, the impact of the conflict on the organization must also be considered. If the conflict ends in the selection and promotion of the better person, then from the organization's viewpoint the effect is good. If, as a result of the competition, the parties have produced more or made improvements within their areas of responsibility, then the effect is also positive. At the same time, there may be several destructive effects which offset the good. The overall work of the organization may have suffered during the conflict. The loser may resign or withdraw as a result of personal failure. The struggle may turn into continuous conflict and inhibit the work of the organization. In extreme cases, the health of one or both of the participants may be adversely affected.

The destructive effects of conflict are generally obvious. The constructive effects may be more subtle. It is essential that the manager be able to recognize these constructive effects and to weigh their benefits against the costs. Some of the useful effects of conflict are:

---

[3] Stuart M. Schmidt and Thomas A. Kochan, "Conflict: Toward Conceptual Clarity," *Administrative Science Quarterly* 17 (1972) pp. 359–70.

[4] Kenneth Thomas, "Conflict and Conflict Management," in *Handbook of Industrial and Organizational Psychology*, ed. Marvin D. Dunnette (Skokie, Ill.: Rand McNally, 1976), p. 891.

[5] K. W. Thomas and W. H. Schmidt, "A Survey of Managerial Interests with Respect to Conflict," *Academy of Management Journal* June 1976, pp. 315–18.

1. Conflict energizes people. Even if not all of the resulting activity is constructive, it at least wakes people up and gets them moving.
2. A structural or strategic conflict usually involves a search for a resolution of the underlying issue. In resolving the conflict, needed changes in the organizational system may be discovered and implemented.
3. Conflict is a form of communication, and the resolution of conflict may open up new and lasting channels.
4. Conflict often provides an outlet for pent-up tensions, resulting in catharsis. With the air cleaned, the participants can again concentrate on their primary responsibilities.
5. Conflict may actually be an educational experience in that the participants may become more aware and more understanding of their opponents' functions and the problems with which they must cope.[6]

The potential for conflict depends on how incompatible the objectives of the parties are, the extent to which the required resources to achieve the objectives are scarce and shared, and the degree of interdependence of task activities.[7] The potential for conflict is great at all levels of the organization. It has been suggested that the occurrence of conflict will become even greater in organizations in the future. This prediction is based on the belief that the objectives and values of employees are continually becoming more and more divergent from the objectives and values of owners and managers.[8]

PROGRESSIVE STAGES OF THE CONFLICT CYCLE

A manager must be aware of conflict's dynamic nature. Conflict does not usually appear suddenly. It passes through a series of progressive stages as tensions build. These stages of development are as follows.[9]

1. Latent conflict: at this stage the basic conditions for potential conflict exist but have not yet been recognized.

[6] Jane Templeton, "For Corporate Vigor, Plan a Fight Today," *Sales Management*, June 15, 1969, pp. 32–36. Dr. Templeton draws heavily upon George R. Bach and Peter Weyden, *The Ultimate Enemy* (New York: William Morrow, 1969). Also, Joseph A. Litterer, "Conflict in Organizations: A Re-Examination," *Academy of Management Journal*, September 1966, pp. 178–86.

[7] Schmidt and Kochan, "Conflict: Toward Conceptual Clarity," *Administrative Science Quarterly*, September 1972, pp. 359–70.

[8] Richard H. Viola, *Organizations in a Changing Society* (Philadelphia, Pa.: W. B. Saunders, 1977), p. 153.

[9] Louis Pondy, "Organizational Conflict: Concepts and Models," *Administrative Science Quarterly*, September 1967, pp. 296–320.

2. Perceived conflict: the cause of the conflict is recognized by one or both of the participants.
3. Felt conflict: tension is beginning to build between the participants, although no real struggle has yet begun.
4. Manifest conflict: the struggle is under way, and the behavior of the participants makes the existence of the conflict apparent to others who are not directly involved.
5. Conflict aftermath: the conflict has been ended by resolution or suppression. This establishes new conditions that will lead either to more effective cooperation or to a new conflict that may be more severe than the first.

Conflict does not necessarily pass through all of these stages. Furthermore, participants in a conflict may not be at the same stage simultaneously. One participant could be at the manifest stage of conflict while the other participant is at the perceived stage.

ANALYZING CONFLICT

Conflict can be analyzed from two basic perspectives. One approach analyzes conflict as a process internal to the individual (intrapersonal conflict). The other approach views conflict as a process that is external to the individual—individual versus individual, individual versus group, group versus group, organization versus organization, or any combination of these. External conflict can be categorized into three general types: structural, interpersonal, and strategic. The following sections examine intrapersonal, structural, interpersonal, and strategic conflict in more detail.

Intrapersonal Conflict

Intrapersonal conflict is internal to the individual and is probably the most difficult form of conflict to analyze. The existence of intrapersonal conflict in organizations has received increasingly greater attention in the 35 years since Elton Mayo concluded that organizational life removes all meaning from work.[10] Many authors have suggested that the objectives of organizational life are in direct conflict with the needs and goals of individual employees, causing them to become frustrated, alienated, and threatened. Chris Argyris contends that as individuals grow and mature, certain basic personal characteristics change.[11] Argyris

[10] Elton Mayo, *The Social Problems of an Industrial Civilization*, (Cambridge, Mass.: Harvard University Press, 1945).

[11] Chris Argyris, *Personality and Organization* (New York: Harper & Row, 1957).

FIGURE 13–1
Development Characteristics

Infancy characteristics	*Adult characteristics*
Passivity	Increased activity
Complete dependence on others	Relative independence
Erratic, casual, shallow interest	Longer, deeper, more consistent interests
Short time perspective	Long time perspective
Subordinate position in family	Equal or superordinate position in family
Lack of awareness of self	Awareness of self

contends that most individuals who are employed by organizations want to express adult characteristics; however, the basic principles of organization create an environment requiring infancy characteristics (see Figure 13–1). Such an environment assumes that concentrating effort on a limited field of endeavor increases quality and quantity of output. The basic principles most frequently criticized by Argyris are task specialization, chain of command, unity of direction, and span of management. If these principles are followed as defined, Argyris contends, individuals will be passive, dependent, short-time oriented, and will exhibit characteristics of children. Thus, Argyris postulates that there is a lack of congruity between the needs of healthy individuals and the demands of the organization (this theory has been labeled Argyris' incongruity model).

Frustration and conflict are some of the predicted results of this basic incongruity. Basically, intrapersonal conflict relates to the need-drive-goal motivational sequence (see Figure 13–2) that was discussed in Chapter 10.

Intrapersonal conflict can result when barriers exist between the drive and the goal. This situation often leads to frustration on the part of the individual involved. Intrapersonal conflict may also result when goals have both positive and negative aspects and when competing and conflicting goals exist. Figure 13–3 illustrates the motivational sequence and how intrapersonal conflict can occur.

Frustration Frustration results when a drive or motive is blocked before the goal is reached. Barriers can be either overt

FIGURE 13–2
The Motivation Sequence

Need ——► Drive or motives ——► Achievement of goals

FIGURE 13–3
Sources of Intrapersonal Conflict

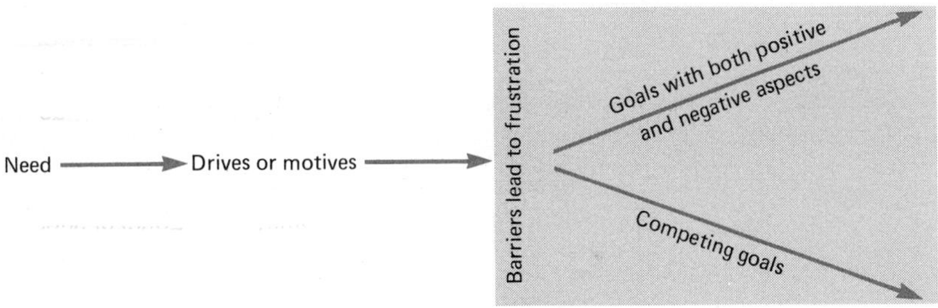

(rules and procedures) or covert (mental hang-ups). When a drive is blocked, people tend to react with defense mechanisms, which are behaviors used to cope with frustration. Figure 13–4 enumerates some typical examples of defense mechanisms.

The responses to frustration are varied and can be expressed as withdrawal behavior (higher absenteeism and turnover rates), aggression (sabotage and other destructive work performance), excessive drinking or drug abuse, and more subtle responses such as ulcers or heart trouble.

Goal conflict Goal conflict occurs when a goal has both positive and negative features, or when two or more competing goals exist. Basically, there are three forms of goal conflict. These are as follows:

1. Mutually exclusive positive goals. This type of goal conflict results when an individual is simultaneously motivated toward two or more positive, mutually exclusive goals. The decision a student makes in selecting an academic major is an example of this type of conflict. Business administration, law, and medicine may all have positive aspects, but all cannot be pursued simultaneously. Generally this form of conflict can be resolved by making a decision rather quickly, thereby eliminating the conflict.

2. Positive-negative goals. In this form of goal conflict, the individual attempts to achieve a goal that has both positive and negative effects. For example, in pursuing a top management position, individuals frequently must make personal sacrifices of their own time and time with their family. Thus, the goal of being a successful business leader has both positive and negative aspects.

3. Negative-negative goals. Here the individual attempts to avoid two or more negative, mutually exclusive goals. Under these circumstances, the individual may choose to abandon the situation and, therefore, not select either of the goals. An example of

FIGURE 13–4
Reactions to Frustrations

Adjustive reactions	*Psychological process*	*Illustration*
Compensation	Individual devotes himself to a pursuit with increased vigor to make up for some feeling of real or imagined inadequacy.	Zealous, hardworking president of the Twenty-Five Year Club who has never advanced very far in the company hierarchy.
Conversion	Emotional conflicts are expressed in muscular, sensory, or bodily symptoms of disability, malfunctioning, or pain.	A disabling headache keeping a staff member off the job, the day after a cherished project has been rejected.
Displacement	Redirecting pent-up emotions toward persons, ideas, or objects other than the primary source of the emotion.	Roughly rejecting a simple request from a subordinate after receiving a rebuff from the boss.
Fantasy	Daydreaming or other forms of imaginative activity provide an escape from reality and imagined satisfactions.	An employee's daydream of the day in the staff meeting when he corrects the boss' mistakes and is publicly acknowledged as the real leader of the group.
Negativism	Active or passive resistance, operating unconsciously.	The manager who, having been unsuccessful in getting out of a committee assignment, picks apart every suggestion that anyone makes in the meetings.
Rationalization	Justifying inconsistent or undesirable behavior, beliefs, statements and motivations by providing acceptable explanations for them.	Padding the expense account because "everybody does it."
Regression	Individual returns to an earlier and less mature level of adjustment in the face of frustration.	A manager having been blocked in some administrative pursuit busies himself with clerical duties or technical details, more appropriate for his subordinates.
Repression	Completely excluding from consciousness impulses, experiences, and feelings which are psychologically disturbing because they arouse a sense of guilt or anxiety.	A subordinate "forgetting" to tell his boss the circumstances of an embarrassing situation.
Resignation, apathy, and boredom	Breaking psychological contact with the environment, withholding any sense of emotional or personal involvement.	Employee who, receiving no reward, praise, or encouragement, no longer cares whether or not he does a good job.
Flight or withdrawal	Leaving the field in which frustration, anxiety, or conflict is experienced, either physically or psychologically.	The salesman's big order falls through and he takes the rest of the day off; constant rebuff or rejection by superiors and colleagues pushes an older worker toward being a loner and ignoring whatever friendly gestures are made.

Source: Timothy W. Costello and Sheldon S. Zalkind, *Psychology in Administration: A Research Orientation* (Englewood Cliffs, N.J.: Prentice-Hall, 1963), pp. 148–49.

this form of conflict exists when an individual dislikes his/her job, but the alternative of quitting and looking for another job may be even less attractive. The likely outcome in this situation is frustration.

Goal conflict forces the individual to make a decision. Decision making often creates a feeling of conflict within the individual. An individual experiencing such a feeling of disharmony, called dissonance, will always attempt to reduce it. Some methods used in reducing dissonance and, hence, goal conflict are summarized below:

> changing a behavioral element, changing an environmental cognitive element, and adding new cognitive elements. For example, suppose that a person owns a car that his friends call a "lemon." One way of reducing or eliminating dissonance would be to sell the car (changing a behavioral element). But perhaps he cannot find a buyer, or he must take a large financial loss. In this case, it might be preferable to try to convince his friends that the car is really a fine piece of machinery (changing an environmental cognitive element). Friends, however, are not always easily convinced; so perhaps he would fail there also. He might then seek favorable opinions of others regarding the quality of the car (adding new cognitive elements). Of course, it is not proposed that an individual is more prone to use one mode of reduction rather than another nor that he systematically tries all methods of dissonance reduction.[12]

Structural or Functional Conflict

Structural or functional conflict exists as a result of the organizational structure and is relatively independent of the individuals occupying the roles within the organizational structure. The marketing department and the production department in Figure 13–5, for example, may experience structural conflict. The mar-

FIGURE 13–5
Functional Organization Structure

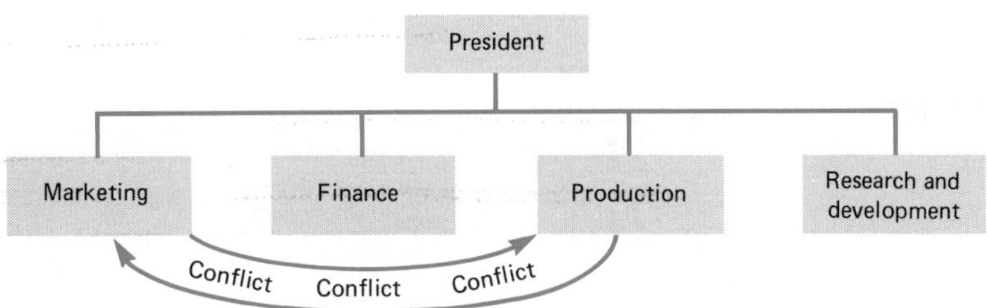

[12] Marvin E. Shaw and Phillip R. Costanzo, *Theories of Social Psychology* (New York: McGraw-Hill, 1970), p. 210.

keting department, being customer-oriented, may believe that some exceptions can and should be made in production for the sake of sales and the generation of future sales. The production department may view such exceptions as completely unreasonable and certainly not in the best interests of the organization. Hence a structural conflict occurs. Various types of structural conflict are discussed in the following sections.[13]

Goal segmentation and rewards. Each functional unit of an organization has different functional goals. These differences can be the basis for conflict which, when it emerges, may appear to result from personality clashes. The classical problem of inventory levels illustrates this dilemma. The marketing department would like to keep finished goods inventories high so that they can supply all of the customers' needs on short notice. The finance department would like to keep inventories low because of the cost incurred in maintaining these inventories.

Another illustration of this dilemma concerns the product line. Marketing would like to carry a product line composed of all shapes, sizes, and colors. Because of the problems involved in producing multiple shapes, sizes, and colors, the production department would prefer one basic product. The end result in either case is often a conflict between departments.

Richard Walton and John Dutton suggest that the reward system is the key to reducing this type of conflict.[14] They believe that a reward system that emphasizes the separate performance of the conflicting departments encourages the conflict. However, a reward system which remunerates the combined efforts of the conflicting departments reduces the conflict.

Mutual departmental dependence. When two departments or units within an organization are dependent on one another for the accomplishment of their respective goals, a potential for structural conflict is present. For instance, the marketing department's sales depend on the volume of production from the production department; at the same time the production department's quotas are dependent on the sales of the marketing department. This type of mutual dependence exists in many organizations and creates a potential for conflict.

Unequal departmental dependence. Frequently, organizational structures exist which cause departmental dependence to be unequal and foster conflict. In most organizations, for instance, staff groups are generally more dependent on line groups.

---

[13] Much of the material from this section is drawn from Richard E. Walton and John M. Dutton, "The Management of Interdepartmental Conflict: A Model and Review," *Administrative Science Quarterly*, March 1969, pp. 73–84.

[14] Ibid., p. 75.

The staff generally must understand the problem of the line, cooperate with the line, and sell their ideas to the line. However, the line does not have to reciprocate.

One tactic that is used in this form of conflict is an attempt by the more dependent unit to interfere with the work performance of the independent group. The more dependent group hopes that the independent group will cooperate once they realize how the dependent group can hinder their progress.

Functional unit and the environment. Functional units obviously perform different tasks and cope with different segments of the environment. Research has shown that the more the environments served by functional units differ, the greater the potential for conflict. Paul Lawrence and Jay Lorsch have developed four basic dimensions for describing these differences: (1) structure—this refers to the basic type of supervisory style employed; (2) environment orientation—this refers to the orientation of the unit to the outside world. (3) time-span orientation—this refers to the unit's planning time perspectives; (4) interpersonal orientation—this refers to the openness and permissiveness of interpersonal relationships.[15]

Lawrence and Lorsch applied their scheme to six organizations in the plastics industry and reported the results shown in Figure 13–6. The environmental differences outlined in Figure 13–6 are a primary cause of structural conflict. Coordinating the activities of departments such as applied research, sales, and production is made more difficult due to these differences.

Role dissatisfaction. Role dissatisfaction may also produce structural conflict. Professionals in an organization unit who receive little recognition and have limited opportunities for advancement may initiate conflict with other units. Purchasing agents in organizations often experience this form of conflict.

Role dissatisfaction and conflict often result when a group that has low perceived status sets standards for another group. For example, within academic institutions, administrators, who may be viewed by the faculty as having less status, frequently set standards of performance and make administrative decisions that affect the faculty.

Ambiguities. Ambiguities in the description of a particulr job can lead to structural conflict. When the credit or blame for the success or failure of a particular assignment cannot be determined between two departments, conflict is likely to result. For instance, improvements in production techniques require the ef-

---

[15] P. R. Lawrence and J. W. Lorsch, *Organization and Environment* (Boston: Harvard Business School Division of Research, 1967).

FIGURE 13–6
Differences Related to Environment of Departments

Departments	*Degree of formality in departmental structure*	*Orientation toward environment*	*Orientation toward time*	*Interpersonal orientation**
Fundamental research	Medium (4)	Techno-economic and scientific	Long	Task (2)
Applied research	Medium (3)	Techno-economic	Long	Relationship (3)
Sales	High (2)	Market	Short	Relationship (4)
Production	Highest (1)†	Techno-economic	Short	Task (1)

*Fiedler's questionnaire discussed in Chapter 14 was used in this analysis.

†Numbers refer to the relative ranking of the departments.

Source: P. R. Lawrence and J. W. Lorsch, "Differentiation and Integration in Complex Organizations," *Administrative Science Quarterly* 12 (1967), pp. 16–22.

forts of the engineering and production departments. However, after the improvements are made, credit is difficult to assign, and thus, conflict often results between these two departments.

Common resource dependence. When two organizational units are dependent on common but scarce resources, potential for conflict exists. This type of conflict often occurs when two departments are competing for computer time. Each department obviously feels that its projects are more important.

Communication barriers. Semantic differences can cause conflict. For instance, purchasing agents and engineers generally use different language to describe similar materials, which can lead to conflict.

Another cause of communication-related conflict occurs when a physical or organizational barrier to effective communication exists. Relationships between company headquarters and branch offices frequently suffer from this problem. The role of communication in the management process was discussed in depth in Chapter 11. Figure 13–7 provides a summary of types of structural conflict.

Interpersonal Conflict

Interpersonal conflict may result from conflicting personalities as well as from structural conflict and many other factors. Interpersonal conflicts most assuredly arise when barriers exist to communication between the involved parties. These barriers are often more difficult to overcome than the communication barriers discussed earlier as structural conflict. Communication barriers often

FIGURE 13–7
Summary of Types of Structural Conflict

Type	*Example*
Mutual departmental dependence	Marketing department's sales are dependent on the volume of production from the production department.
Unequal departmental dependence	Staff departments are generally more dependent on line departments.
Goal segmentation and rewards	Different inventory levels are desired by different functional departments.
Functional unit and environment	The environment faced by an applied research department and a sales department are different and can lead to conflict between these departments.
Role dissatisfaction	Professionals in an organization unit who receive little attention.
Ambiguities	When the credit or blame for the success or failure of a particular assignment cannot be determined between two departments.
Common resource dependence	Two departments competing for computer time.
Communications barriers	Semantic differences. Purchasing agents and engineers may use different language to describe similar materials, and conflict can result from those semantic differences.

give rise to what is called pseudoconflict.[16] Pseudoconflict results from an inability on the part of the participants in a group to reach a group decision because of their failure to exchange information, opinions, or ideas. Although the group may actually be in complete agreement, the situation has all the symptoms of a conflict caused by differences of opinion.

A second major cause of interpersonal conflict occurs when individuals are dissatisfied with their roles as compared to the roles of others. An employee may be compatible with his or her manager and fellow employees, but, when one of the employee's peers is promoted to a management job, the employee may no longer accept his or her position in relation to the former peer.

[16] E. Rhenman, L. Stromberg, and G. Westerlund, *Conflict and Cooperation in Business Organizations* (New York: Wiley Interscience, 1970), pp. 7–8.

Opposing personalities often cause conflict situations. Some people simply rub each other the wrong way. The extrovert and the introvert, the boisterous and the reserved, the optimist and the pessimist, the impulsive and the deliberate, are but a few possible combinations that might bother each other.

Finally there are special prejudices based on personal background or ethnic origin that cause conflict. This, of course, includes racial and religious conflicts, but also other, more subtle, prejudices. Possible examples include the college graduate versus the person without a college education, the married person versus the divorced person, or the experienced employee versus the new hiree.

Unlike structural conflicts in which both parties are actively involved, interpersonal conflicts may be one-sided, with one of the parties being totally unaware of the existing conflict.

Strategic Conflict

usually planned

Intrapersonal, structural, and interpersonal conflicts are usually not planned. They simply develop as a result of existing circumstances. Strategic conflicts are often deliberately instigated and are sometimes fought with an elaborate battle plan. Such conflicts usually result from the promotion of self-interests on the part of an individual or group. There is a clear objective to be attained, and those who stand in the way of reaching the objective are identified as the adversary. The goal is usually to obtain an advantage over the opponent within the performance appraisal and reward system. The potential reward may be a bonus or commission, a choice assignment, a promotion, or an expansion of power. Whatever the reward, the situation is usually such that only one of the participants will receive it (or the greatest portion of it).

The vice presidents of an organization may find themselves in a strategic conflict situation as the retirement of the president of the organization approaches. An overly ambitious vice president, in an attempt to better his or her personal chances for the presidency, may create a strategic conflict with one or more of the other vice presidents. Strategic conflict can also occur between departments within a university when a new course is offered and two or more departments feel that they should be teaching the course.

Strategic conflict does not necessarily imply that the participants are dishonest or unethical. Indeed, rewards are established to be pursued vigorously. Sometimes, however, such conflicts degenerate into unfair play because of the participant's inability to resist temptation.

Because it is usually impossible to isolate a single cause, few conflicts fit neatly into one of the above categories. Nevertheless, these classifications do provide a useful framework for analyzing conflict.

MANAGING CONFLICT

In general, there are five methods of solving interpersonal conflict situations: (1) withdrawal of one or more of the participants, (2) smoothing over the conflict and pretending it does not exist; (3) compromising for the sake of ending the conflict; (4) forcing the conflict to a conclusion by third party intervention; and (5) confrontation between the participants in an effort to solve the underlying source of conflict.[17] Confrontation, or problem solving, has been found to be the most effective method of resolving conflict, while forcing the conflict to a conclusion has been found to be the least effective method.[18]

Much structural conflict results from interdependencies inherent in the organizational structure. Some of the conflict potential resulting from these interdependencies may be removed by decoupling the conflicting parties. This can be accomplished either by reducing their common resource dependencies, by giving each control over their own resources, by introducing large buffer inventories, or by invoking impersonal, straightforward rules for resource allocation. Decoupling may also occur by duplicating facilities for dependent departments. However, this approach may be too expensive for the organization. Lawrence and Lorsch suggest the use of a "linking" position between dependent departments. The purpose of the linking position is to facilitate communication and coordination between interdependent and potentially conflicting departments.[19] Another alternative is to design the work flow so that the system reflects more logical and complete work units where responsibility and authority are more consistent. Lastly, the matrix organization (discussed in Chapter 8) can offer a means for facilitating constructive confrontation which, as stated earlier, has been found to be the most effective method of conflict resolution.

A Model for Conflict Management

Richard Walton and John Dutton have developed a general model, shown in Figure 13–8, for managing conflict in organizations. This model views the conflict situation from two perspectives. The first

---

[17] Ronald J. Burke, "Methods of Resolving Interpersonal Conflict," *Personnel Administration,* July–August 1969, pp. 48–55.

[18] Ibid.

[19] P. R. Lawrence and J. W. Lorsch, "New Management Job: The Integrator," *Harvard Business Review,* November––December 1967, pp. 142–51.

FIGURE 13–8
Model for Conflict Management

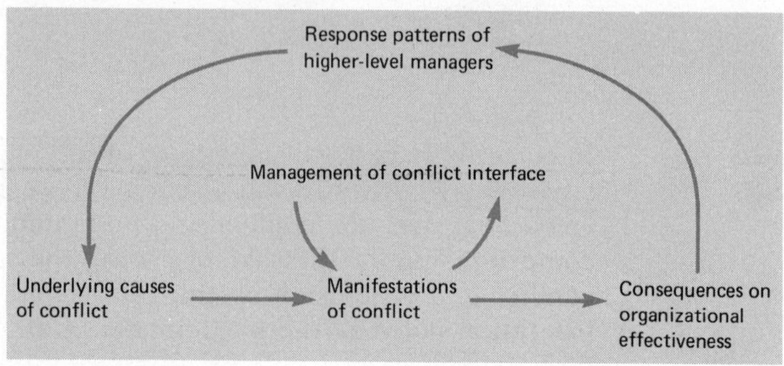

Source: Richard F. Walton and John M. Dutton, "The Management of Interdepartmental Conflict: A Model and Review," *Administrative Science Quarterly*, March 1969, p. 74.

perspective views the manager as an intervening force in the conflict cycle. The second perspective involves the response patterns of higher-level managers.

The conflict interface. Management of the conflict interface is based on monitoring the behavior of the participant(s) as the conflict develops. The objective of the manager is not to resolve the conflict but to act as a referee and counselor in helping the participant(s) reach an acceptable solution. Understanding the type of conflict—intrapersonal, structural, interpersonal, strategic—and the stage of the conflict cycle will aid the manager in the conflict situation. Figure 13–9 presents several key questions that a manager should address when attempting to apply the concepts presented in this chapter to the resolution of a conflict situation.

The manager should also be aware of the following ground rules for verbal confrontations to maximize the constructive aspects of the conflict and to speed its resolution while minimizing the destructive consequences.[20]

1. Review past actions and clarify the issues before the confrontation begins.
2. Communicate freely; do not hold back grievances.
3. Do not surprise the opponent with a confrontation for which the individual is not prepared.

[20] Henry Assael, "Constructive Role of Interorganizational Conflict," *Administrative Science Quarterly*, December 1969, pp. 573–82; Richard E. Walton, "Third Party Roles in Interdepartmental Conflict," *Industrial Relations*, October 1967, pp. 29–43.

FIGURE 13–9

Key Questions to Be Answered in Conflict Resolution

1. What perceived loss or threat of loss has led each party to perceive a conflict?
2. How does each party define the conflict issue?
   - Does each party have an accurate perception of the other's concerns?
   - Is the issue posed superficially rather than in terms of underlying concerns?
   - Would alternative definitions of the issue be more helpful in suggesting integrative solutions to the conflict?
3. How does each party pursue his or her objectives in dealing with the other party?
   - What is his or her underlying orientation in approaching the conflict issue—competitive, collaborative, sharing, avoidance, accommodative?
   - What assumptions underlie the individual's choice of strategies and tactics?
4. How is each party's behavior influenced by the behavior of the other?
   - What ongoing dynamics seem to be producing the escalation or de-escalation?
   - Is each party aware that the other's behavior is partly a response to his or her own?
   - What efforts are the parties making to manage their own conflict?
5. If things proceed as they are, what are apt to be the short-term and long-term results—both substantive and emotional?
   - What foreseeable effects will this episode have upon subsequent episodes?
6. Does the general makeup of either party predispose them toward the use of specific conflict-handling modes?
   - Are those predispositions compatible with the requirements of his or her position?
   - To what extent could a person's behavior be changed through training experiences?

7a. Is either party acting as representative for a larger set of individuals?
   - What expectations do they have of the representative's behavior?
   - How much power do they have over this person?
   - To what extent can they monitor his or her negotiating behavior?

7b. Who are the other, relatively neutral, onlookers?
   - What sort of behavior will they encourage or discourage?
   - How much power do they have over the parties?

8. What is the relative importance and frequency of competitive issues versus common problems in the relationship as a whole?
   - To what extent have resource scarcities created conflict of interest between the parties?
   - In what ways have differentiated responsibilities created conflict of interest?

9a. Are there many rules which dictate or constrain settlements on specific issues?
   - To what extent are the parties free to problem-solve on important issues?

9b. How are the behaviors of the parties shaped by the format of their negotiations?
   - How frequently do the parties interact?
   - When and where are meetings held?
   - What are the number and composition of people present?
   - How formally are the negotiations conducted?

9c. What provisions are there for involving third parties?
   - Are skilled third parties available to help the parties resolve their own disputes?
   - Does the larger system have provisions for terminating conflict episodes by imposing settlements when the parties deadlock?

Source: Kenneth Thomas, "Conflict and Conflict Management," in *The Handbook of Industrial and Organizational Psychology*, ed. Marvin D. Dunnette (Skokie, Ill.: Rand McNally, 1976), pp. 927–28. By permission of the editor.

4. Do not attack the opponent's sensitive spots that have nothing to do with the issues of the conflict.
5. Keep to specific issues; do not argue aimlessly.
6. Maintain the intensity of the confrontation but ensure that all participants say all that they want to say. If the basic issues have been resolved at this point, agree on what steps are to be taken toward resolving the conflict.

Besides acting as a referee in enforcing these rules, the manager of the conflict interface can give valuable assistance to the participant(s) without interfering with the participant(s) responsibility to resolve it. The manager can help the participants understand why the conflict exists and what underlying issues must be resolved. The manager can also help obtain information that may be necessary in order to reach a solution. In interpersonal conflict, the manager can, to some extent, regulate the frequency of contacts between the participants and perhaps establish a problem-solving climate when they meet. The manager's most important contribution, however, is to keep them working toward a true resolution of the conflict. Confrontation of the conflict situation within the guidelines developed above should encourage constructive conflict within the organization.

Responses of higher-level managers. The second level of conflict management concerns the responses of higher-level managers to the consequences of the conflict as it affects the ongoing work of the organization. If the conflict itself or the nature of its aftermath have produced conditions considered intolerable, management must step in and make whatever decisions and changes they deem necessary to restore order. The resulting actions either force a resolution to the conflict or change the solution that has been reached. This intervention is often regarded as arbitrary by the participant(s), especially by those who do not receive a favorable decision. In such cases, it is important that the intervening authority not give the impression that the action has been taken because either or both of the participants have failed but rather because an immediate or different solution is in the best interest of the organization. There should be no doubt that the solution is final and that the conflict has been concluded.

MANAGING CHANGE

Change often causes many of the types of conflict that have been described in this chapter. Successfully managing change increases the likelihood that positive benefits will result from conflict. Resistance to change is natural and normal. It is not a reaction that is reserved only for troublemakers. Some of the most frequently encountered reasons for resistance to change are described below.

Fear of the Unknown

It is natural human behavior to fear the unknown. The problem with many changes is that the outcome of the change is not always foreseeable. If the outcome is foreseeable, the results are often not communicated to all of the affected employees. For example, employees may worry about and resist the installation of a new machine if they aren't sure what the impact of the machine will be on their jobs. Similarly, employees may resist a new manager simply because they don't know what to expect. Another related fear is the uncertainty that an employee may feel about operating under a change. The employee may fully understand a change yet have serious doubts as to whether he or she will be able to handle the change. For example, an employee may resist a change in procedures because of a fear that he or she won't be able to master the new procedure.

Economics

Employees fear any change that they think threatens their jobs or income. The threat may be real or imagined. In either case, the result is resistance to change. For instance, a salesperson will resist a territory change if he or she believes that the change will result in less opportunity. Similarly, production workers will oppose new standards that they believe will be more difficult to achieve.

Inconvenience

Many changes result in personal inconveniences to the affected employees. If nothing else, change often causes employees to have to learn new ways. This may require additional training, schooling, or practice. In either case, the employee will probably be inconvenienced. A common reaction by employees is "it isn't worth the extra effort required."

Threats to Interpersonal Relations

The social and interpersonal relationships between employees can be quite strong. These relationships may appear to be insignificant to everyone but the involved parties. For example, the opportunity to have lunch with a certain group of employees may be very important to the involved employees. When a change, such as a transfer, threatens these relationships, the affected parties often resist. Employees naturally feel more at ease when working with people they know well. Also, the group may have worked out procedures for accomplishing their work based on the strengths and weaknesses of group members. Any changes in the group would naturally disrupt the routine.

REDUCING RESISTANCE TO CHANGE

Most changes originate with management. The manner in which management goes about implementing a change often has a significant impact on the acceptance of the change. Several suggestions for reducing resistance to change are presented in Figure 13–10 and discussed in the following paragraphs.

FIGURE 13–10
Suggestions for Reducing Resistance to Change

- Build trust.
- Discuss upcoming changes.
- Involve the employees in the changes.
- Make sure the changes are reasonable.
- Avoid threats.
- Follow a sensible time schedule.
- Implement in the most logical place.

Build Trust

If the employees trust and have confidence in management, they are much more likely to accept change. If there is an air of distrust, the change is likely to be vigorously resisted. Trust cannot be established overnight: it is built over a period of time. Management's actions determine the degree of existing trust. If employees perceive management as fair, honest, and forthright, trust develops. If they feel that management is always trying to put something over on them, they will not exhibit trust. Managers can go a long way toward building trust if they discuss upcoming changes with the employees and if they actively involve the employees in the change process.

Discuss Upcoming Changes

Fear of the unknown is one of the major barriers to change. This fear can be greatly reduced by discussing any upcoming changes with the affected employees. During this discussion the manager should be as open and honest as possible. The manager should not only explain what the change will be, but should also include an explanation of why the change is being made. The more background and detail the manager gives the more likely that the change will be accepted by the employees. The manager should also outline the impact of the change on each of the affected employees (everyone is primarily interested in how the change will affect them personally). A critical requirement for success is that the manager allow the employees an opportunity to ask questions. Regardless of how thorough the explanation might be, the employees usually have questions. The manager should attempt to answer each of these questions to the fullest extent possible.

Involve the Employees

Another way to reduce resistance to change and build employee trust is to actively involve employees in the change process. While employee involvement is not always possible, it can be extremely effective. It is only natural for employees to want to go along with a change they have helped bring about. A good approach is to solicit employee ideas and inputs as early as possible in the change process. In other words, don't wait until the last minute to ask the employees what they think: ask them as soon as possible. When affected employees have been involved in a change from or near its inception, they will usually actively support the change. The psychology involved here is simple: no one wants to oppose something he or she has helped develop.

Make Sure the Changes Are Reasonable

The manager should always do whatever is possible to ensure that any proposed changes are reasonable. Frequently proposals for changes are generated by upper levels of management. These proposals sometimes are unreasonable because upper management is unaware of all the pertinent circumstances. In this situation it is the manager's responsibility to do what can be done to straighten out the situation.

Avoid Threats

The manager who attempts to implement change through the use of threats is taking a negative approach. Such an approach is likely to decrease rather than increase employee trust. Most people resist threats or coercion. A natural reaction is "this must be bad news if it requires a threat." Even though threatening tactics may get results in the short run, they may be very damaging in the long run. Such tactics will usually have a negative impact on employee morale and attitude.

Follow a Sensible Time Schedule

A manager can often influence the timing of the implementation of changes. There is no doubt that some times are better than others for implementing certain changes. The week before Christmas, for example, would ordinarily not be a good time to implement a major change. Similarly, a major change should ordinarily not be attempted during the height of the vacation season. The manager can often provide valuable insight regarding the proper time for a change. If nothing else, the manager should always use common sense when recommending a time schedule for implementing a change.

Implement in the Most Logical Place

It is not unusual for a manager to have some choice as to where a change will take place. For example, a manager usually decides who will get a new piece of equipment. The manager who makes it a point to know his or her employees usually has a pretty good idea as to who will most likely be flexible and who will not. Changes should, where possible, be implemented in such a way so as to minimize their effect on interpersonal relationships. Attempts should be made not to disturb smooth-working groups. The effect of a change on social relationships should also be given consideration.

MANAGING STRESS

Conflict and change often cause stress in employees. It has been argued that stress is part of living and can contribute to personal growth, development, and mental health.[21] However, excessive and prolonged stress generally becomes quite negative. Stress of this type is said to be related to health problems such as insomnia, asthma, ulcers, and heart disease.[22]

Stress involves an interaction between a person and an environment. The potential for stress exists when an environmental situation presents a demand threatening to exceed a person's capabilities and resources for meeting it, under conditions where the person expects a substantial difference in the rewards and costs resulting from meeting the demand versus not meeting it.[23]

Stress can result from many factors. Some of the more common sources of stress that affect employees are:

---

[21] Hans Selye, *The Stress of Life* (New York: McGraw-Hill, 1956).

[22] C. G. Weiman, "A Study of Occupational Stressor and the Incident of Disease Risk," *Journal of Occupational Medicine*, February 1977, pp. 119–22; M. T. Matteson and J. M. Ivancevich, "Organizational Stressors and Heart Disease: A Research Model," *Academy of Management Review*, July 1979, pp. 347–58.

[23] Joseph E. McGarth, "Stress and Behavior in Organizations," in *Handbook of Industrial and Organizational Psychology*, ed. Marvin D. Dunnette (Skokie, Ill.: Rand McNally, 1976), p. 1352.

MANAGEMENT IN PRACTICE

Executives under Stress

In the final days, the pressure had built up to immense proportions. During his two years as president of Continental Airlines, Alvin Feldman had experienced a long and bitter strike by flight attendants, a nerve-racking hijack attempt and finally an aggressive takeover campaign by a competitor, Texas International Airlines. On Sunday of last week Feldman sadly informed key subordinates that a plan to sell the airline to its employees had fallen through and that Continental would almost surely fall into the hands of its rival, which holds 48.5 percent of Continental stock. Then, only hours later, he lay on a couch in his office and put a bullet through his brain. In his last letters to his children, the 53-year-old executive wrote of the sorrow he had felt since losing his wife to cancer just one year earlier.

"The constant fighting was wearing us all down," recalls a close associate, "but it was worse for him. In the last month he had become extremely tired. He was also alone with the responsibility, and he took that responsibility too far. I think on Sunday he saw that there was no resolution (to the takeover troubles), and he felt he was responsible for letting us down."

Breaking Point

While extreme in its outcome, the Feldman case reads like a clinical case history of the phenomenon known as "executive stress," an insidious sense of helplessness that frequently leads to physical discomfort, and occasionally to alcoholism, heart attacks and even suicide. Some tension, of course, is a useful thing in the workplace, and many executives thrive on the challenge it creates. But researchers have found that every individual has his own breaking point beyond which further pressure only diminishes performance.

"Corporate executives never get a break," says University of Southern California psychologist Milton Holmen. "The twelve-hour days don't necessarily wear down (an executive) personality. It's the specter of the twelve-hour days tomorrow; next week, next year that makes them stressed."

Contrary to popular mythology, it is not the corporate boss who is most likely to fall victim to the pressure. "The people in the middle positions have it the roughest," says Willis Goldbeck, executive director of the Washington Business Group on Health. "There may be 15 people who want to be corporate vice president, but only one can be it. So the other 14 feel like losers, and that's tough to cope with." Top executives, on the other hand, have demonstrated a high tolerance for stress by the very fact of having risen so high, and their lives are made easier by numerous perks.

Isolation

The first sign of excessive strain, says Robert L. Veninga of the University of Minnesota School of Public Health, is a pattern of "sleep disturbances" in which an executive goes night after night either unable to sleep or waking constantly with office problems on his mind. That quickly leads to a lack of enthusiasm, self-doubt, and an inability to make decisions. And finally, in the most serious stage, the executive feels a deep sense of isolation, insisting that no one else can possibly understand what he is going through.

The financial costs of executive stress

are impossible to calculate, but most large companies are beginning to take the problem seriously. Many of them have set up special stress-management programs featuring physical exercise as well as relaxation techniques, and some firms have gone even further. Rand Corp., for example, actually pays bonuses to induce its workaholic researchers to take vacations. Nonetheless, executive stress continues to take its toll, and it is starting to zero in on a new set of victims. As they move up in the corporate structure, female managers are beginning to suffer the hypertension, ulcers and heart attacks traditionally associated with their aggressive male colleagues.

Source: Harry Anderson, Janet Huck, Frank Maier, and Sandra Cavazos, *Newsweek*, August 24, 1981, p. 53.

Common sources of stress:

1. Job or task stress (e.g., job or task is too difficult).
2. Role stress (e.g., ambiguities in the description of a particular job).
3. Stress from human environment (e.g., overcrowding or understaffing).
4. Stress from physical environment (e.g., extreme cold or heat or poor ventilation).
5. Stress from social environment (e.g., interpersonal conflict).
6. Stress that comes from within an individual (e.g., intrapersonal conflict).

As can be seen, these six sources are not mutually exclusive and have considerable overlap.

Burnout

Stress can result in a phenomenon called burnout. In fact, one study reported 56 percent of 5,500 respondents experienced physical and/or mental illnesses as a result of their jobs.[24] Burnout is generally thought to consist of three phases: (1) an increased feeling of emotional exhaustion; (2) a callous and dehumanized perception of others; and (3) a self-evaluation which is negative in terms of one's effectiveness.

Consequences of burnout for the organization are serious. They include deterioration in organizational performance, low worker morale, absenteeism, frequent job turnover, and an increase in the use of drugs and alcohol among employees. A lack of job sat-

[24] Walsh, D. "Classroom Stress and Teacher Burnout," *Phi Delta Kappa*, vol. 61, no. 4 (1979), p. 253.

isfaction is not the same as burnout. In fact, a stressful job can be very satisfying. Job dissatisfaction is frequently found when symptoms of burnout are evident, but a dissatisfied employee is not necessarily burned out.

Some organizations have built exercise rooms to help cope with stress and burnout. Other remedies that have been tried are to shortened hours of direct contact with customers, special leaves or temporary assignments, and early retirement programs. Including employees in the decision-making process has also been used to reduce stress.

Stress can never be entirely eliminated and, as was mentioned previously, some stress actually produces positive results. Effectively using the techniques of conflict resolution and managing change that have been discussed in this chapter should serve as a positive step in reducing the negative aspects of stress.

SUMMARY

Conflict in organizations is often assumed to be an unnatural and undesirable situation that is to be avoided at all costs. Management must realize that conflict exists in all organizations and is not necessarily negative. The goal of management should be to understand and manage conflict in order to obtain the maximum benefits.

Conflict refers to overt behavior arising out of a process in which one part seeks the advancement of its own interests in its relationship with others. Conflict begins when one party perceives that a second party has frustrated, or is about to frustrate, some concern of the first party. In this definition, the parties involved denote social units in conflict and can therefore be referring to individuals, groups, organizations, or nations. The potential for conflict depends on how incompatible the objectives of the parties are, the availability of the resources required to achieve the objectives, and the degree of interdependence of task activities.

Conflict does not usually appear suddenly. The stages of conflict development are: latent conflict, perceived conflict, felt conflict, manifest conflict, and the conflict aftermath.

Conflict was analyzed from two basic perspectives—internal or intrapersonal conflict and external conflict. External conflict can be further divided into three types: structural, interpersonal, and strategic.

A model was presented in which conflict management is viewed from two perspectives. The first perspective views the manager as an intervening force in the conflict cycle. The second perspective concerns the responses of higher-level managers to the consequences of the conflict as it affects the ongoing work of the organization. Several questions were presented which need to be answered in order to resolve a conflict situation.

Change often causes conflict. Resistance to change is natural and normal. Some reasons for resistance to change are: fear of the unknown, economics, inconvenience, and threats to interpersonal relations. Resistance to change can be reduced by building trust, discussing upcoming changes with employees, involving the employees in the changes, making sure the changes are reasonable, avoiding threats, following a sensible time schedule, and implementing the change in the most logical place.

Stress involves an interaction between a person and an environment. The potential for stress exists when an environmental situation presents a demand which threatens to exceed a person's capabilities and resources for meeting it, under conditions where the person expects a substantial difference in the rewards and costs resulting from meeting the demand versus not meeting it. Six common sources of stress were described.

Stress can also result in a phenomenon called burnout. Several approaches used by organizations in dealing with employee burnout were described.

REVIEW QUESTIONS

1. What are two basic viewpoints that can be used to analyze conflict?
2. What causes intrapersonal conflict?
3. What are some typical defense mechanisms used when an individual is frustrated?
4. Describe three forms of goal conflict.
5. Name at least four types of structural conflict.
6. What are some of the causes of interpersonal conflict?
7. What is strategic conflict?
8. Describe some of the useful effects of conflict.
9. Identify the five stages of conflict.
10. What are some methods that can be used to resolve conflict?
11. Describe in detail a model for managing conflict in organizations.
12. Outline some key questions that need to be answered in conflict resolution.
13. Describe some methods a manager can use to overcome resistance to change.
14. Identify six common sources of stress.

DISCUSSION QUESTIONS

1. Discuss the following statement: "Every manager should attempt to avoid conflict at all times."
2. "Conflict is inevitable." Do you agree or disagree? Discuss.
3. How can managers reduce destructive role conflict in organizations?
4. Describe how you would handle the situation in which you have two people working for you who "just rub each other the wrong way."

SELECTED READINGS

Altier, W. J. "Change: The Name of the Game." *Business Horizons,* June 1979, pp. 25–27.

Bedeian, A. G., and A. A. Armenakis. "Path-Analytic Study of the Consequences of Role Conflict and Ambiguity." *Academy of Management Journal,* June 1981, pp. 417–24.

Benson, H., and R. L. Allen. "How Much Stress Is Too Much?" *Harvard Business Review,* September–October 1980, pp. 86–92.

Brief A. P. "How to Manage Managerial Stress." *Personnel,* September–October 1980, pp. 25–30.

Burke, Ronald J. "Methods of Resolving Interpersonal Conflict." in *A Contingency Approach to Management: Readings,* ed. John W. Newstrom et al. New York: McGraw-Hill, 1975, pp. 482–491.

Cochran, D. S., and D. D. White. "Intraorganizational Conflict in the Hospital Purchasing Decision Making Process." *Academy of Management Journal,* June 1981, pp. 324–332.

Cooper, C. L., and A. Melhuish. "Occupational Stress and Managers." *Journal of Occupational Medicine,* September 1980, pp. 588–92.

Drucker, P. "How to Manage in Turbulent Times." *Canadian Business Magazine,* May 1980, pp. 69–70.

Filley, Alan. *Interpersonal Conflict Resolution.* Chicago: Scott, Foresman and Company, 1975.

Harrison, F. "Management of Organizational Conflict." *University of Michigan Business Review,* May 1979, pp. 18–23.

King, D. "Three Cheers for Conflict!" *Personnel,* January–February 1981, pp. 13–22.

Labovitz, G. H. "Managing Conflict." *Business Horizons,* June 1980, pp. 31–37.

Levison, H. "When Executives Burn Out." *Harvard Business Review,* May–June 1981, pp. 72–81.

Likert, Rensis, and June Gibson Likert. *New Ways of Managing Conflict.* New York: McGraw-Hill, 1976.

Phillips, E., and R. Cheston. "Conflict Resolution: What Works?" *California Management Review,* Summer 1979, pp. 76–83.

Pondy, Louis. "Organizational Conflict: Concepts and Models." *Administrative Science Quarterly,* September 1972, pp. 296–320.

Rahim, A. "Management of Intraorganizational Conflicts: A Laboratory Study with Organization Design." *Management International Review* 19, no. 1 (1979), pp. 97–106.

Sheane, D. "When and How to Intervene in Conflict." *Personnel Management,* November 1979, pp. 13–22.

Verheyen, L. G. "Change through Employee Feedback." *Training and Development Journal,* January 1980, pp. 62–65.

Case 13–1

Problems at the hospital

Smith County is a suburban community near a major midwestern city. The county has experienced such a tremendous rate of growth during the past decade that local governments have had difficulty providing adequate service to the citizens.

The Smith County Hospital has a reputation of being a first-class facility, but it is inadequate to meet local needs. During certain periods of the year the occupancy rates exceed the licensed capacity. There is no doubt in anyone's mind that the hospital must be expanded immediately.

At a recent meeting of the Hospital Authority the hospital administrator, Sam Austin, presented the group with a proposal to accept the architectural plans of the firm of Watkins and Gibson. This plan calls for a 100-bed addition adjacent to the existing structure. Sam announced that after reviewing several alternative plans, he believed the Watkins and Gibson plan would provide the most benefit for the expenditure.

At this point, Randolph (Randy) Lewis, the board chairman, began questioning the plan in such a manner that Sam became defensive. Randy made it clear that he would not go along with the Watkins and Gibson plan. He stated that the board should look for other firms to serve as the architects for the project.

The pursuing arguments became somewhat heated and a 10-minute recess was called to allow those attending to get coffee as well as to allow tempers to calm down. Sam was talking to John Rhodes, another member of the Hospital Authority Board, in the hall and said, "Randy seems to fight me on every project."

Randy, who was talking to other members of the board, was saying, "I know that the Watkins and Gibson plan is good but I just can't stand for that guy Austin to act like it's his plan. I wish he would leave so we would get a good administrator from the community who we can identify with."

1. Is Randy's reaction uncommon?
2. What type of conflict exists between Randy and Sam?
3. What methods would you use to reduce or resolve the conflict?

Case 13–2 

The young college graduate and the old superintendent

Situation: You are a consultant to the manager of a garment manufacturing plant in a small southern town. The manager has been having trouble with two employees: Ralph, the plant superintendent, and Barbara, the production scheduler. Ralph is 53 years old and has been with the company since he was released from military duty after World War II. He started as a warehouseman with a sixth-grade education and worked his way up through the ranks. Until recently, Ralph, along with his many other duties, handled the production scheduling function himself. He was proud of the fact that he could handle it all "in his head." As the volume of production and the number of different products grew, however, the plant manager felt that significant savings could be attained through a more scientific approach to scheduling. He believed that he could save on raw materials by purchasing in larger lots and on production set-up time by making longer runs. He also wanted to cut down on the frequency of finished good stock-outs, and when backlogs did occur, he wanted to be able to give customers more definite information as to when goods would be available. He wanted to have a schedule documented for at least two months into the future with daily updates.

Barbara is 24 years old, and grew up in the Chicago area. This is her first full-time job. She earned a master of science in industrial engineering from an eastern engineering school. She jumped right into the job and set up a computer-assisted scheduling system using a time-sharing service with a teletype terminal in her office. The system is based on the latest production scheduling and inventory control technology. It is very flexible and has proven to be very effective in all the areas that were of interest to the plant manager.

Plant Manager: Sometimes I just want to shoot both Ralph and Barbara. If those two could just get along with each other, this plant would run like a well-oiled machine.

Consultant: What do they fight about?

Manager: Anything and everything that has to do with the production schedule. Really trivial things in a lot of cases. It all seems so completely senseless!

Consultant: Have you tried to do anything about it?

Manager: At first I tried to minimize the impact of their feuds on the rest of the plant by stepping in and making decisions that would eliminate the point of controversy. I also tried to smooth things over as if the arguments were just friendly disagreements. I thought that after they had a chance to get accustomed to each other the problem would go away. But it didn't. It got to the point that I was spending a good 20 percent of my time stopping their fights. Furthermore, I began to notice that other employees were starting to take sides. The younger women seemed to support Barbara; everybody else sided with Ralph. It began to look as if we might have our own little war.

Consultant: What's the current situation?

Manager: I finally told them both that if I caught them fighting again, I would take very drastic action with both of them. I think that move was a mistake though, because now they won't even talk to each other. Barbara just drops the schedule printouts on Ralph's desk every afternoon and walks away. Ralph needs some help in working with those printouts, and Barbara needs some feedback on what's actually going on in the plant. Frankly, things aren't going as well production-wise now as when they were at each other's throats. And the tension in the plant as a whole is even worse. They are both good people and outstanding in their respective jobs. I would really hate to lose either one of them, but if they can't work together, I may have to let one or both of them go.

1. Why is this conflict occurring?
2. What method did the manager use in dealing with this conflict situation? Was it effective?
3. Recommend an approach for resolving the conflict.

14 Leadership Behavior

Objectives

1. To define leadership and show its relationship to the management process.
2. To review research that has been conducted on the leadership process.
3. To describe some of the implications of leadership research for organizations and managers.

Chapter Outline

Glossary of Terms

Authority The right to issue directives and expend resources.

Autocratic leader One who makes most decisions for the group.

Contingency approach to leadership An approach to leadership which contends that the most effective style of leadership depends on the situation in which the leader is functioning.

Coercive power Power that is based on fear.

Democratic leader One who guides and encourages the group to make decisions.

Expert power Power that is based on the special skill, expertise, or knowledge of an individual.

Laissez-faire leader A leader who allows individuals in the group to make the decisions.

Leader The individual who occupies the central role in a leadership situation; this person has the ability to influence the behavior of others according to his or her desires in a given situation.

Leader behavior description questionnaire (LBDQ) A questionnaire developed by researchers at Ohio State University and designed to determine how successful leaders carry out their activities.

Leadership Process of influencing the behavior of other members of the group.

Legitimate power Power based on position in an organization; for instance, an individual's boss has a certain amount of legitimate power over an employee.

Managerial grid A two-dimensional classification scheme used to describe an individual's leadership style with regard to concern for people and concern for task accomplishment.

Path-goal theory of leadership States that the role of the leader in eliciting goal-directed behavior is to increase personal payoffs to subordinates for work-goal attainment, to make the path to payoffs easier to travel, and to increase the opportunities for satisfaction in route, and that the effectiveness of the leader's efforts depends on the particular situation.

Power The ability or capacity to influence another to do something that the person would not otherwise do.

Referent power Power based on the charismatic traits or characteristics of an individual.

Reward power Power based on the ability of one individual to provide rewards, either intrinsic or extrinsic, for compliance with this individual's wishes.

Self-fulfilling prophecy (same as Pygmalion in management) Term used to describe the influence of one person's expectations on another's behavior.

Theory X—Theory Y Terms coined by Douglas McGregor to describe assumptions that are made by managers concerning the basic human nature of people.

Trait theory Theory of leadership that is based on certain physical and psychological characteristics, or traits, that differentiate leaders from their groups.

> Concern with leadership is as old as recorded history. Plato's Republic, to give but one early example, speculates about the proper education and training of political leaders, and most political philosophers since that time, have attempted to deal with this problem. Leadership has been a particular concern in democracies, which, by definition, cannot rely upon the accident of birth for the recruitment of leaders. Where there is no hereditary aristocracy, every man is potentially a leader, and society has to give thought to the identification and proper training of men who will be able to guide its institutions.
>
> *Fred E. Fiedler**

Each year, new information is published that explores various facets of leadership. Checklists have been established to determine the style of leadership used by individuals. Questionnaires have been developed to determine the style of leadership used within a particular organization. New teaching aids and devices appear which are designed to improve one's leadership abilities. All of this activity would indicate that today's practicing manager knows a great deal about the leadership process, but this is not true. Many managers appear to experience difficulty performing effectively in leadership roles. As the above quote states leadership is and must be a concern of society and organizations. This chapter is designed as a review of the leadership process and is intended to provide a perspective on leadership styles and processes.

LEADERSHIP—WHAT IS IT?

Leadership is a process of influencing the activities of either formal or informal work groups in their tasks of goal setting and goal achievement. The ability to obtain followers and the ability to influence those followers makes a leader. Generally, influence is the result of an interaction between people in which one person presents information in such a manner as to convince the other members of the group that their situation will be improved if they behave as suggested or desired. A leader is the person who takes the central role in this interaction by influencing the behavior of other members of the group.

*Fred E. Fiedler, *A Theory of Leadership Effectiveness* (New York: McGraw-Hill, 1967), p. 3.

Most managers are in a leadership role because they can influence the behavior of members of the formal work group. However, the fact that the manager is in a leadership role does not mean the manager performs the role effectively.[1] A manager's leadership effectiveness can be measured by the results achieved by the work group in furthering the organization's objectives (such as increased profit or service to customers).

Additionally, the distinction between management and leadership is not always that clear. A manager performs those functions which result in other people executing prescribed formal duties for organizational goal attainment. As was described in Chapter 1, these functions include planning, controlling, organizing, staffing, and motivation. Leadership, on the other hand, is a more restricted type of managerial activity emphasizing the interpersonal interaction between a manager and one or more subordinates, with the purpose of increasing organizational effectiveness.[2] In fact, leadership and the management function of motivation are complementary processes. In most instances, the degree of motivation exhibited by an individual is influenced by leader effectiveness. Thus, both effective leadership and effective motivation are essential for good management and good performance.

Generally, there are two types of leaders in organizations: the formal or appointed leader (manager) who is assigned to the leadership position by the organization, and the informal leader who is chosen by the group itself. Each type of leader relies on different sources of authority in performing the leadership role. It is important to note, however, that appointed leaders (managers) may or may not be informal leaders.

SOURCES OF AUTHORITY

The emergent leader of a group is the one perceived by the group as being the individual most capable of satisfying the group's needs. The authority of the leader can be removed, reduced, or increased depending on the group's perceived progress toward its objectives. The authority of the leader may also be threatened by the emergence of different or additional objectives.

The following simple example illustrates this point. Suppose a group of people were shipwrecked on a desolate island. The

[1] Abraham Zaleznik, "Manager and Leaders. Are They Really Different?" *Harvard Business Review,* May–June 1977, pp. 67–78.

[2] Chester A. Schriesheim, James M. Tolliver, Orlando C. Behling, "Leadership Theory: Some Implications for Managers," *MSU Business Topics* 26, no. 3 (1978), pp. 34–35.

group's first goal would probably be to ensure their security by attaining food, water, and shelter. Using the definition of leadership that has been previously developed, the person selected by the group as the leader would be the person perceived by the group as the one who could best help the group achieve the essentials for survival. However, after satisfying this need, other needs will emerge. The need to escape from the island would probably emerge rather quickly. The person originally selected for the leadership position may not necessarily be the person perceived by the group as the most capable in directing the attainment of these new, emerging needs. In this case, the group might select a new leader. The leadership position might continue to change depending on the group's needs and perceptions. Chapter 12 outlined some of the criteria that informal work groups use in selecting a leader.

The role of the manager and the role of the leader in the previous example are different. The example illustrated more of an elective or emergent style of leadership. Under this system, the leader must perceive the needs of the group and must be perceived by the group as being the most capable in achieving those needs. In other words, the source of authority for the leader is the group being led. In most organizations, however, the source of authority for a manager comes from above rather than below. As was discussed in Chapter 7, lower levels of management are generally appointed by higher levels of management. Thus, a manager's sourcc of authority does not come from the group being managed but rather from higher management.

Little research has been performed regarding the relationship between the leader's source of authority and the leadership process. One research study demonstrated that the continuity of leadership is better maintained in groups where leaders are elected than in groups where leaders are appointed.[3] Another study indicated that a leader's source of authority is perceived and reacted to by the group as an important element in the leadership process.[4]

POWER, AUTHORITY, AND LEADERSHIP

Power is the ability to command or apply force and is not necessarily accompanied by authority. It is through power that an individual can be influenced by another to do something that the

[3] A. M. Cohen and Warren G. Bennis, "Continuity of Leadership in Communication Networks," *Human Relations* 14 (1961), pp. 351–67.

[4] J. W. Julian, E. P. Hollander, and C. R. Regula, "Endorsement of the Group Spokesman as a Function of His Source of Authority, Competence, and Success," *Journal of Personality and Social Psychology* 11 (1969), pp. 42–49.

individual would not otherwise do.[5] The use of power or the desire to have power is often viewed negatively in our society because power is often associated with the capacity to inflict punishment. There are, however, numerous forms of power, as shown in Figure 14–1.[6]

Authority, which exists in the formal organization, is the right to issue directives and expend resources. As discussed in Chapter 7, authority has traditionally been viewed as a function of position in the organizational hierarchy, flowing from the top to the bottom of the organization. Basically, the amount of authority that a manager possesses depends on the amount of coercive, reward, and legitimate power that the manager can exert as a result of occupying a certain position. Alternatively, Barnard's acceptance theory of authority, also discussed in Chapter 7, suggests that the source of a manager's authority lies with the subordinate, because the subordinate has the power either to accept or reject a superior's command: if the subordinate rejects the authority of a superior, it does not exist. Barnard viewed a subordinate's disobeying or ignoring a communication from a superior as a denial of the manager's authority by the subordinate. Basically, Barnard was referring to the degree of legitimate power that a manager commands. It seems logical that the degree of

FIGURE 14–1
Types of Power

Coercive power	Based on fear, the subordinate does what is required to avoid punishment or some other negative outcome. The disciplinary policies of organizations generally are based on this type of power.
Reward power	Based on the ability of one individual to provide rewards, either intrinsic or extrinsic, for compliance with this individual's wishes.
Legitimate power	Based on an individual's position in the organization; thus, when joining an organization, a person accepts the fact that the boss's orders are to be carried out.
Expert power	Based on the special skill, expertise, or knowledge that a particular individual possesses.
Referent power	Exemplified by the charismatic individual who has unusual traits that allow that person to control situations.

[5] T. O. Jacobs, *Leadership and Exchange in Formal Organization* (Alexandria, Va.: Human Resources Research Organization, 1971), p. 216.

[6] John R. P. French and Bertram Raven, "The Bases of Social Power," in *Group Dynamics*, ed. Darwin Cartwright and A. F. Zander, 2d ed. (Evanston, Ill.: Row Peterson, 1960), pp. 607–23.

coercive and reward power a manager can exert would influence the degree of legitimate power that the manager holds.

Leadership has been defined as a process of influencing the behavior of other members of the group. Leaders may use one or several power types in combination to influence group behavior. For instance, some political leaders use referent power; others use a combination of coercive, reward, and referent power, as demonstrated by Adolph Hitler. Informal leaders generally combine expert and referent powers. Some managers rely only on their authority—which is the combination of coercive, reward, and referent power—while others use different combinations. In fact, David C. McClelland and David H. Burnham have extensively explored the relationship between power and effective management. They report as follows:

> Good managers are not motivated by a need for personal aggrandizement or by a need to get along with subordinates, but rather by a need to influence others' behavior for the good of the whole organization. In other words, good managers want power.[7]

However, these same authors also suggest that power can lead to authoritarianism and thus must be tempered by maturity and a high degree of self-control.

LEADER ATTITUDES

In the late 1950s, Douglas McGregor developed two attitude profiles or assumptions concerning the basic nature of people. These two divergent attitudes were termed Theory X and Theory Y and are summarized in Figure 14–2. McGregor maintained that many leaders basically subscribe to either Theory X or Theory Y and that they behave accordingly. A leader subscribing to Theory X would more than likely use a much more authoritarian style of leadership than a leader who believes in Theory Y assumptions. The real contribution coming from McGregor's work was the suggestion that a leader's attitude toward human nature has a large influence on how the person behaves as a leader.

Others have also investigated the relationship between a leader's attitudes and the performance of individuals within the group. Specifically, the relationship between a leader's expectations and the resulting performance have received considerable attention.

J. Sterling Livingston has looked at the relationship between a manager's expectations and the resulting performance demon-

[7] David C. McClelland and David H. Burnham, "Power Is the Great Motivator," *Harvard Business Review,* March–April 1976, p. 100.

FIGURE 14–2
Assumptions about People

Theory X

1. The average human being has an inherent dislike of work and will avoid it if he can.
2. Because of their dislike of work, most people must be coerced, controlled, directed, or threatened with punishment to get them to put forth adequate effort toward the achievement of organizational objectives.
3. The average human being prefers to be directed, wishes to avoid responsibility, has relatively little ambition, and wants security above all.

Theory Y

1. The expenditure of physical and mental effort in work is as natural as play or rest.
2. External control and the threat of punishment are not the only means for bringing about effort toward organizational objectives. Workers will exercise self-direction and self-control in the service of objectives to which they are committed.
3. Commitment to objectives is a function of the rewards associated with their achievement.
4. The average human being learns, under proper conditions, not only to accept but to seek responsibility.
5. The capacity to exercise a relatively high degree of imagination, ingenuity, and creativity in the solution of organizational problems is widely, not narrowly, distributed in the population.
6. Under the conditions of modern industrial life, the intellectual potentialities of the average human being are only partially utilized.

Source: Douglas McGregor, *The Human Side of Enterprise* (New York: McGraw-Hill, 1960), pp. 33–34 and 47–48. Copyright © 1960 by McGraw-Hill, Inc. Used with permission of McGraw-Hill Book Company.

strated by subordinates. If the manager's expectations are high, productivity is likely to be high. On the other hand, if the manager's expectations are low, productivity of the subordinate is likely to be poor. Livingston called this idea "Pygmalion in management." McGregor had earlier called it the "self-fulfilling prophecy." Livingston's findings are summarized as follows:

> What a manager expects of his subordinates and the way he treats them largely determine their performance and career progress. A unique characteristic of superior managers is their ability to create high performance expectations that subordinates fulfill. Less effective managers fail to develop similar expectations, and, as a consequence, the productivity of their subordinates suffers. Subordinates, more often than not, appear to do what they believe they are expected to do.[8]

[8] J. Sterling Livingston, "Pygmalion in Management," *Harvard Business Review*, July–August 1969, p. 82.

Both McGregor and Livingston believe that the attitudes or assumptions made by leaders or managers concerning their subordinates can have a significant influence on the performance of the subordinates.[9]

GENERAL APPROACHES TO LEADERSHIP

Over 300 studies have been conducted on leadership over the past 70 years.[10] Some of the more important studies that have been conducted on leadership are discussed in the following paragraphs.

Trait Theory

Early research efforts devoted to leadership concentrated on what the leader was like rather than what the leader did. Numerous personality traits (e.g., originality, initiative, persistence, knowledge, enthusiasm), social traits (e.g., tact, patience, sympathy), and physical characteristics (e.g., height, weight, physical attractiveness) have been examined to differentiate leaders from nonleaders.[11]

At first glance, a few traits do seem to distinguish leaders from followers. Some of these include being slightly superior in such physical attributes as weight and height and in a tendency to score higher on tests of dominance, intelligence, extroversion, and adjustment.[12] Unfortunately, the differences between leaders and followers seem to be small with considerable overlap. Thus, the research in this area has generally been fruitless, largely because the traits related to leadership in one situation usually did not prove to be predictive in other situations.[13] In fact, numerous studies have shown that leadership characteristics or traits that are effective in one situation may not be effective in other situations.[14] One study even concluded that the likelihood of uncover-

---

[9] For additional information on expectations and their influence, see Robert Rosenthal and Lenorce Jacobson, *Pygmalion in the Classroom* (New York: Holt, Rinehart & Winston, 1968).

[10] Ralph M. Stogdill, *Handbook of the Leadership* (New York: Free Press, 1974), pp. 432–580.

[11] J. D. Barrow, "The Variables of Leadership: A Review and Conceptual Framework," *Academy of Management Review*, April 1977, p. 232.

[12] C. A. Gibb, "Leadership" in *Handbook of Social Psychology* ed. G. Lindzey and E. Aronson, (Reading, Mass.: Addison-Wesley Publishing, 1969), pp. 205–82.

[13] C. A. Gibb, "The Principles and Traits of Leadership," *Journal of Abnormal Psychology* 42, 1947, pp. 267–84; and R. M. Stogdill, "Personal Factors Associated with Leadership: A Survey of the Literature," *Journal of Psychology* 25, 1948, pp. 35–71.

[14] R. M. Stogdill, "Historical Trends in Leadership Theory and Research," *Journal of Contemporary Business*, Autumn 1974, p. 5.

ing a set of universal leadership effectiveness traits is essentially impossible.[15] In general, it can be said that traits may influence the capability to lead to some extent, but these traits must be analyzed in terms of the leadership situation (which is described in detail later in this chapter.)

Basic Leadership Styles

Studies conducted in the 1930s by Kurt Lewin, Ronald Lippitt, and Ralph K. White concentrated on the manner or style of the leader. These studies identified three basic leadership styles: autocratic, laissez-faire, and democratic. The main difference among these styles is the location of the decision-making function. Generally, the autocratic leader makes most decisions for the group; the laissez-faire leader allows individuals within the group to make all decisions; and the democratic leader guides and encourages the group to make decisions. A more detailed description of each of the leadership styles is given in Figure 14–3. It should be noted that Figure 14–3 implies that the democratic style is the most desirable and productive. However, current research on leadership (which will be discussed later in this chapter) does not necessarily support this conclusion. The primary contribution of this early research on leadership was that it identified the three basic styles of leadership.

Dimensions of the Leadership Process

Beginning in 1945, a series of studies was conducted at Ohio State University to find out the most important activities that are performed by successful leaders. The researchers wanted to find out what a successful leader does regardless of the type of group being led: a mob, a religious group, a university, or a business organization. In approaching the problem, they developed a questionnaire called the Leader Behavior Description Questionnaire (LBDQ) which is still used today, either in the original form or in variations.

In applying the questionnaire, two leader activities emerged consistently as being the most important. These were "consideration" and "initiating structure." The term *consideration* refers to the leader activity of showing concern for the individual group members and the satisfaction of their individual needs. The term *initiating structure* refers to the leader activity of structuring the work of group members, and directing the group toward the attainment of the group's goals.

[15] C. A. Schriesheim, J. M. Tolliver, and C. Behling, "Leadership Theory: Some Implications for Managers," *Michigan State University Business Topics*, Summer 1978, p. 35.

FIGURE 14–3
Relationship between Styles of Leadership and Group Members

Autocratic style

Leader

1. The individual is very conscious of his or her position.
2. He or she has little trust and faith in members of the group.
3. This leader believes that pay is a just reward for work and the only reward that will motivate workers.
4. Orders are issued to be carried out, with no questions allowed and no explanations given.

Group members

1. No responsibility is assumed for performance, with people merely doing what they are told.
2. Production is good when the leader is present, but poor in the leader's absence.

Laissez-faire style

Leader

1. He or she has no confidence in his or her leadership ability.
2. This leader does not set goals for the group.

Group members

1. Decisions are made by whomever in the group is willing to do it.
2. Productivity generally is low and work is sloppy.
3. Individuals have little interest in their work.
4. Morale and teamwork generally are low.

Democratic style

Leader

1. Decision making is shared between the leader and the group.
2. When the leader is required or forced to make a decision, his or her reasoning is explained to the group.
3. Criticism and praise are given objectively.

Group members

1. New ideas and change are welcomed.
2. A feeling of responsibility is developed within the group.
3. Quality of work and productivity generally are high.
4. The group generally feels successful.

Source: Adapted from Leland B. Bradford and Ronald Lippitt, "Building a Democratic Work Group," *Personnel* 22, no. 3 (November 1945). Copyright © 1945 by American Management Association, Inc. Reprinted by permission of the publisher.

Subsequent to the Ohio State research, many other studies have been conducted on the relationship between the leader activities of consideration and initiating structure and their resulting effect on leader effectiveness. The major conclusions that can be drawn from these studies are as follows:

1. Leaders scoring high on consideration tend to have more satisfied subordinates than leaders scoring low on consideration.

MANAGEMENT IN PRACTICE

Number 1, and Still Counting

After 315 victories now, after all the history of the past 36 years and after all the hyperbole of the past three weeks, who is this Paul W. ("Bear") Bryant anyway? Let's see. He is a football coach named for a bear (looks a little like a football, a lot like a bear). He is a brilliant coach who was never an innovator. He oversees practices from a tower yet touches each player personally somehow. He is a humanitarian who began accepting black players no earlier than 1970. He is shy, but he is not retiring. He is called the cruelest coach in memory and the kindest man in the world.

It is easier to say what Bryant has done. At Maryland, Kentucky, Texas A & M and—for the past 23 years—Alabama, he has won more football games than any other college coach. Numbers are simple. To catch Babe Ruth, all Henry Aaron had to do was hit 35 homers a year for more than 20 years. To catch Amos Alonzo Stagg, all Bear Bryant had to do was win 10 games a year for more than 30 years.

He finished doing it last Saturday against Auburn, except he is not finished. A trip to the Cotton Bowl is set for January, and then he will start planning for next fall. As time goes on—and Bryant, 68, says he is going on with it—there may be no catching Bear. For now, there may be no knowing him, except through his players and assistants. At least they can share the feeling of knowing him. And not just by their Bear stories, as fun as those are. The stories are as picturesque as he is, and they top him off like his houndstooth hat. But they do not show enough of what is underneath.

Stagg used to say, "No coach ever won a game by what he knows; it's what his players have learned." So perhaps it would be instructive to ask Bryant's players—and his coaches—what they have learned. For instance, Jack Pardee.

The Washington Redskins' and Chicago Bears' former head coach, now the San Diego Chargers' defensive coordinator, is a survivor of that infamous 1954 Junction (Texas) training camp in the Bear's first Texas A & M season. Of 96 players who went to summer camp, 27 were left after 10 days of workouts in up to 110 degree heat. The others quit. "It was an effort to survive," says Pardee. "Each player could tell his own story, but mine was simply to make it to the next practice." The Bryant term for such tests: "gut checks."

Those who did not make it included an all-conference center, "the only good player we had," recalls Pardee. "He didn't want to work one day and was fired. Bryant ran him out."

New Orleans Saints Coach Bum Phillips, one of Bear's assistants at A & M, was awed by Bryant's command. "He'd go into a staff meeting," Phillips says, "and he'd never have to say, 'Let me have you-all's attention.' Hell, he had it. You respected him and you liked him. You didn't do it because you were scared of him, although I was a little scared of him."

Bum enjoys setting the scene in the meeting room, assistants quietly quaking while Bear takes out a cigarette, taps it on his thumb, lights it, and smokes it almost all the way down before the hush is broken. And Phillips laughs. He doubts if Bryant knew how intimidating he was. "That's the beautiful part about him," says Bum. "He just acted natural and, hell, that's the way it came out. I don't think a man could plan to do as many great things as that man has done in handling people."

At Alabama, Joe Namath knew Bryant's discipline. "If you cut classes, you had to take study hall in his office at 4 A.M.," Namath says. "You had to be there waiting for him when he got to work. Nobody wanted to do that. He was frightening." For something worse than cutting class, an infraction never told, Namath was kicked off the team for the last game of the 1963 season (his junior year) and the Sugar Bowl. Joe could have gone to Canada, then and there, to play professional football. He stayed at Alabama. "When he spanked you," says Namath, "you knew it was because he loved you." There's still sting in the Bear's spank. When two of his players were caught carousing on the eve of the Auburn game, he instantly bounced them from the team.

The players, all the different ages of players, growing their hair from a stubble to a stalk, have loved him. Houstin Oiler Quarterback Ken Stabler, who ran away from the Alabama team once, was brought in and told by Bryant: "You don't deserve to be on this football team." After a long pause, Stabler said, "Well, I'm coming out there anyway." That sold Bear on Stabler, and maybe Stabler on Stabler.

To the players, this record isn't larger than life, this man is. "Boy, he's a big awesome devil when he walks in a room," former Dallas Cowboy Linebacker Lee Roy Jordan says. George Blanda, who quarterbacked for Bryant at Kentucky, remembers thinking, "this must be what God looks like." Bryant's only Heisman Trophy winner, halfback John David Crow, was so terrified of the coach that he crossed the street to avoid him. "Now," Crow says, "I love him."

Only one Heisman, but 27 bowls, 12 Southeastern Conference championships (one Southwest Conference) and 6 national titles. Won 315, lost 80 and tied 17.

Not much of all this talking and fussing pleases Bryant, who says little about himself and mumbles that. "The record I'm excited about is our team's record," says Bear, "because all the records are the team's. Thousands of people are part of it. It's a 'we' thing an 'us' thing, it's no 'I' thing." Football coaches are good at saying how bad they are, at minimizing what they have just done for the benefit of the coming opponent. But minimizing this is not going to be easy. It's a gut check, all right.

Source: Tom Callahan: *Time*, December 7, 1981, p. 68.

2. The relationship between the score on consideration and leader effectiveness depends on the group that is being led. In other words, a high score on consideration was positively correlated with leader effectiveness for managers and office staff in a large industrial firm, whereas a high accent on consideration was negatively correlated with leader effectiveness for production foremen.
3. There is also no consistent relationship between initiating struc-

ture and leader effectiveness, but rather the relationship varies depending on the group that is being lead.[16]

Likert's Work

The Institute for Social Research of the University of Michigan was granted a contract in April 1947 by the Office of Naval Research.[17] The purpose of the contract was to discover principles contributing both to the productivity of a group and to the satisfaction derived by group members. The study was conducted at the home office of the Prudential Insurance Company in Newark, New Jersey.

Interviews were conducted with 24 section heads or supervisors and 419 nonsupervisory personnel. Results of the interviews showed that supervisors of high-producing sections were more likely:

1. To receive general, rather than close, supervision from their superiors.
2. To like the amount of authority and responsibility they have in their job.
3. To spend more time in supervision.
4. To give general, rather than close, supervision to their employees.
5. To be employee-oriented rather than production-oriented.[18]

Supervisors of low-producing sections had basically opposite characteristics and techniques. They were production-oriented and gave close supervision.

In 1961, Rensis Likert, then director of the Institute for Social Research at the University of Michigan, published the results of his years of research. His book, *New Patterns of Management,* is a classic in its field.[19] Basically, Likert feels that the patterns or styles of leadership or management employed by a particular organization can be categorized into four styles. He has identified and labeled these styles as follows:

System 1: Exploitative authoritative—Authoritarian form of management that attempts to exploit subordinates.

System 2: Benevolent authoritative—Authoritarian form of management but paternalistic in nature.

[16] Victor H. Vroom, "Leadership," in *Handbook of Industrial & Organizational Psychology,* ed. Marvin D. Dunnette (Skokie, Ill.: Rand McNally, 1976), p. 1531.

[17] Daniel Katz, Nathan MacCoby, and Nancy C. Morse, *Productivity, Supervision, and Morale in an Office Situation* (Ann Arbor: Institute for Social Research, University of Michigan, 1950).

[18] Ibid., p. 69.

[19] Rensis Likert, *New Patterns of Management* (New York: McGraw-Hill, 1961).

System 3: Consultative—Manager requests and receives inputs from subordinates, but maintains the right to make the final decision.

System 4: Participative—Manager gives some direction but decisions are made by consensus and majority based on total participation.

Likert used a questionnaire to determine the style of leadership and management pattern employed in the organization as a whole. The result of his studies indicated that System 4 is the most effective style of management, and that organizations should strive to develop a management pattern analogous to this system.[20]

The Managerial Grid®

In the early 1960s, Robert Blake and Jane Mouton developed a method of classifying the leadership style of a particular individual.[21] Basically, the Managerial Grid®, depicted in Figure 14–4, is a two-dimensional framework characterizing a leader according to concern for people and concern for production. A questionnaire is used to locate a particular style of leadership or management on the Grid. Notice that the leader activities of concern for people and concern for production closely relate to the leader activities identified in the Ohio State studies—consideration and initiating structure.

Blake and Mouton identified five basic styles of management using the Managerial Grid. Authority-Obedience, located in the lower right-hand corner (9,1 position), assumes that efficiency in operations results from properly arranging the conditions at work with minimum interference from other people. The opposite view, Country Club Management, located in the upper left-hand corner (1,9 position) assumes that proper attention to human needs leads to a comfortable organizational atmosphere and work place. Team Management, located in the upper right-hand corner (9,9) combines a high degree of concern for people with a high degree of concern for production. The other two styles on the Grid are Impoverished Management (1,1) and Organization Man Management (5,5).

The Managerial Grid is intended to serve as a framework en-

[20] Rensis Likert, *The Human Organization* (New York: McGraw-Hill, 1967), p. 46.

[21] Robert R. Blake and Jane Srygley Mouton, *The New Managerial Grid*® (Houston: Gulf Publishing, 1978).

FIGURE 14–4
The Managerial Grid®

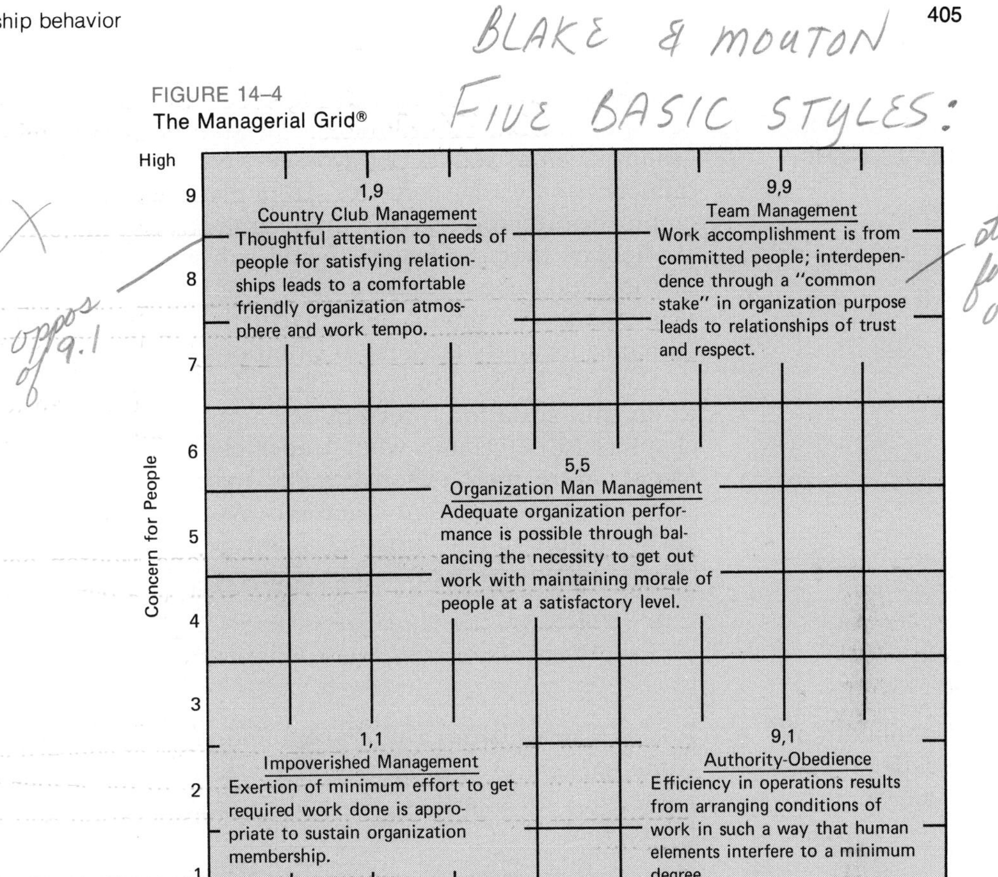

Source: Robert R. Blake and Jane Srygley Mouton, *The New Managerial Grid®*. (Houston: Gulf Publishing, 1978), p. 11. Copyright © 1978 by Gulf Publishing Company. Reproduced by permission.

abling managers to learn what their leadership style is and to develop a plan to move toward a 9,9 team management style of leadership. Subsequent studies on the Managerial Grid suggest that although the Grid assumes that managers are initially unbalanced in their emphasis on people or production, this is not necessarily true. In fact, Frank Harrison has suggested that practicing managers give somewhat equal emphasis to both of these concerns out of necessity, since inadequate emphasis on either one or both will result in reduced managerial effectiveness.[22]

[22] Frank Harrison, "Reshaping the Managerial Grid," *University of Michigan Business Review*, 20, no. 5 (September 1977), p. 24.

SITUATIONAL APPROACHES TO LEADERSHIP

The leadership studies discussed so far are similar in that they do not specifically address the complexities of differences between groups (such as production workers versus accountants) and their influences on leader behavior. To imply that a manager should be employee-oriented rather than production-oriented (Michigan studies) or that the leader should exhibit concern for both production and people (Blake and Mouton) does not say much about what the leader should do in particular situations or offer much guidance for daily leadership situations.[23]

Current leadership research is largely concerned with the leadership situation. Previous attempts (described earlier in this chapter) to determine what leader characteristics or leader behaviors were most effective failed mainly because the relationships varied in different situations. As a result, researchers have not been able to conclude that one type of behavior or one set of characteristics were related to effective leadership.

Continuum of Leadership Behaviors

Tannenbaum & Schmidt

Robert Tannenbaum and Warren Schmidt contend that different combinations of situational elements require different styles of leadership. They suggest that there are three important factors or forces that must be considered in determining what leadership style is most effective: forces involving the manager, forces involving the subordinate, and forces involving the situation.[24] Furthermore, all of the forces are interdependent.

Figure 14–5 describes in detail the forces that affect leadership situations. Since these forces differ in strength and interaction in differing situations, one style of leadership is not effective in all situations.

In fact, as shown in Figure 14–6, Tannenbaum and Schmidt argue that there is a continuum of behaviors that the manager may employ depending on the particular situation. They further concluded that successful leaders are keenly aware of those forces that are most relevant to their behavior at a given time; accurately understand not only themselves but also the other individuals involved in the organizational and social environment; and are able to behave appropriately in light of these perceptions.[25]

---

[23] Vroom, "Leadership," p. 1533.

[24] Robert Tannenbaum and Warren Schmidt, "How to Choose a Leadership Pattern," *Harvard Business Review*, May–June 1973, pp. 162–80.

[25] Ibid.

FIGURE 14–5
Forces in the Leadership Situation

Forces in the manager

Value system:
- How the manager personally feels about delegating
- Degree of confidence in subordinates

Personal leadership inclinations:
- Authoritarian versus participative

Feelings of security in uncertain situations

Forces in the subordinates

Need for independence:
- Some people need and want direction while others do not

Readiness to assume responsibility:
- Different people need different degrees of responsibility

Tolerance for ambiguity:
- Specific versus general directions

Interest and perceived importance of the problem:
- People generally have more interest in and work harder on important problems

Degree of understanding and identification with organizational goals:
- A manager is more likely to delegate authority to an individual who seems to have a positive attitude about the organization

Degree of expectation in sharing in decision making:
- People who have worked under subordinate-centered leadership tend to resent boss-centered leadership.

Forces in the situation

Type of organization:
- Centralized versus decentralized

Work group effectiveness:
- How effectively the group works together

The problem itself:
- The work group's knowledge and experience relevant to the problem

Time pressure:
- It is difficult to delegate to subordinates in crisis situations

Demands from upper levels of management

Demands from government, unions, and society in general

Fiedler's Contingency Approach to Leadership

Fred Fiedler has further refined the idea of a situational approach to leadership by attempting to define the particular style of leadership that is appropriate for a given situation.[26] Fiedler defined two basic styles of leadership—task-motivated and relationship-motivated. The task-motivated style of leadership (similar to earlier discussed ideas of concern for production and initiating structure) fulfills the leader's need to gain satisfaction from the performance of a task. The relationship-motivated style of leadership (similar to concern for people and consideration) fulfills

[26] Fred E. Fiedler, *A Theory of Leadership Effectiveness* (New York: McGraw-Hill, 1967).

FIGURE 14–6
Continuum of Leadership Behavior

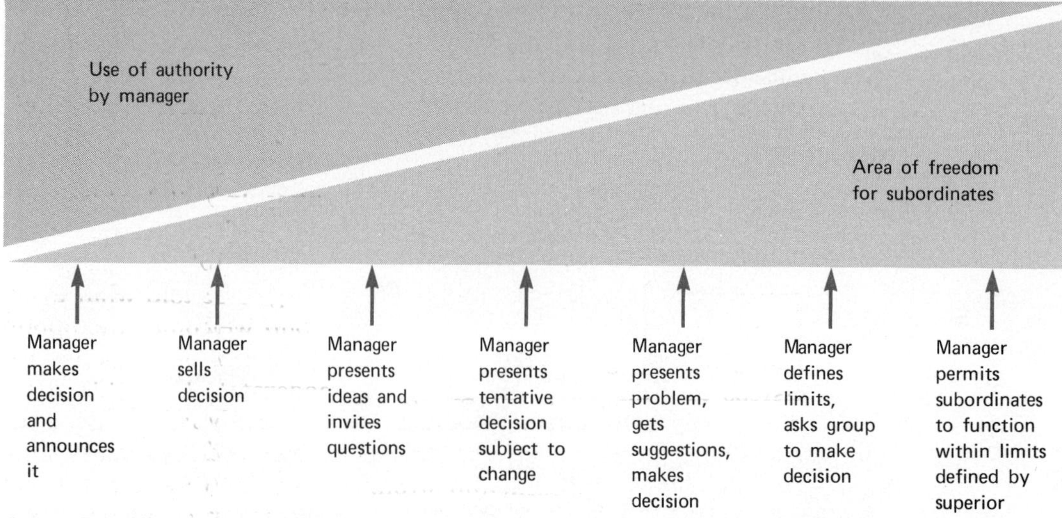
Use of authority by manager
Area of freedom for subordinates
Manager makes decision and announces it
Manager sells decision
Manager presents ideas and invites questions
Manager presents tentative decision subject to change
Manager presents problem, gets suggestions, makes decision
Manager defines limits, asks group to make decision
Manager permits subordinates to function within limits defined by superior

Source: Robert Tannenbaum and Warren H. Schmidt, "How to Choose a Leadership Pattern," *Harvard Business Review*, May–June 1973. Copyright © 1973 by the President and Fellows of Harvard College; all rights reserved.

the leader's need to gain satisfaction from interpersonal relationships.

Fiedler employed a questionnaire to determine the leadership style used by a particular individual. The respondent was asked to describe the person with whom he or she could work least effectively, and the person with whom he or she could work most effectively. A person who describes a least-preferred co-worker in relatively favorable terms is presumably basically motivated to have close interpersonal relations with others; Fiedler classified these people as relationship-motivated leaders. On the other hand, people who reject co-workers with whom they have difficulties are presumably basically motivated to accomplish or achieve the task: they are classified as task-oriented leaders.

Fiedler turned his attention next to the situation in which the leader was operating. He classified leadership situations along a favorable-unfavorable continuum by considering three major dimensions: leader-member relations, task structure, and position power. Leader-member relations refer to the degree that others trust and respect the leader, and to the leaders' congeniality. This is somewhat analogous to referent power. Task structure is the degree to which job tasks are structured. For example, assembly-line jobs are more structured than managerial jobs. Position power refers to the power and influence that go with a job. A manager has more position power if the manager is able to hire, fire, and discipline. Position power is analogous to coercive, reward, and legitimate power. Using these three dimensions, an eight-celled classification scheme was developed. Figure 14–7 (p. 410), illustrates this classification scheme along a favorable-unfavorable continuum.

Figure 14–8 shows the most productive style of leadership for each of the different situational possibilities. In both highly favorable and highly unfavorable situations, a task-motivated leader was found to be more effective. In highly favorable situations the group is ready to be directed and is willing to be told what to do. In highly unfavorable situations, the group welcomes the opportunity of having the leader take the responsibility for making decisions and directing the group. In moderately favorable situations, a relationship-motivated leader was found to be more effective. In situation 7 (moderately poor leader-member relations, unstructured task, and strong position power), the task and relationship style of leadership were equally productive. Thus, Fiedler has gone one step beyond Tannenbaum and Schmidt by demonstrating which particular style of leadership is most effective in a given situation.

PATH–GOAL THEORY OF LEADERSHIP

The path-goal theory of leadership considers the reasoning processes that subordinates use in responding to leader behavior. Basically, the path-goal theory assumes that individuals react rationally in pursuing certain goals because those goals ultimately result in highly-valued payoffs to the individual.

The leader's role is to elicit work-goal directed behavior from individuals by increasing personal payoffs for work-goal attainment, making the path to these payoffs easier to travel by clarifying it and reducing road blocks and pitfalls, and increasing the opportunities for personal satisfaction en route.[27]

Additionally, the path-goal theory implies that the degree to which the leader can be effective in eliciting work-goal directed behavior depends on the situation. The leader can have positive effects in those situations in which there are ambiguities in what is required to reach work goals or in which the leader controls the reward/punishment system. In situations in which tasks are routine and the reward/punishment system is relatively fixed, attempts by the leader to clarify path-goal relationships can in-

[27] Robert J. House, "A Path-Goal Theory of Leader Effectiveness," *Administrative Science Quarterly*, September 1971, p. 324.

FIGURE 14–7

Fiedler's Classification of Situations

Situation	*1*	*2*	*3*	*4*	*5*	*6*	*7*	*8*
Leader-member relations	Good	Good	Good	Good	Poor	Poor	Poor	Poor
Task structure . . .	Structured	Structured	Unstructured	Unstructured	Structured	Structured	Unstructured	Unstructured
Position power . . .	Strong	Weak	Strong	Weak	Strong	Weak	Strong	Weak
	Favorable for leader ←							→ Unfavorable for leader

FIGURE 14–8

Relationship of Leadership Style to Situation

Situation	*1*	*2*	*3*	*4*	*5*	*6*	*7*	*8*
Leader-member relations	Good	Good	Good	Good	Poor	Poor	Poor	Poor
Task structure	Structured	Structured	Unstructured	Unstructured	Structured	Structured	Unstructured	Unstructured
Leader position power	Strong	Weak	Strong	Weak	Strong	Weak	Strong	Weak
	Favorable for leader ←							→ Unfavorable for leader
Most productive leadership style	Task	Task	Task	Relation	Relation	No data	Task or relation	Task

crease performance but generally at the cost of a decrease in level of satisfaction. Finally, leader behavior that reflects concern for people can result in increased performance only to the extent that it facilitates the accomplishment of goals.

IMPLICATIONS OF LEADERSHIP THEORIES FOR ORGANIZATIONS AND MANAGERS

How can all of these leadership theories be made relevant to the organization's need for effective managers? First, given the situational factors that have been discussed throughout this chapter, it appears to be unlikely that selection procedures will be developed to accurately predict successful leaders.[28] The situational forces are further complicated by the dynamic nature of managerial roles which are continuously changing. Even if the initial selection process could select effective leaders, the dynamics of the managerial situation might make the initial selection invalid.

Further, contrary to many of the conclusions drawn from the studies that have been discussed, most leadership training today is conducted on the assumption that there is one best way to lead.[29] However, leadership training designed to help leaders or potential leaders identify the nature of the leadership situation appears to have potential in developing managers into more effective leaders. Training in effective leadership skills is not so much a process of changing individual characteristics but rather one of ensuring that the individual is operating in an appropriate situation or teaching the individual how to act to fit the situation.[30]

In conclusion, the following points can tentatively be made concerning effective leadership:

1. High consideration and initiating structure often provide a successful leadership style.
2. Under emergency or high-pressure situations, emphasis on initiating structure is desirable and often preferred by subordinates.
3. When the manager is the only information source for subordinates regarding their tasks, they often expect the manager to structure their behavior.
4. Subordinates have differing preferences regarding the degree of consideration and initiating structure exhibited by their managers.

---

[28] Steven Kerr, C. A. Schriesheim, C. J. Murphy, and R. M. Stogdill, "Toward a Contingency Theory of Leadership Based upon the Consideration and Initiating Structure Literature," *Organizational Behavior & Human Performance,* August 1974, pp. 62–82.

[29] Schriesheim et al., "Leadership Theory," p. 37.

[30] Ibid., p. 38.

5. Higher management often has set preferences regarding the leadership styles employed by lower level managers.
6. Some managers can adjust their behavior to fit the situation; while others, in attempting to make this adjustment, appear to be fake and manipulative.[31]

SUMMARY

Leadership is a process of influencing the activities of either formal or informal work groups in their tasks of goal setting and goal achievement. Generally, there are two types of leaders in organizations—the appointed leader (manager) and the informal leader. Power is defined as a relationship between people in which an individual can be influenced by another to do something that the individual would not do otherwise. Various types of power are: coercive, reward, legitimate, expert, and referent. Leaders may use one or several power types to influence group behavior.

Several important research studies on leadership were also reviewed. The trait theory focuses on the characteristics or traits of the leader. It was concluded, however, that traits must be analyzed in light of the leadership situation. Studies in the 1930s identified three basic styles of leadership—autocratic, laissez-faire, and democratic. The Ohio State studies in 1945 attempted to describe what successful leaders do. They identified consideration for people and initiating structure as key dimensions of leadership behavior. Using leadership dimensions similar to the Ohio State studies, Blake and Mouton developed the Managerial Grid, which uses a two-dimensional grid for classifying leadership styles. The University of Michigan studies on leadership were designed to study the relationship between leadership style and productivity. Basically, these studies concluded that the employee-oriented manager had more productive workers.

Most current leadership research has been concerned largely with the leadership situation. Tannenbaum and Schmidt contend that different combinations of situational elements require different styles of leadership. Fiedler further refined the idea of a situational approach to leadership by attempting to define the particular style of leadership that is appropriate for a given situation. Finally, the path-goal theory of leader effectiveness was discussed. This theory states that the role of the leader in eliciting work-goal directed behavior consists of increasing personal payoffs to subordinates for work-goal attainment, making the path to those payoffs easier to travel by reducing road blocks, and increasing the opportunities for personal satisfaction en route to the goal.

path-goal theory

[31] Ibid., pp. 38–39.

The final section of the chapter attempted to make the previously discussed theories on leadership relevant to the organization's need for effective managers. Several points were summarized concerning effective leadership.

REVIEW QUESTIONS

1. Define leadership. What is the source of a leader's authority?
2. Describe in detail the following three leadership styles:
   a. Autocratic.
   b. Laissez-faire.
   c. Democratic.
3. What was the purpose of the Ohio State leadership studies? What were the results of the Ohio State studies?
4. What was the purpose of the University of Michigan leadership studies? Explain the results of the Michigan studies.
5. Describe the Managerial Grid.
6. Describe three important forces or factors that Tannenbaum and Schmidt think should be considered in determining what leadership style is most effective.
7. What is Fiedler's contingency approach to leadership?
8. What is the path-goal theory of leader effectiveness?
9. Describe some of the implications of the studies on leadership for organizations and managers.

DISCUSSION QUESTIONS

1. Discuss the following statement: "Leaders are born and cannot be developed."
2. "Leaders must have courage." Do you agree or disagree? Why?
3. Do you think the variance in leadership styles of such people as Adolph Hitler, Franklin D. Roosevelt, and Martin Luther King, Jr., can be explained by any of the theories discussed in this chapter? Elaborate on your answer.
4. "Leaders lead by example." Explain what people mean when they use this statement. Do you believe it? Explain.

SELECTED READINGS

Blake, R. R., and J. S. Mouton. "What's New with the Grid?" *Training and Development Journal,* May 1978, pp. 3–8.

Burke, W. W. "Leadership: Is There One Best Approach?" *Management Review,* November 1980, pp. 54–56.

Carbone, T. C. "Theory X and Theory Y Revisited." *Managerial Planning,* May –June 1981, pp. 24–27.

Davis, T. R. V., and F. Luthans. "Leadership Reexamined: A Behavioral Approach." *Academy of Management Review,* April 1979, pp. 237–48.

Fiedler, Fred. *A Theory of Leadership Effectiveness.* New York: McGraw-Hill, 1967.

Greene, C. N. "Questions of Causation in the Path-Goal Theory of Leadership." *Academy of Management Journal,* March 1979, pp. 22–41.

House, Robert. "A Path Goal Theory of Leadership Effectiveness." *Administrative Science Quarterly* 16 (1970), pp. 321–38.

House, Robert, and Mary L. Baetz. "Leadership: Some Empirical Generalizations and New Research Directions." In *Research in Organizational Behavior, Vol. 1.,* ed. Barry M. Staw (Greenwich, Conn: JAI Press, 1979), pp. 341–423.

Lawrie, J. W. "Guide to Customized Leadership Training and Development." *Personnel Journal* 58 (September 1979), pp. 593–96.

Likert, Rensis. *The Human Organization.* New York: McGraw-Hill, 1967.

———. *New Patterns of Management.* New York: McGraw-Hill, 1961.

McGregor, Douglas. *The Human Side of Enterprise.* New York: McGraw-Hill, 1960.

Peters, T. J. "Leadership: Sad Facts and Silver Linings." *Harvard Business Review,* November 1979, pp. 164–72.

Schriesheim, C. A.; J. M. Tolliver; and O. C. Behling. "Leadership Theory: Some Implications for Managers." *MSU Business Topics,* Summer 1978, pp. 34–40.

Sinetar, M. "Developing Leadership Potential." *Personnel Journal,* March 1981, pp. 193–96.

Stogdill, Ralph. *Handbook of Leadership.* New York: Free Press, 1974.

Tannenbaum, Robert, and Warren Schmidt. "How to Choose a Leadership Pattern." *Harvard Business Review,* May–June 1973, pp. 162–175 ff.

Vroom, Victor H. "Can Leaders Learn to Lead?" *Organizational Dynamics,* Winter 1976, pp. 17–28.

Vroom, Victor, and Philip Yetton. *Leadership and Decision-Making.* Pittsburg: University of Pittsburg Press, 1973.

Zaleznik, Abraham. "Managers and Leaders: Are They Really Different?" *Harvard Business Review,* May–June 1977, pp. 67–78.

Zierden, W. E. "Leading Through the Follower's Point of View." *Organizational Dynamics,* Spring 1980, pp. 27–46.

Case 14–1

Does the congregation care?

Situation: You are talking with a young pastor of an independent church with about 300 adult members. The pastor came directly to the church after graduating from a nondenominational theological school and has been in the job for eight months.

Pastor: I don't know what to do. I feel as if I've been treading water ever since the day I got here, and frankly, I'm not sure that I will be here much longer. If they don't fire me, I may leave on my own. Maybe I'm just not cut out for the ministry.

You: What has happened since you came to this church?

Pastor: When I arrived I was really full of energy and wanted to see how much this church could accomplish. The very first thing I did was to conduct a questionnaire survey of the entire adult membership to see what types of goals they wanted to pursue. Unfortunately, I found that the members had such mixed (and perhaps apathetic) feelings about the goals, that it was hard to draw any conclusions. There were a few who felt very strongly that we should be doing much more in the area of evangelism and charitable service. There were also a few who strongly favored more emphasis on internal things, such as remodeling the sanctuary, developing our music program, and setting up a day-care center for the use of the members. Most of the members, however, didn't voice any strong preferences. A lot of people didn't return the questionnaire, and a few even seemed to resent my conducting the survey.

You: What have you done since you took the survey?

Pastor: To be honest about it, I've kept a pretty low profile, concentrating mainly on routine duties. I haven't tried to implement or even push any major new programs. One problem is that I've gotten the impression, through various insinuations, that my being hired was by no means an overwhelmingly popular decision. Evidently a fairly substantial segment of the congregation was skeptical of my lack of experience and felt that the decision to hire me was railroaded through by a few members of the Pastoral Search Committee. I guess I am just reluctant to assume a strong leadership role until some consensus has developed concerning the goals of the church and I've had more time to gain the confidence of the congregation. I don't know how long that will take, though; and I'm not sure I can tolerate the situation much longer.

1. Can you analyze and explain the situation using any of the theories of leadership discussed in this chapter?
2. What would you recommend that the young pastor do?

Case 14–2

Changes in the plastics division

Ed Sullivan is general manager of the plastics division of Warner Manufacturing Company. Eleven years ago, Ed hired Russell

(Rusty) Means as general manager of the Plastic division's two factories. Ed trained Rusty as a manager and feels that Rusty is a good manager, an opinion based largely on the fact that products are produced on schedule and are of such quality that few customers complain. In fact, for the past eight years Ed has pretty much let Rusty run the factories independently.

Rusty believes strongly that his job is to see that production runs smoothly. He feels that work is work. Sometimes it is agreeable; sometimes, disagreeable. If an employee doesn't like the work, he or she can either adjust or quit. Rusty, say the factory personnel, "Runs things. He's firm and doesn't stand for any nonsense. Things are done by the book or they are not done at all." The turnover in the factories is low, and nearly every employee likes Rusty, feels that he knows his trade and that he stands up for them.

Two months ago, Ed Sullivan retired and his replacement, Wallace Thomas, took over as general manager of the plastics division. One of the first things Thomas did was call his key management people together and announce some major changes that he wanted to implement. These included: (1) bring the operative employees into the decision-making process; (2) establish a planning committee made up of three management members and three operative employees; (3) start a suggestion system; and (4) install as quickly as possible a performance apprisal program agreeable to both management and the operative employees. Wallace also stated that he would be active in seeing that these projects would be implemented without delay.

After the meeting, Rusty was upset and decided to talk to Robert Mitchell, general manager of sales for the plastics division.

Rusty: Wallace is really going to change things, isn't he?

Robert: Yeah, maybe it's for the best. Things were a little lax under Ed.

Rusty: I liked them that way. Ed let you run your own shop. I'm afraid Wallace is going to be looking over my shoulder every minute.

Robert: Well, let's give him a chance. After all, some of the changes he's proposing sound good.

Rusty: Well, I can tell you the factory employees won't like them. Having them participate in making decisions and those other things are just fancy management stuff that won't work with factory employees.

1. What different styles of leadership are shown in this case?
2. What style of leadership do you feel that Wallace will have to use with Rusty?
3. Do you agree with Rusty? Discuss.

SECTION THREE
CASE

Trouble on the line crew*

Theresa Selmants, 27, has a degree in elementary education. Three months ago, City Bell contacted her and informed her she had been selected to begin employment training as a line technician. She had applied for the job last October when she found herself unable to suitably support her two young children on a schoolteacher's salary. Naturally, she was elated when City Bell called her and she was eager to report to work. She was to begin her training with a one-week pole-climbing school.

Theresa's friends were shocked, to say the least. Her only comment with regard to her new job was that she had always wanted to work outdoors and looked forward to learning her new job. She was realistic enough to know that she might be in for some rough times at first. It wasn't that she couldn't handle the job. She knew that she could. The fact of the matter was that City Bell, employing some 37,000 employees throughout the state, had only 630 females in traditionally male jobs, with only 190 employed in semiskilled outside craft jobs like that of line technician. But this did not bother Theresa; she knew that if she could hold her end of the job up and didn't use her sex as a strategic weapon, she would become part of the gang with no real problems.

Her first week in pole-climbing school was largely uneventful. Although she came home dead tired every night, she was able to master everything she was taught. Her instructor had dutifully explained to her, as he did to the other 2 women and 11 men in the class, how to position herself and carry the various tools, equipment, and cable. She had no problems and found that she picked up extra tips from watching the others and listening to the trainer's suggestions as he spoke with the other trainees.

During her first week, she had become fairly close friends with Ellen Mayer, another trainee, who had early in the week confessed to her that she was terrified of heights. Ellen was disturbed by the fact that she had been literally pushed by the employment interviewer to take the line technician's job when she had applied for a job with City Bell. Although she had told the interviewer she did not like the idea of having to climb poles, the interviewer assured her that everyone had those fears and, after all, the pay was worth it. Ellen claimed that she should have paid heed to her doubts about the job and that all the interviewer had been con-

*Much of the information on which this case is based was taken from a story reported by Cathy Frost in the *Detroit Free Press,* March 12, 1979.

cerned with was meeting affirmative action quotas. When Ellen left the training program at the end of the first week, Theresa understood how hard it was for her to finally admit the job wasn't for her.

Upon successfully completing pole-climbing school, Theresa was assigned to a crew working out of the Ansley garage. As a rookie line technician, she was to work with two experienced line technicians: William (Bill) Autrey, 25, and Jimmy Davis, 24. The Ansley garage was staffed with 40 craft employees, only two of which were female. Theresa was the only female craft employee assigned to work outside of the garage.

Ben Holz, supervisor of the Ansley garage, greeted her warmly on her first day at the job. He introduced her to her crew—Bill and Jimmy—and explained that they would "show her the ropes"—how to set up poles, string out cables, and perform basic maintenance and repairs. While Bill and Jimmy left to get their equipment together, Ben took Theresa aside and said, "I really admire you, old girl. You're stepping into some pretty tall shoes. Take it easy on old Bill and Jimmy—they've never had to work along side a pretty lady before. Bill is pretty quiet and won't give you much lip, but old Jimmy—he's a little loose-mouthed. He'll be hard on you like he is on all the rookies—he's already made it clear that he doesn't look forward to 'babysitting a chick', as he put it. Quite frankly, you don't look cut out for it—I'll be surprised if you make it through the first week. But I'm rooting for you, sugar—give it a good try!" With a friendly swat on her behind, Ben sent Theresa off to her crew.

Theresa turned back to Ben before meeting her crew and said, "Mr. Holz, wouldn't you feel funny swatting Jimmy that way?"

Ben, looking at her quizzically, started to chuckle and she continued, "Well then, I'd appreciate your feeling the same way toward me." Walking toward her crew, Theresa took a deep breath and thought, "Boy—he claims Jimmy will be rough to win over—he doesn't even think I can make it!"

The first few days were more than Theresa had bargained for. Jimmy was far worse than she had expected. He continued referring to her as "half-man," "boy," and other names that were far less flattering. While Bill didn't join in the name calling at first, he doubled over laughing when she reminded Jimmy that her name was Theresa.

After her first week as a rookie technician, Theresa felt she had made considerable progress, given her situation. She had been forced to watch Bill and Jimmy work most of the time because they refused to let her become actively involved. She also spent a large part of the time being the butt of their practical jokes. They would rig her equipment making it impossible to get some of the work done and then blame her inability to perform on her being female; or they would sneak away from the work site and drive off, leaving her stranded. She was constantly reminded that if they had a "full crew" they could work at their normal pace. Priding themselves on being top-notch line technicians, both Bill and Jimmy made it perfectly clear they resented having the "token broad" assigned to them.

Theresa desperately kept on trying to learn what she could and ignore the childish treatment she was being subjected to by her alleged trainers. Whenever she asked a question, the usual response was for either Bill or Jimmy to look upward, pretending not to hear—or putting her off by saying that "there isn't time to explain something so simple right now . . . if you can't learn the basics you might as well go back to the kitchen where you belong."

On her 12th day, Theresa finally snapped. She and her crew had gone into a local diner for breakfast, and as usual Bill and Jimmy took two chairs at the counter where the adjacent chairs were already occuped. Theresa, sitting down at a table by herself, almost welcomed the relief from their constant, nasty remarks. After finishing her breakfast, she saw they were still drinking coffee, so she got up and went toward the washrooms. As she passed the counter, Jimmy yelled out above the noise of the crowded diner, "Hey 'half-man' don't take all day in their powdering your nose. We ain't got all day!" She cringed as all eyes turned toward her as she was walking into the ladies' room, her ears ringing with the laughter around her. A few minutes later she emerged to find that Bill and Jimmy had left. Rushing outside, she saw no trace of them. Sitting down on the curb, she waited, fighting back angry tears. They had left her like this before but always came back a few minutes later. After waiting 45 minutes and suffering through the joking comments of customers leaving the diner who had witnessed the earlier scene, she went inside and called a taxi.

Upon returning to the garage, she immediately went to Ben Holz's office. Her voice revealed how angry and frustrated she was as she told Ben what she had put up with the past two weeks.

"Mr. Holz, I've tried—I really have but they're doing everything they can to humiliate me and ensure that I fail as a line technician. But this morning—that was the last straw. I want to be transferred to another crew as soon as possible."

Ben, sitting back with a smile across his face explained, "Now sugar, I warned you it wasn't going to be easy. The boys always break in the rookies. It's part of the training you either can take it, or you leave. Now you're the one who wants to be treated as a equal. Sure, they may be having a little more fun with you than most, but it's all part of the game."

Theresa responded defiantly, "Mr. Holz, what I've been subjected to is not fun and games by any stretch of the imagination. Why, animals are shown more consideration than I've been shown. I cannot—absolutely cannot—learn anything or function effectively while having to work with that crew. I am *not* being given a fair chance to succeed."

Ben got up from his chair, walked over to Theresa, put his arm around her, and said, "Sugar, let me give. . . ."

"Do *not* call me 'sugar!' My name is Theresa—or Miss Selmants—whichever you prefer!," Theresa said, pulling away from Ben's outstretched arm.

"Alright, *Miss Selmants.* As I was starting to say, cry-babies are not looked upon favorably around here. No, as a matter of fact, the cry-babies never make it. Now I won't let on that you came in here all upset, but you'd better learn one thing quick—in a man's world you gotta settle things by yourself. If you can't get along with your crew, you'd just better figure out what you're doing wrong. Honey—I mean Miss Selmants—you can't keep running to me everytime one of the boys looks at you cross-eyed.

"And let me tell you, it isn't going to be different with any of the other boys. There's a big productivity campaign on now—we gotta keep costs down. You just see to it you don't hold those boys back—Bill and Jimmy are the best linemen we've got in the garage."

Theresa left Ben's office even more dejected than before. As she walked behind the storage area into the main garage, she heard Jimmy's voice.

"Yeah—she refused to sit at the same table with us at breakfast. Said we were uncouth and not fit for a lady like her. Bill and I told her we'd had just about enough of her uppity ways—why she doesn't want to get dirty, and she hates to climb poles. You know, I heard she only made it through pole-climbing school because old City Bell has to pacify Uncle Sam. Anyway, she got all red-faced and mad and started crying right there in the diner. Then she stormed out of the diner and took a taxi. We tried to calm her down. Shoot, we had a major repair job over on the west side and couldn't get to it cause we needed a full crew. But you know how broads are when they get upset."

Another voice popped up, "Hey Bill, I raise my bet to $25 that that little —— won't make it to pay day."

The voices silenced as Theresa walked up. Moving past the group of people, she walked toward Jimmy and Bill and said flatly, "We're already late. We'd better get a move on."

Little conversation transpired between the three for the rest of the day. As Theresa was leaving the garage, Bill called out, "By the way, half-man, the next time you go crying to Holz, you'll have more than a taxi fare to complain about." She walked out of the garage pursued by laughter.

As she entered the garage the next day, she saw Ben talking to Jimmy and Bill and a few of the other guys. When she walked up, the group disbanded and she sensed that she had been the major topic of conversation. She knew she had been when Bill turned to her, bowed dramatically and said, "*Ms.* Selmants, would you care to join Mr. Davis and myself on a little jaunt to Clower Street?"

"Ah, cut it out, Bill," she replied. "Let's just go." They arrived at Clower Street and set about repairing the down line. Neither Bill nor Jimmy had much to say to her all day and Theresa wondered what they were up to. After all, Ben hadn't seemed to be too supportive yesterday. She was afraid to hope for the best—that they were finally going to settle down and work with her and not against her.

Things went along remarkably smoothly until she walked over to her equipment box and tripped over a loose piece of cable. Jimmy lunged at her, grabbed her up by the neck, and screamed, "Woman you just better get on the ball. You've been dragging us down for two weeks now. We don't have time for you!" Shaking loose his hand, Theresa shouted, "If you *ever* ever touch me again, I'll have you arrested." With that Bill jerked around, grabbed her shoulder and made a fist, catching himself as he drew it back. "No, that's just what you need. If I hit you, you'll run to Holz crying again. No little lady, you just listen—listen good and clear. No one in the garage wants you. You just hold us down. You're not gonna make it, so why don't you make it easy on yourself and just go back to teaching school—or better yet, stay at home and take care of your children like you're supposed to anyway."

Theresa ran to the truck and drove off. She finally stopped at a wooded area, parked the truck, and got out. Tears were streaming down her face as she sat down on the ground.

"Why is it that you have to put yourself through so much hassle just to get a good job? I like this job. I like being able to care for my family, to give them things other children have. I like knowing I'm financially dependent on no one.

"I knew that linemen were a special breed—all hung up over their macho image. But I have never, never been around men who were such pigs. I know I can handle the job. I've *proven* that. I just can't handle the harrassment, the humiliation. I'm a person, too!"

A few minutes later, Theresa got back in the truck, drove it to the garage, and parked it. She walked straight through the garage to Ben's office. Ben was not in. She placed the keys on his desk and left him a note:

"Mr. Holz, we definitely do have a problem."

1. What types of communication patterns are evident in this case?
2. What effect did the informal work group have in this case?
3. What types of conflict were exhibited in the case?
4. Was Mr. Holz an effective leader? If not, what type of leadership style would be effective? Why?

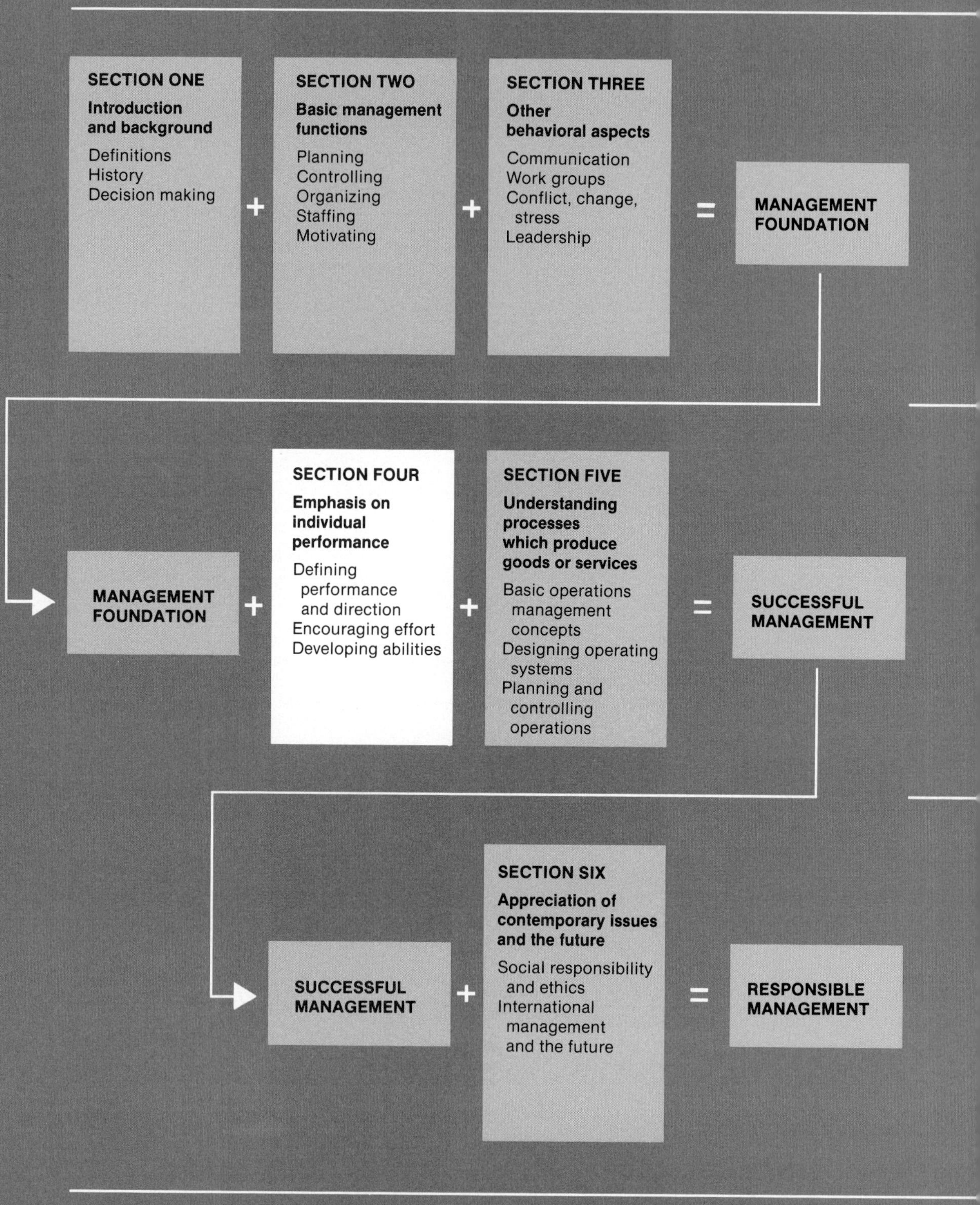

SECTION ONE
Introduction and background
Definitions
History
Decision making

+

SECTION TWO
Basic management functions
Planning
Controlling
Organizing
Staffing
Motivating

+

SECTION THREE
Other behavioral aspects
Communication
Work groups
Conflict, change, stress
Leadership

=

MANAGEMENT FOUNDATION

MANAGEMENT FOUNDATION

+

SECTION FOUR
Emphasis on individual performance
Defining performance and direction
Encouraging effort
Developing abilities

+

SECTION FIVE
Understanding processes which produce goods or services
Basic operations management concepts
Designing operating systems
Planning and controlling operations

=

SUCCESSFUL MANAGEMENT

SUCCESSFUL MANAGEMENT

+

SECTION SIX
Appreciation of contemporary issues and the future
Social responsibility and ethics
International management and the future

=

RESPONSIBLE MANAGEMENT

section four

EMPHASIS ON INDIVIDUAL PERFORMANCE

The first three sections of this text are designed to provide a sound management foundation by outlining what managers do, discussing the basic functions that managers perform in doing their jobs, and developing an understanding of human behavior in organizations. Building on this management foundation, Section Four is based on the realization that if managers are to be successful they must be able to integrate and apply their knowledge *through individuals.* In fact, the success of a manager depends largely on the performance of subordinates. A manager must know how to elicit high levels of performance from them. Section Four shows how to apply the management concepts and principles developed in the earlier sections so as to attain high performance. Performance is discussed and presented as dependent on three major factors—effort, ability, and direction.

The first part of Chapter 15 is devoted to a discussion of performance in general. What determines performance and how to measure it are two questions that are addressed. Several different methods and techniques are presented for setting performance standards in organizations. The last part of Chapter 15 presents several methods for providing direction to employees.

Chapter 16 deals with the effort component of performance. The purpose of the chapter is to explore the relationship between organizational rewards and employee performance.

Chapter 17 emphasizes the importance of developing employees' abilities. The relationship of staffing (discussed in Section Two) to developing individual abilities is discussed. The role of training in modern organizations is explored. Alternative methods for training employees are presented.

15 Defining Performance and Direction

Objectives

1. To develop an appreciation for the importance of measuring individual performance.
2. To identify the major deteriminants of individual performance and to describe the essential requirements of good performance measures.
3. To describe the importance of defining direction for individual organization members.
4. To explore some of the methods that can be used for defining direction within an organization.

Chapter Outline

RECOGNIZING PERFORMANCE
- Determinants of Performance
- Environmental Factors as Performance Obstacles
- The Activity Trap

MEASURES OF PERFORMANCE—CRITERIA
- Subjective Performance Measures

DEFINING EMPLOYEE DIRECTION
- Job Descriptions
- Performance Appraisal
- Disciplinary Systems

Glossary of Terms

Activity trap A trap many managers fall into by focusing on the effort component of performance rather than on performance itself.

Checklist Method of performance appraisal in which the rater completes a series of questions concerning the behavior of the individual being rated answered by checking yes or no.

Conceptual criterion A verbal statement of important or socially relevant outcomes or performance levels based on the general aims of the organization.

Constructive discipline Discipline system in which proper conduct is defined and communicated; employees are given the opportunity to correct improper conduct and are warned that future breaches of proper conduct will result in progressively harsher disciplinary action.

Critical incident appraisal Method of performance appraisal in which the rater keeps a written record of incidents that illustrate both positive and negative behavior of the job holder; the rater then uses this as a basis for conducting the performance appraisal.

Discipline Actions taken against an individual who fails to conform to the rules of the organization of which he or she is a member.

Essay appraisal Method of performance appraisal in which the rater prepares a written statement listing an individual's strengths, weaknesses, past performance, and potential for advancement.

Forced-choice rating Method of performance appraisal that requires the rater to choose from several seemingly equal statements those that best describe the jobholder being rated.

Graphic rating scale Method of performance appraisal that requires the rater to assess an individual on such factors as initiative, dependability, cooperativeness, and attitude.

Hot stove rule A set of guidelines used in constructive discipline which call for administering disciplinary actions quickly, consistently, and impartially.

Job description Written statement which identifies the tasks, duties, activities, and performance results required.

Management by objectives (MBO) A management system in which the superior and subordinate jointly define the objectives and responsibilities of the subordinate's job which the superior then uses as criteria in periodically evaluating the subordinate's performance.

Performance The degree of accomplishment of the tasks that make up an individual's job.

Performance appraisal Process that involves communicating to a person how that person is performing the job and establishing a plan of improvement if necessary.

Ranking method Method of performance appraisal in which the performance of an individual is determined by ranking his or her performance relative to that of others.

Reliability Refers to the reproducibility of results or the degree to which a measuring instrument is consistent or stable.

Validity The degree to which a criterion measures what it purports to measure. The terms *relevance* and *validity* are often used interchangeably.

Work standards approach Method of performance appraisal in which specific output or time standards or both are set for a job, and the jobholder's performance is then evaluated against these standards.

> . . . They are real people in every way except one: they are unclear to what they are trying to accomplish. . . .
>
> It's like finding an opponent's sword sticking out of your chest, then discovering that a duel has been underway for ten minutes and that you have lost.
>
> It's like running in a race with none of the contestants knowing how long it is to be. They can only wonder if it is time to sprint for the wire—it may be a 100-yard dash or it may be the Boston Marathon.
>
> It's like being hit by a falling tree, after which the ax man leans over your broken body to whisper TIMBER!
>
> *George S. Odiorne**

The analogies given above were used by George S. Odiorne in explaining the dilemmas employees face when they don't understand what is expected of them on the job. A critical element in defining what is expected of employees on the job is the establishment of performance measures. Only after measures of good or effective performance have been clearly defined can managers direct their subordinates toward the attainment of these measures. The purpose of this chapter is to discuss the establishment of performance measures and to explore some of the methods that can be used for successfully defining direction within the organization.

RECOGNIZING PERFORMANCE

Performance refers to the degree of accomplishment of the tasks that make up an individual's job. It reflects how well an individual is fulfilling the requirements of a job. Often confused with effort, which refers to energy expended, performance is measured in terms of results. For example, a student may exert a great deal of effort in preparing for an examination and still make a poor grade. In such a case, the effort expended was high yet the performance was low.

Determinants of Performance

Lyman Porter and Edward Lawler have described job performance as being "the net effect of a person's effort as modified by

*George S. Odiorne, *Management and the Activity Trap* (New York: Harper & Row, 1974), p. 29.

FIGURE 15–1
Determinants of Performance

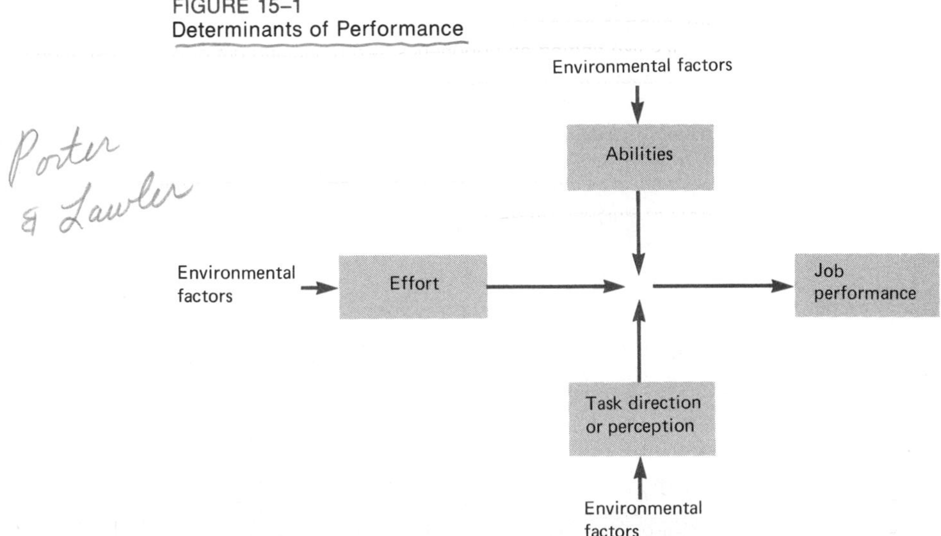

Source: Adapted from Lyman W. Porter and Edward E. Lawler III, *Managerial Attitudes and Performance* (Homewood, Ill.: Richard D. Irwin and The Dorsey Press, 1968), p. 17. Copyright © 1968 by Richard D. Irwin, Inc., and The Dorsey Press.

his abilities and traits and by his role perceptions."[1] This definition implies that performance in a given situation can be viewed as resulting from the interrelationships between effort, abilities, and role (or task) perceptions (see Figure 15–1).

Effort refers to the amount of energy (physical and/or mental) used by an individual in performing a task. Abilities are personal characteristics used in performing a job. Abilities and traits do not fluctuate widely over short periods of time. Role or task perceptions refer to the direction(s) in which individuals believe they should channel their efforts on their jobs. The activities and behaviors that people believe are necessary in the performance of their jobs define their role perceptions.

In order to obtain an acceptable level of performance, a minimum level of proficiency must exist in each of the performance components. Similarly, the level of proficiency in any one of the performance components can place an upper boundary on performance. If individuals put forth tremendous effort and have great abilities but lack a good understanding of their roles, performance will probably not be good in the eyes of their superiors. A

[1] Lyman W. Porter and Edward E. Lawler III, *Managerial Attitudes and Performance* (Homewood, Ill.: Richard D. Irwin and The Dorsey Press, 1968), p. 28. Copyright © 1968 by Richard D. Irwin, Inc., and The Dorsey Press.

lot of work will be produced, but it will be misdirected. Likewise, an individual who puts forth an above-average amount of effort and understands the job, but lacks ability, probably will rate low on performance. A final possibility is the individual who has good ability and understands his or her role but is lazy and expends little effort. This person's performance will also probably be low. Of course, an individual can compensate up to a point for a weakness in one area by being above-average in one or both of the other areas.

Environmental Factors as Performance Obstacles

Other factors beyond the control of the subordinate can also stifle performance. Although such potential obstacles are sometimes used merely as excuses, they are often very real and should be recognized by management.

Some of the more common potential performance obstacles include a lack of time or conflicting demands on the subordinate's time; inadequate work facilities and equipment; restrictive policies that affect the job; lack of cooperation from others; type of supervision; timing; and even luck.[2]

A skillful and motivated machine operator cannot be productive without good machinery and proper raw materials. A salesperson's performance may be hindered by overly restrictive and outdated policies. A research and development project may prove to be fruitless because a competitor perfected the ideas first. It is obvious that the individual worker does not have total control over performance in these situations.

The dynamics of the work group (as discussed in Chapter 12) can also inhibit performance. This occurs when informal group norms are counterproductive to organizational goals. In such instances, the performance of individuals is influenced by their attraction to the group.

Many performance obstacles can be overcome by following good organization principles. In other instances, it may be necessary to redefine the job. However, the first step in overcoming performance obstacles is for management to recognize that they really exist.

Environmental factors should not be viewed as direct determinants of individual performance but as modifying the effects of effort, ability, and direction (see Figure 15–2). For example, poor ventilation or worn-out equipment might very easily affect the effort exerted by an individual. Unclear policies or poor supervi-

---

[2] Charles N. Greene, "The Satisfaction-Performance Controversy," *Business Horizons*, October 1972, p. 36.

FIGURE 15–2
Environmental Factors that Modify Performance

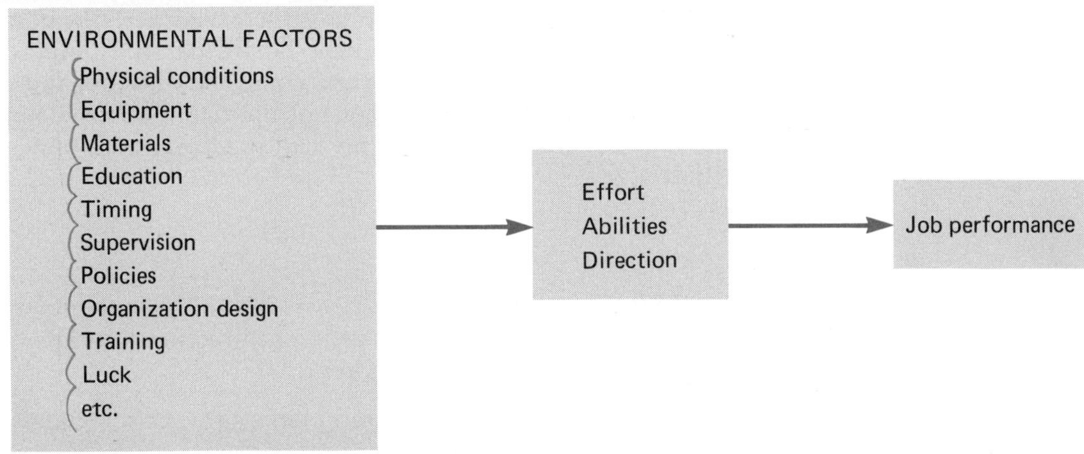

sion can easily produce misdirected effort. Similarly, a lack of training could result in underutilized abilities. One of management's greatest responsibilities is to provide employees with adequate working conditions and a supportive environment in order to eliminate or minimize performance obstacles.

The Activity Trap

One major problem in organizations today is that managers tend to focus on the effort component of performance rather than on performance itself. George Odiorne has referred to this as "the activity trap."[3] Ordiorne has offered the following explanation of what goes wrong in many organizations:

> Most people get caught in the Activity Trap! They become so enmeshed in activity they lose sight of why they are doing it, and the activity becomes a false goal, and end in itself. Successful people never lose sight of their goals, the hoped-for outputs.[4]

The activity described by Odiorne may supplant the effort component of performance. As an activity becomes entrenched, it becomes more meaningful than actual performance. Managers become supervisors of activity rather than performance. Looking busy and generating activity becomes more important than producing results.

As Odiorne explains, the activity trap is a self-feeding mecha-

[3] Odiorne, *Activity Trap.*
[4] Ibid., p. 6.

nism. Top management can lose sight of its purpose and start to enforce activity controls which become increasingly unrelated to any useful purpose. All the while, this increased activity consumes more and more resources (money, labor, materials, and so on) and produces less and less. Style and conformity become more important than performance. "It does not matter whether or not you get results as long as you do it my way," becomes the prevalent attitude.

MEASURES OF PERFORMANCE—CRITERIA

There are many other reasons for measuring individual performance aside from the purpose of providing direction to employees. Measuring performance may serve:

1. As a basis for setting objectives and planning work schedules.
2. As a basis for rewarding workers.
3. As a basis for promotions, separations, and transfers.
4. As a means for evaluating different work methods, different tools and equipment, and different conditions of work.
5. As a basis for estimating and allocating costs.
6. As a means of determining when and if a problem arises.

As evidenced by the foregoing list, measures of job performance are needed in most, if not all, phases of management.

One of the most difficult jobs a manager faces is locating or creating satisfactory measures of job success, called criteria. The difficulties of obtaining satisfactory criteria rise from a variety of problems. There are many jobs that do not readily lend themselves to objective measurement. But even in cases that do, job performance is often influenced by many factors outside the individual's control. A salesperson's performance, for example, is not only a function of the person's own effectiveness but also of the particular sales territory. Similarly, a machine operator's performance may be affected by the physical condition of the machine or the lighting conditions.

Robert Thorndike and Elizabeth Hagen have listed four qualities that should be sought when selecting criteria.[5] Listed in order of importance they are: (1) validity or relevance, (2) freedom from bias, (3) reliability, and (4) availability. Relevance is the primary and absolutely fundamental requirement of a criterion measure. A criterion is relevant if the knowledge, skills, and basic

[5] Robert L. Thorndike and Elizabeth Hagen, *Measurement and Evaluation in Psychology and Education* (New York: John Wiley & Sons, 1955), p. 118.

aptitudes required for success on it are the same as those required for performance of the ultimate task.[6] In other words, relevance addresses the question: To what degree does the criterion represent the characteristics of the job it purports to measure? Unfortunately, relevance can rarely be empirically proven. Therefore, the relevance of a particular criterion usually must be estimated on rational grounds using professional judgment.

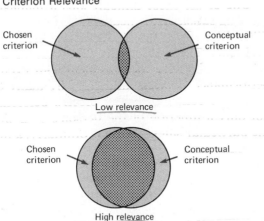

Ordinarily, some ultimate or "conceptual" criterion exists. A conceptual criterion is a verbal statement of important or socially relevant outcomes based on the general aims of the organization.[7] Because the conceptual criterion is rarely directly measurable, substitutes must frequently be used. A conceptual criterion might be the successful performance of a production supervisor. A substitute that might be used for the conceptual criterion is the output of the supervisor's department. Most criteria that are actually used represent only a part of the conceptual criterion.[8] The major problem in criteria selection is choosing the criteria which are most representative of the conceptual criterion. Figure 15–3 depicts a chosen criterion which is not very relevant to the conceptual criterion and a chosen criterion which is highly relevant. The more overlap there is between the chosen criterion and the conceptual criterion, the more relevant is the chosen criterion.

FIGURE 15–3
Criterion Relevance

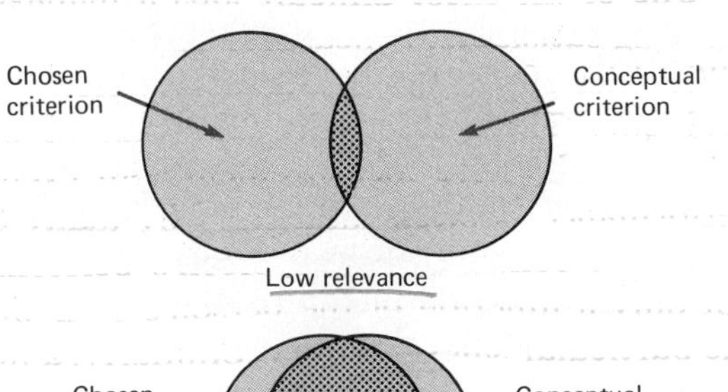

[6] Robert L. Thorndike, *Personnel Selection* (New York: John Wiley & Sons, 1949), p. 125.

[7] Alexander W. Astin, "Criterion-Centered Research," *Educational and Psychological Measurement*, 1964, p. 809.

[8] Thorndike and Hagen, *Measurement and Evaluation*, p. 125.

The second desirable quality of a criterion measure, freedom from bias, requires that each person be provided an equal opportunity to make a good score. For instance, if widgets per hour is the criterion used in evaluating the performance of a certain set of workers, each worker should have identical or equivalent equipment. If some workers have faster machines than others, then the criterion measure is biased.

Reliability refers to the reproducibility of results. Reliability answers the question of how consistently the criterion measures whatever it does measure. A criterion measure is reliable to the extent that the same person working under the same conditions produces approximately the same results at different times. If a machine operator's output is highly dependent on a fluctuating supply of raw materials, then output would probably not be a reliable measure of the worker's performance.

Finally, the criterion measure must be reasonably convenient and available. Practicality in terms of time and cost must be considered, and may dictate the choice of the criterion.

Subjective Performance Measures

As was pointed out in the previous section, objective performance measures should be used wherever and whenever possible. However, objective measures are not feasible, or even possible, in many situations. One method of handling such situations is to measure performance on the basis of larger and larger groups until objective measures can be established.[9] For example, it is difficult to objectively measure the contribution of any one member of a rowing team, but it is not difficult to objectively measure the entire team. A second approach is to use subjective measures on an individual or small group level. The key factor in determining the feasibility of using subjective measures is the degree of trust between the superior and the subordinate. As Edward Lawler has stated, "The more subjective the measure, the higher degree of trust needed."[10] Using subjective performance measures increases the likelihood that the subordinate will not believe that rewards are based on performance unless a high degree of trust exists. Figure 15–4 illustrates the relationship between trust and subjectivity of the performance measure. It should be noted that in Figure 15–4 some amount of trust is required for even the most objective system.

---

[9] Edward E. Lawler III, *Pay and Organizational Effectiveness: A Psychological Review* (New York: McGraw-Hill, 1971), p. 171. This section draws heavily on Lawler's work.

[10] Ibid.

FIGURE 15–4
Relationship of Trust and Objectivity of Performance Measure to Success of the Program

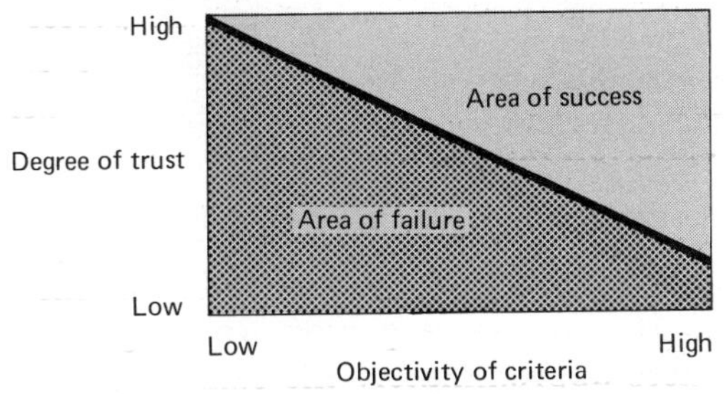

Source: Edward E. Lawler III, *Pay and Organizational Effectiveness: A Psychological Review* (New York: McGraw-Hill, 1971), p. 172.

DEFINING EMPLOYEE DIRECTION

After appropriate measures of good or effective performance have been determined, the manager can begin defining employee direction so that employees properly perceive their job requirements and understand clearly what is expected from them. The powerful influence that a manager's expectations have on an employee's performance was described earlier in Chapter 14.[11]

A manager can use many methods in defining his or her expectations for an employee. Three of these methods are discussed in the remaining sections of this chapter. The first is properly defining the job through a job description. The second is communicating to employees, through a performance appraisal, how well they are doing. The third is through the proper use of discipline.

Job Descriptions

A first step in defining employee direction is the development of a job description. A job description is a written statement which identifies the tasks, duties, activities, and performance results required in a particular job. A job description is developed from a job analysis, which is the process of determining, through observation and study, the pertinent information relating to the nature of a specific job. Many justifiable criticisms have been made concerning job descriptions. Many organizations have made them overly formal and meaningless in content. Furthermore, job descriptions can be misused in order to limit the scope of a job. "It's not part of my job description" is a sentiment too frequently ex-

[11] J. Sterling Livingston, "Pygmalion in Management," *Harvard Business Review*, July–August 1969, pp. 81–89.

pressed. In addition, many organizations do not keep job descriptions current. In order to provide direction, the job description must be relevant in terms of the information it provides, and this requires periodic review and updating. One approach designed to minimize such problems is for the person holding the job to write the job description, subject to management's approval.

Although job descriptions are a necessary step in defining employee direction, care must be taken in order to ensure that they are not misused.

Performance Appraisal

Performance appraisal is a process that involves communicating to an employee how the person is performing the job and, ideally, involves establishing a plan of improvement. Naturally, no type of performance appraisal will work until the performance measures, as discussed in the first part of this chapter, have been established.

Performance appraisal systems are normally designed to meet three basic purposes:

1. They provide systematic judgments to support salary increases, promotions, transfers, and sometimes demotions or terminations.
2. They are a means of telling subordinates how they are doing, and suggesting needed changes in their behavior, attitudes, skills, or job knowledge; they also let employees know where they stand with the boss.
3. They also are being increasingly used as a basis for the coaching and counseling of the individual by the superior.[12]

The importance of evaluating performance cannot be overstated. When properly compiled, appraisal information can be used for adjusting salaries, making promotion decisions, setting organizational and individual objectives, determining development needs of managers and other employees, planning personnel requirements, and validating selection and promotion procedures. Performance appraisal helps the organization maintain control and make efficient use of its human resources while at the same time serving to reduce tension and stress by letting employees know how they are performing. It is important to note that an atmosphere should be avoided in which the evaluator is the judge and the individual being evaluated is the defendant. Perfor-

[12] Douglas McGregor, "An Uneasy Look at Performance Appraisal," *Harvard Business Review,* May–June 1975, pp. 89–94.

mance appraisal should be both a learning and a developing experience for the person being evaluated.

Ideally, performance appraisal should be directly related to the performance criteria of the job. Under this ideal situation, performance appraisal would be relatively simple, requiring only that actual performance be compared to the criteria or standard. However, as noted earlier, setting relevant and objectively measurable criteria is very difficult for many jobs. In such situations performance appraisals are often based on personal characteristics and other subjective criteria.

The assumption made in this type of performance appraisal is that there are certain personal characteristics which lead to increased performance. It is further assumed that these characteristics can be perceived and isolated, can be evaluated, and should be rewarded. These characteristics include integrity, dependability, work quality, attitude, initiative, judgment, responsibility, attendance and potential for growth.

The difficulties of a performance appraisal system based on personal characteristics are numerous. Managers resist the process. The underlying reason seems to be that it places the manager in the position of judge and the employee in the position of defendant. Another problem is the temptation of the appraiser to favor friends and close associates. Because it is natural for one to perceive favorable characteristics in friends, the appraiser may never realize favoritism is interfering. Despite all the problems, the fact remains that performance appraisal systems based on personal characteristics and subjective evaluation are still in widespread use.

The most commonly used performance appraisal methods include:

1. Essay appraisal.
2. Graphic rating scale.
3. Checklist.
4. Forced-choice rating.
5. Critical incident appraisal.
6. Work standards approach.
7. Ranking methods.
8. Management by objectives.[13]

Each of these methods is discussed in detail in the following pages.

[13] Winston Oberg, "Make Performance Appraisal Relevant," *Harvard Business Review*, January–February 1972, p. 62.

MANAGEMENT IN PRACTICE

Performance Assessment: The Real Art of Managing

Perhaps the most unfortunate consequence of the controversy surrounding employee appraisal is the effect it has of shifting managers' attention away from the simple, urgent logic of appraisal—that in order to manage performance one must evaluate it—towards its more esoteric technical aspects.

Managers should be encouraged to stop thinking of performance appraisal as an abstract high technology tool to be mulled over by experts and then periodically reintroduced as a component in business management. Appraising performance is a prerequisite of effective performance management. It is a way of managing employees effectively. It is neither a form nor a system but an integral part of managing.

The manager who understands this can judge effectively, without an appraisal form or a system. The manager who does not understand this will avoid appraising employee performance for as long as possible while awaiting the development of a system that will make it "easier." Not only will this manager be a long time waiting, but in all likelihood, he or she will fail to benefit from such an ideal, technologically rigorous appraisal program.

The true measure of an appraisal program lies not in its apparent technological sophistication nor in its reliability and validity research. The true measure of an appraisal program is in what it does for the manager and the employee, both in terms of the quality of their communication about the work contract and in terms of the ensuing action precipitated by that dialogue.

The real reason that effective employee appraisal is so elusive and so difficult for managers to handle lies not in the appraisal itself, but in the rather deceptive complexity of the task of managing.

A good manager plans, organizes, and directs the work of the staff, sometimes with its participation. In each case, the manager makes the employee's target accomplishments clear. The clearer the target, the more obvious it is to both manager and employee that the achievement of the target is the criterion for measuring results. If a manager is managing effectively, the dimensions of the task which will form the criterion for measuring performance results are already being delineated.

There is nothing very mysterious here. The manager—not the appraisal form or system—makes employee appraisal work. The manager makes clear what results are expected of the employee. The manager defines what "doing a good job" is.

The manager observes the employee in action; gives feedback on progress; helps identify results attained as measured against expectations; identifies problems and offers a diagnosis of what may be behind these problems; acknowledges the employee's achievements; indicates how such judgments are made; and finally, prescribes action, where required, for better performance.

The manager who is unable to execute his responsibility satisfactorily without the appraisal form or system is not managing. A manager, by definition, achieves organizational goals through other people. The manager manages people, or more specifically, the manager manages people's performance.

Source: "Performance Assessment: The Real Art of Managing," by John S. Piamonte, copyright October 1980. Reprinted with the permission of *Personnel Journal,* Costa Mesa, California; all rights reserved.

Essay appraisal The essay appraisal method merely requires the evaluator to write a series of statements concerning an individual's strengths, weaknesses, past performance, and potential for promotion. Letters written by former employers, teachers, or associates concerning an individual's qualifications and past performance are examples of essay appraisals. Letters of this kind are frequently used in selecting candidates to fill managerial and professional jobs. The biggest problem with essay appraisals is that their length and content can vary considerably depending on the evaluator. For instance, one person may write a lengthy statement covering an individual's potential for achievement, but discuss past performance only briefly. On the other hand, another evaluator might write a short memorandum reviewing only the individual's past work. Thus, essay appraisals are difficult to compare.

Graphic rating scale. With this technique, the evaluator assesses an individual on factors such as initiative, dependability, cooperativeness, attitude, and quantity of work. Figure 15–5 presents a typical sample of choices related to the characteristic of dependability.

Even though the graphic rating scale technique often has come under attack, it is one of the more widely-used appraisal methods. Probably the most frequently used argument against it is that many raters have a tendency to evaluate everyone a little above average, making comparison of their ratings difficult. Despite the

FIGURE 15–5
Sample Items and Choices that Might Be Used on a Graphic Rating Scale Evaluation Form

DEPENDABILITY is ability to do required jobs well with minimum of supervision.

( )	( )	( )	( )	( )
Requires close supervision; is unreliable	Sometimes requires prompting	Usually completes necessary tasks with reasonable promptness	Requires little supervision; is reliable	Requires absolute minimum of supervision

criticisms, this method does give comparative data on individuals and is relatively inexpensive to develop.

Checklist. In the checklist method, the rater does not evaluate performance but merely records it. The rater checks yes or no responses on a series of questions concerning the employee's behavior. Figure 15–6 illustrates some sample questions.

FIGURE 15–6
Sample Checklist Questions for Performance Appraisals

	Yes	*No*
1. Does the individual lose his or her temper in public?	______	______
2. Does the individual play favorites?	______	______
3. Does the individual praise employees in public when they have done a good job?	______	______
4. Does the individual volunteer to do special jobs?	______	______

The scoring key for such a system is usually kept by the personnel department. The rater is generally not aware of the values associated with each question, but because the rater can see the positive or negative connotation of each, bias can be introduced. It is difficult to assemble the questions for this method. An additional drawback is that a separate listing of questions must be prepared for different job categories.

Forced-choice rating. There are many variations of the forced-choice rating method, but the most commonly used one requires the rater to choose from several seemingly equal groups of statements those that are most or least applicable to the person being reviewed. The statements are then weighted or scored. Generally, the weights or scores that are assigned to each statement are not known to the raters; thus, in theory, they are not likely to play favorites. After the reviewer describes the individual, someone in the personnel department applies the weights and develops a score. Individuals with higher scores are rated as better employees.

In the forced-choice method, the rater would choose between one of the two following statements:

1. Has complete mastery of all phases of his or her job.
2. Shows superior ability to express himself or herself.

Although the rater may think that both are applicable, the rater must choose the one that best describes the person in question. The reviewer is also required to choose between statements that are equally unfavorable. For instance, the evaluator might have to choose between the following:

1. Requires close supervision.
2. Careless and makes recurrent errors.

By presenting choices that are not obviously distinguishable as to desirability, this method attempts to eliminate bias on the part of the reviewer.[14] However, it does have drawbacks. Winston Oberg reported that "the forced-choice method tends to irritate raters, who feel they are not being trusted."[15] In addition, the cost of developing such a system may be prohibitive if it is to be used for a small number of people.

Critical incident appraisals. Under this approach, the person who does the appraisal is asked to keep a written record on incidents that illustrate both positive and negative behavior on the part of the individual being rated. With this method, the individual's actual behavior, not personality traits, is discussed. Ideally, individuals who are being evaluated are given a chance to present their views of the circumstances of the incident and to know the type of behavior that the rater views as important.

The main drawback to this approach is that the rater is required to jot down incidents regularly; this can become burdensome and time consuming. Also, if the incident that the rater records is minor, the person being rated may have forgotten the circumstances surrounding it by the time the performance appraisal takes place.

Work standards approach. Some organizations set standards for measuring the work of employees after the performance measures have been determined. Generally speaking, work standards should reflect the normal output of a normal person. Work standards attempt to answer the questions: What is a fair day's work? or How good is good enough? Output standards for production workers and for those in lower levels of the organizational hierarchy are usually expressed as pieces per time or time per unit. Standards for management, professional, and staff people generally are broader and more difficult to define. Therefore, the work standards approach is used generally for lower-level employees.

Several methods can be used for setting work standards. Some of the more frequently used methods are described in Figure 15–7.

---

[14] Amiel T. Sharon and C. J. Bartlett, "Effect of Instructional Conditions in Producing Leniency on Two Types of Rating Scales," *Personnel Psychology*, Autumn 1969, pp. 251–53.

[15] Oberg, "Make Performance," p. 64.

FIGURE 15–7
Frequently Used Methods for Setting Work Standards

Methods	Areas of applicability
Average production of work groups	When tasks performed by all individuals are the same or approximately the same.
Standards based on the performance of specially selected individuals	When tasks performed by all individuals are basically the same and it would be cumbersome and time consuming to use the group average.
Time study	Jobs involving repetitive type tasks.
Work sampling	For noncyclical types of work where many different tasks are performed, there is no set pattern or cycle.
The use of expert opinion	When none of the more direct methods (described above) apply.

The advantage to setting work standards is that the performance review is based on factors that usually are more objective than those used in other methods. Of course, in order to be effective, the standards must be viable and fair. The most serious criticism of standards is lack of comparability. Evaluating people on different work standards creates problems when promotions and salary increases are made on a comparative basis.

Ranking methods. When it becomes necessary to compare the performance of two or more individuals, ranking methods are frequently used. The two most commonly used ranking methods are alternative and paired comparison ranking.

Alternation ranking. The names of the individuals who are to be rated are generally listed in random order down the left side of a sheet of paper. The reviewer is then asked to choose the "most valuable" employee on the list, cross this name off, and put it at the top of the column on the right side of the paper. The rater is then asked to select and cross off the name of the "least valuable" employee and move it to the bottom of the right column. The reviewer then repeats this process for all the names on the left side of the paper. The resulting list of names in the right column gives a ranking of the evaluated employees from most to least valuable.

Paired-comparison ranking. This method is best described by an example. Suppose a rater is to evaluate six employees. The names of these individuals are listed on the left side of a sheet of paper. The rater then evaluates the first employee against the second employee on a chosen criterion, such as quantity of work. If the reviewer thinks that the first employee has produced more work than the second employee, a checkmark is placed beside the first employee's name. The first employee would then be compared to each of the other employees. The process is repeated for each worker. The one with the most checkmarks is the most valuable employee, in the rater's opinion. Likewise, the person with the least number of checkmarks is the least valuable. The major problem with the paired-comparison method is that it becomes unwieldy when comparing large numbers of employees.

Management by objectives. Management by objectives (MBO) (which was discussed in Chapters 4 and 6) is similar to the work standards approach to performance appraisal. Whereas the work standards approach is used more often for operative and clerical employees, MBO is usually used for professional and managerial personnel. It is one alternative to resolving the problem of basing performance appraisals of managers and professionals on subjective data.

Frequency of performance appraisals. There seems to be no consensus on the question of how frequently performance reviews should be done. The answer seems to be, as frequently as is necessary in order to let the employee know what kind of job is being done. If performance is not satisfactory, the actions that the evaluator believes are necessary for improvement must be communicated to the employee. For most people, these objectives cannot be accomplished by a performance appraisal given only once a year. Therefore, it is recommended that reviews be conducted three to four times a year for most employees.

Salary recommendations and performance appraisals. Studies have indicated that it is undesirable to deal with salary and promotion recommendations during the formal performance appraisal session.[16] The primary reason for this is that it places the individual being evaluated in a defensive position and prohibits or blocks learning. It should not be inferred that salary increases and promotions must not be based on performance, but annual salary review sessions should be held separately from the actual performance appraisal session.

[16] L. Miller, "The Use of Knowledge of Results in Improving the Performance of Hourly Operators (New York: General Electric, Behavioral Research Service, 1965).

Disciplinary Systems

Organizational discipline is action taken against an employee who fails to conform to the rules established by the organization.[17] Discipline is used to aid the organization in obtaining effective performance from employees and to guarantee their adherence to work rules. Furthermore, discipline serves to guide employee behavior by establishing the minimum standards of performance and behavior that managers expect.

Generally disciplinary action is taken against employees for three types of conduct. Conduct that directly affects job performance such as absenteeism, insubordination, or negligence is subject to discipline. Employees are disciplined for action reflecting "bad organization citizenship" such as fighting, theft of organizational property, or disloyalty. In addition, employees are often subject to discipline for conduct that negatively affects society in general, whether or not it occurs on the job.

While discipline can be used to punish employees for past behavior, it serves more importantly to direct future behavior so that it does not deviate from the expected standards. Rather than being viewed as an end in itself, discipline should be regarded as a learning opportunity for the employee and as a tool for improving productivity and human relations at the work place.[18] Unfortunately, many organizations regard discipline as an end in itself and take an authoritarian approach to disciplinary actions. Such organizations view discipline soley as a punitive measure taken to deter other employees from misconduct. Constructive discipline, on the other hand, views discipline as a learning process and is more appropriate for defining individual direction.

Constructive discipline. As stated above, constructive discipline is intended to be a learning experience so that the future behavior of the individual being disciplined will change. In this regard, discipline should be invoked with the objective of modifying behavior to benefit both the individual and the organization. Under constructive discipline, proper conduct must first be defined and known by all employees. When misconduct does take place under a system of constructive discipline, light penalties are invoked for the first offense and progressively harsher penalties follow for repeated offenses. Generally, after a certain number of offenses, regardless of whether or not they are the same type of offense, the employee is discharged. However, the employee is given fair warning and ample opportunity to correct be-

[17] Dallas L. Jones, *Arbitration and Industrial Discipline* (Ann Arbor: University of Michigan Bureau of Industrial Relations, 1961), pp. 2–3.

[18] Richard F. Gibson, "Discipline: Laying Down the Law—Productively," *Industry Week,* May 17, 1976, p. 51.

havior that violates organizational rules and management expectations. A suggested schedule of steps to be used in dealing with problem employees is as follows:

1. Oral warning that is not recorded in employee's personnel records.
2. Oral warning that is recorded in employee's personnel records.
3. Written reprimand.
4. Suspension.
5. Discharge.

Of course, exceptions occur in the above steps in that some offenses, such as fighting or drinking on the job, are subject to immediate termination. Furthermore, labor organizations play an important role in establishing disciplinary policies.

Applying discipline should be analagous to the burn received when touching a hot stove. Often referred to as the "hot-stove rule," this approach emphasizes that discipline should be directed against the act rather than the person. Other key points of the hot-stove rule are: immediacy, advance warning, consistency, and impersonality. Figure 15–8 outlines the hot-stove rule.

FIGURE 15–8
Hot-Stove Rule

1. The hot stove burns immediately. Disciplinary policies should be administered quickly. There should be no question of cause and effect.
2. The hot stove gives a warning and so should discipline.
3. The hot stove consistently burns everyone that touches it. Discipline should be consistent.
4. The hot stove burns everyone in the same manner regardless of who they are. Discipline must be impartial. People are disciplined for what they have done and not because of who they are.

Immediacy refers to the length of time between the misconduct and the discipline. For discipline to be most effective it must be taken as soon as possible, without being an emotional, irrational decision.

Discipline should also be preceded by advance warning. A manager cannot begin enforcing previously unenforced rules by disciplining an employee as an example. Notation of rules infractions in an employee's record is not sufficient to support disciplinary action. An employee must be advised of the infraction in order for it to be considered a warning. Noting that the employee was warned for the infraction and having the employee sign a discipline form are both good practices. Failure to warn an employee of the consequences of repeated violations of a rule is one reason often cited for overturning a disciplinary action.

A key element in discipline is consistency. Inconsistency lowers morale and diminishes respect for the manager. Striving for consistency does not mean that past infractions, length of service, work record, and other mitigating factors should not be considered when applying discipline. However, an employee should feel that any other employee under essentially the same circumstances would have received the same discipline.

Managers should also take steps to insure that personalities are not a factor when applying discipline. The employee should feel that the disciplinary action is a consequence of what he or she has done, not because of a personality clash with the manager. The manager should avoid arguing with the employee and should administer the discipline in a straightforward, calm manner. Administering discipline without anger or apology and resuming a pleasant relationship aids in reducing the negative effects of discipline.

The manager should also attempt to administer discipline in private. The only exception for public reprimand would be in the case of gross insubordination or flagrant and serious rule violations, where a public reprimand helps the manager regain control of the situation. Even in this type of situation the manager's objective should be to gain control, not embarrass the employee.

Finally, the manager should warn the employee of the result of repeated violations. Sometimes suggestions to the employee on ways to correct his or her behavior are beneficial.

If the hot-stove rule is followed and discipline is applied in a constructive manner, it can serve as an excellent method for not only correcting but also directing the behavior of employees.

SUMMARY

Performance in a given situation results from the interrelationships between effort, abilities, and role perceptions. Effort refers to the amount of energy (physical and/or mental) used by an individual in performing a task. Abilities are the individual's personal characteristics which are used in performing the job. Role or task perceptions refer to the direction(s) in which individuals believe they should channel their efforts on the job.

Measures of job performance are needed in most, if not all, phases of management. Satisfactory measures of job success are called criteria. Four qualities that should be sought in selecting criteria are relevance, freedom from bias, reliability, and availability.

Defining direction so that employees properly perceive their job requirements and what is expected of them is an important element in improving performance in organizations. Job descriptions, performance appraisals, and proper discipline are three effective methods used in defining direction.

A job description is a written statement which identifies the tasks, duties, activities, and performance results required in a particular job. A job description is the end result of job analysis, which is the process of determining, through observation and study, the pertinent information relating to the nature of a specific job.

Performance appraisal is a process involving communicating an evaluation of an individual's job performance and establishing a plan for improvement. Performance appraisal information can be used for adjusting salaries; making promotion decisions; setting organizational and individual objectives; determining development needs of managers and other employees; planning personnel requirements; and validating selection and promotion procedures. The following methods of performance appraisal were discussed in this chapter: essay appraisal, graphic rating scale, checklist, forced-choice rating, critical incident appraisal, work standards approach, ranking methods, and management by objectives.

Disciplinary systems were also discussed as means for defining direction in organizations. Organizational discipline is action taken against an employee who fails to conform to the rules established by the organization. Constructive discipline is a system of discipline in which proper conduct is defined and communicated. Employees are given the opportunity to correct improper conduct in the future and are warned that further breaches of proper conduct will result in progressively harsher disciplinary action. The hot-stove rule is a set of guidelines used in constructive discipline which calls for administering disciplinary actions quickly, consistently, and impartially.

REVIEW QUESTIONS

1. What are the three determinants of performance?
2. What is the activity trap?
3. Define job analysis and job description. How are they used in defining direction?
4. What is performance? Performance appraisal?
5. Describe some of the uses for performance appraisal information in organizations.

6. Describe the following methods of performance appraisal:
   a. Essay appraisal.
   b. Graphic rating scale.
   c. Checklist.
   d. Forced-choice rating.
   e. Critical incident appraisal.
   f. Work standards approach.
   g. Ranking methods.
   h. Management by objectives.
7. Define the following terms:
   a. Organizational discipline.
   b. Constructive discipline.
   c. Hot-stove rule.

DISCUSSION QUESTIONS

1. Discuss the following statement: "Job descriptions for management jobs are a waste of time."
2. Do you think MBO would work for determining the performance of professional athletes? Discuss.
3. Describe which performance appraisal method you think would be most effective for the following jobs:
   a. Secretary.
   b. College professor.
   c. College student.
   d. Executive manager.
4. Why do you think that many managers avoid, or attempt to avoid, appraising the performance of their subordinates?

SELECTED READINGS

Ash, R. A., and E. L. Levine. "Framework for Evaluating Job Analysis Methods." *Personnel,* November–December 1980, pp. 53–59.

Beer, M. "Performance Appraisal: Dilemmas and Possibilities." *Organizational Dynamics,* Winter 1981, pp. 24–36.

Boncarosky, L. D. "Guidelines to Corrective Discipline." *Personnel Journal,* October 1979, pp. 698–702.

Brinkerhoff, D. W., and R. M. Kanter. "Appraising the Performance of Performance Appraisal." *Sloan Management Review,* September 1980, pp. 3–16.

Haynes, Marion. "Developing an Appraisal Program—Part I." *Personnel Journal,* January 1978, pp. 14–19.

———. "Developing an Appraisal Program—Part II." *Personnel Journal,* February 1978, pp. 66–67 ff.

Hoffman, R. R. "MJS: Management by Job Standards." *Personnel Journal,* August 1979, pp. 536–40 ff.

Klingner, D. E. "Does Your MBO Program Include Clear Performance Contracts?" *Personnel Administrator,* May 1979, pp. 65–68.

Lazer, R. I. "Performance Appraisal: What Does the Future Hold?" *Personnel Administrator,* July 1980, pp. 69–73.

Livingston, J. Sterling, "Pygmalion in Management." *Harvard Business Review,* July–August 1969, pp. 81–89.

Ludden, G. L.; D. E. Thompson; and C. R. Klasson. "Performance Appraisal: The Legal Implications of Title VII." *Personnel,* May–June 1980, pp. 11–21.

Moravec, M. "Performance Appraisal: A Human Resource Management System with Productivity Payoffs." *Management Review,* June 1981, pp. 51–54.

Murray, R. S. "Managerial Perception of Two Appraisal Systems." *California Management Review,* Spring 1981, pp. 92–96.

Odiorne, George S. "MBO—Systematic or Mechanistic? Nine Cases with Nine Precepts." *University of Michigan Business Review,* September 1977, pp. 9–13.

Richardson, P. R., and J. R. M. Gordon. "Measuring Total Manufacturing Performance (Canada)." *Sloan Management Review,* Winter 1980, pp. 47–58.

Schneier, Dena B. "The Impact of EEO Legislation on Performance Appraisals." *Personnel,* July–August 1978, pp. 24–34.

Summers, C. W. "Protecting All Employees Against Unjust Dismissal." *Harvard Business Review,* January–February 1980, pp. 132–39.

Sutton, R. H., and R. L. Mathis. "Performance Appraisal." *Journal of Systems Management,* July 1979, pp. 9–13.

Yager, E. "Critique of Performance Appraisal Systems." *Personnel Journal,* February 1981, pp. 129–33.

Zippo, M. "Dealing with the Poor Performer." *Personnel,* January–February 1981, pp. 44–45.

Case 15–1

Can MBO work?

Situation: You are a consultant to the president of a marketing company. It is fairly small and has not grown very rapidly over the years, though it has gained a reputation for innovative and effective approaches to market research and advertising. The organization consists mainly of intelligent and creative people who seem to love their work. The current president was brought in a year ago. The previous president, also the founder and sole owner of the firm, had died and left the company to his two sons. The sons were not interested in getting actively involved with the business, but they wanted to hire someone who had proven ability to stimulate and guide rapid growth of the organization. The current president had previously managed a shoe manufacturing company through a period of fantastic growth. He enjoys a reputation as an extremely effective manager.

President: I am really frustrated and baffled by my inability to meet my objectives since I came here. My goal for the first year was a 25 percent increase in revenue, which I thought would be easily attainable if we combined some good solid management with the talent and fine reputation of our staff. Instead of a 25 percent increase, we suffered an 8 percent decrease, and that's the first decrease this company has ever had. On top of that, morale around here is at low ebb right now. I just can't understand it. I know I'm a good manager; I've proven that. I've been using the same management philosophies and techniques that have worked so well for me in the past.

Consultant: What sorts of philosophies and techniques have you been applying?

President: The very first thing I did when I took over was to get the whole staff together and talk over our objectives for the year. The main objective, of course, was growth. The 25 percent figure was an understanding between the two owners of the company and myself. Looking back on that staff meeting, I must admit that the staff did not seem overly awed or inspired by that objective, but they didn't fight it either.

Consultant: What did you do next?

President: Well, I knew that if I was to be effective in managing this group, we needed to get organized. I could find no written documentation of the organization structure, so I decided to start from scratch. I asked every member of the staff to write his or her own job description. The results were really disappointing. Most of them didn't even know what a job description should consist of, and nobody seemed to put much effort into it. Anyway, the job descriptions showed that the individuals perceived themselves as having very broad and vague responsibilities. There was a lot of overlap, as if everybody thought he or she should be involved in just about everything.

Consultant: What did you do about it?

President: I decided that if we were going to get organized, I would have to develop the structure myself. I put a lot of time and thought into it and came up with a functional division of labor. I set up a client development department (which is really our sales effort), a market research department, and a media systems department (which is really advertising). I assigned individual staff members to the three departments based on my perceptions of their interests and talents and our needs. I designated one person in each department to serve as departmental manager and report directly to me.

Consultant: How was that accepted by the staff?

President: Hard to tell. Nobody said very much at the time.

Consultant: What else have you done?

President: I worked directly with each of the department managers in writing their new job descriptions and had them do the same thing with each person in their departments. Then I introduced an MBO program, in which individuals worked with their immediate superiors in setting personal goals for the remainder of this year, that would contribute to the overall goal of 25 percent growth. I also developed a procedure for following up on performance for each individual on a quarterly basis.

Consultant: How did that work out?

President: Not too well so far, I'm afraid. I can't seem to get the departmental managers to deal in objectively measurable goals for themselves or their subordinates. Everything seems so vague. I would really like your help with some training on the proper application of MBO, and then maybe we can develop some sort of incentive program based on performance measured against objectives.

1. Why do you feel that this MBO program is going wrong?
2. What type of training would you recommend to the president?
3. What can be done to correct this situation?

Case 15–2

Promotions at the university

Dan Andrews, an assistant professor of management at the state university, has just received a call from the dean. Dan had written a letter to the dean asking whether promotions were based on seniority or performance.

The letter had been written because Dan had just been notified that he had not been promoted to associate professor because he did not have five years in grade as an assistant professor. Dan was extremely upset because he had over 20 articles published, had a book in process that was to be published by a leading textbook publisher, and was always rated high on student evaluations.

The dean had told Dan in the telephone conversation that he understood how Dan felt and promised that Dan would be promoted next year when he had the time in grade. In fact, the dean had told Dan that measuring the performance of college professors is extremely difficult and should not be the sole basis for promotion. He asked that Dan meet with him in the near future to discuss the problems of measuring the performance of a faculty member.

1. Do you agree with the dean's analysis of the situation?
2. What suggestions, if any, would you make to the dean?
3. Which of the performance appraisal systems described in the chapter might be appropriate for this situation?
4. Can you think of any situation where you would suggest a system of promotion based on seniority?

16 Encouraging Effort through Organizational Rewards

Objectives

1. To explore the relationship between organizational rewards and employee performance.
2. To develop an understanding of the importance of the entire organizational reward system.
3. To discuss how an organization can get maximum benefit from its compensation system.

Chapter Outline

Glossary of Terms

Cafeteria approach to compensation Reward system in which employees have the opportunity to choose how their compensation will be distributed from a wide range of alternatives.

Extrinsic rewards Rewards that are controlled and distributed directly by the organization and are of a tangible nature.

Incentive pay plans Plans that attempt to relate pay directly to performance or productivity, usually used in addition to the basic wage or salary.

Intrinsic rewards Rewards that are internal to the individual and are normally derived from involvement in certain activities or tasks.

Job evaluation A systematic method of evaluating the value of each job in relation to other jobs in the organization; concerned with jobs, and not the individuals holding the jobs.

Organizational rewards Rewards that result from employment with the organization; includes all types of rewards, both intrinsic and extrinsic.

Organizational reward system Organizational system that is concerned with the selection of the types of rewards that are to be offered and the distribution of these rewards.

> All you have to do is look around you to see that modern organizations are only getting people to use about 20 percent—the lower fifth—of their capacities. And the painful part is that God didn't design the human animal to function at 20 percent. At that pace it develops enough malfunctions to cause a permanent shortage of psychoanalysts and hospital beds.
>
> *Robert Townsend**

In most cases, the organizational reward system is one of the most effective motivation tools that managers have at their disposal. The design and use of the organizational reward system is often interpreted by employees as a reflection of management attitudes and intentions. Also, there are few things that evoke as much emotion as the organization's reward systems.

THE ORGANIZATIONAL REWARD SYSTEM

The organizational reward system consists of the types of rewards that are to be offered and their distribution. A manager may be involved in the selection of the rewards, in the distribution of the rewards, or both. Organizational rewards include all types of rewards, both intrinsic and extrinsic, that are received as a result of employment by the organization. Intrinsic rewards are rewards that are internal to the individual and are normally derived from involvement in certain activities or tasks. Job satisfaction and feelings of accomplishment are examples of intrinsic rewards. Most extrinsic rewards are directly controlled and distributed by the organization and are more tangible than intrinsic rewards. Pay and hospitalization benefits are examples of extrinsic rewards. Figure 16–1 provides examples of both types of rewards.

Though intrinsic and extrinsic rewards are different, they are also closely related. Often the provision of an extrinsic reward provides the recipient with intrinsic rewards. For example, if an employee receives an extrinsic reward in the form of a pay raise, the individual may also experience feelings of accomplishment (intrinsic rewards) by interpreting the pay raise as a sign of a job well done. Organizations can also influence intrinsic rewards through job design (which is discussed at length in Chapter 19).

* Robert Townsend, *Up the Organization* (New York: Alfred A. Knopf, 1970), p. 140.

FIGURE 16–1
Extrinsic versus Intrinsic Rewards

Extrinsic rewards	*Intrinsic rewards*
Formal recognition	Achievement
Fringe benefits	Feeling of accomplishment
Incentive payments	Informal recognition
Pay	Job satisfaction
Promotion	Personal growth
Social relationships	Status
Work environment	

Selection of the rewards that are to be offered is critical if the reward system is to function effectively. As a first step, management must recognize what employees perceive as meaningful rewards. Rewards may include things that are not overly obvious, such as office or work location or the allocation of certain pieces of equipment. Organizations should learn what the employees, and not necessarily what management, perceive as meaningful rewards.

If an organization is going to distribute rewards—and all do—why not get the maximum in return? Just as investors attempt to gain the maximum return on their investments, so managers should try to get the maximum return for the rewards dispersed by the organization. Such a return can be realized only if the desires of the employees are known. Traditionally, managers have assumed that they are fully capable of deciding just what rewards the employees need and want. Unfortunately, this is not always true. Another closely related, and often false, assumption made by managers is that all employees want the same rewards. This is exemplified by the fact that most organizations offer the same mix of rewards to all employees. A 1975 study found that sex, age, marital status, numbers of dependents, years of service, and job title generally appeared to influence employee preferences for certain rewards.[1] For example, older employees usually are much more concerned with pension benefits than are younger employees.

In an attempt to increase their return on the rewards that are dispersed, some organizations have introduced a "cafeteria approach" to rewards. With this approach, employees select how their direct compensation and benefit dollars will be distributed

[1] J. Brad Chapman and Robert Ottemann, "Employee Preference for Various Compensation Fringe Benefit Options," *The Personnel Administrator*, November 1975, p. 34.

from among several options. Each employee is given a certain amount of total compensation that can be collected in the form of a number of options for pay or fringe benefits. For example, a middle-aged employee with several children in school might select benefits differently from a young, single employee. Figure 16–2 lists many potential reward options that can be provided under the cafeteria approach.

Although implementation of the cafeteria approach to compensation and benefits is not simple, the potential gains from it are attractive enough to merit consideration. The cafeteria approach not only better meets the needs of individual employees but also reduces the amount of funds wasted on benefits not valued by the employees.

Another dimension that should be considered when selecting the types of rewards to be offered is the intrinsic benefit that might occur as a result of the reward. All too often, managers and employees alike consider only the tangible benefits associated with a reward. In general, rewards that are directly related to performance result in greater intrinsic benefits to the recipients than rewards that are not based on performance. For example, if every one receives an across-the-board pay increase of seven percent, it is hard to derive any feelings of accomplishment from the reward. However, if pay raises are related directly to performance, an employee receiving a healthy pay increase would more than likely also experience feelings of accomplishment. Unfortunately, many formal rewards provided by organizations are unrelated to performance and thus have little effect on employee effort. Rewards in this category include paid vacations, insurance plans, and paid holidays; these are almost always determined by organizational membership and seniority rather than by performance. Other rewards, such as promotion, can and should be related to performance. However, opportunities for promotion may occur only rarely. When available, the higher positions may be filled on the basis of seniority or by someone outside the organization. Thus, the primary organizational variable that can be used to reward individuals and reinforce performance is pay.

PAY SATISFACTION: IS IT IMPORTANT?[2]

While there is considerable debate concerning the motivational aspects of pay, there is little doubt that inadequate pay can have a very negative impact on an organization. Certainly one does not

[2] Much of this section and the next is drawn from Edward E. Lawler III, *Pay and Organizational Effectiveness: A Psychological View* (New York: McGraw-Hill, 1971), pp. 205–63.

FIGURE 16–2
Potential Compensation Options

Accidental death, dismemberment insurance
Birthdays (vacation)
Bonus eligibility
Business and professional memberships
Cash profit sharing
Club memberships
Commissions
Company medical assistance
Company-provided automobile
Company-provided housing
Company-provided or subsidized travel
Day-care centers
Deferred bonus
Deferred compensation plan
Deferred profit sharing
Dental and eye care insurance
Discount on company products
Education costs
Educational activities (time off)
Employment contract
Executive dining room
Free checking account
Free or subsidized lunches
Group automobile insurance
Group homeowners insurance
Group life insurance
Health maintenance organization fees
Holidays (extra)
Home health care
Hospital-surgical-medical insurance
Incentive growth fund
Interest-free loans
Layoff pay (S.U.B.)
Legal, estate-planning, and other professional assistance
Loans of company equipment
Long-term disability benefit
Matching educational donations
Nurseries
Nursing home care
Opportunity for travel
Outside medical services
Paid attendance at business, professional, and other outside meetings
Parking facilities
Pension
Personal accident insurance
Personal counseling
Personal credit cards
Personal expense accounts
Physical examinations
Political activities (time off)
Price discount plan
Private office
Professional activities
Psychiatric services
Recreation facilities
Resort facilities
Retirement gratuity
Sabbatical leaves
Salary
Salary continuation
Savings plan
Scholarships for dependents
Severance pay
Shorter or flexible workweek
Sickness and accident insurance
Social security
Social service sabbaticals
Split-dollar life insurance
State disability plans
Stock appreciation rights
Stock bonus plan
Stock option plan (qualified, nonqualified, tandem)
Stock purchase plan
Survivors' benefits
Tax assistance
Title
Training programs
Vacations
Wages
Weekly indemnity insurance

Source: David J. Thomsen, "Introducing Cafeteria Compensation in Your Company." Copyright *Personnel Journal,* March 1977, p. 125. Reprinted with the permission of *Personnel Journal,* Costa Mesa, California; all rights reserved.

have to look long to find employees who are not satisfied with their pay. Just how important is it that employees feel satisfied with their pay? Pay dissatisfaction is frequently blamed as the cause of everything from strikes to poor job performance. Figure 16–3 summarizes some of the more frequently mentioned behaviors that are said to result from pay dissatisfaction. Edward Lawler has developed a simple model designed to help explain the impact of pay dissatisfaction.

FIGURE 16–3
Some Consequences of Pay Dissatisfaction

- Poor job performance
- Strikes
- Grievances
- Turnover
- Job dissatisfaction
- Mental disorders
- Look for new job

Source: Edward E. Lawler III, *Pay and Organizational Effectiveness: A Psychological View* (New York: McGraw-Hill, 1971), p. 232.

According to Lawler's model (Figure 16–4), pay dissatisfaction influences an individual's feelings about his or her job in two ways: (1) it increases the desire for more money and (2) it lowers the attractiveness of the job. When individuals increase their desire for more money, they are likely to engage in actions that can increase their pay. These actions might include joining a union, looking for another job, performing better, or going on strike. With the exception of performing better, all of the consequences would generally be classified as undesirable by management. Better performance would happen only in cases where pay is perceived as being directly related to performance. On the other hand, when the job decreases in attractiveness, the individual is more likely to be absent, tardy, and to become dissatisfied with the job itself. After studying compensation systems in Great Britain for more than ten years, Elliot Jacques reported that "underpayment by more than 10 percent brings about enough dissatisfaction to make employees want to act to get their compensation boosted, and that underpayment by roughly 20 percent produces an explosive situation."[3] Thus, while its importance may vary somewhat from situation to situation, pay satisfaction can and usually does have

[3] Elliott Jacques, *Equitable Payments* (New York: John Wiley & Sons, 1961), p. 142.

FIGURE 16–4
Lawler's Model of the Consequences of Pay Dissatisfaction

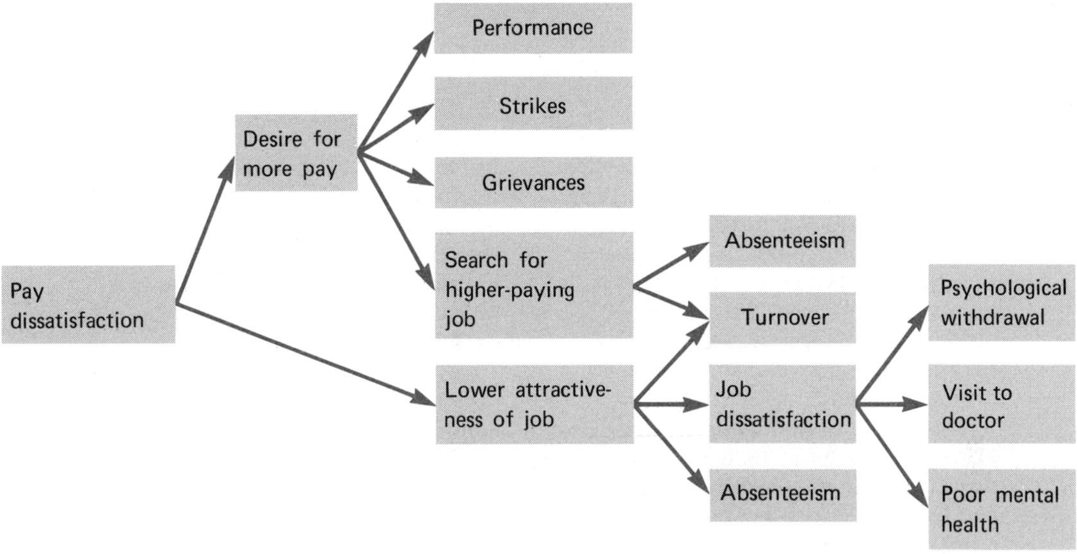

Source: Edward E. Lawler III, *Pay and Organizational Effectiveness: A Psychological View* (New York: McGraw-Hill, 1971), p. 233.

a significant impact on both individual and organizational performance.

Determining Fair Pay

The problem of defining an employee's fair pay is not a new one. Frederick Taylor and his protégés attempted to answer the question through the use of motion and time studies and the establishment of performance standards. Today, wage surveys are frequently used to determine fair wages. The question of fair pay involves two general factors: (1) what the employee is being paid for doing his or her job compared to what other employees are being paid to do their jobs in the same organization (this is referred to as internal equity); and (2) what employees in other organizations are being paid for performing similar jobs (this is referred to as external equity). It is not at all unusual for an individual to feel good about internal equity and bad about external equity or vice versa. For example, employees may feel very good about their pay in comparison to what their friends working in other organizations are making. However, a person may be very unhappy about his or her pay relative to several other people in the same organization. Realizing the differences between internal equity and external equity can help a manager understand why employees may be unhappy about their pay.

MANAGEMENT IN PRACTICE

Want a Raise? Take a Workers' Vote!

Eight years ago, in response to a turbulent eight-week unionization effort by its employees, Romac—a pipefitting plant in Seattle, Washington—initiated a unique employee relations program that has been drawing nationwide attention ever since. The program's unique feature: The employees themselves decide who should get a raise by voting on the matter.

According to Romac president Manfred R. McNeil, the unionization drive came about because management had lost the trust and confidence of the employees. The election ended in a tie vote, and as a consequence the company was in danger of becoming subject to regulation by the National Labor Relations Board. To prevent this from happening, McNeil proposed a new pay plan that would allow production workers to vote on their own pay increases and that would closely tie their own pay increases to gains in productivity. The wage plan has been so successful that the 55 Romac employees think of it as their own custom-made device.

How the Plan Works

A new employee at Romac can request a pay hike after a six-month probationary period by completing a form that includes information about his or her current pay level, previous raise (if any), the requested raise (the average is 20 to 40 cents per hour), and why the employee believes he or she deserves a raise. The employee then "goes on the board." His or her name, hourly wage, and photograph are posted for six consecutive working days, during which time the other employees can observe his or her performance. At election time, the majority rules. Although executives and other top-level managers don't have the right to vote, they can veto any raise granted by the employees. However, McNeil explains, the veto has not been exercised to date.

Along with the privilege of determining who should get a raise, employees learn that the money to pay for these raises comes directly from additional sales dollars generated by increases in productivity.

McNeil says that the employees have managed the wage plan very well over the years, and direct labor costs are not out of line. He also maintains that although the workers seldom say so, they often know better than management who should be promoted, fired, or given a raise. "Somehow we had to get the workers involved so that our problems were also their problems. And I believe that this philosophy has helped our wage plan succeed."

Management Reaction

McNeil admits that at the beginning, many managers at Romac showed little enthusiasm for the plan. One corporate manager told McNeil that the plan wouldn't last more than one year because, by that time, the company would be bankrupt. Another top-level executive said that if there was any real merit to the plan, big corporations would have adopted it long ago. McNeil disagreed.

The main attractions of the plan, he maintains, are involvement and recognition. Workers have told him that they believe immediate recognition should be given individuals for innovative ideas, skills improvement, productivity increases, good attendance, and so on. 'Therefore, a wage increase at Romac . . . says that the employee is doing well in the job—in his or her opinion, in the company's opinion, and in the opinion of the employee's peers. Everyone is involved and gets a chance to reward a co-worker for a job well done."

Source: "Roundup," *Personnel*, September–October 1980 (New York: AMACOM, a division of American Management Associations, 1980), pp. 43–44.

Pay Satisfaction Model

Figure 16–5 presents a model developed by Lawler which outlines the determinants of pay satisfaction. The model is based on the idea that people will be satisfied with their pay when the perception of what their pay is and their perception of what they think it should be are in agreement. This happens when employees feel good about the internal and external equity of their pay.

Naturally, present pay is a primary factor that influences a person's perception of equity. However, the person's wage history and perception of what others are getting also have an influence. For example, people who have historically received high pay tend to lower their perception of present pay. Similarly, the higher the pay of friends and peers, the lower one's individual pay appears. These factors account for the fact that two people might view the same amount of pay in a very different manner.

Lawler's model also shows that a person's perception of what his or her pay should be depends on several other factors, including job inputs, the perceived inputs and outcomes of friends and peers, and nonmonetary outcomes. Job inputs include all the experience, skills, and abilities that an individual brings to the job in addition to the effort the person puts into the job. The perceived inputs and outcomes refer to the individual's perception of what friends and peers put into their jobs and what kind of pay they get in return. The nonmonetary outcomes received refer to the fact that certain nonmonetary rewards can sometimes substitute for pay, at least up to a point.

It is also interesting to note that the model makes allowances for people who feel that their pay exceeds what they think it should. Research has shown that in such cases people often experience feelings of guilt, inequity, and discomfort.[4]

[4] Lawler, "Pay and Organizational Effectiveness," pp. 244–47.

FIGURE 16–5
Model of the Determinants of Pay Satisfaction

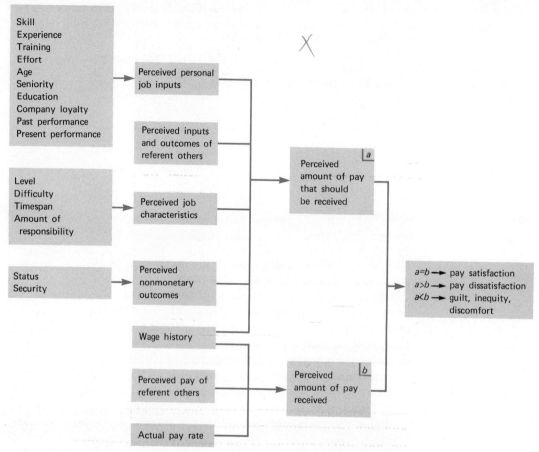

Source: Edward E. Lawler III, *Pay and Organizational Effectiveness: A Psychological View* (New York: McGraw-Hill, 1971), p. 215.

What Can the Manager Do?

Many remedies may be used by managers to minimize real pay inequities and employees' perceptions of pay inequities.[5] Several of these remedies are listed in Figure 16–6 and are discussed below.

Managers can adopt a policy covering pay differentials that reflects the dominant norms of equity of the employees.[6] This ap-

[5] Malcolm S. Salter, "What Is 'Fair Pay' for the Executive?" *Harvard Business Review*, May–June 1972, pp. 6–14, 144–46.

[6] For a detailed discussion of this idea, see Elliott Jacques, *Equitable Payments* (New York: John Wiley & Sons, 1961).

FIGURE 16–6
Remedies to Reduce Pay Dissatisfaction

Adopt a policy covering pay differentials that reflects the dominant norms of equity of the employees.
Ensure consistency of pay brackets through a thorough job evaluation program.
Relate pay to performance.
Disclose pay ranges for different job levels.
Implement a form of "cafeteria compensation."
Raise pay outcomes.

proach contrasts with the traditional view that compensation should reflect top management's judgment. It is based on the assumption that employees at all levels can agree on what constitutes a fair level of pay for the different, respective jobs. For instance, the employees must be able to agree that skilled workers are paid more than unskilled workers. The basic idea is to avoid a situation in which an individual intuitively feels unfairly compensated. Naturally, such a system requires considerable employee input.

Another suggestion is to develop procedures for ensuring consistency of pay brackets for broad levels within the organization, and with respect to similar levels within other organizations. This normally requires a thorough job evaluation program.

Job evaluation is a systematic method or appraising the value of each job in relation to other jobs in the organization.[7] It determines the relative worth of jobs. Job evaluation is concerned with jobs, not performance, personalities, or the individual performing the job. Job evaluation is discussed in the next section.

A third suggestion is to relate pay to performance. As was discussed in Chapter 10 and earlier in this chapter, individuals make judgments concerning the relationship of rewards and performance. If an individual believes that pay is not related to performance, then pay will not serve as a motivator. Also, most people view a situation in which pay is unrelated to performance as being unfair.

A fourth suggestion is to periodically disclose ranges of pay for various job levels in the organization. Pay secrecy makes it difficult for individuals to determine if pay is related to performance. Pay secrecy does not eliminate pay comparisions but it may (1) cause employees to overestimate the pay of their peers and (2)

[7] David W. Belcher, *Compensation Administration* (Englewood Cliffs, N.J.: Prentice-Hall, 1974), p. 88.

cause employees to underestimate the pay of superiors.[8] Both situations can create unnecessary feelings of dissatisfaction. One obvious solution would be to make all pay rates public information. However, many people, and especially high achievers, feel very strongly that their pay is nobody else's business.[9] A good compromise solution is to disclose the pay ranges for various job levels within the organization. This obviously applies only in situations where several employees occupy each of the different job levels.

A fifth action that the organization might take to reduce pay dissatisfaction is to implement a form of cafeteria compensation as discussed earlier in this chapter.

A final suggestion is to raise the pay outcomes for the employees. The old adage, "you get what you pay for" has some applicability here. The key question here is, at what point do pay raises cost more than they buy? The extent to which pay raises result in lower absenteeism, less turnover, fewer strikes and grievances, and higher job satisfaction determines the practicality of increasing pay. Unfortunately, many managers look at pay in a negative fashion and attempt to pay as little as possible. Such an attitude neglects all the positive things that happen when employees are satisfied with their pay. Managers should not look at pay as a necessary evil, but should view it as a tool to help achieve good employee performance.

JOB EVALUATION

Job evaluation (as defined earlier) is a systematic method of appraising the value of each job in relation to other jobs. The process of job evaluation has several essential steps.[10] The first involves a study of the jobs in the organization, accomplished through job analysis. Job analysis is defined as the process of determining, through observation and study, the pertinent information relating to the nature of a specific job. The end results of a job analysis are a job description which identifies and describes the job and a job specification which outlines the skills, abilities, traits, or attributes necessary for successful performance of the job.

The job evaluation process identifies the factor or factors that are to be used in determining the worth of different jobs to the

---

[8] Edward E. Lawler III, "Managers' Perceptions of Their Subordinates' Pay and Their Superiors' Pay," *Personnel Psychology,* Winter 1965, p. 413; and Lawler, "Should Managers' Compensation Be Kept under Wraps?" *Personnel,* January–February 1965, p. 17.

[9] P. Thompson and J. Pronsky, "Secrecy or Disclosure in Management Compensation," *Business Horizons,* June 1975, pp. 67–74.

[10] For an in-depth discussion see Belcher, *Compensation,* pp. 88.

organization. In other words, what factors should be used in determining the pay scale of jobs? Some factors frequently used are skill, responsibility, and working conditions.

The job evaluation process also involves developing and implementing a system that uses the chosen factors for evaluating the relative worth of the different jobs to the organization. Such a system should consistently place jobs requiring more of the factors at a higher level in the job hierarchy than jobs requiring less of the factors. Several existing methods for comparing jobs are available.

Finally, the job evaluation process prices the jobs. Wages and salaries are assigned to jobs according to their position in the job hierarchy. Wage data from other organizations in the same labor market play an important role in arriving at the final price tag for each job.

While the overriding purpose of job evaluation is to establish the relative worth of jobs, a number of other goals may be attained. Figure 16–7 presents a list of potential job evaluation benefits.

Ordinarily, job evaluation should result in a wage range for each job. Performance appraisal is then used to position an individual within the established range. High performers should be placed at the upper end of the range; lower performers in the middle and lower end. Thus, an individual's compensation should be determined by both the value of the job to the organization and the individual's performance in that job.

FIGURE 16–7
Potential Job Evaluation Benefits

1. To provide a more workable internal wage structure in order to simplify and make rational the relatively chaotic wage structure resulting from chance, custom, and such individual factors as favoritism or aggressive tendencies.
2. To provide an agreed-upon device for setting rates for new or changed jobs.
3. To provide a means whereby realistic comparisons may be made of the wage and salary rates of employing organizations.
4. To provide a base for measuring individual performance.
5. To reduce grievances over wage and salary rates by reducing the scope of grievances and providing an agreed-upon means of solving disputes.
6. To provide incentive values to employees to strive for higher-level jobs.
7. To provide facts for wage negotiations.
8. To provide facts on job relationships for use in selection, training, transfers, and promotion.

Source: David W. Belcher, *Compensation Administration* (Englewood Cliffs, N.J.: Prentice-Hall, 1974), pp. 91–92. © 1974 by Prentice-Hall, Inc. Reprinted by permission.

INCENTIVE PAY PLANS

Pay incentives gained wide acceptance in the early 1900s. In the 1970s it was estimated that approximately two thirds of all companies listed on the stock exchanges used some type of pay incentives.[11] With incentive pay plans, pay is related directly to performance or productivity in an endeavor to reward above-average performance rapidly and directly. Although good performance can be rewarded through the normal wage scale either by raising an individual's pay or by promoting the employee into a higher pay grade, these rewards are often subject to delays and other restrictions, such as seniority. Therefore, such rewards often are not viewed by the recipients as being directly related to performance.

Because of minimum wage laws and labor market competition, most incentive plans include a guaranteed hourly wage or salary. Thus, the incentive plans usually function in addition to, not instead of, the basic wages. Incentive plans can be used on an individual or group basis. Normally, individual plans are preferred because of their direct link with the performer. However, many situations (such as an assembly line) require a cooperative effort and, therefore, lend themselves to group incentives.

Lower-level incentive programs are usually a function of production or time and are by definition related to performance. At such levels the only potential hazard is in setting the standard. A time standard has little validity if it is established using inefficient or improper methods. A standard set too high causes people to take a negative attitude and not attempt to achieve the standard. Management incentive programs present a different set of problems. Performance appraisals for managers, being subjective in nature, frequently result in similar ratings for everyone. This all too often leads to everyone receiving the same bonus.

A well-administered incentive program can, under the right circumstances, benefit all parties. However, a poorly administered, inappropriate scheme can result in increased costs, output restriction, and hostility.[12] Because of the potential ill effects, the adoption of an incentive program requires careful planning.

SUMMARY

The organizational reward system is often the most effective motivation-related tool at the manager's disposal. Organizational rewards include all types of rewards, both intrinsic and extrinsic, that are received as a result of employment by the organization.

---

[11] Arch Patton, "Why Incentive Plans Fail," *Harvard Business Review*, May–June 1972, p. 59.

[12] Gene K. Groff, "Worker Productivity: An Integrated View," *Business Horizons*, April 1971, p. 84.

Intrinsic rewards are rewards that are internal to the individual and are normally derived from involvement in certain activities or tasks. Extrinsic rewards are those rewards that are tangible and are controlled and distributed by the organization. Proper recognition and selection of the rewards to be offered are critical if the reward system is to function effectively. Traditionally, managers have assumed that they are fully capable of deciding just what rewards employees want; however this is often not true. Under the "cafeteria approach" to compensation, employees can select from among several options how their direct compensation and benefit dollars will be distributed.

Unfortunately, many formal rewards provided by an organization, such as paid vacations, insurance, and paid holidays, are unrelated to performance and thus have little effect on employee effort. The primary tool that can be used to reward individuals and reinforce performance is pay. Pay satisfaction can have a significant impact on many organizational variables such as job performance, strikes, grievances, turnover, absenteeism, and job dissatisfaction. The question of fair pay involves two general factors: (1) what the employee is being paid, or perceives he or she is being paid, for doing a job compared to what other employees are being paid, or perceived as being paid, in the same organization and (2) what employees in other organizations are being paid, or perceived as being paid, for performing similar jobs. A pay satisfaction model developed by Edward Lawler is based on the idea that people will be satisfied with their pay when the perception of what their pay is and their perception of what it should be are in agreement. Several remedies may be used by the organization to reduce pay dissatisfaction. These include the adoption of a pay policy to reflect the norms of the employees, ensuring consistent pay ranges through job evaluation, relating pay to performance, disclosing pay ranges, implementing a form of "cafeteria compensation," and raising pay outcomes. Incentive pay plans attempt to relate pay directly to performance and are normally used in addition to, not in lieu of, basic wages. Job evaluation is a systematic method of appraising the value of each job in relation to other jobs.

REVIEW QUESTIONS

1. What are organizational rewards?
2. What are the differences between intrinsic and extrinsic rewards?
3. What are some variables that have been found to influence employee preferences for certain rewards?
4. What is the "cafeteria approach" to compensation?

5. What is the primary organizational variable that can be used to reward individuals and reinforce performance?
6. Describe some of the consequences of pay dissatisfaction.
7. What are the two general factors relating to the question of fair pay?
8. Describe Lawler's pay satisfaction model. How is pay satisfaction determined by the model?
9. Name six remedies or organizational actions that can be taken to reduce pay dissatisfaction.
10. What are pay incentives?

DISCUSSION QUESTIONS

1. The XYZ Company has just decided to take all of its 200 employees to Las Vegas for an expense-paid, three-day weekend to show its appreciation for their high level of performance this past year. What is your reaction to this idea?
2. Comment on the following statement: "Employees are not capable of deciding what rewards they should receive."
3. Recently a manager was overheard making the following comment, "Most employees are *never* satisfied with their pay anyway, so why should we even try? I think we should pay as little as possible and just accept the fact that the employees won't like it." If you were this manager's superior, what would you say?
4. Discuss the following statement: "Any employee who is satisfied with his or her pay is not very aggressive."

SELECTED READINGS

Adams, J. S. "Toward an Understanding of Inequity." *Journal of Abnormal and Social Psychology* 67 (1963), pp. 422–36.

Hulme, Robert D., and Richard V. Beron. "The Blue-Collar Worker Goes on Salary." *Harvard Business Review*, March–April 1975, pp. 104, 112.

Jacques, Elliott. *Equitable Payments*. New York: John Wiley & Sons, 1961.

Klein, Stuart M. "Pay Factors as Predictors to Satisfaction: A Comparison of Reinforcement, Equity, and Expectory." *Academy of Management Journal*, December 1973, pp. 598–610.

Lawler, Edward E., III. "Managers" Perceptions of Their Subordinates' Pay and of Their Superior's Pay." *Personnel Psychology*, Winter 1965.

———. "New Approaches to Pay: Innovations that Work," *Personnel*, September–October 1976, pp. 11–23.

London, Manuel, and Greg R. Oldham. "A Comparison of Group and Individual Incentive Plans." *Academy of Management Review*, March 1977, pp. 34–41.

Miner, Mary G. "Pay Policies: Secret or Open? And Why?" *Personnel Journal*, February 1974, pp. 110–15.

Opshal, R. L., and Marvin D. Dunnette. "The Role of Financial Compensation in Industrial Motivation." *Psychological Bulletin* 66 (1966), pp. 94–118.

Patton, Arch. "Why Incentive Plans Fail." *Harvard Business Review*, May–June 1972, pp. 58–66.

Patton, John A. "Wage Incentives: From Failure to Success." *Industrial Engineering*, June 1974, pp. 20–27.

Porter, Lyman W., and Edward E. Lawler III. *Managerial Attitudes and Performance*. Homewood, Ill.: Richard D. Irwin and The Dorsey Press, 1968.

Salter, Malcolm S. "What Is 'Fair Pay' for the Executive?" *Harvard Business Review*, May–June 1972, pp. 6–14, 144–46.

Shuster, Jay R., and Jerome A. Colletti. "Pay Secrecy: Who Is For and Against It?" *Academy of Management Journal*, March 1973, pp. 35–40.

Thomsen, David J. "Introducing Cafeteria Compensation in Your Company," *Personnel Journal*, March 1977, p. 125.

Case 16–1

An informative coffee break

On Monday morning, April 28, George Smith was given the news that effective May 1, he would receive a raise of 13 percent. This raise came two months before his scheduled performance appraisal. He was informed by his manager, Tom Weeks, that the basis for the raise was his performance over the past several months and his potential worth to the company. He was told that this was a very considerable increase.

On the next day, Tuesday, a group of fellow workers in George's office were engaging in their normal coffee break. The course of conversation swung to salary increases. One of the group had received a performance review in April, but no indication of an impending salary adjustment had been given. George made a comment concerning the amount of any such increase, specifically questioning the range of increase percentages. A third individual immediately responded, expressing surprise at having received an "across the board" 12 percent increase the previous Friday. A fourth individual had received a similar salary increase. Definitely astounded, George pressed for information, only to learn that several people had received increases of "around" 11 to 13 percent. George broke up the gathering by excusing himself.

That evening, George wrestled with his conscience concerning the foregoing discussion. His first impression of his raise was that it had been given based on performance. His second impression was decidedly sour. Several questions were bothering him:

1. Why did his boss tender the raise as a merit increase?
2. Is job performance really a basis for salary increases in his department?
3. Did his superior hide the truth regarding the raise?
4. Can he trust his boss in the future?
5. Upon what basis will further increases be issued?

1. What effect do you think that this new information will have on the effort put forth by George Smith?

2. What can Tom Weeks do to regain George Smith's confidence?

Case 16–2 Does money motivate?

About four months ago, Greg Holcomb was promoted to supervisor of the claims department for a large, eastern insurance company. It is now time for all supervisors to make their annual salary increase recommendations. Greg doesn't feel comfortable in making these recommendations since he has only been in his job for a short time. To further complicate the situation, the former supervisor has left the company and is unavailable for consultation.

There are no formal company restrictions on the kind of raises that can be given, but Greg's boss has said that the total amount of money available to Greg for raises would be 8 percent of Greg's total payroll for the past year. In other words, if the sum total of the salaries for all of Greg's employees was $100,000, then Greg would have $8,000 to allocate for raises. Greg is free to distribute the raises just about any way he wants, within reason.

Summarized below is the best information on his employees that Greg can find from the files of the former supervisor of the claims department. This information is supplemented by feelings Greg has developed during his short time as supervisor.

Sam McNally: Sam has been with Greg's department for only five months. In fact, he was hired just before Greg was promoted into the supervisor's job. Sam is single and seems to be a carefree bachelor. His job performance, so far, has been above-average, but Greg has received some negative comments about Sam from his co-workers. Present salary: $11,000.

Tina Strickland: Tina has been on the job for three years. Her previous performance appraisals have indicated superior performance. However, Greg does not feel that the previous evaluations are accurate. He feels that Tina's performance is, at best, average. Tina appears to be well liked by all of her co-workers. Just last year, she became widowed and is presently the sole support for her five-year-old child. Present salary: $12,000.

Evelyn Roth: Evelyn has been on the job for four years. Her previous performance appraisals were all average. In addition, she has received below-average increases for the past two years. However, Evelyn recently approached Greg and told him that she feels she was discriminated against in the past due to both her age and sex. Greg feels that Evelyn's work so far has been satisfactory but not superior. Most employees don't seem to sympathize with Evelyn's accusations of sex and age discrimination. Present salary: $10,000.

Jane Simmons: As far as Greg can tell, Jane is one of his best employees. Her previous performance appraisals also indicate that she is a superior performer. In addition, Greg knows that Jane badly needs a substantial salary increase due to some personal problems. In addition, all of Greg's employees are aware of Jane's problems. She appears to be well respected by her co-workers. Present salary: $11,500.

Bob McClure: Bob has been performing his present job for eight years. The job is very technical, and he would be difficult to replace. However, as far as Greg can discern, Bob is not a good worker. He is irritable and hard to work with. In spite of this, Bob has received above-average pay increases for the past two years. Present salary: $13,000.

1. Indicate the size of the raise that you would give each of these employees.
2. What criteria did you use in determining the size of the raise?
3. What do you feel would be the feelings of the other people in the group if they should find out what raises you recommend?
4. Do you feel that the employees would eventually find out what raises others received? Would it matter?

17 Developing Abilities

Objectives

1. To explore the process of developing individual abilities within organizations.
2. To discuss several specific methods of developing individual abilities in organizations.
3. To introduce the concept of organization development and some methods for implementing it.

Chapter Outline

Glossary of Terms

Abilities An individual's personal characteristics, which are used in performing a job.

Apprenticeship training Supervised training and testing for a minimum time period and until a minimum skill level is reached.

Assessment Center Formal procedure used to evaluate an individual's potential as a manager by using exercises which elicit managerial behaviors by the participant.

Behavior modeling A form of training which involves identifying interaction problems faced by managers, such as overcoming resistance to change; identifying behaviors necessary to resolve these problems; practicing these behaviors in problem interactions; and developing a plan to transfer these learned behaviors back to the job.

Employee development A process concerned with the improvement and growth of the capabilities of individuals and groups within the organization.

Grid training A form of training used in organization development which is designed to make managers and organizations more team-oriented.

Human asset accounting A proposed approach to accounting which attempts to place a value on an organization's human assets.

Management development A type of employee development which is designed to improve managerial performance.

On-the-job training A form of training given by an employee's manager or a senior employee which involves actually showing the employee the job and explaining how it is to be done.

Organization development (OD) Organization-wide, planned effort, managed from the top, with a goal of increasing organizational performance through planned interventions in the organization. OD relies heavily on behavioral science knowledge and techniques.

Orientation Training concerned with introducing the new employee to the organization and his or her job.

Sensitivity training A form of training used in organization development which is designed to make one more aware of oneself and one's impact on others.

Training A process that involves the acquisition of skills, concepts, rules, or attitudes in order to improve present and future performance.

Few organizations would admit that they can survive without it—yet some act as though they could.

Everyone knows what it is—yet management, unions, and workers often interpret it in light of their own job conditions.

It is going on all the time—yet much of it is done haphazardly.

It is futile to attempt it without the needed time and facilities—yet often those responsible for it lack either or both.

It costs money—yet at times there is not adequate budgetary appropriation for it.

It should take place at all levels—yet sometimes it is limited to the lowest operating levels.

It can help everyone do a better job—yet those selected for it often fear it.

It is foolish to start it without clearly defined objectives—yet this is occasionally done.

It cannot be ignored without costing the company money—yet some managers seem blind to this reality.

It should permeate the entire organization and be derived from the firm's theory and practice of management—yet sometimes it is shunted off to one department that operates more or less in isolation from the rest of the business.

*F. A. Phillips, W. M. Berliner, and J. J. Cribbin**

Abilities are an individual's personal characteristics used in performing a job. These characteristics do not fluctuate widely over short periods of time. Because abilities place an upper limit on the performance of an individual regardless of effort and direction, organizations should make a conscious attempt to develop the abilities of its employees. Staffing, as discussed in Chapter 9, involves securing and developing personnel for jobs which are created in the organizing function. However, as the introductory quote points out, there are problems associated with developing the abilities of an organization's personnel. The purpose of this chapter is to explore these problems in depth.

HUMAN ASSET ACCOUNTING

Human asset or human resource accounting involves an attempt to place a value on an organization's human assets. Rensis Likert defines human asset accounting as follows: "Human asset accounting refers to activity devoted to attaching dollar estimates

*F. A. Phillips, W. M. Berliner, and J. J. Cribbin, *Management of Training Programs* (Homewood, Ill.: Richard D. Irwin, 1960), pp. 5–6.

to the value of a firm's human organization and its customer goodwill."[1] Basically, the proponents of human asset accounting feel that the quality of the personnel in an organization should be reflected on the balance sheet of the organization.

Several methods for determining the financial value of an organization's human resources have been suggested. These approaches include:

1. Start-Up Costs—Derive the original costs of hiring and training personnel as well as the costs of developing working relationships.
2. Replacement Costs—Estimate the cost of replacing current employees with others of equivalent talents and experiences.
3. Present Value Method—Multiply the present value of the wage payments for the future five years times the firm's efficiency ratio (which is a measure of the firm's rate of return in relation to the average rate of return for the industry).
4. Goodwill Method—Allocate a portion of the company's earnings in excess of the industry average (goodwill) to human resources.[2]

Human asset accounting is not presently an acceptable accounting practice for financial reporting purposes.[3] However, it must be pointed out that direct costing, which was introduced as a managerial technique in 1939, has become accepted managerial accounting for internal purposes, although it has never been an accepted practice for either tax or financial reporting.[4] Thus, in order for the use of human asset accounting to become widespread, it must first be proven to be useful in practice.

EMPLOYEE DEVELOPMENT

Employee development (which was mentioned in Chapter 9) is a process concerned with altering the work behavior or attitudes of employees in order to increase organizational goal achievement.[5] The primary activities involved in employee development are orientation, training in job skills, modifying attitudes, and the cultivation of managerial skills. Other activities related to employee development include performance appraisal and employee disci-

---

[1] Rensis Likert, *The Human Organization* (New York: McGraw-Hill, 1967), p. 148.

[2] Michael H. Gilbert, "The Asset Value of the Human Organization," *Management Accounting*, July 1970, pp. 26–27.

[3] Jacob B. Paperman and Desmond D. Martin, "Human Resource Accounting: A Managerial Tool?" *Personnel*, March–April 1977, p. 45.

[4] Ibid., p. 45.

[5] John Hinrichs, "Personnel Training," in *Handbook of Industrial and Organizational Psychology*, ed. Marvin D. Dunnette (Skokie, Ill.: Rand McNally, 1976), p. 832.

FIGURE 17–1
Employee Development Process

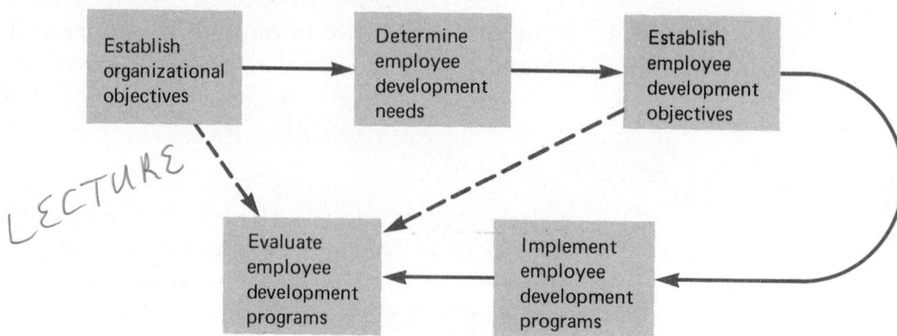

pline. Because this last set of activities relates more directly to defining direction within the organization, they were covered in Chapter 15, Defining Performance and Direction. Figure 17–1 illustrates how the employee development process should work in any organization.

Chapter 4 discussed in detail the process of establishing organizational objectives. This essential step must be accomplished before an overall program of employee development can be implemented because employee development must relate to the organizational objectives.

Employee development objectives are determined by the personnel requirements that are established through the personnel planning process. Organizational objectives and a skills inventory aid management in forecasting the specific abilities that are required. The results of this process enable management to establish objectives for the overall employee development program. Employee development objectives can also be derived from management reports on absenteeism, turnover, production, or safety problems.

After objectives have been established, the appropriate programs can be developed and implemented. Finally, employee development programs should be evaluated by comparing their results with projected employee development objectives.

EMPLOYEE TRAINING

Training is a process involving the acquisition of skills, concepts, rules, or attitudes in order to improve present and future performance. Training is and must be the responsibility of all managers.

Many organizations establish a training department to implement training programs. This department is normally located within the personnel or human resources department. The training department assists the managers of the organization in the following areas: (1) determining training needs; (2) organizing and scheduling formal training classes; (3) providing instructors for training classes; and (4) evaluating the formal training programs.

Orientation

The training process begins on the first day of employment for an individual. This phase of training is known as orientation. Orientation is concerned with introducing the new employee to the organization and his or her job. It is important to remember that all employees receive orientation whether or not there is a formal orientation program. New employees form impressions and attitudes about the organization through their daily contacts on the job. In order for the employee to form accurate impressions, it is desirable that every organization have a formalized orientation program. Generally, the formalized orientation program is administered by the personnel department. Orientation on the job is normally given by the new employee's manager. Both of these forms of orientation are important in shaping the new employee's attitude toward both the job and the organization as a whole.[6] Unfortunately, many organizations underestimate the importance of an orientation program. New employees are all too often given a policy and procedures manual and told to study it until they are given another assignment. At this point, policies and procedures have little meaning to new employees and they quickly become bored. The unfortunate part is that new employees are often not given another assignment for several days—even weeks in some cases. Obviously, the new employee is off to a bad start. Figure 17–2 gives information that should be covered in orientation of new employees. Figure 17–3 shows what is usually covered by the manager if a personnel department is involved in the orientation program.

Methods of Training

Training should be objective-oriented. Regrettably, many training programs have no objectives at all. The adage "training for training's sake" seems to be appropriate for those situations. The following criteria should be considered as guideposts in defining training objectives: (1) training objectives and organizational objectives should be compatible; (2) training objectives should be

[6] John Wanous, "Effects of a Realistic Job Preview on Job Acceptance, Job Attitudes, and Job Survival," *Journal of Applied Psychology*, 58, no. 3 (1973), pp. 327–32.

FIGURE 17–2
Information to Be Covered in Orientation of New Employees

1. A welcome.
2. The objectives and philosophy of the organization.
3. An explanation of the organization's operations, the levels of authority, and how they relate.
4. A brief history of the organization.
5. What is expected of the new employee: attitude, reliability, initiative, emotional maturity, and personal appearance.
6. Job functions and responsibilities.
7. Introduction to his or her department and fellow workers.
8. General office practice and business etiquette.
9. Rules, regulations, policies, and procedures.
10. Why the organization needs the new employee.
11. City, state, and federal laws, if applicable.
12. Skill training.
13. Performance evaluation criteria.
14. Promotional opportunities.
15. Conditions of employment: punctuality, attendance, conduct, hours of work, overtime, termination.
16. Pay procedures.
17. Benefits: salary, job security, insurance, recreational facilities, employee activities, rest periods, holidays, vacation, sick leave, leave of absence, tuition refund, pension.
18. Safety and fire prevention.
19. Personnel policies.
20. Functions of management.
21. Techniques for learning.
22. Encouragement.

Source: Adapted from Joan Holland and Theodore Curtis, "Orientation of New Employees," in *Handbook of Modern Personnel Administration,* ed. Joseph Famularo (New York: McGraw-Hill, 1972), pp. 23–24, 23–25.

realistic; (3) training objectives should be clearly stated in writing; and (4) results should be measurable and verifiable.

In general, training programs are considered successful when participants respond enthusiastically to the program. The opinions and casual observations of participants comprise the extent of most training evaluation. However, enthusiasm cannot be taken as positive evidence of improved ability. Opinions do not always reflect the effectiveness of the training program. If training programs are to contribute to the achievement of organizational objectives, they must be objectively evaluated and the results must be carefully analyzed by management.

When training results are measured objectively, a number of benefits accrue. Less effective programs can be withdrawn from consideration, which saves time and effort. Weaknesses within established programs can be strengthened. Finally, the results of

FIGURE 17–3
Information to Be Covered in Orientation by the Manager if There Is a Personnel Department

1. Welcome the new employee.
2. Introduce the new employee to other employees in the work unit.
3. Familiarize the new employee with his or her duties and responsibilities.
4. Explain the nature of the work and its relationship to the work of co-workers and that of the work unit as a whole.
5. Discuss policies on performance and conduct.
6. Familiarize the employee with the physical surroundings.
7. Discuss safety and fire prevention.

effective training can be promulgated in a meaningful fashion and can be objectively evaluated by management. For instance, one study evaluating the effectiveness of formal training versus informal training found that formally trained blue-collar workers became more competent more quickly than those trained by informal methods, at a lesser cost and with lower scrap loss and higher-quality performance.[7] This type of information not only reinforces the value of training but also facilitates the communication of its value to higher management.

Several different methods are available for achieving training objectives. Some of these include on-the-job training, apprenticeship training, classroom training, and programmed instruction.

On-the-job training is the most common method of training employees, and is normally given by the employee's manager or a senior employee. It merely involves showing the employee the job and demonstrating or explaining how it is done. One commonly used method for structuring on-the-job training is the job instruction training (JIT) system developed during World War II. Figure 17–4 summarizes the steps involved in applying JIT. The advantages of on-the-job training are that no special facilities are required and the trainee is engaged in productive work during the training period. Its major disadvantage is that the pressure of the workplace can lead to haphazard, inadequate instruction.

In job rotation, sometimes called cross training, an employee learns several different jobs and performs each job for a specific length of time. The JIT system can be used in training the employee on each job. The main advantage of cross training is that when a person is absent or leaves, the vacated job can be readily performed by others.

[7] James Cullen et al., "Training: What's It Worth?" *Training and Development Journal,* August 1976, pp. 12–20.

FIGURE 17–4
Steps in the JIT System

Determining the training objectives and preparing the training area
1. Decide what the trainee must be taught so he or she can do the job efficiently, safely, economically, and intelligently.
2. Provide the right tools, equipment, supplies, and material.
3. Have the workplace properly arranged, just as the employee will be expected to keep it.

Presenting the instruction

Step 1. Preparation of the trainee:
1. Put the trainee at ease.
2. Find out what the trainee already knows about the job.
3. Get the trainee interested in and desirous of learning the job.

Step 2. Presentation of the operations and knowledge:
1. Tell, show, illustrate, and question to put over the new knowledge and operations.
2. Instruct slowly, clearly, completely, and patiently, one point at a time.
3. Check, question, and repeat.
4. Make sure the trainee understands.

Step 3. Performance tryout:
1. Test the trainee by having him or her perform the job.
2. Ask questions beginning with why, how, when, or where.
3. Observe performance, correct errors, and repeat instructions if necessary.
4. Continue until the trainee is competent in the job.

Step 4: Follow-up:
1. Put the trainee on his or her own.
2. Check frequently to be sure the trainee follows instructions.
3. Taper off extra supervision and close follow-up until the trainee is qualified to work with normal supervision

Source: Adapted from *The Training within Industry Report* (War Manpower Commission, Bureau of Training, 1945,) p. 195.

Vestibule training is a compromise between on-the-job and off-the-job training. In this type of training, the individual uses procedures and equipment similar to those of the actual job, but located in a special area called a vestibule. Trainees are taught by skilled persons, and are able to learn the job at their own speed without the pressures of production schedules. The primary advantage of vestibule training is that though the trainee is still actually performing the job, proper performance rather than output is emphasized. However, this method is expensive and the trainee must afterward adjust to the actual production environment and its pressures.

Apprenticeship training involves supervised training and testing for a minimum time period and until a minimum skilled level is reached. This approach, dating back to biblical times, is commonly used in skilled trades. Over a period of time, the apprentice has formal classroom training and practical on-the-job experience. During this time, the apprentice is normally paid somewhat less than workers who have completed their apprenticeship.

Formal classroom training is probably the most familiar type of training because most people experience it throughout their own education. Lectures, movies, and exercises are the most commonly used methods of conducting classroom training.

Programmed instruction is one of the newest methods of providing training within organizations. With this method, material is presented in text form, and the student is required to read and answer questions concerning it. If the answers are correct, the student progresses to more advanced material and is retested. Programmed instruction involves such features as "active practice through gradual increase in difficulty levels over a series of small steps, immediate feedback, learning at the individual's own rate, and minimization of error."[8] Programmed instruction generally does not require an instructor or training leader. A current extension of programmed instruction is computer assisted instruction (CAI). Under this method, the same principles are involved, but a computer displays the material and processes the students' answers.

Make the Training Meaningful

Regardless of the type of training used, there are several common pitfalls that a manager should avoid in order to make an employee's training experience more meaningful. Lack of reinforcement is a common error in training. An employee who is praised for doing a job correctly is likely to be motivated to do it correctly again. Too many managers only point out mistakes. Praise and recognition of a trainee can be a very effective means of reinforcing an employee's learning. Similarly, managers often tell people "I'll let you know if you do the job wrong." However, people also want to know when they do the job right. Feedback regarding progress is critical to effective learning. Setting standards of performance for trainees and measuring their performance against them encourage learning.

"Practice makes perfect" definitely applies to the learning process. Too many managers try to explain the job quickly and then expect the person to do it perfectly the first time. Having a trainee perform a particular job or explain how to perform a job focuses their concentration and facilitates learning. Repeating a job or

[8] John B. Miner and Mary Green Miner, *Personnel and Industrial Relations: A Managerial Approach*, 2d ed. (New York: Macmillan, 1973), p. 365.

task several times also helps. Learning is always helped by practice and repetition.

Managers also sometimes have preconceived and inaccurate ideas about what certain people or groups of people can or can't do (the Pygmalion effect). A manager should realize that different people learn at different rates. Some learn rapidly, some learn more slowly. The pace of the training should be adjusted to the trainee. A manager shouldn't expect everyone to pick the job up right away. Also, if a person is not a fast learner, this does not mean that the person will always be a poor performer. The manager should take the attitude that all people can learn and want to learn. Figure 17–5 summarizes several conditions for effective learning. A manager should attempt to develop these conditions for all trainees.

Pygmalion effect

FIGURE 17–5
Conditions for Effective Learning

1. Acceptance that all people can learn.
2. The individual must be motivated to learn.
3. Learning is an active, not passive, process.
4. Normally, the learner must have guidance.
5. Appropriate materials for sequential learning must be provided: hands-on experiences, cases, problems, discussion, reading.
6. Time must be provided to practice the learning; to internalize; to give confidence.
7. Learning methods, if possible, should be varied to avoid boredom.
8. The learner must secure satisfaction from the learning.
9. The learner must get reinforcement of the correct behavior.
10. Standards of performance should be set for the learner.
11. A recognition that there are different levels of learning and that these take different times and methods.

Leslie This and Gordon Lippitt, "Learning Theories and Training," *Training and Development Journal*, April 1966, pp. 2–11.

MANAGEMENT DEVELOPMENT

Formalized management development programs are a subset of the employee development process. Ideally, they should be designed, conducted, and evaluated based on the objectives of the organization. They should also have the total support of top management, be designed around the needs of the organization and the individual needs of each manager, and be periodically evaluated.

It is important to note that there is a real difference between top management support for management development programs and lip-service to these programs. True support for man-

MANAGEMENT IN PRACTICE

For Gino's Trainees, Learning How Things Should Work Is Just a Game

KING OF PRUSSIA, Pa.—It is 10 A.M. on a Thursday, and Ted Goldflies, would-be manager of a Gino's Inc. fast-food outlet, is struggling with a tough question: What is the proper cooking temperature of a Gino's fish sandwich?

This is the sort of challenge that confronts management trainees in every walk of corporate life. It sometimes bores them silly. But Mr. Goldflies isn't bored, he is delighted. By knowing that Gino's fish is cooked at exactly 350 degrees, he has just won 15 points, and avoids paying $15 to his trainee opponent, Michael Beckett.

"Luck, just luck," Mr. Beckett sneers as he proceeds to his turn.

The two are playing "OJT," a computerized board game whose name stands for "on-the-job-training." The board is like Monopoly's except that it simulates a fast-food unit complete with kitchen, counter and dining area. Also like Monopoly, trainees get play money, and try to wind up with the most money. They move counters around the board, roll dice and answer questions. OJT has a computer that beeps when a trainee punches in correct answers and buzzes for incorrect ones. (That way, opponents don't learn the correct answer.)

Crafted to Captivate

OJT was developed by Personel Management Systems, Inc. a Princeton, N.J., management consulting firm that recently designed training games for divisions of Penn Central Corp. and the Pillsbury Company. The games are designed to "captivate the trainees and stimulate their egos," and make them concentrate on the material, says Robert Defamontagne, personnel management president.

Gino's first used OJT in August. Since then, about 100 trainees have used it as part of their nine-week training course. Rustler Steak Houses, another Gino's division, is using a similar game adapted to cafeteria-like steak house operations. Gino's plans to add an advanced game for existing managers next year, says Thomas Harrison, director of management training and development.

Gino's trainees play OJT as excitedly as children. And its "trick" questions have answers that surprise even trainees familiar with the material.

Evidence Destroyed

Trainee Barbara Veith gets a surprise. What should she do, she is asked, if a customer returns a chicken box with only bones left, but complains that the chicken was undercooked? She chooses to refund the money. "It doesn't cost that much, and he'll be satisfied," Miss Veith says. She gets a computer buzz; wrong answer.

She is startled at the seemingly callous solution to the problem: not to refund the customer's money or replace the product. "He ate the evidence: there's nothing to show that the product was bad," says Craig Heizer, who supervised the games.

As QJT is played just before a final written examination, it helps the trainees practice what they have learned, before they get assigned to a restaurant. And for trainees, who studied hard during seven weeks, QJT is a "welcome change from boring lectures," says Mr. Goldflies. He now is an assistant manager in a Philadelphia area Gino's.

Source: Deborah A. Randolph; *The Wall Street Journal,* October 7, 1980.

agement development programs demands the genuine and active interest of top managers and usually includes their participation in part of the programs. It does little good to enlighten lower-level managers if they return to an environment where the learned concepts cannot be applied.

Management development is concerned with developing the experience, attitudes, and skills necessary to becoming, or remaining, effective managers. Management development can be used to reduce the negative effects of managerial obsolescence which exist when an individual no longer holds the skills and knowledge thought necessary for current or future effective performance.[9]

Objectives in Management Development

As with employee training, management development programs must have clearly defined objectives, derived in terms of overall organizational objectives. One classification system for preparing objectives involves setting routine, problem-solving, and innovative objectives.[10] With regard to management development, routine objectives might include objectives related to conducting ongoing supervisory training courses. Specifically, these objectives might incorporate goals relating to the number of trainees, hours of training, cost per trainee, and time required for trainees to reach a standard level of knowledge.

Problem-solving objectives are developed to resolve particular problem areas in an organization. To formulate problem-solving objectives for management development programs, an analysis could be made of management reports on such factors as absenteeism, turnover, safety, and grievances. In addition, managers could be interviewed or polled with questionnaires concerning problems that they feel might be resolved by training.

The purpose of innovative objectives is to obtain higher levels of excellence through new kinds of behavior and new techniques which improve the quality or reduce the cost of training.

The difference between problem-solving and innovative management development objectives can be illustrated by the following example. Suppose that an organization notices a sudden increase in the number of union grievances. To correct this, a new supervisory development program is designed to improve the skills of supervisors in handling these complaints. If, through this pro-

[9] William F. Glueck, *Personnel: A Diagnostic Approach* (Plano, Tex.: Business Publications, 1978), p. 367. Copyright © 1978 by Business Publications, Inc.

[10] George Odiorne, *Personnel Administration by Objectives* (Homewood, Ill.: Richard D. Irwin, 1971), p. 338–51. Copyright © 1971 by Richard D. Irwin, Inc.

gram, the number of grievances returns to normal or is reduced even further, the situation has been remedied. The problem-solving objective has been met. Suppose that, in another company, new supervisors have received most of their training in the form of on-the-job training and that this method appears to be meeting the organization's needs. However, if a new system of home study and programmed learning is introduced and allows new supervisors to build their skills faster or at a lower cost, an innovative objective has been achieved.

The routine, the problem-solving, and the innovative objectives of management development have been discussed from an organizational perspective. Equally important is spelling out the unique career needs of each manager within the organization. Figure 17–6 illustrates the relationship between the individual manager's development needs and those of the entire organization.

FIGURE 17–6
Relationship between Individual Manager's Development Needs and the Organization's Management Development Objectives

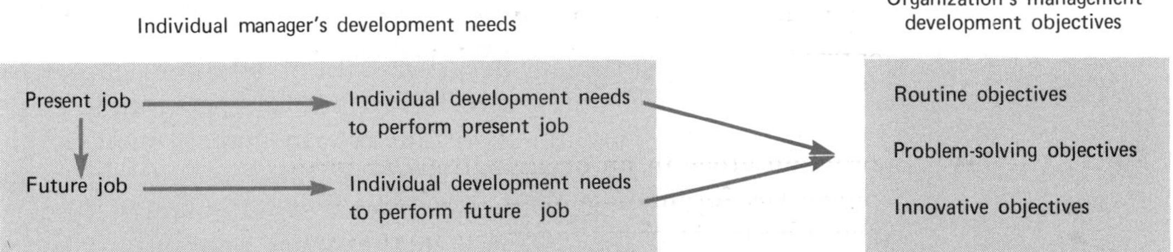

Methods of Management Development

Management development can take many forms. Techniques for management development include coaching, job rotation, individual self-improvement programs, performance appraisals, inhouse training programs, as well as training courses and programs sponsored by universities and other professional organizations.

Coaching is probably the most widely used technique in management development. Under this system, a coach, generally a higher-level manager, is assigned the responsibility of seeing that a manager-trainee learns the skills needed in becoming an effective manager. The assumption is made that the most effective method of teaching good management is for effective managers to teach what they are doing. Coaching often has good results, but not without its problems. First, this method of management development perpetuates current management practices and styles. This may or may not be desirable. In addition, the coach frequently does not have enough time to spend with the trainee and doesn't, therefore, allow the trainee to make mistakes and learn from experience. Since there has been little evaluation of this form of management development, it is difficult to determine the effectiveness of the technique.

Job rotation is the practice of periodically changing job assignments. Job rotation can lead to effective management development, but if it is not properly used, it can do more harm than good. Job rotation can be ineffective in management development if the trainee is merely shifted from department to department within the organization, doing jobs that require little skill and lead to no development.

Individual self-improvement programs merely involve the self-development activities of a manager. These include home study courses or any other related activity that is designed to improve job performance. Ideally, coaching and job rotation should provide the perceptive manager with information and problems that could be used for home study. Obviously, this approach to management development is very unstructured, and the effectiveness of such a program is difficult to determine.

Performance appraisals were discussed in detail in Chapter 15 as they relate to defining direction. However, performance appraisals can also play an important role in management development. One purpose of performance appraisal is to evaluate an individual's actual performance compared to planned performance. Analyzing the results of performance appraisals aids in increasing future performance by identifying both the strengths and weaknesses of the individual. Performance appraisal should involve the following basic components: (1) mutual establishment of performance objectives by superior and subordinate; (2) mutual review of the subordinate's performance; and (3) mutual discussion of development needs necessary to improve performance.

In-house training programs are generally conducted through the personnel or human resources department. Such programs are generally designed to give classroom instruction in such topics as planning, motivating, leadership, communication, and so on. Lectures, movies, games, exercises, role playing, and case studies are frequently used in this form of management development.

Organizational training programs may be supplemented by courses offered by educational or professional groups. Universities and colleges offer a wide range of programs designed to increase the skills of managers. Professional groups such as the American Society for Personnel Administration and the American Management Association also offer a wide range of courses.

In summary, it is unrealistic to assume that the very difficult job of managing complex organizations can be accomplished by untrained managers. There are some managers who have an intuitive and workable approach to the management process—unfortunately, few of them exist. One realistic method of acquiring managerial skills is through effectively planned and conducted management development programs.

ASSESSMENT CENTERS

An assessment center is a formal procedure aimed at evaluating an individual's potential as a manager and his or her developmental needs. Assessment centers are used both in the selection and development of managers. The basic idea of the assessment center approach is to simulate, in a lifelike situation, the problems that a person would face in a particular managerial situation. Presently, more than 2,000 companies use assessment centers, and, because of its validity, its use grows every year.[11]

In the typical assessment center, 10 to 15 participants of approximately equal organizational rank are brought together for three to five days to work on individual and group exercises similar to ones they would be handling in a managerial situation. Management games, situational problems, interviews, and cases are normally used to simulate certain managerial situations. These exercises elicit behaviors on the part of the participants in decision-making, leadership, written and oral communication, planning, organizing, and motivation. The assessors observe the participants and evaluate how well they perform. The assessors then provide feedback to the participants on their performance and developmental needs.

Generally, assessors are selected from management ranks several levels above the participants. Professional psychologists from outside the organization frequently serve as assessors. In order for the program to be successful, the assessors must be rigorously trained in the assessment process, the mechanics of the exercises that are to be observed, and techniques of observation and providing feedback.

ORGANIZATION DEVELOPMENT

Organization development (OD) seeks to improve the performance of groups, departments, and the overall organization. Spe-

[11] L. A. Digman, "How Well-Managed Organizations Develop their Executives," *Organizational Dynamics,* Autumn 1978, pp. 65–66. See also the entire February 1980 issue of *The Personnel Administrator,* which is devoted to an analysis of assessment centers.

cifically, OD is an organization-wide, planned effort, managed from the top, with a goal of increasing organizational performance through planned interventions in the organization. In particular, OD looks at the whole human side of organizations. OD seeks to change attitudes, values, organizational structures, and managerial practices in an effort to improve organizational performance. The ultimate goal of OD is to structure the organizational environment so that managers and employees can use their developed skills and abilities to the fullest.

An OD effort has as its initial phase a recognition by management that organizational performance can and should be improved. Following this initial recognition, most OD efforts include the following phases:

1. Diagnosis.
2. Strategy planning.
3. Education.
4. Evaluation.

Diagnosis means that information is gathered from organization members through the use of questionnaires or attitude surveys. Strategy planning involves developing a plan for organization improvement based on the obtained data. This planning identifies specific problem areas in the organization and outlines steps that are to be taken to resolve the problems. Education consists of sharing the information obtained in the diagnosis with people who are affected by it, and helping them to realize the need for changed behavior. The education phase often involves the use of outside consultants working with individual employees or employee groups. It can also involve the use of management development programs that were discussed earlier. Other techniques that are used in the education phase are examined later in this chapter. The evaluation phase is in effect a repeat of the diagnostic phase. In other words, after diagnosis, strategy planning, and education, additional data is gathered through attitude surveys or questionnaires to determine the effects of the OD effort on the total organization. This information can then, of course, lead to additional planning and educational efforts.

Sensitivity Training

Sensitivity training is frequently used in OD programs and is designed to make one more aware of oneself and one's impact on others. Unfortunately, some people tend to equate sensitivity training and OD. It is important to note, however, that sensitivity training is only one technique that can be used and actually does not have to be used at all in organizational development. In fact, Sheldon A. David, commenting on the OD effort at TRW Systems, stated: "This effort has reached a point where sensitivity training, per se, represents only 10 to 15 percent of the effort in our program. The rest of the effort . . . is in on-the-job situations, working real problems with the people who are really involved in them."[12]

Sensitivity training involves a group, normally called a training group or T-group, which meets and has no agenda or particular focus. Normally the group consists of from between 10 to 15 people who may or may not know each other. Since the group has no planned structure and no prior common experiences, the behavior of individual group members in attempting to deal with the lack of structure becomes the agenda. While engaging in dialogue with the group, each member is encouraged to learn about himself or herself and others in the nonstructured environment. The objectives of sensitivity training are to:

1. Increase self-insight and self-awareness concerning the participant's behavior and its meaning in a social context.
2. Increase sensitivity to the behavior of others.
3. Increase awareness and understanding of the types of processes that facilitate or inhibit group functioning and the interactions between different groups.
4. Heighten diagnostic skill in social, interpersonal, and intergroup situations.
5. Increase the participant's ability to intervene successfully in inter- or intragroup situations so as to increase member satisfactions, effectiveness, or output.
6. Increase the participant's ability to analyze continually his or her own interpersonal behavior for the purpose of helping himself or herself and others achieve more effective and satisfying interpersonal relationships.[13]

Although sensitivity training sessions have no agenda, there is a desired pattern of events. The group meets with no directive leadership patterns, no authority positions, no formal agenda, and no power and status positions. Therefore, a vacuum exists. Nonevaluative feedback received by each individual on their behavior from other group members is the method of learning. From this feedback and from limited guidance given to the group by

[12] Sheldon A. Davis, "Organic Problem-Solving Method of Organization Change," *Journal of Applied Behavioral Science* 3, no. 1 (1969), p. 5.

[13] John P. Campbell and Marvin D. Dunnette, "Effectiveness of T-Group Experiences in Managerial Training and Development," *Psychological Bulletin*, August 1968, pp. 73–104. Copyright © 1968 by the American Psychological Association. Reprinted by permission.

the trainer, a feeling of mutual trust follows. Openness and mutual trust emerge as the members of the group serve as resources to one another. Collaborative behavior develops. Finally, the group explores the relevance of the experience as it relates to its own individual organization.

Sensitivity training has suffered many misconceptions and misunderstandings. Chris Argyris attempted to correct some of the misunderstandings by outlining what sensitivity training is not. Basically he feels that sensitivity training is not:

1. A set of hidden, manipulative processes used to brainwash individuals into thinking, believing, and feeling the way someone might want them to without realizing what is happening to them.
2. An educational process guided by a leader who is covertly in control and hides this fact from the participants by some means.
3. Designed to suppress conflict and get everyone to like one another.
4. An attempt to teach people to be callous, disrespectful of society, and to dislike those who live a less open life.
5. Psychoanalysis, nor intensive group therapy.
6. Necessarily dangerous, but must focus on feelings.
7. A guarantee that a participant who attends a session will change behavior.[14]

In order for sensitivity training to be effective, some guidelines need to be followed. These are summarized below:

1. The trainer(s) providing the training should be closely evaluated.
2. Trainees should be carefully screened.
3. Trainees should know in advance the nature of the training.
4. The training should be administered to each individual participant outside the normal work group.

Finally, sensitivity training has been passionately criticized, and defended, as to its relative value for organizations. In general, the research on sensitivity training indicates that individuals who have attended sensitivity training sessions tend to show increased sensitivity, more open communication, and increased flexibility.[15] However, these same research studies indicate that it is difficult to predict exactly what the outcome of a sensitivity training session will be for any one particular individual.[16] Thus,

---

[14] Chris Argyris, "T-Groups for Organizational Effectiveness," *Harvard Business Review*, March–April 1964, pp. 68–70.

[15] Michael Beer, "The Technology of Organization Development," in *Handbook of Industrial and Organizational Psychology*, ed. Marvin D. Dunnette (Skokie, Ill.: Rand McNally, 1976), p. 941.

[16] Ibid.

the research indicates that the outcomes from sensitivity training are beneficial in general, but the impact of such a session for a particular individual cannot be predicted.

Grid Training

Another approach used in OD is grid training. Grid training is an extension of the Managerial Grid which was discussed in Chapter 14. The methodology used in grid training can be divided into six phases which are summarized below:

1. Laboratory-seminar training—This phase is designed to introduce the participant to the Managerial Grid concepts and material. Each manager determines where he or she falls on the Managerial Grid.
2. Team development—This phase involves establishing the ground rules and relationships necessary for 9,9 management.
3. Intergroup development—This phase involves establishing the ground rules and relationships necessary for 9,9 management for group-to-group working relationships.
4. Organizational goal setting—Management by objectives is used to establish individual and organizational goals.
5. Goal attainment—Goals established in Phase 4 are pursued.
6. Stabilization—Changes brought about by the other phases are evaluated, and an overall evaluation of the program is made.[17]

As with sensitivity training, grid training has had mixed success in organizations. Little research has been conducted on grid training and more is needed before determinations can be drawn regarding the effectiveness of grid training.[18]

Behavior Modeling

A relatively recent approach that can be used in traditional management development programs and in OD involves the use of reinforcement theory (discussed in Chapter 10). This approach is called behavior modeling or interaction management.[19] Basically, behavior modeling involves identifying interaction problems faced by managers such as gaining acceptance, overcoming resistance to change, motivating employees, and reducing tardiness. The sequence of learning activities in behavior modeling then involves:

---

[17] Robert R. Blake, Jane S. Mouton, Louis B. Barnes, and Larry E. Greenes, "Breakthrough in Organization Development," *Harvard Business Review*, November–December 1964, pp. 137–38.

[18] Beer, "Organizational Development," p. 943.

[19] William Byham and James Robinson, "Interaction Modeling: A New Concept in Supervisory Training," *Training and Development Journal*, February 1976, pp. 25–33.

1. A filmed model or demonstration of the skills necessary to solve the problem being applied.
2. Practice in solving the problem through role playing for each trainee.
3. Reinforcement of the correct behaviors in solving the problem during the practice situation.
4. Planning by each trainee in how to transfer the skills back to his or her specific job situation.[20]

While behavioral modeling is a new technique, results have been encouraging. In one study, behavioral modeling resulted in better performance than found with no training or more traditional management development methods.[21]

In summary, many techniques, such as traditional management development programs, sensitivity training, grid training, behavioral modeling, and others are used in OD. Studies conducted to evaluate the effectiveness of the organization development concept have produced both positive and negative results. Much more research work is needed before conclusions can be drawn concerning the most effective methodologies for use in OD and, in fact, concerning the overall effectiveness of OD itself.

SUMMARY

Abilities are an individual's personal characteristics used in performing a job, and as such, they place upper limits on the performance of an individual. Therefore, organizations should make a conscious effort to develop the abilities of their employees.

Human asset accounting involves an attempt to place a value on an organization's human resources.

Employee development is concerned with the improvement and growth of the capabilities of individuals and groups within the organization. The employee development process involves establishing organizational objectives, determining employee development needs, establishing employee development objectives, conducting employee development programs, and evaluating the employee development programs. Employee development programs should be evaluated based on organizational objectives, employee development objectives, and the results produced by the development programs.

Training is a process that involves the acquisition of skills, concepts, rules, or attitudes in order to improve present and fu-

---

[20] Hinrichs, "Personnel Training," p. 857.

[21] Joseph Moses and Richard Ritchie, "Supervisory Relationship Training: A Behavioral Evaluation of a Behavior Modeling Program," *Personal Psychology* 29 (1976), pp. 337–43.

ture performance. Training serves as a supportive function of the organization and should be objective-oriented. The training process begins on the first day of employment. Orientation is concerned with introducing the new employee to the organization and his or her job. Some of the methods available for achieving training objectives are on-the-job training, apprenticeship training, classroom training, and programmed instruction.

Management development is a subset of the employee development process and can take many forms including coaching, job rotation, individual self-improvement programs, performance appraisals, in-house training programs, and educational and professional training courses.

An assessment center is a formal procedure aimed at evaluating an individual's potential as a manager and his or her developmental needs. Organization development (OD) is an organization-wide, planned effort, managed from the top, with a goal of increasing organizational performance through planned interventions in the organization. Sensitivity training is frequently used in OD programs and is designed to make one more aware of oneself and one's impact on others. Grid training, which is an extension of the Managerial Grid, is another approach used in OD. Behavior modeling is a relatively new technique used in OD.

REVIEW QUESTIONS

1. What are abilities?
2. What is human asset accounting?
3. Describe the employee development process.
4. What is training? What are some guideposts in defining training objectives?
5. What is orientation?
6. Describe the following methods of training:
   a. On-the-job.
   b. Apprenticeship.
   c. Formal classroom training.
   d. Programmed instruction.
7. Describe the following techniques for management development:
   a. Coaching.
   b. Job rotation.
   c. Performance appraisals.
   d. Organizational training programs.
   e. Educational and professional training courses.
8. What is an assessment center?
9. What is organization development?

10. Describe the following techniques used in organization development:
    a. Sensitivity training.
    b. Grid training.
    c. Behavioral modeling.

DISCUSSION QUESTIONS

1. "Today's financial statements do not accurately reflect an organization's assets." Do you agree with this statement? Discuss in detail your reasons.
2. Discuss the following statement: "Managers are born, not made."
3. "Why should we train our workers? It is a waste of money because they soon leave and another organization gets the benefit." Discuss.
4. "Everyone needs sensitivity training." Do you agree? Explain.

SELECTED READINGS

Alexander, L. D. "Exploratory Study of the Utilization of Assessment Center Results." *Academy of Management Journal,* March 1979, pp. 152–57.

Argyris, C. "Some Limitations of the Case Method: Experiences in a Management Development Program." *Academy of Management Review,* April 1980, pp. 291–98.

Blake, R. R., and J. S. Mouton. "OD—Fad or Fundamental?" *Training and Development Journal,* June 1979, pp. 110–17.

———. "OD Technology for the Future." *Training and Development Journal,* vol. 33 (November 1979), pp. 54–64.

Cobb, A. T., and N. Margulies. "Organization Development: A Political Perspective." *Academy of Management Review,* January 1981, pp. 49–59.

Craig, Robert L., and Lester R. Bittel. *Training and Development Handbook,* 2d ed. New York: McGraw-Hill, 1976.

Digman, L. A. "Determining Management Development Needs." *Human Resource Management,* Winter 1980, pp. 12–16.

———. "How Companies Formulate Management Development Programs." *Human Resource Management,* Summer 1980, pp. 9–13.

Ezzell, W. "Is Your OJT Fact or Fiction?" *Training and Development Journal,* January 1980, p. 10.

Gorb, Peter. "Management Development for the Small Firm." *Personnel Management,* January 1978, pp. 24–27.

Herzog, E. L. "Improving Productivity via Organization Development." *Training and Development Journal,* April 1980, pp. 36–39.

Jurkus, A. F. "The Uncertainty Factor in Human Resources Accounting," *Personnel,* November–December 1979, pp. 72–75.

Kelsey, H., Jr. "Practicing What They Preach: Successful Management

Development Programs." *Business Horizons,* December 1980, pp. 3–6.

Newstrom, J. W. "Evaluating the Effectiveness of Training Methods." *Personnel Administrator,* January 1980, pp. 55–60.

Ostroff, H. "New Look in Skills Training." *Training and Development Journal,* March 1980, pp. 42–43.

Parker, T. C. "Assessment Centers: A Statistical Study." *Personnel Administrator,* February 1980, pp. 65–67.

Parras, Jerry I., and P. O. Berg. "The Impact of Organizational Development." *Academy of Management Review,* April 1978, pp. 249–64.

Schriescheim, Janet, and Chester Schriescheim. "The Effectiveness of Business Games in Management Training." *Training and Development Journal,* May 1974, pp. 14–17.

Tanaka, H. "Japanese Method of Preparing Today's Graduate to Become Tomorrow's Manager." *Personnel Journal,* February 1980, pp. 109–12.

Tauber, M. S. "New Employee Orietation: A Comprehensive Systems Approach." *Personnel Administrator,* January 1981, pp. 65–69.

This, L., and G. L. Lippitt. "Managerial Guidelines to Sensitivity Training." *Training and Development Journal,* June 1981, pp. 144–50.

Case 17–1

Development—for what?

The Matlock Corporation began an extensive management development program several years ago. The company's personnel director felt that this program would benefit the company by providing a ready source of promotable individuals for filling vacancies as they occurred in the company. Up until this point, promotions had often been filled by personnel from outside the company.

Managers at all levels of the organization became involved in the management development program. They participated in in-company classes on subjects such as general management and time management. In addition, they were encouraged to improve other skills by taking night courses at the local college at company expense. Many of the managers did in fact enroll in several of the courses.

At the time the program was initiated, and at subsequent management development meetings, the participants were advised by top management that the program was designed to improve their management skills and to qualify them for future promotions within the company.

Paul Martin, a section supervisor, has been with the company for over ten years. He has diligently participated in the management development program and has completed several night courses at the local college. Paul originally felt that this diligence on his part would be rewarded by a promotion when an opening developed. However, twice during the last year outsiders had been hired to fill supervisory positions within Paul's department. In each case, Paul and the other section supervisors had applied for the vacancy and felt that their experience plus the additional knowledge gained through the management development program made them better qualified than the outsider who was hired.

At a recent appraisal interview, Paul brought up this problem for discussion with his department manager. He was told that in each case no supervisor within the company was considered to be qualified for the managerial opening. Paul expressed the opinion that the company management development program was a waste of time for the supervisors if the knowledge and experience gained were not recognized by higher-level management. Paul's department manager explained that it takes time to develop a supervisor for higher-level responsibility. He also reminded Paul that individuals are rewarded for their self-improvement efforts by extra merit salary increases during the annual performance appraisals.

1. Do you think that Paul has a legitimate complaint?
2. Do you think the organization is "training for training's sake?"
3. How do you think that Paul's supervisor should have handled the problem?

Case 17–2

The frustrated banker

Mr. Albert Tiech is a graduate of a well-known university. After graduation, he entered the military service and performed admirably as a combat officer, receiving the Bronze Star in recognition of his achievements. Tiech received an honorable discharge upon completion of his tour of duty.

Returning to civilian life, he accepted the position of management trainee with Suburbia Bank. A relatively small banking enterprise, Suburbia serves the local community in the checking, savings, and loan areas.

The organizational structure of Suburbia Bank consists of the president, vice president, loan department, teller department, and bookkeeping department. The president is Mr. Shy, a paternal individual, who has been successful in satisfying the wants and needs of the employees. Mr. Right serves as vice president. He joined Suburbia Bank many years ago upon graduation from high school and has gained much banking experience over the years. He displays an aggressive and arrogant attitude, both on and off the job, and has been given the authority to discipline and terminate employees as necessary. Shy and Right have been good friends since their high school days.

The loan department, teller department, and bookkeeping department are managed by middle-aged women who are high school graduates and have been employed by the bank from one to six years.

When Tiech joined the bank, he believed his training program would be personally handled by the president. His initial assignment was with the bookkeeping department, where he was to become familiar with all its functions, while working directly with the department supervisor. For three months, he spent 90 percent of his time filing cancelled checks. The remaining time was devoted to conferences with the supervisor on departmental procedures. Although Miss Jones, the supervisor, was able to efficiently carry out the functional aspects of her position, she was unable to effectively communicate to Mr. Tiech how or why certain policies and procedures were formulated. Tiech had very little contact with Shy during this time, and any encounters between them were usually paternal in nature.

At the conclusion of this three-month detail, Tiech received a message from Shy's secretary indicating that he was invited to have lunch with the president at the local country club. At lunch, Tiech was informed that as a result of his evaluation from the supervisor of the bookkeeping department his training program would be accelerated. The supervisor's evaluation indicated that Tiech got along well with the people and answered telephone inquiries effectively. The president informed Tiech that his next assignment was to be with the teller department, where he could observe and learn the functions of that important activity.

Tiech was assigned a position directly behind the head teller and observed transfer of monies, checks, and deposits. The head teller was very busy and showed Tiech how things were done but could not, or would not, take the time to explain why. Tiech was then assigned to a teller post, where he worked for a period of four months, carrying out the same activities as other tellers in the department.

Tiech became frustrated, and his frustration manifested itself by frequent trips to the water fountain and to the restroom. Later this pattern accelerated, manifesting itself in late arrival for work and extended lunch periods.

At the conclusion of this work assignment, Tiech requested a conference with the president. He explained to the president that he felt he had sufficient training in the teller department and requested an assignment involving more direct management training. Shy indicated that he was extremely pleased with Tiech's performance in both previous assignments but felt that he should continue in the teller department for a few more months. He informed Tiech he would consider his request and give him a decision in a few days. Approximately a week later Tiech observed that a room which had been used to store office supplies and equipment was being remodeled. Subsequently, he was called by the president and informed that the remodeled room was to be his office. Within a week, Tiech occupied his new office and was assigned a new function involving the collection of bad debts, including the repossession of automobiles and other items involving delinquent loans. This task required about 20 percent of Tiech's time; the balance was to be spent working directly with Right, the vice president, who would teach him all he knew about banking.

Right has had occasional meetings with Tiech during which he expounded on his golf game and various aspects of his personal life. Tiech attempted to steer these discussions toward banking matters; however, Right continually put off answering them until a "later time." Currently, Tiech is sitting in his newly decorated office pondering his dilemma.

1. What do you think of Tiech's training program?
2. How can a person in Tiech's position change the situation?
3. Do you think that Tiech's situation is an exaggeration of the "average" training program?

SECTION FOUR
CASE

Allied's errant subordinate

Bob Alwine, a quiet, introverted 22-year-old statistical clerk, had worked in the accounting department of Allied Products Corporation for approximately 14 months without apparent incident. Just prior to his employment at Allied, Bob had spent several months in a mental hospital but had been discharged with a clean bill of health. He appeared and acted normal in every way and had not tried to conceal his hospitalization at the time of his employment. His training and limited work experience prior to hospitalization had been as an accountant doing simple bookkeeping functions for several small concerns. At no time had he been employed by one organization for more than nine months. When questioned about this prior to his employment at Allied, Bob stated that his health had been poor since shortly after graduation from high school but that "everything seemed to be straightened out now." Recognizing the risk that was being assumed, the personnel director at Allied decided to take Bob on as a temporary employee on a probational status for six months. At the end of that period the reports from Bob's supervisor were favorable and his status was made permanent with the company.

About two months after Bob's first anniversary with Allied, his supervisor, Maxine Montgomery, asked to speak with her boss, Alex Cloud, manager of the accounting branch at Allied. Maxine, appearing quite upset, closed the door to Alex's office and asked Alex to fire Bob. Since this came as a complete surprise to Alex, he asked for the reasons. Maxine proceeded to describe her exasperation with Bob's performance in recent months.

Shortly after Bob's six-month probationary period had been completed, Maxine claimed that she noticed a slight but perceptible change in Bob's attitude toward his work. Bob, for the first time since being employed at Allied, missed one or two of the deadlines for his statistical reports. He also was less punctual in reporting to work. In fact, according to Maxine, Bob was late three times during his first month after the probationary period. On each occasion, Maxine said that she reminded Bob that all employees were expected to be at their work stations by the beginning of working hours—8:30 A.M. When she came down harder on Bob after the third infraction, conditions seemed to improve temporarily. Bob went for five weeks without being tardy but then started to get careless once more. Over the next three or four months, Bob established an irregular pattern of tardiness which was not documented. On most occasions, Maxine would talk with

Bob about his tardiness but when conditions didn't improve, Maxine started keeping a record of each incident of tardiness. She had just started this documentation process at the time of Bob's annual performance evaluation. Despite Maxine's obvious concern and admonitions about tardiness, Bob did not appear to be particularly concerned. During the discussion that occurred at Bob's annual performance evaluation, Bob commented to the effect that he couldn't understand "why everybody was so uptight about a few minutes here or there."

During the two months since Maxine started documenting Bob's tardiness, she had recorded 12 incidents ranging from one to six minutes. Maxine had continued to try to work with Bob to resolve this problem but has become convinced that Bob really is not making much of an attempt to change. Finally, on the last two incidents, Maxine issued a written letter of warning for the official file. Even this did not seem to help.

Considerable pressure was building within Maxine's unit as other employees watched the cavalier attitude demonstrated by Bob. It seemed to his co-workers that Bob was challenging the rules on working hours and getting away with it. When the other employees expressed their concern about why nothing was being done, Maxine explained that she had "appropriately" documented Bob's personnel file to the effect that his tardiness was unacceptable. It was rather obvious to Maxine, however, that her explanation and handling of Bob's situation was not well received by her subordinates. Informal contacts with several of her closer subordinates and information obtained through the grapevine disclosed that a majority of the personnel in her unit strongly resented the preferential treatment they felt was being given to Bob. More and more frequently subordinates were overheard asking, "Why should *I* bother to observe the rules around here?"

Sensing the unrest within her unit, Maxine decided she had to take more drastic action. It was at this point that Maxine had entered Alex's office and asked him to fire Bob.

Alex's first question, after listening to Maxine's description of the circumstances, was, "Do you have a copy of Bob's last performance evaluation?" Maxine replied in the negative, but said that in her opinion, the evaluation report would not be of any assistance since there was nothing unusual about it. Alex, somewhat confused by this statement, asked Maxine how she had rated Bob in the category of dependability on the performance appraisal form. Maxine said she had rated Bob "satisfactory" because she had not documented the tardiness incidents prior to the time she prepared the evaluation report. Besides, Maxine did not want to get into a "messy confrontation" with Bob, especially if she was not prepared to go into all the details on the charges. After all, she explained, "I've seen other supervisors get nailed to the wall around here when they challenge their subordinates on disciplinary issues and overlook some little detail that ends up getting the supervisor in trouble."

Alex showed obvious irritation at this point and exclaimed, "How do you expect me to fire Bob when you haven't even laid the groundwork? You certainly know the procedure we must follow in order to fire employees." Maxine admitted that she really was not familiar with all the details of the company procedure but that she would check it out with personnel and attempt to comply. Alex tried to summarize the major elements of the company procedure, which included appropriate citations on the performance evaluation report, letters of warning, suspensions, and, finally, discharge. He pointed out that Maxine's procrastination in documenting previous infractions would be a problem and asked her to proceed immediately in properly preparing the way for firing Bob.

Maxine wasted no time in visiting the personnel department. She was advised that, according to her account of the incidents involving Bob, there certainly was ample cause for dismissal. It would be necessary, however, to carefully document the case, following prescribed procedures. These procedures are summarized in Exhibit 1.

EXHIBIT 1
Procedure for Handling Unexcused Tardiness of Employees

Step 1—First offense	Oral warning
Step 2—Second offense	If within 30 days of first offense, written warning If beyond 30 days of first offense, oral warning
Step 3—Third offense	If within 30 days of second offense, two-day suspension without pay If beyond 30 days of second offense, written warning
Step 4—Fourth offense	If within 30 days of third offense, five-day suspension without pay, plus warning of possible termination for next offense If beyond 30 days of third offense, letter of censure
Step 5—Fifth offense	If within 30 days of fourth offense and where warning of termination was issued, termination Otherwise, three-day suspension without pay, plus warning of possible termination for next offense
Step 6—Sixth offense	Termination

After studying the official procedure, Maxine asked the manager of the personnel department if it would be necessary to start the process from Step 1 or if she could pick up at one of the later steps in view of the documentation she had initiated in Bob's case within the past several months. She was informed that it would be entirely in order for her to proceed from the second step, her letter of warning having satisfied the requirement for a written warning as a result of a second infraction within a 30-day period after the first offense.

Maxine left the personnel department feeling confident that it would now be merely a matter of time before she could fire Bob. She also felt better because she felt that she would enhance her image in the eyes of subordinates by taking a hard stand on this tardiness issue.

On Tuesday morning, just four days after Maxine's visit to the personnel department, Bob clocked in five minutes late. Maxine immediately prepared a notice to Bob, informing him that, effective the following day, he was to take a two-day suspension without pay and report back to work, on time, Friday morning. Bob initially was highly indignant and very aggressive in protesting this "vindictive" action. Maxine informed Bob that she was following the official procedure for handling cases of tardiness and refused to consider any excuses Bob offered. Bob then turned to emotionalism, broke out in tears, and pleaded for clemency because he was the sole support for his ailing mother. He simply could not afford to lose the income resulting from the suspension. Maxine held her ground, however, and refused to reconsider her position on this issue.

The suspension appeared to have shaken Bob because he made it to work on time for the next six weeks—the longest period without tardiness that Maxine could recall. However, Bob came in three minutes late 54 days after his two-day suspension. Maxine, well versed on the appropriate action dictated by this occasion, responded with a forceful letter of censure. Bob did not show any outward signs of emotion on receipt of the letter. Apparently, he did not view this action to be as severe as the suspension he had previously received. In fact, he clocked in four minutes late again just five days later. Maxine immediately served him with a memorandum informing him of a three-day suspension to be imposed immediately and a warning that the next incident of tardiness would be grounds for termination of employment. Before delivering this memorandum, Maxine cleared it with and received the approval of Alex, her boss.

Bob, once again, reacted violently, claiming that he was detained by extremely heavy traffic on the way to work that day, should not be held accountable for the subsequent delay, and was therefore being treated unfairly. Again, Maxine refused to alter the memorandum. After the suspension Bob demonstrated once more his capability for getting to work on time. It was not until 19 weeks later that he reported five minutes late for work. Maxine immediately served Bob with a notice of termination of employment, signed by Alex and endorsed by the personnel department.

By comparison, all of Bob's previous outbursts paled into insignificance. He became almost hysterical, using abusive language, and threatening violence to Maxine and the organization. Bob claimed that Maxine had been "out to get him for a long time" and that he was going to retain legal assistance to break up the "conspiracy."

1. What do you think was the real problem in this situation?
2. How could the problem have been avoided?
3. How important are performance evaluations in organizations?
4. Do you think Allied pursued the best possible course of action? If not, what would you have done?

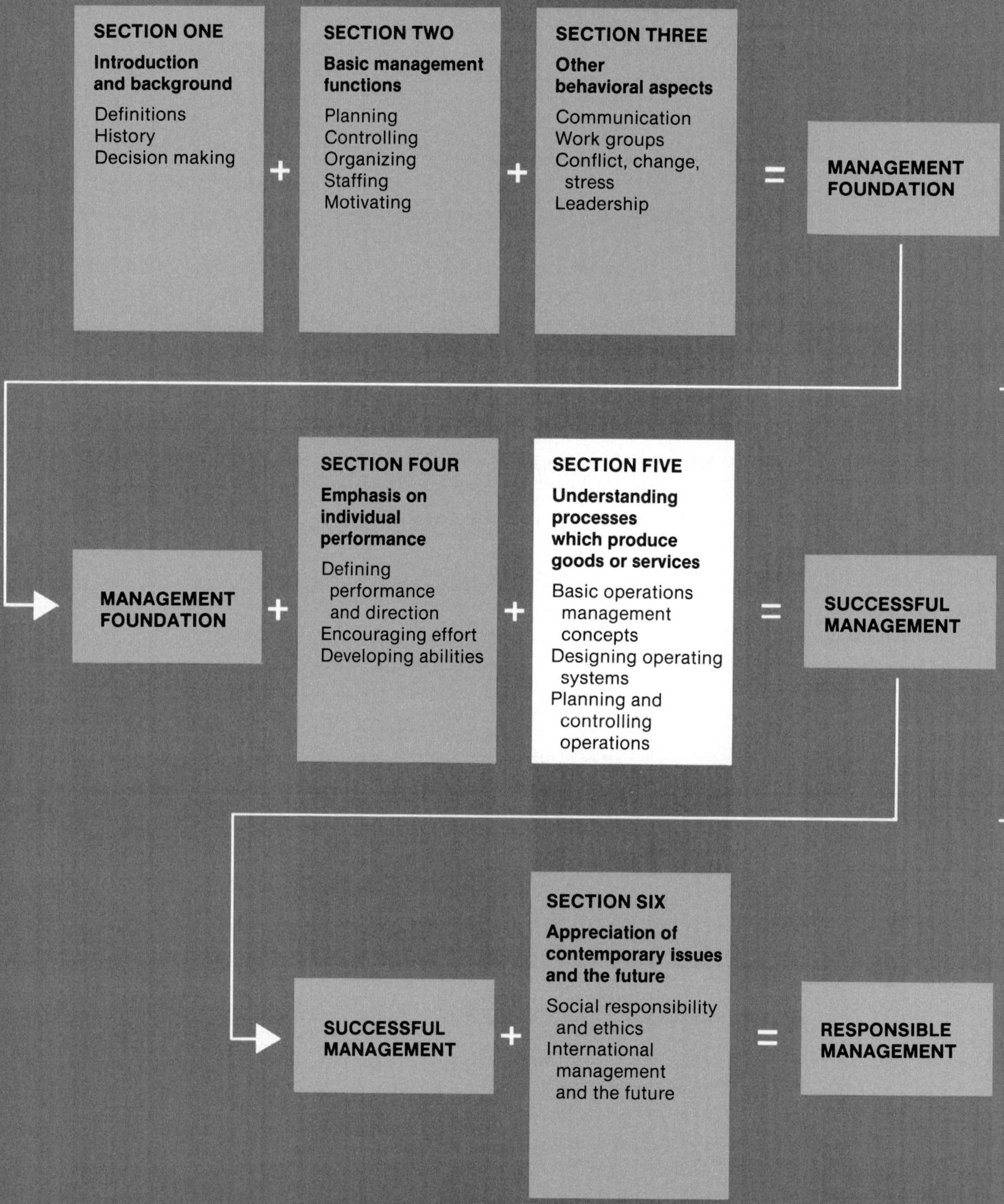

SECTION ONE
Introduction and background
Definitions
History
Decision making

+

SECTION TWO
Basic management functions
Planning
Controlling
Organizing
Staffing
Motivating

+

SECTION THREE
Other behavioral aspects
Communication
Work groups
Conflict, change, stress
Leadership

=

MANAGEMENT FOUNDATION

MANAGEMENT FOUNDATION

+

SECTION FOUR
Emphasis on individual performance
Defining performance and direction
Encouraging effort
Developing abilities

+

SECTION FIVE
Understanding processes which produce goods or services
Basic operations management concepts
Designing operating systems
Planning and controlling operations

=

SUCCESSFUL MANAGEMENT

SUCCESSFUL MANAGEMENT

+

SECTION SIX
Appreciation of contemporary issues and the future
Social responsibility and ethics
International management and the future

=

RESPONSIBLE MANAGEMENT

section five

OPERATIONS MANAGEMENT

The first three sections of this text concentrated on building a sound foundation for understanding the management process. Section Four, which emphasized individual performance, added to that foundation. The next tier which must be added to the foundation in order to provide the ingredients necessary for successful management is an understanding of the goods and/or services producing function of the organization—the operations function. The operations function includes the design, operation, and control of the facilities and resources that are directly involved in the production of the organization's goods and/or services. Because most management personnel are either a part of or interact with the operations phase of the organization, and because the operations phase usually involves the largest portion of an organization's financial assets, personnel, and expenditures, it behooves all managers to have a basic understanding of the operations function.

Chapter 18 introduces the topic of operations management. The operations function and its relationship to the other parts of the organization are defined. The concept of productivity and its importance are discussed.

Chapter 19 concentrates on the design of operating systems. The argument is made that the operating system must first be properly designed if the organization is to be efficient. Product/service design, process selection, site location, physical layout, and job design are all discussed along with several methods and techniques for accomplishing these tasks.

The final chapter in this section, Chapter 20, is concerned with the day-to-day planning and controlling of operations. The point is stressed that the operating system must not only be properly designed but that the day-to-day operations must be properly planned and controlled. Production planning and control, inventory control, and quality control are all covered.

18 Operations Management

Objectives

1. To introduce the major concepts relating to operations management.
2. To explain the role of the operations manager in the organization.
3. To define productivity, develop an appreciation for its importance, and explain specific strategies for achieving high organizational productivity.

Chapter Outline

Glossary of Terms

Operating capabilities Refers to the production capacities and abilities of the organization.

Operating system A system consisting of the processes and activities necessary to transform various inputs into goods and/or services.

Operations management The application of the basic concepts and principles of management to those segments of the organization that produce the goods and/or services.

Productivity Units of output per worker-machine hour or total output/total input.

Technology The systematic application of scientific or other organized knowledge to practical purposes, including new ideas, inventions, techniques, and materials.

As man's capability to produce goods freed him from the threat of starvation and the elements, and society became more complex and interdependent, the demand for services developed. Productive systems were created to deliver education, health care, letters and parcels, fire protection, transportation, financial services, and a tremendous variety of other services. Thus, productive systems are man's unique invention: they are the means by which we create the endless list of goods and services that are needed to sustain modern society. The flow of these goods and services in a gigantic interdependent and intricate system represents the economy as a whole, functioning throughout the world with international flow of goods and services. There are industries within economies and enterprises within industries, and the building block on which the entire structure it established is the productive system. These systems, which are man's mechanism for creating goods and services, deal with the operations phase of all kinds of enterprises (private and public, manufacturing and service), and the management of these productive systems is called "operations management."

*Elwood S. Buffa**

As indicated in the quote above, operations management, which evolved from the field of production or manufacturing management, is concerned with the application of the basic concepts and principles of management to those segments of the organization that produce the goods and/or services of the organization. Traditionally, the term *production* brings to mind such things as smoke stacks, machine shops, and the manufacture of real goods. Operations management is concerned with the management of the producing function in any organization, whether it is private or public, profit or nonprofit, manufacturing or service. Specifically, operations management involves designing the systems of the organization that produce the goods or services and with the planning and controlling of the day-to-day operations which take place within these systems. The overall focus of operations management is the effective integration of resources in the pursuit of organizational goals.[1]

MANUFACTURING VERSUS SERVICE

A manufacturing production system transforms inputs into a tangible product.[2] A service production system is based to a greater

* Elwood S. Buffa, *Operations Management: The Management of Productive Systems* (New York: John Wiley & Sons, 1976).

[1] Wickham Skinner, "New Directions for Production and Operations Management," *Academy of Management P/OM Division Communication 2,* ed. George J. Gore, July 1972, p. 5.

[2] Richard J. Tersine, *Production/Operations Management: Concepts, Structure, and Analysis,* New York: Elsevier-North Holland Publishing, 1980, pp. 5–6.

degree on the processing of knowledge or skills into a product that is not physical in nature.[3] Many organizations represent a mix of manufacturing and service. One might first think that manufacturing and service systems should be approached differently from an operations management viewpoint. However, experience has shown that most types of service systems are not significantly different from manufacturing systems when viewed from an operations management perspective.[4] In other words, the great majority of operations management techniques developed in the manufacturing sector are equally applicable to the service sector. Most operations management techniques were developed in the manufacturing sector simply because this sector has been dominant since before 1900. Secondly, service industries have not, until recent times, been as concerned with efficiencies as have manufacturing industries. Attempts have been made in this chapter (and the next two) to use both manufacturing and service illustrations and examples. Unless otherwise stated, the reader should assume that the methods and techniques discussed are equally applicable to both manufacturing and service systems.

OPERATING SYSTEMS AND ACTIVITIES

Operating systems consist of the processes and activities necessary to transform various inputs into goods and/or services. Operating systems exist in all organizations and are composed of people, materials, facilities, and information. The end result of an operating system is to add value by improving, enhancing, or rearranging the inputs. Often this involves bringing inputs together into a new arrangement in such a manner that the inputs can do something that they could not do separately.[5]

The assembly of an automobile represents a combination of separate parts to form a more valuable whole. At other times, the operating system involves breaking something down from a larger quantity to smaller quantities which hold more value. A metal shop which fabricates smaller parts from larger sheets of metal or a butcher who produces steaks, hamburger, and other cuts from a side of beef both break down a larger quantity into smaller quantities with more value. A third type of operating system is one which produces services by transforming inputs into more useful outputs. In producing services emphasis is usually placed

---

[3] Ibid.

[4] Richard B. Chase and Nicholas J. Aquilano, *Productions and Operations Management*, rev. ed. (Homewood, Ill.: Richard D. Irwin, 1977), p. 17.

[5] John A. Reinecke and William F. Schoell, *Introduction to Business* (Boston: Allyn & Bacon, 1974), p. 183.

more on labor and less on materials. For example, a television repair shop uses some materials but the primary value results from the repairperson's labor. Figure 18–1 presents a simplified model of an operating system.

As can be seen in Figure 18–1 the operating system is broader and more inclusive than just the conversion or transformation process. The operating system includes not only the design and operation of the transformation process but also many of the activities necessary to get the various inputs into the transformation process (such as product design and scheduling) and many of the activities necessary to get the outputs out of the transformation process (such as inventory control and materials distribution).

FIGURE 18–1
Simplified Model of an Operating System

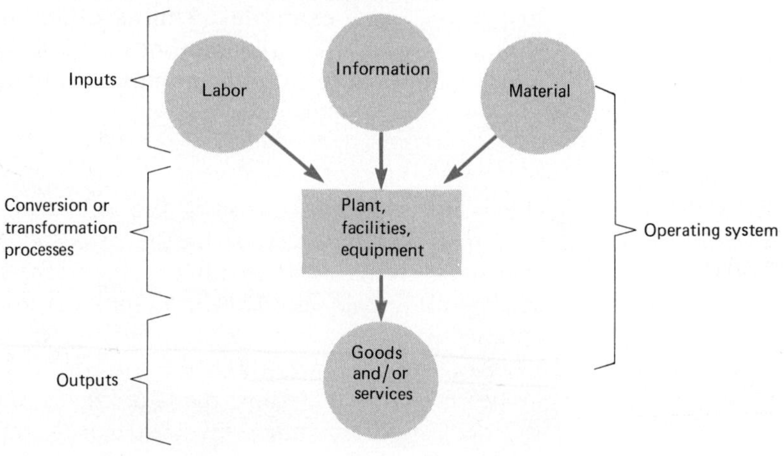

WHAT DO OPERATIONS MANAGERS DO?

Large organizations may employ several operations managers, each having responsibility over some portion of the operating system. There may also be a higher-level operations manager who coordinates and oversees the entire operations function.[6] In small organizations the operations manager typically manages the entire operating system, or at least a large portion of it.

The activities required to manage an operating system can be categorized into two main areas: (1) system design and (2) operations planning and control. The design of an operating system starts with the product/service design. Product/service design

[6] James B. Dilworth, *Production and Operations Management*, New York: Random House, 1979, p. 13.

largely determines the production capabilities needed. Equipment and process selection, site location, physical layout, and design of work methods are all part of the design phase of operations management. It is obviously impossible to design efficient and effective operating systems and facilities without knowing the short- and long-range plans, policies, and strategies of the organization. Therefore, all of the design-related activities of the operating system must be closely coordinated with the overall plans of the organization.

The operations planning and control phase includes planning and maintaining control over the day-to-day operations after the designed system has been put into operation. This includes production control (aggregate output planning, resource allocation, and activity scheduling), inventory control, quality control, cost control and improvement, and facility maintenance. The opera-

FIGURE 18–2
Operations Activities Related to the Basic Management Functions

Basic management function	*Related operations activity*
Planning	Determine product level (aggregate production planning) Process selection Equipment selection Activity, scheduling Resource allocation Product/service design Site location Physical layout
Controlling	Production control Cost control and improvement Facility maintenance Inventory control Quality control
Organizing	Equipment selection Activity scheduling Resource allocation Process selection Physical layout
Staffing	Determine production personnel requirement (aggregate production planning) Job design Process selection Equipment selection Activity scheduling Personnel allocation Physical layout
Motivating	Job design Work methods Work incentives

tions planning and control activities must be closely coordinated with the design activities. For instance, the design objectives of the operating process would most likely dictate the most appropriate control system. Similarly, the design objectives would also impact on the number and types of personnel needed. Figure 18–2 relates specific operations activities to the basic management functions.

The relative importance of the various operating activities varies considerably depending on the nature of the specific operating system. For example, quality control is a much more important factor in producing pharmaceuticals or mechanical parts with close tolerances than when producing toys. Furthermore, not all operations managers work with every component of an operating system. In fact, many operations managers do not come in contact with the operating system until the system has been designed and is already in operation. Of course, this does not prohibit a redesign of portions of the system. For instance, new work methods might be established or a new scheduling system installed after the operating system has been designed and is functioning. Figure 18–3 shows in detail the components of an operating system.

RELATIONSHIP OF OPERATIONS MANAGEMENT TO OTHER AREAS

In addition to the operations function, most organizations require a marketing function and a finance function. The marketing function generally centers around the sale and distribution of the goods or services produced by the operating system. The function of finance is to provide the funds necessary to support the operations and marketing activities. These funds come from the sale of the organization's goods and services, and may also be acquired through loans, sale of stock, investment income, retained earnings, and so on.

Many of the activities of the three functions overlap. For example, product design and packaging are operations functions that directly relate to marketing. Process design and equipment acquisition are operations activities which cannot be undertaken independently of finance. Thus, the operations manager must continually coordinate and communicate with the other functional areas of the organization.

THE IMPORTANCE OF OPERATIONS MANAGEMENT

The production of goods and/or services ordinarily involves the largest portion of an organization's financial assets, personnel, and expenditures. The operations process (which produces a good or service) also usually consumes an appreciable amount of time.

FIGURE 18–3
The Operating System

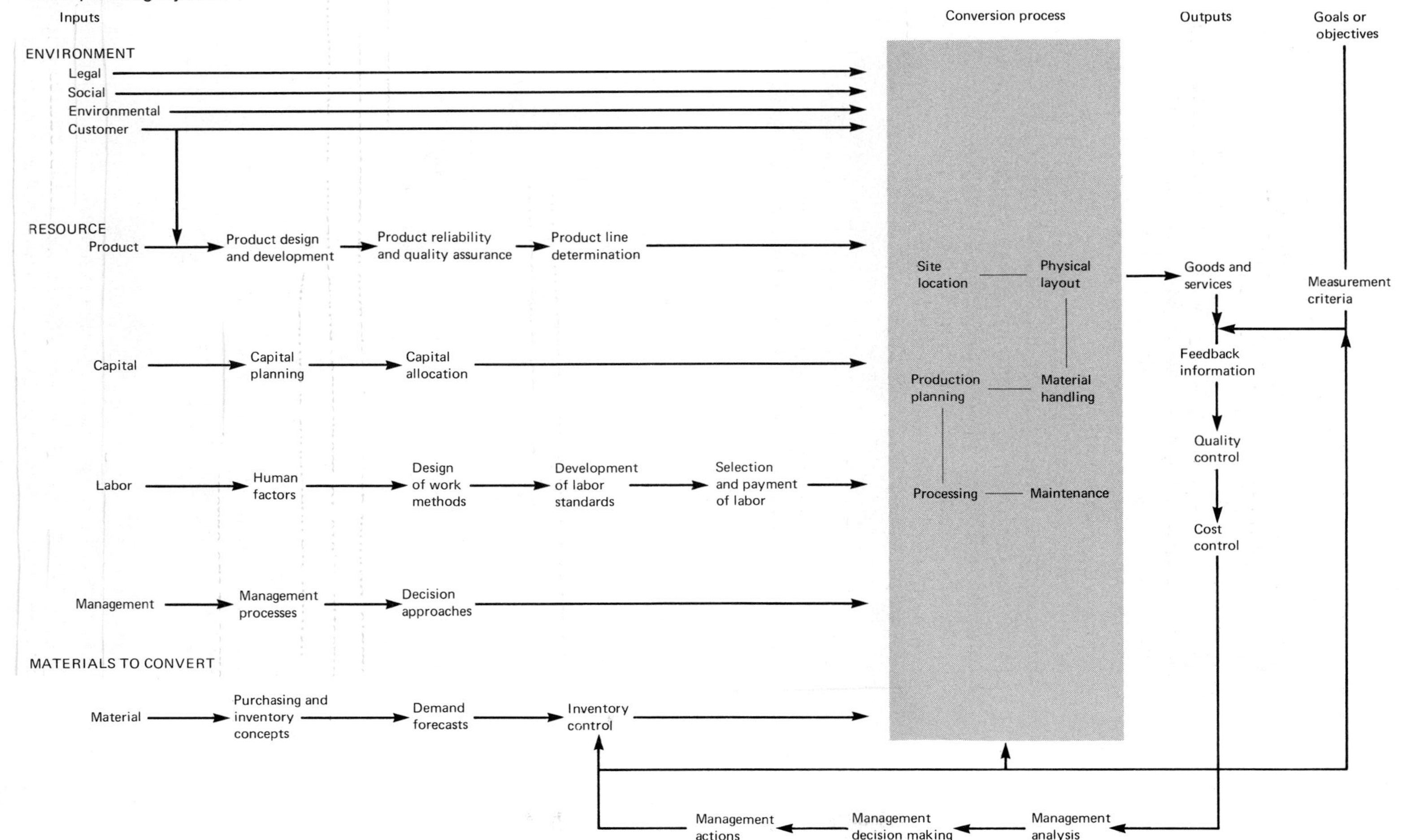

Source: Leonard J. Garrett and Milton Silver, *Production Management Analysis*, 2d ed. (New York: Harcourt Brace Jovanovich, 1973). Copyright © 1973 by Harcourt Brace Jovanovich, Inc. Reprinted and reproduced by permission of the publisher.

Thus, because of the resources and time consumed by the operations function, the management of this function plays a critical role in achieving the organization's goals.

One direct influence on worker output is the effectiveness of operations managers in (1) building group cohesiveness and individual commitment and (2) making sound technical and administrative decisions. Both of these problems have increased in complexity and importance in recent years. Society wants not only improved productivity but also an enriched work environment. At the same time, social changes have increased the cultural gap between new workers and established managers. The human problems confronting operations management have therefore become increasingly important and more difficult.

Most operations managers no longer manage in a stable environment with standard products. Changing technology and a dominant emphasis on low costs have changed the technical and administrative problems confronting the operations manager. The modern operations manager must be concerned not only with low costs but also with product diversity, high quality, short lead times, improved supply dependability, and a rapidly changing technology. As a result, the problems confronting operations managers are now more difficult and require substantially greater managerial talent.

In the past the operations area has suffered from an unglamorous image which has made it difficult for organizations to attract, develop, and retain operations managers capable of high performance. Management cannot wait for these problems to disappear or diminish; positive action—including increased attention and emphasis on operations management—is necessary.

BASIC TYPES OF OPERATING SYSTEMS

Two basic types of operating systems exist. One is based on continuous flows, the other on intermittent flows. Organizations engaging in continuous flow generally have a standardized product or service. This product or service is often advertised, and is immediately available to the customer. The post office, paper mills, petroleum refineries, assembly plants, and fast food outlets with standardized products (such as McDonald's) are examples. The continuous type of operation is characterized by relatively large volumes of identical or similar products/services flowing through similar stages of the operating system.

The second type of operating system, the intermittent (or job shop) type, is used to produce customized products and services. Because of its customized nature, organizations using an intermittent operating system usually do not maintain inventories or finished products and do not offer standardized services. Examples of intermittent flow systems include special order fabrication shops, hospitals, advertising agencies, and dental offices.

As suggested above, the basic type of operating system is generally determined by the certainty of the product or service specifications and by the volume demanded.[7] High volumes are best accommodated by continuous flow systems while low volumes are best handled by intermittent flow systems. The stability or certainty of the product specification and design also affects the most appropriate type of operating system. Table 18–1 depicts the relationships between type of operating system, volume, and product specification.

TABLE 18–1

Type of Operating System, Volume, and Product Specification

Certainty of product specification	*Low market volume*	*High market volume*
High	Intermittent production	Continuous production to stock
Low	Intermittent production to customer orders	Continuous production to customer orders

Source: Adapted from Howard L. Timms and Michael F. Pohlen, *The Production Function in Business*, 3d ed. (Homewood, Ill.: Richard D. Irwin, 1970), p. 23. Copyright © 1970 by Richard D. Irwin, Inc.

Because of economies of scale, specialization of labor, and high equipment utilization, the continuous flow system usually results in lower unit costs than the intermittent flow system. However, continuous flow systems usually require special-purpose equipment which is less flexible and usually more expensive than general-purpose equipment. A continuous flow system therefore usually requires a larger capital investment than does an intermittent flow system.

DETERMINING OPERATING CAPABILITIES

The capabilities developed within an operating system should match the requirements of an organization.[8] The organizational requirements are determined by the organization goals and re-

[7] Howard L. Timms and Michael F. Pohlen, *The Production Function in Business*, 3d ed. (Homewood, Ill.: Richard D. Irwin, 1970), pp. 23–24. Copyright © 1970 by Richard D. Irwin, Inc.

[8] Gene K. Groff and John F. Muth, *Operations Management: Analysis for Decisions* (Homewood, Ill.: Richard D. Irwin, 1972), p. 4. Copyright © 1972 by Richard D. Irwin, Inc.

sources and by the environment. Because almost all organizations (including service and nonprofit organizations) must operate within certain budgetary constraints, almost all are concerned with costs. The extent of their concern for cost is determined for the most part by the technological and competitive characteristics of the firm's environment. Many public service organizations have recently become more cost conscious as private organizations have started to provide direct competition. For example, the number of private hospitals has been increasing. The efficient utilization of resources must be a primary concern of operations managers.

Three general types of operating environments for firms have been identified.[9] The first type of environment is the noncompetitive, monopolistic environment in which success is easily achieved. Even with operating inefficiencies, an organization can thrive in such an environment. Businesses producing patented products often operate in such an environment.

The second type of environment is relatively stable and is characterized by pure competition, a relatively stable technological base, and undifferentiated product designs. The packaging industry, lumber mills, banks, and insurance companies represent organizations operating in a relatively stable environment. Success in this environment is highly dependent on operating efficiencies.

In the third type of environment, organizations are confronted with rapid change and multifirm competition. Survival depends on innovation, not solely on short-run operating efficiency. Because of the rapid rate of change, the operations area must continually improve current capabilities in order to stay competitive. The development of new products and new methods is also essential. The more technical industries, such as electronics and plastics, operate in this type of environment.

Operating Capabilities for a Stable Environment

Environments characterized by stable designs and price competition still exist for many organizations. In such environments, the focus of the operations manager is on efficiency in the form of high productivity and low costs. High productivity is attained through task specialization. Products are standardized wherever possible in order to keep costs low. High-volume production runs are encouraged in order to minimize "changeover" costs. Methods are continually analyzed and perfected. Emphasis in a stable environment is on efficiency and cost-reducing activities.

---

[9]Ibid., pp. 4–10.

Operating Capabilities for a Changing Environment

Organizations operating in a rapidly changing environment must also change if they are to maintain a competitive position. Change in such an environment normally means new products and new processes as well as improvement of existing products and services. All of this must be accomplished while maximizing quality and minimizing costs. Thus, organizations operating in a rapidly changing environment must not only be concerned with efficiency but also with product value as measured by customers. The value attached to a product by the customer is affected by its quality, dependability, delivery time, and its level of technology. In order to attain high product value, emphasis should be placed on research and development and product improvement. The added concern for product value makes the operations manager's job much more complex in a rapidly changing environment than in a stable environment. Figure 18–4 shows specific operating capabilities required by stable and changing environments.

FIGURE 18–4
Operating Capabilities for Stable and Changing Environments

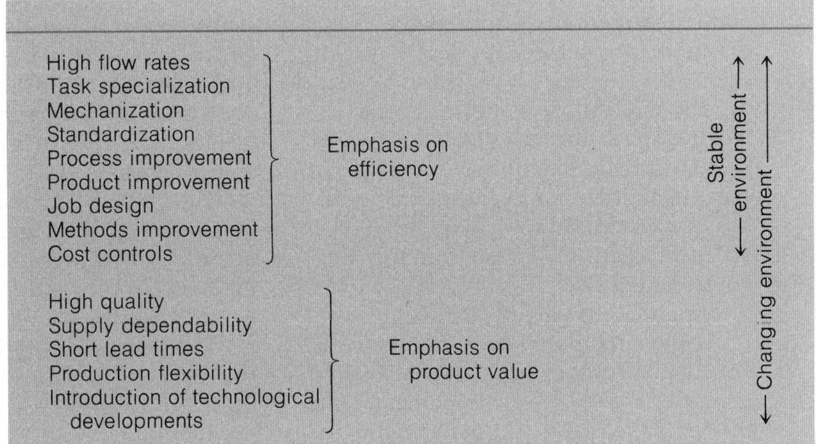

WHY PRODUCTIVITY?

Productivity may be defined as units of output per worker-machine hour. Management and labor leaders alike publicly urge higher productivity yet many people do not understand what it is or why it is important. Speaking in 1972 in reference to his activities as former chairman of the Price Commission, Jackson Grayson, Jr., stated, "I've been actually astonished at how few of the major companies that we've met with even know what productiv-

MANAGEMENT IN PRACTICE

Westinghouse Seeks Rise in Productivity

Baltimore—Westinghouse Defense and Electronic Systems Center, taking a lead from the Air Force's Integrated Computer-Aided Manufacturing (ICAM) program, plans to combine a variety of its management, design, production, information, and communications functions into a coordinated structure called Westinghouse Integrated Computer-Aided Management (WICAM).

Primary goal of the effort is to increase the overall productivity of the group, according to E. M. Migliorisi, WICAM manager. "WICAM is a management concept and organization that combines automation, technology and human resources from many disciplines to increase productivity," he said.

The WICAM concept emerged at Westinghouse during 1979 and achieved the status of an identifiable organization within the group last year, Migliorisi said. He described the program as an "evolution from the Air Force ICAM project," in which Westinghouse is participating.

Enhancing the systems group's ability to meet the needs of its primary customers—the Defense Department and the armed services—is a primary thrust of the WICAM effort, Migliorisi said. By implementing the integrated components of the WICAM structure, the group intends to:

Improve its design-to-cost capability.

Reduce lead times involved in beginning new programs.

Increase production standards.

Enhance its ability to respond to emergency defense mobilization situations.

Cornerstones in the WICAM approach to productivity improvement include matrix management, use of group technology and emphasis on training and worker involvement in production process improvement.

Managers are assigned a dual role in matrix management: to coordinate the activities in their respective areas of responsibility and to stay abreast of technology development in those areas.

The group technology concept centers around use of specifically assembled groups of production machines to manufacture components similar in design or in the means of fabrication. Each machine group is optimized to maintain as much versatility as possible, within the constraint of its having been tailored to produce one variety of similar components.

The group technology concept is emphasized both in engineering and in manufacturing at Westinghouse, and it both encourages and relies on greater flexibility among production workers.

Training programs aim at reducing the limits on manufacturing flexibility that derive from the limitations of production workers. Worker involvement in process and quality improvement is encouraged by promotion of Quality Circle groups—voluntary committees of production workers. Each Quality Circle is composed of workers from a single production area that identify production problems and formulate solutions for suggestion to manufacturing management.

The Quality Circle idea was adopted

from Japanese industry, and it functions on a larger scale and with more organization than the system of individual employe suggestions used widely throughout U.S. industry.

Source: *Aviation Week & Space Technology*, January 26, 1981, p. 65. Reprinted with permission.

ity is. . . ."[10] There is little evidence to indicate that this has changed in the past 10 years.

Historically, America has enjoyed very high productivity relative to other countries. However, in the post-Vietnam era, the country's previously unmatched production capabilities have become a matter of national concern.[11] This concern is based on at least two productivity-related facts.[12] First, our productivity rate has slowed substantially in recent years (see Figure 18–5). Not only has the United States experienced a reduction in the productivity growth rate, but negative rates occurred in 1974 and 1979. The second fact causing concern is that other industrial nations have exhibited comparative buoyancy. Their productivity rates have steadily grown during this same time period. Furthermore, as indicated in Figure 18–6, projected international productivity trends show higher productivity growth rates in the 1980s for Japan and the Western European nations than for the United States.[13]

Productivity Determinants

Unfortunately, when the term *productivity* is mentioned, many people automatically assume that it only means harder work. This is not necessarily the case. As indicated in Figure 18–7, productivity is the result of three separate components—efficiency of technology (equipment, methods, materials, and so on); efficiency of labor; and the effectiveness of management.

As defined here, technology includes new ideas, inventions, innovations, techniques, methods, and materials. Efficiency of labor is a function of the general level of services offered and the motivation to work. Services include health, education, research, and so forth. Given high efficiencies of technology and labor, these

[10] Richard C. Gerstenberg, "Productivity: Its Meaning for America," *Michigan Business Review*, July 1972, p. 1.

[11] Wickham Skinner, "After Seven Lean Years," *Proceedings, 33d Annual Meeting, Academy of Management*, ed. Thad B. Green and Dennis F. Ray, August 1973, p. 557.

[12] *Productivity Perspectives*, Houston: American Productivity Center, 1980, p. 2.

[13] Ibid., p. 48.

FIGURE 18–5
Capital, Labor, and Total Factor Productivity in U.S. Private Domestic Economy, 1948–1979

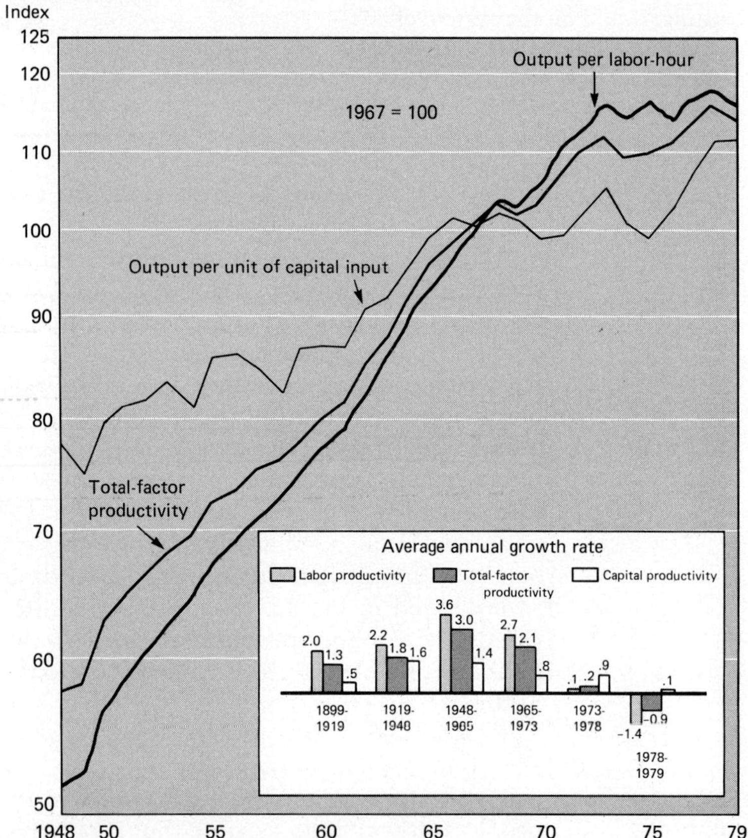

Source: *Productivity Perspectives* (Houston: American Productivity Center, 1980), p. 2.

inputs must be effectively combined by management if high productivity is to result. Thus, productivity is not simply a matter of making employees work longer and harder. The desire to work—often referred to as the puritan work ethic—must not be absent; however, it represents only one of several requirements for high productivity. Richard Gerstenberg, former chief executive officer for General Motors, has said that the real meaning of productivity is "to produce more with the same amount of human effort."[14] Gerstenberg's statement is based on the fact that, over the long run, far greater gains in productivity come from efficiency of labor. For example, the average factory worker in the United States

[14] Gerstenberg, "Productivity," p. 2.

FIGURE 18–6
Projected International Productivity Trends, GDP per Employee

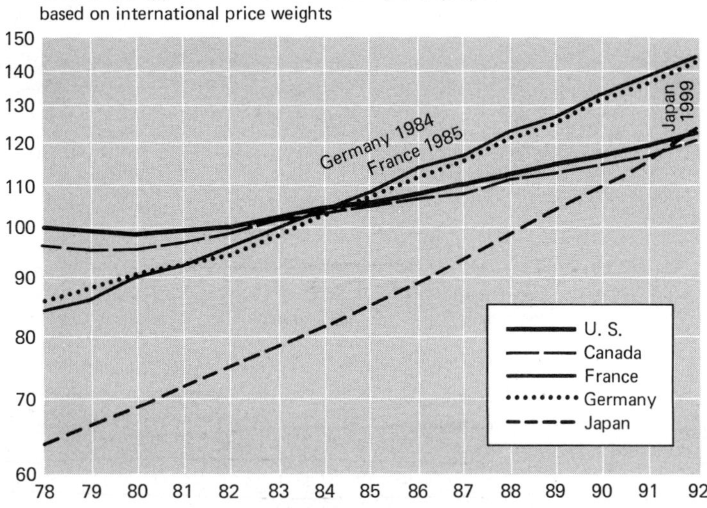

Source: *Productivity Perspectives* (Houston: American Productivity Center, 1980), p. 49.

FIGURE 18–7
Determinants of Productivity

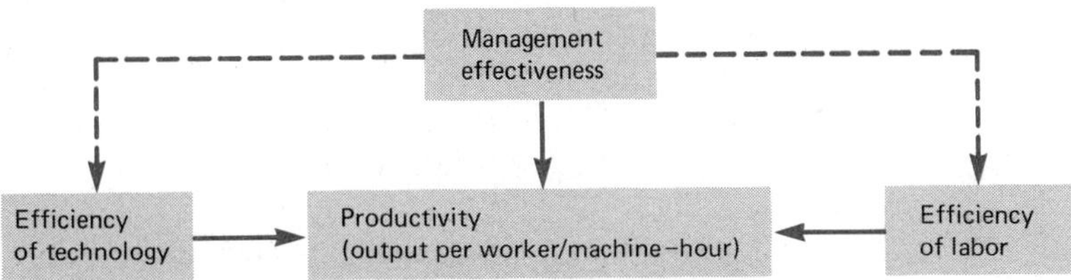

currently produces more than six times as much in an hour as that worker's grandfather produced at the turn of the century and, in most cases, with less effort.[15]

Productivity and Standard of Living

Figure 18–8 diagrammatically shows the basic relationship between productivity and standard of living. Total production depends on the rate of productivity, the quantity of equipment, and the quantity of people willing and able to work. New capital equipment, consumer goods, and services are the result of production. The new equipment is cycled back to industry, while the goods and services are used by the consumer. The level of goods

[15] Ibid., p. 5.

FIGURE 18–8
Productivity and Standard of Living

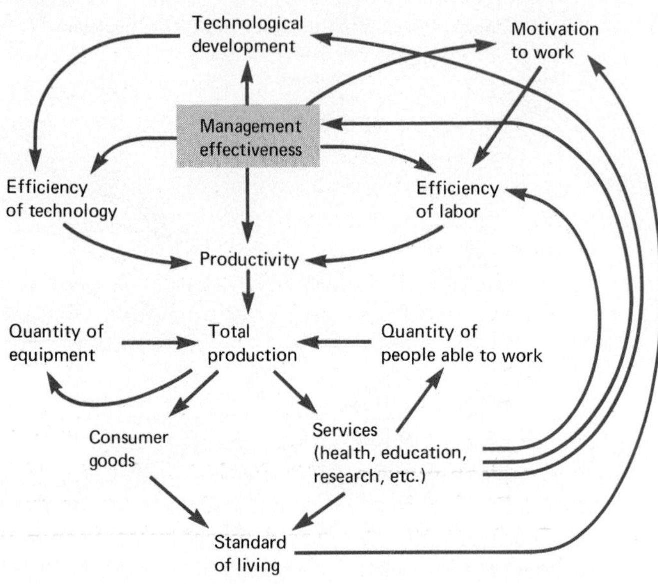

and services used by and available to the consumer determines the overall standard of living. Productivity is central to the quality of our daily lives.

SUMMARY

Operations management is the application of the basic concepts and principles of management to the operating systems of an organization. Operating systems consist of the processes and activities necessary to transform various inputs into goods and/or services. Operating systems exist in all organizations and are composed of people, material, facilities, and information. When viewed from an operations management perspective, most service systems are not significantly different from manufacturing systems. The end result of an operating system is to add value to the inputs by improving, enhancing, or rearranging them.

The activities undertaken while managing an operating system can be categorized into two main areas: (1) systems design and (2) operations planning and control. Product design and selection, equipment and process selection, site location, physical layout and design of work methods are all part of the design phase. Production control (aggregate output planning, resource allocation, and activity scheduling), inventory control, quality control, cost control and improvement, and facility maintenance are all part of the operations planning and control phase of operations management.

Operations management overlaps with other functional areas of an organization; therefore, many of the operations activities should be coordinated with the other functional areas.

There are two basic types of operating systems: one based on continuous flows, the other based on intermittent flows.

The capabilities developed within an operating system should match the requirements of the organization. One factor which influences these requirements is the environment. The operations manager in a stable environment is primarily concerned with efficiency and cost-reducing activities. The operations manager in a changing environment is concerned not only with cost, but also with increasing the value of the product to the consumer.

Because of the relatively large amount of resources and time consumed by the operations function, the management of this function plays a critical role in achieving the organization's goals.

Productivity is a central concern of the operations manager. Productivity also has a direct relationship to the standard of living in a society.

REVIEW QUESTIONS

1. What is operations management?
2. Describe an operating system.
3. What are the activities required to manage an operating system?
4. How does operations management relate to the other functional areas of an organization?
5. Describe the two basic types of operating systems.
6. What are the operating capabilities required for a stable environment? A changing environment?
7. What are the main determinants of productivity?
8. How is productivity related to the standard of living?

DISCUSSION QUESTIONS

1. Explain how you might take a production-line approach (transferring the concepts and methodologies of operations management) to a service organization such as a fast food restaurant.
2. Why should a marketing manager be concerned with the operations or production function of the organization?
3. What in your opinion are the reasons that the rate of increase in productivity has begun to slow in this country?
4. How does the organization's environment affect the needed capabilities of the organization's operating system?

SELECTED READINGS

Adam, Everett E., and Ronald J. Ebert. *Production and Operations Management* 2d ed. Englewood Cliffs, N.J.: Prentice-Hall, 1982.

Boyer, Charles H. "Lockheed Links Design and Manufacturing." *Industrial Engineering,* January 1977, pp. 14–21.

Chase, Richard B., and Nicholas J. Aquilano. *Productions and Operations Management.* 3d ed. Homewood, Ill.: Richard D. Irwin, 1981.

Coates, J. B. "Productivity: What Is It?" *Long Range Planning,* August 1980, pp. 90–97.

Day, Charles R., Jr. "Solving the Mystery of Productivity Measurement," *Industry Week,* January 26, 1981, pp. 61–66.

Gerstenberg, Richard C. "Productivity: Its Meaning for America." *Michigan Business Review,* July 1972, pp. 1–7.

Hamlin, Jerry L. "Productivity Means More Than 'Push the Wheelbarrow Faster,' " *Industrial Engineering,* April 1978.

Kendrick, John W., and Elliot S. Grossman. *Productivity in the United States.* Baltimore: Johns Hopkins University Press, 1980.

Levitt, T. "Production-Line Approach to Service." *Harvard Business Review,* September–October 1972, pp. 61–70.

Lubar, Robert. "Rediscovering the Factory," *Fortune,* July 13, 1981, pp. 52–64.

McConnell, Campbell R. "Why is U.S. Productivity Slowing Down?" *Harvard Business Review,* March–April 1979, pp. 36–60.

Marital, Shlomo, and Noah M. Meltz, eds. *Lagging Productivity Growth.* Cambridge, Mass.: Ballinger Publishing, 1980.

Case 18–1

The lines at Sam's

Sam Baker owns and manages a cafeteria on Main Street in Dawsonville. Sam has been in business for almost two years. During his two years of operation, Sam has identified several problems that he has not been able to solve. One major problem is the line that always seems to develop at the checkout register during the rush hour. Another problem is that customers are constantly complaining that the size of the helpings and the size of the pie slices vary tremendously from customer to customer. A third problem that has been disturbing Sam is the frequency with which the cafeteria runs out of "choice dishes." The final problem perplexing Sam is the fact that every Sunday at noon, when a large crowd arrives after church, Sam invariably runs short of seating space.

Sam has worked at other food establishments for the past 15

years and most of them have experienced similar problems. In fact, these and other related problems have come to be expected and are, therefore, accepted practice for the industry. After all, Sam's former boss used to say, "You can't please everybody all the time." Sam is wondering if he should take the industry's position and just accept these problems as an inherent part of the business.

1. Do you have any suggestions for Sam? If so, what are they?
2. Can you think of other service-oriented industries that seem to take the same view as Sam's industry toward their problems?

Case 18–2

"Milking" the business

Mickey "Mick" Lang is operations manager for the Tremble Company. Tremble was started by Joseph Went, Sr., in 1910 and is still privately owned by the Went family. In fact, Joseph Went III, is now president of Tremble. In recent years, the Went family has been "milking" the profits from the company and has refused to modernize in any respect. For example, Tremble has been in the same building and has been using the same basic equipment for the past 40 years. The company has also been reluctant to grant any employee benefits beyond the minimum requirements of the law.

Recently, the productivity of Tremble began to slip. This, coupled with rising labor and material costs and a soft market, has put Tremble in a precarious position for the first time in its history. As a result, Joseph Went III, has approached Mick and suggested that Mick is not properly motivating his employees. After explaining that numerous machine breakdowns had occurred, Mick received the following reply from Mr. Went: "This equipment has done a good job for the past 40 years and there is no reason why it won't for the next 40 years! You obviously don't understand that motivation is what causes high productivity."

1. Do you agree with Mr. Went?
2. In light of the situation, what should Mick do?
3. How do the long-term prospects look for Tremble?

19 Designing Operating Systems

Objectives

1. To emphasize the importance of operating system design to the overall success of the organization.
2. To discuss the activities involved in designing an operating system.

Chapter Outline

Glossary of Terms

Assembly chart Depicts the sequence and manner in which the various components of a product or service are assembled.

Flow process chart Outlines what happens to a product or service as it progresses through the facility.

Job The aggregate of all the work tasks that the job holder may be asked to perform.

Job content Refers to the make-up of the job. Job content is determined by the specification of individual tasks and by the manner in which these individual tasks are combined in a specific job.

Job design Designates the specific work activities of an individual or group of individuals.

Job methods Refer to the manner in which the human body is used, the arrangement of the work place, and the design of the tools and equipment which are used.

Line balancing A process of deteriming the optimum number of work stations.

Physical layout The process of planning the optimum physical arrangement of facilities which includes personnel, operating equipment, storage space, office space, materials handling equipment, and room for customer or product movement.

Process physical layout A type of physical layout in which equipment or services of a similar functional type are arranged or grouped together.

Process selection Specifies in detail the processes and sequences required to transform inputs into products or services.

Product physical layout A type of physical layout in which equipment or services are arranged according to the progressive steps by which the product is made or the customer is served.

Sociotechnical approach Approach to job design which takes into consideration both the technical system and the accompanying social system.

The Designer bent across his board
Wonderful things in his head were stored
And he said as he rubbed his throbbing bean
"How can I make this thing tough to machine?
If this part here were only straight
I'm sure the thing would work first rate,
But 'twould be so easy to turn and bore
It never would make the machinists sore.
I better put in a right angle there
Then watch those babies tear their hair
Now I'll put the holes that hold the cap
Way down in here where they're hard to tap,
Now this piece won't work, I'll bet a buck
For it can't be held in a shoe or chuck
It can't be drilled or it can't be ground
In fact the design is exceedingly sound."
He looked again and cried—"At last—
Success is mine, it can't even be cast."

*Ken Lane**

The specific product or service produced by an organization establishes both opportunities for and limitations on the design of its operating systems. If the design of the product or service causes extensive systems redesign, equipment alteration, new personnel, and so on, it can drastically alter the attractiveness of the product or service. As suggested by the introductory quote, the design of the product or service can be functionally sound, yet unproducible. Certainly specific functional design objectives must be achieved; however, several alternative designs are often available for attaining these objectives. When such alternatives exist, production costs should certainly be one criterion used in evaluating the alternatives.

Designing an operating system involves selecting the process that is going to be used in producing the product or service, determining the location and layout of the physical facilities, and designing the jobs necessary to produce the product or service.

Process selection, like product design, can have a great impact on the costs and quality of the product or service. Process selec-

* Ken Lane, *As Some Men See Us*. As quoted by J. P. Hahir, "A Case Study on the Relationships between Design Engineering and Production Engineering," Proceedings, Fifth Annual Industrial Engineering Institute, University of California, Berkeley and University of California, Los Angeles, 1953, p. 22.

tion specifies in detail thc processes and sequences required to transform the inputs into products or services. When goods or products are produced, the emphasis of process selection is usually on the specific equipment that is to be used and how it fits together. With service industries the major emphasis shifts to the procedures used.[1]

The location and layout of the physical facilities are also important decisions that affect the organization's capabilities. Not only can site location affect overall costs in terms of wages paid, transportation costs, energy costs, and so on, but it can also affect the ability to service customers adequately. The primary objective of physical layout is to develop an operating system that meets the productive and quality requirements of the organization in the most economical manner.[2]

Job design designates the specific work activities of an individual or group of individuals. Job design determines the depth and scope of the job and is, therefore, influenced by the physical layout and the process selection. As discussed in Chapters 7 and 10, job design can have a significant impact on employee motivation.

There are important interdependencies among each of the different design phases. The operations manager must serve as an integrating force for design decisions and ensure that the final design is effective from a total production standpoint.

PRODUCT/SERVICE DESIGN

The operations manager usually becomes involved with product or service design after many of the preliminary design decisions have been made. Traditionally, after the design engineers and marketing specialists have worked out the basic specifications so that the product or service meets its functional requirements, the operations manager becomes involved. At this point the operations manager begins to select the materials, basic configurations, and the processes that will be used to minimize the production costs. Possible alterations to the design may be necessary due to cost considerations. Experience has shown that in many situations more than one basic design is functionally acceptable. The operations manager and the design engineer must work closely at this point to ensure that the design is sound from both a functional and cost standpoint.

---

[1] Richard B. Chase and Nicholas J. Aquilano, *Production and Operations, Management: A Life Cycle Approach*, rev. ed. (Homewood, Ill.: Richard D. Irwin, 1977), p. 83. Copyright © 1977 by Richard D. Irwin, Inc.

[2] Elwood S. Buffa, *Basic Production Management*, 2d ed. (New York: John Wiley & Sons, 1975), p. 271.

Historically conflict has existed between design engineers and operations managers. Design engineers are technically oriented and sometimes lack concern for production methods and costs. On the other hand, operations managers are more concerned with production costs and requirements than with the functional requirements of the product. Such potentially destructive conflict can be minimized through good communication, which fosters an appreciation by both the engineer and the manager of the common objective of producing a functionally sound product or service at the minimum cost.

PROCESS SELECTION

Process selection encompasses a wide range of decisions including the feasibility of the product design, the basic type of configuration of the process system that is to be used, equipment selection, and product routing. Richard Chase and Nicholas Aquilano have classified process selection decisions into four different categories: (1) major technological, (2) minor technological, (3) specific component, and (4) specific process flow.[3] Figure 19–1 outlines the scope of each type of process selection decision. Major technological decisions answer the basic question of whether or not the product or service can be produced. These decisions do not address the question of whether or not the product can be economically produced. Major technological decisions deal primarily with the physical sciences.

Minor technological decisions choose between the alternative transformation processes available. These decisions include the choice between the use of general purpose and special-purpose equipment; make or buy decisions; or the degree of automation. The overall organizational objectives and plans must be considered in making minor technological decisions. This requires input from both technical specialists and other areas of management.

Specific component decisions refer to the selection of equipment and procedures. Obviously, equipment and procedures decisions should not be made independently of the minor technological decisions. Beyond the normal cost considerations, the following factors should be evaluated in making specific component decisions:

1. Training required for the operators.
2. Maintenance record and potential.
3. Availability of parts and service.

[3] Chase and Aquilano, *Production and Operations*, p. 91.

FIGURE 19–1
Decisions in Process Selection

General-process decision	*Decision problem*	*Decision variables*	*Decision aids*
Major technological decisions	Transformation potential	Product choice Laws of physics, chemistry, etc. State of scientific knowledge	Technical specialists
Minor technological decisions	Selecting among alternative transformation processes	State of the art in equipment and techniques Environmental factors such as ecological and legal constraints Primary task of organization General financial and market strength	R&D reports Technical specialists Organizational objectives Long-run market forecasts Mathematical programs
Specific component decisions	Selecting specific equipment	Existing facilities Cost of equipment alternatives Desired output level	Industry reports Investment analysis, including make-or-buy, brake-even, and present-value methods Medium-range forecasts
Specific process flow decisions	Selecting production routings	Existing layout Homogeneity of products Equipment characteristics	Product specifications Assembly charts Route sheets Flow process charts Equipment manuals Engineering handbooks

Source: Richard B. Chase and Nicholas J. Aquilano, *Production and Operations Management: A Life-Cycle Approach*, 3d ed. (Homewood, Ill.: Richard D. Irwin, 1981, p. 34. Copyright © 1973 by Richard D. Irwin, Inc.

4. Supplier assistance in installation and debugging.
5. Compatibility with existing equipment.
6. Flexibility of equipment in handling product variation.
7. Safety of equipment.
8. Delivery date expected.
9. Warranty coverage.

Specific process flow decisions route the materials and product through the facility. These decisions are highly dependent on the available equipment and space. Although the process flow may appear to be fixed because of certain physical limitations, it should always be carefully analyzed.

Routing involves determining the best path and sequence of operations for attaining a desired level of output with a given mix of equipment and personnel. Routing attempts to make optimum use of the existing equipment and personnel through careful assignment of these resources. An organization may be required to analyze its routing system frequently or infrequently depending on the variety of products or services being offered.

Flow charting and diagrams are used to aid in detecting and eliminating inefficiencies in a process by analyzing a certain sequence of operations in a step-by-step fashion. Most charting procedures distribute the actions which occur during a given process into five classifications: operations, transportations, inspections, delays, and storages. Figure 19–2 defines each of these types of actions. Two charts frequently used are assembly charts and flow process charts.

Assembly charts depict the sequence and manner in which the various components of a product or service are assembled. A flow process chart outlines what happens to the product as it progresses through the operating facility. Flow process charts can also be used to map the flow of customers through a service facility. Figure 19–3 is an example of a flow process chart representing the processing of an examination.

FIGURE 19–2
Flow-Charting Activities

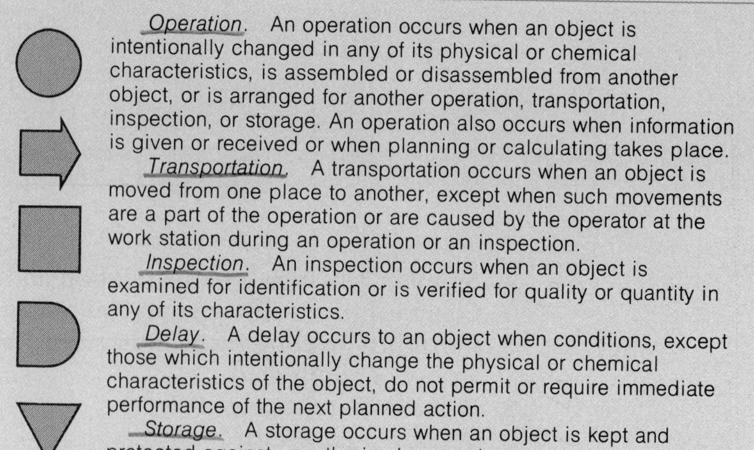

Operation. An operation occurs when an object is intentionally changed in any of its physical or chemical characteristics, is assembled or disassembled from another object, or is arranged for another operation, transportation, inspection, or storage. An operation also occurs when information is given or received or when planning or calculating takes place.
Transportation. A transportation occurs when an object is moved from one place to another, except when such movements are a part of the operation or are caused by the operator at the work station during an operation or an inspection.
Inspection. An inspection occurs when an object is examined for identification or is verified for quality or quantity in any of its characteristics.
Delay. A delay occurs to an object when conditions, except those which intentionally change the physical or chemical characteristics of the object, do not permit or require immediate performance of the next planned action.
Storage. A storage occurs when an object is kept and protected against unauthorized removal.

Source: William R. Mullee and David B. Porter, "Process-Chart Procedures," in *Industrial Engineering Handbook,* 2d ed., ed. H. B. Maynard (New York: McGraw-Hill, 1963), pp. 2–21.

FIGURE 19–3
Flow Process Chart

Flow Process Chart

Analysis				
Why?				
What?	Where?	When?	Who?	How?

Question each detail

No. 231

Page 1 of 1

Summary	Present No.	Present Time	Proposed No.	Proposed Time	Difference No.	Difference Time
◯ Operations	5					
⇨ Transportations	6					
□ Inspections	5					
D Delays	4					
▽ Storages	2					
Distance traveled	530 FT.		FT.		FT.	

Job Prepare, Type, Print examination

Man or Material: Examination

Chart begins: 10:30 a.m. 4/1/81

Chart ends: 5:00 p.m. 4/7/81

Charted by: GFR Date: 4/8/81

Details of method (Present / proposed)	Operation	Transport	Inspection	Delay	Storage	Distance in feet	Quantity	Time	Activity: Eliminate	Activity: Combine	Change: Seque	Change: Place	Change: Person	Activity: Improve	Notes
1. Make up exam problems	●														Instructor
2. Check answers			■												"
3. Carry to typist		➡				35									Secretarial pool
4. Waits in typing backlog				◗											
5. Master copy typed	●														Typist
6. Waits in finished work file				◗											Locked file
7. Picked up	●														Instructor
8. Carried to instructor's office		➡				35									"
9. Proofread exam			■												"
10. Carry to typist		➡				35									"
11. Wait in backlog				◗											
12. Carry to copy center		➡				200									Typist
13. Wait in backlog				◗											
14. Print exam	●						75								Machine operator
15. Check quality of copies			■												" "
16. Carry to collator		➡				10									" "
17. Wait in backlog				◗											
18. Assemble and staple exams	●														Machine operator
19. Count finished copies			■												" "
20. Wait in finished work file				◗											
21. Deliver to instructor		➡				215									Messenger service
22. File until needed					▼										

Source: Roy D. Harris and Richard F. Gonzalez, *The Operations Manager: Role, Problems, and Techniques* (St. Paul, Minn.: West Publishing Co., 1981), p. 125.

The different phases of process selection described above are all interdependent and overlapping. They should not be carried out in a distinct step-by-step fashion but rather in an integrative manner. The overriding objective of process selection is to specify in detail the most economical processes and sequences required to transform the inputs into the desired product or service.

SITE SELECTION

Management should give careful consideration to site-location decisions. It is easy to become overly engrossed in the operating details and techniques and ignore the importance of site location. Location is an ongoing question that does not occur only when a facility is outgrown or becomes obsolete. Location decisions relate to offices, warehouses, service centers, and branches, as well as the main facility. Each site selection decision should consider the total production-distribution system of the organization. Therefore the location of new facilities should not be the only locations examined. The location of present facilities should also be periodically examined to determine the most effective production-distribution system.

Several possibilities exist for expanding capacity when the existing facility is overcowded:

1. Subcontract work.
2. Add another shift.
3. Work overtime.
4. Move operation to a larger facility.
5. Expand present facility.
6. Keep current facility and add another facility elsewhere.

If a decision is made to move the entire operation to a larger facility, or to keep the current facility and add another facility elsewhere, then management is faced with a location decision. Figure 19–4 lists several factors which should be considered by management when locating a new facility. The final site choice will, by necessity, represent a compromise among these factors.

PHYSICAL LAYOUT

Physical layout is essentially the process of planning the optimum physical arrangement of facilities which includes personnel, operating equipment, storage space, office space, and materials

FIGURE 19–4
Factors to Be Considered in Site Location

1. Revenue
   a. Location of customers and accessibility
   b. Location of competitors
2. Operating costs
   a. Price of materials
   b. Transportation costs: materials, products, people
   c. Wage rates
   d. Taxes: income, property, sales
   e. Utility rates
   f. Rental rates
   g. Communication costs
3. Investment
   a. Cost of land
   b. Cost of construction
4. Other limiting factors
   a. Availability of labor with appropriate skills
   b. Availability of materials, utilities, supplies
   c. Union activity
   d. Community attitudes and culture
   e. Political situation
   f. Pollution restrictions
   g. Climate
   h. General living conditions

handling equipment or room for customer service and movement. Physical layout integrates all of the previous planning of the design process into one physical system. Physical layout decisions become necessary for a number of different reasons:

1. Construction of a new or an additional facility.
2. Obsolescence of current facilities.
3. Changes in demand.
4. The development of a new or redesigned product or process.
5. Personnel considerations: frequent accidents, poor worker environment, or prohibitive supervisory costs.

Demand forecasts for the product or service must be considered in establishing the productive capacity of the organization. Management must balance the costs of running short on space and equipment with the costs of having idle space and equipment. A good approach is to match space requirements with estimates of future demand, but purchase equipment only as it is needed. Such an approach provides for quick capacity expansion and avoids the costs of the idle equipment.

MANAGEMENT IN PRACTICE

The American Productivity Center—"Tending to Productivity Levels"

In an effort to practice what it teaches, the American Productivity Center in Houston has not overlooked the need to tend to its own productivity levels. In doing so, it has created a highly productive total environment seemingly planned specifically with the trainer of today and tomorrow in mind.

If the center's design particularly fills the needs of the trainer, it is not by accident, because that, in essence, is the role the Center has carved out for itself. It acts as a catalyst among business, labor, and governmental organizations to create awareness of the productivity problem, then helps establish programs within individual organizations to improve productivity at the grass roots level.

Situated along the banks of Buffalo Bayou on the western edge of Houston's Memorial Park, the Center's wooded setting buffers the staff and associates from the bustling Magic Circle distractions. The total product, then—secluded setting, towering trees, meandering bayou, imaginative design, technologically advanced equipment—allows trainers to think, develop, produce, and effectively present their information to learners.

The focal point for training activities is the semicircular amphitheater, located just off the atrium lobby. Its strategically angled walls and advanced acoustical materials control the direction in which sound bounces, eliminating the waffling effect that is common in most hotel conference and meeting rooms. Even without the balanced sound system and voice-actuated speakers at each chair, speakers and participants can be heard clearly from anywhere in the room.

Satellite communications designed into the building allow teleconferencing, while closed-circuit television facilities allow the center to broadcast programs and information to the adjacent inn, or its conference center, or to the world via satellite.

Virtually all of the state of the art audio-visual aids available are being installed in the center's facility. This includes a color graphics device that allows a trainer to computer-design a chart or graph on a television screen, display it in a variety of formats (bar chart, pie graph, etc.), select the most appropriate one, hit a button, and receive a slide. The slide can be inserted in the multi-projector rear screen capability servicing the facility.

Permanently installed color videotape cameras, individual specially designed "fatigue resistant" Herman Miller furniture, overhead projection coupled through the rear screen, electrically adjustable podiums, and a large clock on the rear wall controlled by the speakers are among the features available to the trainer.

Perhaps most noticeable in this day of solar screens and mirrored glass are the clear windows in each of the two office floors of the four-story building. The windows are tilted outward at 43 degrees, much like an airport control tower.

The inclined glass reflects sound upward to a special ceiling material that absorbs up to 90 percent of the noise reaching it. The angle also allows for a more direct view of the surrounding grounds and bayou by eliminating the need for window coverings.

Displayed in the lobby is a 40-foot, spiral stack of paper. Next to it is a ½-inch thick stack of microfiche which is a chip used in IBM's bubble memory, so small that it must be displayed in a block of lucite to be noticed; yet it can store information equivalent to the microfiche and the paper stack.

A fiber-optics exhibit presents a hologram and displays the fibers—1/50,000th the size of standard communications wire—being used in communications today.

Conspicuous by its absence is the central service core that exists in most buildings. Elevators, stairs, restrooms, and storage closets were moved to the exterior walls to help insure the success of the open-office concept.

The ever-shifting office work station configuration is accommodated by flat wiring borrowed from the space program, adding a new acoustical ceiling material, and developing itinerant electrical, communications, and air conditioning techniques.

Electrical wiring and communications conductors are installed under removable carpet tiles. Telephones and electrical outlets, therefore, may be placed precisely where they are needed and moved as often as necessary. Similar flexibility exists with overhead lighting and air conditioning outlets. Both can be moved within a 10-foot radius in order to be properly positioned over each work area.

Source: *Training and Development Journal*, September 1980, p. 11.

Basic Layout Classifications

Most layouts can be classified as either process-oriented or product-oriented. Process layouts are generally used in intermittent flow operating systems (discussed in Chapter 18). In a process layout, equipment or services of a similar functional type are arranged or grouped together. A process layout is followed when all x-ray machines are grouped together, all reproduction equipment is grouped together, all drilling machines are grouped together, and so forth. Custom fabrication shops, hospitals, and restaurants are usually arranged in this fashion. Under a process layout a product or customer travels from area to area according to the desired sequence of functional operations. When the product or service is not standardized or when the volume of similar products or customers in service at any one time is low, a process layout is preferred because of its flexibility.

Product layouts are usually employed in continuous flow operating systems (also discussed in Chapter 18). In a product layout, equipment or services are arranged according to the progressive steps by which the product is made or the customer is serviced. A product layout is generally used when a standardized product is made in large quantities. The assembly line is the ultimate example of a product layout. Automobile assembly plants, cafeterias, and standardized testing centers are examples which normally are product layout-oriented. In a product layout, all the equipment or services necessary to produce a product or completely serve a customer are located in one area. Figure 19–5 summarizes the major advantages of both process and product layouts.

FIGURE 19–5
Advantages of Process and Product Layout

Advantages of process layout

1. Lower investment in equipment and personnel because of less duplication (do not need the same machine or person doing the same thing in two different areas).
2. Adaptable to demand fluctuations.
3. Worker jobs are not as repetitive or routine.
4. Layout is conducive to incentive pay systems.
5. Allows for the production of a greater variety of products with a smaller capital base.
6. Failures of equipment or people do not hold up successive operations.

Advantages of product layout

1. Relatively unskilled labor may be utilized.
2. Training costs are low.
3. Materials handling costs are usually low.
4. Smaller quantities of work in process.
5. Operations control and scheduling is simplified.

Computer-Assisted Physical Layout

Various computer programs have been developed to aid in designing physical layouts. Most of the computer approaches to designing a process-oriented layout attempt to optimize the relative placement of like components subject to some predetermined criterion or criteria. Materials handling cost is the most frequently used criterion. Computer programs for product-oriented layouts generally attempt to determine the optimum number of work stations to meet certain criteria. This approach is known as *line balancing*. Processing cost is normally the criterion used for line balancing.

JOB DESIGN

Job design specifies the specific work activities of an individual or group of individuals. Job design answers the question of how

FIGURE 19–6
Factors in Job Design

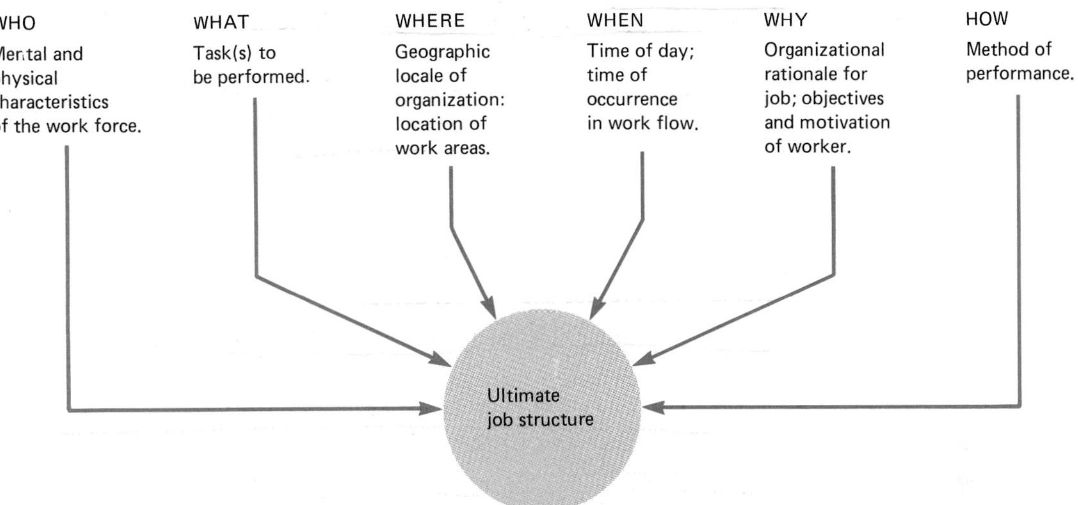
WHO
Mental and physical characteristics of the work force.
WHAT
Task(s) to be performed.
WHERE
Geographic locale of organization: location of work areas.
WHEN
Time of day; time of occurrence in work flow.
WHY
Organizational rationale for job; objectives and motivation of worker.
HOW
Method of performance.
Ultimate job structure

Source: Richard B. Chase and Nicholas J. Aquilano, *Production and Operations Management: A Life-Cycle Approach,* (Homewood, Ill.: Richard D. Irwin, 1981), p. 329. Copyright © 1981 by Richard D. Irwin, Inc.

the job is to be performed, who is to perform it, and where it is to be performed. As shown in Figure 19–6 the ultimate job structure results from job design.

The job design process can generally be divided into three phases:

1. The specification of individual tasks.
2. The specification of the method of performing each task.
3. The combination of individual tasks into specific jobs to be assigned to individuals.[4]

Phases one and three determine the content of the job (which includes both job scope and job depth), while phase two indicates how the job is to be performed. Job scope and job depth were both briefly discussed in Chapter 7.

Job Content

A job is the aggregate of all the work tasks that the jobholder may be asked to perform. Until recently, the prevailing practice in designing the content of jobs was to focus almost totally on the process by which the job was done. This usually meant minimizing

[4] Louis E. Davis, "Job Design and Productivity: A New Approach," *Personnel,* March 1957, p. 420.

short-run costs by minimizing the unit operation time. This approach resulted in the application of the following rules.

For specifying the content of individual tasks:

1. Specialize skills.
2. Minimize skills requirements.
3. Minimize learning time.
4. Equalize work loads and make it possible to assign full work loads.
5. Provide for worker's satisfaction.
6. Conform to the layout of equipment or facilities or, where they exist, to union restrictions on work assignments.

For combining individual tasks into specific jobs:

1. Limit the number and variety of tasks in a job.
2. Make the job as repetitive as possible.
3. Minimize training time.[5]

FIGURE 19–7
Employee-Centered Approaches for Overcoming Job Boredom

1. *Job rotation* is the practice of periodically changing job assignments. It does not require that jobs be redesigned. Personnel are shifted from one job assignment to another.
2. *Job enlargement* makes a job structurally larger by increasing its scope (number of different operations performed). A greater variety of tasks are performed.
3. *Job enrichment* increases both job scope (diversity) and job depth (freedom to plan and organize the work). The employee is given greater responsibility for how to perform his job responsibilities.
4. *Participative management* solicits employee advice on job related decisions. The employee is considered a partner with a valuable input to the decision-making process.
5. *Industrial democracy* places worker representatives on all decision making bodies of the organization. Industrial democracy can encompass much more than job related matters.
6. *Organizational development* attempts to change attitudes and values to improve communication and reduce conflicts. Group processes and sensitivity training are associated with the organizational development approach.
7. *Variable work schedules* permit employees a certain amount of freedom in selecting work hours.
8. *The four-day workweek* consists of four 10-hour days. The worker has a longer weekend for leisure activities.

Source: Richard J. Tersine, *Production/Operations Management: Concepts, Structure, and Analysis*, New York: Elsevier-North Holland Publishing, 1980, p. 273.

[5]Ibid.

The obvious problem with this process-centered approach is that the job can become overly routine and repetitive, which leads to motivational problems in the form of boredom, absenteeism, turnover, and, possibly, low performance.

Figure 19–7 lists many employee-centered approaches that have been developed for overcoming this problem. All of these approaches attempt to add satisfaction to the job through increased participation, job variety, job freedom, and flexibility. The key is to balance the process or technical components of job design with employee (behavioral) considerations. Figure 19–8 presents some specific guidelines that can help achieve this balance without sacrificing technical efficiency.

One fact that complicates the job design process is that different people react differently to similar jobs. Because of this Don-

FIGURE 19–8
Some Practical Guidelines for Designing Jobs

Elements of workers' jobs	*Suggested design guidelines*	*Workers' needs affected*
Workers' job tasks (The work itself—arrangement of machines, workplace layouts, work methods, and sequence of work tasks)	1. Avoid machine pacing of workers. Workers should determine, when possible, rates of output.	Self-control
	2. When practical, combine inspection tasks into jobs so that workers inspect their own output.	Self-control
	3. Work areas should be designed to allow open communication and visual contact with other workers in adjacent operations.	Socialization
	4. When economically feasible and generally desired by workers, combine machine changeovers, new job layouts, setups, and other elements of immediate into workers' jobs.	Self-direction/control
Immediate job setting (The management policies and procedures that directly impinge upon workers jobs)	1. Rotate workers where practical between jobs that are repetitive, monotonous, boring, and short cycled.	Variety and relief of boredom and monotony
	2. Assign new workers to undesirable jobs for fixed periods of time, then transfer them to more preferred jobs.	Equity
	3. Provide workers with periodic rest periods away from repetitive jobs to relieve monotony.	Relief of boredom and socialization
	4. Set higher pay rates for undesirable jobs.	Physiological, security, equity, and achievement

Source: Adapted from Norman Gaither, *Production and Operations Management: A Problem Solving and Decision Making Approach* (Hinsdale, Ill.: Dryden Press, 1980), p. 415. Copyright © 1980 by The Dryden Press, a division of Holt, Rinehart and Winston, Publishers. Reprinted by permission of Holt, Rinehart and Winston, CBS College Publishing.

Donald Schwab and Larry Cummings have suggested a situational approach to job scope.[6] Their contention is that a given employee's reaction to the scope of the job is dependent on several situational factors. This approach would explain why different individuals react differently to jobs of a similar scope. The situational approach to job scope also emphasizes the importance of the staffing process and matching the individual to the job.

Job Methods

Once job content has been determined, the next step is to determine the precise methods that should be used to perform the job. The optimum method of performing a job is a function of the manner in which the human body is used, the arrangement of the work place, and the design of the tools and equipment which are used.[7] The overriding objective of job method design is to find the one best way of performing a particular job. Normally, job methods are determined after the basic process and physical layout have been determined.

Motion study is the primary approach used in designing jobs. Basically, motion study involves determining the necessary motions and movements for performing a job or task and then designing the most efficient method for putting these motions and movements together. Figure 19–9 presents a list of motion-economy principles.

Charts similar to those used in process design are also useful in methods design. The difference is that charts used in methods design show more detailed work elements than do process charts, which represent entire operations.

Traditionally, job methods designers have concentrated their efforts on manual activities. However, the basic concept of finding the one best way is applicable to all types of jobs.

The Physical Work Environment

The physical work environment, which includes factors such as temperature, humidity, ventilation, noise, light, and color, can have an impact on worker performance and safety. While there are studies which clearly show that adverse physical conditions do have a negative effect on performance, the degree of influence varies from individual to individual.

---

[6] Donald P. Schwab and Larry L. Cummings, "A Theoretical Analysis of the Impact of Task Scopes on Employee Performance," *Academy of Management Review*, April 1976, pp. 23–35.

[7] Richard A. Johnson, William T. Newell, and Roger C. Vergin, *Production and Operations Management: A Systems Concept* (Boston: Houghton Mifflin, 1974), p. 204.

FIGURE 19–9
Principles of Motion Economy

A check sheet for motion economy and fatigue reduction

These 22 rules or principles of motion economy may be profitably applied to production and service work alike. Although not all are applicable to every operation, they do form a basis or a code for improving efficiency and reducing fatigue.

Use of the human body:

1. The two hands should begin as well as complete their motions at the same time.
2. The two hands should not be idle at the same time except during rest periods.
3. Motions of the arms should be made in opposite and symmetrical directions, and should be made simultaneously.
4. Hand and body motions should be confined to the lowest classification with which it is possible to perform the work satisfactorily.
5. Momentum should be employed to assist the worker wherever possible, and it should be reduced to a minimum if it must be overcome by muscular effort.
6. Smooth, continuous, curved motions of the hands are preferable to straight-line motions involving sudden and sharp changes in direction.
7. Ballistic movements are faster, easier, and more accurate than restricted (fixation) or "controlled" movements.
8. Work should be arranged to permit easy and natural rhythm wherever possible.
9. Eye fixations should be as few and as close together as possible.

Arrangement of the workplace:

10. There should be a definite and fixed place for all tools and materials.
11. Tools, materials, and controls should be located close to the point of use.
12. Gravity feed bins and containers should be used to deliver material close to the point of use.
13. Drop deliveries should be used wherever possible.
14. Materials and tools should be located to permit the best sequence of motions.
15. Provisions should be made for adequate conditions for seeing. Good illumination is the first requirement for satisfactory visual perception.
16. The height of the workplace and the chair should preferably be arranged so that alternate sitting and standing at work are easily possible.
17. A chair of the type and height to permit good posture should be provided for every worker.

Design of tools and equipment:

18. The hands should be relieved of all work that can be done more advantageously by a jig, a fixture, or a foot-operated device.
19. Two or more tools should be combined wherever possible.
20. Tools and materials should be prepositioned whenever possible.
21. Where each finger performs some specific movement, such as in typewriting, the load should be distributed in accordance with the inherent capacities of the fingers.
22. Levers, crossbars, and hand wheels should be located in such positions that the operator can manipulate them with the least change in body position and with the greatest mechanical advantage.

Source: Ralph M. Barnes, *Motion and Time Study*, 6th ed. (New York: John Wiley & Sons, 1968), p. 220.

The importance of safety considerations in the design process was magnified by the passage of the Occupational Safety and Health Act (OSHA) in 1970. Designed to reduce the incidence of job injuries, the act outlines very specific federal safety guidelines which must be followed by all U.S. organizations.

In general, the work environment should allow for normal lighting, temperature, ventilation, and humidity. Baffles, acoustical wall materials, and sound absorbers should be used where necessary to reduce unpleasant noises. If workers must be exposed to less than ideal conditions, it is wise to limit these exposures to short periods of time so as to minimize the probability that the worker will suffer any permanent physical or psychological damage.[8]

Sociotechnical Approach

The sociotechnical concept was first introduced in the 1950s by Eric Trist and his colleagues at the Tavistock Institute of Human Relations in London, England.[9] The thrust of the concept is that both the technical system and the accompanying social system should be considered when designing jobs. Under the sociotechnical concept, jobs should be designed by taking a "holistic or systems" view of the entire job situation including its physical and social environment. The sociotechnical approach is very situational because few jobs have identical technical requirements and social surroundings. Specifically, the sociotechnical approach requires that the job designer carefully consider the role of the worker in the sociotechnical system, the nature of the task boundaries, and the autonomy of the work group. Using the sociotechnical approach, Louis Davis has developed the following guidelines for job design:

1. The need for the content of a job to be reasonably demanding for the individual in terms other than sheer endurance and yet provide some variety (not necessarily novelty).
2. The need for being able to learn on the job and to go on learning.
3. The need for some minimum area of decision making that the individual can call his own.
4. The need for some minimal degree of social support and recognition at the work place.
5. The need to be able to relate what the individual does and what he produces to his social life.

---

[8] Ibid., p. 206.

[9] Peter B. Vaill, "Industrial Engineering and Socio-Technical Systems," *Journal of Industrial Engineering,* September 1967, p. 535.

6. The need to feel that the job leads to some sort of desirable future.[10]

SUMMARY

The specific product or service produced by an organization establishes limitations on the design of its operating system. Operations managers generally become involved with product or service design after much of the preliminary design has been accomplished by engineering. At this point, the operations manager and the design engineer must work closely to ensure that the optimal design from a functional and production standpoint is found.

Process selection encompasses a wide range of decisions, including the feasibility of product design, the basic type and configuration of the process system that is to be used, equipment selection, and product routing. The overriding objective of process selection is to specify in detail the most economical processes and sequences required to transform the inputs into the desired product or service.

The location and layout of physical facilities are important decisions which also affect the success of the product or service. Plant location has an impact on employee morale as well as on costs. The physical layout integrates all of the planning of the design process into one physical system. Process-oriented and product-oriented are the basic forms of physical layout.

Job design designates the specific work activities of an individual or group of individuals and answers the questions of how the job is to be performed, who is to perform it, and where it is to be performed. Job content is determined by the specification of individual tasks and by the manner in which these individual tasks are combined into a specific job. Job methods specify the precise method of performing each task.

Unlike the more traditional approach to job design, which assumes that the job content is fixed by the requirements of the process or by the organization structure, the sociotechnical approach advocates considering both the task and social environment in designing jobs.

REVIEW QUESTIONS

1. Outline the different phases involved in designing operating systems.
2. Identify the four major categories of process selection decisions.

---

[10] Louis E. Davis, *Job Satisfaction—A Socio-Technical View,* report 515–1–69 (Los Angeles: University of California, 1969), p. 14.

3. What charting procedures are available to aid in process selection?
4. Discuss several factors that should be considered in site location.
5. What is a process-oriented layout? A product-oriented layout?
6. What is the sociotechnical approach to job design? Give some guidelines for job design using the sociotechnical approach.

DISCUSSION QUESTIONS

1. Does process selection in service industries such as restaurants and hotels differ from process selection in manufacturing? If so, how?
2. How do the problems of organizing facilities for a service organization differ from those of laying out the facility for a manufacturing or goods-producing organization?
3. Why should all of the phases involved in designing an operating system be integrated?
4. Discuss the following statement made by a senior engineer: "Why should we be concerned with the product or process design since we know management will make us do it again anyway?"

SELECTED READINGS

Adam, Everett E., Jr., and Ronald J. Ebert. *Production and Operations Management,* 2d ed., Englewood Cliffs, N.J.: Prentice-Hall, 1982.

Chase, Richard B., and Nicholas J. Aquilano. *Production and Operations Management: A Life Cycle Approach,* 3d ed., Homewood, Ill.: Richard D. Irwin, 1981.

Chase, Richard B. "Strategic Considerations in Assembly-Line Selection." *California Management Review,* Fall 1975, pp. 17–23.

Cooper, M. R., et al. "Changing Employee Values: Deepening Discontent?" *Harvard Business Review,* January–February 1979, pp. 117–25.

Cummings, T. G. "Self-Regulating Work Group: A Socio-Technical Synthesis." *Academy of Management Review,* July 1978, pp. 625–34.

Ebert, R. J., and E. E. Adam, Jr. "Behavioral Dimensions of Facility Location Planning." *Business Horizons,* December 1977, pp. 35–42.

Hackman, J. R., et al. "A New Strategy for Job Enrichment." *California Management Review,* Summer 1975, pp. 57–71.

Schmenner, R. W. "Look Beyond the Obvious in Plant Location." *Harvard Business Review,* January–February 1979, pp. 126–32.

Van Der Zwaan, A. H. "The Sociotechnical Systems Approach: A Critical Evaluation." *International Journal of Production Research* 13, no. 2 (1975), pp. 149–63.

Vollman, Thomas E., and Elwood S. Buffa. "The Facilities Layout Problem in Perspective." *Management Science,* June 1966, pp. 345–68.

Case 19–1

A new building for Tot-Two

The Tot-Two Company manufactures clothes for children up to age five. Tot-Two has been growing rapidly for the past several years and is planning to build a new plant in a recently developed industrial park on the north side of town. Charles "Chubby" Shaver, the plant's operations manager, has been assigned the task of drawing up a new physical layout subject to the constraints that the new building cannot exceed 7,000 square feet including office space, and that it must be a perfect rectangle in order to minimize the construction costs. Chubby developed the following list of departments with their respective approximate space requirements:

Shipping (400 square feet)—area for shipping all finished goods.

Receiving (400 square feet)—area for receiving all materials and supplies.

Materials supply room (200 square feet)—storage area for all incoming materials.

Spreading and cutting area (1,600 square feet)—area containing three 40-foot tables for spreading and then cutting the cloth. Many layers of cloth are spread on top of each other and cut at the same time with large portable cutters.

Pattern making area (200 square feet)—area in which patterns are made.

Assembly area (1,200 square feet)—area for sewing together the various clothing parts.

Packing area (400 square feet)—area for packing the finished goods into boxes for shipping.

Finished goods storage (500 square feet)—area for storing finished goods prior to shipping.

Design area (200 square feet)—area occupied by designers.

Office space (800 square feet)—space for secretaries and company officers.

Wash facilities (300 square feet)—area containing men and women's bathrooms.

Lunch/break area (400 square feet)—area with vending machines and lunch tables.

Chubby then drew up an initial layout as illustrated in Exhibit 1.

EXHIBIT 1

Designers (200 sq. ft.)	Office (800 sq. ft.)	Assembly (1,200 sq. ft.)
Lunch/break (400 sq. ft.)		
	Packing (400 sq. ft.)	
Wash facilities (300 sq. ft.)	Finished goods storage (500 sq. ft.)	Spreading and cutting (1,600 sq. ft.)
Shipping (400 sq. ft.)		
Pattern making (200 sq. ft.)	Material supply (300 sq. ft.) / Receiving (400 sq. ft.)	

1. What are the strong points of Chubby's layout? What are the weak points?
2. Redesign the layout based on your answers to Question 1.

Case 19–2

Allocation of office and work space

The Burr Corporation has an office which audits its various divisions and offices throughout the northwestern United States. The Audit Office occupies one entire floor of a relatively small building in a large centrally located city in the Northwest. Much of the audit work is done outside of the city in which the Audit Office is located. When the auditors are on travel status, they are provided office and working space by the divisions and offices being audited.

The Audit Office is run by a director who has four deputy directors. Additionally, the Audit Office has 16 audit managers assigned about equally under the deputy directors. Audit staffs are assigned to the audit managers from a pool of about 125 auditors. Naturally, the job supervisors who work under the audit managers have usually spent a number of years with the office; the other staff members are relatively new.

The floor of the building where the office is located is in a rectangular shape. The director's office is toward the center, with an open entrance hall leading into it. A receptionist and two secretaries are positioned at desks in the open space leading to the director's office. Two of the secretaries do work for one of the deputy directors whose office is positioned directly across from the director's office. In addition to being responsible for directing about 25 percent of the audits, this deputy director is responsible for making audit assignments. The other three deputy directors are assigned to three larger offices in three of the corners of the floor.

In addition to the offices of the deputy directors, there are 22 other sizeable offices around the perimeter of the floor. Nineteen of the offices are occupied by the 16 audit managers, a training coordinator, a recruiter, and a computer specialist. The remaining three offices around the perimeter of the office are left for use by audit teams.

The inner portion of the floor is partitioned into 18 small cubicles, a conference room, a mail and file room, and a library. Therefore there are only the 18 cubicles and the three team rooms for the audit staffs to use when they are working in the office. These spaces are available to the auditors on a first-come, first-served basis, without regard to whether the auditor is a first-year employee or a ten-year supervisor. At times the number of auditors overflows into the library and other areas. Another drawback is that the auditors sometimes lose productive time looking for an unoccupied cubicle.

There have been complaints from the auditors about the situation. Some of the job supervisors also consider it degrading that after many years with the office they do not have even a desk in the office for permanent use.

The director has recognized that space is a problem but has said that the office would have to do the best with what it has. For one thing, there was still a short-term lease on the building.

1. What impact could the described situation have on the morale of the audit staff and the performance of audits?
2. How should the director handle the situation? Has everything been done to help the situation, or are there any other options?

20 Planning and Controlling Operations

Objectives

1. To emphasize the importance of properly implementing and controlling operating systems.
2. To apply the control concepts and principles learned in Chapter 6 to operating systems.
3. To introduce and discuss production control, inventory control, and quality control.

Chapter Outline

Glossary of Terms

ABC classification system A method of managing inventories based on their values.

Acceptance sampling A statistical method of predicting the quality of a batch or large group of products from the inspection of a sample or group of samples.

Activity scheduling Develops the precise timetable to be followed in producing a product or service.

Aggregate production planning A process of determining work force requirements, production rates, and inventory levels over a specified time period for the entire operating system.

Economic order quantity (EOQ) The optimum number of units to order at one time.

Inventory A quantity of raw materials, in-process goods, or finished goods on hand.

Process control chart A time-based graphic display which shows whether a machine or process is producing items that meet certain preestablished specifications.

Production planning and control A form of planning and control concerned primarily with aggregate production planning, resource allocation, and activity scheduling.

Quality circle A group of employees (who are members of the same work unit) that meets on a regular basis to discuss quality problems and generate ideas for improving quality.

Quality control A process of ensuring or maintaining a certain level of quality with regard to materials, products, or services.

Resource allocation Refers to the efficient allocation of people, materials, and equipment in order to meet the demand requirements of the operating system.

Safety stocks Inventory stocks maintained for the purpose of accommodating unexpected changes in demand and supply and to allow for delivery time.

While the achievement of a steady state level of system performance implies that design and startup problems have been solved, it does not mean that the pressure is off the production manager. Regardless of how careful the planning, few systems of any complexity can be expected to operate indefinitely without encountering some type of malfunction that must be corrected. This is true not only for the physical production process but for the production management system that monitors that process as well. Indeed, while machinery may produce scrap or break down, thus necessitating repairs, the operating and control system that governs the use of the machinery may provide faulty information and incorrect decisions, requiring that it, too, be overhauled.

*Richard B. Chase and Nicholas J. Aquilano**

Product design, physical layout, and other design-related topics were discussed in Chapter 19. Unfortunately, designing an effective operating system does not in itself ensure that the system will operate efficiently. As indicated in the introductory quote, after the system has been designed, the day-to-day operations must be properly planned and controlled. The products or services must be guided and scheduled through the system, the system processes must be monitored, quality must be maintained, inventories must be managed, and all of this must be accomplished within cost constraints.

Effective operations planning and control are attained by applying the planning and control concepts discussed in Chapters 4, 5, and 6 to the operations function of the organization, and can be a substitute for resources. For example, good inventory control can reduce the investment cost in inventories. Similarly, good quality control can reduce scrap and wasted materials, thus reducing costs.

PRODUCTION PLANNING AND CONTROL

Production planning and control is a form of planning and control that is concerned with aggregate production planning, resource allocation, and activity scheduling. The overriding purpose of production planning and control is to maintain a smooth, constant flow of work from start to finish, so that the product or service will be completed in the desired time at the lowest possi-

* Richard B. Chase and Nicholas J. Aquilano, *Production and Operations Management: A Life Cycle Approach,* rev. ed. (Homewood, Ill.: Richard D. Irwin, 1977), p. 579. Copyright © 1977 by Richard D. Irwin, Inc.

ble cost. Aggregate production planning is a broad level of planning which determines the general personnel requirements, production rates, and inventory levels over a specified time period for the entire operating system. Detailed routing and scheduling through the production facility are undertaken after the production rates have been determined by the aggregate plan.

Aggregate Production Planning

Aggregate production planning is concerned with the overall operations and with balancing the major segments of the operating system. The primary objective of aggregate production planning is to match the organization's resources with the demands for its goods or services. Specifically, the aggregate production plan should determine the production rates which satisfy demand requirements while minimizing the costs of work force and inventory fluctuations. Aggregate production plans generally span from 6 to 18 months into the future.

The first step in developing an aggregate production plan is to obtain a demand forecast for the organization's goods or services. The second step involves evaluating the impact of the demand forecasts on the organization's resources. The final step in the process is to develop the best plan for using the organization's current and expected resources for meeting the forecasted demand. The aggregate production plan results in the determination of production rates, work force requirements, and inventory levels for the entire operating system over a specified time period.

Resource Allocation

Resource allocation refers to the efficient allocation of people, materials, and equipment in order to meet the demand requirements of the operating system. Resource allocation is the natural outgrowth of the aggregate production plan. The precise materials needed must be determined and ordered; the work must be distributed to the different departments and work stations; personnel must be allocated; and time allotments must be established for each stage of the process.

As a result of resource scarcities the resource allocation process has become increasingly critical in recent times. Materials, personnel, machines and equipment, and utilities are all in short supply compared to earlier times. Increased competition, from both domestic and foreign sources, has also contributed to the importance of resource allocation. Proper resource allocation can result in significant cost savings which can provide the needed competitive edge.

Numerous tools and techniques can be used to assist in resource allocation. Linear programming, critical path method (CPM), and program evaluation and review technique (PERT) are some of the most frequently used resource allocation techniques.

Activity Scheduling

Scheduling develops the precise timetable to be followed in producing the product or service. Scheduling also includes the dispatching of work orders and the expediting of critical and late orders. Scheduling does not involve determining how long a job will take (which is part of job design), but rather determining when the work is to be performed. The process of scheduling is the link between system design and operations planning and control. Once the initial schedule has been established, the system is ready for operation. Of course, scheduling is a continuous activity in the life of an operating system.

A detailed scheduling system cannot be designed without knowledge of the respective operating system for which it is being designed. Scheduling for intermittent systems is very complex because of the relatively large number of individual orders or customers which must flow through the system. Numerous types of scheduling tools—such as the Gantt chart, which was discussed in Chapter 6, have been developed to help the scheduler visualize and simplify the intermittent scheduling problem.

Scheduling for high-volume continuous flow systems generally involves a process of balancing the available resources to match the production rate requirements as outlined by the aggregate plan. Computer simulation has been used successfully to assist in the scheduling of continuous-flow systems by estimating the overall system impact of different scheduling decisions.

INVENTORY CONTROL

Inventories serve as a buffer between different rates of flow associated with the operating system. Inventories can generally be classified into one of three categories depending on their respective location within the operating system: raw material, in-process, or finished goods. Raw material inventories serve as a buffer between purchasing and production. In-process inventories are used to buffer differences in the rates of flow through the various production processes. Finished goods inventories act as a buffer between the final stage of production and shipping. Figure 20–1 illustrates these relationships.

Inventories add flexibility to the operating system and allow the organization to do the following:

1. Purchase, produce, and ship in economic batch sizes rather than in small jobs.

FIGURE 20–1
Inventories as Buffers between Different Rates of Flow

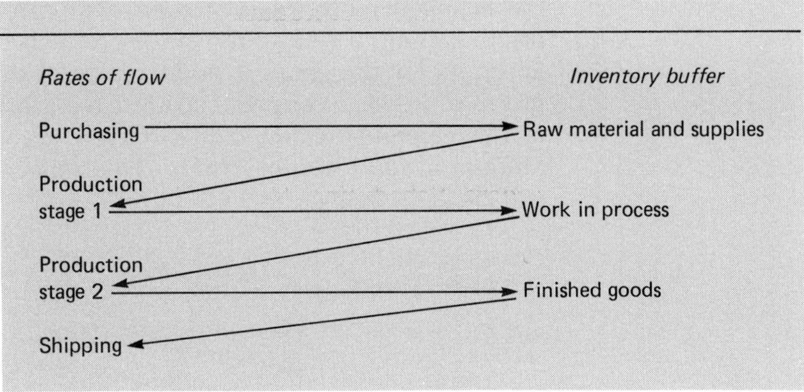

2. Produce on a smooth, continuous basis even though the demand for the finished product or raw material may fluctuate.
3. Prevent major problems when forecasts of demand are in error or when there are unforeseen slowdowns or stoppages in supply or production.

When making inventory decisions, management must answer three basic questions: (1) what items to carry in inventory; (2) how many of the selected items to order and carry; and (3) when to order the items.

If it were not costly, every organization would attempt to maintain very large inventories in order to facilitate purchasing, production scheduling, and distribution. However, inventories often represent a sizeable investment. It is not uncommon for a manufacturing concern to have 25 percent of its total invested capital tied up in inventories.[1]

Potential inventory costs include such factors as insurance on the inventory, inventory or property taxes, storage costs, obsolescence costs, spoilage, and the opportunity cost of the money invested in the inventory. The relative importance of these costs depends on the specific inventory being held. For example, when dealing with women's fashions, the obsolescence costs are potentially very high. Similarly, the storage costs might be very high for dangerous chemicals. Thus, when dealing with inventory decisions, management must continually balance the costs of holding the inventory against the costs of running short of raw materials, in-process goods, or finished goods.

[1] Elwood S. Buffa, *Modern Production Management,* 5th ed. (New York: John Wiley & Sons, 1977), p. 372.

ABC Classification System

One of the simplest and most widely used systems for managing inventories is the ABC system. The ABC approach is a method of managing inventories in accordance with their value. In many organizations, a small number of products or materials, Group A, accounts for the greatest dollar value of the inventory. The next group of items, Group B, accounts for a relatively small amount of the inventory value; and Group C accounts for a very small amount of the inventory value. This concept is illustrated in Figure 20–2.

FIGURE 20–2
ABC Classification System

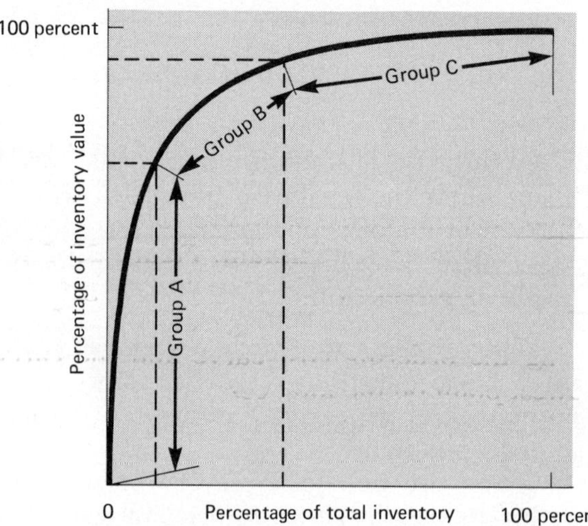

Source: James H. Greene, *Production Control Systems and Decisions* (Homewood, Ill.: Richard D. Irwin, 1965), p. 204. Copyright © 1965 by Richard D. Irwin, Inc.

The purpose of classifying items into these groups is to establish appropriate control over each item. Generally, the items in Group A are monitored very closely; the items in Group B, are monitored with some care; while the items in Group C are only checked occasionally. Items in Group C are usually not subject to the detailed paperwork of items in Groups A and B.

One potential shortcoming of the ABC method is that although the items in Group C might have very little cost value, they may be critical to the operation. It is possible, for instance for a very inexpensive bolt to be vital to the production of a costly piece of machinery. This shortcoming does not make the ABC method unuseable, but it points out the necessity to exercise some minimum control over all items, especially those critical to the operation.

The Order Quantity

After management has decided what items are to be carried in inventory, a decision must be made concerning how much of each item to order. Most materials and finished products are consumed one-by-one or a few units at a time; however, because of the costs associated with ordering, shipping, and handling inventory, it is usually desirable to purchase materials and products in large lots or batches.

When determining the optimum number of units to order, the ordering costs must be balanced against the cost of carrying the inventory. Ordering costs include such things as the cost of preparing the order, shipping costs, and setup costs. Carrying costs include storage costs, insurance, taxes, obsolescence, and the opportunity costs of the money invested in the inventory. The smaller the number of units ordered, the lower the carrying costs (because the average inventory held is smaller) but the larger the ordering costs (because more orders must be placed). The optimum number of units to order, referred to as the economic order quantity (EOQ), is determined by the point where ordering costs equal carrying costs, or where total cost (ordering costs + carrying costs) is at a minimum. Figure 20–3 graphically shows the inverse relationship between ordering costs and carrying costs. The total cost curve in Figure 20–3 is found by vertically summing the ordering cost curve and the carrying cost curve. The lowest point on the total cost curve corresponds to the point where ordering costs equal carrying costs and determines the economic order quantity.

FIGURE 20–3
Inventory Costs versus Order Size

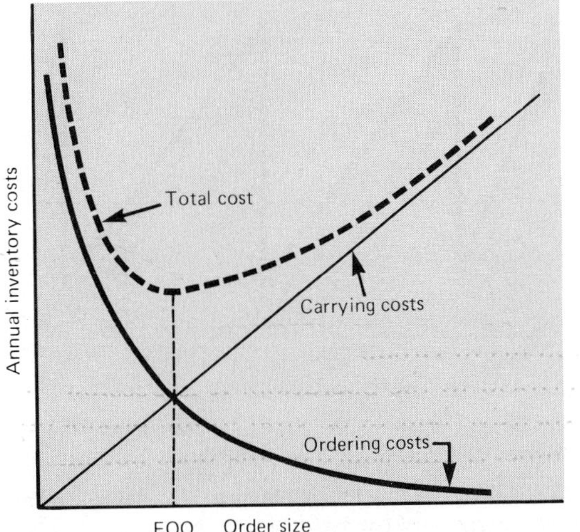

The greatest weakness of the economic order quantity approach is the difficulty in accurately determining the actual carrying and ordering costs. However, research has shown that the total costs associated with order sizes that are reasonably close to the economic order quantity do not differ appreciably from the minimum total costs associated with the EOQ.[2] Thus, as long as the estimated carrying and ordering costs are "in the ball park," meaningful results can be obtained using this approach. Variations of this basic model have been developed for taking into account such things as purchase quantity and other special discounts.

Based on the relationships depicted in Figure 20–3, mathematical formulas have been developed for determining the economic order quantity. Appendix D (at the end of the text) discusses these formulas.

Reorder Point and Safety Stock

The operations manager needs to know not only how much to order, but also when to order. There are two basic methods for determining when to order: the fixed-order quantity method and the fixed-order period method. Under the fixed-order quantity method, which is illustrated in Figure 20–4, orders are placed whenever the inventory reaches a certain predetermined level, regardless of how long it takes to reach that level. With regard to Figure 20–4, orders would be placed at times T_1, T_2, T_3, and T_4

FIGURE 20–4
Fixed-Order Quantity Method of Reordering

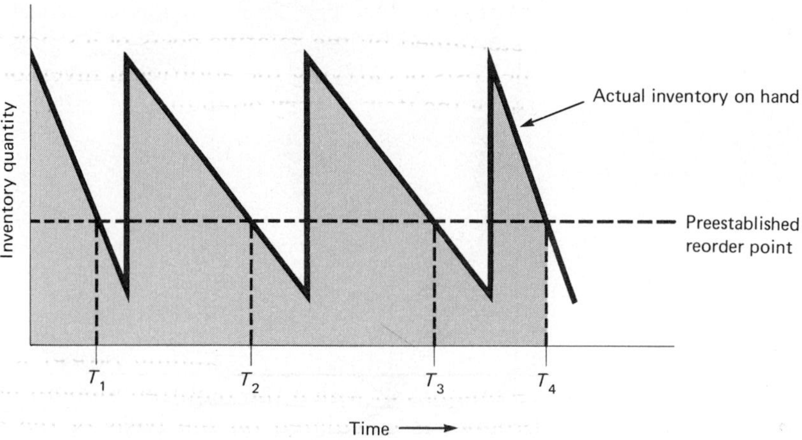

[2] For example, see John F. Magee, "Guides to Inventory Policy: I. Functions and Lot Size," *Harvard Business Review,* January–February 1956, pp. 49–60.

FIGURE 20–5
Fixed-Order Period Method of Reordering

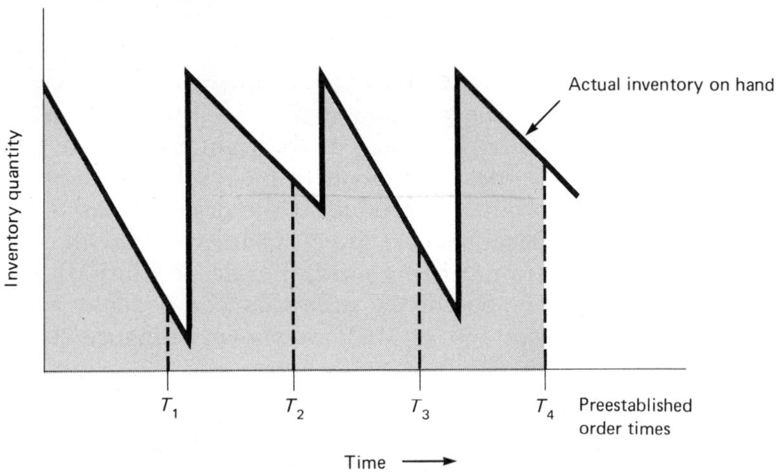

under the fixed-order quantity method. Thus the time between orders can vary depending on the demand. Under the fixed-order period illustrated in Figure 20–5, orders are placed for replenishment at predetermined regular time intervals regardless of how much inventory is on hand. With this method, the amount ordered rather than the time between orders can vary depending on the demand.

Most organizations maintain safety stocks for purposes of accommodating unexpected changes in demand and supply and allowing for delivery time. The optimum size of the safety stock is determined by the relative costs of a stock-out of the item versus the costs of carrying the additional inventory. The cost of a stock-out of the item is very often difficult to estimate. For example, the customer may go elsewhere rather than wait for the product. If the product is available at another branch location, the stock-out cost may be simply the cost of shipping the item from one location to another.

Material Requirements Planning (MRP)

Material requirements planning (MRP) is a system or a set of techniques in which the required amount of each component of a product is calculated on the basis of the amount of the parent product that is to be produced. When each component is needed is determined by the time at which the parent assembly is needed and the lead time at which the component should be incorporated into the assembly.[3] In one sense MRP is so inseparably related to production scheduling that it might seem more logical to treat it as a scheduling technique. However, MRP so drastically affects raw material inventories in manufacturing that it is usually considered as an integral part of inventory planning.[4]

The philosophy behind MRP is to get the right materials to the right places at the right time. MRP is based on the fact that it does little good to have some of the components necessary to produce a product if the organization does not have all of them. Because there are costs associated with carrying components that are not being used, the idea behind MRP is to provide either all or none of the necessary components. Some of the potential advantages of MRP are shown in Figure 20–6.

FIGURE 20–6
Potential Advantages of Material Requirements Planning

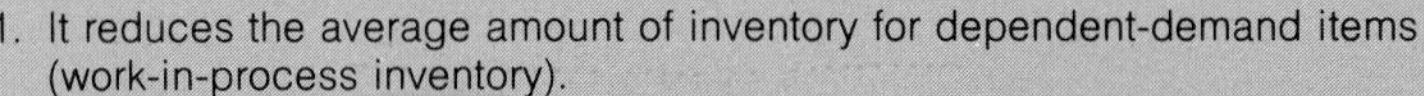

1. It reduces the average amount of inventory for dependent-demand items (work-in-process inventory).
2. It improves work flow, resulting in reduced elapsed time between the start and finish of jobs.
3. It enables delivery promises to be more reliable.
4. It minimizes parts shortages.
5. It keeps priorities of work items up to date so that shopwork is more effective and appropriate.
6. It helps plan the timing of design changes and aids in their implementation.
7. It can simulate and evaluate changes in the master schedule.
8. It tells management ahead of time if desired delivery dates appear achievable.
9. It changes (expedites or deexpedites) due dates for orders.
10. It facilitates capacity requirements planning.

Source: James B. Dilworth, *Production and Operations Management* (New York: Random House, 1979), pp. 189–90.

While not an absolute requirement, almost all MRP utilizes a computer. This is not because there are complex equations to solve, but because of the computer's ability to store and rapidly manipulate large amounts of data.[5] As the number of items in the system begins to increase, it becomes necessary to utilize a computer. Naturally, many versions of MRP programs are available.

---

[3] James B. Dilworth, *Production and Operations Management* (New York: Random House, 1979), p. 188.

[4] Norman Gaither, *Production and Operations Management* (Hinsdale, Il. Dryden Press, 1980), p. 532.

[5] Dilworth, *Production and Operations*, p. 189.

Most MRP programs require three inputs: a master production schedule; a bill-of-materials file; and an inventory records file. The master production schedule specifies the types and quantities of all end items to be produced during the planning horizon. The master production schedule is determined by the aggregate production planning process and accepted as given in MRP. A bill of materials file is a complete list of all finished products to be produced, the quantities of materials required in each product, and the structure (assemblies, subassemblies, parts, and raw materials and their relationships) of products.[6] The inventory status file contains records of the inventory on hand, materials on order, customer orders for each item, lot sizes, lead times, safety stock levels, scrap rates, and so forth.

Once the inputs are provided, the MRP program breaks down the end items stipulated by the master production schedule into the raw materials, parts, subassemblies, and assemblies required for each time period. The net material requirements are calculated after considering the materials available. Three primary outputs result from MRP:[7]

1. Planned order schedules: a plan showing the quantity of each material to be ordered in each time period.
2. Order releases: authorizations to produce the materials identified in the planned order schedules.
3. Changes to planned orders: modifications of previous planned orders.

Other, optional outputs are also possible from most MRP programs. It should be noted that an MRP system is not designed to be used occasionally but rather on a regular basis.

QUALITY CONTROL

Quality is a relative term that means different things to different people. The consumer who demands quality may be talking about a completely different concept than the operations manager who demands quality. The consumer is concerned with service, reliability, performance, appearance, and so forth. The operations manager's primary concern is that the product or service specifications be achieved, whatever they may be. For the operations manager quality is determined in relation to the specifications or standards set in the design stages. Figure 20–7 lists some specific reasons for maintaining quality control.

---

[6] Gaither, *Production and Operations,* p. 536.
[7] Ibid., p. 538.

FIGURE 20–7
Reasons for Maintaining Quality Control

1. Maintain certain standards (such as with interchangeable replacement parts).
2. Meet customer specifications.
3. Meet legal requirements.
4. Find defective products which can be reworked.
5. Find problems in the production process.
6. To grade products (such as lumber or eggs).
7. To provide performance information on individual workers and departments.

When determining the most desirable level of quality, management must attempt to balance the marketability of higher levels of quality versus the cost of attaining this higher quality. Figure 20–8 graphically depicts the general relationship between these factors. As shown in the graph, total revenue is a function of quality. Consumers may not be willing to pay for extremely high levels of quality. A housewife may desire a mixer that has three to five variable speeds and is dependable for five to ten years; however, the same housewife is probably not willing to invest substantially more money to obtain a 20-speed, lifetime guaranteed mixer. The shape of the total cost curve shows that the cost of quality generally is increasing at an increasing rate. Point Q where profit is at a maximum, is the most desirable level of quality.

FIGURE 20–8
Quality versus Cost

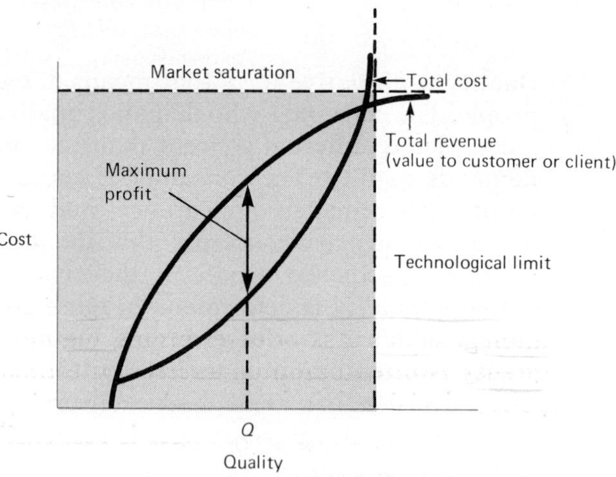

MANAGEMENT IN PRACTICE

The Jaguar Roars Back on Track

It was sleek and expensive, but for years the Jaguar suffered from a reputation for unreliability—a reputation it deserved. "The cars were constantly breaking down," admits Dub Cornelius, sales manager for a Jaguar dealership in Dallas, Texas. "You had to be either a Jaguar devotee or a masochist to buy one." Now there is nothing shoddy about the car, and the company is making a comeback. "I used to receive death threats from my customers," says one New York dealer. "Now I get thanks."

The turnabout came just in time. Jaguar's parent, BL, Ltd., has stopped production of the MG sports car and other models in an attempt to stem mounting losses. Two years ago, BL's chairman appointed a new boss for Jaguar, John Egan, and told him to fix up the company or shut it down. Egan targeted the U.S. market for expansion. In 1980 the company shipped fewer than 3,000 cars across the Atlantic; this year it expects to sell 9,500 in the United States—even though the Jag carries a hefty sticker price of $30,000.

Warranty

The sales boom is the payoff for Jaguar's huge investment aimed at making a better automobile. To upgrade the car's reputation, Egan created quality-control groups modeled after those on Japanese assembly lines. He also induced suppliers to deliver better component parts—and, Egan explains, made them pay not only the cost of the bad products but the cost of lost labor time as well. To cut back overhead, Egan sheared the payroll of about 10,500 employees in 1980 to 6,900, though he recently rehired some of them to cope with the upsurge in orders. Workers were also put on a bonus system, and as a result, Egan claims that over-all productivity has increased by 100 percent.

To call attention to Jaguar's new quality, the company underwrote a widely publicized 36,000-mile warranty on all cars sold in the United States. The strategy has worked. Jaguar's sales have remained steady among its traditional, affluent American clientele, as they have in Britain, where 90 percent of sales are still to companies that buy the car as a perk for top executives. But Jaguar has also begun to appeal to a new class of buyer in the sports-car market. The company made news in Britain recently when that militant man of the people—Arthur Scargill, the left-wing leader of the miners' union—traded in his Rover for a posh new Jaguar.

While the costs represented in Figure 20–8 are very real costs, management's task of determining the most appropriate level of quality is often based on guesses or estimates. However, once a policy decision has been made concerning the desired level of quality, the operations manager is responsible to ensure that the stated level of quality is achieved.

Quality Checkpoints

If the desired level of quality is to be attained in the final product or service, checks or inspections may be required at several different points in the operating system. Figure 20–9 shows some of the more frequent inspection points in an operating system. The first inspection point is when the raw materials are received. The quality of the raw materials must be compatible with the quality desired in the final product. The incoming materials should be checked for quality, quantity, and possible damage.

Depending on the operation to be performed, it may be desirable to inspect the materials again before they enter the operation. This is especially likely if the operation is costly or irreversible (such as with silverplating).

Other checkpoints may take place prior to operations which

FIGURE 20–9
Potential Quality Control Checkpoints

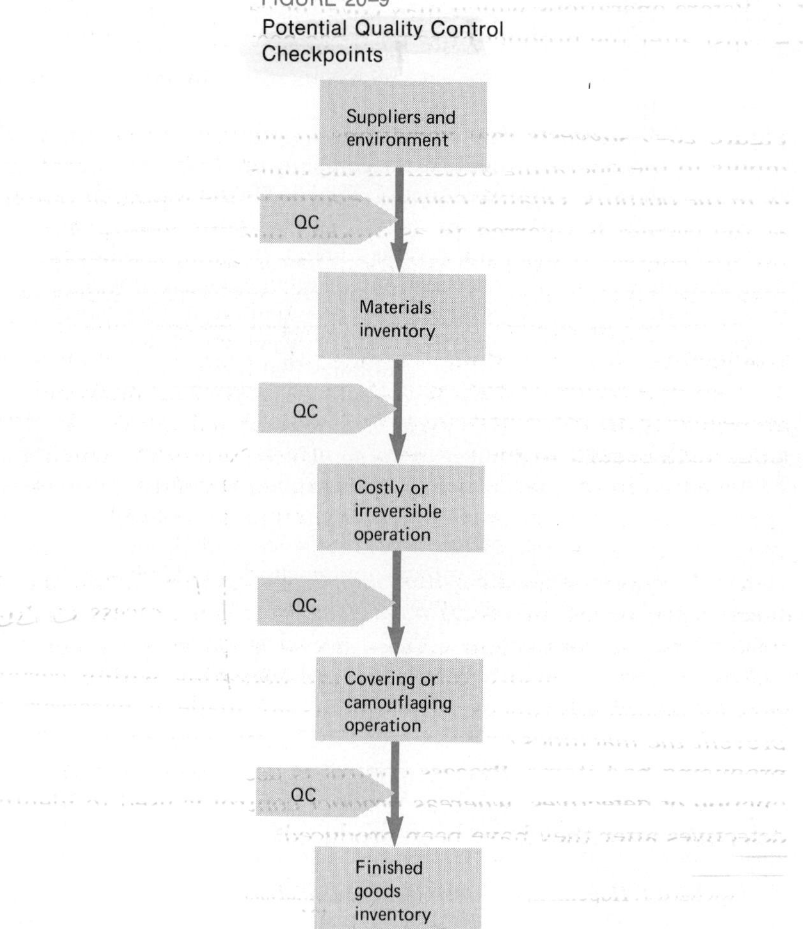

cover or camouflage defects in the process. For example, painting may temporarily camouflage a flaw which resulted from an earlier operation.

A final inspection should take place before the product or service is distributed to the customer. This provides a check on the end product or service. It should be stressed that the optimum location and number of checkpoints depend on two separate costs: inspection cost and the cost of passing a defective. As the number of inspection locations increase, so do the inspection costs; however, the probability of passing on a defect decreases.

In summary, quality checks might appropriately be performed at the following points in the operating system:

1. When the raw materials are received.
2. Before costly or irreversible operations.
3. Before operations which may cover or camouflage defects.
4. Just after the product or service has been completed.[8]

quality check points

Types of Quality Control

Product Quality Control

Figure 20–9 suggests that variations in quality can occur in the inputs to the operating system, in the transformation operations, or in the outputs. Quality control relating to the inputs or outputs of the system is referred to as product quality control. Product quality control is used when the quality is being evaluated with respect to a batch of products or services that already exists, such as incoming raw materials or finished goods. Product quality control lends itself to acceptance sampling procedures in which some portion of a batch of outgoing items (or incoming materials) is inspected in an attempt to ensure that the batch meets specifications with regard to the percentage of defective units which will be tolerated in the batch. Under acceptance sampling procedures, the decision to accept or reject an entire batch is based on a sample or group of samples.

Process (Quality) Control

Quality control relating to the control of a machine or an operation during the production process is called process control. Under process control, machines and/or processes are periodically checked to ensure that they are operating within certain preestablished tolerances. Adjustments are made as necessary to prevent the machines or processes from getting out of control and producing bad items. Process control is used to prevent the production of defectives, whereas product control is used to identify defectives after they have been produced.

[8] Richard J. Hopeman, *Production Concepts Analysis Control,* 2d ed. (Columbus, Ohio: Charles E. Merrill Publishing, 1971), p. 481.

Acceptance Sampling

As defined in the previous section, acceptance sampling is a method of predicting the quality of a batch or large group of products from an inspection of a sample or group of samples taken from the batch. Acceptance sampling is used for one of three basic reasons: (1) the possible losses or costs of passing defective items are not great relative to the cost of inspection (it would not be wise to inspect every match produced by a match factory); (2) inspection of some items requires destruction of the product being tested (as is the case when testing flash bulbs); and (3) sampling usually produces results more rapidly than does a census.

The procedure followed in acceptance sampling is to draw a random sample, of a given size, from the batch or lot being examined. The sample is then tested and analyzed. If more than a certain number (determined statistically) are found defective, the entire batch is rejected as having an unacceptably large percentage of defective items. Because of the possibility of making an incorrect inference concerning the batch, acceptance sampling always involves risks. The risk that the producer is willing to take of rejecting a good batch is referred to as the producer's risk. The risk of accepting a bad batch is referred to as the consumer's risk. Obviously, one would desire to minimize both the producer's risk and the consumer's risk. However, the only method of simultaneously lowering both of these risks is to increase the sample size—which also increases the inspection costs. Therefore, the approach which is usually taken is to decide the maximum acceptable risk for both the producer and the consumer and to design the acceptance sampling plan around these risks.

Process Control Charts

Mean & Range (most common)

A control chart is a time-based graphic display which shows whether a machine or process is producing items that meet certain preestablished specifications. If the machine or process is producing items that do not meet specifications, then the machine or process is said to be out of control. Control charts do not attempt to show why a machine or process is out of control, only if it is out of control.

The most frequently used process control charts are called mean and range charts. Mean charts (also called $\overline{X}$-charts) monitor the mean or average value of some characteristic (dimension, weight, etc.) of the items produced by a machine or process. Range charts (also called R-charts) monitor the range of variability of some characteristic (dimension, weight, etc.) of the items produced by a machine or process.

The quality control inspector, using control charts, first calculates the desired level of the characteristic being measured. The next step is to calculate statistically the upper and lower control limits which determine how much the characteristic can vary from the desired level before the machine or process is considered to be out of control. Once the control chart has been set up, the quality control inspector periodically takes a small sample from the machine or process outputs. Depending on the type of chart being used, the mean or range of the sample is plotted on the control chart. By plotting the results of each sample on the control chart it is easy to identify quickly any abnormal trends in quality. A sample mean chart is shown in Figure 20–10.

FIGURE 20–10
Mean Chart

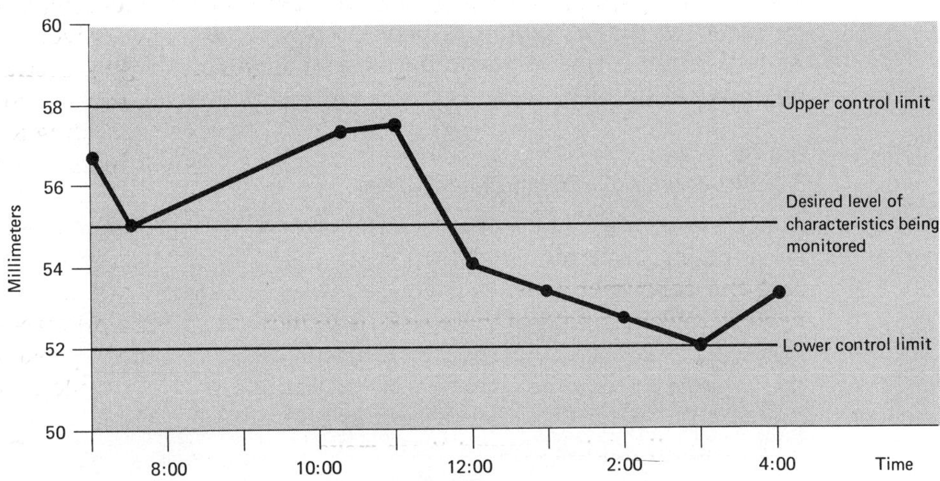

A mean or range chart used by itself can easily lead to false conclusions. For example, the upper and lower control limits for a machined part might be 0.1000 mm and 0.0800 mm respectively. A sample of four parts of 0.1200, 0.1100, 0.0700, and 0.0600 would yield an acceptable mean of 0.0900; yet every element of the sample is out of tolerance. For this reason, when monitoring variables, it is usually desirable to use mean and range charts simultaneously to ensure that a machine or process is under control.

Quality Circles

The relatively new idea of quality circles was originated in Japan. A quality circle is composed of a group of employees (usually from 5 to 15 people) who are members of a single work unit, section, or department. The units' supervisor or manager is usually included as a member of the quality circle. These employees have a common bond in performing a similar service or function by turning out a product, part of a product, or a service. Membership in a quality circle is almost always voluntary. The basic purpose of a quality circle is to discuss quality problems and to generate ideas that might help improve quality.

A quality circle usually begins by exposing the members to specialized training relating to quality. Meetings of a quality circle are normally held once or twice per month and last for one to two hours. After the initial training, a quality circle begins by discussing specific quality problems which are brought up by either management representatives or by the circle members. Staff experts may be called upon by the circle as needed. Figure 20–11 outlines the major, potential benefits of a quality control circle. As with other forms of participative management, the underlying objective of quality circles is to get employees actively involved.

FIGURE 20–11
Potential Benefits of a Quality Control Circle

1. Problems—including some that have existed for years—do get solved.
2. Employees get to participate in changing things for the better.
3. Employees and managers broaden and develop as they receive special training and put it into practice.
4. Morale improves and is maintained as people become involved in helping to improve their work life and fulfill their potential.
5. The channel for upward and downward communication is strengthened.
6. Greater trust is built between levels in the organization and among units.
7. Managers are relieved of many worries and concerns without having any of their authority diluted or releasing control.

Source: Adapted from Rich Tewell, "How to Keep Quality Circles in Motion," *Business*, January–March 1982, pp. 48–49.

SUMMARY

If an operating system is to be effective, its day-to-day operations must be properly planned and controlled. Products or services must be scheduled through the system; the system processes must be monitored; quality must be maintained; inventories must be managed; and all of this must be accomplished within cost constraints.

The purpose of production planning and control is to maintain a smooth, constant flow of work from start to finish, so that the product or service will be completed in the desired time at the lowest possible cost. Aggregate production planning, resource allocation, and activity scheduling are all part of production control. Aggregate production planning is a process of determining work force requirements, production rates, and inventory levels over a specified time period (usually 12 months or less) for the entire operating system.

Inventories can generally be classified as raw materials inventories, in-process inventories, and finished goods inventories. Raw materials inventories serve as a buffer between purchasing and production. In-process inventories are used to buffer differences in the rates of flow through the various production processes. Finished goods inventories act as a buffer between the final stage of production and shipping.

When making inventory decisions, management must answer three basic questions: (1) what items to carry in inventory; (2) how many of the selected items to order and carry; and (3) when to order the items.

The ABC classification system is a simple method for managing inventories in accordance with their value.

The economic order quantity is one method for determining the optimum order size by finding the lot size that minimizes the total ordering and carrying costs of the inventory. The fixed-order quantity and the fixed-order period are the two most common methods for determining the reorder point.

Material requirements planning (MRP) is a system in which the required amount of each component of a product is calculated based on the amount of the parent product that is to be produced. When each component is needed is determined by the time at which the parent assembly is needed and the lead time necessary to incorporate the component.

Quality is defined for the operations manager by the product or service specifications. When determining the most appropriate level of quality, management must balance the marketability of higher quality against the cost of attaining the higher quality. Generally a minimum level of quality is necessary before the product or service can be sold. There is also usually a point of quality beyond which consumers are unwilling to pay.

Quality checks are appropriately performed at several points in the operating system. These points include when the raw materials are received; before costly or irreversible operations are performed; before operations which may cover or camouflage defects; and after the product or service has been completed.

Quality control relating to existing products or services (including raw materials) is referred to as product quality control. Quality control relating to the control of a machine or an operation during the production process is called process control.

A quality circle is a group of employees that meets on a regular basis to discuss quality problems and to generate ideas for improving quality.

REVIEW QUESTIONS

1. What is production planning and control?
2. Define aggregate production planning.
3. What is the difference between resource allocation and activity scheduling?
4. What are inventories?
5. How does the ABC classification system work?
6. What costs affect the economic order quantity?
7. What is the purpose of carrying safety stock?
8. Describe the basic philosophy behind MRP.
9. What are the three primary inputs required by MRP?
10. Define quality.
11. List five possible reasons for quality control.
12. At what points in an operating system might quality checks be appropriately performed?
13. What is a process control chart?

DISCUSSION QUESTIONS

1. Discuss the production control problems that arise when demand is continually changing.
2. Since the cost of a stock-out of an inventory item is usually very difficult to estimate, how can the safety stock level be determined with any accuracy?
3. To what degree do you think the need for a computer restricts the applicability of MRP?
4. Since quality is a relative concept, how does a manager ever know if the quality level is optimum?

SELECTED READINGS

Blank, Lee, and Joyce Solorozano. "Using Quality Cost Analysis for Management Improvement." *Industrial Engineering,* February 1978, pp. 46–51.

Buffa, Elwood S. "Aggregate Planning for Production." *Business Horizons,* Fall 1967, pp. 87–97.

Buffa, Elwood S., and Jeffrey G. Miller. *Production—Inventory Systems: Planning and Control,* 3d ed. Homewood, Ill.: Richard D. Irwin, 1979.

Chardran, Ryan, and Robert Linnerian. "Planning to Minimize Product Liability." *Sloan Management Review,* Fall 1978, pp. 33–45.

Greene, James H. *Production and Inventory Control: Systems and Decisions,* rev. ed. Homewood, Ill.: Richard D. Irwin, 1974.

Hall, Robert W., and Thomas E. Vollmann. "Planning Your Material Requirements." *Harvard Business Review,* September–October, 1978, pp. 105–12.

Ling, Tony, "MRP: The Next Revolution in Manufacturing Management." *Plant Management and Engineering,* April 1981, pp. 22–25.

Orlicky, Joseph. *Material Requirements Planning.* New York: McGraw-Hill, 1975.

Vinson, William D., and Donald F. Heany. "Is Quality Out of Control?" *Harvard Business Review,* November–December 1977, pp. 114–22.

Case 20–1

Production problems

The Braddock Company of Sea Shore City fabricates stamped metal parts used in the production of wheelbarrows. Braddock fabricates two basic styles of wheelbarrow trays: one is for a deep, four-cubic-foot construction model and the other is for a shallow, two-cubic-foot homeowner's model. Braddock's process is simple: raw metal sheets are picked up from inventory (Braddock presently maintains about seven day's worth of the large metal sheets for the construction model and about ten day's worth of the smaller sheets for the homeowner model) and fed into a large machine which bends and shapes the metal into the desired tray. The trays are then inspected and packaged, ten to a box, for shipping.

In the past few days, Braddock has been experiencing quality problems with both tray styles. Undesirable creases have been forming in the corners following the stamping operation. However, the problem with the construction model tray is more pronounced and appeared almost three full days before it did on the homeowner's model.

Several incidents have occurred at Braddock during the past week that Hal McCarthy, the operations manager, thinks may have a bearing on the problem. Shorty McCune, a machine operator and labor activist, was accused of drinking on the job and released a few days before the problem began. Since his release, Shorty has been seen in and around the plant talking to several other employees. About two weeks ago Braddock also began receiving raw metal from a new supplier because of an attractive price break.

Presently the only inspection performed by the company is the postfabrication inspection.

1. What do you think is causing Braddock's problem?
2. Why is the problem more pronounced on the construction model than on the homeowner model?
3. How can Braddock eliminate its problem?

Case 20–2

The purchasing department

The buyers for a large airline company were having a general discussion with the manager of purchasing in her office Friday afternoon. The inspection of received parts was a topic that created a considerable amount of discussion. Apparently, several parts had recently been rejected six months or more after being received. Such a rejection delay was costing the company a considerable amount of money since most of the items were beyond the standard 90-day warranty period. The current purchasing procedures state that the department using the parts is responsible for the inspection of all parts, including stock and nonstock items. The company employs an inspector who is supposedly responsible for inspecting all aircraft parts in accordance with FAA regulations. However, the inspector has not been able to check those items purchased as nonaircraft parts because he is constantly overloaded. Furthermore, many of the aircraft parts are not being properly inspected because of insufficient facilities and equipment.

One recent example of the type of problem being encountered was the acceptance of a batch of plastic forks that broke readily when in use. The vendor had shipped over a hundred cases of the forks of the wrong type. Unfortunately all the purchase order specified was "forks." Another example was the acceptance of several cases of plastic cups with the wrong logo. The cups were subsequently put into use for in-flight service and had to be used since no other cups were available. A final example was the discovery that several expensive radar tubes in stock were found to be defective and with expired warranty. These tubes had to be reordered at almost $900 per unit.

It was apparent that the inspection function was inadequate, and unable to cope with the volume of material being received. Purchasing would have to establish some guidelines as to what material should or should not be inspected after being processed by the material checker. Some of the buyers felt that the material checker (who is not the inspector) should have more responsibility than simply checking quantity and comparing the packing sheet against purchase orders. Some believed that the checker could and should have caught the obvious errors in the logo on the plastic cups. Furthermore, if the inspector had sampled the forks they would have been rejected immediately. As for the radar tubes, they should have been forwarded by the inspector to the Avionics Shop for bench check and then placed in stock. Some buyers felt that the inspector should be responsible for inspection of all material received, regardless of its function or usage. It was pointed out, however, that several landing gears had been received from the overhaul/repair vendor and tagged by the inspector as being acceptable. These gears later turned out to be defective and unuseable and had to be returned for repair. This generated considerable discussion concerning the inspector's qualifications, testing capacity, work load, and responsibility for determining if the unit should be shop checked.

Much of the remaining discussion centered around what purchasing should recommend for the inspection of material. One proposal was that everything received be funneled through the inspection department. Another proposal was that all material be run through inspection except as otherwise noted on the purchase order. Other questions were also raised. If purchasing required all material to be inspected, would this demand additional inspection personnel? Who would be responsible for inspection specifications? Furthermore, who should determine what items should be shop checked?

The meeting was finally adjourned until the following Friday.

1. What do you think of the current system of inspection?
2. Do you think the inspector is incompetent?
3. What would you suggest at the meeting next Friday.

SECTION FIVE
CASE

Ajay corporation—the alloy division

The Ajay Corporation is a medium-sized conglomerate (see Exhibit 1 for organizational structure). Ajay originally had one division, the Alloy Division, which eventually generated sufficient profits to fund acquisitions of other divisions that were totally divorced in operations from the Alloy Division. The Alloy Division is still by far the largest and most profitable division of Ajay. In 1982, income and profits were:

	Income	*Profits*
Alloy Division	$80,000,000	$9,000,000
All other divisions	60,000,000	4,000,000

The company has a bank line of credit of $20 million which has never been used.

The Alloy Division produces and markets various randium metal alloys in raw forms (such as ingots, billets, rods, bars, plates, tubes, strips, and wires). The customers of the Alloy Division are secondary fabricators, stamping houses, machine shops, and plating houses, all of which utilize the raw randium alloy in further processing before the final product reaches the consumer. As a matter of fact, the ultimate user (and demand generator for the Alloy Division's products) rarely comes into direct contact with the division itself.

Randium, in its pure metal state, is demanded by a small and highly technical market. Its primary use is in making various alloys, chiefly nickel. In this application, randium serves as a hardener, providing nickel with mechanical properties nearly equivalent to steel. However, because randium is higher priced than other ferrous metals, it is used only in the most extreme problem areas where high alloy properties (i.e., strength and hardness) are an absolute necessity. Thus, the potential market for randium alloys is limited.

The primary market for randium alloys includes the communication, automotive, and electronics industries. The major uses for randium alloys include (1) springs and contacts used in switches; (2) connectors used in semiconductor circuitry (such as transistors); (3) diaphragms which expand and contract with pressure (such as those used in barometers); (4) rotational measuring devices (such as torsion wrenches used in automotive repairs); and (5) welding materials in various specifications.

EXHIBIT 1
Organizational Structure—Ajay Corporation

- Board of directors
  - President
    - Vice president, finance (Wade Millwood)
    - Vice president, brake/clutch division
    - Vice president, earth moving, scraper blade, manufacturing
    - Vice president, nonmetallic crystals division
    - Vice president, alloy division (John Anderson)
      - Director, marketing (Tom Henderson)
        - Manager, sales administration
          - Field sales manager
            - Territory sales reps (6)
        - Manager, district centers
          - Managers, 4 distribution warehouse
      - Director, research
        - Manager, quality assurance
          - Ohio plant
          - Pennsylvania plant
        - Manager, R&D
      - Director, production
        - Ohio plant
        - Pennsylvania plant
        - Raw material mining-Pennsylvania

The Alloy Division has one plant in Ohio and one in Pennsylvania. "Rough" randium alloy products (i.e., large, heavy products) are manufactured in Ohio. "Finished" or finer products are manufactured in Pennsylvania. Raw materials are mined in western Pennsylvania with distribution warehouses located in New Jersey, Detroit, Chicago, and Los Angeles. Purchase orders may be entered at any of the distribution warehouses and mills. Deliveries may also be made from all six locations.

The Alloy Division's manufacturing process is similar to an integrated steel mill. In general, the manufacturing operation is capital-intensive and highly automated. The randium ore is reduced to a billet (the initial casting before any fabrication is done) in a process involving one smelting furnace and four casting units at the Ohio mill. At this initial stage, either a semicontinuous rolling billet (flat shaped) or an extrusion billet (round or square shaped) is produced. The billets (either flat, round, or square shaped) can be shipped directly to customers or they can be further processed. Exhibit 2 illustrates the total process.

The flat billets initially enter the primary hot and primary cold mill processes, and depending on the gauge (thickness) of the product, the resulting billets will either be shipped or processed further. Flat billets of gauge 0.090 inches or more are shipped directly to the customer. Those with a gauge less than 0.090 inches are sent from the Ohio mill to the Pennsylvania mill for further processing. At the Pennsylvania mill, those billets with a gauge less than 0.020 inches are processed through two different steps. Those with a gauge over 0.020 inches only go through one step before being shipped. The cold mill sendzimer process pulls the material while the cold mill four-high process squeezes it. Both serve to further reduce the thickness of the material.

Round or square billets are initially sent through an extrusion press at the Ohio plant. The extrusion press takes a billet, heats it, and transforms it into a semiplastic state. It is then shaped according to customer specifications. Billets that do not have finer dimensional tolerance specifications are directly shipped to the customer. Those that require finer dimensional tolerances (as a result of customer specifications) are processed by the draw bench, which further shapes the product to customer specifications. If the gauge is over 0.187 inches, the product is shipped directly to the customer. Billets with a gauge of less than 0.187 inches are sent to the Pennsylvania plant where they are further processed on a draw bench, then ultimately shipped to the customer.

The production capacity is directly dependent on three phases of processing: the smelting furnace and four casting units; the primary hot and cold mill processes; and the extrusion press. Of

EXHIBIT 2
Production Process

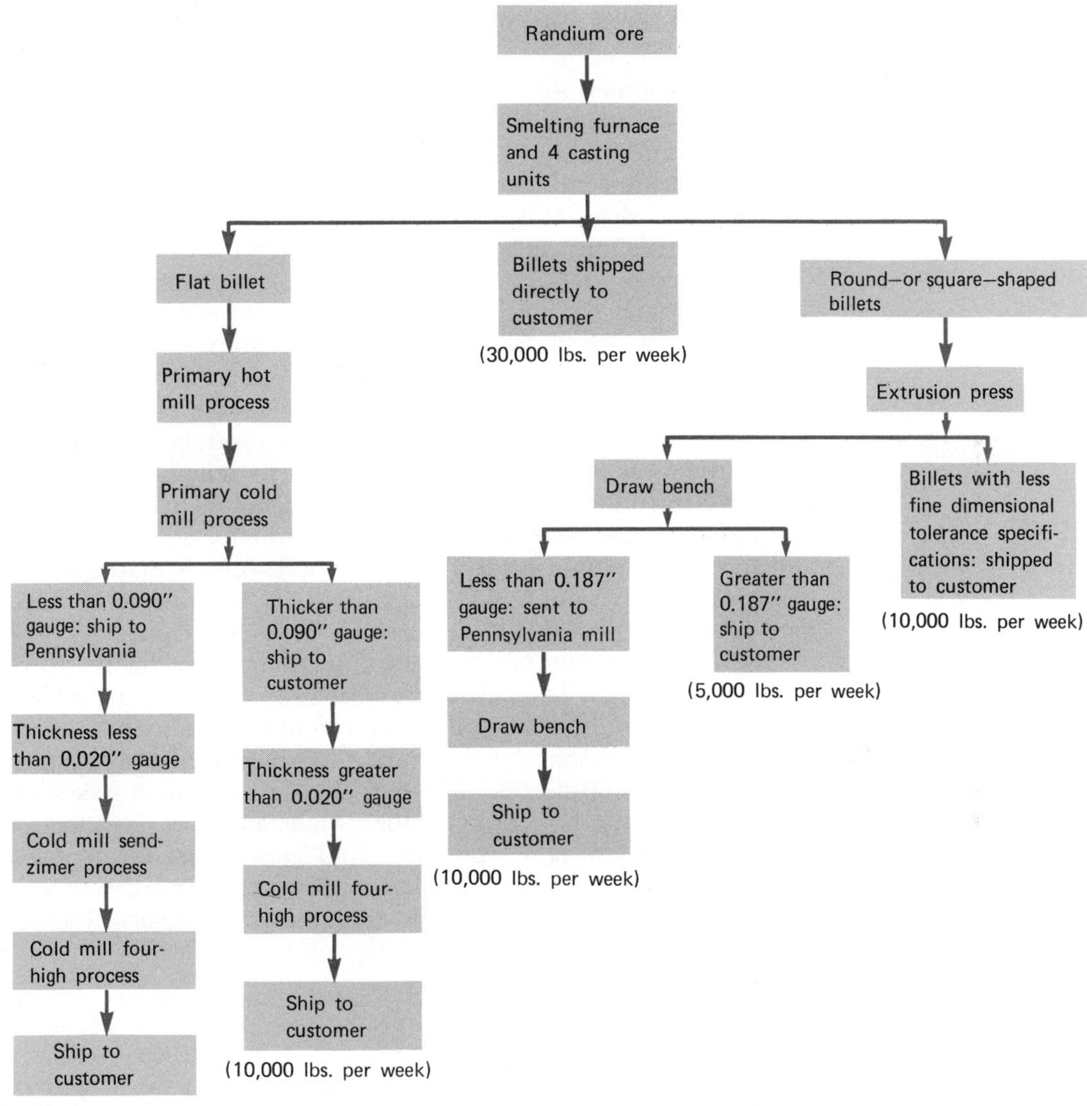

these, the most critical capacity level is that of the smelter complex and four casting units. The normal capacity of these units is 120,000 pounds per week. Normal capacity can be produced by running the entire smelter complex for a 40-hour workweek. It has been further estimated that each hour of operation requires one-half hour of maintenance. Although it can be run more, the smelter complex has been running a 40-hour week for quite some time. However, past experience has shown that if the system is run over 40 hours per week, the maintenance time goes up to about 45 minutes per operating hour. The extrusion press and primary hot and cold mill processes do not present a problem since they are capable of producing about twice as much material as can currently be handled by the Pennsylvania mill. Presently, the Pennsylvania mill can process about 80,000 pounds per week during a one shift, 40-hour workweek. The average weekly production for 1982 for each type of product is shown in Exhibit 2.

Marketing in the Alloy Division is the sole responsibility of the field sales manager. Since demand for Alloy's products is largely determined by the technical developments implemented by Alloy's customers, very little product development or technical innovation occurs within the Alloy Division. Some of the diverse developments that have influenced Alloy's product mix are the miniaturization of electronic components in telephone applications, the introduction of high reliability components in automobile circuitry, the redesign of car bodies to effect "downsizing," and the popularity of color TV. In the past, Alloy's management has traditionally maintained excess capacity in order to be flexible because of the difficulty in forecasting market trends.

The Alloy Division has had one chief competitor for its products. However, the competitor has been slowly cutting back its production since it was acquired by another company four years ago. Thus, Alloy's share of the market has increased from 40 percent in 1978 to 60 percent in 1982. All of this growth has been looked upon quite favorably by John Anderson, vice president of the Alloy Division. However, this rapid growth has also caused John some problems. Tom Henderson, director of marketing, has just walked into John's office and the following conversation occurs:

Tom: John, our salesman on the West Coast just called and has received notice that we have been selected to be the supplier for a large electronics firm out there. The order will be for about 60,000 pounds per week. They want deliveries to start in approximately two years.

John: Tom, that's great. I just hope it doesn't have to go through the Pennsylvania mill.

Tom: Unfortunately, it does!

John: Well we just don't have the capacity there.

Tom: Maybe we can build a mill on the West Coast.

John: Maybe, but we'll have to fight to get the funds from Wade Millwood, vice president of finance. Furthermore, transporting raw materials from Pennsylvania to the West Coast would present a real problem.

Tom: Yes, but we've got to transport the finished product out there if we manufacture it in Pennsylvania. Seems to me we would be better off to find a source of raw materials out West and produce the final product there.

John: Boy, getting a new order can sure create problems!

1. How can the Alloy Division be made to operate more efficiently?
2. How could the Alloy Division solve its problem?

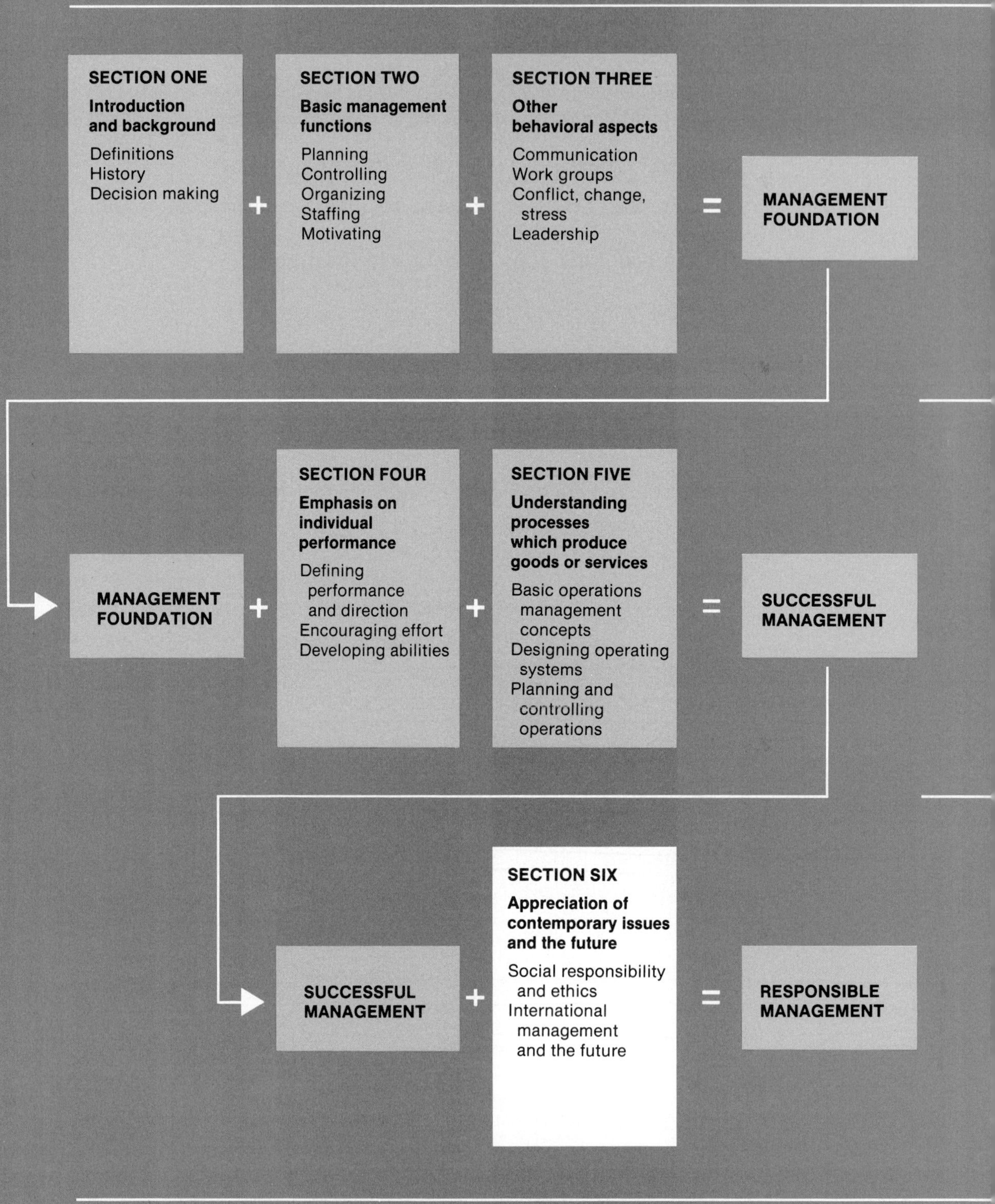

SECTION ONE

Introduction and background

Definitions
History
Decision making

+

SECTION TWO

Basic management functions

Planning
Controlling
Organizing
Staffing
Motivating

+

SECTION THREE

Other behavioral aspects

Communication
Work groups
Conflict, change, stress
Leadership

=

MANAGEMENT FOUNDATION

MANAGEMENT FOUNDATION

+

SECTION FOUR

Emphasis on individual performance

Defining performance and direction
Encouraging effort
Developing abilities

+

SECTION FIVE

Understanding processes which produce goods or services

Basic operations management concepts
Designing operating systems
Planning and controlling operations

=

SUCCESSFUL MANAGEMENT

SUCCESSFUL MANAGEMENT

+

SECTION SIX

Appreciation of contemporary issues and the future

Social responsibility and ethics
International management and the future

=

RESPONSIBLE MANAGEMENT

section six

CONTEMPORARY MANAGEMENT

21. Social responsibility and ethics in management
22. International management and the future

The first five sections of this text concentrated on providing the foundation and ingredients necessary for developing a successful manager. All of the major segments of a manager's day-to-day job were covered. The purpose of this final section is to develop an appreciation for contemporary issues and potential future trends and, thus, develop not only successful managers but also responsible managers.

As a result of the numerous scandals that have occurred in government and large corporations, increasing attention has been focused on the ethics and social responsibilities of managers. Managers' activities are being closely scrutinized in many cases. In today's ever-shrinking world, more and more organizations are conducting business on an international level. This obviously creates the need for an understanding of the basics of international management. Finally the concern of managers for the future is vital. Will organizational life take on drastic changes in the not-too-distant future or will the future be merely an extrapolation of the past? Today's and tomorrow's managers must have an awareness of these issues if they are to be successful and responsible.

Chapter 21 discusses the topics of social responsibility and ethics. Several arguments are presented both for and against organizational actions concerning social responsibility. An argument is also developed that today's organizations need, and should develop, a code of ethics.

The final chapter of this text, Chapter 22, explores international management and the future of management and organizational life. Several potential developments which would affect management in the future are discussed.

21 Social Responsibility and Ethics in Management

Objectives

1. To discuss the concept of social responsibility.
2. To present and analyze arguments for and against social responsibility.
3. To define the concept of ethics as related to organizations.
4. To outline some different approaches for dealing with ethics in organizations.

Chapter Outline

Glossary of Terms

Consumerism Social movement that seeks to increase the power of consumers and buyers in relation to the sellers or providers of goods and services.

Ethics Standards or principles of conduct to govern the behavior of an individual or a group of individuals.

Federal Fair Packaging and Labeling Act of 1967 Regulates labeling procedures for businesses.

Foreign Corrupt Practices Act of 1977 Prohibits American companies operating abroad from bribing foreign officials, political candidates, and party leaders.

Gamesmanship An approach to business ethics which argues that the ethics of business are gamelike and different from the Judaeo-Christian ethic.

Judeo-Christian ethic Generally considered to be the basis of Western ethical codes and has as its primary goal love—including love of God and neighbor.

Social audit Attempt to report in financial terms the expenditures and investments made by an organization for social purposes.

Social responsibility Moral and ethical content of managerial and corporate decisions over and above the pragmatic requirements imposed by legal principle and the market economy.

Truth in Lending Act of 1967 Regulates the extension of credit to individuals.

"Business ethics," the father explained to his son, "is something you couldn't do without. Take today for instance. A man comes in and pays me a hundred dollar bill to clear up his account. After he leaves, I find two bills stuck together. He has paid me two hundred dollars instead of one. Now, son, here comes the question of ethics. Should I tell my partner or shouldn't I?"

*William R. Gerler**

Today organizations are more concerned about social responsibility and about questions concerning ethics in management than they have ever been. The purpose of this chapter is to present an overview of corporate social responsibility and to examine the role of ethics in management.

DEFINING SOCIAL RESPONSIBILITY

Social responsibility is concerned with how individuals and organizations deal with current social issues. However, the general public has a rather broad and all-encompassing definition with regard to the social responsibility of business organizations. The public seems to feel that managers and business organizations should provide leadership in rebuilding cities, wiping out poverty, controlling crime, and cutting government red tape.[1] In short, social responsibility has come to denote participation in a multitude of issues and problems. Presently, no universally accepted definition exists for the term *social responsibility*. However, for the purposes of this book, social responsibility is defined as: "the moral and ethical content of managerial and corporate decisions over and above the pragmatic requirements imposed by legal principle and the market economy."[2]

SOCIAL RESPONSIBILITY—A HISTORICAL PERSPECTIVE

The idea that business has a responsibility other than producing goods and services is not new. In 1919, Henry L. Gantt stated his belief that the community would attempt to take over business if

*William R. Gerler, *Executive's Treasury of Humor for Every Occasion* (West Nyack, N.Y.: Parker Publishing, 1965). Copyright © 1965 by Parker Publishing Company, Inc.

[1] Lloyd L. Byars and Michael H. Mescon, *The Other Side of Profit* (Philadelphia: W. B. Saunders, 1975), p. 4.

[2] Robert H. Bork, "Modern Values and Social Responsibility," *MSU Business Topics*, Spring 1980, p. 7.

the business system neglected its social responsibilities.[3] Another early management writer who discussed social responsibility was Oliver Sheldon. Writing in 1923, Sheldon stressed that management has a social responsibility. His basic philosophy is summarized as follows:

> It is important, therefore, early in our consideration of management in industry, to insist that however scientific management may become, and however much the full development of its powers may depend upon the use of the scientific method; its primary responsibility is social and communal.[4]

However, the concern which these men showed for social responsibility was rare during this early period.

Changes began to occur in the late 1930s and early 1940s. Shorter work weeks and safer working conditions are examples of some of the first changes. Many of these early social responsibility changes were precipitated by labor unions. In effect, labor unions pressured organizations to consider factors other than just profitability.

In 1948, the theme of the annual Harvard Business School Alumni Association meeting was "business responsibility." In 1958, the American Management Association surveyed 700 companies concerning their "managerial creed or statement of basic objectives."[5] Nearly every company expressed the belief that they had a responsibility to society. The 1950s and 1960s saw an increasing number of organizations and managers expressing concern about the social responsibilities of organizations. However, socially responsible programs were actually implemented by very few organizations until the late 1960s. Minority hiring, environmental programs, and loans and technical assistance to minority-owned businesses are all examples of programs that were undertaken by many organizations during the 1970s. It is anticipated that programs such as these will be continued during the 1980s.

Looking back over the years, the attitudes toward social responsibility and value systems of managers seem to have gone through three historical phases. Phase one, which dominated until the 1930s, emphasized the belief that a business manager had but one single objective—to maximize profits. Phase two, which dominated from the 1930s to the early 1960s, stressed that man-

---

[3] Henry L. Gantt, *Organizing for Work* (New York: Harcourt Brace Jovanovich, 1919), p. 15.

[4] Oliver Sheldon, *The Philosophy of Management* (Marshfield, Mass.: Pitman Publishing, 1966), p. xv. (Originally published in London in 1923 by Sir Isaac Pitman and Sons.)

[5] Stewart Thompson, *Management Creeds and Philosophy: Top Management Guides in Our Changing Economy* (New York: American Management Association, 1958), research study no. 32.

FIGURE 21–1

Historical Phases of Attitudes toward Social Responsibility and Value Systems of Managers

Phase one: Profit maximizing management (1800 to 1920s)	*Phase two: Trusteeship management (late 1920s to early 1960)*	*Phase three: Quality of life management (late 1960s to present)*
	Economic	
1. Raw self-interest.	1. Self-interest. 2. Contributors' interest.	1. Enlightened self-interest. 2. Contributors' interests. 3. Society's interests.
What's good for me is good for my country.	What's good for GM is good for our country.	What is good for society is good for our company.
Profit maximizer.	Profit satisficer.	Profit is necessary, but. . . .
Money and wealth are most important.	Money is important, but so are people.	People are more important than money.
Let the buyer beware. (*caveat emptor*)	Let us not cheat the customer.	Let the seller beware. (*caveat venditor*)
Labor is a commodity to be bought and sold.	Labor has certain rights which must be recognized.	Employee dignity has to be satisfied.
Accountability of management is to the owners.	Accountability of management is to the owners, customers, employees, suppliers, and other contributors.	Accountability of management is to the owners, contributors, and society.
	Technology values	
Technology is very important.	Technology is important but so are people.	People are more important than technology.
	Social values	
Employee personal problems must be left at home.	We recognize that employees have needs beyond their economic needs.	We hire the whole man.
I am a rugged individualist, and I will manage my business as I please.	I am an individualist, but I recognize the value of group participation.	Group participation is fundamental to our success.
Minority groups are inferior to whites. They must be treated accordingly.	Minority groups have their place in society, and their place is inferior to mine.	Minority group members are people as you and I are.
	Political values	
That government is best which governs least.	Government is a necessary evil.	Business and government must cooperate to solve society's problems.
	Environmental values	
The natural environment controls the destiny of man.	Man can control and manipulate the environment.	We must preserve the environment in order to lead a quality life.
	Aesthetic values	
Aesthetic values? What are they?	Aesthetic values are OK, but not for us.	We must preserve our aesthetic values, and we will do our part.

Source: Adapted from Robert D. Hay, Edmund R. Gray, and James E. Gates, *Business and Society: Cases and Text* (Cincinnati: South-Western Publishing, 1976), pp. 10–11.

Phase I - Profit maximizing mgmt
II - Trusteeship mgmt
III - Quality of Life Mgmt

agers were responsible not only for maximizing profits but also for maintaining an equitable balance among the competing claims of customers, employees, suppliers, creditors, and the community. Phase three, which is still dominant today, contends that managers and organizations have a responsibility to involve themselves in the solutions of society's major problems. Figure 21–1 describes these three phases in more depth.

SOCIAL RESPONSIBILITY TODAY

Organizations and managers in today's society still have questions concerning the exact nature of their social responsibility. A summary of the major arguments for and against the social responsibility of business organizations is shown in Figure 21–2. In addition, the following sections of this chapter discuss in detail some of the more important arguments.

Arguments for Social Responsibility

It is in the best interest of the business. The future of business organizations depends on maintaining a good relationship with the society in which they operate. If organizations fail to take actions in the area of social responsibility, then society will take action against business organizations. Boycotting the products of an organization, picketing not only the organization but also customers of the organization, and even violence against the organization are examples of actions that can be taken. An extension of this argument is that if public pressure becomes too strong, then government will force the organization to assume the responsibility.[6]

Social actions can be profitable. Research studies designed to determine the accuracy of this statement have produced mixed results. Presently, no clear evidence exists to support a cause and effect relationship between social responsibility and profitability. However, in a more indirect manner, it seems logical to think that donations to higher education, hiring disadvantaged individuals, participating in urban renewal projects, and aiding conservation programs should contribute to the long-term profitability of all organizations.

Being socially responsible is the ethical thing to do. Since business is an integral part of society, many individuals argue that being socially responsible is a moral responsibility of orga-

[6] Harold Williams, "Corporate Accountability—One Year Later," paper delivered at the Sixth Annnual Securities Regulation Institute, San Diego, Calif., January 18, 1979.

FIGURE 21–2
Arguments for and against Social Responsibility

Major arguments for social responsibility:

1. It is in the best interest of the business to promote and improve the communities where it does business.
2. Social actions can be profitable.
3. It is the ethical thing to do.
4. It improves the public image of the firm.
5. It increases the viability of the business system. Business exists because it gives society benefits. Society can amend or take away its charter. This is the "iron law of responsibility."
6. It is necessary to avoid government regulation.
7. Sociocultural norms require it.
8. Laws cannot be passed for all circumstances. Thus, business must assume responsibility to maintain an orderly legal society.
9. It is in the stockholder's best interest. It will improve the price of stock in the long run because the stock market will view the company as less risky and open to public attack and therefore award it a higher price-earnings ratio.
10. Society should give business a chance to solve social problems that government has failed to solve.
11. Business, by some groups, is considered to be the institution with the financial and human resources to solve social problems.
12. Prevention of problems is better than cures—so let business solve problems before they become too great.

Major arguments against social responsibility:

1. It might be illegal.
2. Business plus government equals monolith.
3. Social actions cannot be measured.
4. It violates profit maximization.
5. Cost of social responsibility is too great and would increase prices too much.
6. Business lacks social skills to solve societal problems.
7. It would dilute business's primary purposes.
8. It would weaken U.S. balance of payments because price of goods will have to go up to pay for social programs.
9. Business already has too much power. Such involvement would make business too powerful.
10. Business lacks accountability to the public. Thus, the public would have no control over its social involvement.
11. Such business involvement lacks broad public support. GOOD!

Source: R. Joseph Monsen, Jr. "The Social Attitudes of Management," in *Contemporary Management: Issues and Viewpoints,* ed. Joseph W. McGuire (Englewood Cliffs, N.J.: Prentice-Hall, 1974 © 1974), p. 616. Adapted by permission of Prentice-Hall, Inc.

nizations. The proponents of this argument feel that it is a moral responsibility of organizations to provide safe products, clean up streams, and conserve natural resources. Evidence shows that business decisions generally reflect the ethical system by which a society lives.[7] Thus, if the public at large feels that social respon-

[7] Glenn Gilman, "The Ethical Dimension in American Management," *California Management Review,* Fall 1969, p. 49.

sibility is the ethical thing to do, then it can be expected that businesssmen and organizations will feel the same way.

Arguments against Social Responsibility

It might be illegal. Milton Friedman has argued that the only responsibility of business is to maximize profits for shareholders.[8] This argument assumes that managers are agents of the stockholders and that the diversion of funds to activities that do not contribute to profits may be illegal. This viewpoint was held by most managers and was supported by the courts for a long time. For instance, in 1919, a Michigan court declared that business was to be operated primarily for the profit of stockholders and forced the company to declare a dividend, which it had not done for many years.[9]

However, this argument has been considerably weakened over the years. In 1935, an amendment to the Internal Revenue Code allowed corporations to deduct up to 5 percent of net profits for social purposes. Furthermore, in 1953, the New Jersey Supreme Court upheld the right of the A. P. Smith Company to give funds to Princeton University against the desires of some stockholders. The court stated that "it was not just a right but a duty of corporations to support higher education in the interest of the long-range well-being of their stockholders because the company could not hope to operate effectively in a society which is not functioning well."[10]

Business plus government equals monolith. The proponents of this argument feel that business should make profits and government should spend tax money to attack social problems. They argue that socially motivated business activities sublimate and compromise the profit motive. Theodore Leavitt feels that if business begins to assume more and more social responsibility, then there could ultimately be very little functional difference between business and government.[11] Without this functional difference, society would be dominated by one unopposed and unstoppable monolithy.

GOOD POINT!

Social actions cannot be measured. Milton Friedman has asked, "If businessmen do have a social responsibility other than

[8] Milton Friedman, "Does Business Have a Social Responsibility?" *The Magazine of Bank Administration*, April 1971, p. 14.

[9] George A Steiner, *Business and Society* (New York: Random House, 1971), p. 154.

[10] Committee for Economic Development (CED), "Social Responsibilities of Business Corporations," a statement on national policy by the Research and Policy Committee (Washington, D.C.: U.S. Government Printing Office, June 1971), p. 27.

[11] Theodore Levitt, "The Dangers of Social Responsibility," *Harvard Business Review*, September–October 1958, pp. 41–50.

making maximum profits for stockholders, how do they know what it is? Can they decide how great a burden they are justified in placing on themselves or their stockholders to serve that social interest?"[12] Also, who should decide what is good for society? Proponents of this argument feel that management cannot accurately measure the benefits of social action and that it is fruitless to continue spending money without measuring the return on the investment.

financial (and social?) audits

The financial audit has been used traditionally to measure the profit performance of organizations. The need for measuring an organization's social responsibility has led to the idea of a social audit.

A social audit is an attempt to report, in financial terms, the expenditures and investments made by an organization for social purposes. This is accomplished by categorizing the socially related expenses and investments in terms of income, expenses, assets, and liabilities. However, the problems of placing a dollar measurement on social investments are complex and subject to individual interpretation.[13] Faced with these problems of measurement, some business organizations have used the following methods to present their efforts in socially responsible activities:

1. Narrative disclosure of social responsibility efforts in footnotes of financial statements.
2. The extension of traditional financial statements to include the costs of specific corporate social responsibility efforts.
3. Special reports covering pollution, occupational health, equal employment, and other areas of activity.

ACTIONS NECESSARY TO IMPLEMENT SOCIAL RESPONSIBILITY

The biggest obstacle to organizations assuming more social responsibility is the pressure exerted by owners and managers for steady increases in earnings per share on a quarterly basis. Concern about immediate profit maximization makes it rather difficult to invest in areas that cannot be accurately measured and also have returns which are long run in nature. Furthermore, pressure for short-term earnings has an impact on corporate social behavior because most companies are geared to short-term profit objectives. Budgets, objectives, and performance evalua-

---

[12] "A Changing Balance of Power: New Partnership of Government and Business," *Business Week,* July 17, 1965, p. 90.

[13] Neil C. Churchill and Arthur B. Toan, Jr. "Reporting on Corporate Social Responsibility: A Progress Report," *Journal of Contemporary Business,* Winter 1978, pp. 5–17.

tions are often based on short-run considerations. Management may express a willingness to sacrifice some short-term profit to achieve social objectives. However, managers who sacrifice profit in their own departments and seek to justify it on the basis of corporate social goals may find that their superiors are unsympathetic.

Organizations should also carefully examine their cherished values—short-run profits and others—to ensure that these concepts are in tune with the values held by society. This should be a continuous process because the values held by society are ever-changing.

Organizations should reevaluate their long-range planning and decision-making processes to ensure that they fully understand the potential social consequences. Plant location decisions are no longer merely economic matters. Environmental consequences and impact on employment opportunities for the disadvantaged are examples of other factors that may be considered.

Organizations should seek to help not only governmental agencies but also voluntary agencies in their social efforts. This should include technical and managerial assistance as well as monetary support. Technological knowledge, organizational skills, and managerial competence can all be applied to solving social problems.

FIGURE 21–3
Responsibility of Society to Business in Implementing Social Responsibility Programs

1. *Set rules that are clear and consistent.* Society must define what boundaries organizations should operate within; what minimum standards are to be expected, met, or exceeded; what the performance criteria are. Society must be consistent in its expectations for corporate social responsibility through the various governmental regulations affecting this area.
2. *Keep the rules within the bounds of technical feasibility.* Business cannot do the impossible. However, many of today's regulations are unworkable in practice. Overzealous environmental restrictions have, on occasion, decreed standards surpassing those of Mother Nature.
3. *Make sure rules are economically feasible and recognize that society itself must be prepared to pay the cost—not only of their implementation by business but also their administration by government.* Ultimately, it is the people who must pay either through higher prices or taxes.
4. *Make rules prescriptive, not retroactive.* There is a present trend toward retroactivity in an attempt to force retribution for the past—to make today's rules apply to yesterday's ball game.
5. *Make rules goal seeking, not procedure prescribing.* Tell organizations to devise the best, most economical, and efficient way to get there.

Source: Adapted from Jerry McAfee, "Responsibilities Shared by Corporations and Society," *Credit and Financial Management,* May 1978, p. 31.

Organizations should give attention to the ways in which they can help in solving social problems through the operation of their own business. Many of the social problems that exist stem from the economic deprivation of a fairly large segment of our society. Attacking this problem could be the most significant social undertaking of organizations.

In order for business organizations to successfully implement social responsibility programs, society must also meet certain basic responsibilities. These are summarized in Figure 21–3.

HOW SOCIALLY RESPONSIBLE ARE TODAY'S ORGANIZATIONS?

Regardless of the arguments against social responsibility, organizations—either through their own initiative or through pressures from the government or consumers—are becoming more aware of their social responsibilities. Figure 21–4 summarizes many issues that are now considered to be legitimate social concerns of organizations. The commitments of organizations in three of these areas are discussed below.

FIGURE 21–4
Issues that Are Social Concerns of Organizations

External issues—May or may not have been directly caused by business
1. Poverty
2. Drug abuse
3. Decay of cities
4. Community relations
5. Philanthropy

External issues—Caused by normal economic activity of business
1. Environmental pollution
2. Safety and quality of goods and services (consumerism movement)
3. Social impact of facilities closings
4. Site locations of new facilities

Internal issues—Directly related to economic activity
1. Equal employment opportunity
2. Occupational safety and health
3. Quality of work life

Equal Employment Opportunity

Business has responded to the area of equal opportunity largely as a result of government legislation. Table 21–1 shows the growth of the total number of experienced people employed in the years 1972 through 1979 and also shows the growth in the total number of people employed in managerial or administrative positions categorized by race and sex. Table 22–2 gives a percentage growth

TABLE 21–1
Experienced Civilian Labor Force by Race and Sex

	1972		1979	
	Number employed	*Number employed in managerial and/or administrative positions*	*Number employed*	*Number employed in managerial and/or administrative positions*
White females	27,305	1,311	35,304	2,400
Black and other minority males	4,861	233	5,779	398
Black and other minority females	3,768	86	5,141	174

Note: All numbers are in thousands.

Source: Adapted from *Handbook of Labor Statistics,* U.S. Department of Labor, Bureau of Labor Statistics, December 1980, pp. 46–48.

figure for these same categories. As can be seen, the percentage of people employed in managerial or administrative positions among these categories has grown more rapidly than the percentage increase in the number of people employed in these categories.

In addition, voluntary efforts on the part of business have occurred in the areas of training and hiring the hard-core unemployed and providing assistance to minority business enterprises. However, none of this should be interpreted to mean that business has done all it could or should have done in equal employment opportunity. Much more effort will be required before equal employment opportunity exists for all people.

The Environment

Although many businesses have voluntarily sought to eliminate the environmental effects of air, water, and noise pollution, the

TABLE 21–2
Percentage Growth in Experienced Labor Force by Race and Sex, 1972–1979

	Percent employed	*Percent in managerial and/or administrative positions*
White females	29.3%	83.0%
Black and other minority males	18.9	70.8
Black and other minority females	36.4	102.0

government has enacted a number of environmental protection laws that require business to take specific actions in this area. The two major laws regarding the environment are: the Environmental Policy Act of 1969, which created the Environmental Protection Agency (EPA) to coordinate all federal pollution control programs; and the National Air Quality Standards Act of 1970, which severely restricts the pollution allowed by business, enables the EPA or individuals to sue the pollutant, and subjects violators of the act to maximum fines of $25,000 per day or one year in jail. However, several proposals to limit the powers of the EPA have recently been introduced into Congress.

Consumerism

Consumerism is a social movement that seeks to increase the power of consumers and buyers in relation to the sellers or providers of goods and services. The consumer movement contributed to the passage of the Federal Fair Packaging and Labeling Act of 1966 and the Truth in Lending Act of 1967. The packaging law regulates labeling procedures for businesses while the lending law regulates the extension of credit to individuals.

TABLE 21–3
Areas of Involvement by Industry in Social Responsibility Programs

	Types of organizations (percent involved)				
Area of commitment	*Oil, gas, and mining*	*Manufacturing*	*Transportation, communication, and utilities*	*Wholesale and retail*	*Insurance, finance, and real estate*
Assist charities, welfare, health funds, etc.	56.2%	67.0%	78.9%	83.4%	90.2%
Recruitment and managerial development of racial and ethnic minorities	56.3	56.0	73.7	66.7	58.8
Pollution abatement	100.0	58.2	42.1	0	2.0
Recruitment and managerial development of females	31.2	36.3	36.8	75.0	43.1
Upgrading quality of working life of employees	37.5	31.9	10.5	16.6	29.4
Conserving resources including energy and/or plant and animal life	81.3	23.0	36.8	16.6	7.8
Hiring and training the hard-core unemployed	6.3	20.9	31.6	25.0	19.8
Assisting minority enterprises	6.2	17.6	0	8.3	37.2
Urban renewal and development	0	11.0	0	0	47.1
Consumer protection	12.5	22.0	5.3	50.0	5.8

Source: Sandra L. Holmes, "Corporate Social Performance: Past and Present Areas of Commitment," *Academy of Management Journal*, September 1977, p. 437.

MANAGEMENT IN PRACTICE

Helping Disabled Is Ongoing Effort

Since it produces furniture and related equipment for offices and health-care facilities, Herman Miller Inc. is keenly aware of the needs of handicapped workers. The Zeeland, Mich.-based corporation "can influence in a very tangible way the disabled person's ability to participate fully in the world of work," says Max O. De Pree, its chairman and president.

But "the whole idea of social responsibility in a company ought to be part of a 'red thread' that runs through the entire enterprise," he continues. At Miller the "thread" begins at the payroll office.

Of the 2,400 employees located at company headquarters and other Miller sites in western Michigan, more than 200 (8.33 percent) are handicapped. "Handicapped persons should not be seen as a special minority, but rather as a normal part of a community's population, and every business ought to reflect that normal population," Mr. De Pree contends. (Accordingly, Miller declines to emphasize its handicapped employees through such means as publicity photographs.)

Miller's "thread" also runs into the surrounding community. Last year it sponsored a day-long forum in western Michigan to improve communications between local businesses and administrators of handicapped programs. The motive? Miller's belief that educational and training programs for the disabled are only as effective as industry's acceptance and understanding of the fact that a handicapped person is a valuable human resource.

Still, Mr. De Pree thinks that the majority of the problems confronting disabled persons are solved on a one-to-one basis. One of Miller's foremen, for example, made a special effort to help rehabilitate a young fellow worker critically injured in an auto accident. He invited the young man's parents to come to work with their son, to learn the job he would be relearning. On difficult days the parents were there to help the employee and provide encouragement. The effort paid off.

In May, Miller participated in the President's Committee on Employment of the Handicapped, and it has also been commended by the U.S. Council for the International Year of Disabled Persons for its "initiative and programs."

Source: *Industry Week,* January 11, 1982, p. 41. Used with permission.

These laws attempt to make the consumer more knowledgeable about the product and the terms of purchase. At the same time, the area of product safety has been enhanced for the consumer through the modification of liability laws. The courts have held, in general, that if an organization puts a product on the market it must accept responsibility for it. Table 21–3 indicates the areas of involvement by several different industries in social responsibility programs.

BUSINESS ETHICS

While social responsibility is concerned with how individuals and organizations deal with current social issues, business ethics are concerned with the day-to-day behavior standards of individuals and organizations. Ethics are standards or principles of conduct used to govern the behavior of an individual or group of individuals. Ethics are generally concerned with questions relating to what is right or wrong or with moral duties. Ethics can be developed by an individual, by a group of individuals, or by society. Laws can be viewed as ethics that have been formalized by a society since they are usually concerned with principles of conduct.

Organizational ethics, however, are generally more concerned with the behavior of individuals or groups of individuals that are not covered by the law. Withholding facts, making misleading statements, and padding expense accounts are issues that raise questions about ethical standards.

good point → that is why it is so difficult

Why Is a Code of Ethics Needed?

Because of the adverse publicity that many organizations have received, society is demanding a code of ethics for organizations. Many people believe that if organizations do not voluntarily develop a code of ethics, the issue will be forced by public opinion or even government regulation.[14] In fact, the Foreign Corrupt Practices Act, which prohibits American companies operating abroad from bribing foreign officials, political candidates, and party leaders, was passed in 1977.

Robert L. Heilbroner has summarized several proposals that would aid in forcing a code of ethics on organizations and individuals in organizations. These are summarized in Figure 21–5.

A second reason for developing a code of ethics is to reduce the organizational pressures to compromise personal ethics for the sake of organizational goals. One study indicated that managers feel under pressure to compromise personal standards to achieve company goals.[15] In this study, Archie B. Carroll found that 50 percent of top-level managers, 65 percent of middle-level managers, and 84 percent of lower-level managers feel this pressure.

A third reason for developing a code of ethics is to provide a general standard for measuring performance concerning ethical questions.

---

[14] George K. Saul, "Business Ethics: Where Are We Going?" *Academy of Management Review,* April 1981, p. 275.

[15] Archie B. Carroll, "Managerial Ethics: A Post-Watergate View," *Business Horizons,* April 1975, p. 77.

FIGURE 21–5
Proposals for Legislating a Code of Ethics

Federal incorporation laws to avoid the present welter of differing state requirements and to put the corporation (or at any rate, the large corporation) directly under federal accountability.

Greatly enlarged disclosure requirements, forcing corporations to divulge facts and figures with regard to antipollution expenditures, racial distribution of employees, and so forth.

Public representatives on boards of directors, chosen to represent various constituencies such as suppliers, customers, workers, or simply the public at large.

Stiffer penalties for violation of laws that protect the consumer or the environment, with penalties that include the suspension of responsible executives.

The required appointment of corporate officials charged with responsibility for assuring the compliance of their companies with existing legislation.

Cumulative voting of shares so that small shareowners, who now can cast no more than one vote for or against each director, may concentrate all their voting power for or against one director.

Full availability of corporate income tax returns for public inspection.

Imposition of involuntary "social bankruptcy" for corporations that have failed consistently to abide by existing legislation.

Protection of the rights of corporate employees against corporate retaliation for public testimony with regard to acts of the corporation.

Source: Excerpt from Robert L. Heilbroner, ed., *In the Name of Profit* (New York: Doubleday, 1972), pp. 257–58. Copyright © 1972 by Doubleday and Company, Inc. Reprinted by permission of the publisher.

Judeo-Christian Ethic

The Judeo-Christian ethic is generally considered to be the basis of Western ethical codes and thus might be the basis for an organizational code of ethics. A study committee of the Federal Council of Churches has attempted to define the salient features of the Judeo-Christian ethic. The primary goal of the Judeo-Christian ethic is love—including love of God and neighbor. The committee also outlined several subordinate goals of the Judeo-Christian ethic that are relevant to organizational life. These subordinate goals are summarized in Figure 21–6.

Robert T. Golembiewski has refined the Judeo-Christian ethic into five basic values relevant to organizational life. The numbers in the parentheses refer to the items in Figure 21–6 to which the respective basic value relates.

1. Work must be psychologically acceptable to the individual: that is, its performance cannot generally threaten the individual (1, 3, 8, 10, and 11).
2. Work must allow man to develop his faculties (4, 5, 6, and 7).
3. The work task must allow the individual considerable room for self-determination (3 and 9).

FIGURE 21–6
Subordinate Goals Relevant to Organizational Life

1. *Survival and physical well-being (productivity).* Each individual should have access to the conditions necessary for health, safety, comfort, and reasonable longevity.
2. *Fellowship.* Each individual should have a variety of satisfying human relationships.
3. *Dignity and humility.* Each individual should have the opportunity to earn a position in society of dignity and self-respect.
4. *Enlightenment.* The individual should have opportunity to learn about the world in which he lives. He should be able to satisfy his intellectual curiosity and to acquire the skills and knowledge for intelligent citizenship, efficient work, and informed living.
5. *Aesthetic enjoyment.* The individual should have the opportunity to appreciate aesthetic values in art, nature, and ritual, and through personal relations. Many aesthetic values are attainable through both production and consumption.
6. *Creativity.* The individual should be able to express his personality through creative activities. He should be able to identify himself with the results of his own activity, and to take pride in his achievements; intellectual, aesthetic, political, or other.
7. *New experience.* An important goal of life is suggested by the words variability, spontaneity, whimsy, novelty, excitement, fun, sport, holiday, striving against odds, solving problems, innovation, invention, etc. Each individual should have opportunity for new experience.
8. *Security.* Each individual should have assurance that the objective conditions necessary for attainment of the above goals will be reasonably accessible to him.
9. *Freedom.* Freedom is the opportunity to pursue one's goals without restaint.
10. *Justice.* The Christian law of love does not imply neglect to the self. The individual is to be as concerned about others as he is about himself, neither more nor less.
11. *Personality.* The preceding goals were stated in terms of the kinds of life experiences we wish people to have. These goals can be translated into the kinds of persons we wish them to be. Goals can then be regarded as qualities of human personality; accordingly, a desirable personality would be defined as one that is favorably conditioned toward the various goals.

Source: Chart made up of data of 11 goals from Howard R. Bowen, "Findings of the Study," in *Christian Values and Economic Life,* by John C. Bennett, Howard R. Bowen, W. A. Brown, Reinhold Niebuhr, and Bromley Oxnam (New York: Arno Press, 1954), pp. 50–60. Copyright © 1954 by the Federal Council of the Churches of Christ in America. Reproduced by permission of Harper & Row Publishers, Inc.

4. The worker must have the possibility of controlling, in a meaningful way, the environment within which the task is to be performed (2, 6, and 9).
5. The organization should not be the sole and final arbiter of behavior; both the organization and the individual must be subject to an external moral order (5, 9, and 10).[16]

---

[16] Robert T. Golembiewski, *Men, Management, and Morality* (New York: McGraw-Hill, 1965), p. 65.

Golembiewski has also offered specific suggestions concerning organization structure and managerial techniques that are consistent with the Judeo-Christian ethic. These are summarized in Figure 21–7.

Most of the suggestions offered by Golembiewski are concerned with the application of the Judeo-Christian ethic to the design of jobs and the job environment. They are not concerned

FIGURE 21–7

Organizational Structure and Managerial Techniques Consistent with Judeo-Christian Ethic

1. Work must be psychologically acceptable, nonthreatening	1. Congruence of personality and job requirements *a.* Proper selection to match individual with the job *b.* Compatibility of personalities of members *c.* Self-choice of members
2. Work must allow employees develop faculties	2. Organizing around "work cycles" versus "work units"; job rotation, job enlargement for supervisors and operators
3. The task must allow the individual room for self-determination	3. Managing dependence-interdependence-independence *a.* Wide span of control *b.* Supportive supervision *c.* Motivating by growth versus deficiency
4. Workers must influence the broad environment within which they work	4. "Participation": group decision making. Scanlon plan, multiple management *a.* Monitoring a discrete flow of work versus a process *b.* Organizing around small administrative units at low levels *c.* High supervisory power
5. The formal organization must not be the sole and final arbiter of behavior	5. Decentralization versus centralization *a.* Monitoring a product versus a function *b.* Organizing around small administrative units at high levels

Source: Robert T. Golembiewski, *Men, Management, and Morality* (New York: McGraw-Hill, 1965), p. 73.

with the ethics of individual managers or the ethics between the organization and its stockholders, customers, or other organizations.

Gamesmanship in Business Ethics

Another approach to business ethics is offered by Albert Z. Carr.[17] Carr argues that the ethics of business are game ethics which are different from the Judeo-Christian ethic. For instance, is it considered unethical to bluff in a game of poker? Obviously bluffing in a game of poker does not reflect on the morality of the player. It is merely a strategy of playing the game.

Carr's approach to business ethics is summarized as follows:

> Poker's own branch of ethics is different from the ethical ideals of civilized human relationships. The game calls for distrust of the other fellow. It ignores the claim of friendship. Cunning deception and concealment of one's strength and intentions, not kindness and openheartedness, are vital in poker. No one thinks any the worse of poker on that account. And no one should think any the worse of the game of business because its standards of right and wrong differ from the prevailing traditions of morality in our society.[18]

Carr further asserts that as long as an organization does not violate the rules of the game as set by law, then profit should be the guiding goal of organizational strategy. However, Carr also states that businesses should not take advantage of the situation to the point that employees, competitors, customers, government, or the public at large become hostile. Determining this point is obviously a most difficult task. Furthermore, the gamesmanship approach to ethics does not offer any specific guidelines for making this determination.

The Present Status of Ethics in Business

In 1961, *Harvard Business Review* readers were surveyed concerning their feelings toward business ethics.[19] In 1976, a follow-up study was conducted, again on the *Harvard Business Review* readership, to determine if there had been any substantial changes in views. The 1976 study specifically investigated three major questions:

1. Have business ethics changed since the early 1960s, and if so, how and why?

---

[17] Albert Z. Carr, "Is Business Bluffing Ethical?" *Harvard Business Review,* January–February 1968, pp. 143–53.

[18] Ibid., p. 145.

[19] Raymond C. Baumhart, "How Ethical Are Businessmen?" *Harvard Business Review,* July–August 1961, pp. 6–12.

2. Are codes the answer to the ethical challenges business people currently face?
3. What is the relationship between ethical dilemmas and the dilemma of corporate social responsibility?

Some of the results of the study were as follows:

1. There is substantial disagreement among respondents as to whether ethical standards in business today have changed from what they were.
2. Respondents are somewhat more cynical about the ethical conduct of their peers than they were previously.
3. Most respondents favor ethical codes, although they strongly prefer general precept codes over specific practice codes.
4. The dilemmas respondents experience and the factors they feel have the greatest impact on business ethics suggest that ethical codes alone will not substantially improve business conduct.
5. Most respondents have overcome the traditional ideological barriers to the concept of social responsibility and have embraced its practice as a legitimate and achievable goal for business.
6. Most respondents rank their customers well ahead of shareholders and employees as the client group to whom they feel the greatest responsibility.[20]

A survey conducted among managers at Pitney-Bowes, a large international manufacturer of business equipment, and Uni-Royal, a billion dollar rubber and plastics company, revealed that 90 percent of the respondents supported a code of ethics for business. An overwhelming majority also were in favor of business schools offering courses in ethics.[21] In fact, a 1980 study done by the Institute of Society Ethics and the Life Sciences reported that at least 11,000 courses in applied ethics are presently being offered in undergraduate and graduate business schools throughout the United States.[22] Furthermore, it was reported in 1979 that nearly three fourths of American corporations had written codes of ethics. Unfortunately, this same report stated that only one third of these same corporations distributed the code of ethics to all employees.[23]

At the present time the application of ethics in business seems to be in an evolutionary state. However, the importance of ethics

[20] Steven N. Brenher and Earl A. Molander, "Is the Ethics of Business Changing?" *Harvard Business Review,* January–February 1977, p. 59.

[21] "The Pressure to Compromise Personal Ethics," *Business Week,* January 31, 1977, p. 107.

[22] Liz Horwitt, "Corporate Ethics 101" *American Way,* September 1981, p. 29.

[23] "Company Codes Are Not Uncommon," *Nation's Business,* October 1979, p. 77.

in business is best summarized as follows: "Those who treat management and ethics apart will never understand either one."[24]

James F. Lincoln, founder of the highly successful Lincoln Electric Company, stated one of his management policies as being: "Do unto others as you would have them do unto you. This is not just a Sunday school ideal, but a proper labor-management policy."[25] This also seems to be a very logical starting point for establishing a corporate and personal code of ethics.

SUMMARY

Today's organizations are more concerned about social responsibility and about questions concerning ethics in management than ever before. Social responsibility is concerned with the moral and ethical content of managerial and corporate decisions over and above the pragmatic requirements imposed by legal principle and the market economy.

The basic ideas of social responsibility are not accepted by all organizations, and many arguments exist both for and against social responsibility on the part of business organizations. Arguments for social responsibility are that it is in the best interest of business; social actions can be profitable; and being socially responsible is the ethical thing to do. The major arguments against social responsibility are that it might be illegal; business and government might become indistinguishable; and social actions cannot be measured. Many organizations havc, however, participated in programs attempting to solve social problems.

Ethics are standards or principles of conduct used to govern the behavior of an individual or a group of individuals. Ethics are generally concerned with questions relating to what is right or wrong and with moral duties.

A code of ethics is needed within organizations because society is demanding it and because if it is not done voluntarily by businesses, then government regulation is likely to be passed to ensure that businesses operate with a code of ethics.

The Judeo-Christian ethic is generally considered to be the basis of Western ethical codes and thus might be the basis for a code of ethics for organizations. Another approach to business ethics is the gamesmanship approach which compares business ethics to the strategy of playing a game. At the present time, the applica-

[24] James S. Bowman, "The Management of Ethics: Codes of Conduct in Organizations," *Public Personnel Journal* 10, no. 1 (1981), p. 64.

[25] C. Roland Christensen, Norman A. Berg, and Malcolm S. Salter, *Policy Formulation and Administration,* 8th ed. (Homewood, Ill.: Richard D. Irwin, 1980), p. 591.

tion of ethics in business seems to be in an evolutionary state. However, basic guidelines do exist for the establishment of a corporate and personal code of ethics.

REVIEW QUESTIONS

1. What is social responsibility?
2. Outline three major arguments for social responsibility.
3. Outline three major arguments against social responsibility.
4. What are some obstacles to organizations that desire to become more socially responsible?
5. Categorize the issues that are now considered to be legitimate social concerns of organizations.
6. What is consumerism?
7. What are ethics? Give some reasons why a code of ethics is needed in organizations.
8. Describe the Judeo-Christian ethic.
9. Discuss gamesmanship in business ethics.
10. What is the present status of ethics in business?

DISCUSSION QUESTIONS

1. Do you feel that organizations and managers should be evaluated with regard to social responsibility?
2. "Profits, not social responsibility, must be the primary concern of managers." Discuss.
3. Are most managers ethical? Discuss.
4. Why are numerous unethical practices—such as padding the expense account—accepted by many managers in today's organizational world?

SELECTED READINGS

Ackerman, Robert W., and Raymond A. Bauer. *Corporate Social Responsiveness: The Modern Dilemma.* Reston, Va.: Reston Publishing, 1976.

American Institute of Certified Public Accountants, Committee on Social Measurement. *The Measurement of Corporate Social Performance.* New York: American Institute of Certified Public Accountants, 1977.

Boling, T. E. "Management Ethics Crisis: An Organizational Perspective." *Academy of Management Review,* April 1978, pp. 360–65.

Bork, R. H. "Modern Values and Social Responsibility." *MSU Business Topics,* Spring 1980, pp. 5–17.

Bowman, J. S. "Management of Ethics: Codes of Conduct in Organizations." *Public Personnel Management* 10, no. 1 (1981), pp. 59–66.

Brenner, Steven N., and Earl A. Molander. "Is Ethics of Business Changing?" *Harvard Business Review,* January–February 1977, pp. 57–71.

Buehler, Vernon M., and Y. K. Shetty. "Managerial Response to Social Responsibility Challenge," *Academy of Management Journal,* March 1976, pp. 66–78.

Byron, William J. "The Meaning of Ethics and Businesses." *Business Horizons,* December 1977, pp. 31–34.

Chatov, R. "What Corporate Ethics Statements Say." *California Management Review,* Summer 1980, pp. 20–29.

Friedman, Milton. "The Social Responsibility of Business Is to Increase Its Profits." *New York Times Magazine,* September 1970, pp. 32–33.

Gray, E. R. "Planning for Corporate Social Programs—Problems and Guidelines." *Long Range Planning,* April 1981, pp. 49–53.

Hay, Robert, Edmund R. Gray, and James E. Gates. *Business and Society: Cases and Text.* Cincinnati: South-Western Publishing, 1976.

Heilbroner, Robert L., and Paul London. *Corporate Social Policy Selections from Business and Society Review.* Reading, Mass.: Addison-Wesley, 1975.

Higgins, J. M. "Social Audit of Equal Opportunity Programs." *Internal Auditor,* February 1979, pp. 15–22.

Jones, T. M. "Corporate Social Responsibility Revisited, Redefined." *California Management Review,* Spring 1980, pp. 59–69.

Luthans, Fred, and Richard M. Hodgetts. *Social Issues in Business.* 2d ed. New York: Macmillan, 1975.

Payne, S. L. "Organization Ethics and Antecedents to Social Control Processes." *Academy of Management Review,* July 1980, pp. 409–14.

Saul, G. K. "Business Ethics: Where Are We Going?" *Academy of Management Review,* April 1981, pp. 269–76.

Sonnenfeld, J., and P. R. Lawrence. "Why Do Companies Succumb to Price Fixing?" *Harvard Business Review,* July 1978, pp. 145–56.

Spicer, Barry H. "Accounting for Corporate Social Performance: Some Problems and Issues." *Journal of Contemporary Business,* Winter 1978, pp. 151–70.

Sturdivant, Frederick D. *Business and Society: A Managerial Approach.* Homewood, Ill.: Richard D. Irwin, 1977.

Zenisek, T. J. "Corporate Social Responsibility: A Conceptualization Based on Organizational Literature." *Academy of Management Review,* July 1979, pp. 359–68.

Case 21–1

Bribes and payoffs abroad

A study published by *The Wall Street Journal* gave a cross section of opinion about bribes and payoffs abroad. The survey was conducted by the Conference Board, a nonprofit business research organization based in New York, and included data from 93 executives. Approximately 52 percent of the responding executives felt that U.S. ethical standards should be followed in foreign countries regardless of impact on sales. Approximately 48 percent felt that the ethical standards of the country in which the company is operating should be followed.

Furthermore, only 25 percent of the respondents had written policies concerning unusual payments abroad. Seventy-five percent said their company depended on "unwritten" policies.

1. What future trends do you think will influence this situation?
2. How do you feel companies should operate in foreign countries?
3. Should a company have a written policy on social responsibility and ethics? Describe how such a policy might read.

Case 21–2

Padding the expense account?

Principals:

Rick Bell, residence accounts manager in Midland for United Electric Company. Rick is 25 years old, is considered to have a good potential as a manager, and was promoted to his present job one month ago.

Stan Holloway, district manager for United Electric in Midland. He is 33 years old and has been in his present job two and a half years. His district, Midland, has strong political influence in the company, as the current president of United Electric was raised there. Stan is Rick's boss.

Chester "Chet" House, division manager for United. He is 61 years old and is located at company headquarters, about 30 miles from Midland. He is Stan's boss and is also a close personal friend of the president of United.

At 7:45 A.M. on March 28, Rick Bell was preparing to leave Stan Holloway's office after chatting with him for a few minutes about the week's activities.

Rick: Oh, I almost forgot. As soon as I have my monthly expense voucher typed I'll send it to you for signature so it can be forwarded to disbursing.

Stan: I'm glad you mentioned that. I had meant to talk to you about your voucher this month. I have about $100 worth of items I want you to

> include on your voucher. This month my voucher is really loaded and I hate to submit an extremely high amount in light of the emphasis being placed on personal expense control. Since I have signature authority on your voucher nobody will look at it and when you get your check back you can give me the extra amount to cover my additional expenses. Here is an itemized list of expenses and dates incurred for inclusion.
>
> Also, don't forget that Chet House is coming by today and we are to go to lunch with him.

Rick Bell leaves Stan's office with the itemized list in his hand. During the morning, Rick gives much thought to Stan's request. At about 10 A.M., Stan calls Rick on the intercom and informs him that he (Stan) won't be able to go to lunch with them (Rick and Chet) that day because the local congressman is making an unscheduled stop in Midland to confer with some selected business leaders on some local issues that will be dominant in an upcoming election. He asks Rick to take Chet out to lunch and give him his regrets and to tell Chet that he (Stan) will see them after lunch around 2 P.M. When Chet arrives he and Rick leave for lunch and during the meal, the following conversation ensues:

Rick: Mr. House, What would you do if you were ever approached to include expenses on your expense voucher that were not yours?

Chet: Well son, that's a hard thing to theorize on. I guess the best approach would be to look at the consequences for different courses of action. If you did it and got caught in the yearly audit (a slim but possible chance), you could be reprimanded, or even fired, if the violation were flagrant enough. Of course, if you didn't get caught, you would be home free unless you were repeatedly asked to do it. And if you refuse to do it and the person asking you happens to be your boss, funny things sometimes begin to happen. People get labeled as being uncooperative and nobody wants to be thought of as being uncooperative.

So I guess that every man at some time has to make a decision that determines his survival among the fittest. This situation could be one of them.

Rick and Chet finished their meal in relative silence and went back to the office where they met Stan for their conference. After the conference, Rick went back to his office and gave some thought to the events of the day. That evening after work Rick went back to Stan's office with the results of his decision.

1. What would you have done if you were Rick?
2. Do you agree with Chet's response to Rick?

22 International Management and the Future

Objectives

1. To emphasize the growing necessity for managers to understand the nature of international management.
2. To introduce the basic approaches to and problems associated with international management.
3. To describe some important elements in the Japanese management system.
4. To describe and predict changes that have or will occur with regard to technology, natural resources, and the work force.
5. To analyze how these changes will affect organizations and managers of the future.

Chapter Outline

Glossary of Terms

Electronic data processing system (EDP) Refers to the hardware, software, and personnel that process data into information.

Exporting The selling of an organization's goods or services to another country.

Future shock The reaction of people to the rapid rate of change in society.

Hardware Refers to the computers and various input and output devices that make up a computer system.

Host country The name used for describing the country into which a foreign organization is doing business.

Importing The purchasing of goods or services from foreign countries.

Japanese management Style of management which emphasizes a flow of information and initiative from the bottom up; makes top management the facilitator of decision making rather than the issuer of edicts; uses middle management as the impetus for, and shaper of, solutions to problems; stresses consensus as the way of making decisions; and pays close attention to the personal well-being of employees.

Parent organization The name used for describing an organization that is extending its operations across its nation's boundaries.

Programmer Prepares computer programs based on the specifications of a systems analyst.

Software Programs or sets of instructions that direct the hardware to perform its data processing functions.

Technology The systematic application of scientific or other organized knowledge to practical purposes; includes new ideas, inventions, techniques, and materials.

Technology assessment Appraisal of technological developments in terms of both costs and benefits for individuals, organizations, and society.

Theory Z Name developed by William Ouchi to describe a management system that uses many of the concepts of Japanese management.

In dealing with the future, at least for the purposes at hand, it is more important to be imaginative and insightful than to be 100 percent "right." Theories do not have to be "right" to be enormously useful. Even error has its uses. The maps of the world drawn by the medieval cartographers were so hopelessly inaccurate, so filled with factual error, that they elicit condescending smiles today when almost the entire surface of the earth has been charted. Yet the great explorers could never have discovered the New World without them. Nor could the better, more accurate maps of today been drawn until men, working with the limited evidence available to them, set down on paper their bold conceptions of worlds they had never seen.

*Alvin Toffler**

Predictions about the future generally arouse the interest of most people. Traditionally, references to the future cause most managers to think about growth in profits, growth in the number of employees, and other statistics which forecast the performance of their particular organization. Managers tend to interpret increasing profit and staffing forecasts as justification for the continued application of the same management concepts. Assuming that the future will be like the past and failing to consider the impact of opposing trends or potential discontinuities can be a dangerous pitfall for managers.

Many management textbooks (including the first edition of this book) tend to analyze the future of management in terms of specifics such as the role of middle managers and the structure of future organizations. However, recent developments have indicated that a much more global view of change is required if managers are to cope with tomorrow's world. This is not to say that tomorrow's world will be less desirable, but rather that it will be different.

The purpose of this chapter is to explore some of the major trends that will influence management and organizational life in the future.

MANAGING IN AN INTERNATIONAL ENVIRONMENT

Throughout this text, management has been discussed in terms of American organizations operating in the United States. An important trend of the future is the increasing internationalization of business activity. International business activities range from the exporting of goods to other nations to the establishment of

* Alvin Toffler, *Future Shock* (New York: Random House, 1970), p. 5.

manufacturing operations in other nations. These activities present new challenges and practices to managers.

While not all organizations are directly involved in international business activities, events that significantly impact on the management of American organizations are occurring daily in other nations. This has certainly been evidenced in recent years in the international oil market. Few American organizations have been left untouched by these events. Thus, it is increasingly important that all managers have an understanding of the nature of international business activity.

International Trade

The trading of goods and services across national boundaries results from the principle of comparative advantage. Comparative advantage means that a country produces those products it is relatively more able to produce than other countries. Factors determining a country's comparative advantage in producing goods include the presence of natural resources, adequate quality and quantities of labor and capital, adequate technology, and the costs of these resources.

International Business Involvement

Two objectives: profit stability

Two objectives are generally behind the decision to extend an organization's operations to other countries: profit and stability. In terms of profit, international operations provide organizations with the opportunity to meet the increasing demand for goods and services in foreign countries. In addition, new sources of demand in other countries for an organization's output may have a stabilizing effect on the organization's production process.

Organizations deciding to move into international operations can usually be classified as following one of four basic strategies:[1]

1. *Exploit a technological lead.* When an organization creates a new product, it initially enjoys a distinct competitive advantage. As the product becomes less unique, and this advantage erodes, the organization often attempts to build new markets elsewhere. In addition, as costs begin to play a more critical part in the production of the product, the organization often finds it to its advantage to set up production and/or marketing facilities nearer to the markets it is serving.

2. *Exploit a strong trade name.* A successful product often induces organizations to set up operations on an international basis. Foreign brands often are considered better as a result of snob

[1] Raymond Vernon and Louis T. Wells, Jr., *Manager in the International Economy,* 3d ed. (Englewood Cliffs, N.J.: Prentice-Hall, 1976), p. 5.

appeal or on the basis of superior performance. This is especially evident in the foreign car market.

3. *Exploit advantages of scale.* Larger organizations can assemble the funds, physical assets, and human resources necessary to produce and distribute goods on a larger scale much easier than can smaller organizations.

4. *Exploit a low-cost resource.* When costs of production are of critical concern, an organization may set up international operations in areas where the resource and/or labor costs are relatively lower than they are domestically.

Exporting and Importing

An organization may become involved in international business activities by exporting, importing, or manufacturing in a foreign country.

Exporting refers to the selling of an organization's goods in another country. Importing refers to the purchasing of things from other countries. Some of the more common reasons for exporting and importing are listed in Figure 22–1.

The organization structure used in exporting/importing activities depends on how critical these activities are to the overall organization. Organizations that make a strong commitment to the selling of their products overseas must decide how to organize their exporting/importing activities. The organization may establish its own internal structure. This requires special expertise in international accounting, finance, marketing, and law, and as a result many organizations either cannot or do not desire to establish such divisions. Another alternative is to contract with an outside individual who is sometimes called a combination export-import manager. A combination export-import manager serves a group of exporting/importing organizations and handles all activities involved in the exporting/importing of the organization's goods or services.

Over time, many organizations find that it is economically more feasible to expand their production operations overseas rather than continue exporting goods to their markets abroad. Furthermore, in recent years less-developed countries have sought local production of goods, and as a result American organizations are finding that in order to maintain their overseas markets, they must begin production in these countries.

The ways in which international organizations expand their production activities differ in the degree of control retained by the parent organization (the organization extending its operations across its nation's boundaries). The country in which it is entering is referred to as the host country.

The parent organization may set up assembly operations in a

FIGURE 22–1
Reasons for Exporting and Importing Goods

Why export?	Why import?
1. If the production process requires high volume to reduce cost per unit, the home market may be too small to absorb the output required. Thus, the output may be sold overseas. Stoves, for example, are purchased by households only when needed to replace an old one or when a new home is built. To restrict selling stoves only to the U.S. market would limit the number of stoves demanded below that amount which is cost efficient to produce.	1. The goods may be needed but not available in the importing country (e.g., crude oil).
2. The demand for the firm's product may be seasonal and irregular. By expanding the firm's market to other countries, lower production costs may be gained from more effective production scheduling.	2. Many foreign-made products have prestige value and are demanded by the home market (e.g., French perfumes, sports cars from Germany).
3. All products undergo what is called the product life cycle—when the product is first introduced there is usually a big demand and the introducing firm is the only supplier. As the product reaches maturity, this competitive edge is reduced and can be maintained only by creating new markets where it reenters the growth stage.	3. Some foreign goods are less expensive due to lower production costs.
4. In selling goods overseas, the organization may not face competition as stiff as it does in the United States and thus its marketing costs may be reduced. By selling its established goods in new overseas markets, the organization is also able to increase its profits without risking new product development.	

foreign country whereby parts are exported overseas and the finished product is then assembled. Another arrangement is for the parent organization to contract with a foreign organization to produce its product but retain control over the marketing of the product in that country. Licensing arrangements are an extension

sort of like franchising

of this latter type of expansion under which the parent organization enters into an agreement with a foreign organization, licensing it to produce and market the parent organization's product in return for a specified percentage of resulting sales revenues. Oftentimes the parent organization provides technical and/or managerial support to the foreign organization. The joint venture is similar to the licensing agreement. However, under a joint venture the parent organization has some degree of ownership and control over the foreign organization.

Problems in International Business Activities

When an organization decides to extend its operations abroad, several new problems arise that must be considered if the activities are to be managed effectively.

Tariffs. Tariffs are government-imposed taxes charged on goods imported into or exported from a country. They serve (1) to raise revenues for the country or (2) to protect the country's producers from the competition of imported goods. Since the tariff charged on parts is often less than that charged on finished goods, foreign assembly operations (which were discussed earlier) have become more popular.

Payment for international transactions. As each country has its own form of money, international trade requires exchanging currency from one country into that of another. Foreign exchange rates (the rate of exchange for one currency to another currency; i.e., francs to American dollars) present certain problems as the rates fluctuate in value.

Government control over profits. A firm owning facilities in another country naturally expects to receive profits from its operations. The amount of profits the parent company receives is often controlled by the host country's government, which regulates the access foreigners have to its currency.

Taxation. Firms operating in another country are subject to that country's laws and regulations. As taxes are a primary source of government revenue, many countries tax foreign investments located within their boundaries. These taxes may be quite high since some of these foreign countries have few other businesses to tax.

Culture. International business activities bring people of many different cultures together. This results in problems of language barriers. A more subtle but equally important problem is that of differences in cultural values, tastes, and attitudes.

Countries differ socially, economically, technically, and politically. To be successful in the international business environment requires that these differences be recognized and considered in managing international activities. The implications of failing to consider cultural differences can be revealed in the following examples:

> A U.S. firm in Spain tried to import its company policy of holding picnics sponsored and carried out by management for the workers. The picnic was a fiasco rather than a morale booster as lower-level staff stayed together and felt awkward being served by their superiors. The Spanish attitudes of class distinction and social groups prohibited the mixing and socializing of workers with executives.
>
> A U.S. firm built a pineapple cannery at the delta of a river in Mexico. The plan was to barge the ripe fruit downstream from the plantation located upstream for canning, and load them directly on ocean liners for shipment. However, the time the pineapples were ripe was during the flood stage of the river, prohibiting the back-hauling of the barges upstream. As there was no feasible alternate method of transportation, the firm was forced to close down—selling the new equipment to a group of Mexicans at 5 percent of its original cost. These natives subsequently relocated the cannery and began successful operations.
>
> Goodyear, in marketing its "3T" tire cord in Germany, used its American ad demonstrating the strength of the cord by showing that it could break a steel chain. The German government intervened, as the use of superlatives is not permitted in advertising copy, nor is it legal to imply another product is inferior in Germany.[2]

Japanese Management System

Due to the remarkable success of Japanese organizations, much attention was focused on the Japanese management system during the 1970s. Richard Johnson and William Ouchi have outlined five factors which underlie the success of Japanese management:

1. An emphasis on a flow of information and initiative from the bottom up.
2. Making top management the facilitator of decision making rather than the issuer of edicts.
3. Using middle management as the impetus for, and shaper of, solutions to problems.
4. Stressing consensus as the way of making decisions.
5. Paying close attention to the personal well-being of employees.[3]

---

[2] David A. Ricks, Marilyn Y. C. Fu, and Jeffrey S. Arpan, *International Business Blunders* (Columbus, Ohio: Grid, 1974).

[3] Richard Tanner Johnson and William Ouchi, "Made in America (under Japanese Management)," *Harvard Business Review*, September–October 1974, p. 62.

40¢ on the $ for fringe benefits (predom in U.S & outside of U.S)

MANAGEMENT IN PRACTICE

Leaning from Foreign Management

"What can we learn from American management?" was the question asked all over the world only 10 years ago. Now it is perhaps time to ask: What can American management learn from others in the free world, and especially from management in Western Europe and Japan? For Europe and Japan now have the managerial edge in many of the areas which we used to consider American strengths, if not American monopolies.

First, foreign managers increasingly demand responsibility from their employees, all the way down to the lowliest blue-collar worker on the factory floor. They are putting to work the tremendous improvement in the education and skill of the labor force that has been accomplished in this century. The Japanese are famous for their "quality circles" and their "continuous learning." Employees at all levels come together regularly, sometimes once a week, more often twice a month, to address the question: "What can we do to improve what we already are doing?" In Germany, a highly skilled senior worker known as the *Meister* acts as teacher, assistant, and standard-setter, rather than as supervisor and boss.

Second, foreign managers have thought through their benefits policies more carefully. "Fringes" in the United States are now as wide as in any other country, that is they amount to some 40 cents for each dollar paid in cash wages. But in this country, many benefits fail to help the individual employee. In many families, for instance, both husband and wife are docked the full family health insurance premium at work, even though one insurance policy would be sufficient. And we pay full social security charges for the married working woman, even though married working women under our social security system may never see a penny of their money paid back into their accounts.

Benefits According to Need

By contrast, foreign managements, especially those of Japan and Germany, structure benefits according to the needs of recipients. The Japanese, for instance, set aside dowry money for young unmarried women, while they provide housing allowances to men in their early thirties with young families. In England, a married woman in the labor force can opt out of a large part of old age insurance if her husband already pays for the couple at his place of employment.

Third, foreign managers take marketing seriously. In most American companies marketing still means no more than systematic selling. Foreigners today have absorbed more fully the true meaning of marketing: knowing what is value for the customer.

American managers can learn from the way foreigners look at their products, technology and strategies from the point of view of the market rather than vice versa. Foreigners are increasingly thinking in terms of market structure, trying to define specific market niches for their products, and designing their business with a marketing strategy in mind. The Japanese automobile companies are but one example. Few companies are so attentive to the market as the high technology and high-fashion entrepreneurs of northern Italy.

It is not correct, as is so often

asserted in this country, that Japanese and Western European businesses subordinate profits. Indeed, the return on total assets is conspicuously higher today in a great many foreign businesses than it is in this country, especially if profits are adjusted for inflation. But the foreign manager has increasingly learned to say, "It is my job to earn a proper profit on what the market wants, to buy." We still, by and large, try to say in this country, "What is our product with the highest profit margin? Let's try to sell that and sell it hard."

Incidentally, when the foreign manager says "market," he tends to think of the world economy. Very few Japanese companies actually depend heavily on exports. And yet it is the rare Japanese business which does not start out with the world economy in marketing, even if its own sales are predominantly in the Japanese home market.

Fourth, foreign managements base their marketing and innovation strategies on the systematic and purposeful abandonment of the old, the outworn and the obsolete. In every single business plan of a major foreign company I have seen lately—Japanese, German, French, and so on—the first question is not: "What are the new things we are going to do?" The first question is: "What are the old things we are going to abandon?" As a result, resources are available for innovation, new products, new markets. In too many American companies, the most productive resources are frozen into defending yesterday.

Fifth, foreign managements keep separate and discrete those areas where short-term results are the proper measurement and those where results should be measured over longer time spans, such as innovation, product development, product introduction and manager development. The quarterly P and L is taken as seriously in Tokyo and Osaka as it is in New York and Chicago; and, with the strong role that the banks play in the management of German companies, the quarterly P and L is probably taken more seriously in Frankfurt than it is in the United States. But outside the United States, the quarterly P and L is increasingly being confined to the 90 percent or so of the budget that is concerned with operations and with the short term.

There is then a second budget, usually no more than a few percent of the total, which deals with those areas in which expenditures have to be maintained over a long period of time to get any results. By separating short-term operating budgets from longer-term investment or opportunities budgets, foreign companies can plan for the long haul. They can control expenditures over the long term and get results for long-term efforts and investment.

Sixth, managers in large Japanese, German, and French companies see themselves as national assets and leaders responsible for the development of proper policies in the national interest. One good example may be a group that came to see me six months ago. The chief executive officers of the 40 largest Japanese companies came to discuss how Japan should adjust to demographic changes; official retirement age is still 55 in Japan, while life expectancy is now closer to 80.

"We don't want to discuss with you," said the leader of the group, "what we in Japanese business should be doing. Our agenda is what Japan should be doing and what the best policies are in the national interest. Only after we have thought through the right national policies and have defined and publicized them, are we going to think about the implications for business and for our companies. Indeed we should postpone discussing economics altogether until we have understood what the right social policies are and what is best for the individual Japanese and for the country altogether. Who else besides the heads of Japan's large companies can really look at such a problem from all aspects? To whom else can the country really look for guidance and leadership in such a tremendous change as that of the age structure of our population?"

Any American executive, at all conversant with our management literature, will now say: "What else is new? Every one of these things I have known for 30 years or so." But this is precisely the point. What we can learn from foreign management is not what to do. What we can learn is to do it.

American in Origin

Each of these six practices is American in origin. Every one the foreigners have learned from us in the 20 years they have come to this country to find out how to manage.

The "quality circles" for productivity and quality improvement which are now being touted in American industry as the latest and most advanced "innovation" were brought to Japan in the 50s and 60s by three Americans—Edward Deming and Joseph M. Juran, both then at New York University, and A. V. Feigenbaum of General Electric.

The German *Meister* has ancient roots, but its present form dates back to the 50s and to unashamed imitation of the way IBM, first in this country and then in its European subsidiaries, had restructured the role and job of the first-line supervisor, converting him or her from a foreman into an assistant and teacher.

The Japanese and Germans practice in marketing what every American marketing textbook has been preaching for the last 30 years. The distinction between short-term and long-term budget goes back to Du Pont and General Motors in the 20s. Indeed, each of these practices can be found in any management books written in the late 40s and early 50s including mine. We don't need to learn what the rules are—we invented them. What we need is to put them into practice.

Source: Peter F. Drucker, *The Wall Street Journal*, June 4, 1980, p. 1.

Many American companies have adopted several of the principles of Japanese management. William Ouchi has described this style of management as "Theory Z." Theory Z organizations generally use the following principles:

1. Lifetime employment: This means that employees are not laid-off during recessionary times. Rather, paychecks are paired down for all employees, including management.
2. Evaluaton and promotion: Promotions often only come every 10 years in Japanese companies. However, no one seems to resent this since everyone else is treated the same way.
3. Nonspecialized careers: Japanese managers do not specialize and regularly move from one department to another.

4. Collective decision making: Japanese managers make decisions through a tedious process of collective decision-making.[4]

It is important to note that there are many cultural differences between America and Japan. Determining whether all aspects of the Japanese management system can be applied in the U.S. is still open to question and will require much more research.

FUTURE SHOCK

Rapid changes are currently occurring in technology, values, and other areas that influence individuals and organizations. The following example illustrates the rapid rate of change in transportation.

> It has been pointed out, for example, that in 6000 B.C. the fastest transportation available to man over long distances was the camel caravan, averaging eight MPH. It was not until about 1600 B.C., when the chariot was invented, that the maximum speed was raised to roughly 20 mph.
>
> So impressive was the invention, so difficult was it to exceed this speed limit, that nearly 3,500 years later, when the first mail coach began operating in England in 1784, it averaged a mere ten mph. The first steam locomotive, introduced in 1825, could muster a top speed of only 13 mph, and the great sailing ships of the time labored along at less than half that speed. It was probably not until the 1800s that man, with the help of a more advanced steam locomotive, managed to reach a speed of 100 mph. It took the human race millions of years to attain that record.
>
> It took only 58 years, however, to quadruple the limit so that by 1938 airborne man was cracking the 400-mph line. It took a mere 20-year flick of time to double the limit again. And by the 1960s rocket planes approached speeds of 4,000 mph, and men in space capsules were circling the earth at 18,000 mph.[5]

Exponential rates of change, such as expressed in the quotation above, affect humans not only physically but also psychologically. In 1970, Alvin Toffler coined the term *future shock* to describe the stress and disorientation that result from too much change in too short a time.[6] Organizations and managers must learn to understand and cope with this type of change and the stress that accompanies it.

---

[4] See, for instance, William Ouchi, *Theory Z: How American Business Can Meet the Japanese Challenge* (Reading, Mass.: Addison-Wesley Publishing, 1981). Also see William Ouchi and Alfred Jaeger, "Type Z: Organization Stability in the Midst of Mobility," *Academy of Management Review*, April 1978, pp. 305–14.

[5] Toffler, *Future Shock*, p. 24.

[6] Ibid., p. 2.

THE ROLE OF TECHNOLOGY

The term *technology* often makes people think of sweatshops and clanking machinery. One classic image of technology is the assembly line created by Henry Ford. However, this image does not fully symbolize the nature of technology. As was discussed in Chapter 18, technology also includes new methods and techniques for doing things. For instance, the "invention of the horse collar in the middle ages led to major changes in agricultural methods and was as much a technological advance as the invention of the Bessemer furnace centuries later."[7] New methods of birth control, of planting forests, and of teaching management are all forms of technology. Thus, technology is the systematic application of scientific or other organized knowledge to practical purposes and includes new ideas, inventions, techniques, and materials.

Chapter 18 discussed how technology impacts and significantly affects our current standard of living. As technology has greatly altered life styles, it has also altered many other things, and unfortunately, these alterations have not always been in the best interest of the human race.

In modern history, two major principles have pervaded man's attitude toward technology: (1) if technological expertise is available in a certain area, then it should be applied and (2) output should be maximized.[8] Erich Fromm has suggested that acceptance of the first principle negates humanistic values and allows technology to become the foundation for ethics.[9] Subscribers to this principle would argue that "if it is possible to put men on the moon or to have sky labs in space, these must be done even if it is at the cost of not providing for many social needs."[10] Belief in the second principle, argues Fromm, results in the dehumanization of work and a decrease in individuality. Taken to the extreme, individuals in such a system become numbers without an identifiable personality. Figure 22–2 summarizes some benefits and some disadvantages of technological advancements.

Fortunately, there is evidence that wholesale belief in the above principles is waning and that people are demanding more forethought before technological implementation. In the now classic book, *Limits to Growth,* the authors make a strong plea that new

---

[7]Ibid., p. 23.

[8]Richard H. Viola, *Organizations in a Changing Society* (Philadelphia: W. B. Saunders, 1977), p. 17.

[9]Erich Fromm, *The Revolution of Hope: Toward a Humanized Technology* (New York: Bantam Books, 1968).

[10]Viola, *Organizations.*

FIGURE 22–2
Benefits and Potential Problems Resulting from Technological Development

Benefits	*Potential problems*
Reducing infant and adult mortality rates	Regional overpopulation; problems of the aged
Highly developed science and technology	Hazard of mass destruction through nuclear and biological weapons; vulnerability of specialization; threats to privacy and freedoms (e.g., surveillance technology, bioengineering)
Machine replacement of manual and routine labor	Increased unemployment
Advances in communication and transportation	Increasing air, noise, and land pollution; "information overload;" vulnerability of a complex society to breakdown; disruption of human biological rhythms
Efficient production systems	Dehumanization of ordinary work
Affluence, material growth	Increased per capita consumption of energy and goods, leading to pollution and depletion of the earth's resources.
Satisfaction of basic needs	Worldwide revolutions of "rising expectations"; rebellion against non-meaningful work
Expanded power of human choice	Unanticipated consequence of technological applications; management breakdown
Expanded wealth of developed nations; pockets of affluence	Increasing gap between "have" and "have-not" nations; frustration of the revolutions of rising expectations; exploitation; pockets of poverty

Source: Jean Huston, "Prometheus Rebound: An Inquiry into Technological Growth and Psychological Change," *Technological Forecasting and Social Change,* 9, no. 3 (1976), p. 245. Copyright 1976 by Elsevier Science Publishing Co., Inc.

technological advances be subjected to three basic questions before the technology is widely adopted:

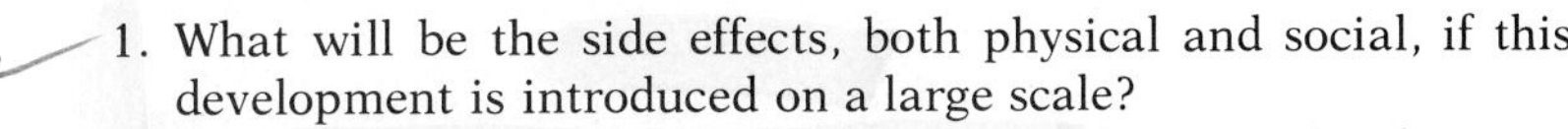

1. What will be the side effects, both physical and social, if this development is introduced on a large scale?
2. What social changes will be necessary before this development can be implemented properly, and how long will it take to achieve them?
3. If the development is fully successful and removes some natural limit to growth, what limit will the growing system meet next?

> Will society prefer its pressures to the ones this development is designed to remove?[11]

As a result of increased awareness and skepticism toward technology, the concept of technology assessment has recently emerged. Technology assessment can be defined as "a cost-benefit analysis of every proposed technological innovation, in which full weight is given to the costs and benefits to society as a whole and to local communities in particular."[12] For example, federal law now requires that an environmental impact statement be filed on certain types of proposed projects.

Computers

One aspect of technology that has significantly influenced organizations in the past and will continue to do so in the future, is computers. Computers are everywhere. Furthermore, as computers get smaller and cheaper they will continue to spread.

Computers are an integral part of management information systems (MIS) which were discussed in Chapter 6. Another frequently used term in computer terminology is EDP (electronic data processing system). An EDP system is the hardware, software, and personnel that process data into information. Hardware refers to the computers and various input and output devices that make up a computer system. Software refers to the programs or sets of instructions that direct the hardware to perform its data processing functions. The personnel in an EDP system fall into three categories—systems analysts, programmers, and operators. Systems analysts design management information systems. Programmers prepare computer programs based on the specifications of systems analysts. Operators run or operate the computers.

SCARCE RESOURCES

Anyone who keeps up with current events is aware of the problem of dwindling resources. A relationship unquestionably exists between changes in technology and the use of resources. New technology can, and frequently does, increase the demand for natural resources. Furthermore, as one resource becomes scarce, new technology is required to shift the demand to other, more available resources.

---

[11] Donella H. Meadows, Dennis L. Meadows, Jorgen Randers, and William W. Behrens III, *The Limits to Growth* (New York: Universe Books, 1972), pp. 154–55.

[12] Louis E. Davis and Albert B. Cherns, *The Quality of Working Life*, vol. I. (New York: Free Press, 1975), p. 36.

Shortages are currently being forecasted not only for the more obvious resources such as petroleum and food but also for the essential resources of water, land, clean air, and many others. The authors of the *Limits to Growth* have stated, "given present resource consumption rates and the projected increase in these rates, the great majority of the currently important nonrenewable resources will be extremely costly 100 years from now."[13] In light of the rise in gasoline prices, this prediction is certainly believable.

Yet, many people may not realize how important and how dependent organizations and people are on resources. For example, food production in America is almost entirely dependent on oil. Agricultural traction, lifting, hauling, and transport depend on oil. The conditioning of the soil through herbicides, pesticides, insecticides, and fungicides is almost totally dependent on petrochemicals.[14] One study concluded that "our mineral inventory developed and ready for immediate extraction is nil in the case of some commodities, and in some cases not equivalent to projected requirements for a decade of U.S. consumption.[15]

Until very recently, many managers have operated on the assumption that supplies of natural resources were unlimited. Furthermore, the management philosophy of most organizations has been based on continued growth. Growth in profits, number of employees, and value of assets has traditionally been high on their list of objectives. The American dream has long been to start your own company and have it *grow* into an industry leader. Yet, with limited resources, there has to be a limit to growth. Zero growth in just population alone would have profound effects upon everyday life. It would be much more difficult for employees to move up in an organization since fewer job openings would exist than in a rapidly growing organization.

The scarcity of resources has led many forecasters to predict that future managers will be forced to change their basic philosophy. These forecasters urge that the new philosophy emphasize "quality of working life" as opposed to "quantity of life." This forecast probably will prove accurate, at least to the extent that managers of the future will have to be much more aware than previously of how scarce resources should be used.

---

[13] Meadows et al., *Limits to Growth*, p. 6.

[14] Ernest W. Grove, "Present and Prehistoric Problems of Natural Resources," *American Journal of Agricultural Economics*, November 1979, p. 618.

[15] G. S. Goudarizi, L. F. Rooney, and G. L. Shaffer, "Supply of Nonfuel Minerals and Materials for the United States Energy Industry 1975–90," U.S. Geological Survey Professional Paper 1006B (Washington, D.C.: U.S. Government Printing Office, 1976), p. B32.

One probable outcome from an economy of near zero growth would be more leisure time, which most people would regard as highly desirable. Ideally, this leisure time would then be devoted to nonconsuming and nonpolluting activities such as art, music, religion, education, research, and athletics. However, such a situation could also present a very unfortunate dilemma as described by Bertrand Russell:

> Suppose that, at a given moment, a certain number of people are engaged in the manufacture of pins. They make as many pins as the world needs, working (say) eight hours a day. Someone makes an invention by which the same number of men can make twice as many pins as before. But the world does not need twice as many pins. Pins are already so cheap that hardly any more will be bought at a lower price. In a sensible world, everybody concerned in the manufacture of pins would take to working four hours instead of eight, and everything else would go on as before. But in the actual world this would be thought demoralizing. The men still work eight hours, there are too many pins, some employers go bankrupt, and half the men previously concerned in making pins are thrown out of work. There is, in the end, just as much leisure as on the other plan, but half the men are totally idle while half are still overworked. In this way it is insured that the unavoidable leisure shall cause misery all around instead of being a universal source of happiness. Can anything more insane be imagined?[16]

The ultimate effect of the changing resource base may not be known for some time to come. Ultimately, however, high-priced, scarce resources could have a dramatic impact on management and organizations.

CHANGING NATURE OF THE WORK FORCE

Since the start of the Industrial Revolution, the trend has been away from agricultural and toward industrial and service occupations. This phenomenon naturally has been accompanied by a decrease in the self-employed work force and an increase in the numbers of workers in large organizations. Most workers must now abide by the rules and policies of these organizations over which the individual may have little control. Figures 22–3 and 22–4 illustrate some of the changes in composition and characteristics of the work force.

The percentage of white-collar employees has grown steadily in recent years. This is primarily due to mechanization of many jobs formerly performed by blue-collar employees. Also, as our

[16] Bertrand Russell, *In Praise of Idleness and Other Essays* (London: Allen and Unwin, 1935), pp. 16–17.

FIGURE 22-3
Trend Away from Agriculture to Industry and Service

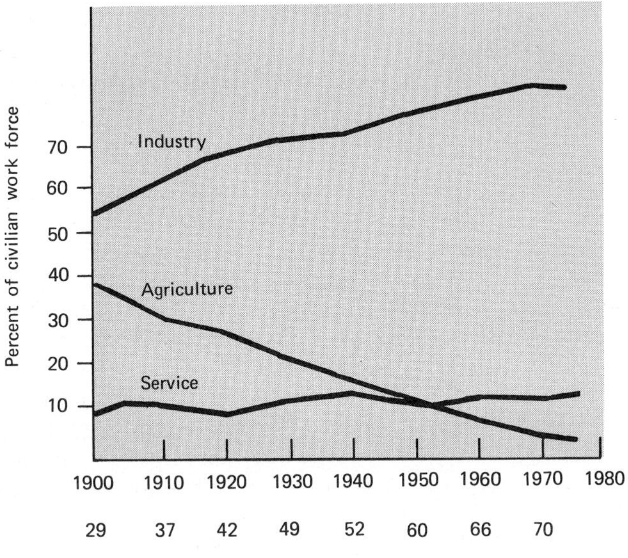

Source: From 1900–1940: U.S. Statistical Abstract—Bicentennial Issue: Colonial Times to Present (series D-182–232), p. 139; 1950–1975: U.S. Statistical Abstract—1975, p. 359. Data prior to 1950 includes workers age 14 and over; subsequent to 1950, data includes workers age 16 and over.

society has become more complex, the demand has increased for professional services, such as legal representation, accounting, and banking.

Another trend, shown in Figure 22–4, involves the employment of women. In the 19th century, generally only unmarried or widowed women worked outside the family business or the home and then usually only as servants, clerks, or factory workers in menial jobs. Figure 22–4 shows that the percentage of males in the work force has decreased from approximately 82 percent in 1900 to approximately 50 percent in 1980. Although women still do not have the same occupational opportunities as men, discrimination based on sex has been declared illegal and attempts to close the gap are being made.

The life expectancy for Americans at birth has lengthened over the past 55 years by almost 20 years. Organizations in the future will be faced with a rising age level of their employees. Employees are also becoming more educated. In 1940, only 4.6 percent of the people in the United States attended college, whereas in 1980 the percentage was approximately 25 percent. In addition, the educational level of the general population has risen.

FIGURE 22–4
Changing Characteristics of the Work Force

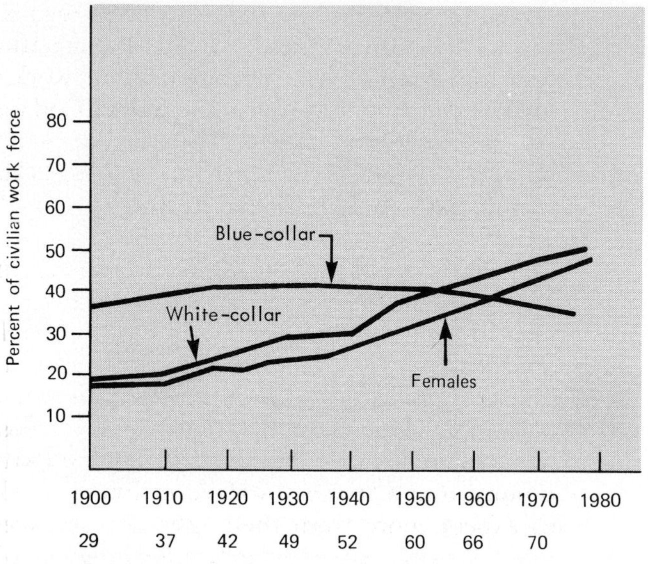

Source: From 1900–1940: U.S. Statistical Abstract—Bicentennial Issue: Colonial Times to Present (Series D-192–232), p. 139; 1950–1975: U.S. Statistical Abstract—1975, p. 359.

The impact of these changes on the work force and the type of work performed can be summarized as follows:

1. Most of the labor force works in large organizations.
2. To coordinate and control the activities of hundreds and thousands of employees, these organizations require obedience to their rules, procedures, and policies.
3. Almost everybody must submit to the formal channels of authority within an organization. With few exceptions, each employee has a boss who tells the employee what to do. Traditionally, the boss is viewed as being "right."
4. Jobs are often narrowly defined; many are so specialized that they may cause boredom.
5. Workers are subjected to pressures not only from the superiors but also from peer groups. Peer pressure can influence tremendously the behavior and performance of individuals.

These changes in the work force have been accompanied by alterations in the attitudes of workers. Some of these changes are discussed in the next section.

Attitudes and Values toward Work

People's views of work have changed appreciably over time. Prior to the Renaissance and the Protestant Reformation, work was reserved for serfs and peasants and was regarded primarily as punishment. However, the Protestant Reformation, led by Martin Luther and John Calvin, advocated that work was neither evil nor undesirable but that it was the will of God for man to work.[17] Out of the Reformation grew the idea that if a person worked hard, he or she would be rewarded accordingly. Max Weber, a German sociologist, labeled this the Protestant ethic.[18]

Work has traditionally been viewed as both necessary and honorable in the United States. However, since the advent of unemployment compensation, social security, and other state and federal welfare programs, work has become less necessary than it once was. Before these programs, people did not really have a choice; they had to work to survive. Because of this, workers were obliged to do as they were told for fear of losing their jobs.

As their lot was improved through education, the influence of unions, and a rising standard of living, workers gradually began to expect more from their jobs. These expectations came to include genuine job satisfaction, feelings of accomplishment, and a sense of challenge. Some researchers have concluded that many employees of today are dissatisfied with their jobs, since many of today's jobs do not provide an opportunity to satisfy these expectations.[19] Other research has indicated, however, that general job satisfaction is high, although in some sections of the work force it is eroding.[20] If this phenomenon of mass job dissatisfaction is real, it would partially explain the increased concern over the quality of working life.

With regard to worker values, one study of 1,058 workers representing various age groups found that substantial differences exist in work value systems held by workers of differing age and educational backgrounds.[21] This is not surprising since today's younger workers grew up in a very different environment with many more educational opportunities than did today's older

---

[17] Robert W. Green, ed., *Protestantism and Capitalism* (Boston: D. C. Heath, 1959).

[18] Max Weber, *The Protestant Ethic and the Spirit of Capitalism* (New York: Charles Scribner's Sons, 1958).

[19] *Work in America,* report of a Special Task Force to the Secretary of Health, Education and Welfare (Cambridge, Mass.: MIT Press, 1973).

[20] Jerome M. Rosow, ed., *The Worker and the Job: Coping with Change* (Englewood Cliffs, N.J.: Prentice-Hall, 1974), p. 75; and George Galley, Jr., "Particularly among Youth: Job Dissatisfaction Growing," speech before the American Management Association, New York, September 11, 1972.

[21] Ronald N. Taylor and Mark Thompson, "Work Value Systems of Young Workers," *Academy of Management Journal,* December 1976, pp. 522–36.

workers. Younger workers were found to value the opportunity to learn and/or the chance to make responsible decisions to a greater degree than did older workers. Pride in work was found to increase as educational and salary levels increased. The importance of money as a reward was found to decline with age. Younger workers showed a greater value for jobs where the opportunities for economic rewards are high than did older workers. Predictably, the younger workers also tended to prefer personally rewarding work tasks and environments to a greater extent than did older workers.

In one survey of opinion on the future environment of organizations, respondents were presented with two opposing ideologies.[22] The first ideology espoused traditional principles of individualism, private property, free competition in an open marketplace, and limited government. The second stressed the idea that the group is more important than the individual and defined the individual as an inseparable part of a community in which the person's rights and duties are determined by the common good. Under this ideology, government would be the planner and implementer of community needs. A total of 1,844 readers of the *Harvard Business Review* returned the questionnaire. While 62 percent thought that the first ideology was dominant in the United States today, 73 percent believed that the second ideology would prevail by 1985. The respondents apparently expect considerable change in values.

MANAGERIAL IMPLICATIONS OF WORLD CHANGES

Having established the fact that many factors in the manager's world are changing rapidly, the obvious question is how will these changes affect managers and the managerial process in the future? Not only is this a difficult question to answer, it is probably impossible. To quote Edgar Fiedler's forecasting rules:

1. It is very difficult to forecast, especially about the future.
2. He who lives by the crystal ball soon learns to eat ground glass.
3. The moment you forecast you know you're going to be wrong—you just don't know when and in which direction.
4. If you're ever right, never let them forget it.[23]

---

[22] William F. Martin and George Cabot Lodge, "Our Society in 1985—Business May Not Like It," *Harvard Business Review*, November–December 1975, pp. 143–52.

[23] Edgar R. Fiedler, "Fiedler's Forecasting Rules," *Reader's Digest*, March 1979, p. 100.

At the same time, however, certain predictions concerning the manager's role can be made with some degree of confidence:

Organizations will continue to become more internationally concerned.

Computers will become even more commonplace.

More emphasis will continue to be placed on quality of life versus quantity of life.

Concern over environmental issues and resource shortages will continue to grow and place limits on organizational growth.

Pressures will exist to broaden the concept of the organization from just a place to work to more of a place to find fulfillment and satisfaction.

Efficiency of operation (productivity) will become more valued.

Fortunately, the changes discussed in this chapter and most of the other changes will not take place overnight. The key to managing successfully in the future is to anticipate and prepare for change. Managers who develop such a future orientation will not view the future merely as an extrapolation of the past but rather will anticipate the inevitable changes: managing tomorrow will be just as exciting as today, but the challenges will be different.

SUMMARY

An important trend of the future is the increasing internationalization of business activity. International business activities include the exporting of domestically-made goods to other nations, the importing of foreign-made goods, and the establishment of American-owned manufacturing operations in other nations.

Organizations generally enter international activities using one of four basic strategies: (1) by exploiting a technological lead; (2) by exploiting a strong trade name; (3) by exploiting advantages of scale; or (4) by exploiting low-cost resources. An organization faces several potential problems in international activities such as tariffs, payment for international transactions, government control of profits, taxation, and different cultures.

During the 1970s, much attention was focused on the Japanese management system. Five factors which underlie the success of Japanese management are: (1) an emphasis on a flow of information and initiative from the bottom up; (2) making top management the facilitator of decision making rather than the issuer of edicts; (3) using middle management as the impetus for, and shaper of, solutions to problems; (4) stressing consensus as the way of making decisions; and (5) paying close attention to the personal well-being of employees.

Technology is the systematic application of scientific or other organized knowledge to practical purposes and includes new ideas, inventions, techniques, and materials. Until very recently, technology had been applied with little appraisal as to its costs versus its benefits. Recently, however, society has begun to demand more forethought and analysis before technologies are implemented. This increased skepticism toward technology has resulted in the evolvement of technology assessment. Technology assessment can be defined as a cost-benefit analysis of every proposed technological innovation, in which full weight is given to the costs and benefits to society as a whole and to local communities in particular. One aspect of technology that has significantly influenced organizations in the past and will continue to do so in the future is computers.

Resource shortages are currently being forecast not only for the more obvious resources, such as petroleum and food, but also for the essential resources of water, land, clean air, and many others. The ramifications of these resource shortages are very significant to organizations and managers of the future; organizations will no longer enjoy unlimited growth.

Several changes have also occurred in the nature of the work force. The percentage of white-collar employees has increased steadily, as has the percentage of working women. Life expectancies have lengthened, and the educational level of the work force has risen. Expectations of workers for genuine job satisfaction, feelings of accomplishment, and a sense of challenge are rising.

One primary result of changes in technology, in resources, and in the nature of the work force is that organizations and managers must increase their awareness of the changes and how they will affect the future.

REVIEW QUESTIONS

1. In what ways may an organization enter into international business activities?
2. Describe four strategies that an organization may follow to move into international operations.
3. Describe some problems faced by organizations in international business activities.
4. What are five factors that underlie the success of Japanese management?

5. What does the term *future shock* mean?
6. What is technology?
7. Describe the basic attitude that society has historically maintained toward the implementation of technology.
8. What is technology assessment?
9. Define MIS and EDP.
10. Describe how the composition of the U.S. work force has changed.
11. How have worker values changed?

DISCUSSION QUESTIONS

1. Do you think that the old saying, "When in Rome, do as the Romans do" applies to international management?
2. Discuss the following statement: "Technology has solved our problems in the past and it will solve the energy problem."
3. "Young people cannot be managed today the same way as people who went through the Great Depression of 1929." Discuss.
4. What predictions can you make regarding organizational life for 1995?

SELECTED READINGS

Carter, A., and N. Foy. "Will 1990 Mark the End of the Will to Work—or the Right to Manage?" *Long Range Planning,* April 1981, pp. 42–48.

Cowan, N. "Personnel Management in the Eighties: Will We Waste Another Decade?" January 1980, pp. 22–25.

Davis, Louis E., and Albert B. Cherns. *The Quality of Working Life.* New York: Free Press, 1975.

Drucker, P. F. "Behind Japan's Success." *Harvard Business Review,* January–February 1981, pp. 83–90.

Fuller, S. H. "How to Become the Organization of the Future." *Management Review,* February 1980, pp. 50–53.

Galbraith, J. K. "Management Problem in the 80's." *Management International Review* 21, no. 1 (1981), pp. 4–6.

Greene, J. P. "People Management: New Directions for the 80's." *Administrative Management,* January 1981, pp. 22–24 ff.

Harbron, J. D. "Why the US Executive Must Change His Ways." *Business Quarterly,* Spring 1981, pp. 10–12.

Hayes, R. H., and W. J. Abernathy. "Managing Our Way to Economic Decline." *Harvard Business Review,* July–August 1980, pp. 67–77.

Ouchi, W. G. "Organizational Paradigms: A Commentary on Japanese Management and Theory Z Organizations." *Organizational Dynamics,* Spring 1981, pp. 36–43.

Peck, W. "Management at Ease: How Coping with Today's Problems will

Determine the Shape of Your Job Ten Years from Now." *Administrative Management,* January 1981, p. 66.

Rehder, R. R. "Japanese Management: An American Challenge." *Human Resource Management,* Winter 1979, pp. 21–27.

———. "What American and Japanese Managers are Learning from Each Other." *Business Horizons,* March–April 1981, pp. 63–70.

Sadek, K. E., and E. A. Tomeski. "Future Challenges for MIS." *Journal of Systems Management,* July 1979, pp. 30–35.

Schwab, B. "Management of Nonrenewable Resources: Will the Free Market System Work?" *California Management Review,* Summer 1979, pp. 5–12.

Sinetar, M. "Management in the New Age: An Exploration of Changing Work Values." *Personnel Journal,* Summer 1980, pp. 749–55.

Talpaert, R. "Looking into the Future: Management in the Twenty-first Century." *Management Review,* March 1981, pp. 21–25.

Thain, D. H. "Improving Competence to Deal with Politics and Government: The Management Challenge of the 80's." *Business Quarterly,* Spring 1980, pp. 31–45.

Weinstein, A. K. "Management Issues for the Coming Decade." *University of Michigan Business Review,* September 1979, pp. 29–32.

Withington, F. G. "Coping with the Computer Proliferation." *Harvard Business Review,* May–June 1980, pp. 152–64.

Zenter, R. D. "2001: Can Management Science Keep Up?" *Interfaces,* February 1981, pp. 56–58.

Case 22–1

Staying at home

With the increased interest in doing business overseas, many large organizations have found it necessary to assign Americans to managerial positions in other countries. The prospect of seeing the world at the company's expense has enticed many Americans to seek overseas assignment in the past. Furthermore, overseas assignment has been used by organizations as a mechanism by which managers are groomed for higher-level positions when they are returned to America. Equally appealing has been the payment of "hardship pay" awarded to these relocated managers to help ease the transition into another society for them and their families. In the past, these managers and their families generally have been relocated in European countries such as England, France, and Belgium.

However, many organizations have found recently that they are having trouble recruiting managers for overseas assignments.

The opportunities, while plentiful, are increasingly being turned down. While some organizations have attempted to solve this problem by resorting to the hiring of people from within the country in which they are operating to fill managerial positions, many others are reluctant to do so. These organizations feel that it is necessary to have managers who understand the workings of the American parent company as well as the complexities of international business. While local people may serve well in lower-level managerial positions, they are hesitant to place them in higher positions of authority. The problem for these organizations is a perplexing one. It is particularly critical in view of the fact that most new foreign position opportunities exist in the Middle East and the underdeveloped countries of the world where capable local human talent does not exist in great quantities. Even if they wanted to use local people to fill these managerial positions, it is unlikely that they would possess the abilities and experience necessary to successfully perform in these positions.

1. Why are firms facing this problem? Why would individuals today be less likely to accept overseas assignments?
2. What considerations would an individual make in deciding whether or not to accept an overseas assignment?
3. Can organizations do anything about this problem—can they make the opportunity of an overseas assignment any more attractive for American managers?

Case 22–2

Threats to management *

In 1957, William H. Whyte, Jr., described his version of the "organization man"—the men and women employed by organizations in the future. He predicted that the Protestant work ethic, characterized by rugged individualism and thriftiness, would be gradually replaced by a social ethic that emphasized the employees' need to conform to the group (organizational) norms and the need to belong (to be accepted).

A little over 20 years later, we are now in a position, through the use of hindsight, to evaluate the accuracy of Whyte's prediction.

* The information on which this case is based was taken from "Big Crusade of the '80s: More Rights for Workers," *U.S. News & World Report,* March 26, 1979, pp. 85–87.

Dan Gellert is a pilot for a large airline, holding a middle management position and describing himself as a "conservative Republican." A few years ago, he found himself in a most uncomfortable position. Dan had repeatedly warned the airline of an aircraft design problem he had found and had gotten nowhere with his warnings. Wrestling with his conscience and professional ideals on one hand and his desire not to rock the boat on the other, Dan finally spoke out publicly about the problem because he felt the airline had ignored his warnings. When Dan was grounded by the airline for his actions, he sued in court and was awarded $1.6 million in damages. He was subsequently reinstated by the airline as a pilot.

A fire fighter in a midwestern town had been repeatedly requested to shave his hairy chest. Not seeing how the hair on his chest affected his ability to fight fires effectively, the young man refused. As a result, he found himself assigned to desk duty. After taking his case to arbitration, the fire fighter was reinstated to his former position, awarded back pay, and was allowed to maintain his chest in its "hairy" condition.

Linda Eaton, also a fire fighter, faces a problem that is growing in importance in today's work force. Due to the nature of her job she has to work many consecutive hours at one time. While this posed no problem before, Linda recently became a mother. When she arranged to have her newborn baby brought to the firehouse so that she could breast-feed him, she was suspended. Linda subsequently won the right to breast-feed her newborn baby through a court decision that concluded that this did not adversely affect her performance on the job.

Personnel files have traditionally been kept off limits to employees whose lives are documented in them. Currently, Michigan, Oregon, Pennsylvania, California, and Maine have laws guaranteeing workers the right to inspect personnel files. Labor unions are pushing for the right of employees to inspect, copy, and challenge documents found in their personnel files.

1. Has Whyte's prediction of the "organization man" held up over the years? Why or why not?
2. What factors have contributed to the growth of this challenging attitude on the part of the workers?
3. What can organizations do in order to deal effectively with this phenomenon?

SECTION SIX
CASE

Nestle S.A.*

On January 16, 1979, Pierre Liotard Vogt, chairman of the board of Nestle S.A., summoned to Vevey, Switzerland the general managers of the infant formula divisions in Third World countries and the general managers of Nestle's U.S. subsidiary. The purpose of the meeting was to discuss the problems that Nestle was experiencing in the infant formula controversy. At that time, Nestle was being blamed by many social and civic organizations throughout the world for the deaths of infants in Third World countries. In fact, some of these organizations were leading a boycott against Nestle's products which had caused a negative impact on Nestle's profits and image.

Nestle is a well-diversified, multinational corporation. Nestle resulted from a merger in 1905 of a condensed milk firm, owned by Charles and George Page, and a milk-food firm, owned by Henri Nestle. Shortly thereafter, Henri Nestle became interested in baby food because of the high infant mortality rate in underdeveloped countries at that time. Studies conducted by Henri Nestle convinced him that there was a need and a market for a milk product that could be used as a substitute for mother's milk. Nestle developed a milk-food product by using Swiss milk concentrated by an air pump at low temperatures.

Nestle's products today include instant drinks, dairy products, culinary products, frozen foods, ice cream, yogurt, chocolates, and pharmaceuticals. It also owns hotels and restaurants. Two of Nestle's subsidiaries in the United States are Libby, McNeil & Libby, which was purchased in 1970, and Stouffer's, which was purchased in 1973. In May 1979, the name of the Nestle Corporation was changed to Nestle S.A.

The Basic Charges against Nestle

"Nestle Latest Killing in the Bottle Baby Market" read a headline in the Summer 1978 edition of the *Business and Society Review*. However, the writer of that article was not referring to a financial killing. He was referring to the actual deaths of infants in several Third World countries. This was not the first time that charges of this type had been made against Nestle S.A. and other infant formula producers. World criticism was directed at the marketing practices of infant formula producers that induced mothers in

*Research for this case was done by Raymond Owes, a graduate student at Atlanta University.

Third World countries to substitute infant formula for breast milk. Critics charged that mothers in Third World countries could not safely use the infant formula and that misuse of the formula had either directly or indirectly led to the deaths of infants.

Critics charged that Nestle S.A. and other companies used billboards, radio, newspapers, magazines, sound trucks, and sales personnel dressed in nurses' uniforms to induce mothers to use infant formula. Free samples were also given away. Critics further charged that in order to use the powdered infant formulas, mothers must be literate enough to read and understand the instructions written on the labels. In Third World countries, a high percentage of mothers are illiterate. Furthermore, unsanitary conditions and insufficient incomes also serve to preclude the safe use of infant formula.

Thus, although Nestle S.A. and its U.S. subsidiary do not market infant formula products in the United States, the Infant Formula Action Coalition (INFACT) was formed in Minneapolis, Minnesota in 1977 for the specific purpose of organizing a nationwide boycott against Nestle's products. INFACT was joined by such organizations as the American Lutheran Church Women, the United Methodist Board of Global Ministries, and the United Presbyterian Church.

Why Nestle?

The primary reason Nestle was at the center of this controversy was that it held 50 percent of the world market in infant formula. This industry has annual sales of more than a billion dollars.

Exhibit 1 gives a geographical breakdown for Nestle's total sales for all its products. Exhibit 2 gives a breakdown of Nestle's sales by product groups.

EXHIBIT 1
Geographical Distribution of Sales (percentage)

	1979	*1978*
Europe	46.7%	46.7%
Africa	4.2	4.4
North America	19.0	20.0
Latin America and Caribbean	15.6	13.7
Asia	12.4	12.8
Oceania	2.4	2.1

EXHIBIT 2
Sales by Product Groups (percentage)

	1979 percent	1978 percent
Dairy products	20.6	20.7
Infant and diet products	6.8	6.7
Infant drinks	30.9	32.6
Chocolate and Confectionaries	8.4	8.4
Culinary and sundry	15.9	15.4
Frozen foods	8.7	8.0
Refrigerated foods	2.0	1.8
Liquid drinks	2.7	2.8
Restaurants and hotels	2.8	2.7
Pharmaceuticals	1.2	0.9
	100.0%	100.0%

Source: *Moody's Industrial Manual*, vol. 2, 1980.

Nestle's Response

In May 1978, the United States Senate held hearings on the infant formula controversy. Among the companies represented at the hearing were Nestle, Abbott Laboratories, Bristol-Myers, and American Home Products. One of the questions asked of the companies was: "Can a product which requires clean water, good sanitation, adequate family income and a literate parent to follow printed instructions be properly and safely used in areas where water is contaminated, sewage runs in the streets, poverty is severe, and illiteracy is high?"

Oswaldo Ballerin, Ph.D., president of Nestle Company of Brazil, was reported to have responded that "Nestle was not responsible for the socioeconomic conditions of an area and that Nestle markets a good product."[1] Ballerin is also reported to have said:

> The United States' Nestle Company has advised me that their research indicates that this is actually an indirect attack on the free world's economic system. A worldwide church organization with the stated purpose of undermining the free enterprise system is in the forefront of this activity.[2]

It has also been reported that Nestle made a steady reduction in its direct consumer advertising for infant formula in the early

[1] "Infant Formula Controversy Report on U.S. Senate Hearings—May 23, 1978", *Food Policy Notes*, Interreligious Task Force on U.S. Food Policy) p. 2.

[2] Colleen Shannon-Thornberry, "Why a Boycott?" Pamphlet produced by the United Methodist Church, p. 13.

1970s and totally terminated its direct consumer advertising for infant formula in 1978.[3]

1. Is Nestle responsible for the socioeconomic conditions in a country in which it sells its products?
2. Do you feel that Nestle has gone far enough in curtailing its advertising?
3. Describe your feelings on the social responsibility of multinational organizations?

---

[3] Leah Rozen, "Nestle Curtails Worldwide Infant Formula Ads," *Advertising Age*, April 23, 1979, p. 28.

APPENDIXES

A. Expected value analysis
B. Break-even analysis
C. Network analysis
D. Economic order quantity (EOQ)

A Expected Value Analysis

INTRODUCTION

The expected value of a random variable is the sum of the products that are obtained by multiplying all possible values of the random variable by their respective probabilities. Mathematical expectation, mean, and average are some common names for expected value.

EXPECTED VALUE FORMULATION

Suppose X represents the value showing when a fair die is thrown. The probability function of X would be as follows:

Values of X	1	2	3	4	5	6
Probability, $f(X)$	1/6	1/6	1/6	1/6	1/6	1/6

The expected value of X, commonly denoted as $E(X)$, is defined to be:

$$E(X) = 1(^1/_6) + 2(^1/_6) + 3(^1/_6) + 4(^1/_6) + 5(^1/_6) + 6(^1/_6)$$
$$= 3.5$$

Thus, if a die is tossed very many times, the expected value or average would be 3.5.

Generalizing from the example above:

$$E(X) = \Sigma x_i f(x_i)$$

Expected value analysis is especially useful for decision makers with situations in which the event in question occurs over and over again. In such situations, the decision maker would definitely be interested in the expected value or mean. However, if the event in question is not repeated a large number of times, the expected value or mean has less meaning to the decision maker.

EXAMPLE PROBLEM

Suppose the probability of having an automobile accident has been calculated to be 0.005. An insurance company offers car insurance of \$10,000 for an annual premium of \$150. What is the insurance company's expected gain?

Let the gain for the company be represented by the random variable X, which has a possible value of \$150 if an accident does not occur, and −\$9,850 if an accident does occur during the year covered by the policy. The probability function of X is:

Values of X	\$ 150	\$−9,850
Probability, $f(X)$	0.995	0.005

$$
\begin{aligned}
E(X) &= \$150(0.995) + (-\$9{,}850)(0.005) \\
&= 149.25 - 49.25 \\
&= \$100.00
\end{aligned}
$$

EXPECTED VALUE PROBLEMS

1. An analysis of historical data has shown that the probability that a 50-year-old female will live another year is 0.985. How much should an insurance company charge a 50-year-old female for a \$10,000 term life insurance policy for a year if the premium should include a profit of \$100?
2. A manufacturer of small motors has found that 2 out of every 1,000 motors sold are returned because of a malfunction before the 90-day warranty expires. If the manufacturer makes \$2 per motor on the sale and it costs the manufacturer \$100 per motor to replace a motor, what is the expected profit for each motor sold?

B Break-Even Analysis

INTRODUCTION

The purpose of this appendix is to illustrate the methodology and application of break-even analysis. A break-even chart is a total revenue chart superimposed upon a total cost chart. Total costs are generally broken down into fixed costs and variable costs.

FIXED COSTS

As stated in Chapter 6, fixed costs are those that do not vary with output or sales in the short run. The rental costs associated with a warehouse that has been leased do not go down if the warehouse is only half occupied. Insurance costs on facilities do not normally vary according to the use of the facilities. Administrative salaries generally do not vary with the level of business activity.

In the long run, fixed costs may go up or down. For instance, the purchase of an additional warehouse or piece of capital equipment would cause fixed costs to go up. In the short run, fixed costs must be paid regardless of what is produced (or not produced).

VARIABLE COSTS

Variable costs are those costs that vary with the level of business activity as measured by sales or output. In a manufacturing situation, the cost of raw materials and direct labor costs depend on output. In the short run, total costs can be reduced only by reducing variable costs.

DETERMINATION OF THE BREAK-EVEN POINT

The break-even point (BEP) is defined as the level of output or sales at which profit is equal to zero. This is also the same point at which total revenue equals total cost.

APPLICATION OF BREAK-EVEN ANALYSIS

Although break-even analysis does not provide the manager with a total understanding of the cost and revenue components, it can assist in decision making. Break-even analysis can aid the manager in evaluating different strategies relating to level of output. It can also be used as a control device to signal when and how far costs are getting out of control, or when and by how much revenues are lagging.

Most specific applications of break-even analysis are related to sales and distribution problems.

EXAMPLE OF BREAK-EVEN ANALYSIS

Suppose the following data have been estimated by the ABC Company for producing a proposed new product, the Blub.

Rent	$1,000 per month
Manager's salary	$1,100 per month
Price of blub	$1.50
Direct labor required	6 minutes per Blub
Wage rate	$2.00 per hour
Materials cost	$1.00 per Blub

Assume that the labor costs are variable and that no expenses, other than outlined above, exist. The marketing department of ABC has estimated that a minimum of 8,000 Blubs can be sold per month. Should ABC put the Blub into production?

$$\text{Profit} = \text{Total revenue } (TR) - \text{Total costs } (TC) \qquad \text{(B–1)}$$

$$\text{Total revenue} = (\text{Price per Blub})\,(\text{Number of Blubs sold})$$

$$TR = (\$1.50)(X) \qquad \text{(B–2)}$$

where

X = number of Blubs sold

$$\text{Total cost} = \text{Variable cost} + \text{fixed cost} \qquad \text{(B–3)}$$

$$\text{Variable cost} = \text{Total materials cost} + \text{total direct labor cost}$$

$$\text{Variable cost} = \$1.00(X) + \left(\frac{6\text{ min/Blub}}{60\text{ min/hr}}\right)(\$2/\text{hr})(X) \qquad \text{(B–4)}$$

where

X = number of Blubs sold

$$\text{Fixed cost} = \text{Rent} + \text{manager's salary}$$
$$\text{Fixed cost} = \$1{,}000 + \$1{,}100 \qquad \text{(B–5)}$$

Substituting equations B–4 and B–5 into equation B–3, yields

$$\text{Total cost} = \$1.00X + \left(\frac{6\text{ min/Blub}}{60\text{ min/hr}}\right)(\$2/\text{hr})(X) + \$1{,}000 + \$1{,}000$$

$$= \$1.00X + \$0.20X + \$2{,}100 \qquad \text{(B–6)}$$

Substituting equations B–2 and B–6 into equation B–1 and setting this equation equal to zero to find the break-even point, yields:

$$\text{Profit} = \$1.50X - (\$1.00X + \$0.20X + \$2{,}100) = 0$$
$$X = 7{,}000 \text{ Blubs per month (break-even point)}$$

Thus, ABC should put the Blub into production since forecasted sales of the product are at least 8,000 per month.

BREAK-EVEN PROBLEMS

1. A small but growing company produced a product which sells for $4 per unit. The costs incurred by the company are as follows:

Manager's salary	$1,000 per month	
Rent on building and equipment	$1,400 per month	
Materials cost	$2.60 per unit	
Salesman's commission	10 percent of sales revenue	
Labor cost:		
	Total cost	*Capacity*
1 worker	$400 per month	1,500 units per month
2 workers	800 per month	3,500 units per month

Production workers are not sent home if they run out of work, and no overtime labor is used. Sketch a break-even chart for this firm and indicate the monthly production volume at which the firm will break even.

2. The Que Company prints personal checks and is located in New York. The company has two options for serving its Washington customers. These options are outlined below:
Option 1. Maintain a sales and customer service office in Washington. Under this arrangement a clerk in the Washington office would receive orders through the mail and telephone them to the New York plant where the order would be produced and shipped directly to the customer. The following costs have been estimated for this arrangement.

Rent for office space	$200 per month
Salary for office person	$480 per month
Furniture and equipment (i.e., typewriter) rental	$200 per month
Telephone expense (WATS line)	$200 per month)
Production cost per order in New York plant	$1.50 per order
Capacity of this method	2,000 orders per month
Price per order	$2.25 per order

Option 2. Open a small plant in Washington. Under this arrangement the following costs have been estimated.

Rent on plant space	$600 per month
Manager's salary	$800 per month
Materials cost	$0.40 per order
Depreciation on equipment	$200 per month
Labor cost:	
1 office clerk	$400 per month
1 typesetter/pressman	$500 per month
1 binding worker	$450 per month
Capacity of this method	3,000 orders per month
Price per order	$2.25 per order

Using break-even analysis, determine what option Que should use throughout the growth of the Washington business and when to change from one method to the next.

C Network Analysis

INTRODUCTION

This appendix is designed to illustrate the basic methodology and computation used in identifying the critical path of a project. It contains some general definitions and guidelines relating to network analysis, as well as a discussion of the Critical Path Method (CPM) and the Program Evaluation and Review Technique (PERT).

DEFINITIONS

The following basic definitions and symbols are commonly accepted and used in network analysis.

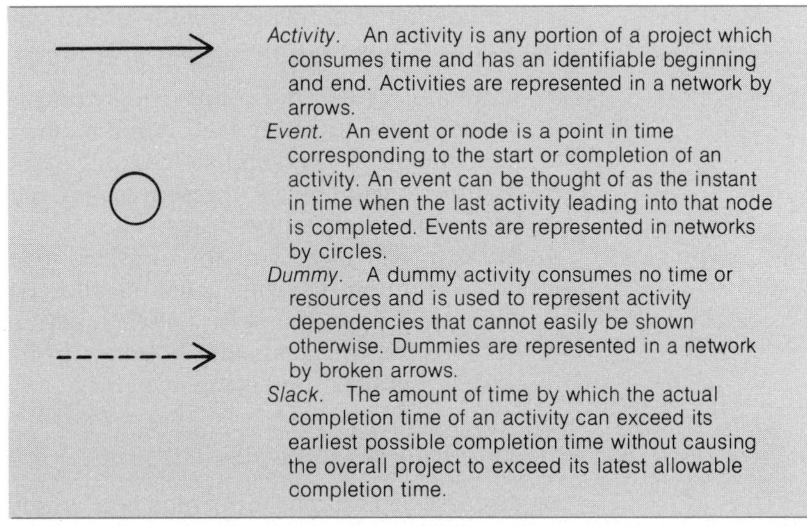

Activity. An activity is any portion of a project which consumes time and has an identifiable beginning and end. Activities are represented in a network by arrows.

Event. An event or node is a point in time corresponding to the start or completion of an activity. An event can be thought of as the instant in time when the last activity leading into that node is completed. Events are represented in networks by circles.

Dummy. A dummy activity consumes no time or resources and is used to represent activity dependencies that cannot easily be shown otherwise. Dummies are represented in a network by broken arrows.

Slack. The amount of time by which the actual completion time of an activity can exceed its earliest possible completion time without causing the overall project to exceed its latest allowable completion time.

NETWORK RULES

An understanding of the following basic rules of network analysis is necessary.

1. Before an activity can begin, all activities or paths leading to the starting event of that activity must be completed.
2. Arrows imply logical sequencing only, and neither the length of the arrow or its "compass" direction have any meaning.
3. Most networks will have only one initial event and one terminal event.

TYPES OF ACTIVITY DEPENDENCIES

When sequencing events, several types of dependencies between and among the activities must be considered:

1. Natural dependencies: These occur when one activity simply cannot take place until another is completed. For example, the roof cannot be put on a house until the frame has been erected.
2. Resource dependencies: These occur when different activities require the use of the same resource and therefore cannot take place simultaneously. For example, if two activities require the use of the same machine they cannot take place simultaneously.
3. Policy dependencies: These occur as the result of an organization policy. For example, it may be a construction company's policy not to begin building until all materials are on site.

ESTIMATING ACTIVITY TIMES

The following statements provide useful guidelines which should be followed when estimating activity times.

1. Estimate activity durations using working days, not man-days.
2. Do not build in safety factors for major contingencies such as fires, floods, strikes, and so forth.
3. Assume normal levels of resources for each activity unless contradictory information exists.
4. Build in considerations for weather, machine down-time, and other common contingencies on an activity-by-activity basis, depending upon the nature of each activity.
5. Account for weekends and holidays in the case of unusual activities (such as the drying of paint).

CRITICAL PATH METHOD (CPM)

As discussed in Chapter 6, CPM is best employed when the project activity durations are relatively well-defined.

Basic Scheduling Computations

The basic scheduling computations involve a forward pass followed by a backward pass through the network. The forward pass computation yields the earliest possible finish time (EPF) for each activity as well as the earliest possible occurrence time (EP) for each event. The backward pass, which cannot be computed until the forward pass has been completed, gives the latest allowable start time (LAS) for each activity as well as the latest allowable occurrence time (LA) for each event.

After both the forward and backward pass have been completed, the slack can be computed for each activity. The critical path is then determined along the path or paths having the least amount of slack.

The following notation is suggested for use in performing network computations.

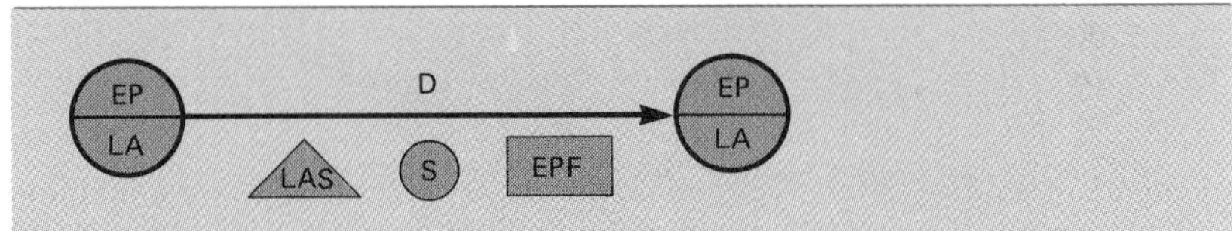

D = Estimated duration of activity.
S = Total slack of activity.
EP = Earliest possible event time.
LA = Latest allowable event time.
EPF = Earliest possible finish time for activity.
LAS = Latest allowable start time for activity.

Forward Pass Rules

The following statements outline the specific rules that are necessary for performing the forward pass computations.

1. The initial project event is assigned an earliest possible event time; usually this is zero.
2. All activities are assumed to begin as soon as all of their predecessor events are completed.
3. The earliest possible finish time (EPF) of an activity is merely the sum of the earliest possible event time (EP) for the event at the start of the activity (tail of the arrow) and the estimated activity duration.
4. The earliest possible event time (EP) is equal to the maximum earliest possible finish time (EPF) of all activities, including dummies, contributing to the respective event.

Example of Forward Pass

Figure C–2 shows the results of the forward pass computations based on the data and network provided in Figure C–1.

FIGURE C–1

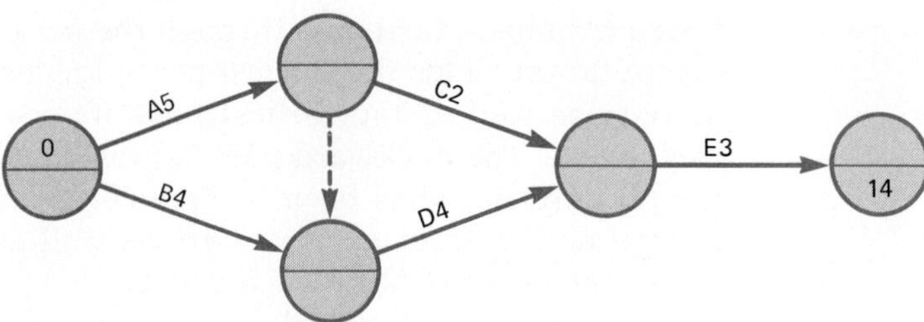

FIGURE C–2

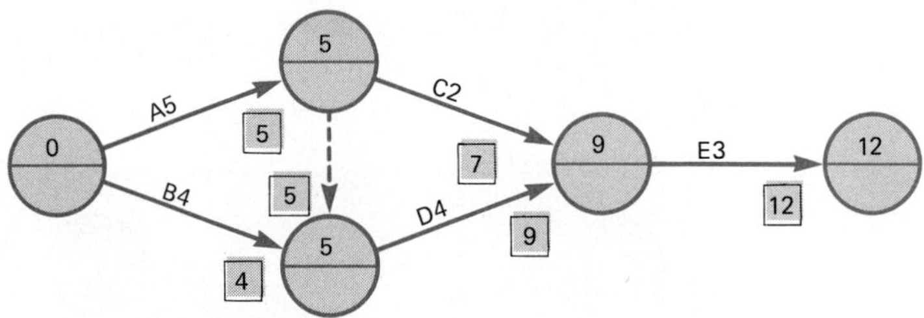

Backward Pass Rules

The following statements outline the specific rules that are necessary for performing the backward pass computations.

1. The latest allowable event time for the project terminal event is equal to its earliest possible event time (EP) as computed by the forward pass unless an arbitrary completion time has been stipulated by management.
2. The latest allowable start time (LAS) for a given activity is equal to the latest allowable event time (LA) for the event at the end of the activity (head of the arrow) minus the activity duration.
3. The latest allowable event time (LA) for a given event is equal to the minimum latest allowable start time (LAS) for all activities, including dummies, that immediately follow (lead from) the respective event.

Example of Backward Pass

Figure C–3 shows the results of the backward pass computations using the data and network provided in Figures C–1 and C–2. In this example management has stipulated that the project must be completed in 14 days.

FIGURE C–3

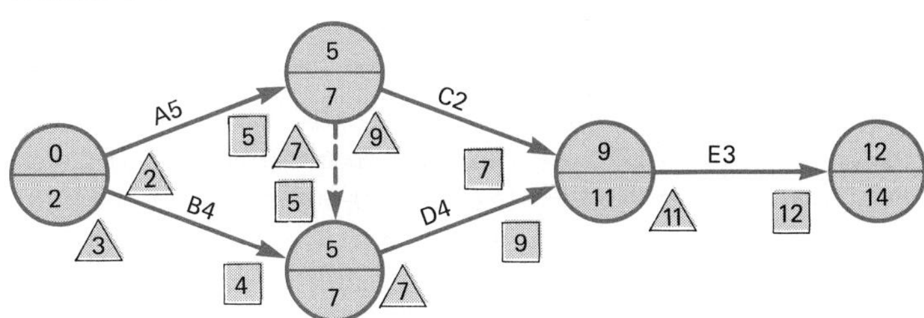

Slack Computations

The total slack for a given activity is equal to the latest allowable event time (LA) for the event at the finish of the activity (head of the arrow) minus the earliest possible finish time (EPF) of the respective activity.

Determination of Critical Path

The critical path(s) falls along those activities (from the initial event of the project to the terminal event of the project) which have the smallest slack value. It should be noted that the slack will be the same for all activities on the critical path. This aspect of the total slack is somewhat misleading in that if one activity on the critical path is delayed, then the slack time of all the following activities on that same path is reduced by the amount of the delay. Thus, there is not as much slack as might first appear.

Example of Determining Slack and Critical Path

Figure C–4 presents the results of the slack computations based on the data and network given in Figure C–3. The heavy lines represent the critical path.

FIGURE C–4

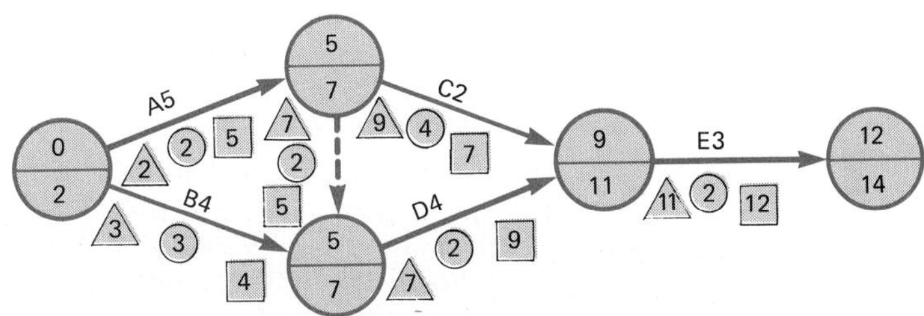

PROGRAM EVALUATION AND REVIEW TECHNIQUE

Program evaluation and review technique (PERT) recognizes that the duration for most activities cannot be stated in advance with total certainty. The PERT procedure attempts to account for this limitation by allowing the networker to state an optimistic, a pessimistic, and a most likely duration for each activity. Using these time estimates, the expected time and the variance of each respective project activity can be calculated. After this analysis has been completed for each activity, an expected completion time and associated variance can be calculated for the entire project. With this information, it is possible to make statements concerning the probability of completing the project within a given amount of time.

PERT Time Estimates

The following statements define the time estimates used by PERT.

Optimistic time (a). The length of time required if exceptionally good luck is encountered during the performance of the activity. Normally the optimistic time is expected to be equaled or bettered only 5 out of every 100 times the activity takes place.

Pessimistic-time (b). The length of time required if exceptionally bad luck is encountered during the performance of the activity. Normally the pessimistic time is expected to be equaled or bettered 95 out of every 100 times the activity takes place.

Most likely time (m). The time required for the activity if normal conditions are encountered. If the activity were repeated a large number of times, the most likely time would be the most frequently occurring time.

The expected time (t_e) for a given activity time is calculated using the following formula which is basically a weighted average of the three estimates:

$$t_e = \frac{a + 4m + b}{6} \qquad \text{(C–1)}$$

The expected time is equivalent to that time estimate which has a 50–50 chance of being completed and is equal to the most likely time only if the optimistic (a) and pessimistic (b) times are equidistant from the most likely time (m). The activity variance (σ^2) is computed according to the following formula:

$$\sigma^2 = \left(\frac{b - a}{3.2}\right)^2 \qquad \text{(C–2)}$$

By using the expected times (t_e) as the activity durations, the same computational procedures and rules used in CPM are used in PERT for performing the forward and backward passes and for determining the critical path.

Example PERT Time Calculations

Assume the following three time estimates have been obtained for a given activity:

$$\text{Optimistic time } (a) = 5 \text{ weeks}$$
$$\text{Most likely time } (m) = 7 \text{ weeks}$$
$$\text{Pessimistic time } (b) = 10 \text{ weeks}$$

Substituting into equations C–1 and C–2, we get

$$\text{Expected time } (t_e) = \frac{5 + 4(7) + 10}{6}$$

$$t_e = 7.17$$

$$\text{Variance } (\sigma^2) = \left(\frac{10-5}{3.2}\right)^2$$

$$= 2.44$$

Thus, the expected time is slightly greater than the most likely time estimate. The variance is 2.44 weeks, which means that if the activity were repeated a large number of times, in 67 percent of the cases the activity should take between 5.61 and 8.73 weeks ($7.17 \pm$ one standard deviation or $7.17 \pm \sqrt{2.44}$).

The variance of the entire project can be calculated by summing the variances of each activity along the critical path. Probability statements can then be made concerning the entire project.

CPM/PERT PROBLEMS

1. Given the following information construct an appropriate network.

Activity	*Immediate prerequisite*
A	—
B	—
C	A,F
D	B
E	C,D
F	—

2. Based upon the following narrative description of a project, draw a CPM logic network that accurately shows the natural dependencies among the activities involved.

   The Sheffield Manufacturing Company is considering the

introduction of a new product. The first step in this project will be to design the new product. Once the product is designed, a prototype can be built and engineers can design the process by which the product will be produced on a continuous basis. When the prototype is completed, it will be tested. Upon completing the process design, an analysis will be made of the production cost per unit for the new product. When the prototype testing and the production cost analysis are both finished, the results will be submitted to an executive committee which will make the final go-ahead decision on the product introduction and establish the price to be charged. Assuming that the committee's decision is positive, several steps can be taken immediately. The marketing department will begin designing sales literature. The production department will obtain the equipment to be used in the manufacture of the new product, hire the additional personnel needed to staff the process, and obtain an initial stock of raw materials. After sales literature has been designed, it will be printed. The new equipment obtained for the production process will have to be modified slightly. The production personnel will be trained as soon as the equipment modifications are complete, all necessary personnel have been hired, and the initial stock of materials has been obtained. When the printing of the sales literature is completed and the production personnel have been trained, the sales literature will be distributed to the salespersons and the product introduction will be considered complete.

3. Perform all forward, backward, and slack computations for the following network and indicate the location(s) of the critical path(s).

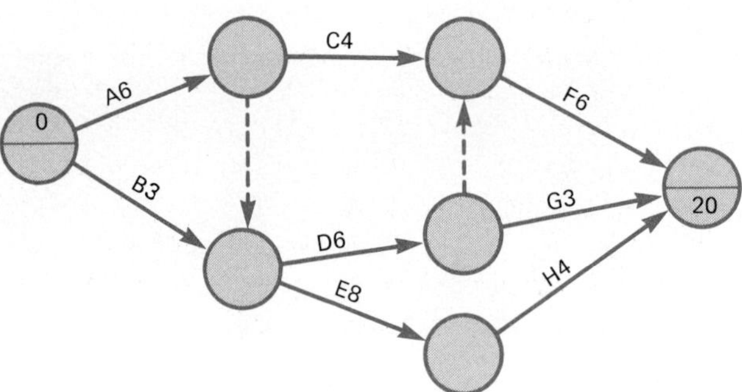

4. Using the network given in problem 3 above, calculate the earliest expected completion time for the project based on the following PERT time estimates.

Activity	*Optimistic* (*a*)	*Most likely* (*m*)	*Pessimistic* (*b*)
A	4	6	8
B	1	3	4
C	3	4	6
D	4	6	8
E	7	8	10
F	4	6	7
G	2	3	4
H	3	4	5

D Economic Order Quantity (EOQ)

INTRODUCTION

The purpose of this appendix is to discuss the methodology and computations used for determining the economic order quantity.

DETERMINING THE ECONOMIC ORDER QUANTITY (EOQ)

As discussed in Chapter 20, the optimum number of units to order (the economic order quantity or EOQ) is determined by two inversely related costs: (1) carrying costs and (2) ordering costs. The lower the number of orders processed, the lower the ordering costs. However, fewer orders mean larger sizes for each order, which results in higher carrying costs. Figure 20–3 in the text graphically depicts the relationship between carrying costs and ordering costs.

The basic idea of the EOQ is to find the order size that minimizes total inventory costs incurred during the period. Total inventory costs associated with a given period are composed of the total carrying cost, total ordering cost, and the actual purchase cost of the inventory. Mathematically, total costs can be expressed as follows:

$$\text{Total costs} = \text{Total carrying cost} + \text{Total ordering cost} + \text{Actual purchase cost of the inventory} \qquad \text{(D–1)}$$

The total carrying cost is determined by multiplying the average inventory on hand during the period by the carrying cost per unit of inventory. Normally the average inventory on hand is approximated by dividing the order quantity (Q) by 2. This assumes a linear usage rate of the items in inventory.

$$\text{Total carrying cost} = (\text{Average inventory during period})(\text{Carrying cost per item}) = (Q/2)(C) \tag{D–2}$$

where

Q = Order quantity
C = Carrying cost per unit

The total ordering cost is equal to the number of orders placed during the period times the cost associated with placing each order. The number of orders placed is equal to the total demand for the period (D) divided by the order quantity.

$$\text{Total ordering cost} = (\text{Number of orders placed during the period})(\text{Cost of placing an order}) = \left(\frac{D}{Q}\right)(P) \tag{D–3}$$

where

D = Period demand
P = Order cost per order

The actual purchase cost of the inventory (the total dollars invested in the inventory) is equal to the demand during the period multiplied by the unit cost.

$$\text{Actual purchase cost of inventory} = (\text{Demand during the period})(\text{Unit cost}) = (D)(U) \tag{D–4}$$

where

U = Unit cost

Substituting equations D–2, D–3, and D–4 into equation D–1, we get

$$\text{Total costs} = \left(\frac{Q}{2}\right)(C) + \left(\frac{D}{Q}\right)(P) + (DU) \tag{D–5}$$

The minimum total costs can then be found by taking the first derivative of equation D–5 with respect to Q, setting the result equal to zero, and solving for Q.

$$\frac{d(\text{Total costs})}{dQ} = \frac{C}{2} - \frac{DP}{Q^2} + 0 = 0 \tag{D–6}$$

$$Q = \sqrt{\frac{2DP}{C}} \tag{D–7}$$

Thus the order quantity (Q) is equivalent to the economic order quantity (EOQ) and can readily be found using equation D–7. Slight variations of equation D–7 are available for accommodating special situations such as quantity discounts.

EXAMPLE EOQ PROBLEM

Suppose the following data have been collected by the AAA Company on a major inventory item:

Annual demand	5,000 units per year
Ordering costs	$25 per order
Carrying costs	$0.50 per unit per year

Determine the economic order cost.

Substituting in equation D–7, we get

$$Q = \sqrt{\frac{(2)(5{,}000)(25)}{0.50}} \tag{D–8}$$

$$Q = 707.11$$

Therefore, the AAA Company should order approximately 707 units at a time.

EOQ PROBLEMS

1. The following data have been collected for an item in inventory:

Annual sales	10,000 units per year
Ordering costs	$32 per order
Item cost	$4 per unit
Inventory holding costs	$0.25 per unit per year

a. Determine the economic order quantity.
b. Determine the annual cost for holding and reordering inventory.
c. If the ordering cost had been erroneously listed at $64 rather than $32, what would the resulting order quantity have

been? How much would this increase the total annual inventory carrying and order costs?

2. The Beta Company purchases widgets from an external supplier. A total of 5,000 widgets are used each year by Beta. Beta figures that it costs $20 in fixed charges for sending purchase orders, receiving goods, and paying bills for each order. Through the years, Beta has found that the carrying costs for most inventory items can be closely approximated by using a figure of 5 percent of the cost of the item. The basic cost to Beta of a widget is $2.
   a. Determine the economic order quantity.
   b. Suppose the fixed cost for sending purchase orders, receiving goods, and paying bills for each order had been erroneously calculated and was actually $40. What effect would this have on the economic order quantity?

Name Index

Subject Index

Q–R

S

This book has been set VIP in 10 and 9 point Aster, leaded 2 points. Section numbers and titles are 24 point Helvetica. Chapter numbers are 60 point Helvetica and chapter titles are 24 Helvetica. The size of the type page is 34½ by 47 picas.